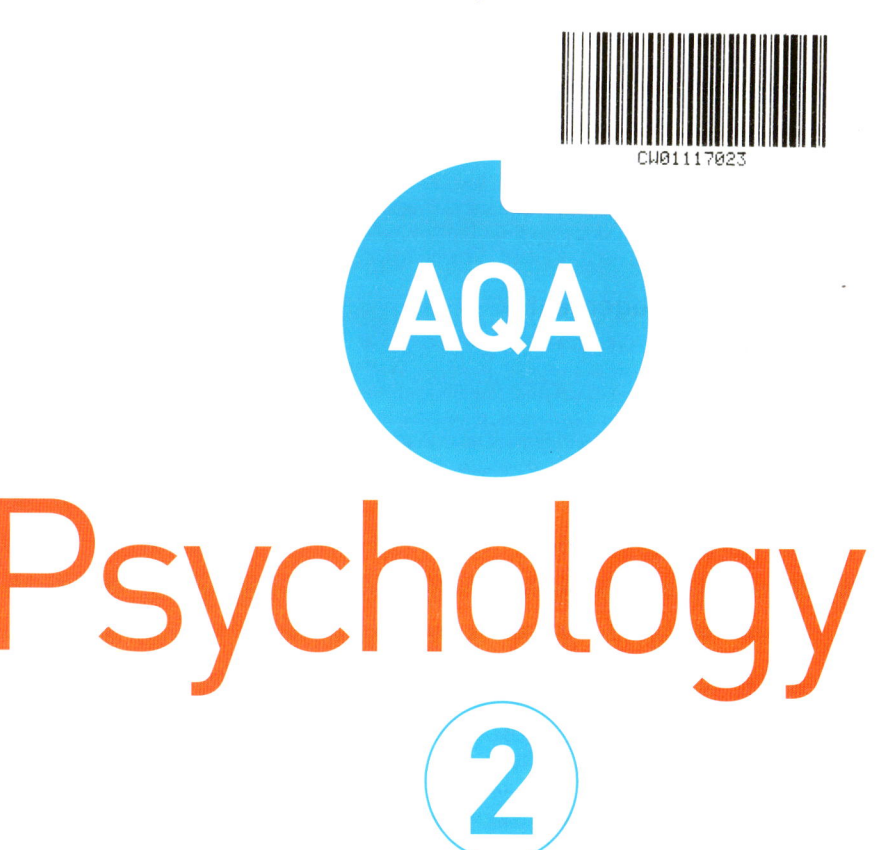

# AQA
# Psychology
## 2

Jean-Marc Lawton
Eleanor Willard

**Approval message from AQA**

This textbook has been approved by AQA for use with our qualification. This means that we have checked that it broadly covers the specification and we are satisfied with the overall quality. Full details of our approval process can be found on our website.

We approve textbooks because we know how important it is for teachers and students to have the right resources to support their teaching and learning. However, the publisher is ultimately responsible for the editorial control and quality of this book.

Please note that when teaching the *AQA Psychology* course, you must refer to AQA's specification as your definitive source of information. While this book has been written to match the specification, it cannot provide complete coverage of every aspect of the course.

A wide range of other useful resources can be found on the relevant subject pages of our website: www.aqa.org.uk.

## Text acknowledgements

**p. 42** Patrick Wintour: Dominic Cummings, as quoted in 'Genetics outweighs teaching, Gove adviser tells his boss' from *The Guardian* (The Guardian, 11 October 2013); **p. 52** www.telegraph.co.uk/news/politics/11078359/Welfare-claimants-to-get-attitude-tests-employmentminister-reveals.html; **p. 55** James Fallon: from *The Psychopath Inside: A Neuroscientist's Personal Journey into the Dark Side of the Brain*, copyright © 2013 by James Fallon. Used by permission of Current, an imprint of the Penguin Publishing Group, a division of Penguin Random House LLC; **p. 86** E. Sahlstein and S. Duck: from 'Interpersonal relations: What we do with relationships' from *The New Handbook of Language and Social Psychology*, ed. P. Robinson and H. Giles (Wiley, 2001); **p. 360** Quentin Tarantino: from *Natural Born Killers*, dir. Oliver Stone (1994).

## Photo acknowledgements

p.1 © Fenton – Fotolia; **p. 2** © Illustrated London News; **p. 5** © Paul Sakuma/AP/Press Association Images; **p. 6** © agsandrew – Fotolia; **p. 11** © Fenton – Fotolia; **p. 13** © Ian Usher; **p. 27** © iagodina – Fotolia; **p. 29** © Alex White – Fotolia; **p. 31** © michaeljayberlin – Fotolia; **p. 34** © laszlolorik – Fotolia; **p. 40** © michaeljung – Fotolia; **p. 48** © iagodina – Fotolia; **p. 56** © vinnstock – Fotolia; **p. 63** © Kalim – Fotolia; **p. 64** © arquiplay77/iStock/Thinkstock; **p. 65** © alswart – Fotolia; **p. 66** *all* © Dr Martin Gruendl, www.beautycheck.de; **p. 68** © nyul – Fotolia; **p. 71** *t* © bst2012 – Fotolia, *b* © shock – Fotolia; **p. 72** © Kalim – Fotolia; **p. 75** © Moviestore Collection/REX; **p. 77** © Peter Steiner/Alamy; **p. 80** © Krasimira Nevenova – Fotolia; **p. 83** © Sashkin – Fotolia; **p. 85** © Agence DER – Fotolia; **p. 87** © kuvona – Fotolia; **p. 89** © WavebreakmediaMicro – Fotolia; **p. 91** © Syda Productions – Fotolia; **p. 94** © Tyler Olson – Fotolia; **p. 97** © Cesar Quiroga/LatinContent/Getty Images; **p. 99** © 2005 TopFoto; **p. 100** *t* © TopFoto, *b* © National Pictures/TopFoto; **p. 107** © ALFRED PASIEKA/SCIENCE PHOTO LIBRARY; **p. 108** © Ken McKay/ITV/REX; **p. 109** © Monkey Business – Fotolia; **p. 110** © Christian Schwier – Fotolia; **p. 112** © The Power of Forever Photography/Getty Images; **p. 113** *l* Courtesy Dan Pharr, *r* © David Ward; **p. 115** © ALFRED PASIEKA/SCIENCE PHOTO LIBRARY; **p. 117** © Pixel Memoirs – Fotolia; **p. 119** *t* © The Granger Collection, NYC /TopFoto, *b* © oksun70 – Fotolia; **p. 121** © Zuzana Egertova/Alamy; **p. 126** © Olga Semicheva – Fotolia; **p. 128** *t* © nickolae – Fotolia, *b* © olga demchishina – Fotolia; **p. 130** © Illustrated London News; **p. 135** © DragonImages – Fotolia; **p. 138** *t* © Michael Ochs Archives/Getty Images, *b* © Laurence Gough – Fotolia; **p. 140** © BBC; **p. 141** © Nancy G Western Photography, Nancy Greifenhagen/Alamy; **p. 144** © Rick Chapman/Corbis; **p. 149** © matka_Wariatka – Fotolia; **p. 150** © Alfred Pasieka/Science Photo Library; **p. 151** *t* © AFP/Getty Images, *b* © cbckchristine – Fotolia; **p. 154** © DragoNika – Fotolia; **p. 159** © Sovfoto/UIG via Getty Images; **p. 160** © auremar – Fotolia; **p. 163** © matka_Wariatka – Fotolia; **p. 165** Courtesy Renee Baillargeon; **p. 169** © lunaundmo – Fotolia; **p. 171** Photo with kind permission by Nicholas Epley; **p. 172** © James Balog/Getty Images; **p. 174** © vetre – Fotolia; **p. 175** © Jeff Morgan 05/Alamy; **p. 178** © willypd – Fotolia; **p. 181** © Robert Taylor, www.taylor-photo.co.uk, Courtesy Cecilia Heyes; **p. 185** © SSilver – Fotolia; **p. 186** © Jean-Marc Lawton; **p. 188** *both* © Terence James Charnley and SANE; **p. 190** © Duane Howell/The Denver Post, MediaNews Group/Getty Images; **p. 193** © vadymvdrobot – Fotolia; **p. 194** © bramgino – Fotolia; **p. 198** © SSilver – Fotolia; **p. 202** © U.S. NATIONAL INSTITUTE OF HEALTH/SCIENCE PHOTO LIBRARY; **p. 204** *t* © Rethink Mental Illness, *b* © gstockstudio – Fotolia; **p. 211** © ROBERT BROOK/SCIENCE PHOTO LIBRARY; **p. 212** © Jb Reed/Bloomberg via Getty Images; **p. 215** © sangiovese – Fotolia; **p. 218** © Jodi Jacobson/Getty Images; **p. 222** © JackF – Fotolia; **p. 227** © Joe Gough – Fotolia; **p. 228** © okyela – Fotolia; **p. 229** © Grafvision – Fotolia; **p. 231** *t* © PETER JOLLY NORTHPIX, *b* © robynmac – Fotolia; **p. 232** © RF Corbis Value/Alamy; **p. 236** © WavebreakmediaMicro – Fotolia; **p. 238** © Joe Gough – Fotolia; **p. 245** © Tatty – Fotolia; **p. 248** © Jacopin/BSIP/Science Photo Library; **p. 252** ©AP / Topfoto; **p. 253** © RioPatuca Images – Fotolia; **p. 256** © Digital Vision/Getty Images; **p. 262** © Apart Foto – Fotolia; **p. 267** © Friedberg – Fotolia; **p. 268** © ADRIAN DENNIS/AFP/Getty Images; **p. 274** *l* Courtesy Janice Kielcolt-Glaser, *r* © Robert Byron – Fotolia; **p. 275** © DR P. Marazzi/Science Photo Library; **p. 278** *t* © Glow Images, Inc/Getty Images, *b* © Monkey Business – Fotolia; **p. 280** © Friedberg – Fotolia; **p. 283** © Picture-Factory – Fotolia; **p. 285** © Rui Vieira/PA Archive/Press Association Images; **p. 286** © Guy Bell/Alamy; **p. 287** © ITV/REX; **p. 292** © Jean-Marc Lawton; **p. 294** © Van D. Bucher/Science Photo Library; **p. 296** © JacobST – Fotolia; **p. 298** © thodonal – Fotolia; **p. 299** © ddp USA/REX; **p. 300** *t* © Owen Franken/Corbis, *b* © ullsteinbild/TopFoto; **p. 301** © spotmatikphoto – Fotolia; **p. 307** © michael luckett – Fotolia; **p. 308** © Adam Pretty/Getty Images; **p. 310** © Fabio Pupin/Visuals Unlimited/Corbis; **p. 314** Courtesy Han G. Brunner; **p. 318** © michael luckett – Fotolia; **p. 321** © Digital Vision/Thinkstock; **p. 324** © ALBERT BANDURA, STANFORD CENTER ON ADOLESCENCE, STANFORD UNIVERSITY; **p. 327** © Getty Images; **p. 330** © igor – Fotolia; **p. 338** © fotandy – Fotolia; **p. 345** © Brian Jackson – Fotolia; **p. 346** © snaptitude – Fotolia; **p. 351** © Brian Jackson – Fotolia; **p. 354** © AP/Press Association Images; **p. 356** © REX; **p. 360** © Mary Evans Picture Library/Alamy; **p. 368** © alphaspirit – Fotolia; **p. 378** © Delphotostock – Fotolia; **p. 381** © Paul Doyle/Alamy; **p. 384** © lassedesignen – Fotolia; **p. 386** © Jörg Hackemann – Fotolia; **p. 391** © nito – Fotolia; **p. 392** © doble.d – Fotolia; **p. 394** © Brent Hofacker – Fotolia; **p. 397** © Mike Marsland/WireImage/Getty Images; **p. 400** © Directphoto Collection/Alamy; **p. 402** © nito – Fotolia; **p. 408** © Eugenio Marongiu – Fotolia; **p. 410** © aleciccotelli – Fotolia; **p. 418** © dalaprod – Fotolia; **p. 424** © Clemens Schüßler – Fotolia.

Every effort has been made to trace or contact all copyright holders, but if any have been inadvertently overlooked the Publishers will be pleased to make the necessary arrangements at the first opportunity.

Although every effort has been made to ensure that website addresses are correct at time of going to press, Hodder Education cannot be held responsible for the content of any website mentioned in this book. It is sometimes possible to find a relocated web page by typing in the address of the home page for a website in the URL window of your browser.

Hachette UK's policy is to use papers that are natural, renewable and recyclable products and made from wood grown in sustainable forests. The logging and manufacturing processes are expected to conform to the environmental regulations of the country of origin.

Orders: please contact Bookpoint Ltd, 130 Milton Park, Abingdon, Oxon OX14 4SB. Telephone: +44 (0)1235 827720. Fax: +44 (0)1235 400454. Lines are open 9.00a.m.– 5.00p.m., Monday to Saturday, with a 24-hour message answering service. Visit our website at www.hoddereducation.co.uk

© Jean-Marc Lawton and Eleanor Willard 2015

First published in 2015 by

Hodder Education,

An Hachette UK Company

Carmelite House, 50 Victoria Embankment

London EC4Y 0DZ

Impression number 3

Year 2016

All rights reserved. Apart from any use permitted under UK copyright law, no part of this publication may be reproduced or transmitted in any form or by any means, electronic or mechanical, including photocopying and recording, or held within any information storage and retrieval system, without permission in writing from the publisher or under licence from the Copyright Licensing Agency Limited. Further details of such licences (for reprographic reproduction) may be obtained from the Copyright Licensing Agency Limited, Saffron House, 6–10 Kirby Street, London EC1N 8TS.

Cover photo © Maya Kruchancova – Fotolia

Illustrations by Barking Dog and Aptara Inc.

Typeset in ITC BERKLEY OLDSTYLE, Book 11/13pt by Aptara.Inc.

Printed in Italy

A catalogue record for this title is available from the British Library

**ISBN 9781471835377**

# Contents

| | |
|---|---|
| **Introduction** | vi |
| **1. The approaches part two** | **1** |
| 1.1 The psychodynamic approach | 2 |
| 1.2 Humanistic psychology | 11 |
| 1.3 Comparison of approaches | 19 |
| **2. Issues and debates in psychology** | **27** |
| 2.1 Gender and culture in psychology | 28 |
| 2.2 Free will and determinism | 33 |
| 2.3 Nature–nurture debate | 40 |
| 2.4 Holism and reductionism | 44 |
| 2.5 Idiographic and nomothetic approaches to psychological investigation | 51 |
| 2.6 Ethical implications of research studies and theory | 55 |
| **3. Relationships** | **63** |
| 3.1 The evolutionary explanation for partner preferences | 64 |
| 3.2 Factors affecting attraction in romantic relationships | 72 |
| 3.3 Theories of romantic relationships | 80 |
| 3.4 Duck's phase model of relationship breakdown | 86 |
| 3.5 Virtual relationships in social media | 91 |
| 3.6 Parasocial relationships | 97 |
| **4. Gender** | **107** |
| 4.1 Sex and gender | 108 |
| 4.2 The role of chromosomes and hormones | 115 |
| 4.3 Cognitive explanations for gender development | 125 |
| 4.4 Psychodynamic explanation for gender development | 130 |
| 4.5 Social learning theory as applied to gender development | 135 |
| 4.6 Atypical gender development | 143 |
| **5. Cognition and development** | **149** |
| 5.1 Piaget's theory of cognitive development | 151 |
| 5.2 Vygotsky's theory of cognitive development | 159 |
| 5.3 Baillargeon's explanation for early infant abilities | 165 |
| 5.4 The development of social cognition | 169 |

# 6. Schizophrenia — 185
- 6.1 Classification of schizophrenia — 186
- 6.2 Biological explanations for schizophrenia — 198
- 6.3 Psychological explanations for schizophrenia — 204
- 6.4 Drug therapies — 211
- 6.5 Cognitive behavioural therapy, family therapy and token economies — 216
- 6.6 The importance of the interactionist approach in explaining and treating schizophrenia — 221

# 7. Eating behaviour — 227
- 7.1 Explanations for food preferences — 228
- 7.2 Neural and hormonal mechanisms involved in the control of eating — 239
- 7.3 Biological explanations for anorexia nervosa — 245
- 7.4 Psychological explanations for anorexia nervosa — 249
- 7.5 Biological explanations for obesity — 256
- 7.6 Psychological explanations for obesity — 259

# 8. Stress — 267
- 8.1 The physiology of stress — 268
- 8.2 The role of stress in illness — 272
- 8.3 Sources of stress — 278
- 8.4 Physiological measures of stress — 285
- 8.5 Individual differences in stress — 289
- 8.6 Managing and coping with stress — 294

# 9. Aggression — 307
- 9.1 Neural and hormonal mechanisms in aggression — 308
- 9.2 The ethological explanation for aggression — 315
- 9.3 Evolutionary explanations for human aggression — 317
- 9.4 Social psychological explanations for human aggression — 321
- 9.5 Institutional aggression in the context of prisons — 330
- 9.6 Media influences on aggression — 335

# 10. Forensic psychology — 345
- 10.1 Problems in defining crime — 346
- 10.2 Offender profiling — 351
- 10.3 Biological explanations for offending behaviour — 360
- 10.4 Psychological explanations for offending behaviour — 366
- 10.5 Dealing with offending behaviour — 378

## 11. Addiction — 391

- 11.1 Describing addiction — 393
- 11.2 Risk factors in the development of addiction — 397
- 11.3 Explanations for nicotine addiction — 407
- 11.4 Explanations for gambling addiction — 409
- 11.5 Reducing addiction — 417
- 11.6 The application of theories of behaviour change to addictive behaviour — 425

**Glossary** — **433**

**Index** — **437**

# Introduction

This book is aimed specifically at those students studying the AQA Psychology A-level specifications, though hopefully it will prove of interest and use to any student of psychology.

The book details the course content as outlined by the AQA specifications, but should also serve as a learning aid in itself and not just be a basic textbook. To create ease of use, there is a standard format throughout the book, with the features designed specifically to help you with your studies.

The book is divided into eleven chapters, reflecting the eleven main topics that make up the second year of the A-level course. Within these chapters is the basic text that describes the relevant theories and explanation required by the specifications, alongside the following regular features, which require some further explanation in order for you to understand and get the most from them. Research Methods is covered in AQA Psychology for A-level Book 1.

## Features

### Understanding the specification

Found at the beginning of each chapter, this feature details the specific elements of topics that need to be studied.

## IN THE NEWS

Written in the style of a newspaper story, this feature highlights topical news items that illustrate central psychological themes of the topics being discussed.

### KEY TERMS

Concise and clear explanations of significant words and words associated with each topic. Key terms are highlighted within the text in the first instance and then fully explained and detailed within the text itself.

### Evaluation

This regular feature can be found after a research section and at the conclusion of explanations/theories and consists of general evaluative and analytical points.

### RESEARCH IN FOCUS

Using examples from the text, this feature gets you to focus on methodological aspects of research studies (how studies are carried out) and asks relevant questions to assist learning and understanding. This knowledge will also be useful for those progressing on to year two of the A-level. It will often be a good idea to reference material in Chapter 7 (Research methods) to get the most out of this feature.

## YOU ARE THE RESEARCHER

This feature also focuses upon research methods, but this time from the viewpoint of the design of psychological studies. This will help to foster a greater understanding of why and how psychologists conduct research and help you to develop the necessary skills to plan your own research.

### On the web

Take your learning and curiosity further by using this feature, which directs you to websites that provide a wealth of further information.

## CLASSIC RESEARCH

As the title suggests, this feature focuses on famous psychological studies, taking you in some detail through the thinking behind such studies, as well as the aims, procedure, findings, conclusions and evaluation.

## CONTEMPORARY RESEARCH

Similar in focus and presentation to the classic research feature, but this time featuring more recent cutting-edge research, providing an up-to-date account of the subject.

### Increase your knowledge

A feature that provides extra learning material to form a useful and relevant source of elaboration for those who wish to take their learning a little further.

### PSYCHOLOGY IN THE REAL WORLD

An occasional feature focusing upon practical applications of psychology that shows its usefulness within real-world settings and which will help to form a valuable source of AO3 evaluative material.

### STRENGTHEN YOUR LEARNING

Found at the end of each element of a topic, this feature is designed to help you focus upon and appraise the material covered within the text. Acting as a form of comprehension exercise, the questions can be used as a means of revision before attempting the questions found at the end of each topic.

## Assessment check

This feature consists of a variety of questions to help you with your studies.

### SUMMARY

Each chapter concludes with a bullet-pointed review of the main points covered within the chapter.

# Assessment checks

## Examination skills

The AQA examinations assess three examination skills. These are Assessment Objective 1 [AO1], Assessment Objective 2 [AO2] and Assessment Objective 3 [AO3].

AO1 assesses level of knowledge and understanding by asking candidates to demonstrate knowledge and understanding of scientific ideas, processes, techniques and procedures, such as by outlining and describing relevant theories/explanations and research studies.

AO2 requires students to apply knowledge and understanding of scientific ideas, processes, techniques and procedures, such as by providing students with some stimulus material and then asking them to apply their psychological knowledge to that material.

AO3 requires students to analyse, interpret and evaluate scientific information, ideas and evidence, such as by assessing the worth and meaning of theories/explanations. For example, by a consideration of what research findings suggest, support/lack of support from other research sources, methodological criticisms, relevant ethical points, as well as practical applications and implications of research.

The assessment check feature presents questions. There are several types of such questions you can be faced with.

1 'Choice' questions require you to select from options provided to complete the answer, for example, see question 1 on page 10 in Chapter 1 The approaches part two.

2 'Scenario' questions describe a situation based on a topic area. Knowledge of that topic area must then be applied to the scenario, for example, see question 2 on page 79 in Chapter 3 Relationships.

3 'Short answer' questions require specific answers, with elaboration (detail) needed to show fuller understanding, for example, see question 3 on page 79 in Chapter 3 Relationships.

4 'Methodology' questions are based upon research studies associated with topic areas. Knowledge of methodology must then be applied, for example, see question 2 on page 10 in Chapter 1 The approaches part two. Some of these questions will require mathematical skills in order to be successfully answered, for example, see question 2 on page 90 in Chapter 3 Relationships.

5 'Essay' questions for the A-level qualification will never be worth more than 16 marks. These may be in the form of 'outline and evaluate', for instance of an explanation or theory, for example, see question 5 on page 134 in Chapter 4 Gender.

# 1 The approaches part two

## Introduction

In Book One the biological, learning and cognitive approaches were covered in detail. This chapter will 'complete the set', covering the psychodynamic and humanist approaches.

The basic assumptions of each approach, plus its key features as highlighted by the specification, will be covered together with relevant research and evaluation of the approach.

All the approaches will be compared at the end of the chapter using six criteria. The book will reflect on the stance of each approach with regard to the criteria and a comparison with the stances of the approaches will be shown along a continuum diagram.

## Understanding the specification

- The basic assumptions of the psychodynamic approach can be asked about specifically in this section of the specification.
- The role of the unconscious, the structure of personality – id, ego and superego – defence mechanisms including repression, denial and displacement, and the psychosexual stages are also mentioned in the specification.
- You will need to know the basic assumptions of humanistic psychology and you also need to be able to evaluate the approach.
- The specific key features in the specification include:
  - free will
  - self-actualisation
  - Maslow's hierarchy of needs
  - focus on the self
  - congruence
  - the role of conditions of worth
  - the influence on counselling psychology.
- The specification mentions that you need to be able to answer questions which require you to draw a 'comparison of approaches'. This means that you need to know how all the approaches compare with each other. It is possible that you may get essay questions asking you to outline and compare two approaches or short answer questions asking you to outline differences/similarities between the approaches.

These are the basic requirements of the specification. However, other relevant material is included to provide depth and detail to your understanding.

# 1.1 The psychodynamic approach

**Figure 1.1** Sigmund Freud, founder of the psychodynamic approach

> 'Unexpressed emotions will never die. They are buried alive and will come forth later in uglier ways.'
> Sigmund Freud (1904)

Sigmund Freud (1856–1939), an Austrian neurologist and psychiatrist, is widely acknowledged to be the founder of the psychodynamic approach. He developed a form of therapy known as psycho-analysis, which deals with the conflicts within the mind that have been developed through traumatic experiences. This approach is called the psychodynamic approach as it deals with the psychodynamics of the mind.

Other psychodynamic psychologists were Anna Freud, Alfred Adler, Carl Jung and Erik Erikson.

## Basic assumptions

As with all the approaches it is important to start with the basic assumptions of the psychodynamic approach. There are three core assumptions:

1 **Unconscious mind.** The psychodynamic approach believes that the driving force behind our behaviour is the **unconscious mind**. It therefore believes that if we have problematic or challenging behaviour then we must access the unconscious mind to sort it out.
2 **Instincts/Drives.** This approach argues that it is instincts or drives that motivate our behaviour. This means that we are driven by instinct to go through a series of stages in development of our behaviour and personality. For example, this approach believes we have a sexual instinct from birth and as we develop we go through a series of five psychosexual stages until we reach the final stage at around 12 years old (see Psychosexual stages on page 6).
3 **Early childhood experiences.** Early childhood is believed to be pivotal in making us the person we are. Most of our psychological development is argued, by this approach, to be formed prior to the age of six.

## The role of the unconscious

As the origin of our behaviour, the unconscious mind is all important. The psychodynamic definition of the unconscious mind can be usefully explained using the iceberg model. This draws an analogy between an iceberg and the mind. The tip of the iceberg above the surface of the water is the **conscious mind**, which is visible to all. However, below the surface is the unconscious mind. There is no clear way of seeing what lies beneath (the unconscious mind), but it is almost certainly greater in influence than the conscious mind.

Freud used three levels of thought to explain behaviour: the conscious, the pre-conscious and the unconscious. As stated, the conscious mind is the

### KEY TERMS

**Unconscious mind** – the thoughts that occur without any conscious awareness

**Conscious mind** – the part of the mind we are aware of

**Pre-conscious mind** – the thoughts that occur just out of conscious awareness

part of our mind we can access. The **pre-conscious mind** is 'just below the surface' and is made up of the thoughts that may surface at any point into the conscious. Many of our memories reside here, as they are accessible, but not in the forefront of our thoughts. However, Freud argued that there are thoughts that will not easily surface, and perhaps may never do so, and these are in the unconscious mind.

The drives or instincts that motivate our behaviour are also in the unconscious and therefore inaccessible. Traumatic or very unpleasant memories are also believed to remain here, not accessible to us but nonetheless driving our behaviour.

# The structure of personality

Our early experiences are believed to be vital in shaping our personality. This approach argues that there are three parts to our personality and the way they develop affects the person we become. The three elements are the **id**, the **ego** and the **superego**. How they influence personality is outlined below.

## Id

This forms from birth to about 18 months old. It is also sometimes referred to as the 'pleasure principle'. This is because the dominant force of the id is to seek pleasure. It is the childlike, selfish and hedonistic part of your personality, which focuses on the self.

## Ego

The ego develops between the ages of 18 months and 3 years and can be referred to as the 'reality principle'. It is able to delay the id's drive for pleasure. It also keeps the balance of influence between the id and the superego (see below) as they are opposite forces. Neither the id nor the superego should become dominant in a personality, otherwise they could adversely affect the behaviour and mental health of the individual. It is the role of the ego to try to ensure this does not happen.

## Superego

The superego is the last element of the three personality influences to develop and does so between the ages of approximately three and six years. Another name for the superego is the 'morality principle'. The role of the superego is to act as an individual's conscience. It is the opposite of the id in that it feels guilt and holds someone back from behaving a certain way if it is thought to be wrong. The superego helps a personality to form a moral code.

These three elements of the personality are shaped through experience and will affect how someone behaves. This approach suggests that much of our behaviour comes from the conflict between the three.

# Defence mechanisms

**Defence mechanisms** are methods we use unconsciously to reduce anxiety. Anxiety weakens the influence of the ego, which needs to be strong to mediate between the id and the superego. It is for this reason that defence

**KEY TERMS**

**Id** – the part of the personality that seeks pleasure

**Ego** – the part of the personality that delays gratification and balances the demands of the id and superego

**Superego** – the part of the personality that stops behaviour and becomes an individual's conscience

**KEY TERM**

**Defence mechanism** – a strategy to reduce anxiety

mechanisms are sometimes called 'ego defence mechanisms'. Defence mechanisms are therefore argued to be helpful.

Anna Freud, daughter of Sigmund Freud, described ten defence mechanisms in her book *The Ego and the Mechanisms of Defence* (1936). There are, however, thought to be more than ten. Sigmund Freud suggested 17. Table 1.1 outlines three – repression, denial and displacement – and their possible everyday effect on behaviour.

**Table 1.1** Defence mechanisms and their possible effects

| Defence mechanism | Outline | Effect on behaviour |
|---|---|---|
| Repression | An unpleasant memory is pushed into the unconscious mind where it is not accessible to the conscious mind and therefore cannot cause anxiety. It does, however, still affect behaviour in the unconscious mind. | There is no recall of the event or situation. |
| Denial | This is a refusal to accept the reality of an unpleasant situation. This reduces anxiety caused by that situation. | Someone may believe that the situation is not negative and that therefore it should not cause anxiety. This is not positive thinking, merely a resistance to accept reality. |
| Displacement | This is when the focus of a strong emotion is expressed onto a neutral person or object. This reduces anxiety by allowing expression of that emotion. | Someone may exhibit very strong emotion but focus it onto an uninvolved person or object. |

### KEY TERMS

**Repression** – highly emotional and unpleasant thoughts are buried deep in the unconscious mind

**Denial** – a refusal to accept the reality of a situation

**Displacement** – a strong emotion is displaced from its target onto a neutral object or person

If applying this to a relatively everyday situation it can be seen how they differ from each other. So, for example, Maria may have a particularly unpleasant boss who makes her angry.

On the one hand, if her unconscious mind used **repression** to protect the ego she would simply not remember when her boss had been unpleasant to her. On the other hand, **denial** would mean that she would believe that what her boss was saying to her was actually pleasant. **Displacement** would prompt her to take out her anger on her friends and family… or slam a door.

# IN THE NEWS

# Ψ The Psychological Enquirer

## The murder of Susan Nason

The idea of memories being repressed and then surfacing has implications for the legal system. In one such case a man was convicted of the murder of an eight-year-old girl thanks to memories remembered 20 years after the crime.

In 1969, an eight-year-old girl called Susan Nason was murdered a few miles from her home in California.

Twenty years later, in 1989, Eileen Franklin-Lipsker reported to the police that she had remembered being present at the murder. She said that the memory had somehow been triggered and that the murderer was her father, George Franklin. She remembered many details of the crime and for that reason George Franklin was arrested.

There was much debate at the trial in 1990 as to whether a repressed memory such as the one Eileen described was reliable. The jury sided with the prosecution that it was and found George Franklin guilty of first-degree murder. The judge sentenced him to life in prison.

However, in 1995 the judgment was overturned. This was due to the prosecution's assertion that because George Franklin had stayed silent it was essentially a confession, which it was not. It was also due to the fact that many of the details Eileen remembered were available at the time in newspapers and that she could have read them or heard discussion about them. This was therefore not a recovered memory as argued by the defence.

It also became apparent, through the testimony of Eileen's sister, that Eileen had recalled the memory through hypnosis, which cast doubt on the reliability. Because the state Supreme Court had by 1995 ruled that testimony based on memories 'recovered' by hypnosis is unreliable, Eileen could have been barred from taking the stand at a new trial. In 1996 George Franklin was released and cannot face trial again for the crime.

Susan Nason's murderer has never been found.

**Figure 1.2** The Supreme Court ruling that memories recovered by hypnosis are unreliable allowed George Franklin to be released from prison.

The idea of **repression** in particular is important because it has arisen in court cases. The defence would usually argue that the memory trace in emotional memories cannot be placed in the unconscious. In support, there is evidence that the **suppression** of memories weakens the memory trace.

## CONTEMPORARY RESEARCH

### Suppressing unwanted memories reduces their unconscious influence – Gagnepain, Henson & Anderson (2014)

Gagnepain and fellow researchers wished to examine whether the act of suppression actually affected the quality of the memory at a later date as this has real-world implications. The fallibility of memory is well documented in eye witness research.

#### Aim
Gagnepain *et al*. were interested in seeing whether suppressing memories into the unconscious mind does influence behaviour or not.

#### Procedure
For the research they concentrated on visual memories as these are often the kinds of memories that sufferers of post-traumatic stress disorder find the most intrusive.

Participants were asked to learn pairs of words and pictures combined. Examples of the objects used were ladders, binoculars and rabbit. This was designed so that when the word was presented to them they would automatically see the picture because of the association. Their brain activity, after the learning process, was measured using a functional magnetic resonance imagery (fMRI) brain scanner. This was done either while the participant was thinking of the picture when given the word, or while they were actively trying to suppress the picture from coming to mind.

#### Findings
To test the effect on the unconscious the researchers asked participants to look at distorted images to identify objects. Ordinarily they would be able to do so quickly and

successfully if they had recently seen the picture that was distorted, and that happened in the no-suppression condition. However, this was not the case when participants had been asked to try to suppress the image.

### Conclusions
This suggests that the memory trace had been weakened by suppression. fMRI scanning of the activity seemed to indicate that the memories had been disrupted, and that behaviour may not be affected by suppressed memories as they cannot be recalled.

### Evaluation
The relevance for this study on repression is important. It would seem to indicate that trying to forget could be a useful strategy to reduce the effects of trauma. It has been argued that repressed memories can exert influence on behaviour from the unconscious, but this research suggests it is not necessarily as great an influence as thought.

Figure 1.3 Can you recall suppressed memories?

> **KEY TERMS**
>
> **Psychosexual stages** – a series of stages that every individual develops through, from birth to puberty
>
> **Fixation** – if a conflict is experienced during development through one of the psychosexual stages, a fixation will affect the personality

## Psychosexual stages

The psychodynamic approach argues that we have drives in our unconscious mind that dictate the stages we experience at varying points in development. The **psychosexual stages** of development are a series of stages every individual progresses through from birth to becoming an adult. The underlying unconscious drive is sexual.

### Oral stage

At birth a child enters the oral stage as the focus for pleasure and gratification is the mouth. A child will get pleasure from biting and sucking, which are oral activities. Freud believed this stage was important in formation of the personality.

Initially (as there are no teeth) Freud said the infant is in a stage called oral passive which is when the pleasure is mostly derived from sucking and swallowing, like breast feeding. Then the infant enters the oral aggressive phase which is when the infant gains their pleasure from biting and chewing, like when a child starts teething.

If a child is weaned from its mother's milk too early or too late, or feeding patterns were erratic it was argued that the child will become fixated at the oral stage. This means that this would have an unconscious effect on the personality. In an adult this **fixation** might mean, if orally passive (non-aggressive), that they are dependent, very passive and they will also be gullible. An orally passive person will believe anything you say.

Conversely an orally aggressive person will be aggressive, and this could be expressed either physically or verbally. Being orally aggressive or passive is dependent on the mother-child relationship.

Overall, people with an oral fixation are thought to be more likely to chew on pens, bite their fingernails and smoke.

### Anal stage

Around 18 months old the child moves into the anal phase of development. The libido (or sexual energy) of the child moves focus from the mouth to the anus. Pleasure is therefore gained from defecating. This is also the age at which the child is potty trained.

If the child loves using the potty and is overly keen to do so, then the child is thought to be in the anally expulsive stage. As an adult fixation this translates to a generous person who is demonstrative with their emotions. They also might have fits of temper.

If the parents are very strict about potty training, the child will become anxious about using the potty and try to hold on to the faeces rather than use the potty. This stage is call anally retentive. An adult with an unconscious fixation at this stage will display personality characteristics like being very organised, very neat and reluctant to spend their money.

## Phallic stage

Around the age of three the child enters the phallic psychosexual stage. The focus for pleasure moves, in this stage, it is argued, to the genitals from the anus. This stage is differentiated by the gender of the child. So, boys experience the Oedipus complex and girls go through the Electra complex.

### Oedipus complex

At this point in his development Freud argued that a boy experiences intense sexual feelings for their mother. His father is then seen, by the small boy, to be a rival and he therefore wants him to leave so that the mother can focus on him. As the father is a lot bigger than the boy, the child feels threatened by his presence and feels potentially he could harm him, as he is a rival for the mother's affections. Freud said that the boy is worried that his father will castrate him as he may see him as a rival and this is called 'castration anxiety'.

In order to combat the anxiety the boy now feels, he has to befriend his father to reduce the anxiety. He does this by acting similarly to the father so he sees him as an ally, rather than a rival for the mother's affections. This is called identification. This reduces the castration anxiety felt by the boy and his Oedipus conflict is resolved.

For this to occur, Freud said that a father figure must be present. In cases where the mother is a single parent and there is no father figure for the boy to identify with, it is argued by psychodynamic theorists that he would be likely to grow up homosexual. In reality, of course, there is no evidence for this.

### Electra complex

For girls at this stage, the realisation that they do not have a penis is very important. They think that the mother has removed it and so, around the age of three, they develop penis envy of males. When that desire is not fulfilled it is expressed through the desire for a baby.

The little girl desires the father in a similar way to boys with their mothers, and so she goes through the identification process in the same way. Fixations at the phallic stage can lead to a jealous and anxious adult.

## Latent stage

At the age of about six, children enter the latent stage. The libido, or sexual energy is displaced throughout the body and it seems that this is a relatively calm time in development with no complexes to resolve or foci for pleasure in the body (according to Freud). The child essentially concentrates on being a child.

Neo-Freudians such as Erik Erikson did not believe that this period is without its problems and he in particular argued that children have all sorts of insecurities and inferiorities to deal with. However, in the theory suggested initially by Freud, this is a quiet period in development and there are no fixations or effects on the adult personality.

## Genital stage

The libido once again is focused in the genitals at this stage, and that is where it stays for the rest of the life. Everyone reaches this stage and from here the child becomes an adult. It is the fixations in the first three stages that have an enduring effect on the adult personality.

A summary of the five psychosexual stages is outlined in Table 1.2. If there is a period of conflict then a fixation may occur which corresponds to the stage the individual is experiencing at that time, depending on their age. This fixation means that the adult may be affected by the fixation that is in their unconscious mind.

**Table 1.2** The five psychosexual stages

| Stage | Divisions within the stage | Age | Effect on behaviour in adults |
|---|---|---|---|
| Oral | Passive | 0–18m | Smoking, dependent |
|  | Aggressive |  | Aggressive behaviour, chew pencils |
| Anal | Expulsive | 18m–3 years | Generous. Open with emotions |
|  | Retentive |  | Organised, neat and mean with money |
| Phallic | Oedipus (boys) or Electra (girls) complex | 3–6 years | Homosexuality |
| Latent | No divisions | 6–11 years | No fixation occurs. No effect on the adult personality |
| Genital |  | 12 years |  |

Much of Freud's work used case studies as he documented the cases he worked with. Little Hans is an example of one such case study.

## CLASSIC RESEARCH

### The Little Hans case study – Sigmund Freud 1909

Herbert Graf was the son of one of Freud's friends, Max Graf. He became the focus of Freud's paper 'The analysis of a phobia in a five-year-old boy', which was published in 1909. Herbert was given the pseudonym of 'Hans' for the paper.

Hans had developed a phobia of horses and Max Graf documented what his son said, and did, in detail and passed the information on to Freud in the form of letters for him to analyse the boy's behaviour. Freud interpreted the boy's behaviour and reported dreams as a problem in the phallic psychosexual stage. It was an in-depth analysis which was written up as about 150 pages.

The key features of the analysis were:
1. Hans' fascination with his 'widdler' (or penis) was important. He noticed that animals, including horses, often had much larger penises than him. This interest was thought to be indicative of the phallic stage of development.
2. Hans' father went away for a while and Hans enjoyed having his mother's attention to himself. When his father returned, Hans resented his presence. This was argued by Freud to be evidence of the Oedipus complex.
3. Hans' little sister, Hannah, was born in this period and was a major influence, Freud thought, on Hans' behaviour. Hans was hostile towards his sister and Freud saw this as an extension of the Oedipus complex.

4 Hans was experiencing a sexual attraction to his mother and his father was therefore a rival for her affections. Hans was experiencing castration anxiety.

The case caused controversy when it was published. The analysis was seen as immoral by some and simply inaccurate by others. However, it also had its supporters.

Hans recovered from his phobia. At the age of 19 Hans met Freud and reported that the phobia had not reoccurred. He even said that when he heard about the case study, he did not realise the report was actually written about him

Key issues and criticisms of the case study

Freud met the boy only once in a therapeutic setting and the information was forwarded by the father, so the source was potentially biased.

Freud had published his ideas about the psychosexual stages prior to his analysis and therefore possibly from a biased perspective. He could have been looking for evidence to support his ideas rather than looking through unbiased eyes.

Hans had seen a horse collapse in the street when he had been out walking one day when he was young. This could have shocked him and thus classically conditioned him. In theory, this could have been the source of the phobia, therefore disproving Freud's analysis.

## Evaluation

- The psychodynamic approach highlights how important childhood experience is to later development. This strengthens the case for children's rights reform. This means that children are, or should be, nurtured as their childhood serves as a precursor to adulthood.
- Freud's ideas are used by some therapists today to treat mental health issues so this would suggest that there is a group of psychologists who feel that the psychodynamic ideas have merit and validity. There are also case studies from Freud's work that seem to show how his patients made a recovery following therapy.
- Freud's ideas are very difficult to test reliably and so this leads to the argument that his ideas are unscientific and cannot be proven. Ensuring that a methodology has actually reached the unconscious mind is problematic.
- Much of the evidence for the psychodynamic approach comes from case studies which lack reliability and cannot be generalised to the general population. The case studies that Freud used were culturally specific and came from the more wealthy people in Viennese society. Both these factors make generalisation difficult.
- It is argued that people recovering from mental illness following psychotherapy could be due to spontaneous recovery over time rather than attendance to therapy. Eysenck (1952) did a meta-analysis of thousands of psychoanalytic patients and found that it worked for some (66 per cent). However, he also found that 70 per cent of people suffering from neurotic disorders and who did not receive treatment also recovered. This would suggest that spontaneous recovery may occur in some cases and that psychotherapy suits some people, but not others.

### STRENGTHEN YOUR LEARNING

1 What is meant by the unconscious mind?
2 What are the three components that form the structure of the personality?
3 What is the difference between the id and the superego?
4 What does a defence mechanism do?
5 What is the difference between denial and displacement?
6 What does repression mean?
7 What are the psychosexual stages?
8 Explain how a fixation at each of the first three stages could affect you as an adult.
9 Explain the strengths and weaknesses of the psychodynamic approach.

# ASSESSMENT CHECK

1. Select from the characteristics A, B, C and D below to complete the table relating to the suggested fixation at a psychosexual stage. One description will be left over. **[3 marks]**

   **A** Laughs a lot

   **B** Homosexuality

   **C** Smokes heavily

   **D** Saves money

   | Psychosexual stage | Characteristic |
   |---|---|
   | Oral | |
   | Anal | |
   | Phallic | |

2. Researchers have examined repression by using longitudinal studies to revisit people who have had trauma in their childhoods and to see whether they have memory for the event.

   What are the ethical and methodological issues of using this as a research methodology? **[4 marks]**

3. Andrea is in a romantic relationship with Mark. Recently he has started to be less attentive towards her, and often does not respond to her texts and calls for a long period of time. She says it is because he is busy or that he has no phone reception. Her friends think he is seeing someone else.

   Identify which defence mechanism would explain Andrea's behaviour and justify your choice. **[3 marks]**

4. Outline what is meant by the ego. **[2 marks]**

5. Outline and evaluate the psychodynamic approach. **[16 marks]**

# 1.2 Humanistic psychology

*'I don't believe in types, I believe in people.'*
Tom Branson (2012)

Humanistic psychology is sometimes referred to as the 'third force' in psychology as it views behaviour in a very different way to many of the other approaches (Maslow, 1962). It was founded in the 1950s. There was a questioning of the influence of the first force, psychodynamic psychology, and the way it focused on unhealthy development in psychoanalysis. The movement also arose from dissatisfaction with the deterministic and overly scientific way behaviourist psychologists (the second force) regarded behaviour.

## Basic assumptions

### Every individual is unique
Humanists believe that we are all different and that we should be treated as such. There is no point in trying to generalise to groups as there are so many differences within each group. This approach is therefore unlikely to try to generalise to groups of people and subdivide the population into clusters which all share a characteristic such as age or gender. This way of viewing people as unique individuals is called idiographic.

**Figure 1.4** Humanists believe that we are all unique, like snowflakes

### Free will
A core assumption of this approach is that we have **free will**. That means we have the ability to choose what we do and we are in control of our behaviour. Ultimately this means that we are in charge of how we develop and progress through life.

The humanistic approach does acknowledge that we have constraints on our free will, in that there are social rules, laws and morals that restrict whether we actually act upon our free will. Ultimately though, if we want to do something, we have the ability to choose to do it.

### KEY TERM
**Free will** – ability of an individual to choose a course of action or to act a certain way

### People should be viewed holistically
Humanists argue that there is no point looking at just one aspect of an individual. If only one part of them is considered then much of what could be affecting them might be missed. For example, if someone is stressed and it is only their work life that is focused upon in therapy, there could be problems in their home life that might be overlooked. Humanists do not agree with focusing on childhood in therapy – they believe the whole life course should be considered. They believe by seeing someone as elements rather than a whole means that much of what is important, and that makes the person who they are, is lost.

### The scientific method is not appropriate to measure behaviour
Humanistic psychology does not describe itself as scientific. It argues the scientific method tries to be too objective (free from opinion and bias) and yet humans are subjective in the way they think and behave.

This therefore means that the methods employed by some approaches in measuring behaviour and thought are inappropriate as they try to measure without acknowledging the subjective experience of the individual.

## Free will

We discussed above that the humanistic approach to explaining behaviour assumes that we have free will. That is, we can decide and choose our course of action. This is unusual as most of psychology believes much of our thought and behaviour is determined, that we have no choice.

This is a difficult concept to prove, but as proof is not important to humanistic psychology, this is not an issue. Humanists believe that we should consider the subjective experience of the individual, and in most circumstances a person will *feel* that they have chosen a course of action. To the humanistic approach this provides evidence of its existence.

An implication of the belief in free will is that this means that a person is responsible for their own behaviour, social or anti-social. In terms of the legal system this places the responsibility with the individual, meaning it is their 'fault'.

Humanists acknowledge that there are constraints on the choices available to an individual at any point, so it is not always the case that a person behaves in the way they would have preferred – they sometimes find their choices restricted by circumstance. This is not against the concept of making a choice, merely a result of the number of options being reduced.

## Self-actualisation

A belief of the humanistic approach is that everyone has an innate drive to achieve their full potential. The achievement of that full potential is a state called **self-actualisation**. Both Carl Rogers and Abraham Maslow believed that individuals self-actualise in their own way and, as with behaviour in general, it is unique to them. The theories behind both Maslow's hierarchy of needs and Roger's focus on the self and congruence are outlined in the sections that follow. Both theorists describe their own ideas on achieving self-actualisation.

When self-actualisation is achieved it can be described as the ultimate feeling of well-being and satisfaction. Theorists argue it is a drive we all have, but we do not all achieve it. The feeling is described in many ways, using the words ecstasy, peak experience, religious or spiritual experience. It is thought to be an intensely strong feeling of 'completeness'.

### KEY TERM

**Self-actualisation** – peak state of existence that any individual can attain

> ### YOU ARE THE RESEARCHER
> Humanistic psychology does not advocate the measurement of individuals. If you were to design a simple study to investigate whether someone is self-actualised or not, how would you do it?
> What research methodology would you choose? How would you analyse the data? How would you classify them?

## IN THE NEWS

# Ψ The Psychological Enquirer

In 2008 Ian Usher, aged 44, split with his wife. He was originally from Darlington, County Durham, but had moved to Australia five years earlier. Following the split from his wife he decided that he needed to change his life as everything reminded him of her, so he put his life up for sale on eBay.

The sale comprised his Perth home with three bedrooms and all his belongings, which included his motorcycle, Mazda car, parachuting gear and a jet ski. The highest bidder would also receive an introduction to his friends and a job as a salesman (which was for a trial period before being made permanent). The winning bid totalled about £193,000.

With the money Ian initially travelled and then bought a Caribbean island and moved there. After a little time alone he met a new partner with whom he settled on the island and spent two very contented years there.

He has now put his Caribbean life up for sale, too, and is travelling the world with no long-term plans in place.

How would someone who is self-actualised appear? How would they act? Is Ian self-actualised? He owns few possessions and is happy exploring the world. His blog is also very positive and he seems content. However, the concept is difficult to test and to categorise someone as self-actualised is problematic.

Bearing in mind that humanistic psychologists do not regard 'proof' and measurement as important or relevant, they do not see a problem with this. For other psychologists this is a flaw in the concept.

**Figure 1.5** Has Ian Usher achieved self-actualisation?

---

Research by Sheffield *et al.* (1995) has shown that there is a positive correlation between an individual's level of self-actualisation and their psychological health. This study was conducted on 185 college undergraduates and the measure for self-actualisation used was the Personal Orientation Inventory developed by Shostrum (1963, 1977). Examples of the measure are shown in Figure 1.6.

### ON THE WEB

You can follow a blog of Ian Usher's life at:

**www.ianusher.com/index.php**

Do his posts support the idea that he may be self-actualised?

| Sample items from Shostrum's Personal Orientation Inventory ||
|---|---|
| Time competence scale | Self-oriented scale |
| 1. (a) I strive to predict what will happen in the future.<br>   (b) I do not feel it necessary always to predict what will happen in the future.*<br>2. (a) I prefer to save good things for future use.<br>   (b) I prefer to use good things now.*<br>3. (a) I worry about the future.<br>   (b) I do not worry about the future.* | 4. (a) My moral values are dictated by society.<br>   (b) My moral values are self-determined.<br>5. (a) I feel guilty when I am selfish.<br>   (b) I do not feel guilty when I am selfish.*<br>6. (a) I am bound by the principles of fairness.<br>   (b) I am not absolutely bound by the principles of fairness.*<br>7. (a) I feel I must always tell the truth.<br>   (b) I do not always tell the truth.* |

**Figure 1.6** Factors affecting the development of self-actualisation. Select one of the two statements. The starred (*) statement scores high for self-actualisation.

## Focus

The theory of flow developed by Csikszentmihalyi in 1990 talks about 'flow' being a state when someone is completely caught up in a task, sport or activity so that they are totally focused on it. An example might be a runner who is fully focused on their performance and not thinking about other everyday matters. This state seems to increase personal growth because the person is driven to improve their performance (Daniels, 1988). They are also more likely to have the sort of peak experiences that are part of self-actualisation.

## Attitude

An outward, more positive attitude means that self-actualisation is more attainable. If someone experiences a negative event, and adopts a negative attitude about it, this will affect their self-concept and prevent personal growth. For example, someone may experience a relationship breakdown and blame themselves. This attitude towards the part they played will impinge on their self-confidence and potentially stop subsequent relationships developing.

> **KEY TERM**
>
> **Hierarchy of needs** – the needs required to be in place before self-actualisation can be realised

## Maslow's hierarchy of needs

*'A musician must make music, an artist must paint, a poet must write, if he is to be ultimately happy. What a man can be, he must be.'*

Abraham Maslow

Maslow considered that self-actualisation could be achieved in a series of stages. These are called the **hierarchy of needs**. He wrote that the five basic needs a person has to meet are physiological, safety, belonging, self-esteem and self-actualisation (growth) needs. They arise in that order and if the first need is not met then all the other needs cannot be fulfilled. This is why the concept is called a hierarchy of needs. This is illustrated in Figure 1.7.

The drive to achieve full potential means that we are all working through these needs in an attempt to self-actualise. It is clear that if you have no food then it will be difficult to move past the physiological needs. Likewise, living in a war zone may mean that you cannot achieve your safety needs. For some people in Western societies, where they are well fed, safe and loved, it can be their self-esteem that prevents them from fulfilling the fourth hierarchy.

The state of self-actualisation is not permanent and if all the five needs do not remain in place, an individual can move out of the state until all the needs are back in place. So, being hungry or being tired, even though a temporary state, will mean that the person is not meeting their needs.

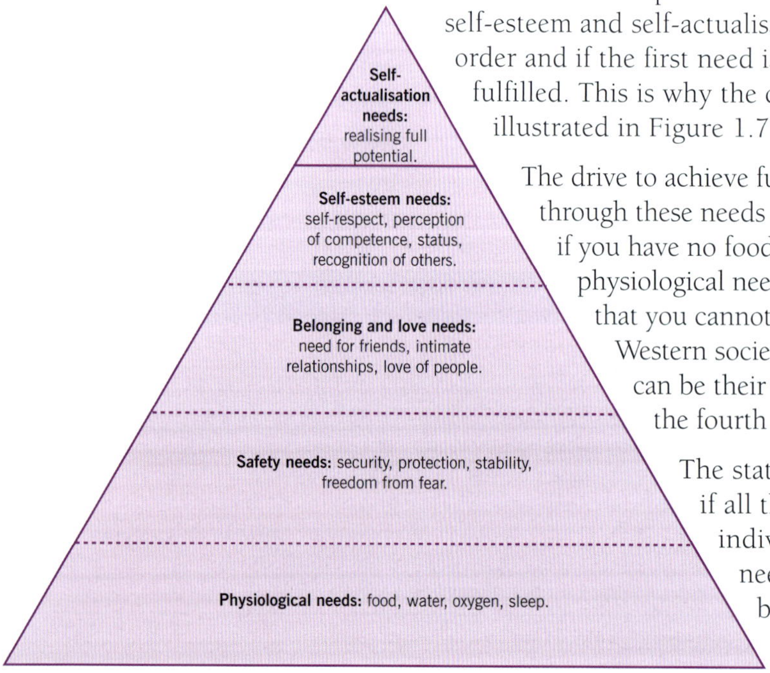

**Self-actualisation needs:** realising full potential.

**Self-esteem needs:** self-respect, perception of competence, status, recognition of others.

**Belonging and love needs:** need for friends, intimate relationships, love of people.

**Safety needs:** security, protection, stability, freedom from fear.

**Physiological needs:** food, water, oxygen, sleep.

**Figure 1.7** Maslow's hierarchy of needs

> *'Whenever two people meet, there are really six people present. There is each man as he sees himself, each man as the other person sees him, and each man as he really is.'*
>
> William James (1892)

## Focus on the self

Carl Rogers' work focuses on the self, or rather the 'selves', of the individual. He suggested that we have three selves which need to integrate to achieve self-actualisation. The three selves are:

- **The self-concept** – this is the self that can be described as the self you feel you are. It is similar to self-esteem and is affected by it. So, if someone has low self-esteem, their **self-concept** will be poor and they will have a distorted view of how capable they are. People may have a distorted view of themselves.

- **The ideal self** – this is the self you wish to be. It is who you are aiming towards becoming. Or, it is possible you are already there! A typical way of knowing whether someone is still working towards their **ideal self** is when you hear someone say, 'I wish I was more…' or 'I wish I was able to…'. This differs from the self-concept in that it is not who you think you are, it is who you wish you were.

- **The real self** – the third self is the **real self**, the person you *actually* are, not who you *think* you are or who you *wish* you were. This is actually a difficult self to demonstrate, as the subjective experience that is so important to humanist theory means that everyone will perceive or judge a person differently. Therefore, this logically means that ascertaining the real self is problematic.

Rogers felt that to be able to reach the state of self-actualisation it is important for the person to be fully functioning. This means that they have the opportunity to strive for self-actualisation and are actually doing so. It is not something that occurs by chance. Being able to pursue your potential means you are fully functional so any barriers that occur in the environment or from within are overcome.

## Congruence

Rogers said that to achieve self-actualisation it is necessary for a person to be congruent. This means that their ideal self and actual experience (self-concept and real self) are the same. It can also be achieved if they are very similar. However, this is difficult to achieve and therefore it means that many people do not realise their full potential and do not become self-actualised.

Rogers believed that an important part of achieving **congruence** is 'unconditional positive regard'. This means that at some point in their lives someone has to be loved for who they are by someone else. They need to be accepted, without proviso. This unconditional positive regard can come from parents or other family members, friends, a partner or, Rogers argues, a therapist. Wherever it comes from, it is essential to be able to reach full potential.

> **KEY TERMS**
>
> **Self-concept** – the way you see yourself
>
> **Ideal self** – the self you wish to be
>
> **Real self** – who you actually are
>
> **Congruence** – when your selves are the same as each other
>
> **Conditions of worth** – requirements an individual believes they must have to be loved

## The role of conditions of worth

**Conditions of worth** are requirements that the individual feels they need to meet to be loved. This is also called conditional positive regard. Conditions of worth can be either real or perceived by the individual.

An example of this might be a child who feels they need to attain high grades in school for their parents to accept and love them. They feel that they will not be loved fully unless they meet that requirement. This feeling could be gained overtly from having been told by parents that they need to get good grades. It could also occur indirectly, if they have witnessed a sibling causing parents disappointment because of poor grades. Either way, if a child feels these conditions of worth it will mean they do not experience **unconditional positive regard** and find self-actualisation even more difficult to attain.

### KEY TERM

**Unconditional positive regard** – total acceptance received from another person

## The influence on counselling psychology

One of the major influences of the humanistic approach is the therapy that has developed from the theory. Carl Rogers developed his client-centred therapy from his ideas. The client–therapist relationship is especially important and it is key that therapists can make their clients feel comfortable and accepted. This is to ensure the client feels unconditional positive regard. If the client feels they are able to say whatever they want to the therapist, and that it will be accepted, then they will be able to be totally honest. This honesty will help them realise potential barriers to becoming congruent, and through working with the therapist will remove those barriers.

The influence of humanistic psychology on counselling was extensive throughout the 1960s and 1970s. However, some argue that this influence waned in the late 1970s. There is now a notably significant influence on counselling which has reoccurred since the 1990s.

The initial decline in popularity was attributed to some extent to the focus on psychology as a science, and as a core assumption of the approach is that scientific measurement is not appropriate for people, there was a conflict with the psychology movement. However, the positive psychology movement, which is influenced by Abraham Maslow's ideas, is gaining influence again. In terms of counselling and psychotherapy the client-centred approach is influencing other therapies, such as cognitive behavioural therapy (CBT). The 'third wave' CBT integrates humanistic ideas of subjective experience (Hayes, 2004) and research by Wampold (1997, 2006) emphasises that all therapies should integrate a client-centred approach, like that of Rogers, to be effective.

Research by Elliott (2002) showed that in a meta-analysis of 86 studies, humanistic therapies prompted a significant improvement in clients when compared with people not receiving treatment. This effectiveness helps to increase the influence of the therapy and consequently the ideas of the humanistic approach.

This seems to suggest there has been a regrowth in the influence of humanistic psychology within counselling psychology over the last two decades.

### Evaluation

- The argument that we are all unique and should be viewed this way by psychology is supported by research that often finds within-group differences to be greater than between-group differences. This is illustrated well by gender research which has, time and time again, found that the difference within men (or women) as a group is greater than the difference between men and women (Hyde, J.S. (2005) The gender similarities hypothesis, *American Psychologist*, Vol. 60, No. 6).

- The ideas of the approach are hard to test scientifically and therefore support with empirical evidence. This is not something that the humanistic approach attempts to do as humanists believe it is inappropriate with humans as we are all unique.

- The subjective experience of the individual is difficult to test, but it is seen as a strength of the approach that it acknowledges the effect it has on the behaviour. As the approach rejects scientific measurement it does not try to be objective.

- The client-centred therapy and other therapies developed from the approach are effective. Although the influence diminished in the 1980s and 1990s, its popularity has increased in recent years. Sexton & Whiston (1994) found they were successful for certain people. There is also an issue in that the measure was subjective (opinion based from the client) so could have been biased. It could be argued, however, that the perception of success is more important than an objective measure of success.

- The acknowledgement of free will is supported by how we feel as individuals. The idea is intuitively correct, but problematic to test.

- Some of the concepts are vague. Describing self-actualisation as a concept is difficult and as a consequence it is difficult to measure. This is not seen to be an issue by the humanistic theorists as they do not feel measurement is appropriate.

- Concepts such as self-actualisation have been widely accepted and the hierarchy of needs itself has been very influential. However, it is criticised for being culture-specific as it is related to well in individualist cultures (where the focus is on the self) but not so well in collectivist cultures (where the focus is on the well-being of others).

- The humanistic theory allows for personal development and change throughout the lifespan and acknowledges that we can change as a consequence of our environment. This is in opposition to the childhood-focused stance of the psychodynamic approach.

### STRENGTHEN YOUR LEARNING

1. What is meant by free will?
2. Explain what self-actualisation is.
3. How does Rogers think an individual achieves self-actualisation?
4. How does Maslow think an individual achieves self-actualisation?
5. What does Rogers say congruence is?
6. What is the role of conditions of worth?
7. What is unconditional positive regard?
8. What part does unconditional positive regard play in humanistic therapy?
9. How has the influence of humanistic ideas on counselling psychology varied over the years?

# ASSESSMENT CHECK

1. Select from the descriptions A, B, C and D below to complete the table relating to the stages of the hierarchy of needs Frances may or may not meet. One description will be left over. **[3 marks]**

   A Frances sometimes wishes she wasn't as shy

   B Frances has lots of friends

   C Frances worries about being mugged

   D Frances is hungry

   | Stage of the hierarchy | Description |
   | --- | --- |
   | Belonging | |
   | Physiological | |
   | Self-esteem | |

2. Discuss two strengths of the humanistic approach. **[4 marks]**

3. Nathan has always worked really hard at school. He is ambitious and wants to become a solicitor. His parents are very proud of him and celebrate his successes. However, of late, his grades at school have slipped. Nathan is feeling miserable and anxious.

   How do conditions of worth explain Nathan's feelings? **[3 marks]**

4. Outline what is meant by free will. **[2 marks]**

5. Outline and evaluate the humanistic approach. **[16 marks]**

# 1.3 Comparison of approaches

This section looks at how the five approaches can be said to be similar, and different, to each other.

A series of six criteria has been chosen to draw a comparison. These are the debates: free will and determinism, nature–nurture, holism and reductionism, idiographic and nomothetic approaches. There is also a comparison on the extent to which the approach can be seen as scientific and whether it extrapolates from animal behaviour to human behaviour.

Each criterion will be dealt with in isolation and all five approaches will be considered with regard to this criterion. There is a diagram showing the approximate position of each approach along the debate continuum, so that it can easily be seen how the approaches compare. It should be noted that the position is approximate. If you feel the approach should be elsewhere, then for the purposes of the exam all you need to do is to be able to justify what you say with evidence.

## Criterion 1: Free will and determinism

**Summary of criterion:** free will is the idea that what we do is voluntary and done through choice. We make our own decisions and choose our own course of action. Determinism is the opposite of this, where an individual's behaviour, choices and thought are determined by internal or external factors.

### What the approaches say

**Biological approach:** this is strongly deterministic as it believes our behaviours are generated from biological roots and therefore outside of conscious control.

**Learning approach:** the behaviourist element is deterministic as it argues that behaviour is due to a stimulus/response reaction. It is even argued that we feel like we have a choice when there is no threat of punishment, but even in those circumstances we are driven to choose whatever gave us pleasure in the past. Social learning argues for a level of choice in whether we imitate or not, but that can still be said to be dictated by experience.

**Cognitive approach:** the way we process information from the environment is determined by our past experiences (schema) but cognitive psychology can be said to argue for an element of free will as cognitive therapy requires the individual to change their thoughts.

**Psychodynamic approach:** the psychodynamic approach has a core assumption that our behaviour and thoughts are dictated by our unconscious mind. As we have no control over our unconscious, it can be argued that the approach is strongly deterministic.

**Humanistic approach:** this is the only approach to fully advocate the existence of free will and the idea that we choose our path in life.

**How do the approaches compare?** See Figure 1.8.

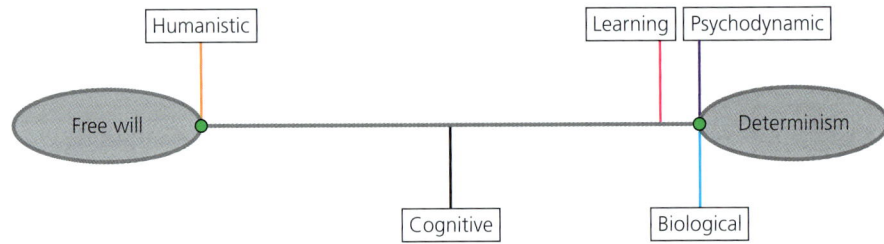

**Figure 1.8** Free will and determinism continuum

# Criterion 2: Nature–nurture debate

**Summary of criterion:** this debate asks whether the way we think, feel and behave is part of our genetic make-up (nature) or due to environmental influences (nurture). See page 40 for more detail.

## What the approaches say

**Biological approach:** one of the core assumptions of this approach is that behaviour can be passed on through the genetic make-up of the individual and therefore this approach is on the nature side of the nature–nurture debate. There is an acknowledgement that the environment does affect development of genetic make-up. This is illustrated by the phenotype of the individual (see Book 1, page 200).

**Learning approach:** behaviourism, in its purest form, believes that everyone is born free of predispositions and that it is their environment that forms their behaviour. For that reason they take an extreme nurture position. This is the same for social learning, as the behaviour is learned from role models in the environment. There is no acknowledgement of the innate and inherited capacities of an individual.

**Cognitive approach:** the cognitive approach accepts both sides of the debate. On one hand it acknowledges that there could be innate thought mechanisms which are important for development of thought and language. However, the cognitive approach also recognises the role of our environment in shaping our thought processes. Processing is based on experience and therefore falls under the nurture side of the debate.

**Psychodynamic approach:** this approach, it can be argued, falls onto neither side of the debate. It argues for the existence of innate drives, represented by the id. However, the way parents raise a child affects the formation of the other elements of the personality and therefore nurture plays a role, too.

**Humanistic approach:** the humanistic stance on the debate is difficult to ascertain, mainly because the humanistic approach does not believe the debate to be valid. It argues that the debate tries to make generalisations to large numbers of people as to whether who they are is innate or learned and therefore the individualism it advocates is at odds with the debate itself. However, looking at the ideas of the approach there seems to be an innate drive to be the best you can be (nature) but that the environment can aid or help that process (nurture). This means that the humanist theories seem to be interactionist.

How do the approaches compare? See Figure 1.9.

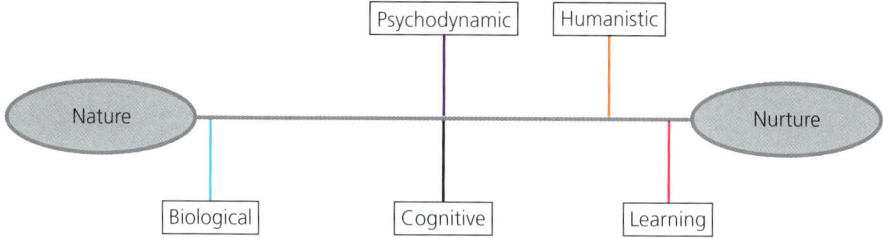

**Figure 1.9** Nature–nurture debate continuum

# Criterion 3: Holism and reductionism

**Summary of criterion:** for any single behaviour there are differing levels of explanation, from the social context to the neuronal level. Reductionism can be defined as the attempt to explain any act by reducing it to a simpler level. Holism, however, is when the interaction of different factors affecting a behaviour is taken into account in an explanation – it does not focus on one specific part of an explanation.

## What the approaches say

**Biological approach:** this approach is the most commonly associated with reductionism. Biological reductionism occurs due to the approach's efforts to explain any act or behaviour as due to a genetic, physiological or biochemical cause.

**Learning approach:** behaviourism is believed to have experimental reductionism due to its focus on stimulus response experimental design. It upholds a scientific approach to investigation and this means isolating elements of behaviours. For that reason it is seen to be reductionist.

**Cognitive approach:** it is argued that the cognitive approach supports experimental reductionism. This is where experiments are carefully controlled to isolate one variable to test. There is also the issue of 'decoupling', which is when one cognitive process is isolated for testing, but in the 'real world' many cognitive functions would be used, so looking in isolation lacks validity. However, there are attempts within the cognitive psychology community to look at context of experiments. This makes them less artificial and less reductionist.

**Psychodynamic approach:** this approach believes that all elements of an individual's behaviour should be taken into account and for that reason is not seen to be reductionist. It also does not employ scientific methods to investigate behaviour so does not display experimental reductionism. However, to say it is purely holistic can be argued to be erroneous due to the focus on drives as underpinning behaviour. As these are a key element they could be seen to be the explanation behind behaviour so therefore reductionist. However, it is widely considered that the psychodynamic approach is more holistic than reductionist.

**Humanistic approach:** the humanistic approach is holistic. It does not believe in reducing behaviour to specific elements and believes that the individual should be regarded as a whole. As it rejects using the scientific method to investigate behaviour it does not have any elements of experimental reductionism.

How do the approaches compare? See Figure 1.10.

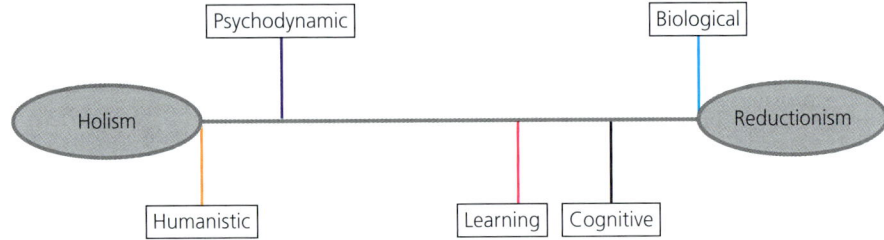

**Figure 1.10** Holism and reductionism continuum

# Criterion 4: Idiographic and nomothetic approaches

**Summary of criterion:** this criterion examines whether an approach is more focused on the uniqueness of individuals (idiographic) or whether it is trying to establish universal rules (nomothetic).

## What the approaches say

**Biological approach:** this approach is nomothetic as it is working on the idea that we share a common physiology and biochemistry and that it is the differences within these that explain the variance in behaviour between people. Although case studies are used, these are to help comparison with typical behaviour and they are used to test general theories.

**Learning approach:** this is also a nomothetic approach as it seeks to establish laws in behaviour such as the law of effect. It believes we have shared processes for learning behaviour and therefore seeks to generalise to all.

**Cognitive approach:** the focus on scientific study of cognitive processing in groups of people together with the comparison of individuals to computers means this approach is nomothetic. It recognises that individuals have vastly differing thoughts but that the processes underlying these can be generalised to all humans.

**Psychodynamic approach:** this approach has elements of being both idiographic and nomothetic. It focuses on the unique childhood of each individual and its favoured method of study (using case studies) focuses on the individual (idiographic), but it does generalise to all by specifying the innate drives we act upon.

**Humanistic approach:** the focus of the humanistic approach on the uniqueness of individuals establishes this approach as firmly idiographic. A humanist psychologist would see no merit in trying to generalise from one individual to another. It could be argued that there are nomothetic elements, such as the hierarchy of needs, but the approach itself would describe itself as idiographic.

How do the approaches compare? See Figure 1.11.

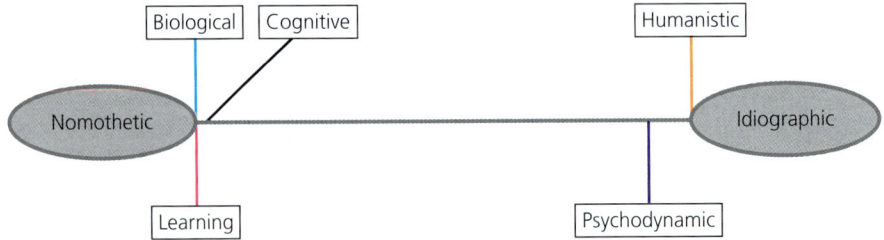

**Figure 1.11** Idiographic and nomothetic continuum

# Criterion 5: Scientific methods

**Summary of criterion:** the core questions for this criterion are: Does the approach use scientific methods for investigating behaviour? Are the research methods used objective and reliable?

## What the approaches say

**Biological approach:** the research methods used by this approach are some of the most scientific in psychology. They include measurement of biochemicals, brain activity using scanning technologies and physical measures such as biofeedback.

**Learning approach:** the behaviourist elements of the learning approaches examine observable behaviour and for that reason are seen to have scientific methods. There is no interpretation involved and so it is more objective than other methods. The cognitive element of the social learning theory is not directly observable so is thus more susceptible to bias and therefore seen as less scientific.

**Cognitive approach:** well-controlled laboratory experiments mean that the data from cognitive experimentation is often reliable and therefore more scientific. However, thoughts are not directly observable, so they can be argued to be biased. This means that the approach is not seen to be as scientific in its methodology as the biological approach.

**Psychodynamic approach:** as the unconscious mind is being investigated in this approach it is, as yet, impossible to measure scientifically. Indeed, it can never be proven that methods designed to uncover the unconscious mind can actually access the unconscious mind. Certainly projective tests and dream analysis cannot prove that they access anything other than conscious thought. The methods are also subjective and require interpretation.

**Humanistic approach:** this approach does not believe that scientific measurement of behaviour is appropriate. Humanists believe that humans are unique individuals and therefore there is no point measuring them scientifically.

**How do the approaches compare?** See Figure 1.12.

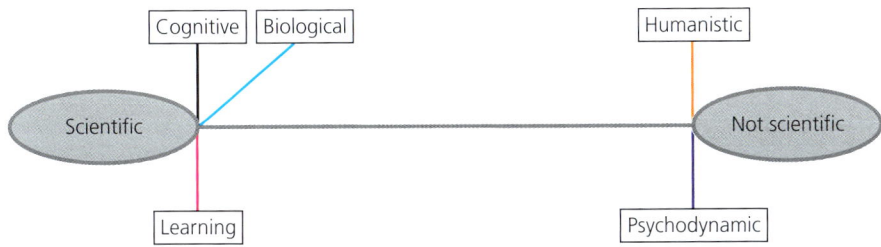

**Figure 1.12** Scientific methods continuum

# Criterion 6: Extrapolation

**Summary of criterion:** extrapolation considers whether an approach uses animal research to provide a test for ideas. This is called extrapolation as there is a core belief that if your ideas relate to animals as well as humans then any behaviour can be generalised across both groups.

## What the approaches say

**Biological approach:** animal research is used widely by this approach as it sees humans as being physiologically similar to animals. Biochemical tests and neurological examinations of animals are therefore appropriate and helpful.

**Learning approach:** behaviourist principles were developed through animal testing as the learning mechanisms humans use are argued to be the same as those of animals. This is not the case, however, for the social learning approach.

**Cognitive approach:** the fact that the cognitive approach is examining thought means that animal research is not appropriate for this approach. As animals cannot communicate through human language, it is difficult to ascertain what they are thinking. Some experiments on perception are run on animals, but this is the exception rather than the rule.

**Psychodynamic approach:** animal research cannot be used by this approach for similar reasons to the cognitive approach. The unconscious mind is difficult to test but would be impossible in animals.

**Humanistic approach:** animal research is conducted in a scientific manner and as this approach does not believe that scientific measurement of behaviour is appropriate, animal research is not used. The ideas of this approach are also focused on human development so there would be no reason to involve animals in the research.

**How do the approaches compare?** See Figure 1.13.

**Figure 1.13** Extrapolation continuum

### STRENGTHEN YOUR LEARNING

1. Which two approaches have opposite views on the existence of free will?
2. Explain how the learning and biological approaches compare with regard to the nature–nurture debate.
3. How do humanistic and cognitive psychologists compare with regard to the nature–nurture debate?
4. Which approaches adopt an idiographic stance?
5. Which approaches adopt a nomothetic stance?
6. Which approaches adopt scientific methods?
7. Which approaches agree with extrapolation to human behaviour from animal behaviour?
8. Name a similarity and a difference between the psychodynamic and the biological approaches.
9. Name a similarity and a difference between the humanistic and the cognitive approaches.

## ASSESSMENT CHECK

1. Explain two similarities between the psychodynamic and the humanistic approaches. **[4 marks]**
2. Outline two differences between the cognitive and the learning approaches. **[4 marks]**
3. Explain how the biological and psychodynamic approaches differ from each other. **[4 marks]**
4. Outline the biological approach and compare it to the learning approach. **[16 marks]**
5. Outline the humanistic approach and compare it to the cognitive approach and/or the biological approach. **[16 marks]**

### Psychodynamic approach

**SUMMARY**

- The psychodynamic approach believes the unconscious mind drives our behaviour and that innate drives motivate our behaviour.
- A key assumption is that early childhood experiences are pivotal in the formation of the adult personality.
- The unconscious mind plays a vital role and therefore the driving force behind our behaviour is difficult to access.
- There are three parts to our personality: the id, the ego and the superego.
- Defence mechanisms such as repression, denial and displacement are used to protect our ego from anxiety.
- Each individual also develops through the psycho-sexual stages of oral, anal, phallic, latent and genital stages.
- The phallic stage differs for males and females — boys experience the Oedipus complex and girls the Electra complex.

### Humanistic approach

- Humanistic psychology assumes each individual is unique and should be regarded holistically.
- The approach also assumes that humans experience free will.
- Humanistic psychologists do not generally accept that measuring behaviour scientifically is appropriate.
- A key drive for an individual is to become self-actualised. This state is difficult to attain and establish.
- Maslow suggested that self-actualisation could be reached through attaining the four needs on the hierarchy of needs: physiological need, safety need, love and belongingness need and esteem need.
- Rogers believed you could become a fully functioning person if your real self, ideal self and self-concept are congruent.
- To be congruent it is necessary to experience 'unconditional positive regard' from another individual.
- Conditions of worth are the conditions someone feels are placed on them to be loved by family and friends.
- The influence of humanistic psychology on counselling psychology dwindled through the 1980s and 1990s but it has become more popular of late due in part to the positive psychology movement.

### Comparison of the approaches

- Comparison of the approaches can be done by considering their stance on the key debates, their methodology and their use of extrapolation from animals.

# 2 Issues and debates in psychology

## Introduction

There are many perspectives and opinions to take into account in psychology and unlike some of the other sciences, there is no proof that any one of those perspectives is correct. This means that agreement is difficult to establish and because psychological ideas are interwoven with philosophy, there are areas of debate for which it is hard to see a resolution in the near future.

In this chapter those areas of debate will be considered in detail. There is no conclusion to the debates in question as there is no 'right' answer. For the purposes of the exam you need to be able to understand what the debate is about and present evidence to support each side.

At the end of the discussion for each debate there will be a table which reviews the topics you will have covered by the end of your second year and how they relate to the debate in question. All nine possible topics will be referred to, but you will have focused on three, so it would make sense to concentrate on understanding those. There will also be reference to the approaches and the first year content if any of it seems particularly relevant to the debate. You can use examples from anywhere in psychology in your essays, so think carefully about what you have learned, and use it!

Psychology has issues as well as debates. There are areas of contention about gender, culture and ethics which need to be considered. These will also be covered, with appropriate examples, in this chapter. Similarly to the debates, there will be a review of the other second year topics to see whether anything you have learned may be used to discuss these issues. You will find them referred to in the same table as the debates after the commentary on each section.

The debates that will be focused upon are:

1 Free will and determinism
2 Nature–nurture
3 Holism and reductionism
4 Idiographic and nomothetic approaches.

The issues that will be considered are:
1 Gender
2 Culture
3 Ethical implications of research.

## Understanding the specification

On Paper 3 you will be asked directly about the content of this chapter. For each debate and issue you need to have an understanding of the key terms and you need to be able to apply them to the other content you have learned.

Key terms that can be asked about on the paper for each debate and issue are as follows:

- **Gender and culture**: you can be asked about androcentrism, alpha and beta bias as they are all key terms named in the specification. For culture the key terms are ethnocentrism and cultural relativism. You will also need to be able to talk about universality and bias in the context of both gender and culture.
- **Free will and determinism**: key terms are hard determinism and soft determinism, biological, environmental and psychic determinism. The specification also mentions the scientific emphasis on causal explanations.
- **Nature–nurture debate**: for this you need to know what the relative importance of heredity and environment in determining behaviour is and how it can be established. You need to understand what the interactionist approach says and its position on the debate.
- **Holism and reductionism**: this requires you to answer a question on levels of explanation in psychology and to be able to define and discuss biological reductionism and environmental (stimulus-response) reductionism.
- **Idiographic and nomothetic approaches**: with this section you need to be able to define idiographic and nomothetic and you need also to be able to give some examples of each from your other topics.
- **Ethical implications of research studies and theory**: for this section, have some examples ready! Some examples need to refer to social sensitivity as it is mentioned in the specification.

This chapter will be subdivided into these six areas and will contain definitions of the key concepts together with examples to aid understanding and to help answer any questions.

These are the basic requirements of the specification. However, other relevant material is included to provide depth and detail to your understanding.

# 2.1 Gender and culture in psychology

*'Wherever you find a great man, you will find a great mother or a great wife standing behind him – or so they used to say. It would be interesting to know how many great women have had great fathers and husbands behind them.'*

Dorothy L. Sayers, *Gaudy Night*

Anatomically men and women are different. This will come as no surprise. However, it is often argued that they also differ psychologically. This can be in terms of cognitive development, their abilities, their personality and the amount of emotion they feel. The general public find research on sex differences fascinating and the culture we live in promotes gender difference. Pink for girls, blue for boys.

There are psychologists who argue that the idea of gender differences is much exaggerated and that the differences within genders are actually much greater than between genders.

# Universality

Universality, when applied to gender as a term, means that all research is assumed to apply equally to both genders. A lot of research is very mindful of the gender perspective so some assumptions of universality are underpinned by rigorous testing across both genders. This means that biased research can occur but assumptions of universality are often well researched.

## Bias

Gender, for the purposes of discussing gender bias in the topic, is the behavioural, cultural and psychological characteristics that distinguish males from females. This is closely related to the biological sex of the individual because that label determines the gender, and therefore all associations that come with it, from birth. This is the case for most individuals. However, there are people for whom the biological sex, and therefore gender, is not appropriate, e.g. transsexuals. These are the minority, but it should be made clear that sex does not equal gender.

**Figure 2.1** The differences between males and females are not always taken into account in psychological research

There are three main ways that gender bias can occur:

1. **Male samples**. Research being conducted on all-male samples and this not being made clear in the subsequent report. It is also the case that some key studies in psychology have had male-only samples and yet the findings have been generalised to women. An example of this is Milgram's research on obedience. The initial study, which is the most often cited, was a male-only sample and Milgram did not hide this fact. However, the findings have been used to explain all obedience to an authority figure, from both males and females.
2. **Male behaviour as standard**. If the behaviour of women differs from that of men the behaviour of women is seen as a deviation from the norm (see Androcentrism, below).
3. **Biological differences emphasis**. Explanations for behaviour that emphasise the biology of the individual also sometimes underemphasise the role of social and external factors. As there are anatomical differences between men and women, any theory that has its roots in biology is liable to implicitly infer that there will be a difference in the behaviour of the two sexes.

# Androcentrism

**Androcentrism** is the stance that the behaviour of men is taken as the norm and that the behaviour of women, if it differs, is therefore atypical. Tavris (1993) argues that most cultures take male behaviour as standard and therefore women make the decision to behave like men or different from them.

While compiling DSM-III-R, a diagnostic manual for mental health, the addition of masochistic personality disorder was proposed. For diagnosis it was argued that the individual should demonstrate behaviours such as self-sacrifice, rejecting opportunity for pleasure and playing the martyr. These could be argued to be examples of the female role and so the behaviour of women was pathologised. This is an example of androcentrism.

### KEY TERM

**Androcentrism** – 'male bias'. Men's behaviour is the standard against which women's behaviour is compared

## Alpha and beta bias

Gender bias as a term is not clearly defined. Hare-Mustin & Marecek (1988) argue that gender bias actually is split into two types, alpha and beta bias.

**Alpha bias** is the attempt to exaggerate the differences between the genders. Examples of this include Freud's theory of moral development. He argued that women have weaker moral codes because they do not fully develop their superego. This means that their conscience and ability to stop behaviour are weaker, leaving them liable to immoral behaviour. Similarly, the socio-biological theory of mate preference states that males look for youth and attractiveness in a partner whereas females look for wealth and status, so it could be argued to overemphasise differences. This therefore could be an example of alpha bias.

**Beta bias** is the attempt to downplay the differences between the genders. The fight-or-flight response is documented as being universal. However, research by Lee & Harley (2012) indicates that women have a slightly different reaction and that they are more likely to 'tend and befriend', i.e. they found that women are more likely to foster social support in response to a stressful situation. It seems that the original assertion of Selye, a psychologist, that the fight-or-flight response was universal, could be beta biased.

> **KEY TERMS**
>
> **Alpha bias** – the attempt to exaggerate the differences between the genders
>
> **Beta bias** – the attempt to downplay the differences between the genders

## Culture

*'Preservation of one's own culture does not require contempt or disrespect for other cultures.'*
Cesar Chavez

Bronfenbrenner (1979, 1989) devised the ecological model to consider a child's development. His model considered the four levels at which interactions can occur:

1. **The microsystem** – this is the immediate context in which a child is involved – for example, face-to-face interaction with its mother.
2. **The mesosystem** – this is the variety of environments that a child encounters, such as school, nursery, grandparents' house and home.
3. **The exosystem** – these are the contexts which affect the child even though he/she does not go there because they interact with the child's microsystems – for example, the interaction between the child's home (mesosystem) and their parents' workplace (which they do not visit, so it is an exosystem).
4. **The macrosystem** – this is the culture in which the child grows up, for example British culture. The macrosystem or culture has a direct effect on the other systems and this section of the topic considers how this is sometimes guilty of skewing research so that there is a bias towards how research is conducted and reported. Researchers have their own macrosystem which can bias how they see the world, and this can affect their objectivity as a researcher.

## Universality

There is an assumption in some research that the findings of their study will generalise globally. This is ethnocentric bias, and as much of the research is carried out in Western culture, the bias in psychology is therefore based on Western culture. However, it should be noted that this is not always the case. Psychological research often considers the perspectives of many cultures and as such the claim for universality can be supported by good research.

# Bias

The scientific tradition of clustering people into groups and formulating laws which apply to them all has meant that cultural bias has occurred in psychology. Much of the research has been conducted in Western universities and as a consequence the results are really applicable to that population only. The assumption of universality from these research studies has meant that findings have been generalised globally and this is a mistake. Cultural differences should have been tested and although it has occurred in some areas, it has not in all. Some biased researchers have assumed that their culture is the norm – this is ethnocentrism.

# Ethnocentrism

**Ethnocentrism** is the assumption that one ethnic group is superior to another, or to all other ethnic groups. It does not necessarily mean that other ethnic groups are seen in a negative light, more that their own ethnic group is normal and that others are strange and abnormal. This is similar to androcentrism in gender research.

# Cultural relativism

**Cultural relativism** is the opinion that there is no global 'right' and 'wrong' and that it is important to consider the behaviour of the individual within their culture before making a judgement. Context is vital. Social norms are culturally relative as what is considered acceptable in one culture may be unacceptable elsewhere.

Mental health disorders are affected by culture greatly. In the case of anxiety disorders the culture seems to determine what situations/objects are likely to cause the anxiety or fear. For example, in Japan there is a syndrome called 'taijin kyofusho'. Sufferers have a fear of upsetting or displeasing others. They also fear blushing and refuse to make eye contact. In the UK this would be diagnosed (along with other diagnostic criteria) as a social phobia, However, in the UK this is usually a fear of embarrassment rather than the fear of upsetting others. This emphasis is culturally determined (see Table 2.1 on page 32).

Syndromes from across the world are culturally driven, such as kayak angst suffered by the Inuit people of western Greenland. The sufferer has acute anxiety about drowning or getting lost at sea. This is observed in seal hunters who often sail alone and the fear they experience is clearly linked to their environmental threats.

> **KEY TERMS**
>
> **Ethnocentrism** – the assumption that one ethnic group is superior to another or all others and that the behaviour in that group is the 'norm'
>
> **Cultural relativism** – the belief that it is essential to consider the cultural context when examining behaviour in that culture. There is no global right or wrong, it varies across cultures

**Figure 2.2** It is important to consider the cultural context of behaviour before making a judgement

**Table 2.1** Gender and culture in psychology in relation to other topics

| Topic | How it relates to gender and cultural bias |
|---|---|
| **Relationships**<br>Mate preference | The evolutionary theory of mate preference emphasises the differences between what each gender looks for in a partner. This can be argued to be an example of alpha bias. Is it not possible that men and women look for similar attributes such as kindness and loyalty in their partner?<br>Culturally there is also difference in attraction and the criteria for choosing a partner. There are cultures and sub-cultures where arranged marriages are successful and in others the emphasis is on wealth from both partners to help support the family. These criteria are far removed from the Western perspective on partner choice. |
| **Gender**<br>Gender bias in biological theory<br>Cultural relativism and gender schemas | There is plenty of material for gender bias within the gender topic, for example the biological theories which could be accused of alpha bias. The work on androgyny could also be accused of beta bias.<br>Culturally the work of Margaret Mead illustrates the differences across cultures and how the Western gender stereotype does not generalise across the world. |
| **Cognition and development**<br>Cultural bias in Vygotsky's work | From the point of view of gender there is little material to use from this section. The biological basis of mirror neurons may mean that sex differences could be emphasised, but as the research does not do this, it cannot be accused of alpha bias.<br>Bronfenbrenner's work on the systems of the child draws attention to the influence of culture on a child's cognitive development. Vygotsky's work was seen as ethnocentric and was criticised for cultural bias. He worked in a collectivist culture and this potentially affected how he emphasised the role of the culture. |
| **Schizophrenia**<br>Gender and cultural bias in diagnosis | The age of diagnosis varies across genders and so do the symptoms presented. Is there actually much of a difference between genders? Could this potentially be an example of alpha bias?<br>Culturally there is an issue with diagnosis of schizophrenia. Auditory hallucinations, seen as a symptom in the diagnostic manuals, are a sign of powers in other cultures and therefore are not indicative of mental illness in those cultures. Cultural relativism should be discussed in relation to diagnosis of schizophrenia. |
| **Eating behaviour**<br>Cultural influences in food preference | The research on anorexia could be accused of being gynocentric (female-centred) as it is based on predominantly female subjects. This is due to the higher prevalence of anorexia in girls and women. However, there are male anorexics and it may be that the disorder has a different root in men.<br>Cultural differences in food preference are covered in the specification and this could be used as an example of how behaviour cannot be generalised across cultures. |
| **Stress**<br>Beta bias in physiological reactions<br>Gender differences in coping with stress | The physiological reaction to stress is documented as being a universal behaviour. However, research has shown that there may be gender differences (fight or flight v. tend or befriend, see above). This can therefore be used as an example of beta bias.<br>The gender differences in coping with stress are part of the specification – could this be used as an example of alpha bias? |
| **Aggression**<br>MAOA gene | The shortened version of the MAOA gene is found in men and the effects on women are not known, which means the theory should not be generalised to all aggression. This gender difference is often underemphasised in reporting of research, so is beta biased.<br>Evolutionary explanations of human aggression imply that the reasons behind aggression are cross-cultural. This is often not the case and aggression can be affected by social norms. |
| **Forensic psychology**<br>Psychodynamic explanations of offending behaviour | The psychodynamic explanation of offending behaviour varies between men and women, with the outcome that women have a weaker moral code. This can be argued to be an example of alpha bias.<br>Defining a crime is problematic due to cultural variations. Legal systems vary across countries, so this can be used to show that cultural relativism should be applied in research. |
| **Addiction**<br>Describing addiction – is there cultural bias? | Theories of addiction and risk factors seem to be seen as universal. However, potentially there may be gender differences, so could this be an example of beta bias?<br>The description of addiction in Western culture is based on the diagnostic manuals, whereas addiction to substances in particular is evident across cultures. However, for some cultures, addiction to opiate derivatives, for example, is not a problem. |

You could consider the androcentric research of Milgram, as his initial studies were carried out on a male sample. The cultural relativism of the definitions of abnormality would make an excellent focus for some commentary, too.

> **Evaluation**
> - It is difficult to look at research through completely objective eyes as we all have a gender and a culture. However, it should be noted that the vast majority of researchers give due consideration to these matters. A recognition that bias can occur is important in ensuring the effect it can have is minimised.
> - There is an issue of reactivity in human research as the gender of the researcher can alter the outcomes of the research. This is also the case depending on whether the researcher is from the ethnic majority or ethnic minority of the culture in which the research is conducted. This makes biases hard to avoid, although, again, an acknowledgement of this reactivity is important to ensure interpretation of the findings is as fair as possible.

**STRENGTHEN YOUR LEARNING**
1. Explain what is meant by universality with regards to gender.
2. What is the difference between alpha and beta bias?
3. Give an example of androcentrism in psychology.
4. Give an example of cultural bias in psychology.
5. What does the term ethnocentrism mean?
6. What does the term cultural relativism mean?
7. Give an example of cultural bias in psychological research.

# 2.2 Free will and determinism

The key question of this debate is: 'Are we in control of what we do?' Many people feel that they are and this supports the idea that we have free will. It certainly feels as though we do. However, most of the work in psychology adopts a more deterministic stance, meaning that we have less control than we feel we do. Indeed, some question the very existence of free will.

## Defining the debate

*'Habits of thinking need not be for ever. One of the most significant findings in psychology in the last twenty years is that individuals can choose the way they think.'*

Martin Seligman (2006)

## Free will

Free will is the ability to behave in the way we want. This means our actions are voluntary and we have freedom of choice. Free will in its purest form means that there are no restraints on choice from the options available. Indeed, we may decide not to choose any of the presented options. This is often how we feel.

**Figure 2.3** Can we behave how we want, or are our actions determined?

## Determinism

This is the opposing view to free will. Determinism is the idea that there is no control or choice on our course of action. Determinants of our behaviour come from a combination of sources, such as biology, learning and thought (see types of determinism below). Due to years of debate, and also in part due to the progression of psychological research, determinism has altered from an extreme stance to varying degrees of determinism, hard and soft.

*'Between stimulus and response there is a space. In that space is our power to choose our response. In our response lies our growth and our freedom.'*

Viktor E. Frankl (1967)

### Hard determinism and soft determinism

The stances within the debate are shown in Figure 2.4. This illustrates that soft determinism takes a less extreme view than hard determinism. Psychology is in the position that much of its theories and research suggest determinism is dominant, yet this does not feel intuitively correct. It is not how people feel, they have a sense of freedom of choice.

**Free will**
This is the idea that we are able to control and choose our course of action. We can make our own decisions and can act in unconstrained ways

**Hard determinism**
This is the view that human behaviour is determined by external forces and the actions are out of control

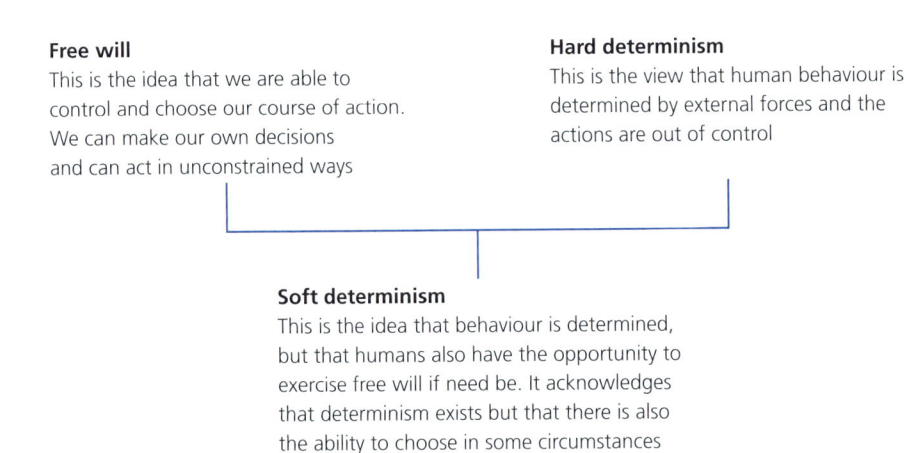

**Soft determinism**
This is the idea that behaviour is determined, but that humans also have the opportunity to exercise free will if need be. It acknowledges that determinism exists but that there is also the ability to choose in some circumstances

**Figure 2.4** Hard and soft determinism

Soft determinism agrees with the idea that we have determinants to our behaviour. These can come from our biological make-up or from learning through experience. However, soft determinism does take note of the subjective feeling that we have an element of control, that we choose. It essentially says that a combination of both ideas is closer to the truth. It is also named 'compatibilism' as it does not deny either side of the debate.

## Types of determinism: biological, environmental and psychic determinism

Determinism advocates the idea that our behaviour is affected by external forces out of our control. So what are those forces? There are thought to be several types of determinants of behaviour and these correspond to the approaches that advocate determinism.

## Biological determinism

The origin of this type of determinism is clear: it is any form of biological influence on the body. Examples of this can be found in the three main biological mechanisms: genetics, brain physiology and biochemistry.

The role of evolution and genetics in determining behaviour exists where there is found to be a genetic influence on behaviour. As research currently stands there is no gene identified where its existence means that a behaviour will definitely occur. Until this happens the hard determinism stance cannot be proven and a softer deterministic viewpoint has to be accepted. Potential areas where genetics may determine behaviour are, among many others, within aggression, addiction and forensic psychology.

Brain physiology can also be seen as a determinant. Areas of localisation (see page 235 in Book 1) in some way indicate that there are specific areas of the brain which affect behaviour, therefore it stands to reason that if that area is damaged, there could be an effect on behaviour which is out of the individual's control.

There is a relationship shown between biochemistry and behaviour. Examples include the dopamine hypothesis in schizophrenia and the role of testosterone in aggression. This is also out of the individual's control, although they can alter the levels through drugs so this becomes less deterministic.

## Environmental determinism

Environmental determinism is the idea that our behaviour is determined by environmental influences. The work of the social psychologists in conformity and obedience illustrates that behaviour can be altered by the environment, and in those cases, the people in someone's environment.

The learning approach is most often associated with environmental determinism. This is because behaviourism in particular advocates a stimulus/response explanation to behaviour, saying that an external trigger prompts a behaviour from the individual. Watson's work actually argued that behaviourism could control behaviour on a large scale and this in itself demonstrates a hard deterministic line.

An example would be classical conditioning (see Book 1, page 115) where a strong association is made between a stimulus that was previously neutral and a strong emotional response. Whenever the stimulus is presented, the strong emotional response is cued, and this is out of the individual's control. This is behaviourism in its purest form and later, more 'diluted' versions adhere to a less deterministic line.

Operant conditioning too is deterministic, as applying the law of effect means that a particular consequence will make a behaviour more likely in future. However, the 'more likely' does imply that there is an element of mediation by the individual and therefore possibly an element of free will.

This idea of interception of thought processes in mediating behaviour is adhered to by the social learning approach. This approach takes a less deterministic line as it acknowledges that reinforcement affects behaviour, but that there are cognitive processes that moderate the response, i.e. whether the person completes the action or not. For example, if the motivation is not there or they are unable to reproduce the behaviour at that time, it will not automatically occur. This is called reciprocal determinism and is a version of soft determinism (see above).

### Psychic determinism

This form of determinism considers the role of the unconscious on conscious thought and how that affects behaviour. This is therefore largely a determinism advocated by the psychodynamic approach.

Freud argued that every action we take has a cause. He also argued strongly that the cause often has its origins in the unconscious. As the root cause was emitted from the unconscious mind the individual would often not be able to say how or why they had followed a course of action. This would only become apparent from psychotherapy.

This idea of psychic determinism means that all behaviour had relevance for understanding an individual's unconscious mind. In therapy, Freud stated that everyday behaviour is also governed by the unconscious and so therefore it also should be examined. Freudian slips – when an individual says the wrong word in conversation seemingly by accident and the word actually demonstrates what is going on in the individual's unconscious mind – are an example of unconscious forces determining everyday behaviour. For example, John F. Kennedy reportedly said that the USA should 'be the breast' and quickly corrected it to 'be the best and the brightest'. Freud would argue he had other things on his (unconscious) mind at the time! These errors in everyday life, which are said to be generated from the unconscious, are called 'parapraxes' and it is argued that they show psychic determinism at work.

## The scientific emphasis on causal explanations

*'I have noticed that even people who claim everything is predetermined and that we can do nothing to change it, look before they cross the road.'*

Stephen Hawking (1993)

Scientism in psychology is the use of methods from the natural sciences to find causal mechanisms for behaviour and thought. Regarding psychology as a science means that this employment of the scientific method is commonplace. To examine a psychological phenomenon a psychologist must do the following:

- They must develop a theory followed by a prediction of what might happen (hypothesis).
- Then they must use empirical methods to test that hypothesis.
- If there is shown to be a significant effect, this is considered to be an indication that there is a causal explanation.

This ability to argue that a behaviour is caused by a particular factor occurs throughout psychology. The idea is that if one factor changes a behaviour in an experiment when all other factors are controlled, then the original factor must be responsible for the change. This can be done only if the research is carried out in a scientifically rigorous way. It is the only way to try to establish causation.

How does the emphasis on causal explanations relate to the free will/determinism debate? Determinism is all about causation. A determinist argument must be able to show that the behaviour has been caused (determined) by something that is not within the individual's or group's control. For example, to focus on biological determinism, if a biopsychologist argues that hormone X causes a change in behaviour Y, they will want evidence. Evidence is thought to be more persuasive if it comes from scientific experimentation. If the research shows that a presence of hormone X is related to someone showing behaviour Y, then this is strong evidence that the two are related. If behaviour Y does not occur when hormone X is not present, this also shows that the two are linked. For some, this would be scientific evidence to support causation, and with causation comes determinism. The biopsychologist would argue that hormone X determines behaviour Y.

The ability to prove this is problematic. It is rare to be able to say that X causes Y. There are always people for whom the effect does not happen. This means that there must be something else that affects whether the behaviour happens or not. Could this be free will (see Table 2.2)?

Table 2.2 Free will and determinism in relation to other topics

| Topic and specific example | How it relates to free will and determinism |
|---|---|
| **Relationships** Evolutionary explanations for partner preferences | The evolutionary argument that our choice of partner is centred around evolutionary advantage is without doubt determinist. It is essentially arguing that we are attracted to people who offer potential to provide and care for healthy offspring and that we have no choice in that attraction. However, elements such as similarity in attitudes and complementarity would suggest we consider what life could be like with them, which suggests an element of free will. A consideration of choice of partner would make good commentary for the free will/determinism debate – how much are we in control of our partner choices? |
| **Gender** Biological and social explanations for gender identity disorder | The biological explanation for gender identity disorder is determinist, arguing that gender identity is fixed at conception. However, there are also social explanations which would suggest an element of cultural influence, and with that the idea that there may be an element of free will (although cultural and environmental influences can still be determinist). You might also want to consider social learning as having a soft determinist stance. There is an element of determinism, but the mediating cognitive factors mean that we do not blindly adhere to gender stereotyping and therefore it can be argued we have some free will. Bem's work on androgyny also supports this less deterministic stance. |
| **Cognition and development** | The innate aspects of Piaget's theories suggest that our cognition and development are determinist. There could also be a determinist drive to learn. It is hard to argue free will in this topic as most developmental thinking appears to be determined by our developmental path, innate or environmentally set. |
| **Schizophrenia** Genetic explanation for schizophrenia Cognitive behavioural therapy as a treatment for schizophrenia | Both the genetic and biochemical explanations for schizophrenia suggest that it is determined. It is hard to understand why someone would opt to adopt schizophrenic behaviours, particularly the negative symptoms. However, in terms of treating schizophrenia, while the drug therapy is deterministic, there are elements of free will in cognitive therapy, so any successes in that area would suggest that schizophrenics can choose to change their thinking. It is important to consider how effective the treatment is if arguing for free will playing a part. |
| **Eating behaviour** Taste aversion Genetic explanation for anorexia | Taste aversion is determinist – whether innate or learned it is beyond our control. The genetic and biological explanations for anorexia also support the determinist stance. Social learning theory, when applied to anorexia, could be argued to have an element of choice as the mediating cognitive factors are used for deciding whether a behaviour is imitated or not. This could be applied as a potential example of free will. |
| **Stress** Physiological reaction to stress v. hardiness | The fact that the autonomic nervous system prompts an automatic response is strictly determinist. However, in less life-threatening but potentially stressful situations, such as traffic jams and workplace pressure, it can be argued that we have an element of choice as to whether we see the situation as stressful or not. The fact that hardiness can be taught would suggest that we can choose to look at such situations in another way. This suggests there may be an element of free will in our perception of stress. |

| | |
|---|---|
| **Aggression**<br>Genetic explanations for aggression | Much of the work on aggression, and especially the biological explanations, support a determinist stance, as if there is no choice in the way aggressive people act. The argument is that it is not all biologically determined, but that the environment determines an aggressive response, such as the situational explanation of institutional aggression. There is little to say that aggression is a choice, although one could argue that it does not feel that way. |
| **Forensic psychology**<br>Genetic explanations for offending behaviour<br>Anger management | This topic lends itself well to the free will/determinism debate. The idea that offenders have no choice in their actions has implications for the culpability of those actions. The explanations for offending, both biological and psychological, suggest a predominantly determinist stance, but when looking at the interventions, such as anger management and restorative justice, it could be argued that there is an element of choice in their behaviour. |
| **Addiction**<br>Genetic vulnerability for addiction<br>Cognitive behavioural therapy for addiction | Addiction as a topic has plenty of evidence for determinism, and the genetic vulnerability for addiction especially so. However, it is possible to argue an element of free will when considering the cognitive interventions. To change how one thinks is hard work, but the success of cognitive behavioural therapy could suggest that it is possible to choose to change one's thought processes, so maybe we have an element of free will, too? |

## Evaluation

- Free will is practically impossible to test. It is a non-physical phenomenon and as such is difficult to quantify and measure. As psychology is a science, the idea that something without a physical presence can affect behaviour is at odds with the discipline. This means that a resolution of the debate is not currently likely. If, at some point in the future, measurement becomes possible, the scientific discipline of psychology may be able to resolve the debate. Of course, the argument is that free will is not measurable because it does not exist.
- The idea of free will feels intuitively correct and it is this experience that means the debate continues. The subjective experience of most people is that they are in control of their own actions and behaviours. The humanistic approach also acknowledges this feeling and argues that we do have free will.

### STRENGTHEN YOUR LEARNING

1. Explain what is meant by determinism in psychology.
2. Explain what is meant by free will in psychology.
3. What is the difference between hard and soft determinism?
4. Give an example of biological determinism in psychology.
5. Give an example of environmental determinism in psychology.
6. Give an example of psychic determinism in psychology.
7. What does the term 'causal explanations' mean?
8. Why is there an emphasis on scientific causal explanations in psychology?
9. Give an example of a causal explanation in psychological research.

## ASSESSMENT CHECK

1 Which two of the following statements describe a strongly ethnocentric viewpoint? **[2 marks]**

   A There is little use conducting cross-cultural research as no differences will occur

   B Data from Europe can be used to explain British behaviour

   C Behaviour varies vastly from culture to culture

   D Work conducted in the UK may not transfer easily to explaining Australian behaviour

   E Generalisations from data in Europe cannot be used to explain behaviour in Africa

2 Briefly outline what is meant by universality in gender research. **[2 marks]**

3 Briefly outline one problem of the free will viewpoint and one problem with the determinist viewpoint. **[4 marks]**

# 2.3 Nature–nurture debate

*'Genes are rarely about inevitability, especially when it comes to humans, the brain or behaviour. They're about vulnerability, propensities, tendencies.'*

Robert Sapolsky (1993)

This debate asks: 'Does behaviour stem from the genetic make-up of the person or do they learn it through experience?' The extreme nature viewpoint is that our behaviour is dictated by our genetic make-up. The extreme nurture viewpoint is that we learn all our behaviour from conception onwards.

## Nature

**Nativism** is the term used to describe a stance that agrees with the nature side of the debate. It was introduced by René Descartes (1596–1650), who suggested that the human soul, when born, is already equipped with an understanding of certain key concepts such as time.

There was no theory of genetics then, so his ideas were unsubstantiated. However, they did form the basis of the nativist point of view that we are born with predispositions and pre-programmed behaviours. The support for the nativist viewpoint today comes from the field of biology and more specifically genetics. Twin studies also offer some support.

## Nurture

**Empiricism** is the opposing extreme viewpoint to nativism which says that we are born without any innate mechanisms and that all we become is due to our experiences. It is therefore another term for the nurture viewpoint. The British philosopher John Locke argued that we are born a 'tabula rasa', which translates to blank slate. He proposed that it is our experience that leads to the formation of the self, i.e. when the slate is written on.

The learning approaches clearly support an empiricist stance. They argue that behaviour is determined by learned experiences and so the role of the environment is all important.

## The relative importance of heredity and environment in determining behaviour

No genetic cause of behaviour has been found so far. This means that the extreme nature viewpoint is widely seen as too extremist. However, there are genes that are related to behaviours, so the key question for the debate is the extent to which genetics affects behaviour, and also how much experience and learning account for what we do. This is a tricky issue – placing a numerical value on the contribution of nature and nurture is very difficult. This is where the debate currently lies. How much is learning? Are your genetics more important? How can we make that decision?.

### KEY TERMS

**Nativism** – the nature side of the debate

**Empiricism** – the nurture side of the debate

**Heredity** – the term for something being inherited, i.e. within the genes

**Figure 2.5** Does our behaviour stem from our genetics or our upbringing?

## Twin studies

A key way that **heredity** is established is through the use of twin studies. Monozygotic (MZ or identical) twins are 100 per cent identical and so, if behaviour was dictated purely by genetics, they would act the same. However, they do not, and so environment must have an influence.

If we compare how likely a behaviour is to occur with identical twins and non-identical twins (who are 50 per cent genetically similar), the difference in genetic similarity gives us an indication of the extent of the genetic influence (see In the news, below). However, the core assumption of twin studies is that the only difference between monozygotic and dizygotic (non-identical) twins is their genetic similarity level. Furnham (1996) argued that this assumption could be erroneous. As monozygotic twins look the same it is possible that their parents treat them more similarly than dizygotic twins. This would mean that the environment differs between the pairs of twins and therefore any difference in likelihood of a behaviour occurring could be due to the treatment from the parents rather than the genetic similarity.

## The QTL method

**Plomin (1994)** argues that we have been too reductionist when looking for genetic explanations. The OGOD (one gene, one disorder) approach has meant that the level of genetic influence could have been underestimated. If only one gene is sought, and none is found, then the role of genes interacting with each other is missed. The alternative viewpoint of how genetics affects behaviour is called QTL (quantitative trait loci) and this research involves the search for multiple genes. Each one of these genes in isolation cannot affect behaviour, but when combined with others the genetic influence on behaviour is greater. Work in this area has increased the potential effect of genetics and environment. Indeed, it is possible that a direct genetic link to behaviour may be found.

## The heritability equation

Geneticists report to have developed a mathematical way of calculating the relative influence of genetics and environment on behaviour. The equation reports to calculate the contribution that each of the two elements makes to the variance of the behaviour (the differences in a population). The formula for this equation is $V = G + E + (G \times E)$. V is variance, G is genetic influence, E is environmental influence and $G \times E$ is the interaction between the genetics and environment.

For a discussion of this equation see In the news, below.

## IN THE NEWS

### Ψ The Psychological Enquirer

## Genetics outweighs teaching, Gove advisor tells boss

Dominic Cummings, an advisor to Michael Gove, then Education Secretary, wrote a 250-page report to his boss stating, among other points, that an individual child's performance is mainly due to genetic influences rather than teaching. This has important implications for education policy.

He stated: 'There is strong resistance across the political spectrum to accepting scientific evidence on genetics. Most of those that now dominate discussions on issues such as social mobility entirely ignore genetics and therefore their arguments are at best misleading and often worthless.'

He used the heritability equation figure for intelligence researched by Shakeshaft *et al.* (2013) of 64 per cent of genetic influence. This figure has been contested, however. Critics have argued that the figure may be relevant to children in the middle classes, but that it probably stands at less than 10 per cent for children from poor families. It is thought that under-resourced families have a less stable environment and this means that the environment has a greater influence on their achievement.

This is an example of how assessing the relative influence of heritability and environment is fraught with problems. There are many factors to be considered and therefore finding a quantitative figure for any on behaviour or condition is very difficult. Caution should be taken in examining figures that claim to have measured the role of nature or nurture.

### The interactionist approach

The interactionist approach takes a stance somewhere between the extreme nature and extreme nurture positions. It argues that the true answer to the nature–nurture debate is, in reality, that both genetics and the environment play a part in behaviour. It seems likely, this approach argues, that genetics gives us a predisposition to certain behaviours, the potential, if you like, to act a certain way. However, that genetic indication is moderated by the environment. The phenotype is the interaction of genetics and environment.

An excellent example of this is intelligence. The interactionist approach argues that we have a genetic predisposition to attain a certain level of intelligence and that we either reach our potential (if the environment is ideal) or we underperform due to environmental factors such as diet, poor education, brain injury, etc. It is unlikely that many people experience an optimum environment that allows them to extend their intelligence to its full potential.

Table 2.3 shows how topics relate to the nature–nurture debate.

**Table 2.3** The nature–nurture debate in relation to other topics

| Topic and specific example | How it relates to nature/nurture |
|---|---|
| **Relationships**<br>The evolutionary explanations for human reproductive behaviour v. cultural differences | The evolutionary stance is nativist, so any evolutionary theory for mate preference is stating the importance of genetics. To combat this viewpoint, it can be argued that the cultural differences found in attractiveness globally would seem to suggest that mate preference is environmentally determined. |
| **Gender**<br>Chromosone v. gender schema theory | There are both biological and psychological arguments for the origin of gender. These arguments can be viewed as potential examples in the nature–nurture debate. In essence, the nature side will argue that our gender is predetermined at birth by our biology whereas the nurture side of the argument is focused on environmental influences such as social learning theory. |
| **Cognition and development**<br>Piaget v. Vygotsky | Piaget argued that the stages of development a child goes through are innate. This supports the nativist argument. However, he did acknowledge the role of the environment and that the child needed to interact with its surroundings to develop properly. This would make Piaget's viewpoint interactionist. Vygotsky, because of his emphasis on cultural influence, takes a more empiricist stance. |
| **Schizophrenia**<br>Genetics v. family dysfunction | Genetic influences on schizophrenia support the nativists' argument as it supports the view that schizophrenia is part of an individual's genetic make-up. Theories such as family dysfunction theory, however, provide evidence for the nurture viewpoint as they stress the importance of the environment in the development of schizophrenia. |
| **Eating behaviour**<br>Psychological explanations for anorexia nervosa: family systems theory v. biological genetic/psychological explanations for obesity | The genetic argument for anorexia nervosa is a firmly nativist stance whereas the family systems theory is focused on the environment and as such is empiricist. Theories of obesity follow a similar pattern, with the psychological explanations arguing for an environmental influence. |
| **Stress**<br>Stress reaction v. individual perception of stress | There can be little argument that the physiological reaction to stress is an innate mechanism that has conferred us with an evolutionary advantage in a life-threatening situation. As such, as a reaction it is support for the nativist viewpoint. However, the perception of everyday stress can be argued to be empiricist. Whether the stress response is engaged or not is down to individual perception of the situation. In life-threatening situations the reaction is automatic, but in reaction to stressors in the workplace, for example, it is the individual who decides whether it is stressful to them or not. Environmental influence such as social support can mediate the reaction. This means that experience of stress is probably interactionist. |
| **Aggression**<br>Genetic factors in aggression v. social psychological theories of aggression | Genetic influences in aggression such as the MAOA gene provide evidence for the nature side of the debate and any evidence for these factors can be used to argue that aggression is an innate drive. Conversely, the social psychological theories such as SLT and de-individuation argue for the environment being the main determinant of aggressive behaviour. |
| **Forensic psychology**<br>Genetic explanations in offending v. psychological explanations of offending | Genetic explanations for offending behaviour are nativist arguments whereas the psychological theories such as the hostile attribution bias and cognitive distortions all suggest environmental influences.<br>Eysenck's theory, due to its biological basis, and the psychodynamic theory with its innate drives can be argued to be interactionist, as they also acknowledge the role of the environment. |
| **Addiction**<br>Genetic vulnerability v. other risk factors | The idea of a genetic vulnerability for addiction is nativist, but the other risk factors in addictive behaviour, such as stress, personality, family influence and peers, are very much contained in the environment. This seems to suggest an interactionist perspective overall would be appropriate. |

## Attachments

The theories of attachment (see Chapter 3 of Book 1) are an ideal topic to refer to when considering the nature–nurture debate. Bowlby's argument is that forming attachments is an innate drive which is something we are born to do. He argued that this is an adaptive behaviour to help survival in the early years when we need care to survive. However, the learning theory is a purely empiricist stance as the theory refers to conditioning processes that are learned from the environment, with no innate input.

> ### Evaluation
> - The nature–nurture debate in recent times has moved from the argument between the extreme circumstances to the general acknowledgement that an interactionist stance is seen to be appropriate. The argument now is based on the relative influence of nature and nurture.
> - Assessing the relative influence of nature and nurture is fraught with difficulties. Even using twin studies is problematic due to the assumption that the only difference between MZ and DZ twins is their genetic similarity. Parenting styles differ in that MZ twins are treated more similarly than DZ twins. This means the difference in concordance rates could be due to nurture rather than nature.
> - Research on the relative heritability of a characteristic varies greatly. This could be due to many things, such as sample size, methodology and age. Indeed, it may possibly be due to the fact that some people are more susceptible to environmental influence than others. This means that consensus is going to be hard to reach.

### STRENGTHEN YOUR LEARNING

1. Explain what is meant by the term nativism in psychology.
2. Explain what is meant by the term empiricism in psychology.
3. What is the difference between the nature and the nurture stances when related to psychology?
4. Give an example of supporting evidence for the nativist perspective in psychology.
5. Give an example of supporting evidence for the empiricist perspective in psychology.
6. What does heredity mean?
7. How can the relative importance of heredity and environment be assessed?
8. What does the term 'interactionism' mean?
9. What evidence is there to support the interactionist approach in psychology?

# 2.4 Holism and reductionism

The essence of this debate is to do with explaining behaviour at different levels. This will be covered in more detail below. The key focus is which level provides the best explanation of behaviour. It is often read that a theory might be too reductionist, as if looking at a specific root cause at, for example, a biological level is a negative thing. In some behaviour it is, but it can equally be argued that in some circumstances it is more appropriate. This is illustrated in 'In the News', below.

## IN THE NEWS

### Ψ The Psychological Enquirer

### Men with eating disorders are failed because conditions are seen as 'women's illnesses', scientists claim

This article in *The Independent* on 22 August 2014 highlighted both the growing numbers of men suffering from an eating disorder and their reluctance to seek help or recognise that they have the illness. This means that numbers could be greater than currently thought.

The research, conducted by Raisanen & Hunt (2014), comprised of interviews with ten men who suffered from an eating disorder. Two key findings were:

- Men were not as aware of the symptoms of an eating disorder, meaning that they did not realise the severity of their illness.
- Eating disorders are seen to be a 'women's illness' and so families and friends did not pick up on the fact that the men had an eating disorder until it was very serious. This misperception also means a man with an eating disorder is less likely to seek help because of the social stigma associated with what is seen as a women's problem. The article goes on to tell the story that a man who went to see his GP about a suspected eating disorder was told to 'man up'.

This research covers a social reason for why there is an issue with diagnosing men with eating disorders and the amount of help they get initially. It would be inappropriate to look for research for this at any other level. However, the reason as to why the men have an eating disorder is different. This can be looked at from many different levels, ranging from the social pressure to be a certain body type, through the thought processes and low self-esteem to the biological level, with genetics, brain physiology and biochemistry all potentially implicated.

For a detailed look at the causes behind eating disorders see Chapter 7.

The **holism/reductionism** debate has important implications for how psychology could develop. If a reductionist stance on the debate is taken, it will inevitably move to a greater emphasis on biological explanations. If it is rejected, then the theories and research will necessarily consider many different factors at many different levels. Like many things in psychology, the debate will probably continue to rage and a stance somewhere between the two will be navigated.

### KEY TERMS

**Holism** – the argument that behaviour should be viewed as a whole

**Reductionism** – an explanation is reductionist when a single explanation or cause is suggested

## Levels of explanation in psychology

If you look at any one behaviour, there are different levels of explanation you can consider to explain it. Figure 2.6 shows the various levels available to consider a behaviour and the realms that psychology deals with. The holism/reductionism asks whether it is appropriate to look at one level specifically or whether more than one level is appropriate.

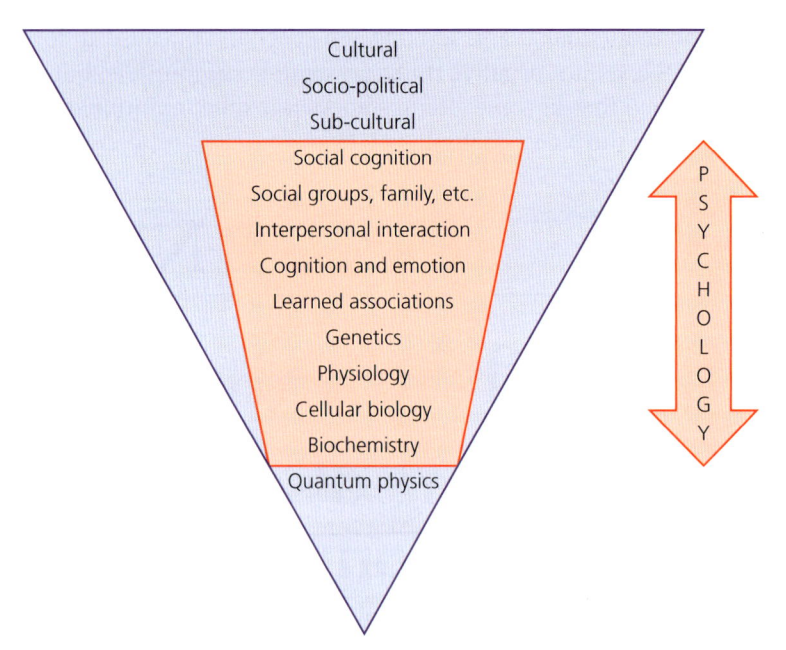

**Figure 2.6** Various levels available to consider a behaviour

The levels of explanation are best illustrated using an example of behaviour: a man physically attacking someone in court who has killed his daughter.

Taking the levels of explanation most often used in the discipline of psychology, the following explanations can be suggested:

- Social cognition: the father may make a dispositional attribution that the attacker is evil and deserves to suffer for what he has done, so he responded with violence.
- Social groups, family, etc.: the father may have witnessed aggressive responses to others as a child, so he responds in a similar way.
- Interpersonal interaction: the father may have received threats from the killer in the past and this prompts him to react aggressively.
- Cognition and emotion: the father reacts with violence because of the extreme emotions of anger and grief.
- Learned associations: the father may have felt that the killer should receive physical punishment for what he has done. Or he may have reacted to an inappropriate comment or action without thinking because he is conditioned to do so.
- Genetics: the father may possess the MAOA or 'warrior' gene.
- Physiology: the father may have brain physiology that means his ability to control himself is diminished, for example frontal lobe damage.
- Cellular biology: the activity in his synapse means that his brain activity with regard to serotonin is affected. Serotonin is implicated in aggression.
- Biochemistry: he may have had alcohol in his bloodstream, which reduced his control and inhibitions.

All these are attempts to explain the behaviour, but at differing levels. Some would have more research evidence to support their suggestion than others, but it should be clear that no one explanation in isolation can be taken as correct, and therefore several explanations at several levels would be more appropriate.

The principle of parsimony suggested by Morgan states that there is no need to explain behaviour in terms of complex processes, and that explanations should be as simple as possible and stay within the evidence in the field of investigation (see Morgan, C.L. (1903) *An Introduction to Comparative Psychology*, 2nd edition, London: W. Scott, p. 59). These are the explanations that may be regarded as reductionist. There are several ways in which reductionism can occur.

## Biological reductionism

Biological reductionism is explaining behaviour using biological systems. This could be genetics, physiology of the body and brain, or biochemistry. It is called biological reductionism because in terms of the levels of explanation, it is as reductionist as psychology goes. If you refer to Figure 2.6 you will see that the four most reductionist levels used by psychology are biological levels.

The final four explanations for the behaviour of the father attacking his daughter's killer, when taken in isolation, would be argued to be biologically reductionist. This is because they do not take into account the higher levels of explanation such as learned associations and the influence of other people.

An advantage of biological reductionism is that it is a more precise and simple explanation, which is a great deal more scientific than the ones at the higher and more general levels of explanation. An explanation that is biologically reductionist can also be tested more easily and more effectively. A desirable consequence is also that it can be used to generate an appropriate treatment, if the condition requires one.

There are issues with being too simplistic, however, and this means that biological explanations are sometimes viewed as incomplete.

## Environmental (stimulus–response) reductionism

Environmental reductionism can be seen in Figure 2.6 as 'learned associations'. This is seen as reductionist because it simplifies a behaviour to a stimulus–response action. This level of explanation is advocated by behaviourist theorists. Classical conditioning is one such example. Essentially a phobia of snakes, for example, can be explained as learned through an experience such as a bite from a snake, where fear and pain are associated with the snake. When the individual then sees a snake after that experience they will avoid it as they experience a strong fearful reaction.

It is evident that this level of explanation can explain many behaviours really well, but there are some for which this is too simple. An example of this would be explaining why someone might kill, as illustrated above. The explanation for this may incorporate many different levels, with a learned association being only one of them.

The simplicity of explanations based on stimulus–response reactions means that it is easier to test the explanation. It also has the advantage of parsimony, which means that by being simple it is argued to be more effective than a complex explanation for the same behaviour. However, as with biological reductionism, the simplicity of the explanations is seen as a flaw and the explanations are inadequate for describing the complexities of human behaviour.

## Holism

Holism advocates looking at the whole person rather than at one specific part to explain behaviour. People who agree with holism as a stance feel that looking at a person at a reductionist level is inadequate. They do not deny the potential influence of genetics or biochemistry but feel that human behaviour is far more complex and that as a consequence it is necessary to take a step back from the detail and consider the person from a less reductionist level. The social context they are in is very important, as are their family and friends in terms of influence. For this reason they are drawn to the higher levels of explanation such as social groups and social cognition.

As a consequence holism is seen as less scientific and it makes behaviour hard to predict, unlike the reductionist explanations. It does have its advantages in that it does not ignore the complexity of human behaviour.

**Figure 2.7** Holism advocates looking at the whole person rather than at one specific part to explain behaviour

## An interactionist perspective

The interactionist stance on the debate believes that several levels of explanation are necessary to explain behaviour ranging from the more reductionist to the more holistic. Interactionists argue that the explanations all have relevance and that, ultimately, it is difficult to establish the explanation with the best explanatory power and that this varies from situation to situation anyway. Table 2.4 shows holism and reductionism in relation to other topics.

**Table 2.4** Holism and reductionism in relation to other topics

| Topic | How it relates to holism/reductionism debate |
| --- | --- |
| **Relationships** | The evolutionary explanation for partner preferences is biologically reductionist because it implies there is some genetic transmission of that behaviour. This therefore argues that why someone chooses a partner is due to their biological make-up. The theories of relationship maintenance and attraction look to an interaction between two people and this is more holistic. |
| **Gender** Chromosomes and hormones v. social stereotypes | Gender provides an interesting contrast as a topic, with some explanations being very reductionist and others being holistic. The chromosomal explanation for gender, which argues that gender-typical behaviour is rooted in biology, contrasts with the gender schema and social learning theory, both of which are more holistic. These attribute gender-typical behaviour to observation of others in the environment. |
| **Cognition and development** | Vygotsky's work considers the role of the tutor in acquiring information and developing thinking, so this is quite holistic. Indeed, most of the content of this section is interactionist, such as Piaget's idea that cognition develops from innate mechanisms and discovery within an environment. It seems there could be several levels of explanation required to explain the development of thinking. The role of the mirror neuron system is probably the most reductionist explanation in the topic, arguing that there is a neural explanation for cognition. |
| **Schizophrenia** Family dysfunction v. genetics | Family dysfunction as an explanation for schizophrenia is a more holistic explanation. It considers the effect of how the family interacts on developing schizophrenia. In contrast, the genetic explanation adopts a biologically reductionist stance and in contrast to family dysfunction theory, argues that the causes of schizophrenia are at the biological level. |
| **Eating behaviour** Genetics v. family systems | The genetic explanation for anorexia is biologically reductionist. It states that the eating disorder has its origins in the genetic make-up of the individual. In contrast, family systems theory considers the home environment and interactions and can therefore be argued to be more holistic as it adopts a higher level of explanation. Contrasting these two is a good example for the debate. |

| **Stress**<br>Cortisol v. workplace stress | Stress as a topic has content that varies greatly in how reductionist it is. The role of cortisol in stress is reductionist in that it argues a biochemical reason behind a stressful experience, whereas in contrast, the explanations of stressors such as life changes and daily hassles take a more holistic stance, considering the context that the individual is in. |
|---|---|
| **Aggression**<br>Genetics v. de-individuation | As with all genetic explanations the genetic argument for the origins of aggression is a good example of biological reductionism. The idea that the MAOA gene can affect aggression is simple and focused at the chromosomal level. However, its expression seems dependent on circumstances in the environment, so perhaps this illustrates the need for consideration of other levels, which is interactionist. The theory of de-individuation considers the influence of the presence of others on the individual's propensity to be aggressive and is therefore more holistic. |
| **Forensic psychology**<br>Genetics v. differential association therapy | The genetics explanation for offender behaviour is clearly biologically reductionist as it argues that criminal behaviour is due to an individual's genetic make-up. This explanation contrasts greatly in terms of reductionism with differential association theory. This alternative explanation focuses on the higher, more holistic explanations for behaviour which concentrates on the groups of people with whom an individual interacts and their social norms. These therefore contrast with each other and would make an excellent example for the reductionism/holism debate. |
| **Addiction**<br>Risk factors for addiction | The risk factors for addiction vary in how reductionist they are. Genetics as a risk factor is a reductionist explanation as it suggests that someone is likely to become addicted to a substance due to their genetic make-up. In contrast, the other risk factors of family influences and peers are more holistic as they consider the context around the individual and how that might influence their behaviour. |

The learning approach, especially behaviourism, has plenty of examples of environmental reductionism as you can use the principles of classical and operant conditioning to illustrate what the term means. See pages 206–216 in Book 1.

## Evaluation

- Biological reductionism can help facilitate development of a biological therapy such as drugs. These do help people suffering from mental health problems. It can also be argued that the development of drug therapy means that a sufferer has access to something which helps them feel better able to tackle the other potential factors through therapies such as psychotherapy or cognitive therapy.
- It is acknowledged by many psychologists that the likelihood that a behaviour has a purely biological route is low. The complexity involved in every behaviour means that a purely reductionist explanation is rarely accepted as sufficient.
- Reductionist explanations mean that an explanation can be tested as there are fewer factors to consider. This means that empirical work can be conducted on an explanation and this gives it academic weight.
- A reductionist explanation may mean that other explanations are ignored and underplayed. In the case of mental illness this could lead to a reoccurrence of the issue as all the factors have not been considered.

## STRENGTHEN YOUR LEARNING

1. Explain what is meant by the term holism in psychology.
2. Explain what is meant by the term reductionism in psychology.
3. What is meant by the term 'levels of explanation' in psychology?
4. Give an example of research or theory of holism in psychology.
5. Give an example of research or theory of reductionism in psychology.
6. What does the term 'biological reductionism' mean?
7. What does the term 'environmental (stimulus–response) reductionism' mean?

# ASSESSMENT CHECK

1. Which two of the following statements describe a strongly nurture viewpoint? **[2 marks]**

    A Behaviour is driven by genetics

    B Behaviour is not affected by family influences

    C Behaviour is affected by peer influences

    D Behaviour is an interaction between the biology of the individual and their environment

    E Behaviour is a product of the individual's environment

2. Briefly outline what is meant by biological reductionism. **[2 marks]**

3. Briefly outline one problem of the nature viewpoint and one problem with the nurture viewpoint. **[4 marks]**

# 2.5 Idiographic and nomothetic approaches to psychological investigation

*'Today you are You, that is truer than true.
There is no one alive who is Youer than You.'*

Ted Geisel (Dr Seuss) (1959)

This debate considers whether **idiographic** or **nomothetic** approaches to research in psychology are appropriate. This ultimately asks the question: 'Is it more important to look at the individual as unique or should you consider them as part of a group and try to establish similarities for that group?'

First it is necessary to consider the terms themselves.

## Idiographic

An idiographic approach to research considers the individual. The word is derived from the Ancient Greek word 'idios', which means one's own or belonging to one's self. This shows, quite clearly, that the emphasis is on the self and on the uniqueness of the individual.

This viewpoint does not seek to generalise to others from research. Indeed, strong supporters of the idiographic stance would be unlikely to conduct large-scale studies or indeed use quantitative methods at all. They believe that an individual is unique and that they should be considered as such. It is therefore irrelevant to try to develop universal laws of behaviour.

Case studies are an illustration of an idiographic approach to research. They document the unique perspective of a person who has in some way illustrated a key behaviour or difference which can be used to help evaluate any theories in the field. Case studies are often criticised for their lack of applicability to the general population because of their uniqueness, but they are useful as a test for a theory. They cannot add much weight to support a theory, but they can show any flaws. It takes only one case study to potentially argue that a theory is wrong as a theory should be able to accommodate all individuals.

The idiographic stance also favours qualitative methods of investigation such as interviews. It traditionally opts to use methods that allow for opinion, attitude and self-reflection, such as self-report measures and qualitative sources like diaries, journals and letters.

## Nomothetic

The word nomothetic is derived from the Greek term 'nomos', which can be translated as 'law'. This approach to looking at behaviour is the opposite to idiographic, as it states we are able to draw conclusions about populations of people and generalise to a wider group than the ones directly involved in research. The nomothetic stance seeks to establish general laws about behaviour that can be applied across any given population.

It is proposed that there are three types of general laws (Radford & Kirby, 1975). These are classification, establishing principles and establishing dimensions and are detailed below.

> **KEY TERMS**
>
> **Idiographic** – when an explanation considers the individual and argues that generalising from person to person is difficult because of their uniqueness
>
> **Nomothetic** – the idea that people can be regarded as groups and theories/explanations are therefore generalisable

## Classification

This is the idea that people can be classified into certain groups according to characteristics, attitudes or behaviour. It is also the foundation on which the diagnostic manuals for mental health are based. ICD10 and DSM-5 both attempt to diagnose people with a mental health disorder by the symptoms they present. This is an attempt at classification.

## Establishing principles

This is the focus on trying to establish laws and principles that can be applied to human behaviour. Behaviourism features highly and Thorndike is known for his proposed law of effect, which is the principle that underpins operant conditioning. Theories generated under this principle are often weakened by evidence from case studies as a law requires application to all and it takes only one person to whom it does not apply to negate it.

## Establishing dimensions

This is the attempt to document continuums upon which an individual can be placed. This allows comparison with others and also facilitates scientific measurement. This focus on establishing dimensions is widely used in personality research where the trait theories state we have a level of a certain trait (for example extraversion) and it is variation in the levels of those traits that influences behaviour.

The nomothetic stance means that quantitative methods of data collection and analysis are seen to be appropriate. It is also the stance taken by natural sciences. Favoured research methods are those that are more objective, such as measurement of biochemicals. The preferred choice for psychologists who adopt a more nomothetic stance is the use of laboratory conditions where variables can be carefully controlled.

The approaches are mostly nomothetic as they seek to apply research across large numbers of people. However, the humanistic approach celebrates the uniqueness of each person and for that reason is seen to be idiographic. For a comparison of the approaches with regard to this debate, see page 22.

### PSYCHOLOGY IN THE REAL WORLD

#### 'Welfare claimants to get attitude tests, employment minister reveals'

The UK government is to pilot the use of psychometric personality and attitude tests on the unemployed in three regions of the country. The idea is that the tests will highlight personality traits and attitudes that might affect whether someone actively seeks employment.

Psychometric tests are based on the idea that we all share common ground in our personalities and attitudes. By administering a test the argument is that unemployed people can be identified as needing intervention if they do not demonstrate the appropriate attitude as a job seeker. Characteristics mentioned as being of particular interest were optimism, self-confidence, self-esteem and eagerness as they would indicate that the person was more likely to have good job-seeking prospects. However, those who demonstrate despondency and apprehension would be highlighted as needing extra input to raise their job-seeking prospects.

*This is a nomothetic approach to intervention, using a measure that generalises across the population. There is an argument that a more idiographic approach should be used as the circumstances faced by each individual are personal and unique, and therefore intervention should be bespoke. This, of course, makes it more costly.*

# Research questions

The research question asked by a researcher and the methodology used are dependent on their viewpoint on this debate. Indeed, this issue underpins much of research practice. Broadly speaking, quantitative methods are seen as nomothetic and qualitative methods are idiographic. This distinction is not clear cut, but while looking at research it is often found to be this way. An example of how the differing viewpoints affect how behaviour is seen is reflected in personality research.

Trait theories of personalities are the attempt to define personality in terms of individual traits. A current theory is the 'Big 5 personality traits'. These describe personality as five particular dimensions: openness, conscientiousness, extroversion, agreeableness and neuroticism. Table 2.5 illustrates possible sources of evidence for the idiographic/nomothetic debate within the A2 topics.

**Table 2.5** Idiographic and nomothetic approaches to psychological investigation in relation to other topics

| Topic | How it relates to idiographic/nomothetic debate |
|---|---|
| **Relationships** All theories v. individual preference | The theories of relationship formation, maintenance and breakdown all take a nomothetic stance. They generalise across people and there is no personalisation. A good example of a nomothetic approach is Duck's phase model of relationship breakdown. |
| **Gender** Psychodynamic v. theories | Gender theories are nomothetic. This includes the psychodynamic theory of gender development. Although work from this approach often has an idiographic stance, the theory of gender development is divided into male and female development and states the stages of the Oedipus and Electra complexes occur in all boys and girls. It therefore comprises aspects of both the nomothetic and idiographic approaches. |
| **Cognition and development** Theorist stages | Cognition and development is comprised of nomothetic research. The primary aim of the developmental psychologists such as Piaget, Vygotsky and Selman was to look for stages that could be generalised across all children. However, the children that do not follow the developmental stages are an argument that an idiographic stance should be adopted. Any research that does not show the stages to be consistent in terms of age or development is an argument that a less nomothetic approach may be more appropriate. |
| **Schizophrenia** Dysfunctional thought processing and biological explanations Drug therapy v. CBT | An area of this topic that lends itself to commentary on this debate is the treatment for schizophrenia. Drug therapies are developed from nomothetic research, which sees the cause of schizophrenia as rooted in the biology of those suffering with it. The biological cause is thought to be the same in all schizophrenics and therefore a drug treatment that addresses biochemical imbalance is appropriate. However, the cognitive behavioural therapy approach to treating schizophrenia is more idiographic and requires a therapist to listen to the patient's individual viewpoint. A comparison of effectiveness of these therapies can help you argue for which approach is the most successful and appropriate. |
| **Eating behaviour** Theories on anorexia – is there an idiographic approach? Distortions and irrational beliefs | The majority of this topic covers nomothetic theory, and the explanations for anorexia are no exception. This refers to both the biological and psychological explanations, although it can be argued that the biological explanations are purely nomothetic whereas the psychological ones, particularly the cognitive ones, are slightly more idiographic. There will be some variation within the mediating cognitive processes in social learning theory and the distortion and irrational beliefs in the cognitive explanation for each case of anorexia diagnosed. These small variations will be dependent on learned experience and therefore have an element of individuality. This makes them less nomothetic than the biological theories. |
| **Stress** Personality types | The physiological reaction to stress is clearly nomothetic as it applies to most humans. This is also the case with the personality types. Stress research is predominantly nomothetic, but where there is some application to this debate is the individual difference in perception of whether a situation is seen as stressful or not. There are factors such as how well supported the person feels (i.e. social support) that affect their reaction. This gives a slightly idiographic angle to the topic. |

| | |
|---|---|
| **Aggression**<br>Media influences | All the neural, hormonal, genetic, ethological and evolutionary work on aggression has a nomothetic stance. This is also true for the psychological explanations. However, research into the effects of computer games on aggression levels is far from conclusive, so it could be argued that individuals react differently. It may be that a more idiographic viewpoint should be taken. This is the case for much of the media influence research. |
| **Forensic psychology**<br>Eysenck v. cognitive distortions | As with many of the topics, forensic psychology is dominated by nomothetic research. The reasons behind offending behaviour, with perhaps the exception of cognitive distortions, are heavily nomothetic as they seek to explain why offenders do what they do and generalise across all offenders with those explanations. It is when considering the treatment of offenders that a more idiographic stance is adopted. Behaviour modification remains firmly nomothetic as it is applying the principles of behaviourism, but anger management is required to look at the individual circumstance of the offender and his or her thought processes, which is more idiographic. Restorative justice programmes consider the unique combination of offender and victim and therefore are more idiographic. |
| **Addiction**<br>Drug therapy v. CBT | The treatment of addiction can be applied to this debate. Drug therapies are clearly nomothetic as they generalise a biochemical root to the addiction. The application of behaviourist principles to all in aversion therapies and other behavioural interventions is also nomothetic. However, cognitive behavioural therapy, although a generalised process, requires the individual thought processes of the addict to be listened to and moderated, which is an idiographic approach. |

The approaches (Chapter 1, pages 2–26) in the first year can be used as examples of the nomothetic approach, as can the commentary on memory. The attachment styles found in Ainsworth's (1970) strange situation research are also very nomothetic.

## Humanistic approach

This approach adopts an idiographic stance and actively rejects any attempts to generalise across all humans. It does not adhere to the scientific principles that much of psychology advocates. However, it would be difficult to write about the idiographic–nomothetic debate without making reference to it.

## Ethical implications of research studies and theory

An important issue within research is not the findings themselves but what should be done with the knowledge gained from that research. For example, an attention-grabbing headline can reach many people, and without considering the findings carefully people can overreact. It is necessary for the researcher to consider not just the ethics of the process but also the wide-reaching effects their research could have.

### Evaluation

- The majority of psychology operates on a nomothetic basis as this means that patterns can be ascertained, which in turn means that interventions can reach many people – in the case of mental health, that many people can be assisted. An idiographic intervention is time consuming and therefore it is difficult for it to be widespread.
- Conversely, a nomothetic stance means that theories are often not an exact fit and adopt a one-size-fits-all approach. This inevitably makes them inappropriate for some. This argument, too, can be applied to interventions and means that people are forced to use interventions that may have only moderate success for them.
- An idiographic stance, such as a case study, is often the seed that prompts an idea for further research. It is looking at behaviour or a phenomenon in detail from an idiographic, in-depth perspective that leads to research ideas. Inevitably, though, a nomothetic stance will be adopted at some point.

> **STRENGTHEN YOUR LEARNING**
> 1. Explain what is meant by the term 'idiographic approach' in psychology.
> 2. Explain what is meant by the term 'nomothetic approach' in psychology.
> 3. Give an example of research or theory with an idiographic approach in psychology.
> 4. Give an example of research or theory with a nomothetic approach in psychology.

# 2.6 Ethical implications of research studies and theory

## IN THE NEWS

### Ψ The Psychological Enquirer

## How I discovered I have the brain of a psychopath

James Fallon is a neuroscientist and has produced work demonstrating that an unusual pattern of low brain function in an area of the frontal lobes commonly associated with empathy and self-control is found in the brain of psychopaths. Psychopaths are not all killers, which is a common misconception, but included among psychopathic traits there is a lack of empathy, manipulation of others and self-orientation.

This work has far-reaching implications. It suggests that by scanning somebody's brain, a diagnosis of psychopathy could be made. This also then provides information that could be used to segregate and persecute those who have that brain activity pattern. This is very socially sensitive research.

The research was highlighted because of an unexpected finding Fallon reported. He states:

'At the same time I'd been studying the murderer's scans, my lab had been conducting a separate study exploring which genes, if any, are linked to Alzheimer's patients as well as several members of my family, who were serving as the normal control group.

'On this same October day, I sat down to analyse my family's scans and noticed that the last scan in the pile was strikingly odd. In fact, it looked exactly like the most abnormal of the scans I had just been writing about, suggesting that the poor individual it belonged to was a psychopath – or at least shared an uncomfortable amount of traits with one. Not suspicious of any of my family members, I naturally assumed that their scans had somehow been mixed with the other pile on the table. I generally have a lot of research going on at one time, and even though I try to keep my work organised, it was entirely possible for things to get misplaced. Unfortunately, since we were trying to keep the scans anonymous, we'd coded them to hide the names of the individuals they belonged to. To be sure I hadn't made a mistake, I asked our lab technician to break the blind code.

'When I found out who the scan belonged to, I had to believe there was a mistake. In a fit of pique, I asked the technician to check the scanner and all the notes from the other imaging and database technicians. But there was no mistake. The scan was mine.'

This highlights yet another issue with socially sensitive research, the idea that the researcher themselves, or those close to them, are in some way affected by the research. What would have happened had James Fallon discovered that the brain scan belonged to his wife, or one of his children?

Consideration of the ethical implications of research and theory is part of the research process. If there is no thought given to how the research process or results could affect those involved in the research process or society in general, the effects can be wide reaching, in a detrimental sense. The degree of social sensitivity of research must be an important part of planning what will be examined.

# Social sensitivity

Social sensitivity refers to any psychological research that has wider ethical implications that impact outside of the research context. The research might affect people or groups in society.

These people/groups could be any of the following:

- The participants in the research. Their friends and families could also be affected as a consequence (see In the news: How I discovered I have the brain of a psychopath).
- The researcher(s) may also be affected. This could also mean that there is an effect in the institution for which they did the work.
- Groups potentially impacted by socially sensitive research include sub-cultures and sub-groups such as those with certain religious and political beliefs, ethnic minorities or groups with a particular sexual preference.

Consideration of the wider implications of research is an imperative and sometimes the potential effects are not considered.

There are three studies included in Table 2.6 which have socially sensitive content. The research and findings will be outlined and the effects explored (you may think of more).

**Figure 2.8** It is important for psychologists to consider the ethical implications of their research, as it can have far-reaching social consequences

**Table 2.6** Socially sensitive research studies

| Name | Details | Potential effects |
|---|---|---|
| **Lowney (1995)** | Participant observations of a group of teenage Satanists in the USA. Lowney recorded their views on life, and their activities, which mainly consisted of a small amount of underage drinking, drug taking and listening to music. She interpreted her findings and suggested that they had become Satanists as they did not agree with the peer groups within their high school and other schools in America. | This research could have made life difficult for the participants following publication, in three ways: <br>• Parental backlash over the behaviour of the young people involved in the study. <br>• Condemnation from the community. <br>• Peer exclusion as the research was directly critical of high school social groups. |
| **Humphreys (1970)** | Research into the social interactions and practices of homosexuals meeting in a public toilet for sex. Humphreys, a heterosexual, acted as a gay man and talked to his participants. He took their car number plates to check their backgrounds and used a contact he had in the police force to find out their addresses. His analysis of his findings suggested that gay stereotypes were false. | The time of the research should be considered for this research. Homosexuality was not widely accepted. There were implications for ethics due to the breach of privacy. The police were informed of the participant identity (via the number plates). There was a large amount of deception and although the research outcome was positive for the gay community, the research was invasive and sensationalised. |
| **Raine (1996)** | This research used brain scans of violent criminals to examine their level of impulse control. Raine found that there was damage in most of the brains, focused around the frontal lobe, which specialises in impulse control. Raine stated that these findings provided a method of identification of people with a predisposition to violent criminal behaviour. He suggested that children could be scanned to help find the potential violent criminals of the future. | The wide-reaching implications of this study are clear. The suggestion that children should have brain scans is problematic. What would then happen if a child was identified as having this pattern of brain activity? What does the child, their parents and society then do with that knowledge? |

Brehm (1992) wrote a great deal about how some topics could not be studied due to their potentially sensitive nature and if they have the potential to cause issues with their participants. The example he gave was 'jealousy between partners participating in laboratory research'. Any experimental design investigating this has the potential to lead to problems within a relationship and this could cause psychological harm to the individuals involved.

The research process will alter the original intentions of the researcher when he or she considers their work. They first have to decide what they want to know and then they should consider what is doable. This will inevitably affect their aim. Finally, even if a piece of research is logistically possible, the wide-reaching ethical implications need to be considered. If the research has the potential to affect themselves, their family and friends, their participants or society in general, then the research should not be conducted, in theory. However, it is important that the potential benefits of research should also be considered. Psychologists argue that some research should be done even if there *is* the potential for harm.

An example of this is some of the work conducted in the 1960s on bystander behaviour. This work was developed following the horrific murder of a young American woman called Kitty Genovese, who was killed in front of more than 30 witnesses. None of the witnesses called for help and Kitty died. The media at the time asked why this might happen in an apparently civilised society and this led to research (Latané & Darley, 1968a, 1968b) to investigate how or why this could have occurred.

The research involved creating mock scenarios where help was required and participants taking part in the research were observed, to try to establish why people do not always act when needed. The scenarios such as filling a room with smoke and hearing someone having an epileptic seizure, although not real, caused distress in participants. This research contravenes current ethical guidelines. However, it was felt at the time that the knowledge that could potentially be gained from the experiment outweighed any cost to participants. Interestingly, participants were asked whether they felt the research was justified and whether they would take part in such research again and they all replied in the affirmative.

Work such as Milgram's electric shock study on obedience has caused controversy over the years for ethical reasons. Justification for conducting a study that deceives and causes harm is problematic, but the argument of the benefits to knowledge it could confer is considered to outweigh the disadvantages. There is some research that necessarily requires deception to work, and Milgram is a prime example of this.

Research is now conducted under strict ethical guidelines by ethics committees within an institution. It is their job to decide who might be affected by the research and how much they may be affected. This is always the main focus of their decision and they try to minimise risk by asking for modifications of the design. However, they inevitably have to decide, if there is potentially any ethical risk, whether the knowledge gained from the research outweighs the risk involved. Table 2.7 outlines ethical implications of research studies.

**Table 2.7** Ethical implications of research studies in relation to other topics

| Topic | How it relates to ethical implications in research |
|---|---|
| **Relationships**<br>The evolutionary explanations for human reproductive behaviour | Relationships as a topic have the potential for research that could affect participants negatively. As outlined by Brehm (1992), research that looks at potential problems in a relationship can be divisive and cause relationship breakdown. Consideration of the costs of the research against the benefits would make excellent commentary. |
| **Gender** | The effect of research into gender identity disorder is potentially socially sensitive as individuals with the disorder are already vulnerable because of the stigma they sometimes face within society. The findings of research could make that stigma worse. |
| **Cognition and development**<br>Mirror neuron system | The work on theory of the mind has obvious implications for people diagnosed with autism and their families. There has been research that has implicated parenting style in the development of autism, but this has been refuted. |
| **Schizophrenia**<br>Reliability and validity of diagnosis | Any research on psychopathology is potentially socially sensitive. It could affect the individual with schizophrenia, the family and society generally. If there is a misdiagnosis there may be issues with safety for the sufferer themselves or others. |
| **Eating behaviour**<br>Psychological explanations for anorexia nervosa: family systems theory<br>Genetic/Psychological explanations for obesity | Research into family systems theory for the origin of anorexia nervosa has obvious implications for the family of the sufferer. Blame for the cause may be directed at family members, so could, for example, upset parents. It could also fall on the individual with the condition, which could exacerbate the issue. |
| **Stress**<br>Gender differences in coping with stress | The argument that women and men react differently to stress can be said to be an example of alpha bias. Is it really to be believed that women are not geared to fight or flight but instead a tend-or-befriend reaction? |
| **Genetic factors in aggression** | The work on the MAOA gene and its connection to aggression has the potential to be socially sensitive for the individual and society in general. The deterministic nature of genetics means that an individual could not be seen as culpable in a criminal act. The legal implications are also socially sensitive as violent crimes could not lead to convictions. There is the prospect of genetic engineering to avoid the gene being transmitted to the next generation. |
| **Forensic psychology**<br>Genetic explanations in offending | The genetic explanations for offender behaviour are socially sensitive. They have implications for both the individual and society. This is for the same reasons as the genetic explanations for aggression (see above in the table under 'Genetic factors in aggression'). |
| **Addiction**<br>Aversion therapy | Treatment for addiction has ethical implications. Aversion therapy can induce short-term harm, and the way that it takes control away from the individual can be seen as ethically unsound. The implication is that addicts are not capable of taking ownership of their own recovery.<br>The genetic vulnerability research also has sensitivity for the reasons highlighted in the forensic psychology and aggression sections of this table. |

The social influence research of Milgram is potentially socially sensitive because of how it could be used to ensure orders are obeyed (see Chapter 1 in Book 1). Genetic and neural explanations of obsessive–compulsive disorder (OCD) are also potentially socially sensitive due to their deterministic nature. The potential for genetic engineering foetuses in the future so that babies are not born with a predisposition to OCD is an implication of research which needs careful consideration and management (see Chapter 4 in Book 1).

## Evaluation

- The code of ethics governed by the British Psychological Society together with university ethics boards means that ethical implications of research have to be considered if research is to be conducted. Stringent guidelines are in place to protect all people who may be involved in the process. The guidelines have become more careful as time has passed so the chances of research causing problems have been reduced.

- Sometimes it is not possible to see what the effects of research might be on the researcher, the participants and society. This makes it hard to judge. It is also not an objective decision, so there is potential for bias from within the decision makers. This means that socially sensitive research still causes problems from time to time.

- The ethical guidelines set for research permission are seen by some to be too strict. There are areas of research which could elicit helpful findings that could benefit a lot of people. However, the research cannot be conducted due to the research process potentially causing issues for the participants or the researcher. Reaching a balance is therefore problematic.

### STRENGTHEN YOUR LEARNING

1 Explain what is meant by the statement 'ethical implications of research'.
2 Explain what is meant by the term 'social sensitivity' in psychology.
3 Give an example of research that is socially sensitive in psychology.
4 Give an example of a theory that is socially sensitive in psychology.

### ON THE WEB

In the UK the British Psychological Society is responsible for governing the ethics of psychological research. They set the guidelines and collaborate with research institutions to ensure the ethics are adhered to. A full version of the Code of Human Research Ethics set out by the society is available here:

**www.bps.org.uk/sites/default/files/documents/code_of_human_research_ethics.pdf**

## ASSESSMENT CHECK

1. Which two of the following statements describe a strongly idiographic viewpoint? **[2 marks]**

   A Theories are useful for explaining the behaviour of specific groups of people

   B Everyone is unique and should be researched as such

   C There are some universal laws of behaviour that apply to all humans

   D Qualitative research is useful in finding out what someone really feels

   E Quantitative research is useful because it can ascertain statistical differences between two groups of people

2. Briefly outline what is meant by social sensitivity in research. **[2 marks]**

3. Briefly outline one problem of the idiographic approach to research and one problem with the nomothetic approach to research. **[4 marks]**

**SUMMARY**

### Gender and culture in psychology

- Universality of gender assumes that all research applies equally to both genders.
- Gender bias can occur in three ways: all-male samples, male behaviour seen as standard and an overemphasis of the biological differences.
- Androcentrism is the belief that male behaviour is the norm or the default and that female behaviour is seen as the non-typical version of behaviour.
- Alpha bias is the overestimation of differences between the behaviour of males and females and beta bias is the downplaying of differences that are found in research.
- Universality in culture is the idea that all behaviours apply equally across the world. Ethnocentrism is the assumption that the behaviour of one ethnic group is the norm. Cultural relativism is the idea that how behaviour can differ cross-culturally is considered within research.

### Free will and determinism

- The free will and determinism debate is a consideration about how much control and choice we have in our behaviour.
- Hard and soft determinism differ in that hard determinism means we have no level of control whereas soft determinism states we have the opportunity to exercise free will if need be.
- Biological determinism is the idea that behaviour is dictated by our biology. Environmental determinism states that our behaviour is elicited by our environment. Psychic determinism suggests that behaviour is determined by unconscious thought processes.
- The focus of scientific proof has led to an upsurge in determinist theories as determinism is thought to be underpinned by causation.

### The nature–nurture debate

- The extreme nature side of the nature–nurture debate asserts that behaviour is genetically pre-programmed, whereas the extreme nurture view believes that we are the end result of our environmental influences.
- The relative importance of heredity and environment can be ascertained, to some extent, through twin studies or the QTL (quantitative trait loci) method.
- The interactionist approach suggests the idea that both genetics and the environment influence behaviour and that neither extreme point of view is valid.

### Holism and reductionism

- Holism is the idea that to explain behaviour it is necessary to look at many levels of explanation at once whereas reductionism focuses on one level of explanation.
- Biological reductionism looks to biological systems to explain behaviour, and environmental reductionism focuses on conditioned stimulus response explanations to account for behaviour.

### Idiographic and nomothetic approaches

- Idiographic explanations consider the individual to be unique and so there is no point in trying to theorise across groups. Conversely, nomothetic explanations try to establish theories and laws that can be used to generalise.

### Ethical implications

- When research is conducted it is vital that the ethical implications are considered. Socially sensitive research can adversely affect the researcher, their family, the participants or wider society. It is essential that careful consideration is given to the research at every stage of the process.

# 3 Relationships

## Introduction

Romantic partnerships and friendships are our main types of relationships, though any situation involving interaction between individuals can be considered a form of relationship, as with colleagues at work or team mates in a sports group. The main psychological focus is upon how relationships are formed, maintained and break down.

Specific focus here will be upon:

1. The evolutionary explanation for partner preference
2. Factors affecting attraction in romantic relationships
3. Theories of romantic relationships
4. Virtual relationships in social media
5. Parasocial (one-sided) relationships.

### Understanding the specification

- The specification requires a knowledge of the evolutionary explanation for partner preferences that includes the relationship between sexual selection and human reproductive behaviour.
- Factors affecting attraction in romantic relationships should include self-disclosure, physical attractiveness (including the matching hypothesis), the filter theory (including social demography) and similarity in attitudes and complementarity.
- Theories of romantic relations must include social exchange theory, equity theory and Rusbult's investment model, along with Duck's phase model of relationship breakdown, as these are specifically named.
- When studying virtual relationships in social media, students need to include self-disclosure in virtual relationships and the effects of absence of gating on the nature of virtual relationships, as again these are specifically listed.
- The study of parasocial relationships needs to focus on three areas: levels of parasocial relationships, the absorption–addiction model and the attachment theory explanation, as these are explicitly listed.

These are the basic requirements of the specification. However, other relevant material is included to provide depth and detail to your understanding.

# IN THE NEWS

# Ψ The Psychological Enquirer

**Figure 3.1** Eternally in love: married for 72 years, Gordon and Norma died within one hour of each other

Gordon Yeager's girlfriend Norma, aged 18, graduated from high school in State Center Iowa, USA, at 10 a.m. on 26 May 1939. At 10 p.m. that night the couple got married. Always together, they went on to have a very full life working as partners in several businesses, socialising and travelling the world. At home they sat side by side in two adjoining chairs, Gordon the outgoing 'hyper' one, who could be seen in his nineties working on the roof of his house, Norma, the supporting, quieter one.

They were married for 72 years until a car accident left them in the intensive care unit of the local hospital, though all the time their concerns were only for each other's injuries.

When it was realised that they would not recover, their beds were moved together so they could hold hands. Gordon stopped breathing and died at 3.38 p.m. on 19 October 2011. But the surprise came when his relatives realised his heart monitor was still functioning. The nurse explained that Gordon was picking up Norma's heartbeat through her hand. Their son Dennis exclaimed, 'Oh my gosh, Mom's heart is beating through him.' Norma died exactly one hour later, at 4.38 p.m. The couple were put in a coffin together holding hands, cremated and their ashes were buried together.

Most people would agree that Gordon and Norma married for love and enjoyed a love that lasted, but there are many factors involved in why people are attracted and form relationships with each other, whether it be for evolutionary, social exchange, equity or financial purposes. Years ago it was not uncommon for people to have penpals they never met, while now people form similar virtual relationships through the internet, with some individuals even forming parasocial (one-sided) relationships with individuals with whom they have no contact. Not everyone is as fortunate as Gordon and Norma – 42 per cent of marriages end in divorce, though 16 per cent of married couples will celebrate their 60th wedding anniversary.

Interestingly, stories like that of Gordon and Norma's death are not that unusual. Bereaved widows and widowers are 30 per cent more likely to die within six months of their partner's death than people of the same age who have not lost a partner. There is even emerging evidence, like that of Ferrer (2013), that romantic partners' heartbeats become synchronised (beat in time with each other) and that is possibly a reason why the number one cause of death for bereaved spouses is sudden cardiac death.

*'Together we cast a single shadow on the wall.'*
Doug Fetherling (1979)

*'Maternity is a matter of fact, paternity a matter of opinion.'*
American proverb

## 3.1 The evolutionary explanation for partner preferences

Charles Darwin (1809–1882) explained that within each animal species, including humans, there is variation, making people not identical. Part of the variation comes from differences in individuals' genes, 50 per cent inherited from each parent, but genes (strands of DNA) can also undergo *mutation*, a random change affecting an individual's physiology and behaviour, which sometimes give individuals an advantage when competing for resources such as food, territories and mates. Such individuals stand more chance of surviving into adulthood and reproducing offspring who will also have the mutated gene, with the characteristic determined by the mutation becoming more widespread over time. This evolutionary process of gradual changes to our genetic make-up is known as natural selection. One important way in which **evolution** works to shape **human reproductive behaviour** is that of **sexual selection**.

## The relationship between sexual selection and human reproductive behaviour

The evolutionary approach, also known as the **socio-biological explanation**, sees males and females as being subjected to different selective pressures, which therefore leads them to use different strategies to maximise their reproductive potentials.

Sexual dimorphism concerns the different characteristics that male and female humans possess – for example, males are generally larger and more muscular than females. Evolution explains sexual dimorphism as developing through the process of natural selection, because the evolution of different features gave an adaptive advantage – that is, it increased the chances of survival into adulthood and sexual maturity, where genes are passed to the next generation.

Sexual selection involves the natural selection of characteristics increasing reproductive success. For example, if muscularity increases a male's chances of being chosen as a mate, the characteristic becomes enhanced as a sexually selected one and over generations males will become progressively more muscular.

Reproductive success involves the production of healthy offspring, surviving to sexual maturity, the offspring reproducing themselves and differences between male and female sexual behaviour will arise, as they are subject to different selective pressures. These differences occur due to anisogamy, the difference between the nature and amount of gametes (sperm and eggs) produced.

Males produce lots of small, highly mobile sperm, about 110 million sperm per ejaculation – around enough to populate Britain twice over – and males can fertilise many females at little cost to reproductive potential. Before the advent of DNA testing, they could not be sure of paternity (that the child is theirs), so natural selection favours male behaviours maximising the number of potential pregnancies, resulting in intrasexual competition between males (where males compete for mating opportunities with females), and polygamy, where one male mates with more than one female. Therefore, a male's best strategy to heighten his chances of reproducing genes into the next generation is to have as much sex as possible with as many females as possible. Various male strategies have arisen, for instance seeking females displaying signs of fertility, such as health, youth and childbearing hips, as mating with fertile females enhances the chances of successful reproduction (see Male strategies, page 67).

Females produce a few, relatively large eggs, each one representing a sizeable reproductive investment, though she is always sure of maternity. Females are fertile for about 25 years – ovulating one egg a month they therefore have only 300 opportunities to reproduce. Males can, in theory, reproduce as many as three times a day and remain fertile for longer – the oldest documented father was Nanu Ram Jogi, an Indian farmer who fathered a child at the age of 90. The oldest documented mother conceiving without hormone treatment

### KEY TERMS

**Evolution** – the process of adaptation through natural selection

**Human reproductive behaviour** – the different mating strategies used by males and females

**Sexual selection** – the selection of characteristics increasing reproductive success

**Socio-biological explanation** – a theory of relationships based on biological determinants

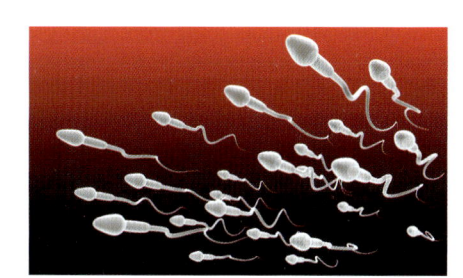

**Figure 3.2** Males produce 110 million sperm per ejaculation – enough to populate Britain twice over

was Dawn Brooke of Guernsey, who gave birth in 1997 aged 59 – her pregnancy was so unexpected it was believed to be cancer. Therefore females must be more selective about who they mate with, as each mating involves a sizeable part of reproduction potential compared with that of males.

Natural selection therefore favours female behaviours, maximising the chances of successful reproduction through various strategies, including careful mate selection, monogamy (having only one sexual partner) and high parental investment. Females seek males displaying genetic fitness, such as strength, status and resources. Females indulge in inter-sexual competition, where females choose males from those available. Females also utilise practices like courtship, which help to select the best male from those available and also serve to make males invest time, effort and resources in them and in any resulting offspring, thus increasing the chances that the male will not desert and will offer more protection and resources to the female and her children (see Female strategies, page 67).

## Attractiveness

**Physical attractiveness** in females is valued by males as an indicator of health and fertility, two of the qualities needed to produce and raise children. Younger women are seen as more attractive, as they tend to be more fertile. Females are more attracted to men, often older, who have access to resources, as this indicates an ability to provide for a female and her children. Although physical attractiveness is less important, females are choosier in selecting mates, as their investment is greater. Females are also attracted to kindness in males, as it indicates a willingness to share resources.

## Body symmetry and waist-to-hip ratio

Body symmetry and waist-to-hip ratio are forms of physical attractiveness that indicate genetic fitness, with males and females possessing near-perfect body symmetry having 2–3 times as many sexual partners as those with asymmetrical bodies. Facial symmetry is especially seen as attractive, as it is regarded as the best predictor of body symmetry. Symmetry is particularly attractive in males, as symmetry requires genetic precision, and only males with good genetic quality can produce it. Generally symmetry itself is not directly attractive, but other characteristics related to body symmetry, like being more dominant or having higher self-esteem, are.

Waist-to-hip ratio is an important aspect of female attractiveness, as females with a larger waist-to-hip ratio are associated with greater reproductive ability – they have 'child-bearing hips'. A small waist also suggests a woman is not carrying another man's child.

### KEY TERM

**Physical attractiveness** – the degree to which an individual's physical characteristics are considered aesthetically pleasing or beautiful

### ON THE WEB

An excellent website for an overview of attractiveness, including the role of waist-to-hip-ratio, leg length and bust size, can be found at:

**www.uni-regensburg.de/ Fakultaeten/phil_Fak_II/ Psychologie/Psy_II/beautycheck/ english/figur/figur.htm**

There are even some interactive experiments about ideal body shape.

**Figure 3.3** Which of these three images is the most attractive? Evolutionary theory predicts the one in the middle with a waist-to-hip ratio of 0.7, compared with 0.6 on the left and 0.8 on the right

*'Courtship – a man pursuing a woman until she catches him.'*
Anonymous

## Male strategies

Several male strategies have evolved seeking to maximise opportunities for mating success, including the following:

- **Courtship rituals** – allow males to display genetic potential, through characteristics and resource abilities.
- **Size** – males evolved to be bigger, demonstrating strength for success in competition against other males. Weaponry evolved in some species, for example antlers in deer.
- **Sperm competition** – natural selection acted on males, making them more competitive by producing larger testicles, bigger ejaculations and faster-swimming sperm.
- **Mate guarding** – males fear being cuckolded (where another male gets their partner pregnant) and spending resources raising another male's child. Males therefore indulge in mate guarding, where they keep an eye on and remain in close contact with female partners to prevent them mating with other males. Buss (1993) believes while men are fearful of partners being sexually unfaithful, females worry about emotional unfaithfulness, due to a fear of their partner spending resources on other females.
- **Sneak copulation** – males mate with females other than their partners if given the opportunity, as it increases their chances of reproductive success. Women gain from this, too, as having different fathers brings a wider genetic diversity to their children, increasing survival chances. Females can also gain an adaptive advantage by being in a relationship with a resource-rich male, while getting pregnant through a sneaky copulation with a genetically fit 'stud', though if found out she risks abandonment and being left to raise the child without male resources. Research is somewhat contradictory, with indications of varying levels of children born through sneak copulations.

*'To catch a husband is an art; to hold him is a job.'*
Simone de Beauvoir (1949)

## Female strategies

Several female strategies have evolved that maximise opportunities for mating success, including:

- **Sexy sons hypothesis** – females select attractive males as they will produce sons with the same attractive features, increasing their sons' and thus their own reproductive fitness.
- **Handicap hypothesis** – Zahavi (1975) believes females select males with handicaps because it advertises ability to thrive despite handicaps, demonstrating superior genetic quality. This may explain females finding males attractive who drink or take drugs in large amounts, as they are demonstrating an ability to handle toxins, a sign of genetic fitness.

> **YOU ARE THE RESEARCHER**
>
> A female's hip-to-waist-ratio is seen as an indicator of her reproductive ability. Therefore evolutionary theory would predict that males will prefer the middle of the three pictures in Figure 3.3 on page 66. Test this out by designing a suitable experiment that uses a systematic sample. Remember that you will need to design the experiment so that you have an IV. What will your DV be?
>
> Previous research suggests the middle picture will be preferred – this should help you decide when composing your experimental hypothesis if you need a one-tailed (directional) or two-tailed (non-directional) hypothesis.
>
> What type of graph would be appropriate to display your data? Justify your decision. Select and carry out an appropriate statistical test to see if your result is significant or not.

- **Courtship** – females use courtship to select males on the basis of reproductive fitness, through males demonstrating strength, health and ability to provide resources. Prolonged courtship rituals also benefit females, as they make males invest time, effort and resources, increasing the chances of males not deserting after successful matings, and so investing more resources in females and their offspring. Thus the human practice of dating, with males investing resources to females.

## CONTEMPORARY RESEARCH

### Sex differences in jealousy: the recall of cues to sexual and emotional infidelity in personally more and less threatening context conditions – Achim Schutzwohl & Stephanie Koch (2004)

**Figure 3.4** Evolutionary theory predicts differences in types of jealousy between males and females

Previous research had indicated men to be more jealous of sexual infidelity and women to be more jealous of emotional infidelity. This study tested the assertion by examining male and female decision times in deciding jealousy choice.

#### Aim
To test **Buss's (1992)** belief that males fear sexual infidelity more, while females fear emotional infidelity more.

#### Procedure
An opportunity sample of 100 male and 100 female German university students formed the sample. Experimental procedures, scenarios and response alternatives were presented on a computer screen.

Participants were presented with four scenarios involving social situations, each with a choice of two alternative responses. Only the responses to scenario four were of interest to the study.

Participants were asked to vividly imagine the scenarios before responding. Participants were told that the scenarios referred to romantic relationships they had been in, were currently in or would like to be in.

Scenario four read as follows:

'Imagine that you discover your partner formed both a deep emotional and a passionate sexual relationship with another person. Which aspect of your partner's involvement would make you more jealous?'

- The deep emotional relationship
- The passionate sexual relationship

The description of sexual and emotional infidelities was counterbalanced across participants. Choices were recorded, along with the times taken to make a decision after scenario presentation.

#### Findings
Both sexes reported more jealousy concerning the partner's emotional involvement, but more males (37 per cent) than females (20 per cent) selected their partner's sexual involvement as making them more jealous.

Women who selected emotional infidelity reached their decision faster than women selecting sexual infidelity.

Men who selected sexual infidelity reached their decision faster than men selecting emotional infidelity.

#### Conclusions
Men who are more jealous of sexual infidelity employ less elaborate decision strategies than men who are more jealous of emotional infidelity, while women who are more jealous of emotional infidelity employ less elaborate decision strategies than women who are more jealous of sexual infidelity.

Men and women who choose their adaptively primary infidelity type – that is, sexual for men, emotional for women – rely on their initial response tendency suggested by their respective jealousy mechanism, whereas men and women selecting their adaptively secondary infidelity type engage in additional considerations that lead them to override their initial response tendency.

#### Evaluation
- Previous results from similar research, suggesting that women who select the emotional infidelity option engage in a more elaborate decision-making process than women selecting sexual infidelity, are refuted by this study.
- The study does not identify the exact nature of the decision processes undertaken, especially by men, when selecting their adaptively secondary infidelity type.

> **RESEARCH IN FOCUS**
>
> Schutzwohl (2004) found a significant difference between male and female jealousy and would thus have been able to accept her experimental hypothesis. However, in doing so there would be a chance of making a type I error.
>
> What is a type I error and under what circumstances would it occur? Explain how a type II error differs from a type I error and under what circumstances it would occur.

## Research

Buss (1989) tested participants from 37 cultures, finding that males prefer young, physically attractive females, while females prefer resource-rich, ambitious, industrious males, supporting the idea that gender-based ideas of attractiveness are biological in nature.

Davis (1990) performed a content analysis of personal advertisements, finding that men look for health and attractiveness, while offering wealth and resources. Females look for resources and status, while offering beauty and youth, supporting the idea of evolutionary-based gender differences in relationship formation. Additional support came from Dunbar (1995), who analysed 900 personal advertisements from four US newspapers, to find that 42 per cent of males sought youthfulness, while only 25 per cent of females did. Of males, 44 per cent sought attractiveness, while only 22 per cent of females did, supporting the socio-biological idea that males and females have different reasons for forming relationships.

Pawlowski & Dunbar (1999) examined the idea that older women do not disclose their true age in personal advertisements because men tend to judge prospective female partners on age, as it correlates with fertility. This was found to be true, especially for women aged 35–50, implying that women disguise their age in order to find high-quality partners before reproductive opportunities are ended by the menopause.

Toma *et al.* (2008), who used personal advertisements to research males, thought it more acceptable to lie about their education and income than females, while Kurzban & Weeden (2005) found females more likely to declare their weight as less than it was. This illustrates how resource richness is seen as attractive in males, while physical attractiveness as a sign of fertility is seen as attractive in females.

Cartwright (2000) found that women with symmetrical breasts were more fertile than more asymmetrically breasted women, supporting the idea that body symmetry indicates reproductive fitness. Additional support comes from Penton-Voak *et al.* (2001), who found that females prefer males with greater facial symmetry, an indication of developmental stability that would be passed on to their sons, increasing reproductive potential.

Langlois & Roggman (1990) used computer-composite images to produce faces of varying symmetrical quality, finding a preference for symmetrical faces, faces identical in shape and form on both sides. This applied to both male and female faces. Cartwright (2000) supported this, finding that men prefer photographs of women with symmetrical faces and vice versa.

> **YOU ARE THE RESEARCHER**
>
> Design a study using a content analysis of personal advertisements (adverts in a newspaper where people seek relationships), to see if the evolutionary predictions that men will offer wealth and resources while seeking health and fertility and that women will offer beauty and youth while seeking resources and status are true. After locating a newspaper with personal advertisements, you will need to create coding units to categorise the qualities you are assessing. Use a random sample of the adverts available. Once you have quantified your data (by counting the number of times each quality appears within your sampled advertisements) you will need to compose a suitable graph and table to display your data in. Select and administer a suitable statistical test to see if your data are significant or not (beyond the boundaries of chance).

It seems that symmetry, which tends to be inherited, equates with fitness. Only individuals with good genes and food supplies develop perfectly symmetrical faces.

Singh (1993) used data from 50 years of beauty contest winners and *Playboy* centrefolds to assess waist-to-hip ratios of attractive women. He found that a small waist set against full hips was a consistent feature of female attractiveness, while breast size, overall body weight and physique varied over the years, suggesting that waist-to-hip ratio is an indicator of reproductive ability.

Swami & Furnham (2006) found that the optimum waist-to-hip ratio of 0.7:1 corresponds closely to supermodels, such as Anna Nicole Smith (0.69), Kate Moss (0.66) and Cindy Crawford (0.69), supporting Singh's findings.

Different studies into children born as a result of human sneak copulations have found differing figures. Peritz & Rust (1972) found a figure of only 0.03 per cent, while Ridley (1993) found a much higher 20 per cent. Simmons *et al*. (2003) gave a questionnaire on lifetime sexual behaviour to 416 Australian women and men, finding 27.9 per cent of males and 22.2 per cent of females admitted to cheating on partners, which suggests a sizeable minority of both sexes use the strategy, supporting evolutionary theory.

### ON THE WEB

Take the BBC 'Lonely hearts advert' test and then read about the evolutionary science behind it at:

www.bbc.co.uk/science/humanbody/mind/surveys/lonelyhearts/index.shtml

Similarly, read about 'The language of love', an evolutionary explanation of relationships by Professor Robin Dunbar, at:

www.bbc.co.uk/science/humanbody/mind/articles/emotions/lonelyhearts.shtml

## Evaluation

- Much early evidence for children born from sneak copulations is based on questionnaires and blood samples and so may not be reliable. Estimates of children born from sneak copulations also vary widely, which may be due to cultural differences, or to the types of samples used – for instance, using DNA data where males had suspicions of non-paternity is more likely to find such evidence. Evidence from supposedly monogamous species in the animal kingdom is supportive though, with Birkhead (1990) using DNA sampling to find that 8 per cent of zebra finch offspring result from females' sneaky copulations with non-partner males.
- Miller (1997) sees evolution as shaping human culture – that is, language, art, humour and music, which act as courtship displays, attracting sexual partners.
- The evolutionary explanation presumes heterosexuality and that all relationships are sexual; it is therefore oversimplified and cannot explain long-distance romantic relationships, like those conducted over the internet. It also cannot explain couples choosing not to have children, as it assumes all relationships are motivated by a desire to reproduce.
- Diamond (1992) believes males, especially in early adulthood, use drugs and indulge in risky behaviours, like bungee jumping, to advertise their reproductive fitness in the face of adversity, providing support for the handicap hypothesis.
- The practice of checking partners' mobile phone records, email accounts, etc. can be regarded as a modern form of mate guarding, where checks are made on partners to see whether they have been sexually/emotionally unfaithful.
- Younger males sometimes desire substantially older women – this goes against evolutionary theory, but may occur due to males wanting to mate with females proven to be fertile.

- Females often alter their appearance through the use of make-up and cosmetic surgery and lie about their age in order to appear younger and more fertile. Males use deceit to exaggerate their resource capabilities and feign love in order to persuade females to mate with them. This supports the idea of males and females using different strategies to maximise reproductive potential.
- Women do not need men in the way they once did and as predicted by evolutionary theory. Females in Western cultures have greater financial security and employment opportunities, and this has occurred simultaneously with a rise in single women having children – according to the Office for National Statistics, 82,000 single women over the age of 30 had babies in Britain in 2006, and 25 per cent of British families are single-parent families (90 per cent are female-led). These statistics are not consistent with women needing male partners to provide for them and their offspring.
- Evolutionary theory explains female choosiness and male competitiveness in terms of maximising reproductive potential. However, this can also be explained by gender role socialisation.

**Figure 3.5** Older females may use make-up and cosmetic surgery to look younger and thus more fertile

### YOU ARE THE RESEARCHER

Test out Pawlowski & Dunbar's claim (see Book 1, Chapter 7) that women disguise their age by using personal advertisements from newspapers to see whether there is a difference in the number of women and men not stating their age (or giving an age range rather than a precise age). If the researchers are correct, more women should not state their age. You will need an equal number of male and female advertisements.

### PSYCHOLOGY IN THE REAL WORLD

**Figure 3.6** Can the art of seduction be learned from evolutionary theory?

One practical application of evolutionary theory of relationships concerns heterosexual men learning skills to seduce women based upon evolutionary theory. The first stage involves creating opportunities to exploit evolved cues of what women find attractive in men, such as demonstrating charm and humour, as these are seen as 'honest' signals of high mate value. Conversation and acts that stress generosity and wealth will also create a good impression. Another male strategy is to befriend an attractive woman and use her as 'bait' to attract other attractive females. Subsequent strategies establish comfort and trust, such as through touch and eye contact to create bonding. Then finally seduction can occur where passion towards sexual activity is created by building intimacy through shared experiences and self-disclosure.

Although such practices may seem ethically questionable, their effectiveness is supported by the comfortable living being earned by a growing number of 'pick-up coaches' who teach such skills. The success of Neil Strauss's best-selling book *The Game: Penetrating the secret society of pick-up artists* (2006) is one such example.

> **STRENGTHEN YOUR LEARNING**
> 1. Explain what is meant by sexual selection.
> 2. Explain why physical attractiveness is valued in females.
> 3. Explain how body symmetry and waist-to-hip ratio can be qualities of attractiveness.
> 4. Outline male and female strategies to maximise opportunities for mating success.
> 5. Outline and evaluate Schutzwohl & Koch's (2004) study of sexual jealousy.
> 6. To what extent does research evidence support the evolutionary explanation of sexual selection and human reproductive behaviour?
> 7. What other evaluative points can be made concerning the evolutionary explanation of sexual selection and human reproductive behaviour?

*'What you seek is seeking you.'*
Jalal ad-Din Muhammad Rumi (1250)

# 3.2 Factors affecting attraction in romantic relationships

Romantic relationships first require attraction – to have a liking or desire for a particular person – and there are several factors that can influence who individuals will be attracted to.

## Self-disclosure

**KEY TERM**

**Self-disclosure** – the revealing of personal information about oneself to another

The idea behind **self-disclosure** is that the revealing of personal information about oneself to another individual is crucial to the development of a closer, more intimate romantic relationship. The concept believes we reveal more personal information to people we like and in turn we like people who reveal more personal information about themselves to us. Self-disclosure generally happens only when sufficient trust has been established so that individuals are relatively certain such information will not be revealed to others as a source of embarrassment.

Altman & Taylor (1973) believe relationships develop through gradual increases in the breadth and depth of self-disclosed information between individuals. They see disclosure of personal information by others as rewarding, as it signals their liking of us and their desire to be more intimate with us. This fits in with the idea of social exchange (see page 80), where individuals are more attracted to those who provide them with rewarding outcomes.

Ajzen (1977) sees self-disclosure more as a product of information processing, where liking someone comes from having positive perceptions of a person. Therefore people who self-disclose personal information to us are seen favourably as likeable, trustworthy and kind.

**Figure 3.7** Self-disclosure of personal information helps to build closer, more intimate relationships

However, self-disclosure is not always seen as rewarding or as leading to having positive perceptions of those doing the disclosing and a number of factors have been identified that influence the relationship between disclosure and attraction.

1. **Appropriateness of the disclosure** – sometimes disclosing personal information is inappropriate, for example doing so on a first date may be viewed as 'over the top', indicating a person is maladjusted and lacking in social skills. Social norms (expected ways of behaviour) seem to exist as to what information is okay to reveal and in what situations/at which times. More attractive people will be sensitive to these norms.

2. **Attributions for the disclosure** – the reasons we believe a person is self-disclosing to us are important. Less attraction occurs if an individual is seen as the kind of person who discloses personal information to everyone, or is someone self-disclosing because the situation is seen as lending itself to self-disclosure. However, more attraction occurs if we believe an individual sees us as someone they especially want to disclose intimate information to.

3. **Gender differences** – women generally are seen as better communicators of and more interested in intimate information, therefore intimate self-disclosures by males may be seen as less appropriate than those by females. Alternatively, self-disclosure by a male may be seen as very rewarding by a female, as it indicates he especially wants to disclose personal information to her. Males, meanwhile, may not be used to and thus feel threatened by females self-disclosing intimate details to them.

4. **Content of the disclosure** – although generally intimate disclosures are seen favourably, disclosure of highly intimate information may be seen as inappropriate and as violating social norms, especially if a relationship is in its early stages. This could decrease attraction, as the recipient of the information may feel threatened and unsure of how to respond. Therefore attraction is generally weaker when self-disclosure is of low intimacy or high intimacy and stronger when self-disclosure is of moderate intimacy.

## Research

Altman & Taylor (1973) reported that disclosing personal information in the initial stages of a relationship, such as at first encounter, was inappropriate and did not enhance attraction, as it suggested the disclosing person was maladjusted and less likeable. This was supported by Derlega & Grzelak (1979), who found that individuals who violated social rules by revealing over-intimate personal information were viewed unfavourably.

Kleinke (1979) found that individuals who were perceived as being selective about who they disclosed personal information to were seen as more attractive, as the recipients of the information felt specially chosen, supporting the idea that attribution for disclosure is an important factor in self-disclosure. This was supported by Wortman *et al.* (1976), who reported that when individuals believed they had been specially selected for intimate disclosure, they felt trusted and admired and thus rated the person disclosing favourably.

**ON THE WEB**

A detailed and comprehensive account of disclosure in virtual relationships by Joinson & Paine (2010) can be found at **www.york.ac.uk/res/e-society/projects/15/PRISD_report2.pdf.**

Derlega & Chaikin (1976) reported that men who disclosed personal information often violated social expectations in doing so and so were judged unfavourably. However, Dindia & Allen (1992) performed a meta-analysis to find females, more than males, regarded intimate disclosure as a development of closeness and thus judged men doing so favourably. Both studies suggest gender differences in self-disclosure, though in different ways.

Brewer & Mittelman (1980) reported that the positive impact of self-disclosure breaks down at extreme levels of intimacy, especially if it occurs between relative strangers, illustrating the importance of the content of self-disclosure as a factor influencing attraction.

Collins & Miller (1994) performed a meta-analysis to find that individuals who give intimate self-disclosure are more attractive than those who give less intimate self-disclosures and that people disclose more to those they are attracted to. Individuals also had increased attraction to those they self-disclosed to, supporting the importance of self-disclosure as a factor affecting attraction.

Kito (2010) assessed how self-disclosure affected different types of relationships in Japanese and American students, finding that self-disclosure was higher in both cultural groups in romantic relationships than in same-sex and cross-sex friendship relationships. This suggests self-disclosure is an important factor in romantic relationships and is a cross-cultural effect.

## Evaluation

- Much of the research into self-disclosure does not distinguish between friendship/companionship and romantic relationships, making it difficult to assess the role of self-disclosure solely in romantic relationships. Also, research that does focus on romantic relationships often does not distinguish between different types, for example relationships that are high in passion, high in intimacy, high in commitment, etc. It may be that self-disclosure makes people more attractive mainly in relationships higher in intimacy.
- It is unlikely that attractiveness of a potential partner would be reliant purely on the level/type of self-disclosure that an individual makes. More likely is that self-disclosure would interact with other considerations, such as level of physical attractiveness, similarity of interests/attitudes, etc.
- An important factor in whether self-disclosure increases the attractiveness of potential partners is that of personality. Individuals who self-disclose intimate information above what is seen as their normal level of disclosure may be viewed as attractive, as it would be more rewarding to the recipient, who would view themselves as having been especially selected to receive such information. The personality of recipients may be important too; different individuals would have different needs for levels of intimacy in relationships and this would affect how attractive they would find intimate self-disclosures.

*'Boys think girls are like books – if the cover doesn't catch
their eye they won't bother to read what's inside.'*
Marilyn Monroe (1955)

# Physical attractiveness

Physical attractiveness plays a significant role in why an individual is initially attracted to someone – it takes time to find out about people's attitudes and values, but physical attractiveness is an immediate and accessible way for potential partners to rate each other. Individuals are not always competent in judging their own level of physical attractiveness, but generally people will agree on the physical attractiveness of a given individual, with greater agreement occurring among men as to the attractiveness of females. This may be because physical attractiveness of females is more important to males in partner selection than it is to females selecting male partners.

Individuals seen as physically attractive tend to create a favourable impression of possessing desirable personality characteristics, such as being trustworthy, optimistic and sociable. This is known as the Halo effect, where a general impression of someone is incorrectly formed from one characteristic. This is one reason why physically attractive people are more desired as dates or romantic partners than less physically attractive people.

Evolutionary theory (see page 65) sees common factors of physical attractiveness as including signs of genetic fitness in males, like facial symmetry and muscularity. Signs of healthy maturity are favoured too, as they suggest resource richness. In females, physical indicators of fertility are preferred, such as signs of health, like lustrous hair, and indicators of youth, like slimness and round, baby-like eyes. However, as well as gender differences in what constitutes physical attractiveness, differences occur across cultures, over time and between individuals. Age can be a factor too, with physical attractiveness of potential romantic partners being more important to younger individuals.

**Figure 3.8** Signs of maturity and resource richness are attractive in males, while youthful signs of fertility are seen as attractive in females

# The matching hypothesis

An important consideration in physical attractiveness is that of Walster *et al.*'s (1966) **matching hypothesis**, which believes that when initiating romantic relationships individuals seek partners who are most like themselves in terms of physical attractiveness. This involves individuals assessing their own level of physical attractiveness and then focusing attention upon potential partners of perceived similar physical attractiveness, as there is seen as being less chance of being rejected. It has also been hypothesised that individuals will feel more secure in a relationship with someone of equal physical attractiveness, due to fears that a more attractive partner might be tempted to end the relationship if a more physically attractive partner became available.

## Research

Brigham (1971) found that physically attractive people are seen as having desirable personality characteristics, including being sociable, interesting, exciting and sexually warm, supporting the idea of the Halo effect, where people's whole personality is judged on the basis that they are physically attractive.

### KEY TERM

**Matching hypothesis** – the idea that individuals are attracted to people of similar perceived attractiveness

Gunnell & Ceci (2010) found that physically less attractive people are 22 per cent more likely to be convicted in courts of law and to get prison sentences of on average 22 months longer than physically attractive people. This supports the Halo effect that physically attractive people are generally seen as more trustworthy than lesser physically attractive people.

Walster & Walster (1969) told students they had been assigned an ideal partner for a forthcoming dance event, though selections had actually been made at random. The students met up before the dance and those who had been paired up with partners of similar physical attractiveness to themselves expressed greater liking of their partners than those who had been paired up with partners of dissimilar levels of physical attractiveness. This supports the matching hypothesis.

Murstein (1972) asked participants to assess from photographs the physical attractiveness levels of genuine couples and non-genuine couples (who had been put together for the purpose of the study). It was found that the real couples were more likely to be judged as of similar levels of attractiveness to each other than the non-genuine couples, thus supporting the matching hypothesis.

Taylor *et al.* (2011) used profiles and photographs from an online dating site to assess the matching hypothesis, finding that initial attraction (assessed by whether communication was requested) was based on levels of physical attractiveness, which did not support the matching hypothesis. However, replies were more likely to be sent to individuals who were judged as of similar levels of physical attractiveness and agreements to 'communicate' were also more likely to occur among couples of similar physical attractiveness. This suggests the matching hypothesis applies more to later stages of the dating process rather than explaining initial attraction.

## ON THE WEB

Watch the matching hypothesis in action as Professor Douglas Kenrick gets people in gender-neutral clothing to make partner choices based on physical attractiveness. Go to **www.youtube.com** and search for 'Attraction: The matching phenomena'.

## Evaluation

- Walster *et al.*'s original matching hypothesis stated that individuals would desire to partner someone as socially desirable as themselves. However, over time the hypothesis has come to be regarded as one focused solely on levels of physical attractiveness, something it was not orientated towards.
- In an earlier study Walster *et al.* (1966) actually found that participants liked people who were more physically attractive and that physical attractiveness was the best indicator by both males and females of wanting to see someone again. This goes against the matching hypothesis, though when asked months later it was found that participants who actually did date their partner again were of similar levels of physical attractiveness, which supports the hypothesis.
- Although physical beauty is an important form of attractiveness, those without it can compensate through complex matching, where they may pair up with a more physically attractive partner by being attractive in other ways, such as through wealth or domestic skills.
- Evolutionary theory suggests that men value physical attractiveness more in women than women do in men, which means it is easier for men to compensate through other means for not being physically attractive.
- In many cultures, such as those practising arranged marriages, senior family members are regarded as better judges of who is compatible as a partner for their children and therefore attractiveness will be judged on factors other than physical attractiveness.

*'You don't always get to choose who you fall in love with.'*
Stephani Hecht (2010)

# Filter theory

## Kerckhoff & Davis (1962)

**Filter theory** believes that choice of partners is affected by factors limiting the availability of those possible to select from. There is a series of filters that serves to 'thin down the field' to those available.

1. Similarity of social demographic variables – focus is upon those individuals we are realistically likely to be able to meet and with whom we will have factors in common. Such individuals will generally be limited to those who live near to us, work with us, socialise with us, etc., with availability further limited to those of similar class, ethnic, religious, educational and economic background to ourselves. Such people will appear attractive, as their similarity will make communication easier, aiding the development of a relationship.
2. **Similarity in attitudes** – focus here is upon individuals meeting and socialising and thus being exposed to each other's beliefs, values and attitudes. Individuals who have similarity of attitudes will be perceived by each other as being more attractive and compatible.
3. **Complementarity** – focus here is upon the degree to which potential partners meet each other's needs, especially emotional ones. Such complementarity helps to make a relationship 'deeper' and thus less superficial and is regarded as the most important factor in establishing commitment towards a long-term relationship.

## Research

Festinger *et al.* (1950) reported that people who lived the closest to the stairways in an apartment block had the most contact with other residents of the block and formed the most friendships with other residents, supporting the idea of social demographic variables affecting the choice of possible partners one could be attracted to. This was further supported by Clark (1952) finding that 50 per cent of citizens of Columbus, Ohio, USA, were married to partners who initially lived within walking distance of their house.

Taylor *et al.* (2010) reported that 85 per cent of Americans who got married in 2008 married someone of their own ethnic group, supporting the social demographic idea that individuals' choice of partners is limited to those of a similar background.

Byrne (1961) found that strangers who had similar attitudes to participants were more liked than strangers with differing attitudes. This supports the idea of similarity of attitudes being a limiting factor in who individuals find attractive. This was supported by Tan & Singh (1995), who got 21-year-old participants to complete a questionnaire concerning their attitudes and then exposed them to fake completed attitude questionnaires of a 'stranger', finding they rated 'strangers' with similar attitudes as more attractive.

Sadalla *et al.* (1987) found that women are attracted to males who are reliable, socially dominant, self-confident and extrovert, as such qualities indicate an ability to achieve a relatively high position in society and thus meet their need for provision of resources. This supports the idea of complementarity being

### KEY TERMS

**Filter theory** – that choice of partners is affected by factors limiting the availability of those possible to select from

**Similarity in attitudes** – the degree of likeness between individuals' viewpoints

**Complementarity** – the ability of individuals to meet each other's needs

**Figure 3.9** Filter theory sees choice of partners as affected by social demographic variables such as religion

an important limiting factor in which individuals are desirable as potential partners. This was further supported by Dijkstra & Barelds (2008), who examined the extent to which individuals were attracted to partners of similar or complementary personality characteristics, finding that complementary personalities were more preferred in both males and females.

### Evaluation

- The relative availability of potential partners due to social demographic reasons changes over time (and across cultures) as attitudes change to relationships between people of different backgrounds. In 1960 in the USA less than 3 per cent of marriages were inter-racial, but this has now risen considerably. There is an age factor here, with younger people more likely to marry outside their ethnic group. However, there are sub-cultural differences too, with white American people more likely to marry Asian and Hispanic partners than black American people are.
- Age is another limiting factor. People tend to socialise in similar age groups and where partners are of different ages, this tends to be between younger females and older men, with a possible evolutionary explanation, as older men tend to be more resource rich and younger females more fertile. The average age difference between partners is 2–3 years, with the female partner being younger.
- Much research into the filter theory focuses on liking and relationships in general, rather than specifically on attraction and romantic relationships, making accurate conclusions difficult to achieve.
- One important consideration in filter theory is that males and females filter out different things, due to having different needs. This applies to age and culture, too. Indeed, filter theory can be accused of cultural bias, as most research was performed in individualistic cultures and therefore may not apply to collectivist cultures where relationships are affected by different limiting factors.

### STRENGTHEN YOUR LEARNING

1. Outline factors that influence the relationship between self-disclosure and attraction.
2. Summarise what research evidence suggests about self-disclosure and attraction.
3. What other evaluative points can be made concerning self-disclosure and attraction?
4. Explain why physical attractiveness makes individuals seem desirable.
5. Explain what is meant by the matching hypothesis.
6. What does research evidence suggest about physical attractiveness in romantic relationships?
7. What other evaluative points can be made concerning physical attractiveness in romantic relationships?
8. Explain how i) **social demography**, ii) similarity of attitudes, iii) complementarity act as filters to limit the field of available partners.
9. Summarise what research evidence suggests about filter theory.
10. What other evaluative points can be made about filter theory?

### KEY TERM

**Social demography** – that choice of partners is limited to individuals of similar class, education and economic background

# ASSESSMENT CHECK

1. Select from the descriptions A, B, C and D below to complete the table relating to the filter theory. One description will be left over. **[3 marks]**

   **A** Where choice of partners is limited by economic background

   **B** The degree to which an individual's physical characteristics are considered pleasing

   **C** The degree of likeness between individuals' viewpoints

   **D** The ability of individuals to meet each other's needs

   | Filter | Description |
   | --- | --- |
   | Similarity in attitudes | |
   | Complementarity | |
   | Social demography | |

2. Freya has decided to use her local newspaper's classified section to find a romantic partner. In her advert Freya describes herself as looking for an older man seeking a long-term relationship, who is well off financially. She describes herself as youthful, slim and attractive and that she enjoys playing sports.

   Making reference to the scenario above, explain Freya's classified advert in terms of evolutionary explanations for partner preferences. **[4 marks]**

3. Research into factors affecting attraction in romantic relationships often uses questionnaires.

   Explain one strength and one weakness of the questionnaire method in researching factors affecting attraction in romantic relationships. **[2 + 2 marks]**

4. Explain what is meant by self-disclosure as a factor affecting attraction in romantic relationships. **[2 marks]**

5. Discuss the relationship between sexual selection and human reproductive behaviour. **[16 marks]**

*'He's Mr Right, but I'm always right.'*
Mara Lawton (2014)

# 3.3 Theories of romantic relationships

## KEY TERMS

**Social exchange theory** – an economic explanation of relationship maintenance based on maximising profits and minimising costs

**Equity theory** – an explanation of relationship maintenance based on motivation to achieve fairness and balance

**Rusbult's investment model** – relationship satisfaction as dependent upon a consideration of perceived benefits, costs and the quality of possible alternative relationships

Theories of romantic relationships attempt to explain the processes by which such relationships are formed and maintained. There are many varying types of theory, but the three featured here are **social exchange theory**, **equity theory** and **Rusbult's investment model**.

*'I told her I'd wait for ever for her, but that was before I found somebody else who'd give me a lift home.'*
Jarod Kintz (2010)

## Social exchange theory

There are different versions of social exchange theory (SET), but underlying all of them is the idea that in any relationship both partners are continually giving and receiving items of value to and from each other and as people are fundamentally selfish, relationships continue only if both partners feel they are getting more out of the relationship than they are putting in.

The theory sees people as perceiving their feelings for others in terms of profit (the rewards obtained from relationships minus the costs). The greater the rewards and the lower the costs, the greater the profit and therefore the greater the desire to maintain the relationship.

Interactions between partners can be 'expensive', as they take time, energy and commitment, and may involve unpleasant emotions and experiences. Therefore, for a relationship to be maintained, individuals must feel they are receiving more than they put in. The theory also sees social interactions as involving an exchange of rewards, such as affection, intimate information and status. The degree of attraction or liking between partners reflects how people evaluate the rewards they receive relative to those given.

Thus SET is an economic theory, explaining relationships in terms of maximising benefits and minimising costs. The 'social exchange' is the mutual exchange of rewards between partners, like friendship and sex, and the costs of being in the relationship, such as freedoms given up. A person assesses their rewards by making two comparisons:

1. The comparison level (CL) – where rewards are compared against costs to judge profits.
2. The comparison level for alternative relationships (CLalt) – where rewards and costs are compared against perceived rewards and costs for possible alternative relationships.

A relationship is maintained if rewards exceed costs and the profit level is not exceeded by possible alternative relationships.

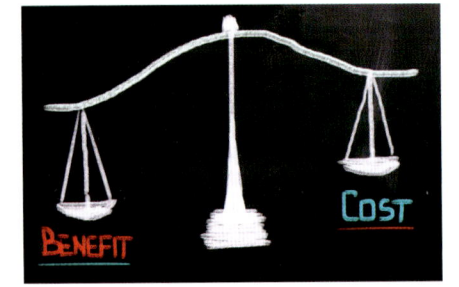

**Figure 3.10** Social exchange theory sees relationships being maintained if benefits exceed costs

Thibaut & Kelley *et al.* (1959) proposed a four-stage model of SET, setting out how relationships could be maintained (see Table 3.1). It perceives that over time people develop a predictable and mutually beneficial pattern of exchanges, assisting the maintenance of relationships.

**Table 3.1** Thibaut & Kelley *et al.*'s four-stage model

| Stage | Description |
| --- | --- |
| Sampling | Rewards and costs are assessed in a number of relationships |
| Bargaining | A relationship is 'costed out' and sources of profit and loss are identified |
| Commitment | Relationship is established and maintained by a predictable exchange of rewards |
| Institutionalisation | Interactions are established and the couple 'settle down' |

## Research

Hatfield (1979) looked at people who felt over- or under-benefited in their relationships. The under-benefited felt angry and deprived, while the over-benefited felt guilty and uncomfortable, supporting the theory by suggesting that regardless of whether individuals are benefited, they do not desire to maintain a relationship if it is unequal.

Mills & Clark (1980) identified two kinds of intimate relationship: the communal couple, where each partner gives out of concern for the other, and the exchange couple, where each keeps mental records of who is 'ahead' and who is 'behind'. This indicates that there are different types of relationships and that SET can be applied to some of them, but not universally to all.

Rusbult (1983) asked participants to complete questionnaires over a seven-month period concerning rewards and costs associated with relationships, finding that social exchange theory did not explain the early 'honeymoon' phase of a relationship when balance of exchanges was ignored. However, later on, relationship costs were compared against the degree of personal satisfaction, suggesting that the theory is best applied to the maintenance of relationships.

Rusbult (1983) found that the costs and rewards of relationships were compared against the costs and rewards of potential alternative relationships in order to decide whether the relationship should be maintained, supporting the social exchange model's idea that people assess rewards by making comparisons.

Rusbult & Martz (1995) found that women who had been physically assaulted by their partners and were living in a women's refuge were likely to return to their abusive partners, as they did not have better alternatives, often due to low levels of education, no job prospects and little access to money. This supports SET, as even though the women were in abusive relationships, the profits were seen to exceed the costs.

### RESEARCH IN FOCUS

Research into relationships, such as Rusbult's (1983) study into the social exchange theory, are written up as psychological reports and subjected to peer review before being published. Such reports have to be written up in a conventional way of different sections in a certain order.

Explain a) what the basic aims of a psychological report are; b) why psychological reports have to be written in a conventional way.

List the basic sections of a psychological report and outline briefly what each section should contain.

### Evaluation

- Rubin (1983) believes that although people are not fundamentally selfish, attitudes towards others are determined to a large extent by how rewarding we think they are for us, supporting the theory.
- Sedikides (2005) claims that people are capable of being unselfish – doing things for others without expecting anything in return. This is most evident in relationships with those emotionally closest to us. Sedikides believes that individuals can bolster their partner's self-esteem when they are faced with failure and other stressful life events. Therefore, the view of humans as being out for what they can get is simplistic and inaccurate.
- Fromm (1962) argues against the theory, defining true love as giving, as opposed to the false love of the 'marketing character', where people expect to have favours returned.
- The social exchange theory was modified into the equity theory, which concerns balance and stability in relationships and is a logical progression.
- Argyle (1988) criticised methodologies that evaluate social exchange theory, declaring them contrived and artificial, with little relevance to real life.
- Research has concentrated on the short-term consequences of relationships rather than the more important, long-term maintenance of relationships.
- The theory applies to people who 'keep score'. Murstein et al. (1977) devised the exchange orientation tool, identifying such scorekeepers, who are suspicious and insecure, suggesting that the theory only suits relationships lacking confidence and mutual trust.

### YOU ARE THE RESEARCHER

Assess social exchange theory by combining the experimental method with a questionnaire to compare two groups of people in romantic relationships, such as people from different age ranges or different genders, by asking them to state what they give and receive in their relationships (see Book One, Chapter 7).

What type of experimental method would this be? What experimental design would you use? What would the IV and DV be? For the questionnaire would you use open or closed questions? How would you compile your data?

Construct a suitable table and graph to display your data. What statistical test would be used to analyse your data? Give three reasons for the choice of this test.

*'Fairness does not mean everyone gets the same. Fairness means everyone gets what they need.'*

Rick Riordan (2005)

## Equity theory

Equity in relationship theory does not mean equality; instead it believes individuals are motivated to achieve fairness in relationships and to feel dissatisfied with inequity (unfairness). Definitions of equity within a relationship can differ between individuals.

Maintenance of relationships occurs through balance and stability. Relationships where individuals put in more than they receive, or receive more than they put in, are inequitable, leading to dissatisfaction and possible dissolution (ending of the relationship). The recognition of inequity within a relationship presents a chance for a relationship to be saved – that is, maintained further by making adjustments so that there is a return to equity.

Relationships may alternate between periods of perceived balance and imbalance, with individuals being motivated to return to a state of equity. The greater the perceived imbalance, the greater the efforts to realign the relationship, so long as a chance of doing so is perceived to be viable.

Walster *et al.* (1978) saw equity as based on four principles, as set out in Table 3.2.

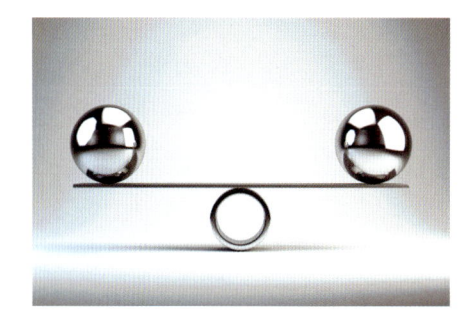

**Figure 3.11** Equity theory sees relationship maintenance occurring through balance and stability

**Table 3.2** The four principles of equity

| Principle | Description |
| --- | --- |
| Profit | Rewards are maximised and costs minimised |
| Distribution | Trade-offs and compensations are negotiated to achieve fairness in a relationship |
| Dissatisfaction | The greater the degree of perceived unfairness, the greater the sense of dissatisfaction |
| Realignment | If restoring equity is possible, maintenance will continue, with attempts made to realign equity |

## Research

Argyle (1977) found that people in close relationships do not think in terms of rewards and costs unless they feel dissatisfied, implying that equity, at least in a conscious fashion, is not a valid explanation of relationship maintenance.

Murstein & MacDonald (1983) supported Argyle, finding that a conscious concern with 'getting a fair deal', especially in the short term, makes compatibility hard to achieve, especially between married couples.

Canary & Stafford (1992) devised the Relationship Maintenance Strategies Measure (RMSM), using it to assess degree of equity in romantic relationships. A link was found between degree of perceived equity and the prevalence of maintenance strategies, implying that equitable relationships are maintained.

Dainton (2003) studied 219 individuals in romantic relationships, finding that those in relationships of perceived inequity had low relationship satisfaction, but were motivated to return to an equitable state to maintain the relationship, suggesting that equity is a main factor in relationship satisfaction and maintenance.

Yum *et al.* (2009) looked at different types of heterosexual romantic relationships in six different cultures. As predicted by equity theory, maintenance strategies differed, with individuals in perceived equitable relationships engaging in most maintenance strategies, followed by those in perceived over-benefited and under-benefited relationships. Cultural factors had little effect, suggesting that equity theory can be applied to relationships across cultures.

### Evaluation

- Equity theory still portrays people as selfish. Many researchers, like Duck (1988), prefer to see people as concerned with an equitable distribution of rewards and costs for themselves *and* their partners.
- Kelley & Thibaut (1978) proposed interdependence theory, which suggests that not all social interactions reflect a shared desire for equity and fair exchange. Intimate relationships are varied and complex, and partners' motives and desires can clash as well as coincide, producing many outcomes, including aggression, altruism, competition, capitulation (giving in), cooperation and intransigence ('digging your heels in'). Interdependence theory goes beyond individual partners, considering the harmony and/or conflict between attitudes, motives, values or goals of people in social relationships.
- Sprecher (1986) believes that close relationships are too complex to allow for precise assessment of various rewards and costs involved in establishing equity.
- Mills & Clark (1982) believe that it is not possible to assess equity in loving relationships, as much input is emotional and therefore unquantifiable, and to do so diminishes the quality of love.
- Equity seems more important to females, suggesting that the theory is not applicable to both genders. Hochschild & Machung (1989) found that women do most of the work to make relationships equitable.
- Some research suggests that equity theory does not apply to all cultures. Moghaddam *et al.* (1983) found that US students prefer equity (fairness), but European students prefer equality, suggesting that the theory reflects the values of US society.

## Rusbult's investment model of commitment

Rusbult's theory attempts to identify the determinants of relationship commitment and is comprised of three factors positively linked with commitment: satisfaction level, the comparison with alternatives and size of investment.

1. **Satisfaction level** refers to the positive v. negative effect experienced in a relationship. Satisfaction is influenced by the degree to which a partner meets an individual's needs, for example the extent to which a partner meets one's emotional and sexual needs.
2. **Comparison with alternatives** refers to the perceived desirability of the best alternative to the current relationship and is based upon the extent to which an individual's needs could be met within that alternative relationship, for example the extent to which a potential alternative partner could meet one's emotional and sexual needs. If such needs could be better met elsewhere then the quality of alternatives is high. If such needs are best met within the current relationship then commitment is stronger.
3. **Investment size** refers to the amount and importance of the resources associated with a relationship and such resources would decline in value or be lost if the relationship was to end. Partners invest directly into relationships, such as the time and effort put into the relationship, as well

as indirect investments, such as shared friends, children and co-owned material possessions. After investments have occurred, commitment is heightened as ending a relationship would then become more costly.

There are also two variables linked to commitment:

- **Equity** is the degree of 'fairness' within a relationship. Inequity (perceived unfairness) leads to distress and lack of satisfaction with a relationship and thus less commitment to it. Such distress can be relieved by ending the relationship.
- **Social support** is the degree of care and assistance available from others, such as from family and friends. If such others approve of a relationship it produces a positive influence that increases commitment to the relationship.

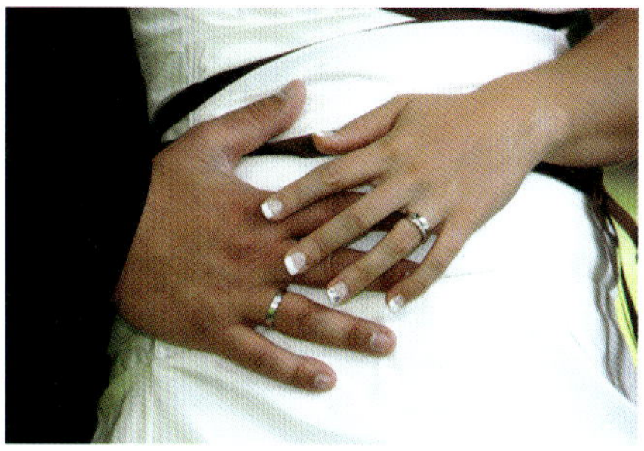

**Figure 3.12** Rusbult's model sees factors of satisfaction level, quality of alternatives and investment as determining relationship commitment

## Research

Lin & Rusbult (1995) found that although findings were inconsistent, females generally reported higher satisfaction levels, poorer scores for quality of alternatives, greater investments and stronger overall commitment. This suggests gender differences may exist, with females demonstrating greater dependence and stronger commitment than males.

Rusbult *et al.* (1998) gave the investment model scale (IMS) questionnaire to student participants in relationships, to find that commitment in relationships was positively correlated with satisfaction level, negatively correlated with the quality of alternatives and positively correlated with investment size, supporting all three factors of Rusbult's model.

Rusbult *et al.* (1998) administered the IMS questionnaire to participants in homosexual relationships, finding support for all factors of the model, as did Duffy & Rusbult (1986) when administering the same questionnaire to individuals in marital relationships, which suggests that the model explains commitment in a variety of relationships.

Van Lange *et al.* (1997) found support for all factors of the model in Taiwanese participants and this was coupled with similar results found by Lin & Rusbult (1995) with Dutch participants, which suggests the model has cross-cultural validity.

### Evaluation

- Research indicates that Rusbult's model with its focus on commitment and what individuals have invested is a better predictor of long-term maintenance in relationships than equity theory.
- Rusbult's model can explain why partners remain in abusive relationships, as the cost of losing what they have invested and committed to in the relationship may be too great, with no possible alternative relationships to turn to.
- The investment model is able to explain infidelity, as such behaviour occurs when there is low satisfaction with a current relationship and high satisfaction with an alternative relationship, with both these factors serving to erode commitment.
- Research that supports the investment model is highly reliant on self-report measures, which may be subject to socially desirable and idealised answers, as well as researcher bias, casting some doubts on the validity of the results.

### ON THE WEB

A fascinating documentary insight into the explanations for relationship formation that focuses on relationships within different cultures can be found online. Go to **www.youtube.com** and search for 'Love and relationships around the world (full documentary)'.

*'Stop going to a dry well for water.'*
Arabic proverb

*'I like my relationships like I like my eggs. Over easy.'*
Jarod Kintz (2010)

# 3.4 Duck's phase model of relationship breakdown

Duck (2001) proposed three general reasons for why relationships break up:

1. Pre-existing doom – incompatibility and failure are fairly much guaranteed from the start of the relationship.
2. Mechanical failure – two compatible, well-meaning people grow apart and find that they cannot live together any longer (this is the most common cause).
3. Sudden death – the discovery of infidelity (cheating) or the occurrence of a traumatic incident (such as a huge argument) leads to immediate ending of a relationship.

Duck proposed several other factors as contributing to relationship **dissolution**:

- Predisposing personal factors – for example, individuals' bad habits or emotional instabilities.
- Precipitating factors – for example, exterior influences, such as love rivals, process features, such as incompatible working hours, emergent properties, such as lack of relationship direction, and attributions of blame, such as perceiving that someone else is to blame.
- Lack of skills – for example, being sexually inexperienced.
- Lack of motivation – for example, perceiving inequity.
- Lack of maintenance – for example, spending too much time apart.

Duck believed that the 'official' reasons given to others, including partners, to justify breaking up are more interesting psychologically than the real reasons. The psychology of break-up involves many individual psychological processes, group processes, cultural rules and self-presentation to others.

As Duck (2001) said:

> *'Truly committed romantic relationships involve the foregoing of other romantic relationships and commitment to only one partner . . . So, the ending of a romantic relationship indicates two people are now legitimately available as partners for other relationships. This requires them to create a story for the end of the relationship that leaves them in a favourable light as potential partners. Romantic relationships are, therefore, typically ended publicly in a way that announces the ex-partners' freedom from the expectations of exclusive commitment.'*

Duck (1982) sees dissolution as a personal process, but one where partners regard how things will look to friends and social networks. Duck therefore suggested an account of dissolution involving four sequential phases. This

**KEY TERM**

**Dissolution** – the process by which romantic relationships break down

**Duck's phase model of dissolution** – that relationship breakdown occurs through a series of stages (also known as Duck's phase model of relationship breakdown)

explanation begins where one partner is sufficiently dissatisfied with the relationship over a long enough period of time to consider ending it.

The four phases are:

1. **Intrapsychic** – one partner privately perceives dissatisfaction with the relationship.
2. **Dyadic** – the dissatisfaction is discussed. If it is not resolved, there is a move to the next stage.
3. **Social** – the breakdown is made public. There is negotiation about children, finances and so on, with wider families and friends becoming involved.
4. **Grave dressing** – a post-relationship view of the break-up is established, protecting self-esteem and rebuilding life towards new relationships.

**Figure 3.13** Duck's theory sees relationship breakdown as occurring in four phases

The thresholds (precipitating factors) and phases are shown in Table 3.3.

**Table 3.3** The main thresholds and phases of dissolving personal relationships (based on Duck, 1982; from Duck, 1988)

| Threshold | Phase | Characteristic behaviours |
|---|---|---|
| 'I can't stand this any more' | Intrapsychic phase | • Personal focus on partner's behaviour<br>• Assess adequacy of partner's role performance<br>• Depict and evaluate negative aspects of being in the relationship<br>• Consider costs of withdrawal<br>• Assess positive aspects of alternative relationships<br>• Face 'express/repress dilemma' – whether you should express your dissatisfaction or keep it to yourself |
| 'I'd be justified in withdrawing' | Dyadic phase | • Face up to 'confrontation/avoidance dilemma'<br>• Confront partner<br>• Negotiation through 'our relationship' talks<br>• Attempt repair and reconciliation?<br>• Assess joint costs of withdrawal or reduced intimacy |
| 'I mean it' | Social phase | • Negotiate post-dissolution state with partner<br>• Initiate gossip/discussion in social network<br>• Create publicly negotiable face-saving/blame-placing stories and accounts<br>• Consider and face up to implied social network effect |
| 'It's now inevitable' | Grave-dressing phase | • Perform 'getting over it' activities<br>• Retrospective, reformative post-mortem attribution<br>• Publicly distribute own version of break-up |

## Research

Kassin (1996) found that women are more likely to stress unhappiness and incompatibility as reasons for dissolution, while men blame lack of sex. Women wish to remain friends, while males want a clean break, suggesting gender differences that Duck's model does not consider.

Argyle (1988) found that women identified lack of emotional support as a reason for dissolution, while men cited absence of fun, again suggesting gender differences that the model does not explain.

Hatfield *et al.* (1984) reported that when an individual experiences initial dissatisfaction with a relationship they are burdened by resentment and feelings of being 'under-benefited', which leads to social withdrawal so that the individual can consider their position, thus supporting the notion of an intrapsychic phase.

Akert (1992) found that the person who instigated the break-up suffers fewer negative consequences than the non-instigator, suggesting individual differences in the effects of dissolution that the model does not explain.

Tashiro & Frazier (2003) performed a survey of 92 students about their experiences after relationship breakdowns, finding a number of personal growth factors that helped with future relationships, such as feeling stronger, more independent and better off emotionally. Participants also felt they had gained wisdom that would help them with future relationships and that their relationships with friends had strengthened. This supports Duck's idea that through grave-dressing processes people are able to recover and move on after relationship dissolution.

### YOU ARE THE RESEARCHER

Design an interview that investigates the reasons why romantic relationships fail and the stages that breakdowns occur by. Will you use a structured, semi-structured or unstructured interview technique and open or closed questions or a mixture of the two? Once you have decided, compose your questions. How will you deal with possible interviewer effects when interviewing both males and females? Finally you will need to decide how to assess and present your data.

### Evaluation

- The theory has face validity as it is an account of relationship breakdown that most people can relate to their own and/or others' experiences.
- The view of dissolution as a process, rather than an event, is widely accepted. This view applies to the breakdown of friendships as well as sexual relationships, including marriages. However, the theory applies mainly to romantic relationships because these are exclusive in a way that friendships generally are not.
- The theory does not focus exclusively on individual partners, but takes their social context into account. As Duck (2001) says: 'Break-up involves not only the individual creating the break-up, but the psychological sense of integrity of the person to whom it all happens . . . But a lot that happens is done with an eye on the group that surrounds the person.'
- The theory does not take into account why dissatisfaction occurred in the first place; its starting point is where dissatisfaction has already set in. Therefore it fails to provide a complete picture of dissolution.
- Duck's four phases are not universal – they do not apply in every case of relationship breakdown – nor do they always occur in the order described.
- The model does not usually apply to homosexual relationships which may not involve some of the decisions over children that heterosexuals have to consider. Additionally it does not apply to heterosexual couples who decide not to have children.

- The model is simplistic as it does not account for relationships such as casual affairs and friendships.
- Rollie & Duck (2006), responding to criticisms, modified the theory to add a fifth phase of resurrection after that of grave dressing, which represented a period of reconfiguration of self and preparation for new relationships. They also added a new element whereby communication patterns within each phase could result in a reversion to an earlier, more positive state of the relationship rather than progressing on to the next phase of the break-up.

## PSYCHOLOGY IN THE REAL WORLD

A practical application of research into relationship formation and dissolution is that of relationship counselling, such as that offered by the organisation Relate. Advice, sex therapy, workshops and mediation are provided for individuals of all ages and persuasions, and even assistance with separating and divorcing, including counselling for children.

Relate helps 150,000 people a year in Britain, with 80 per cent of respondents reporting that the organisation strengthened their relationships. Relate's success can be attributed to the fact that everything the organisation does, including the training of staff, is based on solid psychological facts established through properly conducted research. Therefore Relate's high profile and the valuable work it does are a shining example of the practical applications that psychology can have in the real world, greatly benefiting and enhancing people's lives.

**Figure 3.14** Relationship counselling is a practical application of research into relationship formation and dissolution

## STRENGTHEN YOUR LEARNING

1. Summarise the main points that describe social exchange theory (SET).
2. To what extent does research evidence support SET?
3. What other evaluative points can be made about SET?
4. Summarise the main points that describe equity theory (ET).
5. To what extent does research evidence support ET?
6. What other evaluative points can be made about ET?
7. For Rusbult's investment model of commitment, a) explain what is meant by i) satisfaction level, ii) quality of alternatives, iii) investment size; b) explain how i) equity, ii) social support are linked to commitment.
8. To what extent does research evidence support Rusbult's theory?
9. What other evaluative points can be made about Rusbult's theory?
10. Outline a) the general reasons Duck gives for relationship dissolution, b) other contributory factors for dissolution, c) the four phases of dissolution.
11. To what extent does research evidence support Duck's theory?
12. What other evaluative points can be made about Duck's theory?

# ASSESSMENT CHECK

1. Select from the characteristics A, B, C and D below to complete the table relating to the phases of Duck's theory of dissolution. One description will be left over. **[3 marks]**

   **A** Discussion of situation with friends

   **B** Consideration of the costs of dissolution

   **C** Confrontation with partner

   **D** Performance of 'getting over it' activities

   | Phases of Duck's theory | Characteristic |
   | --- | --- |
   | Social phase | |
   | Intrapsychic phase | |
   | Dyadic phase | |

2. To investigate the investment model of relationships a researcher used an Investment Scale questionnaire, which gave an investment score for each participant on a scale of 0–30, with 0 representing no investment in relationships and 30 representing extreme investment in relationships. The calculated measures of central tendency for the investment scores were for the mean, 10.7, for the median, 11.8 and for the mode 15.

   Sketch a graph to show the distribution of investment scores. Label the axes and mark on the positions of the mean, median and mode. **[4 marks]**

3. Derek is in a long-term relationship with Catherine. Derek used to find the relationship very rewarding, as Catherine gave him a lot of affection and attention. However, more recently Derek feels he puts more into the relationship than he is getting out of it and he also feels he has given up a lot, like not seeing his friends as much as he used to.

   Explain how Derek views his relationship with Catherine in terms of the social exchange theory. **[3 marks]**

4. Research into self-disclosure often uses self-reports. Explain one limitation of self-reports in investigating self-disclosure. **[2 marks]**

5. Outline what is meant by the quality of alternatives within Rusbult's investment model. **[2 marks]**

6. Outline and evaluate the equity theory of romantic relationships. **[16 marks]**

*'The internet is the ultimate singles' bar – without the noise, the drunks, and the high cost of all those not-so-happy hours.'*

Eric Shipmon (2012)

# 3.5 Virtual relationships in social media

The internet and social media have become key factors in the relationships of many individuals in the modern world, involving both romantic and friendship relationships. The internet has created a great opportunity for people to seek and create relationships. According to the Pew Research Internet Project (2013), 11 per cent of all Americans and 38 per cent of those single and looking for a partner have used online dating sites or mobile dating apps. Online dating is most apparent among the 20–45-year-old age group, which is to be expected as this age group has either grown up with or experienced their adult life at a time that coincides with the introduction and growth of social media. Of Americans using online dating sites, 66 per cent have gone on to physically meet up with someone they found through a dating site, with 23 per cent claiming to have met a long-term partner through such means. Internet dating sites have benefited greatly from the advent of picture and video sharing, which are important for creating personal profiles and allowing more choosiness in deciding whether to pursue a virtual relationship with someone.

An early drawback of **virtual relationships** was that such relationships had no visual or audio element to them and were not conducted in real time. The multiple techniques face-to-face interactions use, such as vocal inflections and body language cues, were not present, meaning that such relationships were less rich in communication and presented more opportunities for misreading communications. However, advancements in technology that now allows virtual relationships to be conducted visually in real time with webcams mean that the quality of communication in virtual relationships is greatly advanced.

Online dating is credited with facilitating an increase in inter-racial relationships and spreading the acceptance of homosexual relationships. Dating sites also allow sexual minorities greater access to possible partners. Virtual relationships may allow individuals to explore and experiment with aspects of their sexuality that they never would have in face-to-face relationships.

Social networking services can give greater access to virtual relationships, as they allow individuals to seek and find others with whom they have characteristics in common, such as location, hobbies, age, etc. Individuals can access information about others through their profiles, allowing selection of individuals for possible virtual relationships.

Many individuals also form virtual relationships through online gaming sites, such as World of Warcraft, which allow players to interact and form gaming groups, leading to opportunities for further communication, interaction and even romantic relationships. Such interactions and relationships can also form through online forums and chat rooms.

### KEY TERM

**Virtual relationships** – non-physical interactions between people communicating via social media

**Figure 3.15** The growth of the internet and other social media has seen a huge increase in virtual relationships

Virtual relationships are considered to have produced greater levels of intimacy between individuals, especially those who are less socially skilled, as virtual relationships circumvent barriers that face-to-face relationships can have. Such relationships may also help socially inept people to learn social skills that will aid their ability to form and maintain face-to-face relationships.

A danger of forming virtual relationships is people misrepresenting themselves and that due to the anonymous nature of such relationships people, especially females, become harassed or threatened in ways that would be unlikely to occur in face-to-face relationships. This is known as trolling or cyber-bullying. Individuals are harassed due to the anonymity that social media provides. The virtual nature of the relationship means that bullies or trolls become divorced from the consequences of their actions. Cyber-stalking also occurs where online predators groom victims by misrepresenting themselves, with examples of such relationships becoming physical and abusive.

An interesting aspect of virtual relationships is whether internet affairs are as serious as 'real' affairs. Evolutionary theory predicts that females should be more critical of such conduct, as they have more to lose through emotional infidelity (which is what internet affairs involve), while males should be less critical, as they have more to lose through sexual infidelity, which internet affairs do not involve (see The evolutionary explanations for partner preferences, page 64).

## Research

Mesch & Talmud (2006) surveyed 987 Israeli teenagers to find that they had known their online friends for shorter lengths of time than their physical friends and participated in fewer activities with them, tending to communicate only about specific interests. They also had fewer discussions with virtual friends and on less personal topics. Overall, virtual friendships were perceived as less close, which suggests that for the majority virtual relationships are not as integrated with everyday life as face-to-face relationships are.

Stephure et al. (2009) reported that most people indulging in virtual relationships were seeking fun, companionship and someone to talk to. A majority were also interested in developing casual friendships and dating relationships. However, very few reported seeking such relationships to specifically find sexual or marital partners. This suggests that any long-term physical relationships that develop from virtual relationships are mainly a secondary effect of such relationships.

Mishna et al. (2009) found that the vast majority of 16–24 year olds considered virtual relationships to be as real as their physical relationships and that the internet played a crucial role in sexual and romantic experiences of adolescents, illustrating the importance and acceptance of virtual relationships by the younger generation.

Smith & Duggan (2013) report that 54 per cent of people using online dating sites believe they have been involved with someone misrepresenting themselves and 28 per cent have been contacted in a way that made them feel harassed or uncomfortable. This was more apparent among females (42 per cent) compared with males (17 per cent). The findings back up the view that social media presents more dangers of misrepresentation and harassment than face-to-face relationships do.

> **RESEARCH IN FOCUS**
>
> A lot of the research into virtual relationships is conducted with interviews and questionnaires. Explain why the findings of such research can be invalid due to participants giving idealised and socially desirable answers.

Cornwell & Lundgren (2001) surveyed 80 chat room users to find that 28 per cent admitted to misrepresenting their physical appearance, 23 per cent their age and 18 per cent their background, illustrating the widespread use of misrepresentation in virtual relationships.

Parker & Wampler (2003) found that both males and females considered internet affairs to be less of an affair than a physical affair. Internet affairs primarily involve emotional rather than sexual infidelity, which goes against evolutionary theory that females would be more jealous and therefore more critical of such conduct (see The evolutionary explanations for partner preferences, page 64). This is supported by the researchers also finding that females find involvement in online porn more objectionable than males, again refuting evolutionary theory about gender differences concerning infidelity.

**ON THE WEB**

Watch a fascinating BBC 2 programme about Kira and Nick and how their virtual relationship became an intimate face-to-face relationship, with even their marriage taking place in cyberspace. Go to **www.youtube.com** and search for 'Wonderland – virtual relationships'.

### Evaluation

- 'Real' relationships can have a virtual side to them. Lenhart & Duggan (2014) reported that 25 per cent of Americans who are married or in long-term partnerships have texted their partner when both were at home together. Indeed, 21 per cent of mobile phone and internet users in committed relationships report that they have felt closer to their partners as a result of online or text exchanges and 9 per cent have resolved arguments online or by text that they were having trouble resolving in person. These effects are even higher with younger people. However, 8 per cent of people in committed relationships believe their relationship has suffered due to their partner's virtual relationships with others.
- Virtual relationships may be stopping people from committing to long-term non-virtual relationships because social media supplies them with a never-ending supply of people to form relationships with.
- The ways in which virtual relationships form and are conducted will continue to evolve as different forms of social media emerge. For example, Facebook is a relatively new phenomenon with no guarantee that it will last long term or not be replaced by other social media, in the same way that Bebo and Myspace are now less popular than they were.
- Although online interactions have been calculated to take four times longer than face-to-face interactions, this gives users time to evaluate what has been communicated to them and time to consider a 'perfect' response, making the quality of interactions potentially superior to that of face-to-face communications.

*'On the internet all you reveal is your heart.'*
Anonymous

## Self-disclosure in virtual relationships

Self-disclosure involves revealing of personal information about oneself to another individual. Psychologists are interested in determining whether this differs between virtual relationships and face-to-face relationships.

The anonymity of virtual relationships means that individuals can reveal intimate personal information with less fear of being socially embarrassed by such information being leaked to people who know them. This is similar to Rubin's (1975) 'strangers on a train' phenomenon, where individuals reveal more

**Figure 3.16** The anonymity of the internet allows for greater self-disclosure in virtual relationships

personal information to a stranger as they do not have access to the individual's social circle. Unlike strangers who only meet once, virtual relationships allow for continued interactions, meaning that a relationship can be built.

Because of the greater ease of self-disclosure in virtual relationships, closeness and intimacy develop more quickly than with face-to-face relationships and are based on more meaningful factors, such as shared attitudes and interests, rather than more superficial factors found with face-to-face relationships, like physical attractiveness. Also, because of the anonymity of virtual relationships, self-disclosure tends to be about one's 'true' self rather than a publicly presented 'false' self and such real intimacies help to build a stronger, more meaningful relationship. As virtual relationships have a tendency, through intimate self-disclosure, to be stronger and more meaningful, this means they also have the potential to be long-lasting, unlike more superficial face-to-face relationships.

Self-disclosure creates high levels of affection that are sustained if people in virtual relationships actually meet. This occurs due to a lack of physical information, which can help form initial impressions of individuals who are resistant to change. As deep, virtual relationships form without physical information, such information will not be that influential when people meet.

A recent phenomenon of self-disclosure in virtual relationships is sexting, the sending of sexually explicit photos/videos. This occurs as probably people feel less inhibited in their behaviour in social media than in real life, but there are dangers, such as being blackmailed or coerced into such behaviour against one's will. Self-disclosure in virtual relationships also carries a danger of dishonest individuals misrepresenting themselves in order to appear favourable so that they can successfully exploit people, for example for financial gain or sexual purposes.

## Research

Yum & Hara (2005) found that American participants reported that greater disclosure in virtual relationships was associated with more trust, while Korean participants reported greater disclosure led to less trust, while greater disclosure was not a factor with Japanese participants. This suggests that the effect of disclosure on virtual relationships is mediated by cultural factors.

Peter *et al.* (2005) found introverts were motivated to communicate online to compensate for their lack of social skills, which increased their motivation to make friends online, which in turn led to more self-disclosure and thus more intimate virtual relationships. This suggests that quieter, shy people are more attracted to self-disclose in virtual relationships. However, it was also found that extroverts self-disclosed more in virtual relationships, which helped to develop their relationships further too, illustrating again how personality mediates virtual relationships.

Schouten *et al.* (2007) found that people high in social anxiety revealed greater self-disclosure in virtual relationships due to the lack of non-verbal cues in online communications, supporting the idea that people who have problems socialising in the physical world are able to self-disclose more in virtual relationships.

McKenna & Bargh (2000) surveyed 568 internet users to find that 54 per cent had gone on to physically meet virtual friends and 63 per cent had talked on the phone. In a two-year follow-up study, 57 per cent revealed their virtual relationships had continued and increased in intimacy. Romantic relationships fared even better, with 70 per cent of relationships formed online enduring beyond two years compared with more than 50 per cent of physical relationships that fail within two years. The results illustrate how virtual relationships can develop into physical ones and their often enduring nature.

Data from the Pew Research Internet Project (2014) shows that 9 per cent of American mobile phone owners have sent a sext, with individuals in relationships just as likely to do so as single people. This suggests that this form of uninhibited self-disclosure is a quite common occurrence.

## Evaluation

- The fact that people who lack social skills are especially attracted to virtual relationships suggests a practical application in using virtual relationships as a therapy for the socially inept to learn social skills useful for shaping social relationships in the real world. Such a therapy could also be used to help those with social phobias (fear of social situations) overcome their fears.

- One of the dangers of self-disclosure in virtual relationships is that individuals may be presenting their ideal self to their virtual partner, rather than their real self, faults and all. Therefore the intimacy created can lead to idealisation of a virtual partner, which the person cannot live up to in reality.

- Research has not really discriminated between different types of intimacy and the effects these have on the degree of attraction an individual feels towards a partner. For example, the intimate physical nature of sexting is very different to the intimate revelations of one's inner thoughts and feelings.

- The internet and other forms of social media may be creating social pressure upon individuals to conform to certain levels of intimate disclosures that they are not truly happy with. This is especially true of sexting where many individuals, often female, report pressure on them to send sexts.

# Effects of the absence of gating on the nature of virtual relationships

The creation of virtual relationships is not subject to the usual limiting factors that affect the formation of face-to-face relationships. Visible features, such as level of physical attractiveness, a tendency to stutter, social inadequacy/shyness, etc., are not apparent, which means less physically beautiful and socially skilled individuals have a greater chance to build relationships to the point where intimate self-disclosure can occur. The idea is that once relationships have progressed on to a deeper, more intimate level, then revelations about lack of physical beauty, etc. will not be as damaging to a relationship as they would have been initially in the 'real' world.

As gating can create barriers to less physically attractive and socially inept individuals forming relationships, such individuals often have a stronger, unrealised need to self-disclose in a more intimate and honest fashion, thus revealing their 'true' self and building closer and more meaningful relationships than they would in face-to-face situations. Such individuals therefore regard their virtual relationships as more identity-important, as it is where they reveal their 'true' self.

**ON THE WEB**

A comprehensive and detailed account by Nguyen, Bin & Campbell (2012) of gating in internet and non-internet relationships, including theoretical aspects as well as research studies, can be found at **www.researchgate.net/ profile/Yu_Sun_Bin/publication/ 51750501_Comparing_online_ and_offline_selfdisclosure_a_ systematic_review/links/ 0fcfd506a4f4bd71ae000000.pdf.**

## Research

McKenna *et al.* (2002) got participants to either interact with a partner in person for 20 minutes on two 'real' occasions or via an internet chat room first before meeting face to face. In the final condition participants interacted with one partner in person and another via an internet chat room, but unbeknown to both partners they were actually the same participants (the order in which people met in this final condition was counterbalanced). Each participant was paired with an opposite-sex partner on ten occasions. It was found that partners were liked more when they met via the internet than face to face in all situations because communications were seen as more intimate. This supports the idea that in face-to-face interactions, superficial gating features, like degree of physical attractiveness, dominate and overwhelm other factors that lead to more intimate disclosure and greater attraction.

Bargh *et al.* (2002) found that intimacy developed more quickly with virtual than face-to-face relationships because of a lack of gating features that typically prevent intimate disclosures in face-to-face relationships. This supports the idea that a lack of gating helps virtual relationships to grow more quickly and intimately than face-to-face ones.

McKenna (2002) found that the removal of physical gating features, such as level of physical attractiveness, allowed certain disadvantaged people, such as those with a lack of physical beauty, to bypass the usual obstacles that hinder them from developing intimate relationships in face-to-face settings. This illustrates why a lack of gating features makes virtual relationships so desirable to those who find establishing face-to-face relationships difficult.

Rosemann & Safir (2006) used questionnaires to find that the online environment allowed individuals to experiment with and reveal non-conventional identities to others that would not be possible via face-to-face interactions due to inhibiting gating features. This illustrates how virtual relationships allow people to develop intimate relationships based more upon their true selves than face-to-face relations would.

### KEY TERM

**Absence of gating** – the lack of limiting factors upon the formation of virtual relationships that form barriers to the creation of physical relationships

### Evaluation

- As well as direct gating features that concern visible features of an individual, such as their shyness, lack of physical attractiveness, etc., gating features that limit self-disclosure can be more indirect ones, like the fear associated with face-to-face relationships of disclosed intimate details being revealed to one's social circle.
- The **absence of gating** features in virtual relationships means that there is a much wider potential group of people to form relationships with people online, as virtual relationships will, from the start, be focusing more upon common interests, attitudes, etc. rather than being limited by more superficial but dominant gating features, such as level of physical attractiveness.
- Research has not really considered that limiting gating features may differ between groups of people, for instance age and level of physical attractiveness are probably more of gating factors for females seeking male partners than for males seeking female partners.
- The majority of studies carried out so far into the lack of gating in virtual relationships have used self-reports, which may be prone to idealised and socially desirable answers and thus not be providing valid data.

## STRENGTHEN YOUR LEARNING

1. Summarise the main points regarding virtual relationships in social media.
2. What does research evidence suggest about virtual relationships in social media?
3. What other evaluative points can be made concerning virtual relationships in social media?
4. Explain how self-disclosure can affect virtual relationships in social media.
5. What does research evidence suggest about how self-disclosure affects virtual relationships in social media?
6. What other evaluative points can be made concerning how self-disclosure affects virtual relationships in social media?
7. Outline how an absence of gating can affect virtual relationships in social media.
8. What does research evidence suggest about how an absence of gating affects virtual relationships in social media?
9. What other evaluative points can be made concerning how an absence of gating affects virtual relationships in social media?

*'You can't ever be your heroes, but you can love their gifts.'*
John Piper (2011)

# 3.6 Parasocial relationships

**KEY TERM**

**Parasocial relationships** – one-sided relationships occurring with media personalities outside of an individual's real social network

**Parasocial relationships** are one-sided relationships that occur with media personalities outside of an individual's real social network, generally without the personality's knowledge, such as with hero worship of a celebrity. Parasocial encounters occur when individuals experience a media personality through media presentations, such as on a TV show. Individuals can come to feel that such encounters are the same as face-to-face meetings – they feel they 'know' the personality and are really meeting them. Parasocial relationships resemble physical interpersonal relationships, like friendships, in several ways, for example they are voluntary, have a personal focus, provide companionship and are preceded by attraction.

Parasocial relationships occur in all age groups, but peak between 11 and 17 years of age, then decline slowly afterwards. Level of education is also a factor – the less education, the greater the level of attraction to media personalities. There are gender differences, with males usually more interested in sports stars, while females are generally more interested in the entertainment world.

Parasocial relationships were originally perceived as abnormal and thought to have originated from factors such as neuroticism, isolation, loneliness, fear and a lack of social interactions and to be basically a substitute for inadequate relationships. However, a more recent idea is that parasocial relationships may actually serve to help people, especially young people, with identity formation, through observation and imitation of positive role

**Figure 3.17** Parasocial relationships are one-sided relationships occurring with media personalities outside of an individual's real social network

models. Parasocial relationships may even be related to mood states, for example interacting through media with a certain personality, as doing so is associated with having positive feelings.

## Research

Rubin *et al.* (1985) found little correlation between loneliness and the strength of TV viewers' parasocial relationships with onscreen characters, which refutes the idea that parasocial relationships are a dysfunctional substitute for inadequate relationships.

Turner (1993) found that parasocial relationships, like friendships, tend to form with media personalities with perceived similar attitudes, which supports the idea that parasocial relationships are similar to real interpersonal relationships, though no similarity was found between levels of physical attractiveness and background, which often occurs with face-to-face relationships.

Giles (2000) found that younger people were more attracted to media personalities than older people, supporting the idea that parasocial relationships are affected by age factors.

McCutcheon *et al.* (2002) found a negative correlation of −0.4 between amount of education and amount of celebrity worship, suggesting that those with less education have a more intense interest in celebrity.

Thompson (2006) reported that parasocial relationships satisfy many of the main needs fulfilled by real relationships – the need for relatedness (being connected to someone), competence (a sense of mastery and achievement) and independence. This supports the idea that parasocial relationships resemble face-to-face relationships in many ways.

Gabriel (2008) gave students a questionnaire measuring self-esteem and asked them to write an essay about their favourite celebrity, followed by the same questionnaire. Participants initially scoring low on self-esteem scored much higher after writing the essay, suggesting that they incorporated the celebrities' characteristics into themselves, thus boosting self-esteem, possibly something they could not do in real relationships as the fear of rejection stops them getting close to people. This illustrates how parasocial relationships can have beneficial qualities.

## Evaluation

- Level of education may be a factor in parasocial relationships, as educational high-achievers may perceive the majority of media personalities as less educated than themselves and therefore less worthy of positive regard.
- Younger people may be more attracted to media personalities because they have less involvement in face-to-face social networks and spend more time interacting with media sources than older people.
- Research into parasocial relationships generally uses questionnaires, which can be affected by socially desirable and idealised answers and therefore lack validity. Findings also tend to be in the form of correlations, which do not show causal relationships and may be affected by other variables. For instance, the relationship between low levels of education and high levels of fandom may actually concern levels of intelligence. McCutcheon *et al.* (2004) argue that low levels of education are associated with high levels of parasocial relationships because education is related to intelligence, and thus more intelligent people are better able to see the inadequacies of worshipping media personalities.
- West & Sweeting (2002) recommend media training in schools to highlight the dangers of idolising media personalities, such as developing eating disorders by indulging in extreme dieting to try to attain the super-slim body images of some media personalities.

> *'Stalking is when two people go for a long romantic walk together but only one of them knows about it.'*
>
> Anonymous

## Levels of parasocial relationships

People interact with many forms of media, such as TV, films, music, etc. where they encounter people represented by such media, like actors and musicians. Through media presentations individuals form impressions of these people, some of whom are attractive through the personal qualities that they appear to demonstrate. Feelings about such media personalities generally grow stronger with subsequent parasocial encounters and over time an individual may develop feelings of intimacy towards a media personality.

As such relationships grow stronger, individuals may immerse themselves in increased media presentations to 'maintain' the relationship (such as repeatedly watching a singer's performance on YouTube). Such media consumption can become ritualistic in nature, for instance viewing at certain times of day for certain amounts of time. Individuals may even try to intensify the relationship and show their affection by attempting to communicate with the personality (for example by fan mail) and purchasing memorabilia and products associated with the personality. Individuals may even move increasingly out of touch with their real world and deeper into their imagined world involving their relationship with the personality.

**Figure 3.18** Parasocial relationships are intensified by purchasing memorabilia relating to a media personality

McCutcheon *et al.* (2002) developed the Celebrity Attitude Scale, which measures items within three levels of parasocial relationships:

1. Entertainment-social sub-scale – measures social aspects of parasocial relationships, like discussing media personalities with friends.
2. Intense-personal sub-scale – measures strength of feelings and levels of obsession about media personalities.
3. Borderline-pathological sub-scale – measures levels of uncontrollable feelings and behaviour about media personalities.

It was concluded that parasocial relationships have a single dimension, with lower-scoring individuals showing a keen interest in media personalities, such as reading about them, while high-scoring individuals tend to over-identify with and become obsessive about them.

The differing levels of parasocial relationships are best explained through the **absorption-addiction model**.

## The absorption-addiction model

The absorption-addiction model proposed by McCutcheon (2002) believes that most individuals know that their degree of admiration for a media personality is because of their entertainment/skill level and this degree of admiration will progress no further than that. However, some people may seek a more intense parasocial relationship with a media personality to fill the dissatisfaction they feel in their own lives. For example, an individual who feels they are a low achiever may become fanatical about a media personality who is perceived as successful. In doing so they hope to 'absorb' some of the success.

In extreme cases, however, involvement in a parasocial relationship becomes addictive and an individual's behaviour may become extreme, bordering on the abnormal, and may even involve criminal behaviour. This might take the

### KEY TERM

**Absorption-addiction model** – where an individual's fascination with a media personality progresses to a delusion of a real relationship

form of celebrity stalking, an obsessive-addictive disorder where individuals may develop an illusion that they genuinely are in an intimate relationship with the media personality. Very occasionally such behaviour can result in physical violence towards a media personality (see Figure 3.19).

Giles & Maltby (2006) described how progression through the absorption-addiction model occurs in three levels:

1. Entertainment-social – individuals are attracted to media personalities because they are interesting.
2. Intense-personal – individuals feel a connection with the media personality, for example feeling that they are 'soul mates' with the celebrity.
3. Borderline-pathological – individuals in this category have uncontrollable behaviours and obsessive fantasies about their media personality which are completely divorced from reality and which prevent them living a normal life.

**Figure 3.19** John Lennon was murdered in 1980 by obsessed fan Mark David Chapman, whose idolisation of Lennon turned into an obsession with killing him

### ON THE WEB

An informative article by David Giles and John Maltby on parasocial relationships called 'Praying at the altar of the stars', which includes discussion activities and contact details for the researchers can be found at:

**http://thepsychologist.bps.org.uk/volume-19/edition2/praying-altar-stars**

## CONTEMPORARY RESEARCH

### Celebrity worship syndrome – McCutcheon & Houran (2003)

**Figure 3.20** Celebrity worship syndrome involves a fascination with the lives of the rich and famous

Celebrity worship syndrome (CWS) is a fascination with the lives of the rich and famous that can become addictive and cross the border from harmless fun to abnormal obsession. At its extremes CWS can develop into mentally disordered behaviour, involving delusions and stalking. The researchers were interested in assessing how common CWS is within the general population, and for what reasons individuals develop such a fascination.

#### Aim
To assess whether interest in media personalities divides into pathological and non-pathological cases.

#### Procedure
600 participants completed a personality test and were interviewed about their degree of interest in media personalities.

Participants rated statements, such as 'If he/she asked me to do something illegal as a favour, I would probably do it.'

#### Findings
One third of the participants exhibited CWS.

20 per cent followed media personalities for entertainment-social reasons, with such people tending to be extroverts.

10 per cent had intense-personal attitudes towards media personalities, bordering on addiction, and often believed they had a special bond with a celebrity. Their personalities tended to be neurotic, tense, emotional and moody.

1 per cent were classed as borderline-pathological, displaying impulsive, antisocial, self-centred behaviour indicative of psychosis. This group included celebrity stalkers and people willing to hurt themselves or others in the name of their idol.

#### Conclusions
The findings refute the view that celebrity worship is divisible into pathological and non-pathological cases (harmless

fun and obsession). Instead, they indicate a 'sliding scale', in which celebrity devotees become progressively more fascinated with their idols.

Individuals with intense attitudes towards celebrities are significantly more likely to suffer from anxiety, depression and social dysfunction.

Worshipping media personalities does not make people dysfunctional, but increases the chances of them becoming so.

Evaluation
- The three types of individuals with CWS correspond to Eysenck's three personality dimensions of extroversion, neuroticism and psychosis, though in unequal amounts.
- There is no indication whether certain personality types develop different forms and intensities of CWS, or whether being obsessed with celebrities causes self-esteem to diminish, which then develops into depression, anxiety and even psychosis.

## Research

Meloy (1998) reported that stalkers often have a history of failed sexual relationships and are usually not in sexual relationships at the time of the stalking. Stalking in such cases is a reaction to social incompetence, social isolation and loneliness, which suggests that the borderline pathological level of parasocial relationships is related to personal factors.

Purcell et al. (2002) found female stalkers were of a nurturing disposition, were searching for intimacy and stalked people they physically knew, offering a reason for why celebrity stalking is mainly a male pursuit.

Maltby et al. (2003) used Eysenck's personality questionnaire to find that individuals in the entertainment-social level scored highly on extroversion, while those in the intense-personal level scored highly on neuroticism. This suggests that an individual's level of involvement in parasocial relationships is mediated by personality factors.

Maltby et al. (2004) found that those in the entertainment-social category were mentally healthy, but those in higher categories were prone to poor mental and physical health, suggesting that different parasocial levels are associated with different levels of mental stability.

MacDougal (2005) believes the adoration given to dead celebrities by some fans is like that found in charismatic religions, suggesting that religious worship and extreme levels of parasocial relationships may fulfil similar needs in some individuals.

### Evaluation

- Maltby's (2002) entertainment-social dimension of parasocial relationships is consistent with Stever's (1991) observation that fans are attracted to media personalities due to their perceived ability to entertain.
- Research into the absorption-addiction model suggests people tend to become interested in celebrities at times when they are looking for direction in life, such as in their teenage years, and that such an interest can develop into addiction at a time of crisis, such as the loss of a loved one.
- Research into stalking may help to understand the behaviour, leading to the formation of effective therapies. Suggested treatments include psychotherapy to address underlying causes, with a role also for drug treatments, to reduce obsessive tendencies.
- Legal interventions, like trespassing orders, are the most effective way of dealing with celebrity stalkers, but can make stalkers even more obsessive, malicious and persecutory towards their targets.

> **RESEARCH IN FOCUS**
> Research into parasocial relationships often uses questionnaires. What strengths and weaknesses are there to this method of collecting data? In what ways would a) an interview, b) an experiment be i) superior, ii) inferior to using a questionnaire?

## Attachment theory explanation

An alternative explanation for parasocial relationships is that of **attachment theory**. People form different types of attachments to caregivers in infancy and these attachment types are seen as affecting relationships in later life. Those with insecure-resistant attachment type (see Book One, Chapter 3) are seen as most likely to form parasocial relationships because such individuals have a need for close emotional relationships, but ones in which there is reduced risk of rejection. In a parasocial relationship an individual can believe they have a close intimate bond to a media personality, but as the media personality is not aware of this relationship, there is no chance they will reject the individual.

People with secure attachments are able to develop loving, two-way relationships in real face-to-face relationships and thus have little need for parasocial relationships. People with insecure-avoidant attachments have difficulties trusting others and therefore indulge in behaviours designed not to create intimacy and thus are less likely to foster close emotional ties in either face-to-face or parasocial relationships.

### Research

Kienlen *et al.* (1997) found that 63 per cent of stalkers experienced a loss of primary caregivers during childhood, usually due to parental separation, while more than 50 per cent reported childhood emotional, physical or sexual abuse by primary caregivers. This supports the idea that disturbed attachment patterns are related to extreme forms of parasocial relationships.

Cole & Leets (1999) found that adolescents with insecure-resistant attachments were more likely to have parasocial relationships with television media personalities than those with secure and insecure-avoidant attachments, supporting the idea that those with insecure-resistant attachments are more attracted to parasocial relationships.

McCutcheon *et al.* (2006) measured attraction to celebrities, finding that adults with insecure attachment types had positive attitudes towards obsessive behaviours and stalking, and also that pathological attachment types have a tendency to stalk, implying that stalking behaviour is related to childhood attachment patterns.

McCutcheon (2006) found no relationship between childhood attachment patterns and mild forms of celebrity worship, suggesting that it is only more intense forms of parasocial relationships that are related to attachment types.

**KEY TERM**

**Attachment theory** – the tendency for parasocial relationships to be formed by those with insecure childhood attachments

## Evaluation

- Ross & Spinner (2001) have indicated that there is variation in attachment styles across significant relationships. If this also applies to parasocial relationships it would mean linking a specific attachment pattern to such relationships is not valid.
- Stever (2013) proposes the existence of parasocial attachment, an additional form of attachment to infant–carer attachments and adult romantic attachments, which is progressed to through parasocial interaction (PSI) and then parasocial relationships (PSR). Such attachments are often formed by adolescents to media personalities to allow for the safe exploration of romantic feelings with a partner who will not place any demands on the teenager.
- The idea of attachment being related to parasocial relationships is supported by a key component of attachment theory, that of seeking proximity to the attachment figure. Those in parasocial relationships will often seek 'closeness' to their admired media personality.
- Individuals look to attachment figures as a 'safe base' and this can be seen as a feature of many parasocial relationships where an individual regards a media personality as such a safe base. Stever (2009) cites examples where individuals who have experienced loss of a loved one found comfort in parasocial relationships, for instance with pop stars who 'speak to them' through their lyrics.

### STRENGTHEN YOUR LEARNING

1. Describe what is meant by parasocial relationships.
2. What has research suggested about parasocial relationships?
3. What other evaluative points can be made concerning parasocial relationships?
4. Outline McCutcheon's (2002) Celebrity Attitude Scale.
5. Summarise the main points of the absorption-addiction model.
6. Outline and evaluate McCutcheon & Houran's (2003) study of celebrity worship syndrome.
7. What does other research evidence suggest about the absorption-addiction model?
8. What other evaluative points can be made concerning the absorption-addiction model?
9. Summarise the main points of the attachment theory explanation.
10. What does research evidence suggest about the attachment theory explanation?
11. What other evaluative points can be made concerning the attachment theory explanation?

# ASSESSMENT CHECK

1. Select from the descriptions A, B, C and D below to complete the table relating to levels of parasocial relationships. One description will be left over. **[3 marks]**

   A Individuals have obsessive fantasies about a media personality

   B Individuals stop using social media

   C Individuals are attracted to media personalities because they are interesting

   D Individuals feel an emotional connection with a media personality

   | Level of parasocial relationship | Description |
   | --- | --- |
   | Entertainment–social | |
   | Intense–personal | |
   | Borderline–pathological | |

2. Outline two ethical issues researchers would need to consider when conducting research into virtual relationships. **[2 + 2 marks]**

3. Manon is shy and not confident in social situations. This and the fact that she is not considered physically attractive has prevented her from ever having an intimate face-to-face romantic relationship. Recently though she met Doug online and easily felt able to disclose honest personal information about herself, resulting in an intimate, meaningful relationship quickly developing.

   Refer to features of the situation above to explain the effects an absence of gating has upon the nature of virtual relationships. **[3 marks]**

4. Outline and evaluate the absorption-addiction and/or attachment theory explanation of parasocial relationships. **[16 marks]**

5. Explain why it may be easier for individuals to self-disclose in virtual rather than face-to-face relationships. **[2 marks]**

## SUMMARY

- The evolutionary explanation for partner preferences sees a relationship between sexual selection and human reproductive behaviour, with different strategies for males and females due to different selective pressures.
- Several factors affect attraction in romantic relationships, such as the level of self-disclosure, where personal information is relayed between partners.
- Another factor is that of physical attractiveness, with the matching theory proposing that individuals of similar perceived beauty are suited to each other.
- The filter theory sees choice of partners as affected by factors limiting the availability of people to select from, such as social demography, similarity in attitudes and complementarity.
- Theories of romantic relationships include the social exchange theory, an economic explanation of relationship maintenance based on maximising profits and minimising costs, equity theory, based on motivation to achieve fairness and balance, and Rusbult's investment model of commitment, which views relationship satisfaction as dependent upon a consideration of perceived benefits, costs and the quality of possible alternative relationships.
- Duck's model of relationship dissolution sees the breakdown of relationships as occurring in a series of intrapsychic, dyadic, social and grave-dressing phases.
- Virtual relationships are formed by non-physical interactions between people communicating via social media, with higher levels of self-disclosure and lower levels of gating compared with face-to-face relationships.
- Parasocial relationships are one-sided relationships occurring with individuals outside of a person's real social network that can occur in different levels of involvement.
- The absorption-addiction model explains how parasocial relationships can progress from fascination with a media personality to a delusion of a real relationship.
- The attachment theory of parasocial relationships perceives a tendency for parasocial relationships to be formed by those with insecure childhood attachments.

**The evolutionary explanation for partner preference**

**Factors affecting attraction in romantic relationships**

**Theories of romantic relationships**

**Virtual relationships in social media**

**Parasocial (one-sided) relationships**

# 4 Gender

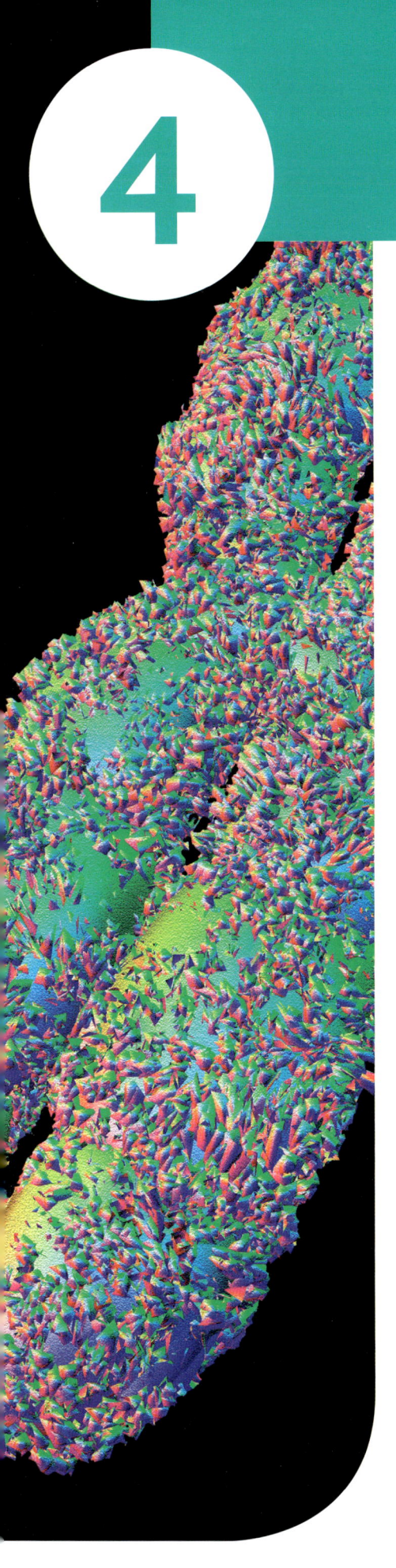

## Introduction

Sex concerns whether individuals are biologically male or female, while gender involves the social and psychological characteristics that go with being male or female. Interest has centred on sex roles, biological, cognitive, psychodynamic and behaviourist explanations of gender, along with atypical gender development.

Specific focus here will be upon:

1. Sex and gender
2. The role of chromosomes and hormones
3. Cognitive explanations for gender development
4. Psychodynamic explanation for gender development
5. Social learning theory as applied to gender development
6. Atypical gender development.

## Understanding the specification

- The specification requires a knowledge of sex and gender that focuses on sex-role stereotypes, as well as androgyny and measuring androgyny, including the Bem Sex Role Inventory, as these elements are explicitly named.
- When studying the role of chromosomes and hormones in sex and gender, testosterone, oestrogen and oxytocin must be included, as these are specifically listed, as are Klinefelter's syndrome and Turner's syndrome when studying atypical sex chromosome patterns.
- Cognitive explanations of gender development need to focus on Kohlberg's theory of gender identity, gender stability and gender constancy, as well as gender schema theory, as these are all explicitly listed.
- Study of the psychodynamic explanation of gender development needs to concentrate on Freud's psychoanalytic theory, Oedipus complex, Electra complex, identification and internalisation, as these again are explicitly listed.
- The social learning theory as applied to gender development should focus upon the influence of culture and media on gender roles, as again these elements are specifically named.
- The specification additionally requires a study of atypical gender development that focuses upon gender identity disorder, especially biological and social explanations, which are explicitly referred to.

These are the basic requirements of the specification. However, other relevant material is included to provide depth and detail to your understanding.

*'All through life there were distinctions – toilets for men, toilets for women; clothes for men, clothes for women – then, at the end, the graves are identical.'*

Leila Aboulela (2005)

## IN THE NEWS

# The Psychological Enquirer

**Figure 4.1** DJ Stephanie (formerly Simon) Hirst

Simon Hirst was a 39-year-old British DJ who hosted a popular breakfast radio show for 11 years until in September 2014 he disappeared from the airwaves without warning. Had he suddenly become unpopular? Been taken ill? Accused of some terrible crime? No, the simple fact was that Simon, who had known since about the age of eight that although physically male he felt psychologically more female, had decided to undergo gender reassignment treatment. His employers 'did not think gender reassignment was suitable or commercially viable content' for radio shows.

Simon, half-way through his treatment, is now known as Stephanie and is doing well. Although numerous sources say Stephanie was suspended from work when she disclosed that she wanted to be a woman, Stephanie says 'everyone was supportive' and that she 'feels genuinely alive', while before she felt like 'a square peg in a round hole'. Her former employers argue they were only thinking of Stephanie's well-being and being 'on air' was not in her best interests.

Stephanie is an example of someone with gender identity disorder, a condition in which individuals have the opposite physical sexual characteristics to the gender they feel they really are. Gender reassignment treatment for the condition is becoming more common – in 2009 143 surgeries were carried out in Britain compared with only 54 in 2000. Since 2000 865 state-funded sex change operations have been carried out, which suggests society is becoming more accepting of and sympathetic towards people with the condition. However, the true number of people with the condition is thought to be a lot higher, possibly a prevalence rate of 1 in every 5,000 people, with many individuals reluctant to publically admit their condition due to a fear of rejection and intimidation.

Hopefully the completion of Stephanie Hirst's treatment will see her return as a radio DJ to become a positive role model for others with the condition.

## 4.1 Sex and gender

*'One is not born, but rather becomes, a woman.'*

Simone de Beauvoir (1949)

**KEY TERMS**

**Sex** – whether an individual is biologically female or male

**Gender** – the social and psychological characteristics of males and females

**Sex** and **gender** are not the same thing, although they do overlap. Sex concerns whether individuals are biologically male or female, while gender concerns the social and psychological characteristics that relate to males and females. Androgyny is the idea that individuals can possess male and female characteristics and attempts have been made, as with the Bem Sex Role Inventory, to measure individuals' level of masculine and feminine features (see below, pages 111–114).

*'The emotional, sexual, and psychological stereotyping of females begins when the doctor says, It's a girl.'*

Shirley Chisholm (1973)

## Sex-role stereotypes

Sex-role beliefs concern the types of qualities and characteristics expected of members of each sex and these beliefs become **sex-role stereotypes** when they are applied as 'rules' to be followed by all individuals. Because these sex-role stereotypes are shared by a lot of people they come to be seen as 'expected' and 'proper' qualities to be exhibited. Individuals are born biologically male or female, but sex-role stereotypes teach them what qualities are seen as masculine and feminine and thus create norms (expected forms of behaviour and attitudes) that people feel pressured to conform to. Therefore much of what is considered as masculine and feminine is learned as a result of socialisation processes (the passing on of beliefs, attitudes and behaviour from one generation to another).

Traditionally sex-role stereotypes for females involve being nurturing, co-operative, domestic, emotional, passive (non-aggressive) and pretty, while males are expected to be strong, independent, physical, aggressive and unemotional. Perceived examples of stereotypes exhibited by members of a gender tend to be overstressed, for example males being aggressive while instances of aggression by females are downplayed. The holding of sex-role stereotypes also leads to an overemphasis of differences between genders, such as males being seen as more competitive and females as more co-operative.

Sex-role expectations are taught from an early age, such as in the way children of different genders are handled, with males being treated more physically. Different games/types of play are also seen as expected of different genders – girls playing quietly with dolls and boys playing more raucously with toy weapons, for instance. Boys and girls pick up sex-role stereotypes very quickly and not only conform to expected roles but also 'police' other children's roles. Individuals perceived as exhibiting incorrect stereotypes are subjected to hostility and pressure to assume 'correct' sex roles. At school boys and girls experience pressure to study 'gender-suitable' subjects, such as mathematics for boys and home economics for girls (indeed, it is noticeable how psychology is perceived as a more 'for girls' subject). Such expectations stretch into later life, with certain careers seen as more suitable for different genders, for instance nursing for females and engineering for males.

The ways in which males and females are portrayed in the media, such as on TV and in magazines, etc., are powerful sources of sex-role stereotyping, both of children and of adults. The role of culture in socialising sex-role stereotypes is also strong, but although many stereotypes are common across cultures, such as males being aggressive and females being passive, considerable differences between cultures also exist, with even behaviours and attitudes regarded as masculine in one culture being seen as feminine in another culture. (For research studies concerning media and cultural influences that could be used to answer questions on sex-role stereotyping, see Section 4.5, Social learning theory as applied to gender development, page 135.)

### KEY TERM

**Sex-role stereotypes** – types of qualities and characteristics seen as appropriate for each sex

**Figure 4.2** Generally our sex-role stereotypes suggest to us that nurses should be female, while in reality there are many male nurses

## Research

Seavey et al. (1975) told one in three adult participants that a three-month old baby dressed in a yellow jumpsuit was a boy, said it was a girl, or did not reveal the baby's gender. They were left to play with the baby in a room containing a ball (stereotypically male toy), a doll (stereotypically female toy) and a plastic ring (non sex-role stereotypical toy). Both male and female adults gave the baby the doll to play with if they believed it to be female, but were more likely to give it the non-stereotypical toy if they thought the baby was a boy. When the baby's gender was not known, female adults handled the baby more and both male and females adults tried to assess the baby's gender on the basis of its perceived strength. The results suggest that males and females react to babies differently according to what gender they believe them to be.

Langlois & Downs (1980) compared peers' and mothers' reactions to preschoolers' play with opposite-gender toys. When boys played with girls' toys, mothers accepted this, but male peers ridiculed and even hit them, demonstrating the intolerance of male peers for cross-gender behaviour, and thus the strength of their influence on establishing gender roles. This was further supported by Archer & Lloyd (1982) reporting that three-year-old children who played the opposite sex's games were ridiculed by peers and ostracised, supporting the idea that peers police sex-role stereotyping.

Urberg (1982) told children aged 3–7 years stories that stressed sex-role stereotypical characteristics, such as bravery or caring, but without specifying the gender of the child in the story. After each story children had to state whether the characteristic illustrated was typical of girls, boys or neither. It was found that responses favoured sex-role stereotypes, such as bravery being a male characteristic and caring a female one. There was a tendency, which peaked at age five, for children to attribute positive characteristics to their own gender and negative ones to their non-gender. Older children showed an increasing tendency to see characteristics as both male and female. The results imply that children learn sex-role stereotypes at an early age, but that they change with age.

Eccles et al. (1990) reported that children were encouraged by their parents to play with gender-typical toys, supporting the idea that parents reinforce sex-role stereotypes. This was supported by Lytton & Romney (1991) finding that parents praised sex-role stereotypical behaviour in boys and girls, such as what activities they participated in.

Renzetti & Curran (1992) found that teachers gave reinforcements such as praise to boys for instances of 'cleverness', while girls received praise for 'neatness', supporting the view that teachers enforce sex-role stereotypes. This was further supported by Colley (1994) finding that in secondary schools pupils had a tendency to view individual subjects as either masculine or feminine, illustrating a further instance of sex-role stereotyping in education.

Sood et al. (2014) reported that only 12 per cent of British primary school teachers and 3 per cent of nursery teachers are male, due to early years teaching being seen as a female profession, their nurturing abilities and the unsuitability of males thanks to their perception as intimidating and threatening. The findings illustrate how sex-role stereotypes affect adult career choices.

**Figure 4.3** Only 12 per cent of British primary school teachers are male

### Evaluation

- The fact that sex-role stereotypes can differ substantially cross-culturally suggests that the characteristics associated with sex roles are culturally transmitted, which implies that environmental learning experiences are stronger than biological forces in determining sex-role stereotypes (see Mead (1935), page 141).
- As evidence suggests that sex-role stereotypes are mainly learned through environmental experience, it implies that negative sex-role stereotyping could be addressed by providing learning experiences for children that reinforce the idea of positive sex roles being equally applicable to males and females.
- One difficulty in addressing negative sex-role stereotyping, such as females being inferior due to their lack of strength and emotional nature, is that examples of stereotypes tend to be over-emphasised as 'typical behaviour', for instance girls crying, while similar behaviour in males is under-stressed as non-typical. Such 'typical' differences are then perceived as 'natural' differences, thus reinforcing the stereotype, making it harder to break down.
- The media are subjected to criticism of their stereotypical presentation of sex roles and so their portrayals have become less stereotyped. However, some argue such portrayals are still stereotyped, but more subtly so, and continue to exert harmful effects, especially in their presentation of negative female sex-role stereotypes.
- Although cultural influences result in different forms of sex-role stereotypes in different cultures, with globalisation and the breaking down of cultural beliefs and practices we may see a movement towards uniform sex-role stereotypes in all cultures.
- Categorising behaviours, occupations, qualities, etc. as either masculine or feminine may place restrictive barriers on positive roles that both males and females could play in society, like males having a primary role in the nurturing of children (only 3 per cent of nursery teachers are currently male) or females making contributions as scientists (only one British woman has ever won a Nobel prize for science).

> 'Androgyny is not trying to manage the relationship between the opposites, it is simply flowing between them.'
> Dr June Singer (1976)

# Androgyny

**Androgyny** involves having both male and female characteristics, which is beneficial, as individuals may act in a masculine way in some situations, such as being domineering in the workplace, and feminine in other situations, such as being nurturing at home, or they may simultaneously blend elements of both.

### KEY TERM

**Androgyny** – co-existence of male and female characteristics within the same individual

**Figure 4.4** Androgyny involves having both male and female characteristics

Traditionally, individuals were seen as masculine or feminine, and it was assumed that those with a good fit with their gender role – that is, masculine males and feminine females – were better adjusted and psychologically healthier. Many psychological tests built assumption into them, making it impossible to score as highly masculine *and* highly feminine, i.e. to be androgynous.

Olds (1981) believed that androgyny is a higher developmental stage reached only by some, while Bem (1983) argued that androgynous individuals have a different cognitive style and adopt behaviours, when necessary, that are independent of gender concepts. Therefore, in terms of cognitive schema theory (which explains how sex-role stereotypes are maintained and transmitted to other members of a culture), androgynous people are gender aschematic (not influenced by sex-role stereotypes), in line with Old's explanation, as individuals can become androgynous only when they perceive the world without gender stereotypes.

Orlofsky (1977) has a behavioural explanation for androgyny, seeing it as learned through reinforcement, allowing individuals to acquire masculine and feminine qualities applicable to different situations. Therefore androgyny is seen more in behavioural than in cognitive terms.

Perhaps because young children's ideas about sex roles are rigid, there is little sign of androgyny among children before nine years of age. But from 11 years onwards signs of androgyny appear, with children showing variation in what they believe masculinity and femininity are.

## Bem Sex Role Inventory

By the early 1970s the view that individuals were either exclusively masculine or feminine was being challenged, and masculinity and femininity were argued to be independent dimensions rather than opposite ends of the same continuum (range). Bem (1975) developed the androgynous hypothesis, which saw androgyny as a positive and desirable condition. A different kind of test was needed to incorporate this notion and the **Bem Sex Role Inventory** (BSRI), designed to measure androgyny, was introduced. This self-report consists of 60 items rated on a seven-point scale: 20 items relate to stereotypically masculine characteristics, 20 to stereotypically feminine characteristics, and 20 are gender-neutral filler items. Individuals score separately for masculinity and femininity to calculate their overall type. The test was revised in 1977 to create four categories of person:

1 **Masculine** – high masculinity, low femininity.
2 **Feminine** – low masculinity, high femininity.
3 **Androgynous** – high masculinity, high femininity.
4 **Undifferentiated** – low masculinity, low femininity.

A prediction derived from the BSRI is that androgyny is a better indicator of psychological well-being/mental health than just having masculine or feminine qualities and evidence supports this view.

### KEY TERM

**Bem Sex Role Inventory** – a self-report measure of masculinity–femininity and gender role

### ON THE WEB

Want to know how androgynous you are? Then take a self-marking BSRI internet test that supplies a score for masculinity, femininity and androgyny. Find the test at:
http://garote.bdmonkeys.net/bsri.html

## CLASSIC RESEARCH

### Psychological androgyny and personality adjustment in normal and clinical populations – Carol Burchardt & Lisa Serbin (1982)

Androgyny involves having masculine and feminine characteristics, which, in her androgyny hypothesis, Sandra Bem saw as desirable. The researchers in this investigation were interested in testing this by investigating the relationship between androgyny and mental health – if Bem was correct then androgyny would be positively correlated with good mental health.

**Figure 4.5** Dr Lisa Serbin, along with her co-researcher Carol Burchardt, provided evidence that androgyny is associated with good mental health

### Aim
To see whether androgyny was associated with positive mental health in both normal and psychiatric populations.

### Procedure
The participants were 106 female and 84 male undergraduates, and 48 female and 48 male psychiatric inpatients.

All participants were administered the BSRI and the Faschingbauer Abbreviated Minnesota Multiphasic Personality Inventory, in order to be classified as masculine, feminine, androgynous or undifferentiated personalities.

### Findings
Androgynous females scored significantly lower for depression and social introversion than feminine females, and in the college sample were also lower on the schizophrenia and mania scales than masculine females.

In the hospitalised male sample, this pattern was partially sustained, with androgynous and masculine participants significantly less deviant than feminine males, and lower on depression.

In the group of college males, androgynous males scored lower on social introversion than feminine males.

### Conclusions
Being androgynous is positively correlated with good mental health, especially concerning levels of depression.

### Evaluation
The results indicate that sex-role conformity may relate differently to personality development and psychological functioning for males and females.

Androgynous personalities score well in mental health terms, but masculine types scored equally well, which suggests that masculinity also assists positive mental health.

## Research

Bem (1974) used the BSRI to measure androgyny, finding 34 per cent of males and 27 per cent of females to be androgynous, which suggests a sizeable minority of people are predominately androgynous rather than being masculine or feminine.

Flaherty & Dusek (1980) found that androgynous individuals have a higher degree of self-esteem, a better sense of emotional well-being and more adaptable behaviour, backing up the idea of psychological androgyny indicating psychological well-being. This was supported by Lubinski *et al.* (1981) finding that androgynous individuals report greater emotional well-being.

Taylor & Hall (1982) suggested that masculinity, in males and females, is a better predictor of psychological well-being than androgyny, which was supported by Taylor (1986) reporting that psychological well-being is more strongly related to masculinity than femininity on the BSRI (a view supported by Burchardt & Serbin (1982) – see Classic research above).

Peters & Cantrell (1993) used the BSRI to find that androgynous females had the best quality of relationships, supporting the idea of androgyny being a positive condition and being associated with higher interpersonal functioning than individuals who are predominately masculine or feminine.

Rose & Montemayor (1994) found that 25–30 per cent of US high school students defined themselves as androgynous, with more girls than boys showing this pattern, and more girls falling into the masculine category than boys into the feminine category. This supports the idea that sex roles are less rigid in older children.

### Evaluation

- The BSRI test has good test-retest reliability, as it produces consistent results when used on different occasions with the same participants, but there are some doubts about its validity – it was created from data generated by American students in the 1970s about what they perceived as desirable characteristics in men and women. The test may therefore lack external validity in terms of being relevant today and to people from other cultures.
- Bem saw androgyny as positive and desirable, but androgyny might not always be positive, as androgynous individuals can exhibit negative masculine characteristics (such as being over-aggressive) and feminine characteristics (being too timid) in certain situations.
- Although Olds (1981) states that androgyny is a higher stage of development, no explanation is given as to why this occurs only in some individuals, or how such development occurs in these individuals.
- Bem argues that androgyny is a psychologically healthy state. However, it could equally be argued that androgyny is not psychologically healthy as it pressurises individuals to reach levels of adequacy in terms of both masculinity and femininity, rather than on a more traditional single level of competence, i.e. being either masculine or feminine.
- It may be that because of the masculine bias in Western cultures, where masculine qualities like independence and competitiveness are more valued than feminine ones such as co-operation and nurturing, masculine qualities are seen as superior even within androgynous individuals. This would fit research findings of masculinity being found to be at least equally associated with positive mental health in comparison with androgyny.
- Reducing masculinity and femininity down to single scores is over-simplistic. More contemporary approaches to androgyny attempt to measure additional aspects of gender-related behaviour, such as interests and abilities, rather than simply personality characteristics.

### YOU ARE THE RESEARCHER

Design a questionnaire on androgyny, by devising ten questions assessing the level of femininity in males and females and ten questions assessing the level of masculinity in males and females.

Make questions concise, clear and unambiguous.

How would each question be scored? How would the data be interpreted to make sense of it?

> **STRENGTHEN YOUR LEARNING**
> 1. What is the difference between sex and gender?
> 2. Give one example of a sex-role stereotype for both males and females.
> 3. Where do sex-role stereotypes come from?
> 4. Summarise what research studies suggest about sex-role stereotypes.
> 5. What other evaluative points can be made concerning sex-role stereotypes?
> 6. How might being androgynous be beneficial to a person?
> 7. Outline Bem's Sex Role Inventory.
> 8. Outline and evaluate Burchardt & Serbin's (1982) study of androgyny and mental health.
> 9. Summarise what research studies suggest about androgyny.
> 10. What other evaluative points can be made concerning androgyny?

*'The test for whether or not you can hold a job should not be the arrangement of your chromosomes.'*

Bella Abzug (1984)

*'He suffers from TMT – too much testosterone.'*

Robert L. Slater (2014)

# 4.2 The role of chromosomes and hormones

Humans have 23 pairs of **chromosomes**, each pair carrying genes that control different characteristics. Biological sex is determined by the sex chromosomes X and Y (on the 23rd chromosome pair), with XX combination for females and XY combination for males (see Figure 4.6). Sex chromosomes contain genetic material that controls development as a male or female. During this process, sex **hormones**, such as **testosterone**, **oestrogen** and **oxytocin**, are produced that direct the majority of sexual development.

## The role of testosterone

Testosterone is a steroid hormone that stimulates development of male secondary sexual characteristics. Although it is found predominately in males, females also produce testosterone, with about 10 per cent of the amount of that found in males. The influence of testosterone on sexual differentiation of a foetus begins early in pregnancy and involves internal and external genitalia, as well as the brain and behaviour. The gonads are sex glands, testes in males and ovaries in females, and these are originally identical in both XY and XX embryos. However, in XY individuals, genetic information on the Y chromosome causes the gonads to become testes, and by week 8 of gestation they produce hormones, particularly the primary androgen, testosterone. If the gonads do not become testes, they become ovaries, which do not produce significant amounts of hormones prenatally.

**KEY TERMS**

**Chromosomes** – structures of nucleic acids and protein found in the nucleus of most living cells that contain genetic information

**Hormones** – chemical messengers that are released into the bloodstream from glands

**Testosterone** – a steroid hormone that stimulates development of male secondary sexual characteristics

**Oestrogen** – a group of steroid hormones which promotes the development and maintenance of female characteristics in the body

**Oxytocin** – a polypeptide hormone which acts also as a neurotransmitter that controls key aspects of the reproductive system

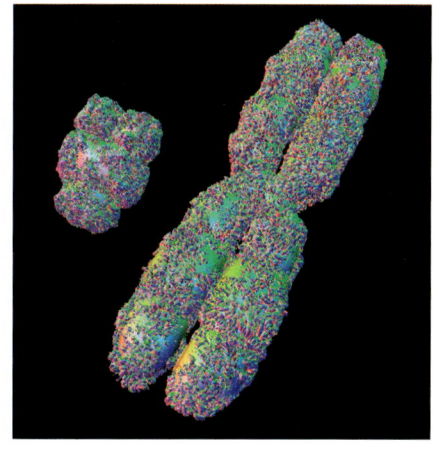

**Figure 4.6** The sex chromosomes X and Y determine human biological sex

The SRY gene on the Y chromosome controls whether gonads become ovaries or testes. Consequently, XY foetuses have higher levels of testosterone than XX foetuses, particularly between 8 and 24 weeks of gestation. Between then and birth, gonadal hormone levels are low in both sexes, but a surge of testicular hormones after birth makes testosterone once again higher in boys than in girls, for about the first six months. When released, testosterone causes the development of male sex organs, but also acts on the hypothalamus; without this, the brain develops as a female type.

Testosterone is associated with masculinisation of the brain, such as the development of brain areas linked to spatial skills. Testosterone is also associated with male-type behaviours such as competitiveness and aggressiveness.

There are differences in the hypothalamus of males and females, with the sexual dimorphic nucleus bigger in males. It is believed that these differences occur through the action of sex hormones, such as testosterone, though this is not a universal view.

## Research

Young (1966) gave male hormones, including testosterone, to female mice (and female hormones to male mice). The effect was an irreversible change in usual gender-related behaviours, suggesting that hormones like testosterone have a key role in determining gender behaviour. Testosterone may alter the sexually dimorphic nucleus (SDN) in the brain, as male rats had a larger SDN than females. Further support came from Edwards (1968), who found that injections of testosterone in neonate female mice made them act like males with increased aggression when given testosterone as adults. However, control females only given testosterone as adults did not react in this way, suggesting that testosterone masculinises androgen-sensitive neural circuits underlying aggression in the brain.

Money & Ehrhardt (1972) reported on a sample of girls whose mothers took drugs containing testosterone during pregnancy. The girls exhibited male-type behaviours, for instance playing energetic sports, and an absence of female-type behaviours, like playing with dolls, which suggests that testosterone has a strong influence on gender behaviour.

Deady et al. (2006) measured testosterone levels and gave the BSRI to women between 25 and 30 years of age, asking additional questions about maternal personality, such as the importance of having children, maternal broodiness, reproductive ambition and the importance of a career. High testosterone levels negatively correlated with low measures of maternal personality and reproductive ambition, which suggests females' maternal drive is affected by testosterone.

Goel & Bale (2008) gave testosterone injections to female mice postnatally (after birth) and/or just before puberty, finding reduced physiological and behavioural stress responses compared with female mice not given testosterone injections. As anxiety and depressive disorders are more common in females and the onset of anxiety and depressive disorders occurs at key developmental times when the brain is sensitive to the influence of hormones, the results suggest that sex differences in stress levels may be due to lowered testosterone levels in females.

### RESEARCH IN FOCUS

Deady et al. (2006) used testosterone levels and the BSRI to find a correlation between high testosterone levels and low measures of maternal personality and reproductive ambition in females.

What type of correlation was this? What conclusion could be drawn from these findings? What were the co-variables in this particular study? What type of graph would be used to display the data?

A weakness of correlations is that they lack causality; what does this mean? How could you carry out this study as an experiment – remember you'd need to have an IV and a DV.

> **RESEARCH IN FOCUS**
>
> Deady *et al.*'s (2006) study was a correlational study of maternal personality and testosterone levels.
>
> What is a correlational study?
>
> The results indicated a positive correlation. Explain in the context of this study what this means.
>
> Why can a correlation not show causality?
>
> The study was reliant on a question-and-answer technique. What disadvantages are there to this method? How could these disadvantages be overcome?

## The role of oestrogen

Oestrogen is a group of steroid hormones, such as oestradiol, oestrone and oestriol, which promotes the development and maintenance of female characteristics of the body and is seen later to regulate menstruation. Although primarily a female hormone, small amounts of oestrogen are produced in males. Aside from influencing physical changes to the body, such as the development of breasts, oestrogen also has psychological and behavioural effects, such as premenstrual tension (PMT), which is associated with emotionality, irritability and irrational behaviour, as well as lapses in self-control that can lead to anti-social behaviour and can even result in acts of criminality. The diminishing of oestrogen levels is associated with the onset of menopause in women. As with testosterone having a role in masculinisation of the brain, similarly oestrogen plays a role in feminising the brain, with oestrogen promoting neural interconnections for a more 'distributed' female brain (equal use of both hemispheres). Oestrogen is also associated with female-type behaviours, such as sensitivity and co-operation.

**Figure 4.7** Oestrogen plays a role in premenstrual tension

### Research

Albrecht & Pepe (1997) found that increasing oestrogen levels in pregnant baboons led to heightened cortisol production, which assisted the development of organs and tissues in foetuses and led to reduced levels of miscarriage by regulating progesterone levels. This suggests that oestrogen plays a key role in maintaining and promoting pregnancy.

Fitch & Denenberg (1998) found that suppressing production of oestrogen by removing ovaries from female rats as late as 16 days after birth led to an increased corpus callosum brain area (a sexually dimorphic cortical brain structure) in adults, though treatment with oestrogen reduced this effect. The findings suggest that there is a later sensitive period for oestrogen-regulated feminisation of the brain compared with testosterone-regulated masculinisation.

Alonso & Rosenfield (2002) reported that oestrogen is necessary for the normal development of body areas and tissues, like the neuroendocrine–gonadal axis, associated with puberty in both males and females. This supports the idea that oestrogen is associated with the transformation into being sexually active and able, not just in females but in males, too.

Finkelstein (2013) gave 400 men aged 20–50 years with normal testosterone levels injections that reduced their testosterone levels to pre-puberty levels. Half the participants then took various doses of testosterone for 16 weeks, while the other half took similar doses also for 16 weeks, but took an additional drug to block the conversion of testosterone into oestrogen. Participants with lower levels of oestrogen had a reduced libido (sex drive), which suggests that male sexual desire is actually related to oestrogen, more commonly perceived as a female hormone.

## The role of oxytocin

Oxytocin is a polypeptide hormone that acts also as a neurotransmitter and is produced in (and outside of) the brain by both males and females to control key aspects of the reproductive system. Its action is greater in females as it synergises (combines) with oestrogen to enhance each other's effect. Oxytocin helps facilitate childbirth (by helping to stimulate contractions) and breastfeeding (by stimulating the 'let down' reflex); it also increases five-fold during sex (though it drops in males immediately after orgasm, which explains males' sudden loss of intimacy at this point). Oxytocin also affects female social behaviour, such as mate selection, 'nesting' behaviour (preparing the house for new offspring), monogamy and pair bonding, as well as the nurturing, acceptance and protection of offspring.

### Research

Van Leengoed et al. (1987) injected an antagonist of oxytocin into female rats shortly after birth to inhibit oxytocin production. Mothers treated in this way showed a delay in maternal behaviours, such as picking up and grooming their pups. When the effects of the antagonist wore off, normal maternal behaviour was seen. The findings support the idea of oxytocin being involved in the promotion of maternal behaviour.

Elbourne et al. (2001) assessed the administration of oxytocin in 3,000 participants during the third stage of labour (a time associated with birth complications, especially during delivery of the placenta), to find evidence of reduced blood loss, highlighting the role oxytocin plays in achieving successful childbirth.

Insel (2001) found that administering oxytocin to female prairie voles, a species known to be monogamous (exclusive pair-bonds), led to them forming long-term mating partnerships, while similar administration of oxytocin to female montane voles, a species known to be promiscuous (having multiple sexual partners), produced no such effect. This suggests oxytocin helps promote pair-bonding in monogamous species such as humans.

White-Traut et al. (2009) measured oxytocin levels in saliva produced by females before, during and after breastfeeding. Oxytocin levels were highest immediately before feeding, decreased at initiation of feeding and rose again 30 minutes after feeding, illustrating oxytocin's important role in promoting breastfeeding.

## Evaluation

- Much of the research on the role of hormones in sex and gender is conducted on animals, but the extent to which results can be generalised to humans is debatable. The physiology of humans and animals, like rats and mice, especially in terms of brain functioning is very different and human development and behaviour are much more subject to social and cultural influences.
- Animal experimentation is often conducted, as similar studies with humans would be unethical. However, ethical concerns are raised with animal experiments, like van Leengoed et al.'s (1987) study which delayed maternal care of young. Such studies may be justifiable in terms of a cost–benefit analysis, for example that such research leads to useful practical applications.
- It is simplistic to think of testosterone being a male hormone and oestrogen and oxytocin being female hormones; research shows all three exert important influences on both males and females.
- It is also simplistic to perceive single hormones as having exclusive effects upon sex and gender. Hormones are often part of biological mechanisms that exert multi-faceted and complex actions upon the body and behaviour, for example the interaction of sex chromosomes, the SRY gene and gonadal hormones.
- A main difficulty in researching the role of hormones on sex and gender in humans is doing so in a non-invasive way. However, White-Traut et al.'s (2009) use of measuring salivary hormonal levels offers such a method, as long as baseline measurements are established so that comparisons can be made after hormone levels are manipulated.
- Isotocin is a type of oxytocin found in non-mammals, such as birds, which causes females to respond to male mating songs. Its action in humans is not known, but as it acts primarily on auditory rather than visual stimuli in females it may explain why women are attracted to male 'crooning' singing voices, such as that of Nat King Cole.

**Figure 4.8** Is the crooning of Nat King Cole attractive to females due to the action of oxytocin?

### PSYCHOLOGY IN THE REAL WORLD

Research into the role of hormones in sex and gender has led to beneficial practical applications. For example, the administration of oxytocin during childbirth reduces haemorrhaging (bleeding), decreasing mortality rates in both mothers and infants. Oxytocin also helps to start and keep labour going, as well as assisting in secreting milk to allow mothers to breastfeed.

Testosterone is given to men with problems attaining and maintaining an erection or with a low libido. Testosterone also increases libido in women, especially those whose sex drive lessens after having a hysterectomy or who are post-menopausal.

Oestrogen supplements offer increased protection to those at risk of strokes and are often given to post-menopausal women to protect against osteoporosis. There is research being undertaken into the ability of oestrogen to protect against Alzheimer's. Oestrogen also helps boost male libido and so is used in sex-drive therapies.

All hormone therapies carry risks of side effects and should be administered only on medical advice.

**Figure 4.9** One beneficial use of oxytocin is in secreting milk in breastfeeding mothers

# Atypical sex chromosome patterns

Most humans are born with XX (female) or XY (male) sex chromosomes, therefore any combinations of sex chromosomes other than these are atypical. Both Klinefelter's and Turner's syndromes are examples of such atypical sex chromosome conditions.

## Klinefelter's syndrome

**Klinefelter's syndrome** (KS) is a genetic condition, which affects about 1 in every 750 males and involves having an extra X chromosome (thus they are XXY). The condition is named after Dr Harold Klinefelter, who reported the condition in the USA in 1942. Males with this condition have small testes that produce insufficient amounts of testosterone before birth and during puberty, which results in normal male sexual characteristics not developing fully. Typically, sufferers lack the ability to grow facial and pubic hair, develop breast tissue, have low muscularity and low fertility levels (see Figure 4.10). There is also a tendency for long legs and arms in ratio to their torso. Psychological effects include poor language skills, which affects reading ability, and a noticeably passive (quiet) temperament, as well as attention problems and an increased risk of anxiety disorders and depression.

Mosaic Klinefelter's syndrome (MKS) involves males having the extra X chromosome in only some of their cells. Sufferers tend to be less affected (how affected depends on how many cells have the extra X chromosome). About 1 in 10 KS sufferers are MKS sufferers (about 1 in 7,500 men). Very rarely males with KS can have several extra copies of the X chromosome, or even extra copies of both X and Y chromosomes in all their bodily cells, for example XXYY or XXXYY, etc. Symptoms are more severe in these cases.

Although a genetic condition, KS is not inherited from parents but occurs during meiosis, the process of cell division that produces egg and sperm cells. An error in cell division called nondisjunction causes an egg or sperm cell to have an extra copy of the X chromosome, leading to the embryo produced at conception having an extra copy of the X chromosome in each of its body cells (a process known as sex chromosome trisomy). MKS occurs similarly, where problems with cell division occur during early development in the womb leading to some body cells having an extra copy of the X chromosome.

Medical complications can arise from KS, such as cardiovascular, circulatory and respiratory conditions, as well as diabetes and renal problems.

Older parents are more likely to have a child with KS and sufferers are generally treated with testosterone supplements, allowing them to live relatively normal lives, though with below-average lifespan.

## Research

Simpson *et al.* (2003) found that behavioural and language difficulties resulting from having KS could be successfully treated with androgen therapy, such as testosterone supplements, and psychological counselling, with greater improvements seen the earlier the treatment was given. This supports the idea that some of the detrimental effects of KS can be successfully counteracted.

**KEY TERM**

**Klinefelter's syndrome** – a chromosomal condition that affects male physical and cognitive development

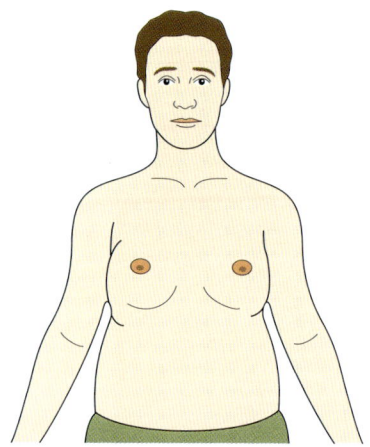

**Figure 4.10** Boys with Klinefelter's syndrome often develop breast tissue

Swerdlow *et al.* (2005) investigated mortality in men diagnosed with KS in Britain from 1959 to 2003, finding 461 of 3,518 patients had died (13 per cent), which was at a greater level than for similar non-KS patients. Major causes of death were from cardiovascular, nervous system and respiratory diseases, as well as diabetes, epilepsy, renal and circulatory disorders, which suggests KS patients have raised mortality levels from several specific causes that reflect hormonal and genetic mechanisms.

DeLisi *et al.* (2005) subjected 11 KS participants and 11 non-KS controls to a psychiatric interview, cognitive tests and an MRI scan. Ten of the KS males had some form of psychiatric disturbance and generally KS males had smaller frontal lobes, temporal lobes and superior temporal gyrus brain areas, which might explain the language deficits noted in the KS participants. This suggests a biological basis to the problems experienced by some KS males.

Stochholm *et al.* (2012) investigated criminal patterns in 1,005 Danish men with standard KS and the XYY version, finding men with KS had higher conviction rates for sexual abuse, burglary and arson and lower conviction rates for traffic and drug offences than non-KS controls and these findings were greater for those with the XYY version of KS. However, when adjustments were made for socioeconomic variables (level of education, fatherhood, cohabiting with a partner, etc.), conviction levels were similar to controls (apart from sexual abuse and arson). This suggests that KS is associated with increased criminality but as a result of poor socioeconomic conditions endured by sufferers rather than the condition itself.

## Turner's syndrome

**Turner's syndrome** (TS) is a genetic condition that affects about 1 in 2,200 females. The condition is named after Dr Henry Turner, who reported the syndrome in 1938, and involves having only one complete X chromosome in each cell; the second X chromosome is either missing or incomplete. The condition occurs at conception, indeed most conceptions occurring with one X chromosome missing end in miscarriage (one in ten miscarriages in the first trimester (third) of pregnancy are due to TS). Mosaic types of TS also exist (MTS) where one copy of the X chromosome is missing or incomplete in some but not all cells.

Prenatally lymphoedema can occur, where fluid leaks into tissues causing swelling, particularly in the neck, hands and feet. Physical effects that emerge after birth are short stature, down-slanting eyes and a short, webbed-like neck, as well as a broad chest, lots of moles and organ abnormalities, especially of the heart and kidneys.

The main deficiency though is non-functioning ovaries, which results in girls with TS not developing breasts during puberty, not having periods and being infertile. However, about one third of girls with the condition have some typical changes during puberty and about 1 in 200 with the condition can get pregnant naturally and most will have a normal vagina and uterus and will enjoy a normal sex life.

Medical complications can arise from TS, such as heart conditions, high blood pressure, urinary complaints, vision and hearing problems and osteoporosis (thinning of the bones). There are few psychological problems with TS, aside from potential problems with social adjustment due to physical appearance (for instance, possible bullying) and a few girls having minor learning difficulties (indeed, some girls may even have advanced reading ability).

### ON THE WEB

The Klinefelter's Syndrome Association UK hosts a website that offers useful information about the condition, links to other related sites, news articles, etc. Find them at:

**www.ksa-uk.net/**

### KEY TERM

**Turner's syndrome** – a chromosomal condition that affects female physical development

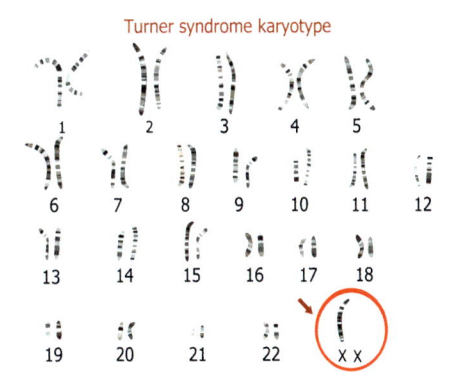

**Figure 4.11** The chromosones for Turner's syndrome

TS is not more common in girls born to older women and it is rare to have a second child with Turner's syndrome. Treatment usually consists of administering growth hormone, as well as oestrogen and progesterone supplements, which allows sufferers to live relatively normal lives with only slightly reduced average life span.

## Research

Price *et al.* (1986) performed a longitudinal study for 17 years of 156 females with TS who survived infancy, finding that 15 died in that time (9 per cent), compared with an expected 3.5 deaths in matched non-TS females. The major causes of death were cardiovascular and circulatory conditions, with the findings confirming the notion that TS sufferers have a shorter than average lifespan.

Brown *et al.* (2002) performed MRI scans of 26 girls with TS and 26 gender- and age-matched non-TS girls, finding that girls with TS had smaller posterior cerebral and cerebellar brain areas. There were no differences between TS girls who had a maternally inherited or a paternally inherited X chromosome. The results suggest that TS affects growth of certain brain areas, which may in turn be related to the developmental effects seen with the disorder.

Hewitt *et al.* (2013) reported that 30 pregnancies had resulted from cryopreservation (extraction and freezing) of eggs taken from females with TS, but only if they were extracted from pre-pubertal girls. The progressive ovarian atresia (shrinking of the ovaries) that occurs with TS females means egg extraction does not result in successful pregnancies in post-pubertal females.

Quigley *et al.* (2014) gave 123 girls with TS either oestrogen supplements or a placebo from ages 5 to 12. There were no differences in physical development between the two groups before age 8.5 years, but between 8.5 and 12 years those given oestrogen had earlier and greater breast development compared with non-TS girls, though no other differences in puberty developments were noted. The findings suggest oestrogen supplements are beneficial between ages 8 and 12 and have a great psychosocial benefit in normalising breast development for girls with TS.

### ON THE WEB

The Turner Syndrome Support Society hosts a website containing up-to-date information about the condition, news articles, web links, etc. Find them at:

**http://tss.org.uk/**

### Evaluation

- The extraction of eggs from pre-pubescent girls with TS offers a means of them later attaining pregnancy and the enhanced psychosocial benefits that would bring. However, from an ethical point of view, care must be taken to fully brief individuals about the technique and to gain informed consent from all involved parties.
- The comparison of people with typical and atypical chromosome patterns allows researchers to see what aspects of biological development and behaviour are under the influence of genetics and chromosomes.
- Research into patients with KS and TS has seen the development of therapies to improve the quality and duration of their lives. For example, treating the stunted physical growth often seen with TS by the application of growth hormone and the treatment of KS with testosterone, which has seen those with the condition develop a less passive nature.

- Although the effects of both KS and TS originate directly from biological influences of genes and chromosomes, some effects are more environmental in nature. For instance, higher criminality is often seen in males with KS, but this may be due to a lack of maturity through not achieving fatherhood or having a long-term partner. Similarly, females with TS may suffer psychologically through not being able to have children.
- Both KS and TS can be diagnosed prenatally based on cytogenetic analysis of a foetus. However, this can be regarded ethically as a socially sensitive area, as such a diagnosis may incur a demand for or bring pressure upon prospective parents to ask for an abortion.
- As both KS and TS are biological conditions caused by atypical chromosome patterns, research into them is justifiable on the basis that it could bring about effective gene therapies to correct the conditions.

### ON THE WEB

Watch a video of Dan, someone with Klinefelter's syndrome, talk about his experience of dealing with the condition at **www.youtube.com**. Search for 'Project 47XXY, Turner's Syndrome Diaries'.

There is also a video produced by the Turner Syndrome Foundation, where Susan, Suzanne, Kym, Jean and Sam talk about their experiences with the condition. Find it at **www.youtube.com**. Search for 'Overview, Turner's Syndrome'.

You can watch Emily talk about her experiences with having the syndrome at **www.youtube.com**. Search for 'My Story – Emily Tarbox'.

### STRENGTHEN YOUR LEARNING

1. Explain how biological sex is determined by sex chromosomes.
2. Outline the role of i] testosterone, ii] oestrogen, iii] oxytocin in sex and gender.
3. Summarise what research suggests about the role of i] testosterone, ii] oestrogen, iii] oxytocin in sex and gender.
4. What other evaluative points can be made concerning the role of chromosomes and hormones in sex and gender?
5. What practical applications have been formed from research into the role of hormones in sex and gender?
6. What causes Klinefelter's syndrome? What behavioural and psychological effects does it have? How does mosaic Klinefelter's syndrome differ from the condition?
7. Summarise what research suggests about Klinefelter's syndrome.
8. What causes Turner's syndrome? What behavioural and psychological effects does it have?
9. Summarise what research suggests about Klinefelter's syndrome.
10. What other evaluative points can be made about Klinefelter's and Turner's syndromes?

# ASSESSMENT CHECK

1. Harold, aged 24, is a shy young man who has never had to shave as he doesn't grow facial hair. He has been told by doctors that he is infertile and can never father children. Harold struggled at school as his reading ability is quite poor. Medical tests have revealed him to have a sex chromosome pattern of XXY.

    **a)** Name the atypical sex chromosome syndrome that Harold has. [1 mark]

    **b)** With reference to the scenario above, explain how this syndrome occurs. [3 marks]

2. Which two of the following definitions A, B, C and D concerning chromosomes and hormones is correct?

    **A** Oestrogen is mainly a female hormone, but small quantities are produced in males

    **B** Chromosomes are chemical messengers that are released into the bloodstream from glands

    **C** Testosterone is made of nucleic acids and protein found in most living cells

    **D** Oxytocin is a hormone, which also acts as a neurotransmitter, that controls key aspects of the reproductive system [2 marks]

3. The following table contains scores for masculinity and femininity for participants taking the Bem Sex Role Inventory test.

| Participant | Score for masculinity (out of 140) | Score for femininity (out of 140) |
| --- | --- | --- |
| 1 | 100 | 110 |
| 2 | 65 | 80 |
| 3 | 40 | 70 |
| 4 | 80 | 60 |
| 5 | 70 | 70 |
| 6 | 65 | 80 |
| 7 | 45 | 90 |
| 8 | 55 | 80 |

   **a)** Calculate the mean score for masculinity. [1 mark]

   **b)** Calculate the median score for masculinity. [1 mark]

   **c)** Calculate the mean score for femininity. [1 mark]

   **d)** Calculate the modal score for femininity. [1 mark]

4. Explain what is meant by androgyny. [2 marks]

5. Discuss sex-role stereotypes. [16 marks]

*'Sugar and spice and all things nice, that's what little girls are made of,
frogs and snails and puppy dogs' tails, that's what little boys are made of.'*
Roud Folk Song Index, early 1800s

# 4.3 Cognitive explanations for gender development

Cognitive explanations of gender development focus on how children's thinking about gender develops, with thinking occurring in qualitatively different stages. Gender identity is seen to result from children actively structuring their own experiences, rather than being a passive (non-interactive) outcome of social learning. **Kohlberg's theory** of gender constancy sees thinking and understanding as the basis behind gender identity and gender role behaviour. Kohlberg perceives children as developing an understanding of gender in three distinct stages, with gender role behaviour apparent only after an understanding emerges that gender is fixed and constant. **Gender schema theory** shares the same cognitive view of gender understanding, but perceives children having schemas for gender at an earlier stage than Kohlberg.

An important difference between the two theories is that schema theory believes that children only need gender identity to develop gender-consistent behaviours, while Kohlberg sees the acquisition of gender constancy as necessary first.

> **KEY TERMS**
>
> **Kohlberg's theory** – an explanation of gender development that perceives children as developing an understanding of gender in stages, with gender-role behaviour apparent only after an understanding emerges that gender is fixed and constant
>
> **Gender schema theory** – an explanation of gender development that sees gender identity alone as providing children with motivation to assume sex-typed behaviour patterns

## Kohlberg's theory of gender constancy (1966)

Other theories of gender role development, such as social learning theory (SLT), assume that children know which gender they are and proceed to learn appropriate roles. Kohlberg sees such knowledge arising from children actively constructing an understanding of the world through interacting with it.

Kohlberg's theory was influenced by Piaget's cognitive development theory, which saw children progressing through stages of understanding as their level of biological maturity allowed them to do so. Gender concepts are seen as occurring through environmental interactions, restricted by biologically controlled mental capabilities at a given time.

Children's discovery that they are male or female causes them to identify with members of their own gender, not the other way round, as SLT and psychoanalytic theories suggest. Kohlberg sees children acquiring an understanding of the concepts 'male' and 'female' in three stages, where they understand increasingly more sophisticated gender concepts, with a new stage appearing only after thinking has matured to a certain point. Consequently, children understand gender differently at different ages, with gender concepts developing as children actively structure their social experiences. It is not, therefore, a passive social learning process occurring through observation and imitation.

It is only after gender constancy is reached, at about the age of seven, that children start to develop gender concepts to suit their own gender. Table 4.1 on page 126 outlines the stages of gender identity.

Table 4.1 Stages in the development of gender identity

| |
|---|
| **Stage 1: Gender labelling (basic gender identity)**<br>Occurs between 18 months and 3 years, and refers to children's recognition of being male or female. Kohlberg sees an individual understanding their gender as a realisation that allows them to understand and categorise their world. This knowledge is fragile, with 'man', 'woman', 'boy' and 'girl' little more than labels, equivalent to personal names. Children sometimes choose incorrect labels and do not realise that boys become men and girls become women. |
| **Stage 2: Gender stability**<br>By the age of 3 to 5 years, most children recognise that people retain gender for life, but rely on superficial, physical signs to determine gender. If someone is superficially transformed – for example, a woman having long hair cut short – children infer that the person has changed gender. |
| **Stage 3: Gender constancy (consistency)**<br>By about age 6–7 years, children realise that gender is permanent, e.g. if a woman has her head shaved, her gender remains female. Gender constancy represents a kind of conservation, an understanding that things remain the same despite changing appearance. Gender understanding is complete only when children appreciate that gender is constant over time and situations. |

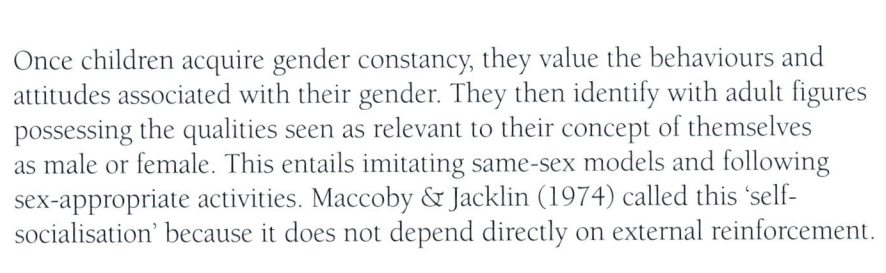

**Figure 4.12** A child with gender constancy understands that a woman with a shaved head is still female

Once children acquire gender constancy, they value the behaviours and attitudes associated with their gender. They then identify with adult figures possessing the qualities seen as relevant to their concept of themselves as male or female. This entails imitating same-sex models and following sex-appropriate activities. Maccoby & Jacklin (1974) called this 'self-socialisation' because it does not depend directly on external reinforcement.

# Research

Slaby & Frey (1975) gave questions to 2–5-year-old children to assess their level of gender constancy and then several weeks later showed them a film of a man and woman performing gender-stereotypical activities. Children with high levels of gender constancy paid more attention to same-sex models than children with low levels of gender constancy, which suggests that high gender constancy children watch their own gender to acquire information about gender-appropriate behaviour, supporting Kohlberg's theory that gender development is an active process. The results also support Kohlberg's claim that gender constancy is a cause, rather than an effect, of the imitation of same-sex models.

Rabban (1950) found, by asking questions about gender, that children's thinking changes as they age. By three years most children demonstrated gender identity, but did not have an understanding of what gender they would grow into. By five years of age, 97 per cent demonstrated gender stability, supporting the stages of Kohlberg's theory.

Thompson (1975) found that by two years, children given pictures of boys and girls could select same-sex ones, demonstrating that children could self-label and identify the gender of others. By three years, 90 per cent showed gender identity, compared with only 76 per cent of two year olds, showing the developmental nature of the concept in line with Kohlberg's theory.

McConaghy (1979) found that if a doll was dressed in transparent clothing so its genitals were visible, children of 3–5 years judged its gender by its clothes, not its genitals, supporting Kohlberg's belief that children of this age use superficial physical indicators to determine gender.

Frey & Ruble (1992) informed children that certain toys were either 'boy' or 'girl' toys. Boys who had achieved gender constancy chose 'boy' toys, even when they were uninteresting. Girls of the same stage exhibited similar tendencies to a lesser degree, giving some support to Kohlberg's theory.

### Evaluation

- Research evidence suggests that the concepts of gender identity, stability and constancy occur in that order across many cultures, lending support to Kohlberg's theory and suggesting a biological mechanism.
- A problem for Kohlberg's theory is that it predicts little or no gender-specific behaviour before children acquire gender constancy. But even in infancy, boys and girls show preferences for stereotypical male and female toys. Children generally demonstrate gender-appropriate behaviours and reward gender-appropriate behaviours in peers before they have reached gender constancy, casting doubt on Kohlberg's idea of universal stages of development.
- Kohlberg underestimated the age at which gender cognition occurs. Bem (1981) believes that children have an awareness of gender and gender-specific behaviours from around two years, due to the development of gender schemas.
- The theory concentrates on cognitive factors and overlooks important cultural and social factors, such as the influence of parents and friends.
- Kohlberg's theory is mainly descriptive – it outlines the process of gender development but does not really explain how developments occur and as such lacks depth of explanation.
- Kohlberg's theory of gender development is more of a holistic than a reductionist theory, as it combines social learning and biological developmental factors.

### YOU ARE THE RESEARCHER

Design an experiment to assess whether children of different ages have gender constancy.

Information from psychological theories should give you some indication of what age groups to use.

How would you assess whether gender constancy had been attained? What would be the IV and the DV? What steps would you take to ensure that the study is ethical?

## Gender schema theory

### Martin & Halverson (1981), Bem (1981)

Gender schema theory sees gender identity alone as providing children with the motivation to assume sex-typed behaviour patterns. The difference between this approach and Kohlberg's is that for initial understanding of gender to develop, children need not understand that gender is permanent. Like SLT, this approach sees children learning 'appropriate' patterns of behaviour by observation. But, similarly to Kohlberg, children's active cognitive processing of information also contributes to sex typing.

Gender schema, an organised grouping of related concepts, begins to develop at 2–3 years, and once children have gender identity, they accumulate knowledge about the sexes, organising this into gender schemas. Such schemas provide a basis for interpreting the environment and selecting appropriate forms of behaviour, and thus children's self-perceptions become sex-typed. In-group schemas are formed concerning attitudes and expectations about one's own gender, and out-group schemas about the other gender. Toys, games and even objects become categorised as 'for boys' or 'for girls' (see Figure 4.13).

Maccoby (1998) believes that because gender is clearly an either/or category, children understand very early that this is a key distinction and it serves as a 'magnet' for new information. Alternatively, adults and other children emphasise gender differences in countless small ways. Whatever the origin of early schema, once established many experiences are assimilated (fitted into existing schemas) and children show preference for same-sex playmates and for gender-stereotyped activities, actively ignoring the other gender. However, gender schemas undergo developmental change as children's general cognitive abilities develop.

**Figure 4.13** Dolls can be categorised as toys 'for girls' and trucks as toys 'for boys'

## Developmental changes in children's gender schema

- Preschoolers learn distinctions about what kinds of activities and behaviour go with each gender by observing other children and through reinforcements received from parents – for example, 'men have short hair' and 'girls play with dolls'. They also learn gender 'scripts', sequences of events that go with each gender, such as 'cooking dinner' (female) and 'building with tools' (male).
- From the age of 4–6 years, children learn subtle and complex sets of associations for their own gender: what children of the same gender like and do not like, how they play, how they talk, what kinds of people they spend time with. Not until age 8–10 do children develop schemas of the opposite gender matching the complexity of the same-gender schema.
- When gender constancy develops at 5–6 years, children's understanding of 'what people like me do' becomes more elaborated. This 'rule' is treated as absolute.
- By late childhood and early adolescence, it is understood that 'rules' are just social conventions and gender-role schemas become more flexible. Teenagers abandon the automatic assumption that what their own gender does is preferable, and a significant minority of teenagers define themselves as androgynous.

## Research

Masters *et al.* (1979) found that children aged between four and five years selected toys by their gender label (boy toy/girl toy) rather than which gender was seen playing with the toy, illustrating the application of gender schemas.

Martin & Halverson (1983) asked children to recall pictures of people, finding that children under the age of six recalled more gender-consistent ones – for example, a male footballer – than gender non-consistent ones – for example, a male nurse – in line with gender schema theory predictions.

Martin & Little (1990) found that preschool children have gender stereotypes about what is appropriate for boys and girls before they develop much understanding about gender, supporting the idea of the formation of gender schemas.

Campbell (2000) found that even the youngest infants between 3 and [?] months had a preference for watching same-sex babies and by 9 months [?] showed an increasing tendency to pay attention to 'boy toys'. This [sh]ows that young children pay more attention to their same-sex group, [sup]porting the idea of gender schemas forming early on.

[Po]ulin-Dubois *et al*. (2002) found girls as young as two years could [ch]oose a doll to carry out stereotypical male or female jobs, demonstrating a schema for gender-appropriate tasks. By 2.5 years, boys showed the behaviour too, suggesting that young children learn from models on the basis of their own sex.

Aubry *et al*. (1999) performed a longitudinal study into preferences for gender-related items. Once a belief had taken hold that an item was for the opposite sex, a reduced preference for that item developed, illustrating how gender schemas affect behaviour.

### Evaluation

- The theory explains why children's attitudes and behaviour concerning gender are rigid and lasting. Children focus only on things that confirm and strengthen their schemas, ignoring behavioural examples that contradict the theory.
- Gender schema theory explains why children are more likely to model gender-appropriate behaviour rather than imitating a same-sex model demonstrating non-gender-appropriate behaviour.
- There is much research evidence supporting gender schema theory, but some studies show that children act in a gender-typical way before they develop gender schemas. Eisenberg *et al*. (1982) found that children aged 3–4 justified their gender-specific choice of toys without reference to gender stereotypes. Schaffer (1996) argues the influence could be in the opposite direction, children's monitoring of their own and others' behaviour leading to the development of gender schemas.
- The theory predicts that as gender schemas develop, children should display behaviour consistent with perception of their own gender. Some research agrees, but there is contradictory evidence, too. Campbell *et al*. (2002) found that two-year-old boys and girls who possessed high levels of gender knowledge did not display preferences to play with gender-specific toys.
- When children perform activities not normally stereotypical of their gender, like a boy cooking, they adjust their thinking so the activity becomes acceptable. This implies that thinking is affected by behaviour, while cognitive schema theory predicts the opposite. This weakens the theory somewhat.
- Gender schema theory is reductionist, as although it offers a plausible compromise between social learning and cognitive developmental theories, the theory neglects the influence of biological factors, assuming that all gender-orientated behaviour is created through cognitive means.

> **STRENGTHEN YOUR LEARNING**
> 1. What is the main difference between Kohlberg's theory of gender constancy and gender schema theory?
> 2. Explain what is meant by i) gender labelling, ii) gender stability, iii) gender constancy.
> 3. What are gender schemas and what do they allow children to do?
> 4. Outline developmental changes in gender schemas.
> 5. Summarise what research evidence suggests about gender schemas.
> 6. What other evaluative points can be made concerning gender schemas?

*'The great question that has never been answered, and which I have not yet been able to answer, despite my thirty years of research into the feminine soul, is "What does a woman want?"'*

Sigmund Freud (1925)

# 4.4 Psychodynamic explanation for gender development

The psychodynamic explanation of gender development centres on the work of Sigmund Freud (1856–1939). Freud saw conscious behaviour as motivated by unconscious drives, with the structure of the mind consisting of the id, ego and super-ego, the three components of personality. The ego, which is based in reality, has to balance the unreal opposing demands of the id, which is constantly seeking selfish pleasure, and the super-ego, which constantly seeks to be morally perfect. Conflicts between these structures of mind occur in each of five stages of psychosexual development – the oral, the anal, the phallic, the latent and the genital – after which the adult personality is formed. The key stage in relation to gender development is that of the phallic stage.

## Freud's psychoanalytic theory of gender

Freud saw children as experiencing an unconscious conflict as they passed through each stage of psychosexual development (see page 2). In the first two stages, the oral and anal stages, a child is perceived as bisexual, as gender identity is not seen as existing and there is no visible difference between the behaviour of boys and girls. However, when a child enters the phallic stage between three and five years of age its libido (life force) is seen as increasingly focused upon its genitals and it is in this stage that a child's gender identity develops through the resolution of either the **Oedipus complex** (for boys) or the **Electra complex** (for girls).

*'If this gun was real I could shoot you and sleep in the big bed with mummy.'*

The Happy Flowers (Homestead Records) (1990)

### Oedipus complex

Oedipus was a mythical Greek king who accidentally killed his father and married his mother. Freud used the term to describe how a boy's first sexual desires are directed at the opposite-sex parent: his mother. This occurs during

**Figure 4.14** Freud developed the psychoanalytic theory of gender development

**KEY TERMS**

**Freud's psychoanalytic theory of gender** – an explanation of gender development that sees gender identity and role as acquired during the phallic stage where the focus of libido moves to the genitals

**Oedipus complex** – the arousal in boys of unconscious sexual desire for their mother and fear and dislike of their father

**Electra complex** – the arousal in girls of unconscious sexual desire for their father and dislike of their mother

the phallic stage of psychosexual development (3–5 years of age), so called as the libido's sexual energy is directed into the phallus (penis). The feeling of attraction for his mother is accompanied by loathing of his father, whom he sees as having access to his mother, the object of his desires. The son also fears his father, as he believes if his father realises the son's desire for his mother, he will remove the boy's penis, a fear known as castration anxiety.

## Male identification and internalisation

To resolve the conflict between his desire for his mother and his fear of his father a boy gives up his desire for his mother and identifies with his father, a process known as **identification** with the aggressor. Identification with his father allows a boy to incorporate his father into his own personality, permitting him to internalise his male gender. Thus, by resolving his Oedipus complex, a boy begins to have a sense of male identity. If a boy was not to satisfactorily resolve his Oedipus complex, Freud believed he would be confused about his sexual identity and could become homosexual.

> *To her the name of her father was another word for Love.*
> Fanny Fem (1853)

> **KEY TERMS**
>
> **Identification** – the process of acquiring the characteristics of the same-sex parent
>
> **Internalisation** – the incorporation of the same-sex parent into an individual's personality

## Electra complex

In Greek mythology Electra was a daughter of King Agamemnon who, with her brother Orestes, plotted against and killed their mother Clytemnestra, to avenge their father's murder. The term (actually coined by Carl Jung in 1913) is used to describe how a girl's first sexual desires are directed at the opposite-sex parent, her father, which, as with the Oedipus complex, occurs during the phallic stage of psychosexual development. In this stage a girl, according to Freud, believes she does not have a penis, as she has been castrated. As her mother also does not have a penis, she gets the blame for the daughter not having a penis. The girl desires a penis, as it is a symbol of male power, a concept known as penis envy. Therefore she desires her father as he has what she wants. Unable to have a penis of her own, penis envy is converted into a desire for a baby, a concept known as the penis-baby making project.

## Female identification and internalisation

A daughter believes herself to be in competition for possession of her father, a feeling she represses for fear of losing the love of her mother. This conflict is resolved by identification with her mother, allowing a girl to incorporate her mother into her own personality and permitting her to internalise her female gender. Thus, by resolving her Electra complex, a girl begins to have a sense of female identity. Because a girl thinks she has already been castrated, Freud saw girls as not as fearful as boys are (who have more to lose) and thus believed female identification was not as strong as male identification. Freud believed that if a girl was not to satisfactorily resolve her Electra complex she would be confused about her sexual identity.

Freud saw girls as only passively identifying with their mothers, while boys more strongly actively identify with their fathers, thus boys are seen as casting off the passivity of their earlier bisexual stage to become active and dominant males, while females take on the passivity of the earlier bisexual stage to become timid and submissive. Indeed, Freud saw women as sexually inferior to men, with male development being the norm and female development being a deviant form of development.

## Research

Freud (1909) performed a case study of 'Little Hans', a five-year-old boy with a phobia of horses, especially ones with black bits around their mouths, which Freud interpreted as horses being representative of the boy's father (the black bits being his moustache). Therefore Hans was actually scared of his father, not horses, which was seen to fit the concept of the Oedipus complex, whereby Hans was fearful of his father castrating him for Hans desiring his mother. Hans was also seen to have overcome his Oedipus complex by having two fantasies, one where a plumber came and exchanged his bottom and 'widdler' (penis) for larger ones, and a second one where he fathered several children. This fitted Freud's theory as Hans was seen as having identified with his father and internalised his male gender.

Hyman (1921) reported that 22 of 31 female manic-depressive patients were diagnosed as suffering with an unresolved Electra complex, with 12 of the 22 having regressed to an earlier stage of psychosexual development, providing some support for Freud's theory.

Malinowski (1922) reported that boys in the Trobriand Islands exhibited the signs of hostility Freud described in his Oedipus complex, however not at their fathers but instead at their maternal uncles, who in Trobriand Islands culture are given the role of family disciplinarian. This opposes Freud's theory as it suggests that boys' hostile relationships with their fathers may be a reaction to the discipline fathers exert rather than being sexual jealousy over their mothers.

Friedman (1952) found that when a story began with a child doing something nice with their opposite-sex parent and then being joined by the same-sex parent, children produced a sadder end to the story than when a story began with a child doing something nice with their same-sex parent and then being joined by the opposite-sex parent. This supports the idea within both the Oedipus and Electra complexes of children having more attraction to opposite-sex parents and more hostility towards same-sex parents.

Snortum et al. (1969) reported that 46 males exempted from military service for being homosexual had more close-bonding and controlling mothers and rejecting, detached fathers than a comparable sample of heterosexual men. This lends support to the idea that males who fail to resolve their Oedipus complex by identifying with their fathers could become homosexual.

Wiszewska et al. (2007) asked female participants to rate the attractiveness of pictures of different kinds of men and to assess the quality of their relationships with their fathers. The researchers also compared the similarity of the images females found attractive to those of their fathers, finding that women who had been well treated by and had close relationships with their fathers as children were attracted to men who resembled their fathers physically. This supports Freud's idea of the Electra complex, where girls' desires become centred on their fathers.

> **RESEARCH IN FOCUS**
>
> The scientific process uses empirical methods, involving the formation and rigorous testing of hypotheses under controlled conditions and without bias or expectation by the researcher. Research should also be replicable to check the validity of results, with hypotheses capable of being seen to be false.
>
> Explain why Freud's theory psychoanalytic theory of gender is widely criticised for not fitting the scientific process.

### Evaluation

- Freud's case study of 'Little Hans' can be criticised for being subjectively interpreted to fit the idea of the Oedipus complex. The boy's father (who supplied Freud with the details of the study) was an avid supporter of Freud and thus biased. Even if Hans did have an Oedipus complex it does not prove, as Freud believed, that this is universal to all individuals.

- There is little scientific support for the theory and where research support does exist, there is generally a majority of studies that do not add support. For instance, Snortum *et al.*'s (1969) findings of homosexual men having unresolved Oedipal complexes is refuted by countless studies that show the incidence of homosexuality in individuals raised only by a same-sex parent is no different to those raised with an opposite-sex parent.

- Evidence that supports Freud can also be interpreted in ways that do not. For example, Wiszewska *et al.*'s (2007) findings of well-treated females being attracted to males resembling their fathers can equally be interpreted as such fathers creating a learned template for good male partners.

- Freud's theory of gender development is mainly male-orientated, which is probably a product of the time period in which it was constructed. The theory sees females as inferior to males, reflecting the standing in which females were held at the time. The concept of the Oedipus complex was created first, with the addition of the Electra complex coming later, almost as an after-thought. Freud was unhappy with it himself, claiming women to be 'a great mystery'.

- Although Freud's theory is of historical importance and stimulated research and interest in gender development, most contemporary psychologists do not consider his ideas to have serious merit.

- Freud's ideas are difficult to assess scientifically – concepts such as the libido, Oedipus and Electra complexes are impossible to measure and thus cannot be tested in any real empirical way.

#### STRENGTHEN YOUR LEARNING

1. Explain how a] a boy goes through and overcomes his Oedipus complex, b] a girl goes through and overcomes her Electra complex.
2. Summarise what research evidence suggests about Freud's psychoanalytic theory of gender development.
3. What other evaluative points can be made concerning Freud's theory?

# ASSESSMENT CHECK

1. Which of the four following presentations, A, B, C or D, correctly puts Kohlberg's stages of gender constancy in the order in which they occur? **[1 mark]**

   A Gender labelling/Gender constancy/Gender stability

   B Gender stability/Gender labelling/Gender constancy

   C Gender constancy/Gender stability/Gender labelling

   D Gender labelling/Gender stability/Gender constancy

2. Elaine is five years old and has a close relationship with her father of whom she is very fond. However, Elaine often has arguments with her mother and refuses to play with her or do as she is told. There are no such problems with her father whom she likes to play with and obeys immediately.

   a) Refer to the scenario above to explain why Elaine may have developed an Electra complex. **[3 marks]**

   b) Explain how Elaine might resolve her Electra complex. **[2 marks]**

3. A researcher got some children who had been assessed as being either of 'low gender constancy' or 'high gender constancy' to watch a film where on one side of a room a man was sawing a plank while on the other side a woman was washing some dishes. The amount of time children spent watching the man and the woman was recorded.

   The following table shows scores for mean percentage time spent watching the man rather than the woman.

   | Sex of participant | Low gender constancy | High gender constancy |
   | --- | --- | --- |
   | Boys | 48% | 70% |
   | Girls | 58% | 40% |

   a) Name an appropriate graph to display the data and give one reason for selecting this type of graph. **[1 + 1 marks]**

   b) Sketch the graph, making sure it is titled and the axes are correctly labelled. **[3 marks]**

4. In terms of the psychoanalytic explanation of gender development, explain what is meant by i] identification, ii] internalisation. **[1 + 1 marks]**

5. Outline and evaluate gender schema theory. **[16 marks]**

*'Children are great imitators. So give them something great to imitate.'*
Anonymous

# 4.5 Social learning theory as applied to gender development

**Social learning theory** (SLT) perceives gender roles being learned through observation and imitation of socialising agents, such as parents and peers, and the **influence of media** and **culture**. Socialising agents model examples of appropriate and inappropriate gender behaviour and the consequences of conforming or not conforming to gender norms. Children observe models being reinforced or punished for gender-appropriate or gender-inappropriate behaviours and so they imitate behaviours they see being reinforced and do not imitate those they see being punished. Through such observational learning, children acquire knowledge regarding gender roles without actually 'doing' anything themselves.

> **KEY TERMS**
>
> **Social learning theory** – explanation that sees gender development as occurring through the observation and imitation of models
>
> **Influence of media** – the effect of mass communication upon gender development
>
> **Influence of culture** – the effect of society upon gender development

*'We've begun to raise daughters more like sons... but few have the courage to raise our sons more like our daughters.'*
Gloria Steinem (1992)

## The influence of parents

SLT sees girls and boys learning dissimilar gender roles, as parents react to them differently. When children imitate gender-appropriate behaviour they are reinforced with praise and affection. Parents also give boys and girls different toys, speak to and handle them differently and even decorate their bedrooms differently. Fathers seem to reinforce sex-typed behaviours more than mothers, especially in sons. SLT also perceives same-sex models as more influential in being more likely to be imitated. Children, by a gradual process of immersion, take on parents' gender schemas.

## Research

Block (1979) found that boys are positively reinforced more for imitating behaviours reflecting independence, self-reliance and emotional control, while girls are reinforced for dependence, nurturance, empathy and emotional expression. This suggests that SLT can explain why males and females acquire different gender roles.

Huston (1983) found that parents believe they respond equally to aggressive acts by sons and daughters, but actually respond more frequently and quickly to girls being aggressive, demonstrating how parents treat children in gender-biased ways.

Quiery (1998) found that fathers interact in a more goal-seeking and achievement-orientated way and give more attention to sons, while mothers attend equally to sons and daughters. This supports the idea that fathers reinforce sex typing more than mothers do.

Fagot & Leinbach (1995) found that four year olds displayed more gender-role stereotyping and used gender labels earlier in 'traditional' families where the dad worked and mum cared for children at home than in 'alternative' families where parents shared childcare. This suggests that parents do act as gender role models for their children.

**Figure 4.15** Fathers reinforce sex-typed behaviours more than mothers

Wood *et al.* (2002) performed a meta-analysis that found parents tend to class more toys as gender-neutral than non-parents of a similar age. This suggests that parents become aware of the limitations that gender stereotyping places upon children's creative explorations and thus come to hold less rigid views.

Friedman *et al.* (2007) found that middle-class mothers who held gender-neutral attitudes often made descriptive stereotypes (descriptions of general 'truths' about each gender), such as 'girls like dolls'. This implies that there are subtle ways in which parents influence gender-stereotyped behaviour.

Rafferty (2013) found that compared with children raised by heterosexual parents, homosexual parents were less likely to endorse gender stereotyping, which suggests that different parenting styles exert different influences upon children's perceptions of gender. This was supported by the additional finding that when homosexual parents adopted more 'traditional' roles, with one as the main wage earner and one as the primary caregiver, children were more likely to express more gender-stereotyped views.

*'So if your mate said jump off a cliff, you'd do that too, would you?'*
Gwlenis Maureen Lawton (1964)

## The influence of peers

Peers (individuals of equal status) act as role models for gender-role stereotypes, with children more likely to imitate same-sex models. Gender differences develop in social situations like peer settings, more than in individual settings, with children soon displaying preferences for same-gender playmates and dividing themselves into mainly same-gender groups, where they resist attempts to interact with the opposite gender. Peers reinforce gender stereotypes, for instance by praising gender-appropriate behaviour and ridiculing non-appropriate behaviour, and are intolerant of cross-gender behaviour, for example boys playing with girls.

The observational learning that occurs through interaction with peers, especially after a child's gender identity and gender-role stereotypes have developed, is a more powerful influence on gender development than interactions with and reinforcements from parents and older others.

However, once children have internalised, through social learning, which behaviours are appropriate for males and females, their own behaviour becomes no longer dependent on external rewards and punishments. Instead, children self-direct their behaviour to satisfy their internalised standards, feeling pride on achieving gender role-consistent behaviour even without external praise, such as from their peers.

### Research

Langlois & Downs (1980) found that peers were less tolerant than mothers of preschoolers playing with opposite-gender toys, supporting the idea of peers being a stronger influence on gender development than parents.

Archer & Lloyd (1982) reported that three year olds playing the opposite sex's games were ridiculed by their peers and shunned, supporting the idea that peers police gender roles.

Lamb & Roopnarine (1979) found peers reward sex-appropriate play in preschool children and ridicule sex-inappropriate play, demonstrating the strong influence that peers have in reinforcing gender behaviour.

Maccoby (1990) reported that children quickly associate with playmates of the same sex, congregating and dividing themselves into same-gender groups and resisting attempts to interact with opposite-gender children. This supports the idea that gender differences emerge as a result of interaction in peer settings.

Bussey & Bandura (1992) found that children aged three years disapproved of gender role-inconsistent behaviour by their peers, such as girls playing football, but rated their own feelings about masculine and feminine toys equally. However, four-year-old children disapproved of gender role-inconsistent behaviour in their peers while also being self-critical in their feelings about playing with gender role-inconsistent toys. This supports the idea that while social sanctions for gender-typed behaviour are evident in young children, self-regulation becomes more important with age.

Francis (2000) found that in school, boys were pressurised to be active, aggressive, competitive and heterosexually inclined. Girls were often referred to in sexual ways and interest in academic pursuits attracted ridicule. Girls, however, constructed themselves as opposite to boys in being sensible and selfless, thus indicating the continued strong influence of peers upon gender, which seems to have more negative consequences for boys' school performance.

Renold (2001) found that final-year primary school girls who sought academic success were bullied and ostracised by both boys and girls and that such girls had problems establishing a feminine role that did not revolve around boys and presenting their body in certain ways. This illustrates how peers play a strong role in policing stereotypical gender roles.

### Evaluation

- SLT cannot explain gender changes with age; indeed, it assumes there are no developmental stages, which evidence suggests do exist.
- SLT cannot explain gender differences between same-sex siblings. Two brothers may be raised by the same parents in the same way, but one turns out to be more 'masculine' than the other, which would suggest more of a biological influence on gender development.
- SLT cannot explain how new gender behaviours arise, for instance the emergence of more child-caring types of men. SLT only explains the observation and imitation of existing gender behaviours. For example, the influence of peers seems often to just be that of reinforcing existing gender-role stereotypes.
- SLT cannot explain why children's willingness to imitate behaviour depends more on whether the behaviour is seen as gender appropriate than the sex of the model demonstrating the behaviour. This suggests cognitive factors are at play, as children seem to be actively selecting which behaviours to imitate.
- Studies of SLT lack gender bias, as such research focuses on the effects of peer influences upon both girls and boys.
- Peers may have a stronger role than adults in shaping gender development, as children interact more with peers in social situations and tend to police gender behaviours more, such as not accepting children who display non-gender-stereotypical behaviour. Parents tend to exert more influence when children are younger, but peers become more important as children age and increasingly interact with each other.

*'I don't want to be a supermodel; I want to be a role model.'*
Queen Latifah (1993)

## The influence of media on gender roles

Media forms, such as television, magazines, social media and pop music, influence the acquisition, shaping and maintenance of gender roles. Males are more represented in most TV programmes, including children's programmes. Males are also portrayed in a wider range of and higher-status roles than females.

Both sexes are portrayed in gender-stereotypical ways and even within shared formats gender roles are apparent, for instance in the composition of pop groups, with females as singers and males as musicians (see Figure 4.16).

Media influences provide children with a constant source of information as to which gender behaviours to imitate. Children who 'consume' the most media, for example those who watch a lot of television, develop stronger and more extreme perceptions of gender roles. More recent media influences, such as social network sites like Facebook, suggest they are more female dominated, but still reinforce traditional gender roles. Nevertheless, there is some contradictory evidence that social network sites can help break down traditional gender stereotypes.

**Figure 4.16** The group Blondie conformed to the gender-stereotypical format

### CONTEMPORARY RESEARCH

**Gender stereotypes of scientist characters in television programmes popular among middle school-aged children – Jocelyn Steinke *et al.* (2008)**

**Figure 4.17** Does TV portray females as scientists?

As more opportunities now exist for females to become scientists, the researchers were interested in seeing whether there was a gender difference in the way in which scientists were portrayed in children's TV programmes (see Figure 4.17).

#### Aim
To examine gender stereotyping in portrayals of scientist characters in television programmes popular with middle school-aged children.

#### Procedure
Fourteen popular television programmes watched by 12–17 year olds with a scientific element to them were selected.

Eight episodes of each programme broadcast between April and May 2006 were randomly selected for analysis – in all, 112 episodes.

Criteria for identifying scientist characters were constructed – for example, conducting experiments – and inter-rater reliability was established by using two raters.

196 scientist characters were identified and the following characteristics listed: sex, race, age group, scientific status, marital status and parental status.

Each character's behaviour was coded for gender-stereotypical and non-gender-stereotypical behaviour.

#### Findings
Of 196 scientist characters, 113 (58 per cent) were male, 83 (42 per cent) were female.

Male scientists were no more likely than females to be portrayed as high status.

Of 42 married scientist characters, slightly more were male.

Of 13 scientist characters with children, slightly more were male.

Female scientist characters were not more likely than males to be portrayed with feminine qualities of dependence and being caring and romantic.

Male scientist characters were more likely than females to be portrayed with masculine qualities of independence and dominance, but not athleticism.

### Conclusions

Popular children's TV programmes portray more male than female scientist characters.

Male scientist characters are more likely to be portrayed with stereotypically masculine characteristics.

### Evaluation

- Progress has been made in presenting scientific characters in children's TV programmes in a non-biased way. Earlier studies, like Steinke & Long (1996), found females more likely to be portrayed as assistants.
- Most programmes featuring female scientist characters were educational ones funded by the National Science Foundation, implying that mainstream media providers are more to blame for gender-stereotyping portrayals.

---

**RESEARCH IN FOCUS**

In Steinke et al.'s (2008) study, criteria for identifying scientist characters were constructed and inter-rater reliability was established by using two raters. Explain in the context of this study the purpose of establishing behavioural criteria.

What is inter-rater reliability and how would it be established using two raters?

---

## Research

Huston & Wright (1998) found that in US TV programmes males almost always outnumber females, especially in children's programmes, with men shown in dominant roles and higher occupational status and women in a narrow range of inferior roles and less able to deal with problems, illustrating the differences in gender-role presentations.

Bee (2000) found that books, including picture books and early reading books, are gender stereotyped and that boys' TV commercials are fast, sharp and loud compared with those for girls, which are slower, gentle and quiet, suggesting that media gender-role portrayals and influences differ for boys and girls from an early age.

Gunter (1986) found that children categorised as 'heavy' viewers of television hold stronger stereotyped beliefs than 'lighter' viewers, a fact Huston (1990) did not find surprising, as by age 18 the average American child has spent more time in front of the TV than in a classroom, demonstrating the potential strength of media influences on gender development.

Kivran-Swaine et al. (2013) examined the relationship between language and gender on social media by analysing 78,000 Twitter messages, to find strong evidence of gender-driven language. Females used more emotive language and had higher usage of emoticons, especially in communications with other females, illustrating how gender influences styles of communication on social media, which are very much in line with traditional patterns of gender roles.

Pew Research Internet Project (2011) found that unlike most social media sites, LinkedIn, with more than 100 million users, was male dominated, men making up 63 per cent of users compared with 37 per cent of users being female. This may be because the site caters for more male-dominated professional occupations. However, females on LinkedIn had created 70 per cent of the connections, which suggests females in traditionally male-dominated industries have become more involved than their male counterparts, with females being seen as more knowledgeable. This illustrates how social media can help to break down typical gender stereotypes.

Martinez-Aleman & Wartman (2009) found that although female dominated, stereotypical gender roles tend to be portrayed on the social media site Facebook, with men conforming to traditional views of masculinity and females to traditional views of femininity. This supports the idea that although a modern phenomenon, social networking sites still reinforce traditional gender roles.

### Evaluation

- The fact that 'heavy' TV watchers hold stronger gender-stereotyped beliefs is merely correlational evidence, not necessarily indicating TV to be the cause of such attitudes. It may simply be that gender-stereotypical children watch lots of TV because it confirms their gender stereotypes.
- It is simplistic to see children as passive recipients of media messages of gender stereotypes. Children actively select particular characters and events to respond to, which suggests more of a cognitive input than a purely social learning effect.
- If media influences do have a negative influence in establishing and reinforcing traditional gender stereotypes, equally they should be able to create and promote positive non-gender-role stereotypes, like female scientists and sports stars. Johnston & Ettema (1982) showed 12 year olds a television programme designed to counter gender stereotypes, and both sexes showed reduced gender stereotyping.
- Media influences on gender development may be exaggerated, as much gender development occurs before four years of age when media influences are weak. Later on, media influences probably reinforce existing gender beliefs rather than create them.

### PSYCHOLOGY IN THE REAL WORLD

SLT shows how the media creates and maintains negative gender stereotypes, but equally SLT should be able to promote positive gender stereotypes through creating opportunities for observation and imitation of positive role models. For example, Steinke et al.'s (2008) study highlights the improvement in how female scientists are presented in children's TV shows, such as 'Nina and the Neurons' (see Figure 4.18).

However, the majority of positive gender stereotyping occurs in educational programmes and it will only be when mainstream TV programming follows suit that real progress in breaking down negative gender stereotyping will be seen to occur. This is highly desirable, for as Steinke argues, if the huge potential for science is to be tapped into, with its positive benefits for society, then greater participation by women is essential.

**Figure 4.18** TV shows like 'Nina and the Neurons' promote positive gender stereotypes of females that ultimately benefits all of society

*'As the traveller is wiser than he who has never left his own doorstep, so a knowledge of other cultures sharpens our ability to scrutinize more steadily, to appreciate more lovingly, our own.'*

Margaret Mead (1949)

# The influence of culture on gender roles

Studying cultural influences on gender roles allows psychologists to assess the extent to which gender is a biological or a social construct. If gender was biological in nature then the different cultural influences that people are subjected to around the world would have no influence on gender development – it would be the same in all cultures. If, however, different cultural influences result in differences in gender roles between cultures this would infer gender to be socially constructed.

## Research

Mead (1935) conducted research into gender differences between tribes in Papua New Guinea. In the Arapesh, both males and females exhibited feminine, caring behaviours. In the Tchambuli, the men exhibited what would be seen in Western culture as female behaviours, while women exhibited traditional (Western) male behaviours. In the Mundugumor, both men and women exhibited masculine aggressive personalities. This indicates gender roles to be socially constructed rather than biological in nature.

Barry *et al.* (1957) found that in non-Western cultures nurturing was seen as a dominantly feminine characteristic, while self-reliance was regarded similarly for males. As these findings reflect those of Western cultures, it therefore suggests a biological basis to gender roles. Further support came from Whiting & Edwards (1988) finding that it was fairly universal cross-culturally for girls to be encouraged into domestic and child-caring roles, while boys are socialised into tasks involving responsibility, like looking after animals.

La Fromboise *et al.* (1990) conducted observations and interviews to find that gender roles among various North American tribes were different from those in Western cultures. For example, women were often warriors, which illustrates that aggressive roles are not universally male, indicating gender to be more of a social construction.

Williams & Best (1990) found that there was universal agreement across cultures about which characteristics were masculine and feminine, with men perceived as dominant and independent, and women as caring and sociable, with children from these cultures also exhibiting the same attitudes. This implies attitudes to gender roles to be universal and therefore biological in nature.

**Figure 4.19** A Native American teenage boy

### Evaluation

- Conducting cross-cultural research is prone to the problem of an imposed etic, where researchers use research methods and tools relevant and applicable in their own culture but alien and non-applicable to other cultures, which can result in flawed conclusions being drawn. Many replications of Western cultural studies in other cultures have involved an imposed etic.
- As gender stereotypes and gender roles are fairly consistent across human populations, it initially seems that gender is more biological.

However, there is also evidence of gender roles varying considerably across cultures, indicating some influence of social learning.

- Globalisation may be contributing to the lessening of cultural differences, and there has been a global reduction in the differences between masculine and feminine gender roles, implying that social influences are stronger than biological ones.
- Margaret Mead's initial beliefs of gender roles being cultural constructions were influential, but she later came to believe that gender roles were predominantly biological in nature. This dramatic conversion is argued by Booth (1975) to have occurred due to Mead marrying a man with very 'traditional' views on the roles of men and women, and to her having her own child. This suggests that the personal viewpoints investigators bring to their research have strong effects on the conclusions they ultimately draw. This is supported by Errington & Gewert's (1989) study of the Tchambuli, which did not find the gender role reversals that Mead did.
- Rather than seeing gender roles as simply a product of nature (biological influences) or nurture (environmental influences), they may be better understood from an interactionist point of view, where initial gender roles are biologically constructed and then later modified by social influences. This would explain the basic cross-cultural similarities in gender roles and gender stereotypes, but also why there is cross-cultural variety, especially in the types of activities to which gender roles are applied.

## STRENGTHEN YOUR LEARNING

1. Explain how gender roles may be learned through socialising agents.
2. Explain how social learning of gender roles can occur through the influence of i) parents, ii) peers.
3. Summarise what research evidence suggests about the learning of gender roles through the influence of parents and peers.
4. What other evaluative points can be made concerning the social learning of gender roles?
5. How might media influence gender roles?
6. To what extent does research suggest media influences gender roles?
7. What other evaluative points can be made concerning the influence of media on gender roles?
8. Outline and evaluate Steinke *et al.*'s (2008) study of gender stereotypes of scientist characters in television programmes.
9. Why are psychologists interested in studying how cultural influences affect gender development?
10. Summarise what research evidence suggests about the influence of culture on gender roles.
11. What other evaluative points can be made concerning the influence of culture on gender roles?

*'No one has the right to demand that your body be something other than what it is.'*
Agnostic Zetetic (2013)

# 4.6 Atypical gender development

Atypical gender development is referred to in the classification system DSM-IV by the clinical label of **gender identity disorder** (GID), an abnormal condition where individuals experience their gender identity – the psychological experience of being male or female – as not fitting their phenotype, the external sex characteristics of the body. In other words, it occurs where a person, who biologically is male, with male genitalia, feels they are female, or a person who is biologically female feels they are male. The personal experience of this discomfort is referred to as gender dysphoria. (Indeed, the more recent DSM-5 classification system now refers to GID as gender dysphoria in order to remove the damaging label of people with the condition as 'disordered'.)

Prejudice and negative feelings of anxiety and distress are experienced, leading to depression, self-harm and sometimes even suicide. GID affects males more than females, and although prevalence rates are hard to calculate, as many are reluctant to admit to having the condition, it is estimated that up to 1 in 5,000 people may have the condition. Indications of the condition may occur fairly early, with children unhappy wearing clothes of their biological gender or playing gender-stereotypical games. Most gender dysphoria occurs in childhood, and for the majority of such children it does not persist after puberty. However, those for whom it does persist tend to have stronger gender dysphoric symptoms in childhood. Often, because of the distress and disgust with the bodily signs of their 'wrong' sex, gender dysphorics may assume the gender role of the desired sex, wearing gender-typical clothes and adopting gender-stereotyped behaviours. This helps them to feel better about themselves. Masculinising or feminising hormones can be taken to alter physical features, with the ultimate remedy being gender reassignment surgery. Since 2000, 865 gender reassignment surgeries have been performed by the NHS (see In the news, page 108).

Early explanations centred on psychological factors, such as maladaptive learning experiences, maladaptive cognitive processes and psychodynamic fixations occurring in childhood development. However, biological explanations, such as genetics and hormones, have become increasingly favoured and supported by research evidence.

## Social explanations for gender identity disorder

**Social explanations for gender identity disorder** perceive GID as being learned, for example by operant conditioning, where individuals are reinforced (rewarded) for exhibiting cross-gender behaviour. Many young children 'experiment' with gender role behaviour, for instance infant boys wearing frocks and jewellery, or girls being 'dad' when playing 'house'.

### KEY TERM

**Gender identity disorder** – a condition whereby the external sexual characteristics of the body are perceived as opposite to the psychological experience of oneself as male or female

**Figure 4.20** Gender identity disorder affects individuals unhappy with their biological sex

### KEY TERM

**Social explanations for gender identity disorder** – the perception that gender identity disorder is a condition learned via socialisation processes

Learning theory argues that parents of gender dysphorics may have reinforced the condition by encouraging and complimenting their children for such behaviour. Such family reactions could contribute to the conflict between anatomical sex and acquired gender identity. This presumably occurs more with males, as gender dysphoria is associated more with boys than girls.

Social learning may also play a part, with the disorder being learned by observation and imitation of individuals modelling cross-gender behaviour (see Figure 4.21).

## Biological explanations for gender identity disorder

**Biological explanations for gender identity disorder** are more recent than social explanations and more supported by evidence. The genetic explanation sees the condition as an inherited abnormality, while the biochemical explanation sees a role for hormonal imbalances during foetal growth in the womb and in later childhood development. It may be that the two explanations combine, with hormonal imbalances being genetically influenced.

To investigate the genetic explanation, gene-profiling studies are performed to try to identify genetic material common to those exhibiting the condition. Attention has centred on gene variants of the androgen receptor, which influences the action of testosterone and is involved in the masculinisation of the brain. Other research methods have utilised twin studies to assess the heritability of the condition and post-mortem studies to search for structural brain differences in those with GID.

A hormonal explanation centres in males upon the release during the third month of pregnancy of significant amounts of male hormones from the newly formed male testes, with an additional release between two and twelve weeks after birth. Such male hormonal surges must occur at the right time and in sufficient amounts for masculinisation of an infant to develop. It may be that if this process is not carried out successfully, through a disorder in the mother's endocrine (hormonal) system, maternal stress or an illness that interferes with hormonal levels, GID may eventually arise. A similar process may occur in females, though with more involvement for oestrogen.

### Research

Gladue (1985) reported that there were few, if any, hormonal differences between gender-dysphoric men, heterosexual men and homosexual men, as evidence against the influence of hormones on gender dysphoria. As similar results are found with women it suggests a social explanation may be more fitting.

Rekers (1995) reported that in 70 gender-dysphoric boys there was more evidence of social than biological factors, but there was a common factor of a lack of stereotypical male role models, suggesting that social learning factors play a role in the condition.

Beijsterveldt *et al.* (2006) used self-report data supplied by mothers to assess cross-gender behaviour in 14,000 Dutch twins at ages seven and ten. At both ages the prevalence for cross-gender behaviour was greater in MZ (identical) than DZ (non-identical) twins and the use of statistical modelling techniques showed that 70 per cent of the variance in the tendency for

**Figure 4.21** A small boy wearing a girl's outfit is an example of cross-gender behaviour

#### KEY TERM

**Biological explanations for gender identity disorder** – the perception that gender identity disorder is physiologically determined

cross-gender behaviour was due to genetic factors in both ages and for boys and girls. This suggests a biological explanation. This was supported by Coolidge *et al.* (2002), who using data from a different twin sample found 62 per cent of variation was due to biological factors and 32 per cent to environmental factors.

Zucker *et al.* (2008) performed a longitudinal study on gender-dysphoric females between two and three years of age who had been referred to a clinic. Only 12 per cent were still gender dysphoric at age 18. A study on equivalent males found that 20 per cent were still gender dysphoric as adults, again supporting the idea that the majority of people exhibiting gender dysphoria do so only in the short term.

Hare *et al.* (2009) examined gene samples from male gender dysphorics and non-dysphorics. A correlation was found between gender dysphoria and variants of the androgen receptor gene, implying the gene to be involved in a failure to masculinise the brain during development in the womb, supporting a biological explanation.

Garcia-Falgueras & Swaab (2008) compared post-mortem data from 17 deceased individuals who had undergone gender reassignment surgery with 25 controls, to find that the hypothalamic uncinate nucleus brain area was similar in male-to-female gender-reassigned participants to female controls and was similar in the one female-to-male gender-reassigned participant to male controls. This supports the idea of GID having a biological origin, with such structural differences possibly occurring due to abnormal hormonal activity during masculinisation and feminisation of the brain.

### Evaluation

- Conditioning experiences may explain why more children than adults are identified as gender dysphoric. Early life experiences are dominated by the family, where cross-gender behaviours are tolerated or even encouraged, but as the individual grows up, others outside the family exert an influence, making it more likely that an individual will be punished for behaving in 'inappropriate' ways.
- Hines (2004) argues that the strong, persistent desire to change sex, and the willingness to undergo surgery and hormone treatment despite formidable obstacles, such as prejudice, bullying and even job loss, points to a biological explanation.
- Increasingly, evidence suggests that the influence of hormones and genetics is the main cause of GID, but there is little evidence to suggest a totally biological explanation and other interacting psychological factors are likely to be involved, too. More research is needed, especially to identify what types of psychological factors are required to elicit an influence, and the biological processes through which genetic effects may be operating.
- Bennett (2006) points out that while SLT explains the development of cross-gender behaviours, it cannot explain the strength of beliefs that individuals possess concerning being the wrong sex, or the resistance of such beliefs to therapy. This would indicate a biological explanation.
- GID is a sensitive area in which to conduct research and care must be taken when investigating the phenomenon to not cause psychological harm to what are often confused and vulnerable individuals.

- The fact that the vast majority of people with GID who are given hormonal therapies to reduce the dissonance (lack of harmony) experienced of feeling they were of opposite gender to their biological sex see their treatment as successful supports the idea of a biological basis to the disorder. Green & Fleming (1990) found that treatment of individuals with GID by hormonal therapy was 87 per cent successful in females reporting gender dysphoria and 97 per cent in males.

### ON THE WEB
The Gender Trust is a support group for people affected by gender identity issues. They run a website containing information about the condition, links to other groups, a glossary of terms, etc. Find them at:

**http://gendertrust.org.uk/**

### STRENGTHEN YOUR LEARNING
1. Why is gender identity disorder now known more commonly as gender dysphoria?
2. Describe the key features of gender identity disorder.
3. Outline how gender identity disorder may be accounted for by i) social explanations, ii) biological explanations.
4. To what extent does research evidence support social and biological explanations of gender identity disorder?
5. What other evaluative points can be made about social and biological explanations of gender identity disorder?

### RESEARCH IN FOCUS
Experiments into gender often use quasi experiments where the IV is whether participants are male or female. Why then do some psychologists regard a quasi experiment as not being a true type of experiment? How does a quasi experiment differ from a natural experiment?

# ASSESSMENT CHECK

1. Which one of the statements A, B and C below relates to the social learning theory of gender development? **[1 mark]**

   A Gender development occurs during the phallic stage of psychosexual development

   B Gender development occurs through surges of hormones in the womb

   C Gender development occurs through observation and imitation of models

2. When he was a young boy Gary liked to play at 'dressing up' and sometimes used to wear one of his sister's dresses and jewellery and he was praised for doing so by his parents. When he became older Gary often felt that even though he was biologically a male, he felt more as if he should be female and he has now been diagnosed with gender identity disorder.

   Refer to the scenario above to show why a social explanation might be the reason that Gary has gender identity disorder. **[3 marks]**

3. Research into the biological explanation of gender identity disorder often uses laboratory experiments. Explain one strength and one weakness of conducting research by this method. **[2 + 2 marks]**

4. Outline and evaluate the influence of culture and media on gender roles. **[16 marks]**

5. Outline the biological explanation of gender identity disorder. **[4 marks]**

**Sex and gender**

**SUMMARY**

- Sex relates to whether an individual is biologically male or female, while gender concerns the social and psychological characteristics of males and females.
- Sex-role stereotypes concern the types of qualities and characteristics seen as appropriate for each sex.
- Androgyny involves having both feminine and masculine characteristics, with androgynous individuals not influenced by sex-role stereotypes.
- The Bem Sex Role Inventory is a self-report method of measuring androgyny in terms of masculinity–femininity and gender roles.

**The role of chromosomes and hormones**

- Biological sex is determined by the sex chromosomes X and Y that contain genetic material that controls development as male or female.
- Testosterone, oestrogen and oxytocin are hormones involved in the development of sexual characteristics.
- Klinefelter's and Turner's syndrome are atypical chromosomal conditions that affect male and female gender development.

**Cognitive explanations of gender development**

- Kohlberg's theory of gender development perceives children as developing an understanding of gender in stages.
- Gender schema theory sees gender identity alone as providing children with motivation to assume sex-typed behaviour patterns.

**Psychodynamic explanations of gender development**

- Freud's psychoanalytic explanation of gender development, gender identity and role is explained as being acquired during the phallic stage.
- The Oedipus and Electra complexes concern the arousal of sexual desire for one's opposite-sex parent and dislike of one's same-sex parent.

**Social learning theory as applied to gender development**

- The social learning theory sees gender development as occurring through the observation and imitation of models, with both culture and media being important influences on gender roles.

**Atypical gender develpoment**

- Gender identity disorder concerns a perceived mismatch between one's external sexual characteristics and the psychological experience of being male or female.
- Biological explanations for gender identity dysphoria have greater research support than social explanations.

# 5 Cognition and development

## Introduction

Cognition concerns the mental processes involved in acquiring knowledge and understanding. It is especially important to comprehend how cognition develops in order to establish the best means of educating children, as the majority of cognitive development occurs in early life, with Piaget, Vygotsky and Baillargeon being three important theorists who attempted to explain such cognitive development.

Social cognition focuses on the role that mental processes play in human social interactions, with important roles perceived here for perspective-taking, the theory of mind and the mirror neuron system.

Specific focus will be upon:

1. Piaget's theory of cognitive development
2. Vygotsky's theory of cognitive development
3. Baillargeon's explanation for early infant abilities
4. The development of social cognition.

### Understanding the specification

- The specification requires study of Piaget's theory of cognitive development with a focus upon schemas, assimilation, accommodation, equilibration and stages of intellectual development, as these are specifically listed. There is also a need to study characteristics of these stages, including object permanence, conservation, egocentrism and class inclusion, as again these are specifically listed.
- Vygotsky's theory of cognitive development must similarly be covered, including focus upon the zone of proximal development and scaffolding.
- There is a requirement to study Baillargeon's explanation of early infant abilities, as this includes knowledge of the physical world and violation of expectation research.
- When studying the development of social cognition, Selman's levels of perspective-taking need to be focused on, as it is specifically listed, as is theory of mind, including theory of mind as an explanation for autism, the Sally-Anne study and the role of mirror neurons in social cognition.

These are the basic requirements of the specification. However, other relevant material is included to provide depth and detail to your understanding.

*'If the mind was simple enough to be understood – we would be too simple to understand it!'*
Marvin Minsky (1970)

# IN THE NEWS

## The Psychological Enquirer

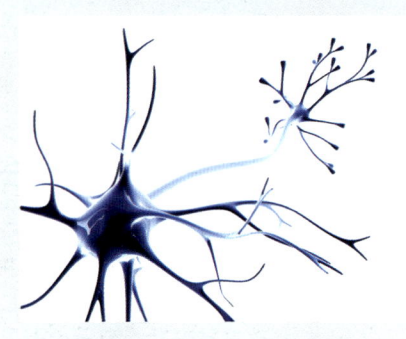

**Figure 5.1** How much of a scientific breakthrough is the discovery of mirror neurons?

How often have you sat watching a romantic movie mopping up the tears with a firmly clutched handkerchief? Probably more times than you care to admit. And how many times have you sat peeping through gaps in your fingers, petrified at some scary scene in a horror movie? And yet why do we love such experiences so? Perhaps mirror neurons are the answer.

Mirror neurons are nerves in the brain that are active not only when we perform certain behaviours ourselves but also when we observe them being performed by others, which allows individuals to share the feelings of others without them having to think about it. This could be the reason, then, why we become so emotionally involved in films, because we 'mirror' the feelings apparently being experienced by the actors and actresses in front of us.

But is this true? It reads as though it could be true, but where is the evidence? Mirror neurons were discovered by Italian scientists studying monkeys in the 1990s and the popular press has promoted the view that their discovery was a 'great scientific breakthrough', with all kinds of claims being promoted as 'truths'. Neuroscientist V.S. Ramachandran, for instance, stated that mirror neurons underpin what it is to be human and that they are responsible not just for empathy but also for language and the evolution of culture, including the use of tools and fire. He even goes as far as to say that when mirror neurons don't work, the result is autism. However, researchers have found it difficult to identify and interpret mirror neuron activity in humans and there are many types of mirror neurons with apparently different functions. Also, humans can understand the intentions of others even when they have never performed such actions themselves. Mirror neurons are an exciting discovery, but only through patient scientific research will the true significance of any observed phenomena be revealed and any true student of psychology should remember this.

## Theories of cognitive development

Theories of cognitive development attempt to explain the growth of mental abilities. Piaget's theory sees thought processes as undergoing qualitative changes as children age, with biological processes directing these changes. Vygotsky, however, sees learning experiences as the major influence upon cognitive development, while Baillargeon believes that children have more of an intuitive ability to reason and learn about events.

*'It is with children that we have the best chance of studying the development of logical knowledge, mathematical knowledge, physical knowledge, and so forth.'*
Jean Piaget (1968)

# 5.1 Piaget's theory of cognitive development

Jean Piaget (1896–1980) is regarded by many as the greatest, most influential psychologist of all time. He certainly has had a great impact on education, where his theories have been applied most. A brilliant academic, publishing his first paper at the age of 10 and getting his PhD at 22, he was originally a biologist and expert on water snails, but had a long-standing curiosity about psychology because of his mother's poor mental health. His interest in cognitive development came from working on intelligence tests and later from observing the intellectual development of his own children, upon whom he performed many experiments. This ultimately led to his theory of cognitive development, which took 30 years of studying and refining, with a main focus upon how children's intelligence changes, a process he called genetic epistemology. Piaget's theory was created through a series of experiments, which allowed him to conclude that cognitive development occurs through the interaction of inborn abilities and environmental events that proceed through a series of stages of intellectual development.

Piaget therefore saw intelligence as a process, with individuals learning about the world around them and how to interact with it, and intelligence being a state of balance or equilibrium achieved by an individual when they are able to deal adequately with the data before them. But it is not a static state; it continually changes by adapting itself to new environmental stimuli.

Humans therefore adapt to their environment, constructing an understanding of reality by interacting with the environment. Knowledge is actively discovered by using mental structures known as:

1 **Functional invariants** – structures that stay the same throughout the developmental process, which assist in the discovery and understanding of knowledge. There are two of these:
   i) the process of adaptation – involves accommodation and assimilation (see below)
   ii) the process of equilibration – involves swinging between equilibrium and disequilibrium (see below).
2 **Variant structures** – structures that change and develop as knowledge is discovered. There are two of these:
   i) **schemas** – units of intelligence/ways of understanding the world
   ii) **operations** – strings of schemas assembled in a logical order.

A baby's earliest schemas are inborn reflexes, such as sucking. These give babies something to interact with the environment and thus help discover knowledge with.

Early schemas are external and physical, while later schemas are more internal and cognitive (mental). These are the earliest forms of thinking. Over time they become less reflex and more deliberate and under the infant's control.

Cognitive development can be seen through the example of the innate schema of sucking. At first babies suck everything they come into contact with in the same inborn manner. This is called **assimilation** (part of the process of adaptation) and involves fitting new environmental experiences

**Figure 5.2** Jean Piaget was possibly the most influential psychologist of all time and his theory of cognitive development is still held in high regard

### KEY TERMS

**Schemas** – ways of understanding the world
**Operations** – strings of schemas assembled in a logical order
**Assimilation** – fitting new environmental experiences into existing schemas

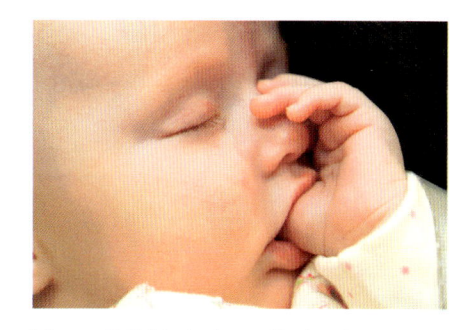

**Figure 5.3** A baby's earliest schemas are innate reflexes such as sucking

## KEY TERMS

**Equilibrium** – a pleasant state of balance

**Equilibration** – the process of swinging between equilibrium and disequilibrium

**Disequilibrium** – unpleasant state of imbalance that motivates a return to equilibrium

**Accommodation** – altering existing schemas to fit in new experiences

into existing schemas. If this is possible, infants are in a state of **equilibrium** (part of the process of **equilibration**), a pleasant state of balance.

When infants find something new so that they cannot suck in the usual way, such as drinking from a cup, they experience **disequilibrium** (the other part of the process of equilibration), an unpleasant state of imbalance. Children are naturally motivated to return to the balanced state of equilibrium, achieved by **accommodation** of the new experience (the other part of the process of adaptation). This involves altering existing schemas to accommodate (fit in) new experiences, such as using new lip shapes to drink/suck out of different things.

Therefore, cognitive development involves constantly swinging between equilibrium and disequilibrium, through continuous series of assimilation (fitting knowledge into new schemas) and accommodation (altering schemas to fit in new knowledge). When new schemas are formed, assimilation allows for the practice of the new experiences until they are automatic. This process continues through life, but is most apparent in the first 15 years.

## Stages of cognitive development

Piaget noticed that children give similar wrong answers at similar ages, which suggests that they progress through different stages of cognitive development. He saw these stages as invariant and cross-cultural – that is, all children go through the same stages, in the same order, at roughly the same age, all over the world. This indicates that the stages and development of intellect are genetically controlled.

There are also transitional periods, in which children's thinking is a mixture of the stage they are moving out of and the stage they are moving into.

### 1 Sensorimotor stage (birth to 2 years)

Piaget described the sensorimotor stage, which lasts from birth to about 2 years of age, as a time of rapid cognitive growth. At the start of the stage, babies only 'think' when perceiving or acting on objects. They have no internal representation of objects or events that adults would recognise as thinking. Therefore, when an object is not being perceived or acted on, it does not exist – that is, the baby has no **object permanence**. Infants at this point are highly egocentric, as they have no understanding of the world other than their own, but gradually during this stage they come to realise that objects exist and events occur independent of their behaviour; they can then be said to have acquired object permanence. Initially between one and four months of age, babies will look at the place where objects disappear from for a few moments, but will not search for them. Then babies start to reach for partially hidden objects, suggesting that they realise that the rest of the object is attached to the visible part. At the age of one, babies search for hidden objects, but only where they were last seen. Object permanence is not fully formed until two years of age.

The other development in the sensorimotor stage is the establishment of the general symbolic function (GSF). This occurs in the final part of the stage, involving the development of mental images to represent objects that children have experienced. Children are no longer dependent on physical manipulation of objects to 'think' about them; they can 'think' inside their heads, marking a transition of schemas to being internal rather than external.

## KEY TERM

**Object permanence** – an understanding that objects that are not being perceived or acted u0pon still exist

The stage itself can be divided into six sub-stages, each characterised by the development of a new skill.

1 Reflexes (0–1 month)
A child here can only understand its world through innate reflexes such as sucking.

2 Primary circular reactions (1–4 months)
This sub-stage involves co-ordinating sensations and new schemas, with infants deliberately repeating actions that are pleasurable.

3 Secondary circular reactions (4–8 months)
A child here focuses more on its world, attempting to manipulate its environment by repeating actions to deliberately trigger a response.

4 Co-ordination of reactions (8–12 months)
Children start to display intentional actions and may also combine schemas to gain desired results. Increased exploration of the environment occurs and infants will imitate the observed actions of others. It is at this point that an understanding of objects begins, with certain objects as seen as having specific qualities.

5 Tertiary circular reactions (12–18 months)
In this sub-stage children engage in trial and error experimentation, such as trying out different actions to see their effects.

6 Early representational thought (18–24 months)
Children can now use symbols to represent objects and events in the environment and so move towards understanding the world through mental operations rather than just through actions.

## 2 Pre-operational stage (2 to 7 years)

The GSF continues to develop, but children are still influenced by how things seem rather than by logical principles or operations, hence, 'pre-operational'. Piaget subdivided the stage into the pre-conceptual and intuitive sub-stages.

### Pre-conceptual (two to four years)

Several developments occur here:

- **Centration** – children cannot classify things in a logical manner.
- **Transductive reasoning** – relationships between two objects are based on a single attribute, for example a dog has four legs, a cat has four legs, therefore a cat is a dog.
- **Animistic thinking** – the belief that inanimate objects are alive.
- **Seriation** – children find it hard to put items in order, for example of size; they can perceive only biggest or smallest.

### Intuitive (four to seven years).

Intuitive children can think in relative terms but find it difficult to think logically, such as understanding the relationship between the whole of something and its parts. Children are egocentric, meaning that they can see things from their point of view only and not from the viewpoint of others. For example (to a boy):

*Question: Do you have a brother?*

*Answer: Yes.*

*Question: Does your brother have a brother?*

*Answer: No.*

### KEY TERM

**Conservation** – an understanding that changing the appearance of something does not affect its mass, number or volume

Children in this stage do not have **conservation**, an understanding that changing the appearance of something does not affect its mass, number or volume, because they fail to realise that things remain the same in amount even if they change their appearance. For instance, intuitive children believe a stretched-out row of seven objects has more objects in it than a more compact row of seven objects.

## 3 Concrete operational stage (7 to 11 years)

The main development in this stage is the growth of conservation, with children developing a mental structure known as an operation, an action performed mentally. At this stage, it can be done only if objects are physically present, hence 'concrete'. Conservation is an example of an operation, with concrete operational children able to understand the relationship between the whole of something and its parts.

Some types of conservation are mastered earlier than others and the order in which this occurs is invariant (the same for everybody). Liquid quantity develops by age 6–7, substance/quantity and length by 7–8 years, weight by 8–10 years and volume by 11–12 years. This step-by-step acquisition of new operations is called decalage.

### KEY TERMS

**Egocentrism** – an inability to see a situation from another's point of view

**Decentring** – a movement away from egocentrism where children are increasingly able to see things from the viewpoint of others

**Class inclusion** – an understanding that some sets of objects or sub-sets can be sets of other larger classes of objects

With conservation, decalage is horizontal, as there are inconsistencies *within* the same kind of ability or operation – for example, a seven year old can conserve number but not weight. There is also vertical decalage, which refers to inconsistencies *between* different abilities or operations – for example, children may master all kinds of classification but not all kinds of conservation.

**Egocentrism** declines, with children increasingly able to see things from the perspective of others. This process is called **decentring**.

**Class inclusion** also occurs in this stage, where children develop an understanding that some sets of objects, or sub-sets, can be sets of other larger classes of objects. Therefore they are able to classify objects as belonging to two or more categories simultaneously, such as a Pointer being a dog and being a mammal at the same time.

## 4 Formal operational stage (11+ years)

Manipulating objects concerns first-order operations, but children in the formal operations stage can now perform second-order operations where they manipulate ideas. Hypothetical situations can be thought about – that is, possibilities, not actualities. Children develop the ability to manipulate things in their head without any need for an object to be physically viewable, for example mathematical sums can be performed mentally without any need for physical manipulation of objects. Inferential reasoning can now also take place where conclusions can be drawn about things that haven't actually been experienced. For example, if a child knows that person A is taller than person B and that person B is taller than person C, it can be concluded that person A is taller than person C even though persons A and C have never been experienced together.

**Figure 5.4** With class inclusion children can classify objects as belonging to two or more categories simultaneously, such as a Pointer being both a dog and a mammal

Abstract reasoning of concepts and ideas with no physical presence also becomes apparent and children can consider possible outcomes of situations rather than having to rely on previous experience. This is important for being able to form long-term plans and goals

This stage is not as uniform as others. Some reach it by age 15, others by age 20, some maybe not at all, and different individuals develop formal operations in different areas of ability and experience. This stage therefore seems not to be as genetically controlled as others. Some researchers believe as few as one third of people reach this stage.

Table 5.1 outlines the various stages.

**Table 5.1** Piaget's stages of cognitive development

| Sensorimotor stage (birth to 2 years) | New schemas arise from matching sensory to motor experiences<br>Object permanence develops |
|---|---|
| Pre-operational stage (2 to 7 years) | Internal images, symbols and language develop<br>Child is influenced by how things seem, not logic |
| Concrete operational stage (7 to 11 years) | Development of conservation (use of logical rules), but only if situations are concrete, not abstract<br>Decline of egocentrism |
| Formal operational stage (11+ years) | Abstract manipulation of ideas (concepts without physical presence)<br>Not achieved by all |

*'People think I'm egocentric, but that's enough about them.'*

Lily Allen (2009)

## CLASSIC RESEARCH

### The Swiss Mountain Scene Study

### Piaget & Inhelder (1956)

Piaget observed that pre-operational children, aged between two and seven, show errors in logic, as they are egocentric (they can see the world from their own point of view only). This was demonstrated in this study by children only being able to select pictures of a view they could see themselves (see Figure 5.5). The study, though, is not without its criticisms.

Figure 5.5 A child looking at a mountain scene

#### Aim
To see whether children below seven years are able to see the mountain scene model from their own viewpoint only.

#### Procedure
Children aged between four and eight years were presented with three papier-mâché mountains of various colours, each with something different on the top: a red cross, a covering of snow or a chalet. Children walked round the model, exploring it, then sat on one side while a doll was placed on one of the other sides. Children were then shown ten pictures of different views of the model, including the doll's and their own. They were asked to select the picture representing the doll's view.

#### Findings
Four year olds chose the picture matching their own view. Six year olds showed some understanding of other viewpoints, but often selected the wrong picture. Seven and eight year olds consistently chose the picture representing the doll's view.

#### Conclusions
Four year olds are unaware that there are viewpoints other than their own. Children under seven years are subject to the egocentric illusion, failing to understand that what they see is specific to their position. Instead, they believe that their own view represents 'the world as it really is'.

#### Evaluation
- Swiss mountains are outside of most children's experience; therefore, what Piaget witnessed, due to his

poor methodology, was not egocentrism but a lack of understanding. Hughes (1975) found that 90 per cent of children aged between 3.5 and 5 years could hide a doll in a 3D model of intersecting walls where a police doll could not see it, but they could see it, as they used their experience of playing hide-and-seek to do so, suggesting that young children are not egocentric (see Figure 5.6). Similarly, Gelman (1979) found that four year olds adjust their explanations of things to a blindfolded listener to make them clearer and use simpler forms of speech when talking to two year olds. This would not be expected if they were egocentric.

- The study is not actually an experiment, as it has no independent variable, but instead is a 'controlled observation'.

### ON THE WEB

To view demonstrations of conservation experiments, go to **www.youtube.com** and search for 'Piaget – Conservacoes'. You can find links to many other Piagetian-style experiments, too.

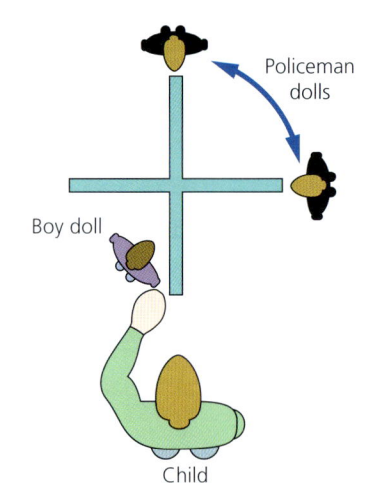

**Figure 5.6** Hughes (1975) found most young children are not egocentric by using a scenario based on hide-and-seek, a situation they were familiar with

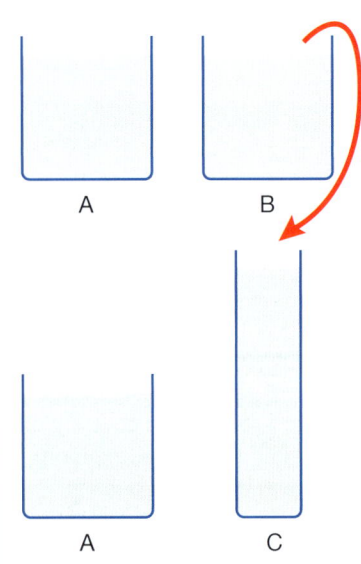

**Figure 5.7** The same amount of liquid in different shaped beakers can appear different in size

### RESEARCH IN FOCUS

Piaget conducted many research studies into cognitive development, such as his 1958 study into formal operational thinking with Inhelder. Such research would be subjected to peer review before it could be published in an accepted psychological journal.

Explain what is meant by peer review and the reasons why peer review is conducted. What are the strengths and weaknesses of peer review?

## Research

Bower & Wishart (1972) found that one-month-old babies show surprise when toys disappear, suggesting that Piaget witnessed immature motor skills, not a lack of object permanence.

Piaget & Szeminska (1941) showed children 18 brown and 2 white wooden beads and asked them i) whether all the beads were wooden, ii) whether there were more brown than white beads and iii) whether there were more brown or wooden beads. Pre-operational children (below the age of seven) answered the first two questions correctly, but thought there were more brown than wooden beads. Concrete operational children (over the age of seven) got all three questions right. The findings suggest that pre-operational children do not have class inclusion, as they presume if brown beads belong to one class, and they are the majority, then they must have more members than any other class.

Piaget (1952) got seven-year-olds to agree that two identically shaped beakers A and B contained equal amounts of liquid (see Figure 5.7). Having witnessed beaker B being poured into beaker C, a taller, thinner beaker that contains the same amount, the children state C contains more, which suggests they cannot conserve. However, Donaldson (1978) argues that as the same question is asked twice, the children think a different answer is required, suggesting that Piaget's methodology was not suitable for such young children.

In another conservation task of number, Piaget (1960) laid out two equally spaced rows of counters and pre-operational children agreed that there was the same number in both rows. One of the rows, in sight of the child, was compressed (the counters were moved closer to each other) and children stated that the longer line had more. McGarrigle & Donaldson (1974) repeated the study and children again initially agreed that the two rows contained the same number. Then 'naughty teddy', a glove puppet, 'secretly' pushed one of the rows together and children stated they still contained the same number. The researchers argue that children believe, from experience, that adults are always changing things, so a different answer is needed when adults meddle with the counters. Similarly, Berko (1960) argues that children misinterpret the words 'more' and 'less' as meaning 'taller' and 'shorter', again suggesting Piaget's findings were due to poor methodology.

Inhelder & Piaget (1958) got participants to consider which of three factors (the length of some string, the heaviness of some weights or the strength of push)

was the most important in assessing the speed of swing of a pendulum. The solution is to change one variable at a time, e.g. try different lengths of string with the same weight, and children in the formal operational stage were able to do this, but younger children could not, as they tended to try several variables at once. This suggests that children in the formal operational stage can think logically in an abstract manner in order to see the relationships between things.

### Evaluation

- Piaget stimulated interest in cognitive development, with his theory becoming the starting point for many later theories and research. Schaffer (2004) believes it to be the most comprehensive account of how children come to understand the world, even though it has declined in importance in more recent years.
- Piaget was not rigid in his beliefs, adapting his theory constantly in response to critical evidence. For example, in later life he referred to his stages of development as 'spirals of development' to reflect evidence that there were transitional periods in which children's thinking was a combination of the stage they were leaving and the stage they were progressing on to.
- As cross-cultural evidence implies that the stages of development (except formal operations) occur as a universal, invariant sequence, it suggests cognitive development is a biological process of maturation.
- However, Dasen (1977) believes that as formal operational thinking is not found in all cultures, this stage is not genetically determined. Also, the fact that not all individuals seem to acquire formal operational thinking, and those that do, do at different ages, suggests this stage is uniform and invariant as others, which additionally suggests it is not biologically determined.
- A major criticism of the theory is that Piaget neglected the important role of emotional and social factors in intellectual development and in doing so overemphasised cognitive aspects of development.
- Piaget saw language ability as reflecting an individual's level of cognitive development, while theorists like Bruner argued it was the other way round, with language development preceding cognitive development.
- Piaget's often poor methodology, such as using research situations that were unfamiliar to children, led him to underestimate what children of different ages could achieve.
- Piaget believed the rate at which a child's cognitive development occurred could not be accelerated (as it was under biological control). However, Meadows (1988) found that direct tuition could speed up development, which suggests Piaget's belief that children could not progress intellectually until they were biologically ready may be wrong.
- Meadows (1995) argues that Piaget saw children as being independent from others as they constructed their knowledge and understanding of the physical world and thus excluded the contribution of others to cognitive development. This important omission of the social nature of learning (how it is influenced by others) is a major feature of Vygotsky's theory.

### STRENGTHEN YOUR LEARNING

1. Explain functional invariants in terms of the process of adaptation and the process of equilibration.
2. Explain variant structures in terms of schemas and operations.
3. Summarise the main developments that occur within Piaget's four stages of cognitive development.
4. Outline and evaluate Piaget & Inhelder's (1956) Swiss mountain scene study.
5. Outline two other studies that Piaget conducted, which support his theory.
6. Explain, with reference to relevant research, why Piaget's poor methodology may have led him at times to reach the wrong conclusions about children's cognitive development.
7. What other evaluative points can be made concerning Piaget's theory?

### ON THE WEB

A website run by the Jean Piaget Society that features a biography and other details of the eminent psychologist, including links to other sources of information, can be found at:

www.piaget.org/aboutPiaget.html

# ASSESSMENT CHECK

1. Select from the descriptions A, B, C, D and E below to complete the table relating to Piaget's stages of cognitive development. One description will be left over. **[4 marks]**

   **A** Internal images, symbols and language develop

   **B** The ability to manipulate ideas develops

   **C** Neurons develop that allow other people's actions to be understood

   **D** Object permanence develops

   **E** Conservation skills develop

   | Stage of cognitive development | Description |
   |---|---|
   | Formal operational stage | |
   | Pre-operational stage | |
   | Concrete operational stage | |
   | Sensorimotor stage | |

2. Nine-year-old Tim and his four-year-old brother Marco watched the recent football match between Sporting Torpedo and Dynamo Lokomotiv from the West Stand, while their grandfather watched it from the East Stand on the opposite side of the ground. After the game, Tim was able to identify the photograph showing the view his grandfather had of the goal that won the game, something Marco could not do, as he picked out a photograph showing his own view of the goal.

   Referring to the above scenario and using your knowledge of Piaget's theory of cognitive development, explain why Tim but not Marco could select the photograph showing the view their grandfather had of the goal. **[4 marks]**

3. Piaget performed a study where seven year olds agreed that two identically shaped beakers A and B contained equal amounts of liquid, but then having witnessed beaker A being poured into beaker C, a taller, thinner beaker that contained the same amount, thought beaker C contained more, which suggests children of this age cannot conserve.

   Explain how test-retest reliability could be established for this study. **[2 marks]**

4. Explain what is meant by i] assimilation, ii] accommodation. **[2 + 2 marks]**

5. Outline and evaluate Piaget's theory of cognitive development. **[16 marks]**

'A word devoid of thought is a dead thing, and a thought unembodied in words remains a shadow.'

Lev S. Vygotsky (1934)

# 5.2 Vygotsky's theory of cognitive development

Lev Vygotsky (1896–1934) was a Russian psychologist whose work was controversial within his home country and was overlooked in Western cultures until the 1970s when it was 'rediscovered'. Although his theory was not fully formed, as he died young at the age of 38 from tuberculosis, it is regarded as an important theory of cognitive development, which has been especially influential in education.

Vygotsky and Piaget's theories are in agreement that knowledge is constructed from a child's active interaction with their environment, but Vygotsky mainly saw cognitive development as a cultural construct – that is, affected by the learning of norms and attitudes of whichever culture a child is raised within. For Vygotsky, therefore, cognitive development is a social process and he aimed to explain how higher mental functions – reasoning, understanding, etc. – arise out of children's social experiences by considering development mainly in terms of cultural and interpersonal levels.

**Figure 5.8** Lev Vygotsky's work was relatively unheralded in his lifetime, but is now regarded as a major contribution to our understanding of cognitive development

## The cultural level

Children are seen as benefiting from the knowledge of previous generations, which they gain through interactions with caregivers, thus passing cultural attitudes and beliefs from one generation to another, developing them further, then handing them on to the next generation.

Each child is believed to 'inherit' a number of cultural tools:

- technological (such as clocks, bicycles and other physical devices)
- psychological (involving concepts and symbols, like language and theories)
- values (such as efficiency and power).

The internet is a recent example of a cultural tool and through such cultural tools, children learn to live in socially effective and acceptable ways and understand how the world works.

For Vygotsky, the most essential cultural tool is language.

## The interpersonal level

At the interpersonal level, culture and the individuals meet. Cognitive development occurs first on a social level, through interaction between people (interpsychological), and second on an individual level within a child (intrapsychological). Even higher-level cognitive functions and concepts were seen by Vygotsky as originating through interactions between individuals.

## Internalisation and the social nature of thinking

The ability to think and reason by and for oneself is called inner speech or verbal thought. Infants are born as social beings capable of interacting with others, but able to do little practically or intellectually by themselves. Gradually, children become more self-sufficient and independent, and by participating in social activities their abilities develop.

For Vygotsky, cognitive development involves active internalisation of problem-solving processes, taking place as a result of mutual interaction between children and people they have social contact with. This therefore replaces Piaget's 'child as a scientist' idea (that children construct and test out their own theories about the world) with the 'child as an apprentice' idea, where cultural skills and knowledge are gained through collaboration with those who possess them.

*'The mind is not a vessel to be filled, but a fire to be kindled.'*
Plutarch (AD 46–AD 120)

## The zone of proximal development

The **zone of proximal development** (ZPD) is the distance between current and potential ability. Cultural influences and knowledgeable others push children through the ZPD and on to tasks beyond their current ability.

Mentors (trusted advisors) with understanding of an area encourage and assist children in their learning. The mentor's role in regulating performance gradually reduces, as a child becomes more able, with the child being given increased opportunity to perform the task independently.

## Scaffolding

**Scaffolding** is a concept that sees cognitive development as being assisted by sensitive guidance, with children being given clues as to how to solve a problem, rather than being given the actual solution – for example, being advised to create the border of a jigsaw first and then fill in the interior. At first a child will need such guidance, but as it increasingly masters a task, the scaffolding is removed so that the child can stand alone to complete the task itself. With scaffolding, learning first involves shared social activities until individuals can self-scaffold, with learning eventually becoming an individual, self-regulated activity.

Several processes have been identified that help create effective scaffolding:

1 Ensuring a task is easy.
2 Gaining and maintaining a child's interest in a task.
3 Demonstrating the task.
4 Keeping a child's level of frustration under control.
5 Stressing elements that will help create a solution to a task.

> **KEY TERMS**
>
> **Zone of proximal development** – the distance between current and potential intellectual ability
>
> **Scaffolding** – tuition given by more knowledgeable others

**Figure 5.9** Scaffolding involves children being assisted by mentors who give clues as to how to solve a problem rather than giving actual solutions

## Semiotics

Semiotics involves the use of signs and symbols to create meaning. Vygotsky saw semiotics as assisting cognitive development through the use of language and other cultural symbols, which act as a medium for knowledge to be transmitted, turning elementary mental functions into higher ones.

At first, children use pre-intellectual language for social and emotional purposes, where words are not symbols for the objects they represent but instead reflect properties of the objects, with pre-linguistic thinking occurring without the use of language. From around two years of age, language and thinking combine so that speech and thought become interdependent (dependent on each other), with thinking thus becoming an internal conversation. Such development occurs in several phases:

- Social speech (birth to 3 years) – involving pre-intellectual language.
- Egocentric speech (3–7 years) – involving self-talk/thinking aloud.
- Inner speech (7+ years) – where self-talk becomes silent and internal, and language is used for social communications.

## Concept formation

Vygotsky (1934) gave children blocks with nonsense symbols on them and they had to work out what the symbols meant. Four different approaches were observed, from which Vygotsky proposed four stages of concept formation (see Table 5.2).

**Table 5.2** The four stages of concept formation

| Vague syncretic | Trial-and-error formation of concepts without comprehension of them<br>Similar to Piaget's pre-operational stage |
|---|---|
| Complex | Use of some strategies to comprehend concepts, but not very systematic |
| Potential concept | More systematic use of strategies, with one attribute being focused on at a time – for example, weight |
| Mature concept | Several attributes can be dealt with systematically – for example, weight and colour<br>Similar to Piaget's formal operations |

### ON THE WEB

To watch an informative video about Lev Vygotsky, including demonstrations of scaffolding and the zone of proximal development, go to **www.youtube.com** and search for 'Vygotsky's Developmental Theory: An introduction (Davidson Films, Inc.)'.

## Research

Wood & Middleton (1975) observed mothers using various strategies to support four year olds in building a model that was too difficult for the children to do themselves. Mothers who were most effective in offering assistance were ones who varied their strategy according to how well a child was doing, so that when a child was progressing well they gave less specific help, but when a child struggled they gave more specific guidance until the child made progress again. This highlights the concept of the ZPD and shows that scaffolding is most effective when matched to the needs of a learner, so that they are assisted to achieve success in a task that previously they could not have completed alone.

Wood *et al.* (1976) conducted a study that assessed tutoring support mothers gave to four and five year olds, ranging from simple encouragement, through verbal instruction, to a full demonstration of how to do the task – fitting wooden blocks together to make a pyramid. A full demonstration frustrated the children due to adults imposing a solution, and verbal instructions that were too difficult were also ineffective. Children learned best with 'sensitive guidance', where mothers provided assistance when children got stuck, so they were not overwhelmed. This supports Vygotsky's idea of the ZPD, that knowledgeable mentors can assist children on to levels beyond their current ability.

Wertsch *et al.* (1980) found that the amount of time children under the age of five spent looking at their mothers when assembling jigsaws decreased with age, illustrating the progression through scaffolding to self-regulation.

McNaughton & Leyland (1990) observed mothers giving increasingly explicit help to children assembling progressively harder jigsaws, which illustrates how scaffolding and sensitivity to a child's ZPD aid learning.

Freund (1990) got three- and five-year-old children to help a puppet decide what furniture should be put in different rooms of a doll's house. Half the children worked alone, while half worked with their mothers providing guidance. The results showed that children given guidance performed best, which suggests that Vygotsky's idea of scaffolding, where children work with guidance, is superior to Piaget's idea of **discovery learning**, where children learn through independent exploration.

Gredler (1992) reported that in New Guinea the symbolic use of fingers and arms when counting among natives limited learning, supporting the idea of cultural influence on cognitive development.

Berk (1994) found that children talked to themselves more when doing difficult tasks, supporting the idea of egocentric speech. This decreased with age in line with Vygotsky's idea of progression to inner speech.

### KEY TERM

**Discovery learning** – learning that occurs through active exploration

> ### YOU ARE THE RESEARCHER
> Design an experiment that compares the ability of five-year-old children to build model aeroplanes either on their own or with scaffolding in the form of guidance from a mentor. Would this be a laboratory, field or natural experiment?
>
> What would be your IV? DV? What extraneous variables would need to be controlled?
>
> Consider what type of experimental design and what level of data you would have in deciding which statistical test to use.

### Evaluation

- Different cultures emphasise different skills and learning goals and yet Vygotsky's concepts of sensitive guidance, scaffolding and ZPD are applicable in all cultures, suggesting his concepts to be 'culture-fair'.
- There are strong central similarities between Piaget's and Vygotsky's theories, and it has been suggested that combining the two may be feasible and desirable to gain a fuller understanding of children's cognitive development.
- Vygotsky's theory is known more for its emphasis on the social, language-driven nature of cognitive development and its emphasis upon the cultural and interpersonal levels at which individuals learn, while Piaget's theory is known more for its emphasis on cognitive development in stages. However, Vygotsky also identified, from research focused upon sorting blocks of different colours and shapes, several stages of concept formation (see Table 5.2), which are often overlooked.
- Unlike Piaget's theory, Vygotsky's theory can explain the influence of the social environment, through culture and language, upon cognitive development.

- Similarly to Piaget, Vygotsky's theory has stimulated much research and the generation of practical applications. For example, Bruner took his concepts of scaffolding and peer tutoring and applied them to education.
- Although there is relatively less research evidence to support Vygotsky's theory, the fact that it focuses more upon the processes involved rather than the outcomes of cognitive development makes it harder to test.
- Schaffer (2004) criticises Vygotsky's theory for failing to include important emotional factors, such as the frustrations of failure and the joys of success, as well as failing to identify the motivational factors children use to achieve particular goals.
- Vygotsky's theory was developed within a collectivist culture and is more suited to such cultures, with their stronger element of social learning than individualistic Western cultures. The theory can also be accused of overemphasising the role of social factors at the expense of biological and individual ones. Learning would be faster if development depended on social factors only.

### ON THE WEB

There is a web archive about Lev Vygotsky that contains a biography, images, his obituary, all of his works and references for further reading, including a 1962 paper by Piaget about Vygotsky. Go to:

**www.marxists.org/archive/vygotsky/**

### PSYCHOLOGY IN THE REAL WORLD

**Figure 5.10** Teaching methods based on Piaget's theory emphasised discovery learning

Both Piaget's and Vygotsky's theories have practical applications in education.

Piaget's theory contributed to the following:
1. The concept of readiness, which believes children should only be taught things that reflect their level of cognitive development.
2. The idea of curriculum, which believes certain things should be taught at certain ages, thus reflecting a child's level of cognitive development.
3. Discovery learning, which sees children learning by themselves through interaction with their environment.

Therefore, for Piaget the role of a teacher was to assess what level of cognitive development a child was currently at and to provide them with relevant learning opportunities.

Vygotsky's zone of proximal development clearly links to education through its capacity for teachers, as knowledgeable others, to guide children from what they can currently do to what they can do with help and thus will be able to do by themselves in the future.

Vygotsky's theory also contributed to collaborative learning, where children of similar levels of ability work together, promoting the use of language to bring about cognitive development, with knowledge being socially constructed by working collectively on common tasks.

Therefore the role of the teacher is to guide children by mentoring, scaffolding them on to ever greater competence.

### STRENGTHEN YOUR LEARNING

1. Explain what is meant by *cultural* and *interpersonal* levels of development in Vygotsky's theory.
2. Explain what Vygotsky meant by:
   a) inner speech/verbal thought
   b) the zone of proximal development
   c) scaffolding
   d) emiotics.
3. Outline Vygotsky's four stages of *concept formation*.
4. Summarise research evidence that supports Vygotsky's theory.
5. What other evaluative points can be made concerning Vygotsky's theory?

# ASSESSMENT CHECK

1. Place an 'x' next to the following two descriptions that relate to Vygotsky's theory of cognitive development. Two descriptions will be left over. **[2 marks]**

   A Vygotsky saw cognitive development as occurring through the ability to understand the behaviour and feelings of others

   B Vygotsky saw cognitive development as affected by the learning of norms and attitudes of whichever culture a child is raised within

   C Vygotsky saw cognitive development as arising from children's social experiences

   D Vygotsky saw cognitive development occurring by being able to attribute false beliefs to others

2. Four-year-old Asmah was given a jigsaw puzzle as a birthday present, but it was too difficult for her to do on her own. However, when her older sister Priti gave her some guidance by showing Asmah how to make the border of the jigsaw first, she found that she was able to complete it successfully.

   With reference to the scenario above, use your knowledge of Vygotsky's theory of cognitive development to explain how Asmah was able to complete her jigsaw. **[3 marks]**

3. A researcher assessed three- and five-year-old children's ability to help a puppet decide what furniture should be put in different rooms of a doll's house. Half the children worked alone, while half worked with their mothers providing guidance. Each child was given a score out of 10 that described their ability to perform the task, with a score of 0 representing very poor ability and 10 very high ability. A table of mean, modal and median scores was constructed.

   |        | Three year olds | Five year olds |
   |--------|-----------------|----------------|
   | Mean   | 3.0             | 7.5            |
   | Mode   | 4.0             | 6.0            |
   | Median | 2.0             | 7.0            |

   a) Sketch an appropriate graph to show the mean scores for three and five year olds, taking care to label the axes correctly. **[3 marks]**

   b) Give one reason for your choice of graph. **[1 mark]**

4. Explain what is meant by the zone of proximal development. **[2 marks]**

5. Compare and contrast Piaget's and Vygotsky's theories of cognitive development. **[16 marks]**

*'No one is so brave that he is not disturbed by something unexpected.'*
Julius Caesar (52 BC)

# 5.3 Baillargeon's explanation for early infant abilities

Renée Baillargeon, born in 1954 in Quebec, was the third child of French-Canadian parents and is currently a Professor of Psychology at Illinois University in the USA.

Inspired by research that appeared to suggest children develop object permanence at a much earlier age than Piaget believed, such as Bower & Wishart's (1972) study that found one-month-old babies show surprise when toys disappear, Baillargeon was able to assess Piaget's beliefs about the ages at which children reach various levels of cognitive development by creation of her **violation of expectation technique** (VOE). This works on the basis that infants will look for longer at things they have not experienced before. The technique works by repeatedly showing a child a scenario that is new to them until they demonstrate, by looking away, that it is no longer a novel experience. At this point the child is shown an example of the scenario that is impossible (such as a solid object appearing to pass through another solid object without either being damaged) and the time they look at it is compared with an example of the scenario that is possible.

Baillargeon, either solely or in collaboration with others, has gone on to perform a series of experiments based upon her violation of expectation technique that uses scenarios familiar to or understandable by very young infants to consistently find results that challenge Piaget's ideas and suggest that children much younger than he thought demonstrate object permanence and have an intuitive knowledge concerning the properties of objects and their relationships to each other.

Baillargeon's research has helped to investigate a major aspect of the **core knowledge theory** (CKT), that of object representation. The CKT believes that humans are born with a small number of systems of core knowledge that serve to represent inanimate objects and their relationships with each other. The idea of object representation is that infants have an inborn ability to perceive the boundaries of objects, to be able to still perceive objects when they move partially or completely out of view and to be able to predict the movements of objects. So just like animals such as horses have an innate ability to stand and walk, humans are seen to have an innate ability to understand objects. Thus humans are seen to possess an understanding of object permanence at a far younger age than Piaget believed, possibly even from birth, and this understanding allows them to learn quickly from environmental experiences, which has an evolutionary survival value.

Recent research, however, has cast doubt on the conclusions drawn by Baillargeon, thus reducing support for CKT and the idea that children from a very early age possess a sense of object permanence.

**Figure 5.11** Professor Renée Baillargeon devised the 'violation of expectation' technique that tests at what age children develop object permanence

### KEY TERMS

**Violation of expectation technique** – a research method that uses the tendency for infants to look for longer at things that are not expected to test their knowledge of the properties of objects

**Core knowledge theory** – the belief that humans have an innate understanding of inanimate objects and their relationships with each other

## RESEARCH IN FOCUS

Baillargeon performed a series of studies into whether children have an innate sense of object permanence, believing that the surprise infants showed at impossible situations (violation of expectation) showed that they do have such an ability. However, Cara Cashon argues Baillargeon is drawing conclusions beyond what the data suggests (Cashon argues infants are merely attracted by interesting stimuli). Explain how Baillargeon's conclusions may be occurring due to the investigator effect of researcher bias. How could the risk of researcher bias may be minimised in studies like this?

## Research

Baillargeon *et al.* (1985) familiarised five-month-old infants with a drawbridge that moved through 180 degrees. A coloured box was then placed in the path of the drawbridge. The infants then either witnessed a 'possible event' where the drawbridge stopped at the point where its movement would be stopped by the box, or an 'impossible event' where the drawbridge appeared to pass through the box and ended up lying flat, with the box apparently having disappeared. It was found that the infants spent longer looking at the impossible event, which suggests the infants were surprised that their expectations (about the properties of physical objects) were violated and that they knew a solid object cannot pass through another solid object. This supports the idea that children develop an understanding of the properties of objects at a much younger age than Piaget thought.

Baillargeon (1987) familiarised three-month-old infants with a scenario where a truck rolled down a ramp and went behind a screen. The screen was then raised and a block was placed either where the truck would roll past it or where it would stop the truck's movement. The screen was then lowered and the truck rolled down the ramp again and emerged from behind the screen. It was found that the infants looked for longer at the impossible event, which suggests they knew the block still existed, despite being behind the screen, and that it should have stopped the movement of the truck. This again supports the idea that children develop an understanding of the properties of objects at a much younger age than Piaget believed.

Baillargeon & DeVos (1991) got three-and-a-half-month-old infants to watch a scenario of either a tall or a short carrot sliding along a track, with the centre of the track hidden by a screen that had a large window in its upper half. The short carrot did not appear in the window when passing through the screen, which was to be expected, as it was not tall enough, but the tall carrot also did not appear in the window even though it was clearly tall enough to do so. It was found that the infants looked longer at the tall rather than the short carrot scenario, which suggests they were able to assess the existence, height and pathway of the carrots when behind the screen and so were surprised at the non-appearance of the tall carrot in the window (see Figure 5.12). This supports the idea of children younger than Piaget claimed having a sense of object permanence, as they realise objects continue to exist even when hidden.

**Figure 5.12** Children expect to see the top of the tall carrot in the window – when they don't it violates their expectation and they stare at that scenario longer

Aguiar & Baillargeon (1999) familiarised two-and-a-half-month-old infants to a toy Minnie Mouse that moved sideways, going behind a screen and then re-emerging at the other side (see Figure 5.13). A scenario was then presented where there was a large window in the middle of the screen, with again Minnie Mouse moving sideways to pass behind the screen. In one window scenario (the high-window event), the window was in the screen's upper half and so Minnie was not visible as she passed through, as she was too short to do so. In a second window scenario (the low-window event), the window was in the screen's lower half and Minnie should have been visible as she passed through, as she was tall enough to do so, but she was not seen, though she then appeared on the other side of the screen as if she had passed through – an impossible occurrence. It was found that the infants looked longer at the impossible low-window event, which suggests they knew Minnie still existed when she passed behind the screen, but were surprised that she wasn't visible when she passed by the low window. This again supports the idea that children develop object permanence at a much earlier age than Piaget stated, which is reinforced by the results of a control condition where the screen was lowered briefly each time before Minnie made her sideways journey, to reveal two identical mice, one standing behind the left edge and one behind the right edge of the screen. The findings here were that the infants looked for equal amounts of time at the high- and low-window events, as their expectation was not violated – there was no impossible occurrence to witness.

Cashon & Cohen (2000) familiarised eight-month-old infants with one of four Baillargeon-type scenarios, which involved a screen rotating in either a 180 or 120 degree arc and a block that was either placed in the path of the rotating screen or was absent from the scenario. It was found that infants looked for longer at scenarios that were more interesting (had more novelty) than ones that were 'impossible', which reduces support for the idea that young infants have object permanence and that humans have an innate understanding of object representation.

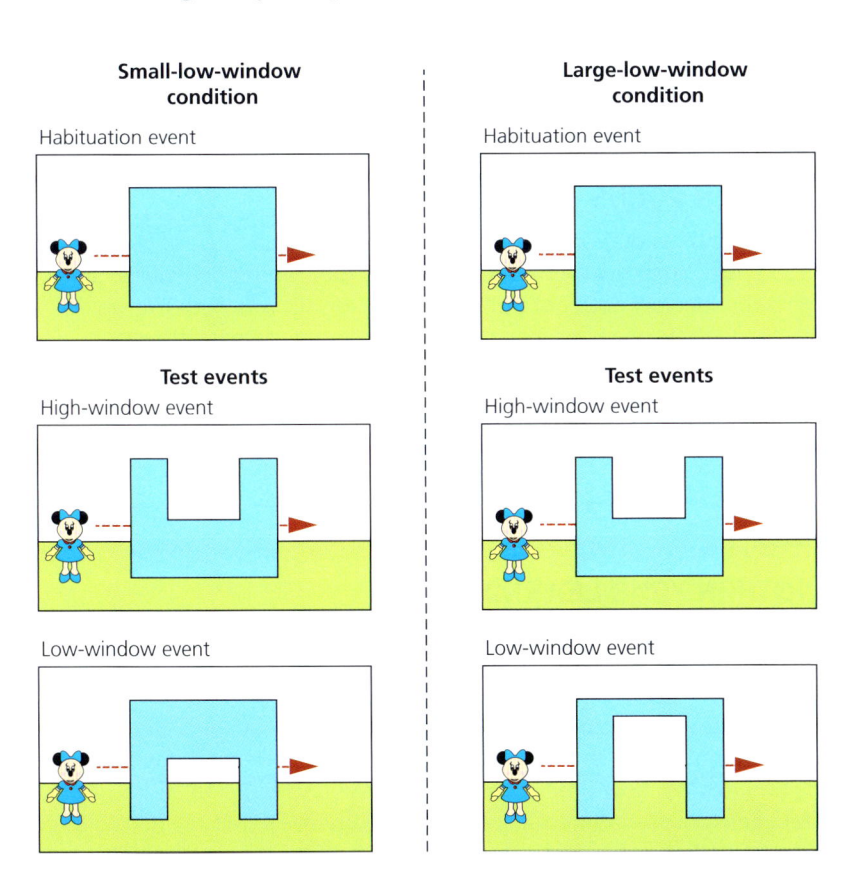

**Figure 5.13** Aguiar & Baillargeon's Minnie Mouse study uses an example of her 'violation of expectation' technique to assess whether children develop object permanence earlier than Piaget believed

## Evaluation

- Baillargeon's violation of expectation technique has become a paradigm method, that is to say the accepted method of assessing children's understanding of the physical properties of objects, which is a testimony to the high regard in which the procedure is held.
- Aguiar & Baillargeon's (1999) Minnie Mouse study is a clever method of investigating the inability of children under three months of age to show surprise at the failure of the tall carrot to appear in the window in the upper half of the screen in Baillargeon & DeVos's (1991) study. Baillargeon wondered whether children of that age did not have a sense of object permanence or instead had not learned that when an object moves behind something that obscures its bottom half, the height of the object determines whether it will be visible in the top half of the window. In the Minnie Mouse study only her bottom half should be visible, something that two-and-a-half-month-old children understood, suggesting they did have a sense of object permanence.
- Investigating the cognitive developmental abilities of infants is problematic as such children cannot communicate verbally what abilities they have. Therefore Baillargeon's paradigm technique is extremely useful, as it allows insight into what skills very young children possess.
- Research based on Baillargeon's methodology produces consistent results and the CKT has come to be widely accepted as a valid explanation. However, some believe Baillargeon draws conclusions that go beyond what the data shows. Schöner & Thelen (2004) argue that all that violation of expectation studies illustrates is that infants notice a *difference* between the 'possible' and 'impossible' scenarios they have been shown, which does not necessarily mean they are *surprised* by what they have witnessed. For instance, in the drawbridge study infants may be attracted to the fact that the 'impossible' scenario has more movement in it than the 'possible' scenario. Therefore, what Baillargeon sees as evidence of infants having innate knowledge of object representation may actually be just the effects of confounding variables. This viewpoint is supported by research such as Cashon & Cohen (2000).

### ON THE WEB

Watch Renée Baillargeon explain her research methods, with emphasis on her drawbridge experiment, at **www.youtube.com**. Search for 'Object permanence rctctom'.

You can also see her 'truck rolling down a ramp' study at **www.youtube.com**. Search for 'Object Concept VOE Ramp Study Baillargeon'.

For the disappearing doll, go to **www.youtube.com** and search for 'Object Concept VOE Screen Task Baillargeon'.

### RESEARCH IN FOCUS

Research using the violation of expectation technique conducted by Baillargeon and Cashon & Cohen reached very different conclusions, so you might wonder how both got published in scientific journals. However, this is quite customary, so long as their research papers pass the peer review system.

Explain i] the purpose of the peer review system, ii] how peer review is conducted and iii] criticisms of the peer review process.

### STRENGTHEN YOUR LEARNING

1. Explain Baillargeon's *violation of expectation* research study method.
2. Outline the *core knowledge theory*.
3. Outline the aims, procedures, results and conclusions from two of Baillargeon's violation of expectation studies.
4. Outline Cashon & Cohen's (2000) *violation of expectation* research study and explain how the findings can be used to criticise Baillargeon's explanation of early infant abilities.
5. What other evaluative points can be made concerning Baillargeon's explanation of early infant abilities?

*'To truly travel is to see the world from someone else's eyes if even only for a second.'*
Aboriginal proverb

# 5.4 The development of social cognition

**Social cognition** relates to the mental processes by which individuals process and understand information relating to themselves and others and by which behaviour is conducted. Social cognition is thus involved with explaining how individuals develop the ability to make sense of their social world. A major element in this is the development of **perspective-taking**, as documented in Selman's levels of perspective-taking, where individuals gradually come to understand the viewpoints of others. **Theory of mind** (ToM) is another important factor, involving the ability to comprehend that others have a mind too, which may differ from our own. ToM has even been offered as a possible explanation for **autism**, with the **Sally-Anne test** being a prime research method in the investigation of ToM. More recent research has focused upon mirror neurons, a system of nerves in the brain that may permit the perception of behaviour observed in others as if it were our own (see page 180).

*'I have wanted you to see out of my eyes so many times.'*
Elizabeth Berg (1996)

> **KEY TERMS**
>
> **Social cognition** – the understanding of information relating to members of the same species
>
> **Perspective-taking** – the ability to understand from another's point of view
>
> **Theory of mind** – the ability to attribute mental states to oneself and others
>
> **Autism** – a developmental disability characterised by problems in communicating and building relationships with others and in using language and abstract concepts
>
> **Sally-Anne test** – a method of assessing an individual's social cognitive ability to attribute false beliefs to others
>
> **Mirror neuron system** – a network of nerves in the brain that allows individuals to experience the actions of others as if they were their own
>
> **Role-taking theory** – an explanation that sees perspective-taking developing through adopting the outlook of others in order to understand their feelings, intentions and thoughts

## Selman's levels of perspective-taking

Perspective-taking concerns the ability to assume another person's perspective (viewpoint) and understand their thoughts and feelings. Being able to differentiate between other people's perspectives and one's own enhances the understanding of others and oneself.

Very young children do not appreciate that other people have experiences and feelings different to their own, but Selman (1980) devised **role-taking theory** to explain the development of perspective-taking, where adopting the perspective of others allows an individual to comprehend their feelings, thoughts and intentions. The theory was developed through research involving interpersonal dilemmas, such as the story of eight-year-old expert tree-climber Holly, who one day falls out of a tree, which leads to her promising her father she will not climb trees any more. However, Holly and her friends then go on to meet Shawn, whose kitten is stuck in a tree and may fall at any moment. Only Holly has the climbing skills to save the kitten. Should she climb a tree to save the kitten?

The theory has five levels, developed from children's answers to questions about such dilemmas. As children mature, they are seen to take more information into account, coming to realise that people can react differently to the same situation. They develop the ability to analyse people's perspectives from the viewpoint of an objective, neutral bystander, and come to realise how different cultural and societal values affect the perception of the bystander.

**Figure 5.14** Selman conducted research based on interpersonal dilemmas, such as that of Holly who breaks her promise not to climb trees in order to save a cat

### Stage 0: Egocentric (undifferentiated) viewpoint (3 to 6 years)

Children understand that other people can have different thoughts and feelings from their own, but often will confuse the two. Children are able to correctly label others' overt (visible) feelings, but cannot see the cause and effect relationship between reasons and social actions. For example, a child may predict that Holly will rescue the kitten, as she does not wish to see it harmed and believes Holly's father will feel the same as she does about climbing the tree.

### Stage 1: Social informational role taking (6 to 8 years)

Children are aware that others have access to different information and thus possess perspectives based on their own reasoning, which may or may not be similar to theirs. Children in this stage tend to focus on one perspective rather than combining different viewpoints. For example, a child will believe that if Holly's father doesn't know about the kitten then he will be angry, but if Holly shows him the kitten he might change his opinion.

### Stage 2: Self-reflective role taking (8 to 10 years)

Children can 'step into each other's shoes' and perceive each other's perspective, and understand that this awareness influences their own and the other's views of each other. Putting oneself in the other's place is a way of judging their intentions, purposes and actions. Children can form a co-ordinated chain of perspectives, but cannot yet simultaneously see each other's perspectives. For example, a child will believe that Holly's father won't punish her as he will understand why she climbed the tree. The child recognises that Holly's father can see the situation from Holly's point of view and thus knows why she broke her promise to not climb trees.

### Stage 3: Mutual (third-party) role taking (10 to 12 years)

Children realise that both self and others can view each other mutually and simultaneously. Children can also step outside of a two-person situation and imagine how they and another would be viewed from the perspective of a third, unbiased person. For example, a child will believe that Holly will think that she shouldn't be punished only if she can get her father to understand why she climbed the tree. In order to realise this, the child has to be able to stand aside from the situation and view Holly's and her father's perspectives simultaneously.

### Stage 4: Social and conventional system role taking (12 to 15 years and over)

Individuals realise that third-party perspective-taking can be influenced not just by mutual, simultaneous perspective-taking but by larger societal values, which are understood by all members of a cultural group (the generalised other) regardless of their position, role or experience. For example, a person believes Holly shouldn't be punished, as the ethical requirement to treat animals humanely justifies Holly breaking her promise and Holly's father will understand this and thus not punish her.

### Research

Selman (1971) got 40 children aged four to six years to predict a child's behaviour after being given information about a situation that was not available to the child in question. Participants, especially the younger ones, tended to make a prediction based on the information they had been given. This suggests

---

**YOU ARE THE RESEARCHER**

Design a study to investigate perspective taking. First you will have to create your own interpersonal dilemma (Selman used the story of tree-climbing Holly). Then you will have to decide how you are going to assess your data to determine which of Selman's five stages a child is in. What type of research study is this? You would be using children of different ages so how would you obtain informed consent to perform the study?

they were in the egocentric viewpoint stage in line with Selman's theory, as they could not see the situation from the child's perspective.

Selman & Byrne (1974) presented children aged between four and ten with two interpersonal dilemmas and then in interviews got them to discuss the perspectives of the different characters involved in each dilemma. Children aged four to six years tended to show evidence of having an egocentric viewpoint, perceiving things from their own perspective, while children aged between six and eight years tended to show evidence of being in the social informational role-taking stage, understanding that people have different viewpoints, but were able to consider only one viewpoint at a time. Children aged eight to ten were increasingly able to see things from different people's perspectives. The results support Selman's theory, as they imply that perspective-taking increases with age in set stages.

Gurucharri & Selman (1982) performed a five-year longitudinal study, using Selman's methodology of interpersonal dilemmas, to assess the development of perspective-taking abilities in 41 children. It was found that 40 of the children developed perspective-taking in the way dictated by Selman's stages, supporting the validity of his theory.

Schultz & Selman (1990) found that the transition from self-centred perspectives to an ability to perceive from others' perspectives is related to the development of enhanced interpersonal negotiation skills and concern for others, suggesting that perspective-taking plays a key role in social maturation.

Epley *et al.* (2004) used children aged 4 to 12 years and adults as participants to assess egocentric bias, interpreting perceptions from one's own viewpoint, by use of a director and a participant sitting on either side of a 5 × 5 grid of 25 boxes, some of which contained objects (see Figure 5.15). Four of the boxes were hidden to the director. The participant moved objects as instructed by the director. One critical instruction referred to one specific object visible from the director's viewpoint, but to two possible objects visible from the participant's viewpoint (one of which was in one of the four boxes hidden to the director). The solution for a participant is to disregard their egocentric viewpoint (what they can see) and interpret the instruction from the director's viewpoint. The number of egocentric errors made was recorded, along with participants' eye movements. It was found that adults made fewer egocentric errors and that egocentric errors were correlated with age, younger children making more egocentric errors than older children. The critical finding, though, was that participants did not differ in the speed at which they looked at the egocentric hidden object, but older participants were quicker to disregard it and look at the mutually visible object. This suggests that egocentrism is not something that is outgrown, but that experience teaches people they can see something from another person's perspective only by learning to disregard their own, which implies there is no change with age in how humans process information.

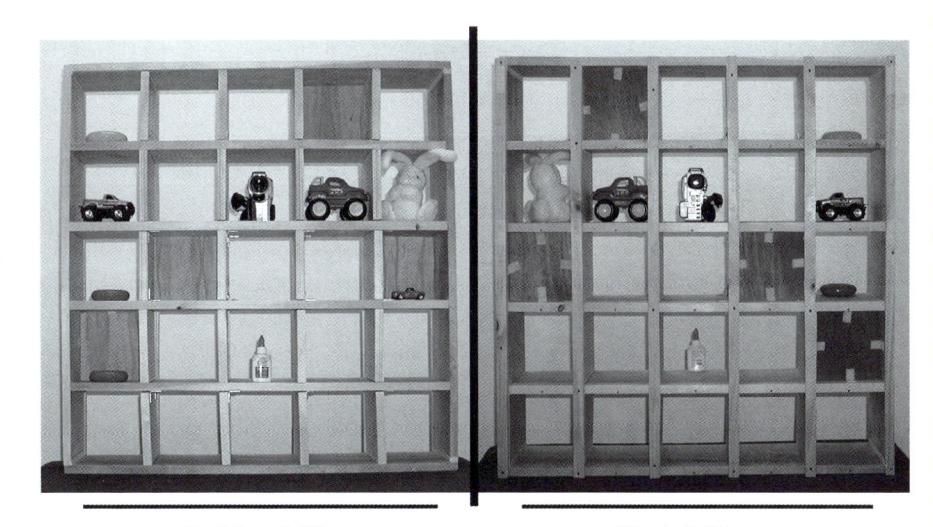

**Figure 5.15** Epley *et al.* (2004) used a 5 × 5 grid of objects to assess perspective-taking

## Evaluation

- The developmental claims of Selman's model are supported by research evidence – individuals progress gradually to higher stages over time, with little evidence of any regression to lower stages.
- Selman's use of interpersonal dilemmas has provided researchers with an objective means of assessing social competence that has become a paradigm (accepted) method of studying the development of perspective-taking.
- Selman's theory has a practical application in physical education, as it has been used to ascertain the ages at which children can understand others' viewpoints and roles within competitive team sports. There is little point in trying to teach team sports to children before they are less egocentric and can appreciate others' viewpoints.
- Selman's theory has been criticised for focusing too much on the effect of cognitive development on perspective-taking and social cognition and downplaying the role of non-cognitive factors. For example, social factors such as arguments between friends have been seen to promote perspective-taking skills, and mediation from others in settling disagreements plays a similar role.
- There are parallels between Selman's theory and Piaget's cognitive development theory. Egocentrism is a central feature of Piaget's idea of pre-operational thinking (see page 152) and forms the basis of Selman's egocentric viewpoint, while decentring, the ability to perceive the world from more than one perspective, is a central feature of Piaget's idea of operational thought and of Selman's later stages. In general, Selman's stages 1 and 2 are seen as relating to Piaget's pre-operational stage, stages 3 or 4 to his concrete operational stage and stages 4 or 5 to his formal operational stage.
- Perspective-taking has practical applications as a means of conflict resolution. Walker & Selman (1998) used perspective-taking to reduce aggression levels by getting individuals to empathise with other people's feelings and viewpoints.
- Research into perspective-taking may be culturally biased, as research was carried out mainly on children from Western cultural backgrounds and therefore findings may not be applicable to children of other cultures. Quintana *et al.* (1999) criticised Selman's work as disregarding the development of perspective-taking in ethnic sub-cultural groupings.

### YOU ARE THE RESEARCHER

Selman used interpersonal dilemmas to devise his role-taking theory. Create an interpersonal dilemma of your own to use with children aged three and over. How would children's answers to this dilemma be rated to decide which level of perspective-taking individuals were in?

It would be important to have inter-rater reliability when analysing answers. What is inter-rater reliability and how would it be established?

*'Do not judge a man until you have walked two moons in his moccasins.'*
Old Native American proverb

## Theory of mind

Understanding the thoughts and emotions of other people is an ability found in few animal species and is seen as indicating higher intelligence. Indeed, the term 'theory of mind' was first used by Premack & Woodruff (1978) when describing the cognitive abilities of chimpanzees. They defined ToM as the ability to attribute mental states, knowledge, wishes, feelings and beliefs to oneself and others. Signs of ToM in humans can be seen in expressions of language where another person's mental state is referred to, such as, 'I think she is upset'.

An important aspect of understanding the concept of mind is the realisation that other people have feelings, desires and beliefs too – that is, that they also have a mind. Equally important is the understanding that other people's beliefs and so on may differ from our own. Research into ToM indicates that this ability is not present at birth but develops over time.

**Figure 5.16** Theory of mind was first used to describe the cognitive abilities of chimpanzees

ToM is investigated by presenting children with false belief tasks. This involves witnessing a scene and being asked to interpret it from the viewpoint of one of the characters in the scene. If they can do this, they are seen as having developed a ToM. If children instead interpret the scene from their own egocentric viewpoint they are not seen as having a ToM (see Sally-Anne study, page 175). Such research generally indicates that children of around the age of four give egocentric answers (have a false belief) and thus have not developed a ToM, while by six years of age most children can perform the task and thus do have a ToM.

ToM is similar to Piaget's idea of egocentrism, with ToM not developing until decentring (see page 154) occurs, at around four years of age. A more recent view emphasises modularity, where specific brain areas, such as the amygdala and basal ganglia, are associated with ToM processing, with a set sequence of development occurring and with ToM reasoning being inferred from other knowledge.

With the development of ToM comes the ability to manipulate and deceive others by hiding one's emotions and intentions. This occurs from three years of age. It is possible that there is a more primitive earlier version of ToM, called shared attention mechanism (SAM), developing between 9 and 18 months of age, which allows two people to realise that they are witnessing the same thing.

## Research

Wimmer & Perner (1983) used models to act out a story to four, six and eight year olds about a boy called Maxi who put some chocolate in a blue cupboard. While Maxi was absent, the children saw his mother transfer the chocolate to a green cupboard. The children were asked where Maxi would look for the chocolate. Most six and eight year olds gave the correct blue cupboard answer, while most four year olds said that he would look in the green cupboard. They thought he would act on the basis of his false belief, implying that they had not developed a ToM.

Shatz *et al*. (1983) reported that children under four years of age can differentiate between mental states. At the age of two they can name emotional states, and by the age of three they can demonstrate knowledge of what thinking is, suggesting that acquisition of a ToM is a developmental process.

Flavell *et al*. (1986) found that three year olds who handled a sponge that looked like a rock called it a rock, while four year olds called it a sponge, suggesting that the development of a ToM requires an appreciation of what is false and that a lack of ToM is a cognitive deficit.

Bartsch & Wellman (1995) found that ToM acquisition follows a common developmental pattern in both US and Chinese children, suggesting that as it is cross-cultural, the ability is biologically controlled.

Harris (1989) reports that at around the age of four, children become aware of their emotions and use them to pretend to be someone else, permitting them to be aware of others' thinking, suggesting that this is a pivotal age in realising that others think differently.

Avis & Harris (1991) found that children in both developed and non-developed countries realise that at four years of age people can have false beliefs, supporting the idea of biological maturation.

### RESEARCH IN FOCUS

Avis & Harris (1991) found that four-year-old children in developed and non-developed countries realise that people can have false beliefs. This laboratory experiment was looking for a difference between two conditions, had data of nominal level and used an independent groups design – therefore what statistical test would be appropriate? If the data had been of ordinal level what test would have been appropriate then? And if the data had been of interval/ratio level?

Frith & Frith (1999) found that the amygdala, basal ganglia, temporal cortex and frontal cortex showed heightened rates of activity when participants had to consider other people's mental states, suggesting that these brain areas are associated with ToM.

> ### Evaluation
>
> - ToM appears in childhood, though there is disagreement as to whether this occurs suddenly at the age of four or more gradually from two years of age and upwards.
> - A lack of ToM is similar to Piaget's idea of egocentrism, coinciding at similar ages, and suggesting that the two concepts are linked.
> - Younger children may fail to understand false belief tasks such as that used by Wimmer & Perner (1983), not because they do not have a ToM but because the language of the questions is too complex. For instance, 'Where will he look for the chocolate?' could be taken by a child to mean 'Where is the chocolate?' Therefore, similarly to Piaget, results may be due to poor methodology.
> - Bloom & German (2000) argue that passing a false belief task involves having more than a ToM. Even if young children do understand that beliefs can be false, the task given in many studies is very complex, such as following the actions of two characters in a scenario, remembering what events have occurred and understanding the specific meaning of the question asked of them. Such requirements may be beyond young children, even if they do have a ToM. They also argue that there is more to having a ToM than passing false belief tasks. Children below the age of two, who tend to fail false belief tests, can initiate pretend play and understand the pretending of others, which would suggest an ability to understand the mental states of others.
> - The modularity view of ToM, which sees the ability as located within specific brain areas, suggests that ToM is an innate, biological process, which matures in set stages at set times and is not affected by learning. Interestingly, studies of ToM find the ability appears at around the same age in children of different cultures, which supports the idea of there being a biological mechanism at work.

*'The eyes are useless when the mind is blind.'*
Anonymous

## Theory of mind as an explanation for autism

Autism is a developmental disability characterised by problems in communicating and building relationships with others and in using language and abstract concept. Autistic children often appear self-absorbed and engrossed in their 'own little world' and often have problems relating to other people and seeing things from their point of view. For this reason an absence of ToM has been suggested as a possible explanation for the disorder. Frith (1989) was the first to suggest that children with autism may not be able to understand that other people, and indeed themselves, have a 'mind'. Frith argued that autism was

**Figure 5.17** Theory of mind has been suggested as an explanation for autism, though the theory has its critics

associated with mind-blindness, an inability to understand what other people were thinking and feeling.

Baron-Cohen (1993) then used the idea of ToM to explain such mind-blindness, as ToM seemed to offer a plausible reason as to why autistic children have problems in seeing things from another's perspective and yet are unaffected in other areas of cognitive functioning (indeed, autistic people can often be autistic savants, displaying highly advanced cognitive talents). Baron-Cohen explored this possibility with his Sally-Anne study (see below), which provided a degree of support for the explanation.

Leslie (1987) proposed the idea of a theory of mind mechanism (ToMM), which saw ToM as an innate ability that biologically matures in most children by around two years of age, but that physiological damage, either shortly before or after birth, hindered development of the mechanism so that cognitive impairments, such as those found in autistic children, occurred.

**Figure 5.18** Simon Baron-Cohen devised the Sally-Anne test to see whether autistic children have a theory of mind

## CLASSIC RESEARCH

### The Sally-Anne study – Simon Baron-Cohen, Alan Leslie, Uta Frith (1985)

The idea of a ToM is that children develop the ability to realise that others have a mind with a viewpoint that may be different to theirs. The researchers wanted to see whether autistic children had a theory of mind by using a false belief study. They adopted Wimmer & Perner's (1983) use of puppets to study false beliefs (see page 173), but in a shorter, simpler and more appropriate way for use with children. The researchers believed that rather than using story-telling, the use of dolls to act out a scenario would be more realistic and thus easier for the children to relate to (see Figure 5.19).

#### Aim
To assess whether a lack of a ToM could be an explanation for autism.

#### Procedure
The study was a natural experiment, as it used a naturally occurring independent variable of three types of children: autistic, with Down's syndrome and normally developed. The dependent variable was the percentage of children correctly completing the false belief task.

The participants were:
- 20 autistic children of average age of 12 years and average verbal mental age of 5.5 years
- 14 Down's syndrome children of average age 11 years and average verbal mental age of 3 years
- 27 normally developed children of average age 4.5 years and average verbal mental age of 4.5 years.
- The normal and Down's syndrome children served as control groups, with the autistic children as the experimental group.

Each child witnesses a scenario played out with the Sally and Anne dolls. The naming question: each child is checked to ensure that they know which doll is Sally and which is Anne. Sally places a marble in her basket and leaves the scene, and Anne transfers the marble and hides it in her box. When Sally returns, children are given the Sally-Anne test: success or failure depends specifically on their response to the third of three questions:

1. Where is the marble really? (*Reality question*)
2. Where was the marble in the beginning? (*Memory question*)
3. Where will Sally look for her marble? (*Belief question*)

The correct answer requires a child to attribute a false belief to Sally (she will look in the wrong place). The first two questions act as control questions to ensure that the child has attended to and knows the current location of the marble, and also that they remember where it was before.

#### Findings
All children passed the naming question, as well as the reality and memory questions.

20 per cent of autistic children passed the false belief question, compared with 85 per cent of normal children and 86 per cent of Down's syndrome children.

#### Conclusions
Autistic children do not have a ToM and therefore cannot attribute beliefs to others, which disadvantages them when trying to predict others' behaviour.

An inability to develop a ToM is a plausible explanation for autism.

#### Evaluation
- The failure of autistic children to attribute beliefs to others is a specific deficit, as it cannot be explained in terms of the general effects of mental retardation, since the more severely retarded Down's syndrome children performed slightly better than even the normally developed children.

- The Sally-Anne test is not suited to assessing whether adults have a ToM, as it was intended specifically as a means of examining the cognitive skills of 4–6 year olds.
- The study can be accused of lacking ecological validity, as a scenario involving dolls lacks relevance to real-life situations.

Maybe autistic children don't attribute beliefs to dolls, as they realise dolls can't have thoughts and beliefs. However, Leslie & Frith (1988) repeated the study with human actors rather than dolls and gained similar results, which suggests the findings are generalisable to real-life settings.

**Figure 5.19** The Sally-Anne study tests whether participants will view a scenario from their own viewpoint or that of the dolls in the scenario

### ON THE WEB

To see children being tested on false belief tasks, including the Sally-Anne test, go to **www.youtube.com**. Search for 'Theory of mind – Smarties task and Sally-Anne task'.

## Research

Happe *et al.* (1996) compared PET scans from a previous study of normally developed individuals performing a ToM task with five patients with Asperger's syndrome (a mild variant of autism) performing the same task. During the task, brain activity was highlighted in the left medial prefrontal cortex brain area in the normally developed participants, but not in those with Asperger's syndrome, though normal activity was detected in adjacent brain areas. This suggests that a very specific brain area is associated with the understanding of one's own and other people's minds.

Ruffman, Garnham & Rideout (2001) performed a variation of the Sally-Anne test that added a third possible location for the marble – in the pocket of the researcher. It was found that autistic children and children with moderate learning disabilities answered the belief question equally well, but that children with moderate learning disabilities tended to look at the correct location of the marble, while autistic children did not, even if they had first answered the question correctly. Those with the most severe autistic characteristics looked least to the correct location. This suggests that eye gaze is a better indication of social deficits in autistic children than verbal responses.

Gernsbacher & Frymiare (2005) reviewed studies that assessed whether autistic participants 1) lacked a ToM and 2) lacked the capacity to process faces. It was found that autistics performed poorly on ToM tasks, due to their impairment in communication abilities, and that they were less likely to fixate the eye region of facial photographs, with a positive correlation found between the amount of time spent fixating the eye region and the amount of activation in the fusiform gyrus brain area, which is associated with the processing of visual information about human faces. This suggests that the tendency of autistics to not have ToM is related to their inability to process facial information.

Tager-Flusberg (2007) reviewed false belief task studies done with autistic children to find that in all studies there were examples of children with autism who passed false belief tasks, which therefore casts doubts on ToM being a complete explanation for autism.

## Evaluation

- A lack of ToM provides plausible reasons for many symptoms of autism. For example, not being able to understand other people's thoughts could be seen to lead to the difficulties autistic children often have with communicating via language.
- A lack of ToM can also explain the lack of pretend play exhibited by autistic children, through autistic children not being able to reflect on their own thoughts. When a child pretends to be a mother to a doll, the child must be capable of simultaneously holding in their mind two contradictory sets of beliefs; the child knows it is a child and that the doll isn't real, but must think the opposite – that they are a mother and the doll is a baby. Without a ToM it is not possible to do this, as autistic children often demonstrate.
- A problem with using ToM as an explanation for autism is that it would be expected that the apparent problems autistic children have in reflecting on their own thoughts would affect their ability to perform complex cognitive actions, such as solving mathematical problems, but some autistic children have advanced mathematical skills.
- Even when autistic children pass false belief tasks, they often perform poorly in tasks requiring use of social stimuli. Even in the first year of life social interactions require recognition of and appropriate responses to vocal and facial expressions and autistic children display early evidence of being unable to do this. ToM is unable to explain such social deficits.
- If ToM was the main explanation for autism, three predictions would be met: that autistics fail tests of ToM, that ToM is innate and that ToM relates to a specific brain region. However, many autistics pass ToM tests, while non-autistics with specific language impairments fail them, so ToM is neither universal in nor specific to autism. Also, tutoring in mind-reading and grammar improves performance on ToM tests, suggesting it is not innate, while brain scanning studies have failed to isolate a specific brain region.

### PSYCHOLOGY IN THE REAL WORLD

Interior frontal gyrus

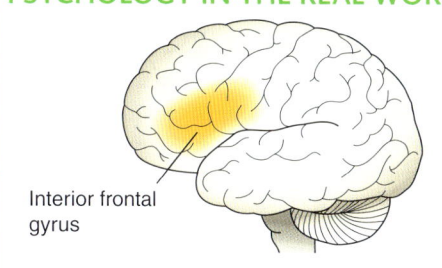

**Figure 5.20** Could a therapy centred on activating mirror neuron activity in the inferior frontal gyrus brain area help autistic children develop empathy?

If ToM can explain autism as a form of 'mind-blindness', an inability to understand what other people are thinking and feeling, then it offers the possibility of a therapy for the disorder that is aimed at developing empathy in sufferers. Such a therapy would probably centre on Leslie's (1987) idea of a theory of mind mechanism, an innate ability that is seen as not biologically maturing in autistic children.

There is also the possibility of a therapy centred on the mirror neuron system, which normally allows individuals an understanding of their own and others' mental states. However, research such as Dapretto et al.'s (2006) study indicates no mirror neuron activity in the inferior frontal gyrus (pars opercularis) brain region of autistic participants, so a therapy focused on rejuvenating mirror neuron activity in this particular brain area would seem sensible.

However, evidence for ToM and a damaged mirror neuron system as explanations for autism is not convincing and if it turns out that ToM is not a plausible explanation and that mirror neurons play only a secondary and not a central role in understanding the actions of others, then a lot of time and effort may have been spent looking in entirely the wrong area for causes (and treatments) of autism that would have been better directed elsewhere.

## STRENGTHEN YOUR LEARNING

1 Explain what is meant by social cognition.
2 Explain how Selman used *interpersonal dilemmas* to investigate perspective-taking.
3 Summarise the main developments that occur within Selman's levels of perspective-taking.
4 Summarise research evidence relating to Selman's levels of perspective-taking.
5 Explain what is meant by *theory of mind* and how it is assessed using *false belief tasks*.
6 Summarise what research evidence suggests about theory of mind.
7 What other evaluative points can be made concerning theory of mind?
8 Explain how theory of mind can be used as an explanation for autism.
9 Outline the aims, procedure, results and conclusion of the Sally-Anne study.
10 What evaluative points can be made concerning the Sally-Anne study?
11 Summarise what other research studies have suggested about theory of mind as an explanation for autism.
12 What other evaluative points can be made concerning theory of mind as an explanation for autism?

*'Empathy is about finding echoes of another person in yourself.'*
Mohsin Hamid (2012)

# The role of the mirror neuron system in social cognition

Mirror neurons are nerves in the brain that are active when specific actions are performed or observed in others, therefore allowing observers to experience the action as if it were their own. Mirror neurons may permit individuals to share in the feelings and thoughts of others by empathising with and imitating others, and thus allow them to have a ToM.

Mirror neurons were discovered, somewhat by accident, in the 1990s by Professor Giacomo Rizzolatti and his colleagues from the University of Parma, Italy, who noticed that when they reached for food, neurons began to fire off in the premotor cortex of monkeys in the same brain area as when the monkeys made the same hand movement, even though the monkeys' hands were not moving and they were merely observing the researchers.

The action of mirror neurons is such that when individuals experience an emotion such as disgust, or view an expression of disgust on another person's face, the same motor neurons are activated. This allows an observer and the person being observed to have direct experiential understanding of each other, thus explaining how people empathise with each other (understand each other's feelings). Before mirror neurons were discovered, psychologists believed individuals used logical thought processes to interpret and predict the behaviour of others, but mirror neurons indicate the possibility that humans understand other people not by thinking but by feeling. In other words, mirror neurons may allow individuals to simulate other people's behaviour and the motivation and feelings behind their behaviour. Therefore, when disgust is observed in another person, the mirror neurons for disgust fire up also in the individual observing that person, creating a sensation within the mind of the feeling associated with disgust, allowing an individual to immediately empathise with what the other person is experiencing.

**Figure 5.21** Do mirror neurons allow humans to directly experience other people's feelings and thoughts?

Research with macaque monkeys also suggests that mirror neurons permit the understanding of others' intentions, as well as their behaviour. For example, different brain areas associated with mirror neurons fire off when observing an individual pick up a cup from a table to drink from it than when they pick it up to clear it away.

Mirror neurons are found in brain areas involved in social cognition, especially motor-related areas (areas concerned with planning and executing movement), such as the inferior frontal, premotor and inferior parietal cortices brain areas.

Mirror neurons may be the biological mechanism by which the understanding of our own and the mental states of others occurs, and defective mirror neuron systems could explain conditions of social communication and interaction deficiencies, such as autism.

## CONTEMPORARY RESEARCH

### Understanding the emotions in others – Dapretto et al. (2006)

Mirror neurons may allow observers to directly experience the behaviour of others, which could explain how humans empathise with each other. Professor Mirella Dapretto and her co-workers from the University of California, Los Angeles, were interested in seeing whether specific brain areas are related to mirror neuron ability. As autistic children often lack the ability to empathise with others, their brain activity was compared with that of normally developed children to see whether specific brain areas could be identified.

#### Aim
To examine mirror neuron ability in autistic and normal children using fMRI scanning.

#### Procedure
Participants were ten high-functioning autistic children and ten normally functioning children aged between 10 and 14 years.

Participants and their parents gave informed consent in line with the Ethics Review Board of the University of California.

Eighty facial expressions representing five different emotions – anger, fear, happiness, neutrality and sadness – were presented for two seconds each in a random sequence.

fMRI scans were used as participants either observed or imitated the faces presented (counterbalanced within each group).

#### Findings
Both groups of children observed the stimuli and imitated the facial expressions.

However, children with autism showed no mirror neuron activity in the inferior frontal gyrus (*pars opercularis*) brain region.

The relationship between activity in mirror neuron brain areas and symptom severity of the autistic children was examined, using scores on the Autism Diagnostic Interview-Revised Scale. A negative correlation was found between activity in the *pars opercularis* brain area and the autistic children's scores.

Activity in the insula and limbic structures, brain areas underlying emotional understanding, was also negatively correlated with symptom severity.

#### Conclusions
There are differences in the neural pathways used by typically developing and autistic children. Typically developing children rely on a right hemisphere mirror neuron mechanism, which interfaces with the limbic system via the insula brain area, whereby the meaning of an observed emotion is directly understood. In autistic children this mirroring mechanism is not engaged, thus the emotional significance of observed emotions is not understood.

Mirror neurons underlie the ability to read others' emotional states from facial expressions.

#### Evaluation
- The lack of mirror neuron activity during the observation and imitation of emotional expressions in autistic children provides support for the idea that early dysfunction in the mirror neuron system is a key factor of the social deficits seen in autism.
- The research suggests a biological foundation to the development of social cognition in humans and also to the development of autism.

## RESEARCH IN FOCUS

In Dapretto *et al.*'s (2006) study the presentation of the 80 faces was done in a random sequence. Explain i] what is meant by a random sequence, ii] how such a random sequence could be constructed, iii] why it was considered important to randomise the sequence.

The study was conducted with the permission of the Ethics Review Board of the University of California. Explain what ethical board/committees are and what their purpose is.

### ON THE WEB

Watch and listen to the Italian psychologist Marco Iacoboni, one of the original and leading researchers of mirror neurons, as he makes the case for mirror neurons allowing us to share in the feelings and intentions of others. Go to **www.youtube.com** and search for 'Intersubjectivity and mirror neurons'.

## Research

Rizzolatti *et al.* (1996) placed electrodes in the brains of macaque monkeys to find that neurons in the frontal and parietal lobes brain areas behaved in the same manner when observing other monkeys pick up food as when the monkey did it itself, which suggests these neurons function to allow the monkeys to experience the other monkeys' movements as if they were their own.

Stuss *et al.* (2001) reported that individuals with damage to their frontal lobes were often unable to empathise with and read other people's intentions and were easy to deceive, which suggests damage to the mirror neuron system and emphasises its importance to normal human social cognition.

Gallese (2001) used fMRI scanning to find that the anterior cingulate cortex and inferior frontal cortex are active when individuals experience emotion or observe another person experiencing the same emotion, supporting the idea of mirror neuron-type activity occurring in humans.

Rizzolatti & Craighero (2004) used a range of physiological measuring techniques, such as EEGs and PET and fMRI scans, on the brains of human participants to find a network of neurons in the frontal and parietal brain areas that appeared to work as mirror neurons similarly to those seen in monkeys, thus providing additional support for the idea of mirror neurons existing in humans.

Wicker *et al.* (2003) found that smelling a horrible aroma activated the anterior cingulate and insula brain areas, but observing another person's facial expression of disgust also activated these brain areas, suggesting that mirror neuron activity allows empathy with other people's emotions.

Iacoboni *et al.* (2005) recorded the activity of single neurons in the inferior parietal lobule, to find that different neurons fired off when a monkey grasped an object to eat it as opposed to grasping an object to place it, even though both required similar hand movements. This suggests mirror neurons allow intentions of others' behaviour to also be understood.

### Evaluation

- For practical reasons there is a methodological problem in studying mirror neurons in humans, as it is not possible to study the actions of single neurons. Therefore it is arguable as to whether the findings from studies on macaque monkeys can be generalised to humans – for example, adult macaques cannot learn by imitation (although infant macaques can do so for a limited period), while human adults can. However, studies using fMRI scans have found evidence of mirror neuron systems in humans and in the same areas as in macaques, though fMRI scans also suggest a wider network of brain areas is involved, including the somatosensory cortex, which may help an observer perceive what it feels like to perform a certain action.

- Social cognition seems to exist only in species of animals that live in fairly complex social groupings, with indications of mirror neuron systems being found in primates, elephants and dogs, which suggests a biological basis to social cognition that has evolved due to its adaptive survival value. However, Atkins *et al.* (2002) have found evidence of a mirroring system in birds, namely Japanese quail, which implies the ability may be more widespread in the animal kingdom.

- Research into mirror neurons has indicated a possible biological explanation for autism, and greater understanding may pave the way for developing methods of counteracting the social deficits associated with the disorder, although evidence linking autism and defective motor neuron systems is far from conclusive as yet. Hickok (2009) argues that it isn't clear whether mirror neurons really are a separate class of cells with no other function, or indeed whether mirror neuron activity is a specific type of response or simply part of the workings of the motor system. He does not doubt the existence of mirror neurons, nor that they provide a mechanism for attaching meaning to actions such as hand and speech gestures, but disputes whether the meanings of actions are *coded* into motor systems – in other words, it is not proven that mirror neurons directly allow understanding of the meaning of actions.
- Kosonogov (2012) raises the point that if individuals can understand the motivation behind other people's actions by mirror neurons firing off when observing a goal-directed action or a pantomime of a goal-directed action (such as someone acting in a film), then how is it possible to know when an action is real and not a pantomime of an action (for example, telling the difference between someone really crying and someone pretending to cry)?
- Heyes (2012) argues that even if mirror neurons do exist, it has not been established yet whether they actually have evolved purely to permit the understanding of actions through the process of natural selection, or whether they are merely a biological by-product of social interaction between individuals.

**Figure 5.22** Professor Cecilia Heyes of Oxford University

### STRENGTHEN YOUR LEARNING

1. Explain how mirror neurons may allow individuals to experience the actions of others as if they were their own.
2. How did Rizzolatti *et al.* discover mirror neurons?
3. Outline and evaluate Dapretto *et al.*'s (2006) study of mirror neurons.
4. Summarise what other research studies have suggested about the role of mirror neurons in social cognition.
5. Explain the criticisms of the role of mirror neurons in social cognition made by:
    a) Gregory Hickok
    b) Vladimir Kosonogov
    c) Cecilia Heyes.
6. What other evaluative points can be made concerning the role of mirror neurons in social cognition?

## ASSESSMENT CHECK

1. Select whether option A, B or C correctly places Selman's levels of perspective-taking in order. **[1 mark]**

   **A** Social informational role taking/self-reflective role taking/egocentric (undifferentiated) viewpoint/mutual (third-party) role taking/social and conventional system role taking

   **B** Self-reflective role taking/egocentric (undifferentiated) viewpoint/social informational role taking/mutual (third-party) role taking/social and conventional system role taking

   **C** Egocentric (undifferentiated) viewpoint/social informational role taking/self-reflective role taking/mutual (third-party) role taking/social and conventional system role taking

2. Isaac's mother Marina has a habit of putting food in the fridge and forgetting about it. Yesterday, while playing outside, Isaac observed his mum through the kitchen window and saw her take a container of fish out of the fridge that she had put in there a few weeks ago. When she opened it the rotting smell made her screw up her face in disgust and Isaac immediately screwed up his face too as he knew exactly what she was experiencing.

   Referring to the scenario above, use your knowledge of the mirror neuron system to explain how Isaac was able to experience his mother's sense of disgust when smelling the rotting fish. **[3 marks]**

3. From Baron-Cohen *et al.*'s (1985) Sally-Anne study:

   a) Identify i] the independent variable, ii] the dependent variable. **[1 + 1 marks]**

   b) Explain why the study may lack ecological validity. **[2 marks]**

4. Outline the theory of mind as an explanation for autism. **[3 marks]**

5. Outline and evaluate Baillargeon's explanation of early infant abilities. **[16 marks]**

## SUMMARY

**Piaget's theory of cognitive development**

- Piaget's theory of cognitive development sees knowledge as being actively discovered through mental structures known as functional invariants and variant structures.
- There are two functional invariants, the process of adaptation, involving accommodation and assimilation, and the process of equilibration, involving equilibrium and disequilibrium.
- There are two variant structures, schemas and operations.
- Cognitive development is seen as occurring through invariant stages: the sensorimotor stage (during which egocentrism is apparent and object permanence develops), the pre-operational stage, the concrete operational stage (during which conservation and class inclusion develop) and the formal operational stage.

**Vygotsky's theory of cognitive development**

- Vygotsky saw cognitive development as a social process where higher mental functions arise out of children's social experiences through cultural and interpersonal levels.
- The cultural level sees children benefiting from the knowledge of previous generations, which they gain through interactions with caregivers.
- The interpersonal level sees cognitive development occurring on a social level, through interaction between people and on an individual level within a child.
- The zone of proximal development concerns the difference between what a child can currently do unaided and what it can do with assistance.
- Scaffolding concerns the idea that children can be assisted by sensitive guidance to arrive at the solution to a problem.
- Vygotsky saw concept formation occurring in four stages: vague syncretic, complex, potential concept and mature concept.

**Baillargeon's explanation for early infant abilities**

- Baillargeon developed the violation of expectation technique, which tests at what age object permanence appears in children.
- Baillargeon's research suggests that object permanence appears at an earlier age than that suggested by Piaget.

**The development of social cognition**

- Social cognition concerns how individuals develop the ability to use mental processes to make sense of their social world.
- Selman used interpersonal dilemmas to identify five stages involved in the development of perspective-taking: egocentric viewpoint, social informational role taking, self-reflective role taking, mutual role taking and social and conventional system role taking.
- The theory of mind (ToM) concerns the ability to attribute mental states to oneself and others.
- ToM has been offered as an explanation for autism as sufferers often have problems seeing from another person's perspective.
- The Sally-Anne study assesses an individual's social cognitive ability to attribute false beliefs to others.
- The mirror neuron system is a network of nerves in the brain that may allow individuals to experience the actions of others as if they were their own.

# 6 Schizophrenia

## Introduction

Schizophrenia is an extremely debilitating disorder that costs £2 billion a year in Britain in treatment and care costs, so it is important it is understood in order for effective treatments to be constructed. Many theories, both biological and psychological, are offered as explanations, though no one theory accounts solely for the disorder.

There are biological and psychological treatments for schizophrenia. Drugs are used to suppress the effects of the disorder, while psychological therapies attempt to deal with the causes to effect a recovery.

Specific focus will be upon:

1. The classification of schizophrenia
2. Biological explanations for schizophrenia
3. Psychological explanations for schizophrenia
4. Drug therapies
5. Cognitive behavioural therapy, family therapy and token economies
6. The interactionist approach in explaining and treating schizophrenia.

### Understanding the specification

- The specification requires that study of the classification of schizophrenia includes positive symptoms of the disorder, including hallucinations and delusions, negative symptoms, including speech poverty and avolition, as well as reliability and validity in diagnosis and classification of schizophrenia that includes reference to co-morbidity, culture and gender bias and symptom overlap.
- Biological explanations should include genetics, the dopamine hypothesis and neural correlates, as these are explicitly listed.
- Psychological explanations should include family dysfunction and cognitive explanations, including dysfunctional thought processing, as again specific reference is made to them.
- When studying drug therapies, typical and atypical antipsychotics should be covered.
- Psychological treatments that require study due to the explicit reference to them in the specification are cognitive behavioural therapy and family therapy, as well as token economies as a means of managing schizophrenia.
- The specification also states a need for the diathesis-stress model to be studied as an interactionist means of explaining and treating schizophrenia.

These are the basic requirements of the specification. However, other relevant material is included to provide depth and detail to your understanding.

*'If you talk to God, you are praying. If God talks to you, you have schizophrenia.'*
Thomas Szasz (1973)

# IN THE NEWS

## Ψ The Psychological Enquirer

**Figure 6.1** Anthony Phillips made a full recovery from a severe episode of schizophrenia

Anthony Phillips was a 40-year-old keen sportsman with an active social life and a successful long-term career in advertising. Anthony had no history of mental disturbance, so it was surprising when he experienced a severe schizophrenic episode. He had hallucinations where voices in his head claimed they were witches who had placed surveillance devices in his clothing and 'mind-melded' him to access his thoughts. This turned into a terrifying delusion that the voices had murdered his girlfriend and parents and raped a former girlfriend and planted evidence so the police would think he had done it. The voices also said that anyone he told about this would die.

So convinced was Anthony of the reality of all of this that he dared not go home, plus the voices said they were going to shoot him. Fortunately, concerned friends convinced Anthony to admit himself into psychiatric care where he was given antipsychotic drugs and within a short time he had recovered, with no need to continue taking medication. He returned to work and years later has never had a repetition of his illness.

Anthony is an example of someone who experienced one incident of schizophrenia and made a complete recovery. The fact that other sufferers do not recover at all, or can establish a reasonably normal level of functioning only by continual use of medication, suggests there may be more than one type of schizophrenia. Some sufferers have a family history of the disorder, suggesting a genetic link, but Anthony's experience seems to be related to his substance abuse and the high levels of stress he had been experiencing immediately before becoming ill. This indicates there may be several causes of schizophrenia. Having schizophrenia at age 40 is unusual and it is rare to have a first onset after this age. The time of highest vulnerability is between the late teens and late 20s.

What is striking about Anthony is that his case illustrates that schizophrenia can affect anyone, not just 'outsiders' who have problems fitting into society. Perhaps one reason that Anthony made a strong recovery was his ability to use his experience in a constructive manner – he created an art installation about his experience that attracted favourable reviews.

**ON THE WEB**

To watch a short film of Anthony giving an explanatory tour of his art exhibition that details what it's like to have a schizophrenic episode (which includes some swearing and references to drugs), go to www.youtube.com and search for 'The ghosts in my clothes'.

# 6.1 Classification of schizophrenia

*'Schizophrenia is a generic name for a group of disorders, characterised by a progressive disintegration of emotional stability, judgement, contact with and appreciation of reality, producing considerable secondary impairment of personality, relationships and intellectual functioning.'*
David Stafford-Clark (1964)

People from all cultures and levels of society develop **schizophrenia** – 1 per cent of people suffer worldwide, but with differences in prevalence rates of between 0.33 per cent and 15 per cent. Schizophrenia is the world's most common mental disorder, accounting for up to 50 per cent of all mental patients. It is difficult to compile accurate statistics, due to inadequately agreed criteria for diagnosis, but there are between 24 million and 55 million people with schizophrenia worldwide.

Schizophrenia affects thought processes and the ability to determine reality. Degree of severity varies between sufferers: some encounter only one episode, some have persistent episodes but live relatively normal lives through taking medication, while others have persistent episodes, are non-responsive to medication and remain severely disturbed. Schizophrenia may be a group of disorders, with different causes and explanations. Clinicians refer to **Type I schizophrenia**, an acute type characterised by **positive symptoms** and better prospects of recovery, and **Type II schizophrenia**, a chronic type characterised by **negative symptoms** and poorer prospects for recovery:

- **Positive symptoms** – involve the displaying of behaviours concerning loss of touch with reality, such as **hallucinations** and **delusions**. These generally occur in acute, short episodes, with more normal periods in between, and respond well to medication.
- **Negative symptoms** – involve the displaying of behaviours concerning disruption of normal emotions and actions. These occur in chronic, longer-lasting episodes, and are resistant to medication. Negative symptoms contribute most to sufferers not being able to function effectively in society, such as in relationships or at work.

To be diagnosed with schizophrenia, two or more symptoms must be apparent for more than one month, as well as reduced social functioning. Other differentiations are chronic onset schizophrenia, where sufferers become increasingly disturbed through gradual withdrawal and motivational loss over a prolonged period, and acute onset schizophrenia, where symptoms appear suddenly, after a stressful incident.

Schizophrenia commonly occurs between 15 and 45 years of age, with an equal incidence rate between males and females, though males show onset at an earlier age.

## Symptoms

Schneider (1959) detailed first-rank symptoms of schizophrenia, subjective experiences based on patients' verbal reports. Most are positive symptoms.

1. Passivity experiences and thought disorders: thoughts and actions are perceived as under external control – for example, by aliens. Sufferers may believe that thoughts are being inserted, withdrawn or broadcast to others.
2. Auditory hallucinations: sufferers experience voices, often insulting and obscene, inside their head, which form running commentaries, or discuss the sufferer's behaviour, anticipate their thoughts or repeat their thoughts out loud. These often occur with simultaneous delusions.
3. Primary delusions: sufferers usually experience delusions of grandeur, believing they are someone important – for example, Jesus Christ reborn. Later, delusions become delusions of persecution, where sufferers believe someone wants to hurt them. Some sufferers experience only one type of these delusions.

### KEY TERMS

**Schizophrenia** – a mental disorder characterised by withdrawal from reality

**Type I schizophrenia** – acute form characterised by positive symptoms and responsive to medication

**Positive symptoms** – the displaying of behaviours involving loss of touch with reality

**Type II schizophrenia** – chronic type characterised by negative symptoms and unresponsive to medication

**Negative symptoms** – the displaying of behaviours involving disruption of normal emotions and actions

**Hallucinations** – the perception of something being real that does not truly exist

**Delusions** – a false belief that is resistant to confrontation with the truth

### KEY TERMS

**Speech poverty** – a negative symptom of schizophrenia, characterised by brief replies to questions and minimal elaboration

**Avolition** – a general lack of energy resulting in loss of goal-directed behaviour

Slater & Roth (1969) added four symptoms, observed directly from behaviour. Most are negative symptoms:

1. Thought process disorders: sufferers wander off the point, invent new words and phrases, stop mid-sentence, muddle their words, interpret language literally (for example, proverbs) and indulge in **speech poverty**, which is characterised by excessively brief replies to questions with minimal elaboration.

2. Disturbances of effect: sufferers appear uncaring of others, display inappropriate emotional responses – for example, giggling at bad news – or display sudden mood swings.

3. Psychomotor disturbances: sufferers adopt frozen, 'statue-like' poses, exhibit tics and twitches and repetitive behaviours – for example, pacing up and down.

4. **Avolition**: sufferers display an inability to make decisions, have no enthusiasm or energy, lose interest in personal hygiene and lack sociability and affection.

### ON THE WEB

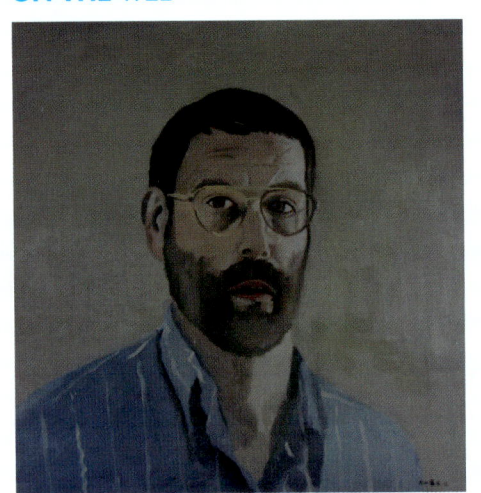

**Figure 6.2** Painting number 1

**Figure 6.3** Painting number 9

Bryan Charnley was an artist and a schizophrenic. In an attempt to portray the experience of the disorder he reduced the medication on which he depended for stability and painted a series of 17 self-portraits as he descended into a world of inner torment. The final portrait was found on the easel in his studio where he committed suicide. A video presentation of the portraits, alongside entries from Bryan's diary, can be found at **www.youtube.com**. Search for 'Bryan Charnley: The self portrait series'.

There is also a website about Bryan and his paintings at:

**www.bryancharnley.info**.

*'Diagnosis is not the end but the beginning of treatment.'*
Martin H. Fischer (1944)

### KEY TERMS

**Diagnosis** – identification of the nature and cause of illness

**DSM-5** – diagnostic classification system produced in the USA

**ICD-10** – diagnostic classification system produced by the World Health Organization

## Diagnosis of schizophrenia

Mental disorders are **diagnosed** by reference to classification systems that are based on the idea, similarly to physical illnesses, that a group of symptoms can be classed together as a syndrome (mental disorder), with an underlying cause and separate from all other mental disorders. The two commonly used classification systems are the **DSM-5** produced in the USA, and the **ICD-10** produced by the World Health Organization. Schizophrenia therefore is seen as a separate mental disorder with a distinct set of symptoms that allows it to be diagnosed in a reliable and valid way.

## Reliability

**Reliability** concerns the consistency of symptom measurement and affects diagnosis in two ways:

1. Test-retest reliability – occurs when a clinician makes the same diagnosis on separate occasions from the same information.
2. Inter-rater reliability – occurs when different clinicians make identical, independent diagnoses of the same patient.

> **KEY TERM**
>
> Reliability – consistency of diagnosis

## Research

Beck *et al.* (1962) reported a 54 per cent concordance (similarity) rate between experienced practitioners' diagnoses when assessing 153 patients, while Sőderberg *et al.* (2005) reported a concordance rate of 81 per cent using the DSM classification system. This suggests that classification systems have become more reliable over time. Interestingly, Nilsson *et al.* (2000) found only a 60 per cent concordance rate between practitioners using the ICD classification system, implying the DSM system is more reliable.

Read *et al.* (2004) reported test-retest reliability of schizophrenia diagnosis to have only a 37 per cent concordance rate, and noted a 1970 study in which 194 British and 134 US psychiatrists provided a diagnosis on the basis of a case description – 69 per cent of the Americans diagnosed schizophrenia, but only 2 per cent of the British did so. This suggests that the diagnosis of schizophrenia has never been fully reliable.

Seto (2004) reported that the term 'schizophrenia' was relabelled 'integration disorder' in Japan, due to the difficulty of attaining a reliable diagnosis, suggesting that schizophrenia, as a separate, identifiable disorder, does not exist.

Jakobsen *et al.* (2005) tested the reliability of the ICD-10 classification system in diagnosing schizophrenia. One hundred Danish patients with a history of psychosis were assessed using operational criteria, finding a concordance rate of 98 per cent, demonstrating the high reliability of clinical diagnosis of schizophrenia using up-to-date classifications.

### Evaluation

- The DSM classification system is regarded as more reliable than the ICD because the symptoms outlined for each category are more specific.
- The reliability of schizophrenia diagnosis, assessed at 81 per cent, is superior to that for anxiety disorders, at 63 per cent. The reliability of schizophrenia diagnosis is also generally considered superior to the **validity** of schizophrenia diagnosis.
- Even if reliability of diagnosis based on classification systems is not perfect, they do provide practitioners with a common language, permitting communication of research ideas and findings, which may ultimately lead to a better understanding of the disorder and the development of effective treatments.
- Evidence generally suggests that reliability of diagnoses has improved as classification systems have been updated.

> **KEY TERM**
>
> Validity – accuracy of diagnosis

> **ON THE WEB**
>
> How difficult is it to diagnose schizophrenia? To watch a film that focuses on the diagnosis of four patients through their symptoms, go to **www.youtube.com** and search for 'How is schizophrenia diagnosed – four patients'.

## Validity

Validity concerns how accurate diagnosis is. For valid diagnoses to occur, schizophrenia should be a disorder separate from all other disorders, as categorised by symptoms through the use of classification systems. There are several ways in which validity can be assessed:

1. Reliability – a valid diagnosis must first be reliable, though reliability in itself does not guarantee validity will occur, it is just the first step towards establishing validity.
2. Predictive validity – if diagnosis leads to successful treatment, then diagnosis is seen as valid.
3. Descriptive validity – to be valid, patients with schizophrenia should differ in symptoms from patients with other disorders.
4. Aetiological validity – to be valid, all schizophrenics should have the same cause for the disorder.

## CLASSIC RESEARCH

### CLASSIC RESEARCH
#### 'On being sane in insane places' – Rosenhan (1973)

**Figure 6.4** David Rosenhan's classic study brings the validity of schizophrenia diagnosis into question

It would be expected that psychiatrists make valid diagnoses – that is, correctly identify the mental disorders people suffer from. However, Dr David Rosenhan, in his famous study, showed this was not necessarily true.

#### Aim
To test the validity of schizophrenia diagnosis using the DSM-II classification system.

#### Procedure
Eight volunteers who did not suffer with mental illness presented themselves to different mental hospitals, claiming to hear voices. All were admitted and acted normally. Time taken to be released and reactions to them were recorded.

Later, a hospital was informed that an unspecified number of pseudo-patients would attempt entry over a three-month period. The number of suspected impostors was recorded.

#### Findings
The eight volunteers took between 7 and 52 days to be released, diagnosed as schizophrenics in remission. Normal behaviours were interpreted as signs of schizophrenia. However, 35 out of 118 actual patients suspected that the volunteers were sane.

During the subsequent three-month period, 193 patients were admitted, of whom 83 aroused suspicions of being false patients.

No actual pseudo-patients attempted admission.

#### Conclusions
The diagnosis of schizophrenia lacks validity, as psychiatrists cannot distinguish between real and pseudo-patients.

#### Evaluation
- It is not usual for people to fake insanity to gain admission to mental hospitals, and clinicians are there to help people, not turn them away. This could explain the admission of the original eight volunteers. The original results can also be explained by an expectation effect: the doctors expected them to be ill and looked for evidence to verify this. Their nervousness of the situation they found themselves in contributed to this.
- Being diagnosed as schizophrenic is a 'sticky label' – difficult to remove, with serious consequences – and yet it is manufactured by psychiatrists with low degrees of accuracy.

## RESEARCH IN FOCUS

How does Rosenhan's study suggest that the diagnosis of schizophrenia may lack validity?

Explain also why diagnoses have first to be reliable to be valid and why reliability of diagnosis does not guarantee a diagnosis being valid.

What are the difficulties in establishing whether diagnoses of schizophrenia are reliable and valid?

## Research

Mason *et al.* (1997) tested the ability of four different classification systems of diagnosis to predict the outcome of the disorder (over a 13-year period) in 99 schizophrenic patients, finding more modern classification systems had high predictive validity, especially if only symptoms that lasted at least six months were considered. This suggests that predictive diagnosis has improved over time, as classification systems have been updated.

Birchwood & Jackson (2001) argue that as 20 per cent of schizophrenics recover and never have another episode, but 10 per cent are so affected they commit suicide, there is too much variety in the outcomes of schizophrenia for predictive validity to be supported.

Jäger *et al.* (2003) found that it was possible to use ICD-10 to distinguish 951 cases of schizophrenia from 51 persistent delusional disorders, 116 cases of acute and transient psychotic disorders and 354 schizoaffective disorders, with schizophrenic patients having more pronounced negative symptoms and lower overall functioning. This suggests that diagnosis has high descriptive validity.

Baillie *et al.* (2009) surveyed 154 British psychiatrists to find that other than an agreement as to the influence of genetics, biochemical abnormalities and substance abuse, they had widely differing views on the causes of schizophrenia. This suggests that the aetiological validity of schizophrenia is low, though that of depression was even lower.

Allardyce *et al.* (2006) reported that because there is a lot of difference between patients in what groupings of symptoms they experience, it is not possible to diagnose schizophrenia as a separate disorder, which suggests diagnoses are not valid. This was supported by Jansson & Parnas (2007), who reviewed 92 studies that applied different definitions of schizophrenia to the same patient samples to find that both ICD-10 and DSM-IV, while showing moderate levels of reliability, indicated only low measures of validity, again suggesting schizophrenia may not exist as a separate condition.

## Evaluation

- The predictive validity of schizophrenia diagnosis can be argued to be low because different sufferers experience such a wide range of symptoms.
- The incidence of schizophrenia is 1 per cent, while for OCD it is 3 per cent. However, the incidence of schizophrenia with co-morbid (simultaneous) OCD is much higher than probability would suggest, which implies the existence of a separate schizo-obsessive disorder

- and that the validity of schizophrenia diagnosis is low, as schizophrenia is not a disorder separate from all other disorders.
- Bentall (2003) claims that the diagnosis of schizophrenia says nothing about its cause, implying diagnosis to be invalid. Diagnosis also says nothing about prevalence rates, which differ widely from rural to urban environments, again suggesting diagnosis to be invalid.
- Being labelled schizophrenic has a long-lasting, negative effect on social relationships, work prospects, self-esteem, etc., which seems unfair when diagnoses of schizophrenia are seemingly made with little evidence of validity.
- Although there is an argument for abolishing diagnoses of schizophrenia as scientifically invalid and damaging to those diagnosed as sufferers, Kendell & Jablensky (2007) argue that diagnostic categories are justifiable, as they give clinicians an agreed framework to investigate and discuss people's clinical experiences, so that a greater understanding can be reached and effective therapies developed.

## Co-morbidity

**KEY TERM**

**Co-morbidity** – the presence of one or more additional disorders or diseases simultaneously occurring with schizophrenia

**Co-morbidity** is where one or more additional disorders or diseases occur simultaneously with schizophrenia and can create problems with reliability of diagnosis, as there may be confusion over which actual disorder is being diagnosed. Schizophrenics often suffer from forms of depression, as well as schizophrenia, at the same time. Co-morbidity also raises issues of descriptive validity, as having simultaneous disorders suggests that schizophrenia may not actually be a separate disorder.

## Research

Sim *et al.* (2006) reported that 32 per cent of 142 hospitalised schizophrenics had an additional mental disorder, illustrating the problem that co-morbidity can create in achieving reliable and valid diagnosis of schizophrenia.

Goldman (1999) reported that 50 per cent of schizophrenics had a co-morbid medical condition, such as substance abuse or polydipsia (excessive thirst), making reliable and valid diagnosis of schizophrenia problematic.

Buckley *et al.* (2009) reported that an estimated 50 per cent of schizophrenics had co-morbid depression, 15 per cent co-morbid panic disorder, 29 per cent post-traumatic stress disorder and 23 per cent obsessive-compulsive disorder, with an additional 47 per cent of sufferers diagnosed with co-morbid substance abuse. This again illustrates the difficulties in reliably and validly diagnosing schizophrenia.

### Evaluation

- Jeste *et al.* (1996) state that schizophrenics with co-morbid conditions are excluded from research and yet form the majority of patients, which suggests that research findings into the causes of schizophrenia cannot be generalised to most sufferers. This also has a knock-on effect as to what treatments such patients should receive.
- The high levels of certain co-morbid disorders found in schizophrenics have led to some arguing that such co-morbidities are actually separate sub-types of the disorder.

- The biggest problem in reliably diagnosing schizophrenia is differentiating it from bipolar disorders (manic depression). Schizophrenia-related changes in mood often include mania and depression, but such changes often do not meet classification system criteria for diagnosis of separate bipolar conditions.
- Alcohol, cannabis and cocaine are substances frequently abused by schizophrenics and not only does such co-morbid substance abuse make reliable and valid diagnosis of schizophrenia difficult to achieve, it also leads to lower levels of functioning, increased hospitalisations and lower compliance with medication, which makes effective treatment more difficult to achieve.

# Culture bias

**Culture bias** concerns the tendency to over-diagnose members of other cultures as suffering from schizophrenia. In Britain, for example, people of Afro-Caribbean descent are much more likely than white people to be diagnosed as schizophrenic. Also Afro-Caribbean schizophrenics in Britain are more likely to be compulsorily confined in 'closed' (secure) hospitals than white schizophrenics, with the accusation being that most British psychiatrists are white and thus more likely to perceive black schizophrenics as more 'dangerous' than white schizophrenics. There is also the possibility that the heightened stress levels people from ethnic minorities experience, from poverty and racism for instance, may actually contribute to higher levels of schizophrenia in such cultural groups.

## Research

Cochrane (1977) reported the incidence of schizophrenia in the West Indies and Britain to be similar, at around 1 per cent, but that people of Afro-Caribbean origin are seven times more likely to be diagnosed with schizophrenia when living in Britain. This suggests either that Afro-Caribbean people living in Britain have more stressors leading to schizophrenia, or that invalid diagnoses are being made due to cultural bias.

McGovern & Cope (1977) reported that two thirds of patients detained in Birmingham hospitals were first- and second-generation Afro-Caribbeans, the other third being white and Asian, suggesting a cultural bias to over-diagnose schizophrenia in the black population.

Ineichen (1984) reported that 32 out of 89 confinements in 'closed' wards in Bristol hospitals were of non-white patients, which is a much greater proportion than that of non-white people in general society, suggesting a tendency to see non-white schizophrenics as more dangerous than their white counterparts.

Whaley (2004) believes the main reason for the incidence of schizophrenia among black Americans (2.1 per cent) being greater than among white Americans (1.4 per cent) is cultural bias, where ethnic differences in symptom expression are overlooked or misinterpreted by practitioners. This suggests a lack of validity in diagnosing schizophrenia cross-culturally.

> **KEY TERM**
>
> **Culture bias** – the tendency to over-diagnose members of other cultures as suffering from schizophrenia

**Figure 6.5** Are heightened levels of schizophrenia in some ethnic minorities due to cultural bias in diagnosis?

### Evaluation

- Fernando (1988) argues that people from ethnic minorities experience greater levels of racism, poverty, etc. than the white population and so higher levels of schizophrenia, triggered by such stressors, should be expected. However, this view is weakened as Cochrane (1983) points out that the only ethnic minority to experience higher levels of diagnosed schizophrenia in Britain are Afro-Caribbean people. One possibility is that Afro-Caribbean people have little immunity to flu (an illness not common in their countries of origin) and children born to mothers who had flu while pregnant have an 88 per cent increased chance of developing schizophrenia.
- Rack (1982) points out that in many cultures it is normal to see and hear recently deceased loved ones (it is part of the grieving process), but people exhibiting such behaviour in Western culture are liable to be diagnosed as schizophrenic.
- Cochrane & Sashidharan (1995) argue that the racism and social deprivation immigrants suffer are bound to negatively affect mental health, but that clinicians wrongly attribute their behaviour to their ethnicity.

## Gender bias

There is some disagreement between psychologists over the gender prevalence rate of schizophrenia. The accepted belief was that males and females were equally vulnerable to the disorder. However, some argue that clinicians, the majority of whom are men, have misapplied diagnostic criteria to women, and more recent studies show that there may be up to 50 per cent more male sufferers.

There is also a **gender bias** in the fact that when making diagnoses, clinicians often fail to consider that males tend to suffer more negative symptoms than women and have higher levels of substance abuse and that females have better recovery rates and lower relapse rates.

Clinicians also have tended to ignore the fact that there are different predisposing factors between males and females, which give them different vulnerability levels at different points of life.

There are gender differences in the classification of schizophrenia, too, with first onset occurring earlier in males, at between 18 and 25 years, than for females, at between 25 and 35 years. First onset for females is generally between 4 and 10 years later than in males. There are two peaks for male schizophrenia, at ages 21 and 39, while there are three peaks for females, at 22, 37 and 62 years of age.

### Research

Lewin *et al.* (1984) found that if clearer diagnostic criteria were applied, the number of female sufferers became much lower, suggesting a gender bias in original diagnosis. This was supported by Castle *et al.* (1993), who found using more restrictive diagnostic criteria that the male incidence of the disorder was more than twice that of females.

Reichler-Rossler & Häfner (2000) reported that males have more severe negative symptoms, which was reinforced by Galderisi *et al.* (2012) finding

### KEY TERM

**Gender bias** – the tendency for diagnostic criteria to be applied differently to males and females and for there to be differences in the classification of the disorder

**Figure 6.6** Females tend to have first onset of schizophrenia at a later age than males

males scored higher for negative symptoms. This, coupled with Hambrecht & Häfner (2000) finding male sufferers had higher levels of substance abuse and Haro *et al.* (2008) reporting that relapse rates are higher in males but recovery rates are higher with females, suggests a gender bias in clinicians not considering such important factors when making diagnoses.

Kulkarni *et al.* (2001) found that the female sex hormone *estradiol* was effective in treating schizophrenia in women when added to antipsychotic therapy, which suggests there may be different protective and predisposing factors in male and female vulnerability to schizophrenia which clinicians are not considering at diagnosis.

### Evaluation

- The fact that females also tend to first develop schizophrenia on average between four and ten years later than males and that women can develop a much later form of post-menopausal schizophrenia suggests there are different types of schizophrenia to which males and females are vulnerable, calling into question the validity of diagnosis.
- Research findings indicate that there is a case to be made for different diagnostic considerations when diagnosing males and females. However, this would cast doubts on the validity of schizophrenia as a separate disorder.
- Differences in the ages at which males and females experience schizophrenia may be related to differences in the types of stressors both sexes experience at different ages and to age-related variations in female menstrual cycles.

## Symptom overlap

In diagnosing schizophrenia, symptoms of the disorder are often also found with other disorders, which makes it difficult for clinicians to decide which particular disorder someone is suffering from. **Symptom overlap** especially occurs with bipolar disorder, where depression is a common symptom, as well as hallucinations. Symptom overlap can also occur with autism, as well as with cocaine intoxication.

### KEY TERM

**Symptom overlap** – the perception that symptoms of schizophrenia are also symptoms of other mental disorders

## Research

Serper *et al.* (1999) assessed patients with co-morbid schizophrenia and cocaine abuse, cocaine intoxication on its own and schizophrenia on its own. They found that although there was considerable symptom overlap in patients with schizophrenia and cocaine abuse, it was possible to make accurate diagnoses.

Konstantareas & Hewitt (2001) compared 14 autistic patients with 14 sufferers of schizophrenia to find none of the schizophrenics had symptoms of autism, but 7 of the autistics had symptoms of schizophrenia, showing some support for the idea of symptom overlap.

Ophoff *et al.* (2011) assessed genetic material from 50,000 participants to find that of seven gene locations on the genome associated with schizophrenia, three of them were also associated with bipolar disorder, which suggests a genetic overlap between the two disorders.

### Evaluation

- The fact that there is genetic overlap between mental disorders suggests that gene therapies might be developed which simultaneously treat different disorders.
- One recently developed method of ascertaining which particular disorder someone is suffering with is to examine the grey matter content of the brain, as schizophrenics can experience a decrease of grey matter, while bipolar sufferers do not.
- Ketter (2005) reports that misdiagnosis due to symptom overlap can lead to years of delay in receiving relevant treatment, during which time suffering and further degeneration can occur, as well as high levels of suicide.

### STRENGTHEN YOUR LEARNING

1. Describe *Type I* and *Type II* schizophrenia.
2. Summarise *positive* and *negative* symptoms of schizophrenia.
3. Outline possible sub-types of schizophrenia.
4. Explain how classification systems categorise mental disorders.
5. Refer to research evidence to assess the extent to which diagnoses of schizophrenia are i] reliable, ii] valid.
6. What other evaluative points can be made about the reliability and validity of schizophrenia diagnoses?
7. Explain how co-morbidity creates problems with reliability and validity of schizophrenia diagnoses.
8. For what reasons might people of Afro-Caribbean origin be seven times more likely to be diagnosed with schizophrenia when living in Britain?
9. In what ways might gender bias be applicable to the classification and diagnosis of schizophrenia?
10. What types of symptom overlap can occur with schizophrenia?

### PSYCHOLOGY IN THE REAL WORLD

The use of gene mapping to identify genes associated with schizophrenia opens up the possibility of gene therapies to treat the disorder. Mei *et al.* (2013) found that by targeting the expression of the gene neuregulin 1, which is over-expressed in humans with schizophrenia, they could reverse behavioural and brain abnormalities in mice exhibiting schizophrenia features (they interacted less and performed poorly on tasks requiring thinking). The gene is known to make a protein important for brain development.

Researchers are excited by the prospect of a treatment that may actually 'cure' the disorder by permanently removing all signs of schizophrenic symptoms, rather than merely suppressing them through drug therapies. However, we shouldn't get too excited yet, as there is a big difference between removing 'schizophrenia-like' features in mice and actually removing schizophrenic symptoms in humans.

# ASSESSMENT CHECK

1. Janelle has been diagnosed as suffering from schizophrenia. It began when she started hearing voices in her head criticising her behaviour and she became convinced that she been chosen by alien beings for a special purpose. Friends noticed that it became increasingly difficult to make sense of Janelle's speech and she would give only brief answers to their questions. She also became untidy and unenthusiastic about life in general, spending hours pacing up and down her room.

   Make reference to the scenario above concerning Janelle to identify negative and positive symptoms of schizophrenia. **[4 marks]**

2. Place a letter 'R' next to the two statements in the following list that relate to reliability of diagnosis and a letter 'V' next to the two statements that relate to validity of diagnosis. One statement will be left over. **[4 marks]**
   - Where a clinician makes the same diagnosis on separate occasions from the same information.
   - Where patients with schizophrenia differ in symptoms from patients with other disorders.
   - Where patients with schizophrenia all have the same cause for their disorder.
   - Where patients with schizophrenia are given combinations of treatments.
   - Where different clinicians make identical, independent diagnoses of the same patient.

3. In reference to schizophrenia, explain what is meant by co-morbidity. **[2 marks]**

4. Explain why, when researching symptom overlap in schizophrenia, it may be difficult to obtain informed consent from patients. **[2 marks]**

5. Outline and evaluate culture and gender bias in the diagnosis and classification of schizophrenia. **[16 marks]**

*'Schizophrenia cannot be understood without understanding despair.'*
R. D. Laing (1960)

*'After a century of studying schizophrenia, the cause of the disorder remains unknown.'*
Thomas R. Insel (2010)

**KEY TERM**

**Genetic explanation** – transmission of abnormality by hereditary means

**ON THE WEB**

To watch an absorbing documentary about schizophrenia and its possible causes, including a focus on a pair of identical twins where one has the disorder and one does not, go to **www.youtube.com** and search for 'Schizophrenia: Stolen minds, stolen lives'.

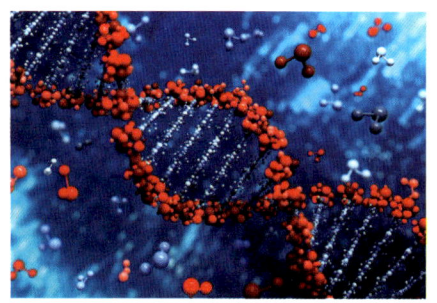

**Figure 6.7** Several genes are suspected of being involved in the development of schizophrenia

# 6.2 Biological explanations for schizophrenia

There are several biological explanations for schizophrenia, which see the disorder as determined by physiological means. The biological factors focused on here are genetics, abnormal dopamine functioning and neural correlates. Although causes of schizophrenia are not fully understood, research does indicate that biological factors play a major role in the development of the disorder.

## Genetics

The **genetic explanation** sees schizophrenia as transmitted through hereditary means, i.e. through the genes passed on to individuals from their families. It is not believed that there is a single 'schizophrenic gene', but that several genes are involved, which increase an individual's overall vulnerability to developing schizophrenia.

Research traditionally used twin, family and adoption studies to assess concordance rates of developing schizophrenia between people with different levels of genetic relatedness, but more recently gene-mapping studies have been used that look for genetic material commonly found among sufferers. Such research has identified a number of genes that seem to exert an influence.

### Research

Gottesman & Shields (1976) reviewed five twin studies and reported a concordance rate of between 75 per cent and 91 per cent for MZ (identical) twins with severe forms of schizophrenia, suggesting that genetics plays a larger role with chronic forms of the disorder. Torrey *et al.* (1994), reviewing evidence from twin studies, found that if one MZ twin develops schizophrenia, there is a 28 per cent chance that the other twin will do so too, supporting the idea that schizophrenia is inherited.

Kety & Ingraham (1992) found that prevalence rates of schizophrenia were ten times higher among genetic than adoptive relatives of schizophrenics, suggesting that genetics plays a greater role than environmental factors.

Varma & Sharma (1993) found a concordance rate of 35 per cent for first-degree relatives of individuals with schizophrenia, compared with 9 per cent in first-degree relatives of non-schizophrenics, indicating a role for genetic factors. Additionally, Parmas *et al.* (1993) conducted a longitudinal family study of schizophrenia, finding that 16 per cent of children whose mothers had schizophrenia developed the disorder, compared with 2 per cent of children whose mothers did not have schizophrenia, again suggesting a genetic link.

Gurling *et al.* (2006) used evidence from family studies indicating that schizophrenia was associated with chromosome 8p21-22 to identify a high-risk sample. Using gene mapping, the PCM1 gene was implicated in susceptibility to schizophrenia, providing more evidence for genetics. Additionally, Benzel *et al.* (2007) used gene mapping to find evidence suggesting that NRG3 gene variants interact with both NRG1 and ERBB4 gene variants to create a susceptibility to developing schizophrenia, suggesting an interaction of genetic factors.

Avramopoulos *et al.* (2013) sequenced genes associated with the neuregulin signalling pathway, which relays signals within the nervous system. They found that some families with high levels of schizophrenia had multiple neuregulin signalling-related variants while others had none. Schizophrenics with neuregulin signalling variants experienced more hallucinations but less impairment than the other schizophrenia patients. The findings suggest that individually harmless genetic variations, which affect related biochemical processes, may unite to increase vulnerability to schizophrenia, but additionally provide support for the idea that schizophrenia is not a single disease at all but a group of related disorders. Patients without neuregulin signalling-related variants have variants in a different pathway and thus different symptoms.

The Schizophrenia Working Group of the Psychiatric Genomics Consortium (2014) analysed the DNA of 36,989 schizophrenics and 113,000 non-schizophrenics, to identify 128 independent genetic variations at 108 locations on the human chromosomes that contribute most to developing schizophrenia. Of these, 83 had not been identified before. Associations were higher in genes expressed in the brain and in tissues with important roles in immunity, supporting the overall idea of biological causation, but especially illustrating a link between the immune system and schizophrenia.

## Evaluation

- Twin studies suggest a genetic factor in the onset of schizophrenia, but do not consider the influence of social class and socio-psychological factors between twins. Twin and family studies also fail to consider shared environmental influences.
- Sorri *et al.* (2004) performed a longitudinal study over 21 years on Finnish adoptees with biological mothers with schizophrenia, comparing them with adoptees whose biological mothers did not have schizophrenia, but also considered family rearing styles among adoptive families. Adoptees with a high genetic risk of developing schizophrenia were more sensitive to non-healthy rearing patterns, suggesting that environmental factors are important, too.
- If genes caused schizophrenia on their own, concordance rates between MZ twins would be 100 per cent, which they are not. Twin studies also produce confusing evidence, with heritability estimates ranging from 58 per cent for MZ twins down to as low as 11 per cent.
- Leo (2006) argues that Kety's adoption study evidence is not convincing as sample sizes were small, making generalisation difficult, and many of the biological relatives with schizophrenia were distant relatives, such as half-siblings, with low biological similarity.
- Hedgecoe (2001) believes that scientists have portrayed schizophrenia as a genetic disease by using evidence from twin and adoption studies in a biased way to 'produce a narrative about schizophrenia which subtly prioritises genetic explanations'.
- Findings from genetic studies provide evidence for the diathesis-stress model, where individuals inherit different levels of genetic predisposition to developing schizophrenia, but ultimately it is environmental triggers that determine whether individuals go on to develop schizophrenia.
- Gene mapping offers the possibility of developing tests to identify high-risk individuals, though this raises socially sensitive and ethical concerns.

> **YOU ARE THE RESEARCHER**
>
> Design a study using identical twins to assess the genetic explanation of schizophrenia. What type of study would this be? What would the hypothesis be for this study? What type of graph would be used to plot your data?
>
> Would it be possible to establish causality in this study? Explain your answer.

## The dopamine hypothesis

The **dopamine hypothesis** centres on the idea that the neurotransmitter dopamine is linked to the onset of the disorder. Dopamine acts to increase the rate of firing of neurons during synapse (a process where neurotransmitters help transmit signals across gaps between nerve fibres), which enhances communication between neurons. However, Snyder (1976) argued that if too much dopamine is released during synapse it can lead to the onset of schizophrenia. The theory developed after it was discovered that phenothiazines, antipsychotic drugs that lessen the symptoms of schizophrenia, seem to work by decreasing dopamine activity. Also, the dopamine-releasing drug L-dopa creates schizophrenic symptoms in non-schizophrenics. Other drugs influencing the dopaminergic system, such as LSD, a hallucinogenic, also create schizophrenic-like behaviour in non-schizophrenics and heighten symptoms in sufferers. It is probable that genetic factors are linked to faulty dopaminergic systems in those with schizophrenia.

Davis *et al.* (1991) updated the theory because high levels of dopamine are not found in all schizophrenics, and the modern anti-schizophrenic drug clozapine, with very little dopamine-blocking activity, works effectively against the disorder. Davis *et al.* suggested that high levels of dopamine in the mesolimbic dopamine system are associated with positive symptoms, while high levels in the mesocortical dopamine system are associated with negative symptoms.

The neurotransmitter glutamate may be involved, too, as there is reduced function of the NMDA glutamate receptor in people with schizophrenia, with dopamine involved, as dopamine receptors restrict the release of glutamate.

### Research

Randrup & Munkvad (1966) created schizophrenic-like behaviour in rats by giving them amphetamines, which activate dopamine production, and then reversed the effects by giving them neuroleptic drugs, which inhibit the release of dopamine, supporting the dopamine hypothesis.

Iversen (1979) reported that post-mortems on people who had had schizophrenia found excess dopamine in the limbic system, suggesting that the neurotransmitter is involved in the disorder.

Kessler *et al.* (2003) used PET and MRI scans to compare people with schizophrenia with non-sufferers, finding that the schizophrenics had elevated dopamine receptor levels in the basal forebrain and substantia nigra/ventral tegemental brain areas. Differences in cortical dopamine levels were also found, suggesting that dopamine is important in the onset of schizophrenia.

**KEY TERM**

**Dopamine hypothesis** – that the development of schizophrenia is related to abnormal levels of the hormone and neurotransmitter dopamine

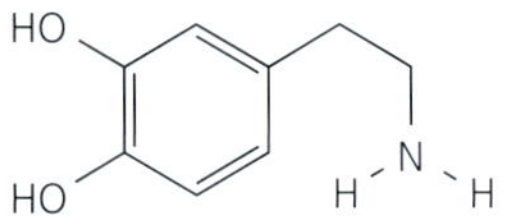

**Figure 6.8** The dopamine molecule – the neurotransmitter dopamine has been linked to the onset of schizophrenia

Javitt *et al.* (2000) found that glycine, a glutamate receptor agonist, reversed phencyclidine hydrochloride-induced psychosis (which closely resembles schizophrenia) in rats and brought about improvements in people with schizophrenia, lending support to the glutamate theory.

Javitt (2007) reported that the drugs phencyclidine and ketamine induce schizophrenic symptoms in non-sufferers by blocking neurotransmission at NMDA-type glutamate receptors, which leads to abnormal dopamine system functioning in striatal and prefrontal brain areas, supporting the idea of a connection between dopamine and glutamate in the onset of schizophrenia.

### Evaluation

- Overall the evidence is inconclusive, as there is no consistent difference in dopamine levels between drug-free schizophrenics and non-sufferers.
- Several neurotransmitters may be involved in the development of schizophrenia. Along with dopamine and glutamate, newer anti-schizophrenic drugs implicate serotonin's involvement, too.
- Healy (2000) believes that pharmaceutical companies were keen to see the dopamine theory promoted, as they would make huge profits from manufacturing anti-schizophrenic drugs that inhibited dopamine production.
- The theory cannot explain why sufferers only recover slowly when given neuroleptic drugs, when the medication has an instant effect on dopamine levels.
- Lloyd *et al.* (1984) believe that even if dopamine is a causative factor, it may be an indirect factor mediated through environmental factors, because abnormal family circumstances can lead to high levels of dopamine which in turn trigger schizophrenic symptoms.
- Differences in the biochemistry of schizophrenics could just as easily be an effect rather than a cause of the disorder.
- Dopamine seems to be associated more with positive symptoms, so it may contribute only to certain aspects of the disorder. Alternatively, this could also suggest that there are several types of schizophrenia, with dopamine linked to certain types only.
- The dopamine hypothesis can be accused of being over-simplistic, as many other neurotransmitters may also be involved in the development of schizophrenia.

## Neural correlates

The idea of **neural correlates** is that abnormalities within specific brain areas may be associated with the development of schizophrenia. Originally evidence was limited to post-mortems conducted upon the brains of dead schizophrenics, but research now uses non-invasive scanning techniques, such as functional magnetic resonance imagery (fMRI), which gives a picture of the brain in action through use of magnetic fields and radio waves. In this way the functioning of the brains of schizophrenics can be compared with that of non-sufferers, to identify brain areas that may be linked to schizophrenia. This is best achieved by giving tasks to participants associated with types of functioning known to be abnormal in schizophrenics, for example social cognition, thought processing and working memory tasks.

### KEY TERM

**Neural correlates** – that the development of schizophrenia is related to structural and functional brain abnormalities

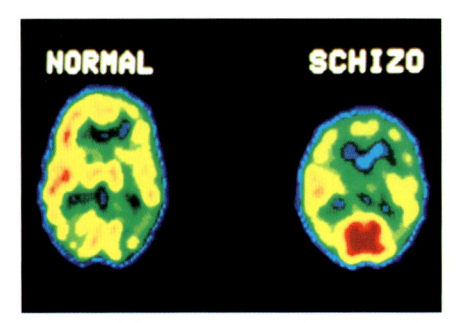

**Figure 6.9** Scans can reveal structural differences between schizophrenics' and non-schizophrenics' brains

One important consideration is whether brain abnormalities found in schizophrenics are caused by genetic factors or are a result of the disorder itself. This can be investigated by comparing the brains of sufferers with non-schizophrenic family members; if similar brain abnormalities are found in non-suffering family members as well as those with the disorder, it suggests a genetic link.

Early research attention was focused on schizophrenics having enlarged ventricles (the fluid-filled gaps between brain areas) (see Figure 6.9). Enlarged ventricles are especially associated with damage to central brain areas and the prefrontal cortex, which more recent scanning studies have also linked to the disorder. Such damage has often been associated with negative symptoms.

## Research

Johnstone *et al.* (1976) found that schizophrenics had enlarged ventricles, while non-sufferers did not, which suggests schizophrenia is related to a loss of brain tissue. Weyandt (2006) reported that enlarged ventricles are associated with negative symptoms only, which implies enlarged ventricles cannot explain all symptoms and incidences of schizophrenia.

Tilo *et al.* (2001) gave fMRI scans to six schizophrenics and six non-schizophrenics while they looked at and spoke about Rorschach ink-blots. In the schizophrenic patients it was found that the severity of thought disorder, a core symptom of schizophrenia, was negatively correlated with the level of activity in the Wernicke brain area, a region associated with the production of coherent speech, supporting the idea of abnormal functioning in specific brain areas being related to schizophrenia.

Li *et al.* (2010) performed a meta-analysis of fMRI studies investigating the difficulties schizophrenics often have in processing facial emotions, to find that although both schizophrenics and non-sufferers activate the bilateral amygdala and right fusiform gyri when processing facial emotions, the activation was severely limited in schizophrenics. This suggests that abnormal brain functioning in schizophrenics may explain their difficulties in processing facial emotions.

Boos *et al.* (2012) performed MRI scans on 155 schizophrenics, 186 of their non-schizophrenic siblings and 122 non-related schizophrenics, to find schizophrenic participants had decreased grey matter density and cortical thinning compared with the other participants. This suggests brain tissue differences in schizophrenics are an effect of having the disorder rather than being due to genetic factors.

Yoon *et al.* (2013) used fMRI scans to examine the brains of 18 schizophrenics and 19 non-schizophrenics performing a memory task. Schizophrenic participants had heightened activity in the substantia nigra, decreased activity in the prefrontal cortex and diminished connectivity between these brain regions. Also, the higher the level of connectivity between the substantia nigra and the striatum, the stronger the symptoms of schizophrenia were. This suggests that abnormal functioning of the prefrontal cortex–basal ganglia brain circuit may be related to the cognitive deficits experienced by schizophrenics.

### Evaluation

- Some non-schizophrenics have enlarged ventricles, while not all schizophrenics do, which goes against the idea of schizophrenia being linked to loss of brain tissue.
- It appears to be schizophrenics who do not respond to medication who mainly exhibit enlarged ventricles. This could mean that it is an effect of suffering from schizophrenia over a long period that leads to physical brain damage rather than brain damage leading to schizophrenia.
- When assessing the role that brain abnormalities play in the development of schizophrenia, consideration must also be given to environmental factors, such as substance abuse and stress levels, which may also be having a damaging influence upon brain tissue.
- It may be that schizophrenic patients who do not respond to medication do not do so because structural brain damage does not allow anti-psychotic medications to have a therapeutic effect in reducing symptom levels.
- Structural brain damage is often evident at first onset of schizophrenia, but only by performing longitudinal studies would it be possible to assess whether damage progressively worsens as the disorder continues. Ho *et al.* (2003) performed MRI scans on recent-onset schizophrenics and re-scanned them three years later. They found evidence of brain damage in the recent-onset patients, which worsened over time (even though they received medication), especially in the frontal lobes, which correlated with an increase in the severity of their symptoms. This suggests brain damage does increase in schizophrenics over time.

### STRENGTHEN YOUR LEARNING

1. What methods are used to assess the genetic explanation? How does each of these methods work?
2. To what extent does research evidence support the genetic explanation?
3. What other evaluative points can be made concerning the genetic explanation?
4. Explain how dopamine may be involved in the experience of schizophrenia.
5. To what extent does research evidence support the dopamine hypothesis?
6. What other evaluative points can be made concerning the dopamine hypothesis?
7. What methods are used to investigate possible associations between neural correlates and schizophrenia?
8. Summarise what research evidence suggests about neural correlates and schizophrenia.
9. What other evaluative points can be made concerning neural correlates and schizophrenia?

## PSYCHOLOGY IN THE REAL WORLD

**Figure 6.10** Rethink Mental Illness

Although many forms of clinical therapy exist, one of the best sources of help for people with schizophrenia can be self-help support groups, such as Rethink Mental Illness. Such groups are encounter or personal growth associations, like Alcoholics Anonymous, that provide a setting in which people who share similar experiences come together to offer practical and emotional support in a non-critical, sharing and mutually beneficial manner. They are based on humanistic psychology (see page 11), an approach perceiving humans as inherently good and motivated to improve themselves. Such groups benefit from the growth of the internet, where vulnerable people can discuss their problems, support each other and get advice in a virtual environment without having to meet physically. Internet groups are often the first step to joining a physical group.

Some believe that self-help support groups actually maintain and even trigger mental disorders, but many self-help support groups have provided the route by which people have sought and obtained psychological help, and without them many disturbed individuals' futures would be a lot worse.

### KEY TERMS

**Family dysfunction** – the idea that dysfunctional family relationships and patterns of communication are related to the development of schizophrenia

**Cognitive explanations** – the idea that the development of schizophrenia is related to maladaptive thought processes

**Dysfunctional thought processing** – the idea that the development of schizophrenia is related to abnormal ways of thinking

### ON THE WEB

Rethink Mental Illness is a charity that believes a better life is possible for people affected by mental illness. For more than 40 years we have brought people together to support each other. We run services and support groups that change people's lives and we challenge attitudes about mental illness. Find them at: **www.rethink.org**.

*'When you treat a disease, first treat the mind.'*
Chen Jen (2010)

## 6.3 Psychological explanations for schizophrenia

There are several psychological explanations for schizophrenia. Here we focus on **family dysfunction** and **cognitive explanations**, including **dysfunctional thought processing**.

### Family dysfunction

The family dysfunction explanation sees maladaptive relationships and patterns of communications within families as sources of stress, which can cause or influence the development of schizophrenia (see Figure 6.11).

Parents of schizophrenics often display three types of dysfunctional characteristics:

1. High levels of interpersonal conflict (arguments).
2. Difficulty communicating with each other.
3. Being excessively critical and controlling of their children.

**Figure 6.11** Dysfunctional families are associated with high levels of schizophrenia (photo posed by models)

Bateson *et al.* (1956) coined the phrase double bind to explain the contradictory situations children could be placed in by parents, where a verbal message is given but opposite behaviour is exhibited. For example, a parent may tell a child to 'be more spontaneous', but if the child is then spontaneous, it becomes confused and uncertain, as by doing what the parent said it is clearly not being spontaneous. This leads to a negative reaction of social withdrawal and flat effect (a lack of emotional expression) in order to escape double bind situations.

Another feature of the theory is that of expressed emotion, where families who persistently exhibit criticism and hostility exert a negative influence, especially upon recovering schizophrenics, who when returning to their families react to expressed emotion by relapsing to an active phase of the disorder and experience severe positive symptoms of hallucinations and delusions of persecution.

## ON THE WEB

An informative review by Paul Gibney of Bateson's 'double bind hypothesis' 50 years on from when it was first proposed can be found at **www.psychotherapy.com.au/fileadmin/site_files/pdfs/TheDoubleBindTheory.pdf**.

## Research

Tienari *et al.* (2004) found that the level of schizophrenia in adopted individuals who were the biological children of schizophrenic mothers was 5.8 per cent in those adopted by healthy families compared with 36.8 per cent for children raised in dysfunctional families, which supports not only the family dysfunction theory but also the idea that individuals with high genetic vulnerability to schizophrenia are more affected by environmental stressors.

Patino *et al.* (2005) established seven problems associated with family dysfunction: poor relationship between adults in the household, lack of warmth between parents and child, visible disturbance of the mother–child, father–child or sibling–child relationship, parental overprotection and child abuse. They found that migrants who had experienced at least three of these seven problems had four times the normal level of vulnerability to developing schizophrenia, compared with the double level of risk for migrants not experiencing family dysfunction. This suggests that family dysfunction increases the likelihood of life stressors triggering the onset of schizophrenia.

Bateson (1956) reported on a case study where a recovering schizophrenic was visited in hospital by his mother. He embraced her warmly, but she stiffened, and when he withdrew his arms she said, 'Don't you love me any more?' To which he blushed and she commented, 'Dear, you must not be so easily embarrassed and afraid of your feelings.' She then left and he assaulted an aide and had to be restrained. This gives support to the idea of double bind.

Kavanagh (1992) reviewed 26 studies of expressed emotion, finding that the mean relapse rate for schizophrenics who returned to live with high expressed emotion families was 48 per cent compared with 21 per cent for those who went to live with low expressed emotion families. This supports the idea that expressed emotion increases the risk of relapse for recovering schizophrenics. This was further supported by Butzlaff & Hooley (1998), who performed a meta-analysis of 26 studies to find that schizophrenics returning to a family environment of high expressed emotion experienced more than twice the average rate for the return of schizophrenic symptoms.

> **Evaluation**
> - Having a schizophrenic within a family can be problematic and stressful on family relationships. Therefore, rather than dysfunctions within families causing schizophrenia, it could be that having a schizophrenic within a family leads to dysfunctions.
> - The family dysfunction theory is supported by the fact that therapies which successfully focus on reducing expressed emotions within families have low relapse rates compared with other therapies.
> - Bateson's idea of double bind was initially popular among clinicians, but some have accused him of selective bias in focusing only on aspects of interviews with schizophrenics that supported his claims. This, coupled with more recent evidence supporting a genetic link, has lessened support for the idea.
> - A problem with the family dysfunction theory is that it fails to explain why all children in such families often do not go on to develop schizophrenia.
> - Although there is a lack of general support for family dysfunction as a causal factor of schizophrenia, research evidence into expressed emotion does suggest that family dysfunction plays a major role in maintenance of the disorder.

## Cognitive theories

Cognitive theories focus upon maladaptive thought processes as a central feature of schizophrenia, with Beck & Rector (2005) proposing a cognitive model that combines a complex interaction of neurobiological, environmental, behavioural and cognitive factors to explain the disorder. Abnormalities within brain functioning are seen as increasing vulnerability to stressful life experiences, which in turn lead to dysfunctional beliefs and behaviours. Cognitive deficits occur, where sufferers experience problems with attention, communication and information overload. Sufferers are also seen as being unable to deal with inappropriate ideas, such as misperceiving voices in their head as people actually trying to speak to them, rather than perceiving them more sensibly as 'inner speech', which most people experience.

With positive symptoms, delusions are seen as occurring because of active cognitive biases (thinking in irrational ways), such as external attributions like individuals believing that they are being persecuted. Hallucinations, meanwhile, are understood in terms of biased information processing, while the cognitive deficits experienced by schizophrenics are referred to as alien control symptoms, where sufferers believe that external people and forces are exerting influence over their thoughts and behaviour.

Negative symptoms are seen as occurring due to the use of cognitive strategies to control the high levels of mental stimulation being experienced. Schizophrenics may actually experience a greater level of emotion than they physically display, as not expressing emotions is one strategy that can be used to try to control the levels of emotion being experienced internally.

# Research

O'Carroll (2000) reviewed available evidence to report that cognitive impairment is found in 75 per cent of schizophrenics, particularly in memory, attention, motor skills, executive function and intelligence, supporting Beck & Rector's cognitive model. Cognitive impairments often pre-dated illness onset, did not occur as a result of substance abuse and were related to social and functional impairments.

Elevag & Goldberg (2000) reported that schizophrenia is better characterised by cognitive deficits rather than symptoms and that cognitive deficits are enduring features of schizophrenia that are not specific to sub-types of the disorder, with memory and attention being the main cognitive deficits forming the core dysfunction of the disorder. This provides support for the cognitive explanation of schizophrenia.

Knoblich *et al*. (2004) got schizophrenics and non-schizophrenics to draw circles on a writing pad connected to a PC monitor and asked them to continuously monitor the relationship between their hand movements and the visual consequences. It was found that the schizophrenics were impaired in their ability to detect a mismatch between self-generated movement and their consequences, which suggests that a cognitive inability to self-monitor may underlie the core symptoms of schizophrenia.

Bowie & Harvey (2006) reviewed evidence to find that cognitive impairments are the core feature of schizophrenia mainly affecting attention, working memory, verbal learning and executive functions. These impairments pre-date the onset of the disorder and are found throughout the course of the illness. This supports Beck & Rector's cognitive model, with additional support coming from the fact that effective therapies seem to reduce cognitive deficits.

Takahashi *et al*. (2013) compared electrical brain activity in 410 schizophrenics and 247 non-sufferers exposed to auditory tones, to find that the ability to detect changes in tone was severely limited in the schizophrenics. This inability to detect changes in sounds may explain the cognitive deficits that schizophrenics experience, such as not being able to direct attention properly, or rapidly encode new information, as changes in the tone of speech convey complex information concerning emotional meaning and content. It may also explain why they experience auditory hallucinations and delusions.

> **RESEARCH IN FOCUS**
> Takahashi *et al*. (2013) compared electrical brain activity in schizophrenics and non-sufferers exposed to auditory tones, finding the ability to detect changes in tone was severely limited in the schizophrenics. What type of experimental design was used in this laboratory experiment? Explain two strengths and two weaknesses of this type of experimental design. Why would it not be possible to use a different type of experimental design?

## Evaluation

- Cognitive theories in themselves do not explain what led to the cognitive dysfunctions seen in schizophrenics and thus cannot be seen as explaining the causes of schizophrenia.
- If schizophrenia is better characterised by cognitive deficits that are not specific to sub-types of the disorder rather than its symptoms, it suggests that it may be possible to construct a specific cognitive deficit profile to better diagnose the disorder.
- A strength of the cognitive explanation is that it can account for both positive and negative symptoms.
- A further strength of the cognitive explanation is that it can be combined with other explanations, such as biological ones, to give a fuller understanding of the causes and maintenance of the disorder.

# Dysfunctional thought processing

The idea of dysfunctional thought processing, where schizophrenics exhibit maladaptive ways of thinking, is an important part of the cognitive explanation of schizophrenia.

All humans use metacognition, the cognitive monitoring of one's own thought processes, which includes the ability to detect errors in cognitive processing, such as cognitive distortions. Metacognition also includes thinking about feelings and the behavioural reactions triggered by thoughts and feelings. Overall metacognition allows individuals to 'view' their own mental states and the wishes and intentions of others, allowing them to make sense of their lives and deal with their ever-changing environments. However, schizophrenics are seen as experiencing metacognitive dysfunction, resulting in them experiencing dysfunctional thought processes.

Dysfunctional thought processes are especially seen as affecting executive functioning, the higher-level cognitive processes that control and manage other cognitive and behavioural processes. Therefore dysfunctional thought processing in schizophrenics can lead to serious impairments in goal-directed behaviour, attention, memory, cognitive flexibility, self-monitoring, inhibition of inappropriate responses and physical motor control of the body.

## Research

Joshua *et al.* (2009) used the Hayling Sentence Completion Test to compare 39 schizophrenics with 40 bipolar disorder patients and 44 healthy control participants, to find that the schizophrenics had slower response times and slower suppression of inappropriate responses, indicative of impaired executive functioning. This supports the idea that dysfunctional thought processing is an important factor in the development of schizophrenia.

Evans *et al.* (1997) gave the Behavioural Assessment of the Dysexecutive Syndrome test, as well as IQ and memory tests, to 31 schizophrenics, 35 brain-injured patients and 26 healthy participants. It was found that the schizophrenic and brain-damaged patients had impaired executive functioning, with the schizophrenics showing especial impairments in memory functioning, thus illustrating the role of dysfunctional thought processing in schizophrenia.

Betall *et al.* (1991) found that schizophrenics struggled to identify words belonging to a certain category, such as birds, that they had read earlier, created themselves or had not seen before, supporting the idea that schizophrenics have meta-representation problems.

Lysaker *et al.* (2008) used the Metacognition Awareness Test and the Delis Kaplan Executive Function System test to assess the metacognitive function of 49 male schizophrenics. It was found that schizophrenic symptoms were linked to an inability to have awareness of one's thoughts and feelings and other people's needs, supporting the idea that metacognitive impairments are linked to the disorder.

Brune *et al.* (2011) reviewed 20 years of evidence to report that many symptoms of schizophrenia and the consequent impairments in social functioning result from poor metacognition, especially the ability to self-reflect and empathise with others, supporting the idea that metacognition dysfunction is an important part of schizophrenia.

### RESEARCH IN FOCUS

Lysaker *et al.* (2008) used a correlational study to assess the metacognitive function of male schizophrenics. Read the details of the study and then name the two co-variables in the study. Why could causality not be established in this type of study? In what way may the study lack external validity? If the data was of ordinal level what statistical test could be used to analyse the data? And if the data was of interval/ratio level?

### Evaluation

- The highlighting of metacognition as an important factor in the development of schizophrenia indicates that therapies for the disorder will need to concentrate on improving metacognitive abilities in sufferers in order to be effective. Indeed, therapies could be targeted at specific areas of metacognitive impairment.
- Research suggests that dysfunctional thought processing in schizophrenics occurs before the onset of the disorder and therefore is not an effect of being schizophrenic. Dysfunctional thought processing though is not necessarily a causative factor, but may instead itself be an effect of abnormal brain functioning, which in turn leads to dysfunctional thought processing.
- Garety *et al.* (2001) believe that schizophrenia is best understood by linking different explanations, both biological and psychological, with cognitive explanations, such as dysfunctional thought processing, being the vital link in the chain.
- Although dysfunctional thought processing seems linked to impairments in memory ability, research indicates that deficits occur only in specific areas of memory functioning, especially the central executive component of working memory and specifically tasks for which the visuospatial system is needed for central executive control. The phonological system seems to be less affected (see Chapter 2, 'Memory', in Book One).

### STRENGTHEN YOUR LEARNING

1. What types of dysfunctional characteristics are often shown by parents of schizophrenics?
2. Outline what is meant by i] *double bind*, ii] *expressed emotion* in relation to family dysfunction and schizophrenia.
3. Summarise what research evidence suggests about family dysfunction and schizophrenia.
4. What other evaluative points can be made about family dysfunction and schizophrenia?
5. Summarise the main features of Beck & Rector's (2005) cognitive model of schizophrenia.
6. To what extent does research evidence support Beck & Rector's model?
7. Explain how dysfunctional thought processing affects *metacognition* and *executive functioning* in schizophrenics.
8. What does research evidence suggest about dysfunctional thought processing and schizophrenia?
9. What other evaluative points can be made about dysfunctional thought processing and schizophrenia?

# ASSESSMENT CHECK

1. Noel is a young man who has had several schizophrenic episodes. Every time he seems to be recovering, leaves hospital and returns to his family he relapses within a short period of time. His family members have trouble communicating with each other properly and are constantly arguing. Both his parents are very critical and controlling of their children.

   Refer to the above scenario to explain the family dysfunction explanation of schizophrenia. **[4 marks]**

2. Give one limitation of research into biological explanations for schizophrenia that uses non-human animals. **[2 marks]**

3. Which one of the three following statements best explains the genetic explanation for schizophrenia? **[1 mark]**
   - That abnormal levels of neurotransmitters are linked to the onset of the disorder.
   - That abnormalities within specific brain areas are associated with the development of schizophrenia.
   - That schizophrenia is passed on through family members by hereditary means.

4. Explain what is meant by dysfunctional thought processing in schizophrenia. **[2 marks]**

5. Discuss the cognitive explanation for schizophrenia. **[16 marks]**

*'Never go to a doctor whose office plants have died.'*
Erma Bombeck (1979)

# Therapies for the treatment of schizophrenia

Many therapies have been developed for treating schizophrenia over the years, with varying degrees of success. Therapies can be broadly divided into biological and psychological ones, though it is often possible to combine therapies to form more effective, long-lasting treatments.

*'Drugs are not always necessary. Belief in recovery always is.'*
Norman Cousins (1991)

# 6.4 Drug therapies

The prime treatment for schizophrenia is the use of antipsychotic drugs, the first being chlorpromazine, introduced in 1952, which quickly had a major effect by enabling many people with schizophrenia to live relatively normal lives outside of mental institutions. Antipsychotics do not cure schizophrenia, but they dampen symptoms so that a degree of normal functioning can occur.

Antipsychotics can be taken in tablet form, as a syrup or by injection, and are divided into **typical antipsychotics** (first-generation) and **atypical antipsychotics** (second-generation) varieties. Atypical drugs were introduced as they were supposedly more effective than typical ones and incurred fewer side effects. However, there is much discussion as to how much these claims are true.

Symptoms such as hallucinations and feelings of agitation tend to reduce within a few days and delusions after a few weeks. After about six weeks many patients see a lot of improvement, though there are wide individual differences in levels of and types of response to taking antipsychotics. Patients often have to take several types before they find the best one for them. Some sufferers have to take a course of antipsychotics only once, while others have to take regular doses in order to prevent schizophrenic symptoms reappearing. There is also a sizeable minority of patients who do not respond to drug treatment. Antipsychotics can also be used as a combination therapy, where drugs are administered to reduce the symptoms of the disorder so that other psychological treatments, such as CBT (see page 216), can be more effective.

Typical antipsychotics, like chlorpromazine, work by arresting dopamine production through blocking the receptors in synapses that absorb dopamine, thus reducing positive symptoms of the disorder, such as auditory hallucinations and delusions. However, it is now thought that typical antipsychotics may also affect other neurotransmitter systems such as the cholinergic, alpha-adrenergic, histaminergic and serotonergic mechanisms. There are a number of side effects associated with the neurotransmitter systems that they affect, for instance their anti-cholinergic side effects include dry mouth, urinary problems, constipation and visual disturbance, while their effects on noradrenergic mechanisms lead to low

### KEY TERMS

**Drug therapy** – chemical treatment of abnormality through tablets and intravenous means

**Typical antipsychotics** – the original neuroleptic drugs created in the 1950s to treat schizophrenia

**Atypical antipsychotics** – a class of neuroleptic drugs produced later used to treat schizophrenia

**Figure 6.12** The main treatment for schizophrenia is the use of antipsychotic drugs

blood pressure, problems with sexual function and nasal congestion. Long-term use leads to 15 per cent of sufferers developing tardive dyskinesia (TD), which causes uncontrollable muscle movements, especially around the mouth. In some sufferers this condition will become permanent.

Atypical antipsychotics introduced in the 1990s, such as clozapine, work by acting on serotonin as well as dopamine production systems, affecting negative symptoms of the disorder, such as reduced emotional expression. However, it is not known specifically how they relieve symptoms and although atypical drugs incur reduced levels of TD and have fewer side effects, there are some side effects specific to taking atypical antipsychotics, such as weight gain, neuroleptic malignant syndrome (a life-threatening neurological disorder whose symptoms include high fever, sweating, unstable blood pressure, stupor and muscular rigidity), increased risk of stroke, sudden cardiac death, blood clots and diabetes. Sufferers can also develop muscle tremors similar to those experienced by Parkinson's disease sufferers.

### ON THE WEB

Listen to and watch Dr Colin Ross talk about treating schizophrenia with antipsychotic drugs, including typical and atypical versions, at **www.youtube.com**. Search for 'How do antipsychotic drugs work? How effective are medications for schizophrenia and psychosis?'.

## CONTEMPORARY RESEARCH

### A systematic review of atypical antipsychotic drugs in schizophrenia – Bagnall *et al.* (2003)

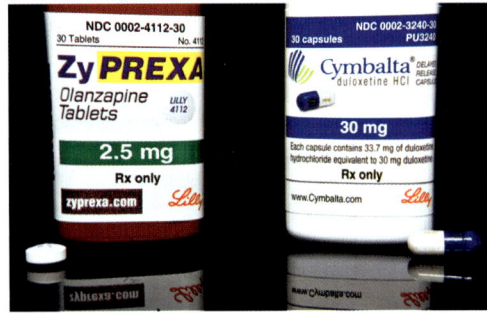

**Figure 6.13** Are atypical drugs more effective and less harmful than typical ones?

Atypical antipsychotics were introduced with claims of being more effective and less harmful than the traditional typical antipsychotics. However, these claims have been disputed. In this meta-analysis, atypical antipsychotics were compared with typical antipsychotics, with drugs of both types being individually assessed, as well as both types being more broadly compared.

### Aim

To compare the clinical effectiveness, safety and cost-effectiveness of typical and atypical antipsychotic drugs in the treatment of schizophrenia.

To assess the effectiveness of typical and atypical treatments against 'treatment-resistant' schizophrenia, as well as 'first-onset' schizophrenia.

### Procedure

Data was compiled from 171 randomly controlled trials and 52 non-randomised trials of the effectiveness of drug treatments on schizophrenia.

Data was additionally compiled from 31 economic evaluations of antipsychotic drug treatments for schizophrenia.

Data was analysed by two independent researchers to establish inter-rater reliability.

### Findings

**Effectiveness.** The atypical drugs risperidone, amisulpride, zotepine, olanzapine and clozapine were all more effective than typical drugs in reducing symptoms of schizophrenia. Quetiapine and sertindole were no more or less effective than typical antipsychotics in reducing overall symptoms of psychosis.

Clozapine was more effective than typical antipsychotic drugs in improving negative symptoms in treatment-resistant forms of schizophrenia. Zotepine also seemed to be more effective on negative symptoms.

No real differences were noted between typical and atypical antipsychotics in treating first-onset schizophrenia.

There was no difference in the effectiveness of atypical v. typical drugs for patients with concurrent substance abuse problems or co-morbid mental illnesses such as depression.

**Dropout rates.** Fewer patients taking atypical drugs left trials early than those from typical drugs groups, the exceptions being those taking ziprasidone and zotepine, which suggests that patients generally found atypical antipsychotic drugs more acceptable.

**Side effects.** All atypical antipsychotic drugs caused fewer movement disorders than typical ones.

Olanzapine, amisulpride, sertindole and risperidone caused less drowsiness than typical drugs. Other atypical drugs were no more or less sedating than typical drugs.

With autonomic effects, clozapine and sertindole increased salivation, temperature and nasal congestion, while quetiapine increased incidence of dry mouth. Olanzapine had fewer autonomic effects than typical antipsychotics, but other atypical drugs had similar amounts of effects to typical drugs.

All atypical drugs had similar levels of inducing nausea and vomiting as typical drugs, except ziprasidone, which increased such effects, and olanzapine, which lessened them.

Amisulpride, risperidone and sertindole caused more weight gain than typical drugs, but ziprasidone, zotepine, clozapine and olanzapine did not.

Typical drugs and the atypical antipsychotics amisulpride, risperidone and sertindole were associated with infertility and impotence.

The atypical drugs sertindole and clozapine were associated with sudden cardiac death.

**Cost effectiveness.** Amisulpride was the most cost-effective atypical antipsychotic drug. Olanzapine was the cheapest atypical antipsychotic drug but may be less effective than the others, as side effects were not included in the assessment. Atypical drugs are more expensive than typical ones.

### Conclusions

Atypical drugs generally seem more effective than typical drugs, though there are differences in effectiveness between individual drugs.

No one drug can be considered superior in terms of symptom reduction, side effects and cost-effectiveness.

All antipsychotics, typical and atypical varieties, have their criticisms. Different drugs suit different patients better, though this can be determined only by trial and error.

### Evaluation

- In most trials, the effect of new atypical antipsychotic drugs on negative symptoms was not assessed, which is surprising given manufacturers' claims about their effectiveness in treating these symptoms.
- Sertindole was removed as a prescription drug in 1999 due to its association with death through cardiac failure.
- Evidence for the effectiveness of the newer atypical antipsychotic drugs compared with the older typical drugs was, in general, of poor quality, based on short-term trials and difficult to generalise to all schizophrenics.

## Research

Davis *et al.* (1989) performed a meta-analysis of more than 100 studies that compared antipsychotics with placebos, finding drugs to be more effective, with over 70 per cent of sufferers treated with antipsychotics improving in condition after six weeks, while fewer than 25 per cent improved with placebos, suggesting that antipsychotics have a beneficial medical effect.

Marder (1996) reported that the atypical antipsychotic clozapine is as effective as typical antipsychotics in relieving the positive symptoms of schizophrenia, and is effective in approximately 30–61 per cent of patients who are resistant to typical antipsychotics, suggesting it to be a superior form of treatment.

Lieberman *et al.* (2005) examined the effectiveness of typical and atypical antipsychotics in treating 1,432 individuals with chronic schizophrenia, finding that 74 per cent of patients discontinued their treatment within 18 months due to intolerable side effects. Discontinuation rates and time to discontinuation were similar between typical and atypical antipsychotics, though for different reasons, with discontinuation of atypical drugs being more associated with muscular disorders, and discontinuation from atypical drugs more associated with weight gain and metabolic effects.

Schooler *et al.* (2005), comparing the effectiveness of typical and atypical antipsychotics, found both effective in treating schizophrenia, with 75 per cent of patients experiencing at least a 20 per cent reduction in symptoms. However, 55 per cent of those receiving typical antipsychotics suffered relapses, compared with only 42 per cent for typical treatment, with relapses occurring earlier in those taking typical drug treatments. Side effects were fewer with atypical antipsychotics. This implies that atypical drugs are superior.

Kahn *et al.* (2008) compared typical with atypical antipsychotics in their effectiveness of treating first-instance schizophrenia, finding that antipsychotics were effective for at least one year but that atypical drugs were not necessarily any more effective than typical ones, casting doubt on the idea that atypical drugs are superior. This was further supported by Stargardt *et al.* (2008), who used data from 3,121 patients to compare atypical and typical drugs in terms of effectiveness, finding no difference between the two drug types in terms of relapse rates, though atypical drugs were superior in treating more severe cases. This suggests that the higher costs for atypical antipsychotics were not justified in terms of them being generally more effective, again casting doubts on the claims of atypical drugs being superior.

## Evaluation

- Antipsychotics are effective, as they are relatively cheap to produce, easy to administer and have positive effects on many sufferers, allowing them to live relatively normal lives outside of mental institutions. Less than 3 per cent of people with schizophrenia in the UK live permanently in hospital.
- One problem with antipsychotics is the high relapse rate – around 40 per cent in the first year after treatment and 15 per cent in later years – generally due to patients stopping treatment because of side effects and the reduced quality of life they can bring.
- Typical antipsychotics incur side effects, such as muscle tremors. Atypical antipsychotics were introduced to reduce such problems, which they do, but they incur serious side effects of their own, some of which are fatal, such as sudden cardiac death.
- Although antipsychotics produce relatively minor side effects for most patients, for instance constipation and weight gain, some sufferers incur serious neurological symptoms that can lead to coma and death.
- There are many within the psychiatric community who see the widespread use of antipsychotics as being fuelled by the powerful influence of the drug-producing companies, which stand to make enormous profits from their use, especially the replacement of typical with atypical drugs, which bring even bigger profits (see Psychology in the real world, page 215).

## RESEARCH IN FOCUS

When testing antipsychotic drugs researchers tend to give half the participants a drug and the other half a **placebo** (a harmless sugar pill). A **double-blind technique** is also usually used, where participants and researchers do not know who is receiving the drug or the placebo.

What is the purpose of using a placebo and a double-blind technique in studies like these?

## PSYCHOLOGY IN THE REAL WORLD

Schizophrenia is a seriously debilitating mental disorder. However, serious questions exist over the use of drug therapies.

Typical antipsychotics had a major effect in allowing many schizophrenics to live relatively normal lives outside of mental institutions, but incurred serious side effects. When drug companies introduced atypical antipsychotics with claims of greater effectiveness and fewer side effects, the future looked good. But then came accusations that drug companies were more motivated by money than patient welfare.

In 2011, 3.1 million Americans were prescribed antipsychotics, generating $18.2 billion (£11.6 billion) in profits. Prescriptions for atypical antipsychotics increased by 93 per cent between 2001 and 2011, though the rate of incidence of schizophrenia and depression for which they are given remained the same. Atypical antipsychotics cost about £75 per prescription compared with only £17 for typical varieties and research has not really backed up claims that they are more effective. Although they reduce side effects associated with typical drugs, they incur serious side-effect risks of their own, which drug companies were not keen to admit to. The Johnson & Johnson pharmaceutical company was fined $2.2 billion (£1.4 billion) in the USA after allegations of 'purposely withholding findings' about antipsychotics it sold increasing risk of strokes, diabetes and being associated with breast growth in males. Accusations have also been made about research into such drugs being largely controlled by drug companies that influence which findings are published.

Drug companies are also accused of marketing new 'improved' drugs only when their patents for older drugs run out. But are such drugs improvements? Invega was approved in 2007 as an improvement on Risperdal, the drug of which it is a metabolite, but research suggests it is no more effective, even though it is costly. When patents run out, other companies can introduce cheaper generic drugs, severely eating into drug companies' profits.

And what of other drugs? Pedersen (2012) found cannabidol, an active ingredient in marijuana (which does not contain THC, an ingredient of cannabis associated with triggering schizophrenia), worked just as effectively as antipsychotics, but with far fewer side effects. However, the suspicion is that as it is much cheaper to produce it would not generate great profits, so the drug companies will not be overly keen to produce it.

**Figure 6.14** Might cannabis be a better treatment than antipsychotics for schizophrenia, but one that drug companies would not be keen to promote?

## STRENGTHEN YOUR LEARNING

1. Antipsychotic drugs do not cure schizophrenia. Explain what their actual role is in the treatment of the disorder.
2. Outline possible side effects of i) typical antipsychotics, ii) atypical antipsychotics.
3. Outline and evaluate Bagnall et al's. (2003) meta-analysis of antipsychotic drugs.
4. Summarise what research evidence suggests about the use of antipsychotic drugs to treat schizophrenia.
5. What other evaluative points can be made about treatment with antipsychotics?

# 6.5 Cognitive behavioural therapy, family therapy and token economies

**KEY TERM**

**Cognitive behavioural therapy** – treatment of abnormality that modifies thought patterns to alter behavioural and emotional states

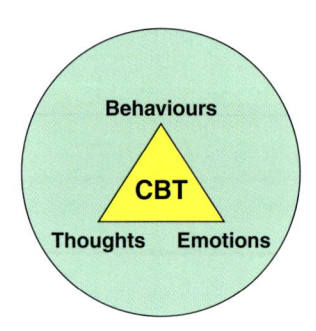

Figure 6.15 Cognitive behavioural therapy is a common psychological treatment of schizophrenia, but how effective is it?

**Cognitive behavioural therapy** (CBT) is the main psychological treatment used with schizophrenia. The idea is that beliefs, expectations and cognitive assessments of self, the environment and the nature of personal problems affect how individuals perceive themselves and others, how problems are approached, and how successful people are in coping and reaching goals. CBT thus aims to help schizophrenics by changing the maladaptive thinking and distorted perceptions seen as underpinning the disorder in order to modify hallucinations and delusional beliefs.

Antipsychotics drugs are usually given first to reduce psychotic thought processes, so that CBT can be more effective. CBT is then undertaken around once every 10 days, for about 12 sessions, to identify and alter irrational thinking. Drawings are often used to display links between sufferers' thoughts, actions and emotions. Understanding where symptoms originate from can be useful in reducing sufferers' anxiety levels.

One CBT approach is personal therapy (PT), involving detailed evaluation of problems and experiences, their triggers and consequences, and strategies being used to cope. Cognitive techniques are developed between patient and therapist, such as:

- distractions from intrusive thoughts
- challenging the meanings of intrusive thoughts
- increasing/decreasing social activity to distract from low moods
- using relaxation strategies.

PT is also used to tackle problems faced by schizophrenics discharged from hospital, taking place in small groups or as a one-to-one therapy. Patients are taught to recognise small signs of relapse, which can build up to produce cognitive distortions and unsuitable social behaviour.

Rational emotive therapy is also used to teach sufferers that emotional instability is a common feature of schizophrenia that they must live with. Patients use muscle relaxation techniques to detect gradual anger build-ups and then apply relaxation skills to control emotions.

## Research

Tarrier *et al.* (2000) found that people with schizophrenia receiving 20 sessions of PT in 10 weeks, coupled with drug therapy, followed by four booster sessions during the next year, did better than sufferers receiving drug therapy alone or supportive counselling. One third of patients receiving PT achieved a 50 per cent reduction in psychotic experiences, with 15 per cent free of all positive symptoms, compared with 15 per cent in the counselling group, with 7 per cent free of all positive symptoms. No patients in the drugs-only group were symptom-free. One year later, similar differences still existed, but at a two-year follow-up the PT group's advantage over the counselling group had vanished, though both groups still outscored the drugs-only group.

McGorry *et al.* (2002) found that after six months of treatment 36 per cent of individuals with a high risk of first-onset schizophrenia who received supportive psychotherapy had developed schizophrenia, compared with only 10 per cent who received drugs and CBT. This suggests CBT is more effective than psychotherapy in preventing first-onset schizophrenia.

Tarrier (2005) reviewed 20 controlled trials of CBT using 739 patients, finding persistent evidence of reduced symptoms, especially positive ones, lower relapse rates and a speedier recovery rate of acutely ill patients. These were short-term benefits, however, with follow-ups needed to assess CBT's long-term benefits.

Zimmerman *et al.* (2005) performed a meta-analysis of 14 studies of CBT published between 1990 and 2004 involving 1,484 patients, and found CBT significantly reduced positive symptoms and that the treatment was especially beneficial to those suffering a short-term acute schizophrenic episode. This implies that CBT is more appropriate when treating certain aspects of the disorder.

Jauhar *et al.* (2014) performed a meta-analysis of 50 studies of CBT for schizophrenia conducted over the last 20 years, finding only a small therapeutic effect on symptoms, including positive symptoms, such as delusions and hallucinations, which CBT mainly targets. Even this small effect disappeared when only studies using blind testing (where researchers are not aware which patients have received CBT) were considered. This strongly questions whether CBT should be used as a treatment for schizophrenia.

### Evaluation

- Evidence suggests that CBT plus antipsychotics is effective in treating schizophrenia and more effective than drugs or CBT alone, supporting the case for combined treatments.
- For CBT to be effective, training of CBT practitioners is essential, successful treatment being dependent on developing empathy, respect, unconditional positive regard and honesty between patient and practitioner. This was supported by Rathod *et al.* (2005) finding that non-Afro-Caribbean therapists had less success using CBT with Afro-Caribbean than white ethnic patients, as empathy between such clinicians and patients was harder to establish.
- CBT is not suitable for all patients, especially those too disorientated, agitated or paranoid to form trusting alliances with practitioners. It may be more suitable for those refusing drug treatments, though such patients are often so highly disturbed it is difficult to effectively undertake CBT.
- Blind testing, where the investigators who make the assessments do not know which group of patients received the therapy, is routinely used in trials of medical treatment but has not always been employed in studies of CBT for schizophrenia, making assessment of the treatment difficult.
- CBT has fewer side effects than antipsychotic drugs but is a more expensive treatment, with cost a key factor at a time of reduced health-care budgets.
- Trower *et al.* (2004) reported that CBT did not actually reduce the intensity of hallucinations but made them seem less of a threat by persuading sufferers that they 'outranked' the voices in their heads. This suggests that rather than treating the symptoms of schizophrenia, CBT teaches patients strategies for dealing with them.

*'When the "I" in illness is replaced with "we" it becomes wellness.'*
Anonymous

## Family therapy

**Family therapy** (also known as family-focused therapy) is a form of psychotherapy based on the idea that as family dysfunction (see page 204) can play a role in the development of schizophrenia, altering relationship and communication patterns within dysfunctional families, and especially lowering levels of expressed emotion, should help schizophrenics to recover. Therefore the treatment involves the whole family, not just the member with schizophrenia, with the family becoming the patient's support network.

### KEY TERM

**Family therapy** – treatment of schizophrenia by alteration of communication systems within families

The main aims of family therapy are:

1. Improve positive and decrease negative forms of communication.
2. Increase tolerance levels and decrease criticism levels between family members.
3. Decrease feelings of guilt and responsibility for causing the illness among family members.

**Figure 6.16** Family therapy aims to alter relationship and communication patterns to treat schizophrenia within dysfunctional families

Therapists meet regularly with the patient and family members, who are encouraged to talk openly about the patient's symptoms, behaviour and progress with their treatment and how the patient's illness affects them. Family members are also taught to support each other and be caregivers, with each person given a specific role in the rehabilitation of the patient. There is an overall emphasis on 'openness', with no details remaining confidential, though boundaries of what is and is not acceptable are drawn up in advance, as part of a document of informed consent.

Family therapy, similarly to CBT, is given for a set amount of time, usually between nine months and a year, with a focus on reducing symptoms and allowing family members to develop skills that can be continued after the therapy has ended.

### Research into family therapy

Leff *et al.* (1985) compared family therapy with routine outpatient care for schizophrenics with families high in expressed emotion, finding in the first nine months of treatment 50 per cent of those receiving routine care relapsed, compared with 8 per cent of those receiving family therapy. This rose after two years to 75 per cent relapsing who received routine care compared with 50 per cent for the family therapy patients. This suggests family therapy is a comparatively effective theory, especially in the short term.

Xiong *et al.* (1994) randomly allocated 63 Chinese schizophrenics to either standard drug care or standard drug care plus family therapy, finding that after one year 61 per cent of the standard care patients had relapsed (36 per cent being rehospitalised) compared with 33 per cent of the standard care plus family therapy patients (12 per cent of whom were rehospitalised). This suggests family therapy forms an effective combined treatment when twinned with antipsychotics.

Pilling *et al.* (2002) performed a meta-analysis of several forms of psychological treatment for schizophrenia, including 18 studies of family therapy with 1,467 patients, finding family therapy had the smallest number of patients who relapsed and the lowest number of hospital readmissions, as well as the highest number of patients who complied with their medication regime, though CBT had the best success rate with treatment-resistant forms of schizophrenia. This suggests family therapy is effective, especially for those in contact with their families.

McFarlane *et al.* (2003) reviewed available evidence to find that family therapy results in reduced relapse rates, symptom reduction in patients and improved relationships among family members, which leads to increased well-being for patients. This suggests that family therapy is an effective treatment, with an indication that better family relationships are the key element.

### Evaluation

- With the emphasis on 'openness' there can be an issue with family members being reluctant to share sensitive information, as it may cause or reopen family tensions. Some family members may also be reluctant to talk about, or even admit, their problems, lowering the effectiveness of the treatment.
- Family therapy can be useful for patients who lack insight into their illness or cannot speak coherently about it, as family members may be able to assist here. Family members have lots of useful information and insight into a patient's behaviour and moods and are often able to speak for them.
- As well as decreasing relapse rates and lowering the need for hospitalisation, family therapy can educate family members to help manage a patient's medication regime, decreasing the need for clinicians to do this, thus making the treatment more cost effective.
- Younger patients who still live at home with their families especially may be in a position to benefit from family therapy.
- Although a combination of drug and family therapy treatments is desirable, due to cost restraints it is often not possible to offer patients such treatments.
- The Schizophrenia Commission (2012) estimates that family therapy is cheaper than standard care by £1,004 a patient over three years, suggesting it is a relatively cost-effective treatment.

### YOU ARE THE RESEARCHER

Design a study to compare the relative effectiveness of CBT and family therapy. What kind of study would this be? What criteria would you assess these therapies on and how would you measure them?

How would participants be assigned to conditions and what steps could be taken to ensure researcher bias does not occur? Create an appropriate table and graph to plot your results and state what statistical test would be used to analyse the data. Give three reasons for your choice of test.

**KEY TERM**

**Token economies** – a method of behaviour modification that reinforces target behaviours by awarding tokens that can be exchanged for material goods

Figure 6.17 Token economies involve earning tokens for demonstrating desired behaviours, which can later be exchanged for goods or privileges

# Token economies

**Token economies** are a behaviourist therapeutic approach to the management of schizophrenia, where tokens are awarded for demonstrations of desired behavioural change. Introduced in the 1970s the technique is mainly used with long-term hospitalised patients to enable them to leave hospital and live relatively independently within the community. Token economies are particularly aimed at changing negative symptoms of schizophrenia, such as low motivation, poor attention and social withdrawal.

The technique uses operant conditioning principles, where patients receive reinforcements in the form of tokens immediately after producing a desired behaviour. The tokens can then later be exchanged for goods or privileges. Desired behaviours can be things like examples of self-care, adherence to medication regime and social interaction.

## Research

Ayllon & Azrin (1968) found token economies a successful technique when used with female schizophrenic patients hospitalised for an average of 16 years. Rewarded with tokens that could be exchanged for viewing a film or visiting the canteen for behaviours such as brushing their hair and making their beds, the average number of daily chores completed rose from 5 to 42, illustrating the success of token economy in getting patients to take more responsibility for themselves.

McMonagle & Sultana (2000) conducted a meta-analysis of token economy programmes involving 110 schizophrenics, finding slight evidence for improved mental state, especially with negative symptoms. This gives a degree of support to the treatment.

Dickerson et al. (2005) reviewed 13 studies of token economy, finding the technique generally useful in increasing the adaptive behaviour of patients, which implies it to be an effective treatment. Token economy worked best in combination with psychosocial and drug therapies, though the specific benefits of the technique when used as a combination treatment were not identified, suggesting an area for future research.

Silverstein et al. (2009) found that schizophrenics living in the community often have trouble performing jobs where they are paid on a long-term basis, such as monthly, as they have difficulty engaging in events to obtain distant rewards, but engage quite readily in situations using token economies where they are rewarded hourly or daily. This suggests that schizophrenics need to be paid on a more short-term basis when in employment.

### Evaluation

- Token economies work best in unison with antipsychotic drugs and other personalised psychotherapeutic treatments. This should therefore not be seen as a treatment for schizophrenia in itself.
- A negative effect of long-term hospitalisation for schizophrenics is institutionalisation, where patients lack motivation and become apathetic, attracting the contempt of nursing staff. So one unforeseen advantage of token economies is patients becoming more independent and active, which has the knock-on effect of nurses' increased regard

- for the patients, leading to the patients becoming even more motivated and developing positive self-regard.
- Another unforeseen advantage of token economies is that their use facilitates a safer and more stable therapeutic environment. Staff and patient injuries reduce, thus decreasing staff absenteeism and emergency incident levels.
- The problem with token economies is desirable behaviour becomes dependent on being reinforced; upon release in the community, reinforcements cease, leading to high re-admittance rates.
- A strength of token economies is that they can be tailored to meet the individual requirements of different patients, as the technique uses the same principles but to target different behaviours. This means that the technique has flexibility, allowing it to be used in a variety of settings.
- Token economies are not favoured by all clinicians, due to perceptions that participation in them is humiliating and that their benefits do not generalise to real-life settings.

### STRENGTHEN YOUR LEARNING

1. Explain how i] *personal therapy*, ii] *rational emotive therapy* are used to treat schizophrenia.
2. What does research evidence suggest about the effectiveness of CBT as a treatment for schizophrenia?
3. What other evaluative points can be made about CBT as a treatment for schizophrenia?
4. For family therapy, state i] its main aims, ii] how it is applied.
5. What does research evidence suggest about the effectiveness of family therapy as a treatment for schizophrenia?
6. What other evaluative points can be made about family therapy as a treatment for schizophrenia?
7. What are the main aims of token economies in managing schizophrenia?
8. Use research evidence and other evaluative points to summarise the strengths and weaknesses of token economies in the management of schizophrenia.

# 6.6 The importance of the interactionist approach in explaining and treating schizophrenia

## Interactionist explanations

There are many explanations and treatments for schizophrenia, both biological and psychological, but rather than trying to assess which is the 'correct' explanation and which is the 'best' treatment, it is probably better to perceive

### KEY TERMS

**Interactionist approach** – the idea that schizophrenia results from a combination of psychological, biological and social factors

**Diathesis-stress model** – the idea that individuals have varying genetic potentials for schizophrenia that combine with the degree of environmental stressors in their lives to form their actual amount of vulnerability to the disorder

**Figure 6.18** The flu theory of schizophrenia perceives the disorder as occurring due to an interaction of biological and environmental factors

schizophrenia as developing through several interacting factors, and to view combinations of different therapies as the best form of treatment.

The **interactionist approach** encompasses the **diathesis-stress model**, where schizophrenia is perceived as resulting from a combination of biological and environmental factors. A schizophrenic episode is seen as being triggered or worsened when environmental stressors (stress) combine with a biological diathesis (vulnerability).

As previously outlined, research indicates schizophrenia has a biological component, with several genes identified that seem to increase vulnerability to developing the disorder (see genetic explanation, page 198). It also seems likely that genetic factors are linked to faulty dopaminergic systems in those with schizophrenia and to abnormal functioning of other neurotransmitters in schizophrenics. However, genes on their own do not cause the disorder, but instead increase the likelihood that environmental stressors can trigger off a schizophrenic episode. Interestingly, research seems to indicate that neural correlates of schizophrenia are an effect of being schizophrenic, rather than being due to genetic influences (see Boos *et al.* (2012), page 201).

Psychological triggers for schizophrenia can be such things as family dysfunction, substance abuse, critical life events, etc. and those most genetically at risk of developing the disorder will be most vulnerable to such triggers. Cognitive deficits and dysfunctional thought processing are again seen as being effects of schizophrenia rather than being causes or triggers of the disorder.

## Research

Walker (1997) reported that schizophrenics have higher levels of cortisol than non-sufferers and that cortisol levels are related to severity of symptoms, with stress-related increases in cortisol levels heightening genetic-influenced abnormalities in dopamine transmission that underpin vulnerability to schizophrenia, triggering the onset of the disorder. This illustrates the interaction of biological and environmental factors in the development of schizophrenia in line with the diathesis-stress model.

Murray (1996) reported that children who were born after flu epidemics where their mothers had contracted the disease while pregnant, especially in the second trimester (pregnancy months 4–6), had an 88 per cent increased chance of developing schizophrenia than children born in the same time period whose mothers had not contracted flu. Exposure to flu during the second trimester is suspected of causing defects in neural development, which leads to increased vulnerability to schizophrenia due to brain damage, which has a knock-on effect on dopamine functioning. This again illustrates how schizophrenia could result from an interaction of factors.

Cannon *et al.* (2002) reviewed available evidence, to find a positive correlation between birth complications and a later vulnerability to developing schizophrenia, with some indication of damage to hormone and neurotransmitter systems, as well as the immune system. This again supports an interactionist explanation of schizophrenia, where biological vulnerabilities interact with later stressors to trigger the disorder.

Barlow & Durand (2009) reported that a family history of schizophrenia, indicating a genetic link, coupled with being part of a dysfunctional stressor elevated the risk of developing schizophrenia, supporting the diathesis-stress model, with the diathesis being the genetic tendency and the stress being the dysfunctional family.

### Evaluation

- To counter the criticism that elevated cortisol levels may be an effect rather than a precipitating factor of schizophrenia, Walker (1997) reports that cortisol levels are higher immediately before onset of schizophrenia rather than during recovery, which suggests elevated cortisol levels trigger schizophrenia rather than being a consequence of it.
- Stressors that may contribute to a risk of developing schizophrenia include biological, environmental, psychological and social factors. However, it is not known precisely how these risks contribute to the diathesis-stress interaction for any one person because specific causes for schizophrenia may differ between individuals.
- The differential susceptibility hypothesis extends the diathesis-stress model to include positive as well as negative environments. An individual person may have a biological vulnerability that combined with a stressor leads to schizophrenia. However, the same individual if exposed to a positive environment, such as a loving family background, could have better outcomes that reduce the chances of them becoming schizophrenic.
- Genes cannot determine outcomes on their own; they need a particular environment in which to express themselves. Therefore genes that predispose someone to have increased vulnerability to schizophrenia cannot on their own cause the disorder; instead they need particular stressors to be present to trigger the potential of the genes to bring about the disorder, in line with the diathesis-stress model.

## Interactionist treatments

Researchers assess the relative efficiency of different treatments for schizophrenia by comparing treatments. Although effectiveness of treatments is dependent upon factors such as cost, relapse rates, degree of side effects, etc., as well as symptom reduction, it is noticeable that research indicates combination treatments, where more than one treatment is administered simultaneously to patients, are generally most effective. Which particular combination of treatments is best though is affected by each patient's individual circumstances and needs – for example, family therapy will only really suit schizophrenics who have problems with dysfunctional family relationships and who have a great deal of contact and interaction with their families. Generally, treatment with antipsychotics is given first to reduce symptoms, so that psychological treatments will then have greater effect, though antipsychotics will generally still be given while these treatments are administered.

### RESEARCH IN FOCUS

Explain how research which produces therapies and treatments for schizophrenia can have implications for the economy. Select two specific research studies of therapies and treatments for schizophrenia and explain the aspects of them that suggest positive implications for the economy.

## Research

Hogarty *et al.* (1986) assessed relapse rates in 103 schizophrenics from high expressed emotion families receiving various treatments, finding first-year relapse rates of 19 per cent for family therapy plus drugs, 20 per cent for social support therapy plus drugs, 41 per cent for drug treatment alone and 0 per cent for family therapy, plus social support and drug therapies. This supports the idea of combining treatments to increase their effectiveness. However, a follow-up study suggested the combined treatment only delayed relapse rather than prevented it.

Guo *et al.* (2010) reported that patients in the early stages of schizophrenia who receive a combination of antipsychotics and a psychological therapy have improved insight, quality of life and social functioning and are therefore less likely to discontinue treatment or relapse than those taking antipsychotics alone, illustrating the value of a combined treatment.

Sudak (2011) reports that antipsychotic drug medication combined with CBT strengthens adherence to drug treatment, as the CBT gives the patient rational insight into the benefits of adhering to their drug treatment, increasing their chances of improvement. This again illustrates a benefit of combining treatments.

Morrison & Turkington (2014) reported that drug treatment plus CBT produced better rates of symptom reduction and relapse than drug treatment or CBT alone, demonstrating the effectiveness of an interaction of treatments.

### Evaluation

- A combination of behavioural and cognitive therapies is often effective as cognitive therapies address disordered thinking, allowing behavioural therapies to then be effective in teaching functional social skills and when to apply them in real-life situations. Without the cognitive restructuring patients are too disordered for behavioural therapies to be of any use.
- Although combining therapies increases the cost of treatment, the greater effectiveness of treatment can make combination therapies more cost effective in the long term.
- As schizophrenia often has both biological and psychological components, combined treatments are often desirable, where biological treatments such as drugs address the biological elements and psychotherapeutic treatments address the psychological elements.
- Combination treatments can have a downside, too – patients receiving CBT sometimes interpret the side effects of simultaneous drug treatment in a delusional manner, increasing their mistrust and resistance to further treatment.

### STRENGTHEN YOUR LEARNING

1. Outline how the *diathesis-stress model* explains the development of schizophrenia.
2. Summarise what research evidence suggests about an interactionist approach (including the diathesis-stress model) to explaining schizophrenia.
3. What other evaluative points can be made about an interactionist approach to explaining schizophrenia?
4. To what extent does research evidence suggest that combination treatments for schizophrenia are effective?
5. What other evaluative points can be made about the use of combination treatments?

# ASSESSMENT CHECK

1. One problem when conducting research to assess the effectiveness of antipsychotic drugs is that of demand characteristics.

    a) Explain what is meant by demand characteristics. **[2 marks]**

    b) Explain how a single blind procedure can be used to reduce the risk of demand characteristics. **[2 marks]**

2. Sally's schizophrenia has been so severe that she has been hospitalised for a considerable time and there have been problems in getting Sally to interact with staff and other patients and to take her medication regularly. She also does little to take care of herself, has low motivation and cannot pay attention to anything for very long.

    With reference to the scenario above, explain how the technique of token economy could be used to improve Sally's behaviour. **[4 marks]**

3. In the statements below referring to treatments for schizophrenia, place a letter 'C' next to the statement that relates to cognitive behavioural therapy and a letter 'F' next to the statement that relates to family therapy. There will be one statement left over. **[2 marks]**

    - A therapy that acts upon serotonin as well as dopamine production systems to reduce negative symptoms of the disorder ☐
    - A therapy that changes maladaptive thinking and distorted perceptions in order to modify hallucinations and delusional beliefs ☐
    - A therapy that improves positive and negative forms of communication and reduces levels of expressed emotion ☐

4. Outline one difference between typical and atypical antipsychotic drugs for the treatment of schizophrenia. **[2 marks]**

5. Discuss the importance of an interactionist approach in explaining and treating schizophrenia. **[16 marks]**

| | **SUMMARY** |
|---|---|
| The classification of schizophrenia | • Schizophrenia is classified in terms of its symptoms, both positive ones, such as hallucinations and delusions, and negative ones, such as speech poverty and avolition. |
| | • Schizophrenia is diagnosed in terms of its symptoms by reference to classification systems such as ICD-10 and DSM-5. |
| | • Reliability of diagnosis concerns whether symptoms are measured in a consistent way, while validity of diagnosis concerns whether symptoms are measured in an accurate way. |
| | • Co-morbidity involves additional disorders or diseases simultaneously occurring with schizophrenia. |
| | • Culture bias concerns the tendency to over-diagnose members of other cultures as suffering from schizophrenia and to hospitalise them more readily than white patients. |
| | • Gender bias concerns the tendency for schizophrenic diagnostic criteria to be applied differently to males and females and for there to be gender differences in the classification of the disorder. |
| Biological explanations of schizophrenia | • Biological explanations include the genetic explanation, which stresses the heritability of the disorder, the dopamine hypothesis, which sees the development of schizophrenia as related to abnormal levels of dopamine, and neural correlates, which sees the development of schizophrenia as related to structural and functional brain abnormalities. |
| Psychological explanations of schizophrenia | • Psychological explanations include family dysfunction, which sees dysfunctional family relationships and patterns of communication as related to the development of schizophrenia, and cognitive explanations, which see the development of schizophrenia as related to maladaptive thought processes, including dysfunctional thought processing, which sees the development of schizophrenia as related to abnormal ways of thinking. |
| Drug therapies | • Drug therapies include the typical first-generation antipsychotics and atypical second-generation antipsychotics. |
| Cognitive behavioural therapy, family therapy and token economies | • Cognitive behavioural therapy treats schizophrenia by attempting to modify thought patterns in order to alter behavioural and emotional states. |
| | • Family therapy treats schizophrenia by attempting to alter communication systems within families. |
| | • Token economies attempt to modify schizophrenics' behaviour by reinforcing target behaviours through awarding tokens exchangeable for material goods or rewards. |
| The interactionist approach in explaining and treating schizophrenia | • The interactionist approach to explaining schizophrenia sees schizophrenia as resulting from a combination of psychological, biological and social factors and as best handled by combining treatments. |
| | • The diathesis-stress model sees biological tendencies to be schizophrenic combining with environmental triggers to determine an individual's level of vulnerability to the disorder. |

# 7 Eating behaviour

## Introduction

Eating is necessary to stay alive, but eating behaviour involves several areas of psychological interest, with an emphasis on biological and psychological factors concerning normal eating behaviour and the development and maintenance of eating disorders.

Specific focus will be upon:

1. Explanations for food preferences
2. Neural and hormonal mechanisms involved in the control of eating behaviour
3. Biological explanations for anorexia nervosa
4. Psychological explanations for anorexia nervosa
5. Biological explanations for obesity
6. Psychological explanations for obesity.

## Understanding the specification

- The specification requires both the evolutionary explanation (including reference to neophobia and taste aversion) and the learning explanation (including social and cultural influences) of food preferences to be studied.
- Neural and hormonal mechanisms involved in the control of eating behaviour must also be covered, including the role of the hypothalamus, ghrelin and leptin.
- There is a requirement to have studied biological explanations of anorexia nervosa, which must include genetic and neural explanations.
- Psychological explanations of anorexia nervosa should focus on three areas: 1) family systems (including enmeshment, autonomy and control); 2) social learning theory (including modelling, reinforcement and media); 3) cognitive theory (including distortions and irrational beliefs).
- When studying biological explanations for obesity students need to include genetic and neural explanations, as these are specifically named.
- When studying psychological explanations for obesity students need to include restraint theory, disinhibition and the boundary model, as well as explanations for the success and failure of dieting, as again these are specifically listed.

These are the basic requirements of the specification. However, other relevant material is included to provide depth and detail to your understanding.

> 'A store of grain, Oh king is the best of treasures. A gem put in your mouth will not support life.'
> The Hitopadesha (1373)

# IN THE NEWS

## The Psychological Enquirer

**Figure 7.1** Elephants can experience salt hunger

Sixty miles north of Lake Victoria in Kenya sits Mount Elgon, home to a special herd of elephants. Animals often travel long distances to 'salt licks', salt-rich pieces of ground, to satisfy their need for salt, but on Mount Elgon the only source of salt is very remote and the elephants make an incredible journey to get access to it (see Figure 7.1). For deep inside the volcanic mountain are natural caves rich in salt-encrusted rocks and the elephants have learned to enter the pitch-black caves in a long line. Once inside the caves the elephants excavate the salt with their tusks, hacking off chunks that they devour with gusto.

The elephants have mined salt here for centuries, enlarging the caves as time passes. Other animals, such as hyenas and buffalo, have also learned to enter the caves to devour the salt crumbs left by the elephants. Unfortunately, poachers attack the elephants at the caves' entrance, killing them for their ivory. A conservation project is now in place to protect this remarkable group of animals.

Many herbivores (plant eaters) experience 'salt hunger', as their diet does not contain enough salt, a foodstuff essential for maintaining neural and muscular activity, therefore they seek out other means of gaining salt, as the elephants of Mount Elgon do. The desire for salt can be seen as an evolved food preference, due to salt's adaptive (survival) value – a preference that is genetically transmitted from one generation to another.

**ON THE WEB**

Videos of the salt-mining elephants can be seen at **www.youtube.com**. Search for 'Fooled by nature – Elephant salt miners'.

A two-part BBC documentary about the elephants can be seen at **www.youtube.com**. Search for 'BBC: The need for salt – Elephant Cave' and for part two 'BBC: Nocturnal highway – Elephant Cave'.

## 7.1 Explanations for food preferences

### The evolutionary explanation

Evolutionary theory sees humans as having genetic variability between individuals. Specific genes are handed down to individuals by their parents and if a particular individual's genes suit the environmental conditions they find themselves in, then they have an advantage, as they will be more able to exploit their environment and thus survive to reproduce themselves into the next generation. By this process of natural selection, such genes become more widespread throughout the population. Therefore individuals with genetic variability that help locate sufficient amounts of safe, nutritious foods would have a selective advantage, allowing them to survive and pass on the advantageous genes to their children. This, according to evolutionary theory, is how human eating behaviours were shaped.

Most human evolution is believed to have occurred during the **Pleistocene era**, between 10,000 and 2 million years ago, a period also known as the Environment of Evolutionary Adaptiveness (EEA). The Pleistocene era was a time of nomadic hunter-gatherers who lived in small, closely related groups. Risk of death was high – humans faced a daily battle to find enough food to survive. Many foodstuffs were available only periodically and required much skill to obtain. Therefore it made sense to evolve preferences for certain foods, such as energy-rich ones, the consumption of which increased survival chances. It also made sense to evolve methods of detecting and avoiding poisonous foods. Individuals with preferences for such foods would be more able to survive to sexual maturity, reproduce and pass on their **food preferences** to their offspring. Over many generations these preferences became more widespread through the population and are still apparent today. It also made sense from a survival point of view to overeat these foods when they were available, with excess energy being stored as fat to be used for times when such foodstuffs were not available.

> *'I want to have a good body, but not as much as I want dessert.'*
> Jason Love (2008)

> **KEY TERMS**
>
> **Pleistocene era** (also known as the Environment of Evolutionary Adaptiveness or **EEA**) – time era when food preferences are seen as having evolved
>
> **Food preferences** – bias towards the consumption of certain foodstuffs

## Sweet taste preference

Evolutionary theory sees a preference for sweet-tasting foods becoming widespread, as sweetness is associated with high-energy, non-poisonous content and therefore sweet foods aid survival. This was acted upon by natural selection to become a universal food preference.

### Research

Desor *et al.* (1973) and Steiner (1977) using choice preferences and facial expressions found neonates (new-born babies) prefer sweet foods to bitter ones, implying the preference is innate.

Meiselman (1977) found people of all ages prefer sweet foods to other tastes. This was supported by Capaldi *et al.* (1989), who found this was also true for other species such as horses, bears and ants.

Logue (1991) found the human tongue has specific receptors for detecting sweetness. This is not the case with other tastes, which are detected by non-specific receptors, and there are also more receptors for detecting sweetness than other tastes, implying sweet tastes are more important and that the preference has a genetic component shaped by evolution.

Zhao *et al.* (2008) found the genetic component of sweetness preference is due to two genes, T1r2 and T1r3, which code for proteins that combine to form the sweetness taste receptor. T1r3 is also activated in the presence of high-sugar concentrations, but not by low concentrations of artificial sweeteners. This may explain why artificial sweeteners are not perceived as being as sweet as sugar. A genetic component to sweetness preference implies that human variation in sweetness preference is explained by variability within the T1r2 and T1r3 genes instead of culture differences, lending support to the **evolutionary explanation** of food preferences.

> **KEY TERM**
>
> **Evolutionary explanation** – that certain foods are preferable as they have an adaptive survival value

Figure 7.2 There is a preference for sweet foods as they are associated with high-energy, non-poisonous content

> **Evaluation**
> - The idea of an evolutionarily determined preference for sweet tastes has much research support, including cross-cultural evidence. For example, Bell (1973) reported that Inuit people, who had never tasted sweet foodstuffs before, accepted them on their first presentation. However, Stefansson (1960) reported that Copper Eskimos were disgusted at their first taste of sugar, going against the notion of sweetness being universally preferred.
> - A fondness for sweetness is found throughout the animal kingdom, indeed animals go to great trouble to obtain sweet-tasting foods. Bears endure stinging by bees to eat the honey inside their hives, lending support to sweetness being an evolutionary preference.
> - Neonate studies suggest an innate sweetness preference, but interpreting neonates' facial expressions is subjective and may not produce reliable results.
> - Read & McDaniel (2008) point out that genes alone are not thought to be responsible for the variations in sweetness reception in humans. The protein hormone leptin has an inhibitory effect on taste reception cells, reducing the amount of sweetness signals transmitted to the brain. During times of food scarcity, less leptin is produced, making sweet foods appear less attractive.

*'Some seek not gold, but there lives not a man who does not need salt.'*
Cassiodorus (519AD)

## Salty taste preferences

Salt is necessary for maintaining neural and muscular activity and water balance. Salt contains sodium chloride, essential for hydration, though too much salt is harmful. The concentration of salt in the blood must remain at a specific level and regularly needs topping up, as small amounts are lost through sweat and the action of the kidneys. Salt deprivation causes salt cravings and animals travel huge distances to find deposits of salt (see In the news, page 228). For early humans, salt was a commodity exchanged for other goods, with huge industries arising out of salt mining and trading.

### Research

Denton (1982) found an innate preference for salt in many animal species, suggesting the preference has a survival value and is evolutionarily determined.

Beauchamp (1987) found that people with sodium deficiency (salt starved) have an innate response to ingest salt and find it more tasty, less horrible in high concentrations and eat more of it than related family members. This appears to be an evolutionary determined mechanism that helps to maintain sodium levels in the body, which suggests it has a high adaptive survival value.

Dudley et al. (2008) found that ants in inland areas in salt-poor environments prefer salty solutions to sugary ones, seemingly an adaptive response to maintain their evolutionary fitness. This was supported by the fact that carnivorous ants did not have such a preference, as they get ample salt supplies from prey they consume.

### Evaluation

- Humans are not born with an apparent innate preference for salt and cannot taste salt very well until four months old, when they show a preference for salty foods. At two years of age children reject foods that do not contain an expected amount of saltiness and this preference for salt is universal and not restricted to cultural experiences. This suggests that salt preference is maturational (developed genetically), with taste buds developing to be able to detect salt in time for weaning.
- There are individual differences in salt preference, which is puzzling, as evolution would predict a standard universal preference. Zinner (2002) found 23 per cent of neonates had a salt preference and had higher blood pressure than other babies and at least one grandparent with hypertension (indicative of high salt consumption). This suggests a genetic basis to individual differences in salt preferences.
- Deer in the Scottish Highlands satisfy salt cravings in winter by licking salt from gritted roads (see Figure 7.3), even though 7,000 are killed by cars each year. Other animals such as tigers do not seek salt licks as they gain sufficient salt from their kills.

**Figure 7.3** Deer lick salt off Scottish roads in winter to satisfy their salt cravings

#### RESEARCH IN FOCUS

The best way to test salt preferences in infants is to give them ever increasing amounts, then assess facial expressions. Explain why from an ethical viewpoint it is not possible to do this, with infants instead being given only small doses upon their tongues. Also, what problems are there in evaluating a preference for salt by assessing infants' facial expressions?

#### PSYCHOLOGY IN THE REAL WORLD

Although salt preference has an adaptive survival value, food companies exploit this evolutionary inheritance by producing over-salty food, as they know people will buy and overeat it, increasing the food companies' profits. 75 per cent of salt ingested is salt that manufacturers add to food. Americans consume around 4,000 milligrams of sodium per day, twice the recommended amount, which leads to serious long-term health implications, such as heart disease and strokes.

**Figure 7.4** Food manufacturers exploit our preference for salt

## Bitter and sour tastes

An ability to detect and reject bitter and sour tastes makes evolutionary sense as such tastes indicate the presence of poisons. Plants produce toxins to discourage being eaten and therefore it is evolutionarily beneficial to develop an ability to dislike bitter and sour tastes. Herbivorous animals eat plants only and have evolved high tolerance levels to the toxins contained within such foodstuffs, by having livers that can break down and neutralise poisonous compounds.

Humans have an innate ability to detect bitter tastes, possessing around 30 genes that code for bitter taste receptors, and as each receptor is able to interact with several compounds, this means humans can detect a wide variety of bitter-tasting substances. Children are especially sensitive to bitter tastes, making evolutionary sense, as young children have not had sufficient environmental experiences to develop learned and culturally acquired taste preferences.

## Research

Liem & Mennella (2003) investigated children's and adults' preferences for sour tastes using five- to nine-year-old children and their mothers. 35 per cent of the children, compared with hardly any adults, had a preference for extreme sour tastes, indicating sour taste preferences are heightened during childhood because children are less food neophobic and more willing to try new foods. They also eat a greater variety of fruits. The results suggest sour taste preferences indicate a greater interest in trying new foods, which would have a selective advantage.

Go *et al.* (2005) looked at the prevalence of the bitter taste receptor genes T2R in humans and 12 other primate species to test for an evolutionary ability to detect bitter tastes. The results showed humans have accumulated more pseudogenes (dead genes) than other primates, indicating that humans' bitter-tasting capabilities have deteriorated more rapidly. T2R molecules play a key role in the avoidance of bitter, toxic substances, so the modification of the T2R gene may reflect different responses to changes in the environment resulting from species-specific food preferences during evolution. Perhaps due to environmental changes, natural selection is acting to reduce humans' ability to detect bitter tastes.

Merrit *et al.* (2008) tested human ability to detect bitter tastes by using a bitter, synthetic compound called phenylthiocarbamide (PTC) and found that people with a PTC taster gene can taste a wider range of toxic, bitter compounds, giving them an evolutionary survival advantage. Since individuals have two copies of all their genes, combinations of the bitter taste gene variants determine whether someone finds PTC intensely bitter, somewhat bitter, or without taste at all.

**Figure 7.5** Children often do not like bitter vegetables, as bitter tastes can indicate toxins

### Evaluation

- Many medicines are naturally bitter tasting and thus revolting to children, who are especially sensitive to such tastes. Children given such medicines vomit them back up as their bodies reject the poison they believe they have eaten. Therefore many children's medicines are sweetened so they can be swallowed. This suggests there is an evolutionary ability to detect, and reject, bitter-tasting compounds.
- If the ability to taste bitter compounds brings a selective advantage, then non-PTC tasters should have died out. Although PTC tasters are found worldwide, the ratio is roughly 75:25 between PTC tasters and non-tasters. It is thought non-PTC tasters may possibly have the ability to taste another bitter compound.
- The fact that there are only two taste receptors for sweet tastes but 27 for bitter tastes suggests an evolutionarily determined need to discriminate between sweet-tasting, energy-rich foods and bitter-tasting toxic foods. This implies the need to avoid poisonous foods is more important to survival than finding edible foods, i.e. being hungry is preferable to being dead.
- It makes evolutionary sense for humans to have different levels of bitter/sour food preferences. As bitter/sour tastes are indicative of toxins, most humans will have evolved the ability to detect and reject such tastes. However, it is also beneficial to have some humans who do not have such neophobic reluctances, so that new foodstuffs can be tested and adopted by the general population if proven to be safe and nutritious.

> *'Meat is murder.'*
> Morrissey (1985)

# Meat eating

Humans do not have an innate tendency to eat meat. It is introduced into children's diets at a relatively late stage of development and many children are reluctant to eat it. Children from cultures that practise vegetarianism do not suffer ill-health effects due to lack of meat, nor do they exhibit a later preference for meat.

Humans are omnivores, capable of digesting both plants and flesh. Some meat eating occurs among other primates, like chimpanzees, while others, like gorillas, are vegetarians. The evidence for when and how meat eating in humans occurred is sketchy and leads to much debate, due to theoretical links to the development of intelligence. Evidence from prehistoric sites suggests meat eating occurred 1.5 million years ago and the use of fires to cook meat probably led to its consumption becoming more widespread, and safer, and by smoking meat it could be preserved for later use. Through natural selection, the tendency towards eating meat would have seen an emerging predominance of humans more able to digest meat and have resistance to harmful pathogens contained within it.

The advantages of meat were derived from it being rich in fat and thus high in energy, and as it was available all year round it had an advantage over seasonal plant foods. Some argue meat eating led directly to advances in intelligence through providing energy to allow brain growth, while others see it as having a more indirect effect, due to the development of intelligence for hunting skills and inter-group living. The disadvantages of meat eating are the dangers associated with hunting it, the toxins that can be contained within it and the dangers of transmissible diseases across species. There is a popular viewpoint that the HIV virus was transmitted to humans from monkeys through the consumption of 'bush meat' (eating monkey meat).

## Research

Dunn (2012) reports that in common with other primates, humans evolved to eat plants that were abundant in the EEA and that human dental structures, digestive systems and other physiological traits are more similar to herbivores than carnivores. This suggests consuming plants is more natural for human bodies and that humans do not have an innate preference for meat.

Goudsblom (1992) found archaeological evidence that controlled fires allowed greater meat eating, as cooking made meat more edible and smoking meat preserved it for later eating.

Foley & Lee (1991) compared primate feeding strategies with brain size, finding evidence that meat eating led directly to larger, more complex brains, suggesting meat eating was evolutionarily favoured.

Finch & Standford (2004) believe humans adapted to eat diverse foods, including meat, as it allowed exploitation of new environments, especially harsh ones devoid of abundant plant foods, suggesting an adaptive advantage to meat eating.

**ON THE WEB**

Additional material on evolutionary food preferences, including why some Africans have less aversion to bitter tastes (clue: malaria), can be found at **www.youtube.com**. Search for 'Evolution of food preferences – Chad Johnson'.

> **Evaluation**
> - Kendrick (1982) studied cultural groups noted for longevity, finding a common factor was their vegetarianism, which suggests there is a price to pay for meat eating: that of having a shorter life span.
> - Meat eating may have become more common when plants became too scarce to sustain life on their own. This is supported by the fact that meat, unlike other human foodstuffs, is not naturally edible. Dunn (1990) points out that real carnivores eat meat raw, guts and all, and it is only humans who have to cook it and smear it in spices and sauces to make it palatable.
> - The American Academy of Paediatrics (1998) reports that neonates can ingest only one food type, milk, with evidence for an innate preference for sweet tastes and distaste for bitter tastes. However, meat has to be introduced into youngsters' diets, suggesting there is no evolutionarily determined preference for meat eating.
> - The fact that meat eating can be dangerous, but has been adopted by most cultures, suggests the benefits of consuming meat override the disadvantages. This suggests the tendency was shaped by evolutionary forces, due to its survival value.

# Neophobia

**KEY TERM**

**Neophobia** – a dislike of new or unfamiliar foodstuffs

Food **neophobia** involves an innate tendency to avoid new foods. From an evolutionary point of view this seems contradictory, as humans need a varied diet to obtain sufficient nutrition to live. But neophobia has a protective function, as new, unknown foods could be toxic. Better to go hungry than die. However, learning experiences, coupled with innate predispositions to learn certain food preferences, can change an initial neophobic reaction to a new food into a preference. New-born infants consume only milk and neophobia begins at weaning when solid foodstuffs are introduced into an infant's diet, where there may be initial reluctance to try them. However, neophobic reaction to a new food will diminish with repeated exposure to the foodstuff and the infant learns it is safe. Reduction in neophobia also generalises to similar-tasting new foods.

## Research

Birch *et al.* (1987) found that two year olds given the most exposure to unfamiliar fruits and cheeses reduced their neophobia of the foodstuffs more quickly. This effect occurred as much with opportunities to smell the food as eat it, which suggests that it is learning that new foods are not toxic that reduces neophobia, supporting the idea of neophobia having an adaptive survival value.

Collectively Pliner & Loewen (1997) and Pliner & McFarlane (1997) compared neophobia in 3–8 year olds, 10–20 year olds and adults, finding that neophobia was minimal in infancy, a time period when infants' access to food was controlled by adults and so neophobia was less necessary for survival. Neophobia then increased through early childhood, a time period when children would forage more for themselves and so be more vulnerable to poisoning by unknown toxic foodstuffs, and then declined into adulthood by which time learning experiences provided knowledge about which foods were safe.

Birch *et al.* (1998) found that there was a neophobic reaction when introducing a new vegetable into an infant's diet, but that this declined with further presentations of the vegetable. On average, 30 grams was consumed at the first feeding but 60 grams at the second feeding. This supports the idea that neophobia declines with repeated exposure to the foodstuff. The researchers also noticed that the neophobic reduction generalised to other unfamiliar vegetables, but not to unfamiliar fruits.

### Evaluation

- Some children appear less neophobic than others and this has an adaptive value, as such children would be more willing to eat unfamiliar foods and thus act as 'guinea pigs' to test out such foodstuffs. If they found them non-toxic their behaviour would be observed and imitated by more neophobic children.
- If neophobia is related to the risk of toxicity in unfamiliar foodstuffs, then we should expect to find more neophobia of eating foodstuffs in cultures where those particular foodstuffs have a heightened risk of being toxic, for example of meat eating in hot countries where meat easily becomes rotten and thus poisonous.

## Taste aversion

**Taste aversion** occurs when individuals eat a foodstuff and become ill, resulting in them avoiding that foodstuff in the future because they associate it with being ill. This effect requires only one experience of illness being associated with that foodstuff and is very resistant to extinction. However, the effect still occurs even if an individual knows that it was not the foodstuff that made them ill, for example they realise they caught a stomach bug from someone else.

Initially taste aversions seem a prime example of classical conditioning, where a previously neutral conditioned stimulus (the food) becomes paired with an unconditioned stimulus (the illness) to produce an unconditioned response (vomiting), causing an individual to avoid that foodstuff in the future. However, often vomiting may not occur straight after eating the food but several hours later, which contradicts classical conditioning. What actually happens is what psychologists call biological preparedness, which entails humans (and other animals) being biologically predisposed through evolution to form certain associations between certain stimuli more easily. These associations involve stimuli essential for survival, such as avoiding toxic foodstuffs. In other words, we are primed by evolution to learn through experience to avoid foodstuffs that make us ill, as this has an adaptive survival value.

### Research

Rzoska (1953) found that rats given poison bait-balls ate small, sub-lethal amounts of them and quickly developed a long-lasting aversion to them, demonstrating the strength of taste aversion.

Garcia & Koelling (1966) illustrated biological preparedness in non-human animals by pairing a sweet-tasting liquid attractive to rats, with an injection containing lithium chloride, which made them ill. The rats quickly learned

### KEY TERM

**Taste aversion** – an innate ability to dislike and avoid certain foodstuffs

to associate the sweet-tasting liquid with being ill and declined to drink it because they were biologically predisposed to do so, i.e. it is a natural adaptive behaviour. However, when the sweet-tasting liquid was paired with an electric shock, the rats continued to drink the sweet-tasting liquid. They had not developed a taste aversion, as rats have no natural biological predisposition to avoid things paired with electric shock.

Bernstein & Webster (1980) demonstrated taste aversion in humans by finding that adults given ice cream before receiving chemotherapy developed a subsequent aversion to eating ice cream as they had a biological preparedness to associate the nausea with food they had eaten rather than the chemotherapy that had actually caused the nausea.

### ON THE WEB

See a video presentation of an experiment into taste aversion with lambs at **www.youtube.com**. Search for 'Food aversion learning – animal behaviour'.

Also, a presentation of how cockroaches use taste aversion to avoid eating sweet-tasting poison at **www.youtube.com**. Search for 'Cockroaches evolve to avoid traps'.

### Evaluation

- A practical application of taste aversion is used by farmers to protect livestock. Dead sheep are laced with lithium chloride to make coyotes and wolves ill. Subsequently the predators refuse to approach sheep and instead display submissive behaviour to them, rolling onto their backs to expose their stomachs.
- Behaviourism traditionally saw all behaviour as learned through experience, with no innate influence. However, taste aversion shows how learning via experience can actually be underpinned by biological genetic influences shaped via evolutionary forces.

### KEY TERMS

**Social influences** – the impact of others upon an individual's food preferences

**Cultural influences** – eating practices that are transmitted to members of cultural groupings

## The role of learning in food preferences

Learning experiences reduce food neophobia, but learning via **social** and **cultural influences** also has a major role to play in shaping food preferences.

## Social influences

Eating is generally a social event, so others influence children's eating habits. When an infant moves on to solid foodstuffs, the mother's eating behaviour strongly affects her child's eating behaviour. Indeed, evidence suggests that the food a mother eats during pregnancy and in the period following birth impacts on her child's eating habits during the transition to eating solid food. Flavours that a mother eats are transmitted to her unborn child via amniotic fluid and after birth through breast milk. For instance, if a pregnant woman eats garlic, the flavour of garlic will be present in the amniotic fluid that nourishes her unborn child and this can lead to a preference for garlic when the child is older.

Social learning also has a part to play, as research indicates that observing what others eat is imitated by children. This plays a role in breaking down food neophobias. The social learning effect carries on into later childhood, with favoured adults and peers being important models for children to observe and imitate. The importance of role models in coaxing children to eat new foods depends upon the relationship between a child and a model. Older children are more influential role models than younger ones and parents are more influential than strangers.

**Figure 7.6** Foods eaten during pregnancy can influence a child's later food preferences

Operant conditioning through reinforcements also plays a part. When children are given foods as rewards for approved behaviours, greater preference for those foods occurs. Interestingly though, if children are given rewards for eating new foodstuffs, for example vegetables, the foods eaten to gain the reward become less preferred. Also, if adults try to shape youngsters' eating habits by restricting what they view as undesirable foodstuffs, the restricted food becomes more desirable to children when they are available.

Overall, children's food preferences and eating habits come to resemble that of their parents, because they share their genetic food preferences transmitted by evolutionary forces, as well as learning their parents' food preferences by sharing the same environmental influences.

## Research

Birch (1992) found that mothers' eating behaviours, attitudes and child-feeding practices influence children's food preferences and eating behaviour when they move on to solid foodstuffs, illustrating the importance of social influences in shaping food preferences.

Mennella & Beauchamp (1996) reported that foodstuffs that mothers ate during pregnancy and while breastfeeding affected infants' early experience of food flavours and shaped their food preferences when older, illustrating how learning of food preferences occurs in the womb.

Harper & Sanders (1975) found that observing the eating practices of mothers was more influential than observing those of strangers, supporting the idea that children's relationship with models is important in influencing food preferences.

Zimmerman *et al.* (1980) found that giving children foodstuffs as rewards for approved behaviour increased preference for those foodstuffs, showing the role that operant conditioning via reinforcements plays in shaping food preferences. However, Newman & Taylor (1992) found giving rewards for eating approved foodstuffs, such as vegetables, reduced preference for those foodstuffs.

### Evaluation

- Animal studies are often used to investigate learning processes, such as social learning in shaping food preferences, but a problem with this is that it is difficult to generalise findings to humans, who have more complex cognitive processes, which affect their eating behaviour.
- There is an adaptive survival value to observing and imitating others' eating practices. If others are seen to safely consume novel foods, this indicates that those foodstuffs are safe to eat, which additionally helps break down food neophobias.
- A practical application of research into social influences upon food preferences is that of pregnant women being advised to not consume potentially unhealthy foodstuffs, as this could transfer into later unhealthy food preferences for their unborn children.

**ON THE WEB**

To read an interesting account of research into how pregnant mothers' food preferences influence their unborn children's food preferences go to **www.theguardian.com/lifeandstyle/wordofmouth/2014/apr/08/child-food-preferences-womb-pregnancy-foetus-taste-flavours**.

The conclusion is that although some food preferences are innate, others are learned, with the learning process beginning in the womb; amniotic fluid being seen as children's 'first food'. One practical application of this is to advise mothers not to eat junk food during pregnancy or else risk the unborn child developing a preference for such food.

*'The trouble with eating Italian food is that five or six days later you're hungry again.'*
George Miller (2006)

*'To eat well in England you should have breakfast three times a day.'*
W. Somerset Maugham (1950)

**Figure 7.7** Cornish pasties are an example of local cuisine

# Cultural influences

Eating is influenced through cultural circumstances, as cultural and sub-cultural groups have different eating practices. These are transmitted to children, via reinforcement and social learning, and include the consumption of different foodstuffs and differences in traditions of preparation and eating practices, such as extended families eating together and eating practices marking special occasions, for instance eating pancakes on Shrove Tuesday. Cultural eating practices are also found in local cuisine, for example Cornish pasties.

Certain cultural practices lead to restrictions, like excluding pork. Cultural influences are, however, generally flexible and newcomers often adopt particular food habits of the local culture.

Overall, culture influences eating behaviour directly, but usually has a moderating role on other variables to determine individual food preferences and eating practices.

## Research

Bourdieu (1984) reported that working-class people's preference for sweet, filling and fatty food was a result of a 'taste of necessity', driven by their lack of food choice and money, as well as a need to feel full, demonstrating how sub-cultural influences shape food preferences.

Schiller (1980) reported that in cultures where chilli is an important flavour, observing adults eating it played a large role in persuading children to eat chilli-flavoured food, showing how cultural influences in the form of social learning shape food preferences.

Menella *et al.* (2005) found that although genetic influences shaped children's food preferences, by adulthood cultural influences over-rode genetic ones, especially in the degree of preference for sweet-tasting foods. This suggests that genetic influences shape early food preferences but culture influences later ones.

Lanfer *et al.* (2013) used sensory tests to assess the food preferences of 1,700 children aged 6–9 years from eight European countries. Common food preferences were not generally found, for example 70 per cent of German children preferred biscuits with high fat content compared with only 35 per cent of Cypriot children, illustrating how food preferences are shaped by cultural influences.

### Evaluation

- A practical application of the fact that food preferences differ between cultures is that different dietary advice needs to be given in different countries to shape healthy eating practices.
- Culture influences eating behaviour directly, but more often plays a moderating role on other variables, such as genetic ones, to determine individual eating practices.
- Cultural eating practices often reflect local environmental conditions, for instance the seasonal or non-availability of certain foods, coupled with the ability to transport and keep foodstuffs in hygienic conditions. For instance, it makes sense not to eat meat in cultures where meat easily goes off and becomes poisonous.
- With the increase in world population mobility, developments in transport systems and modern food hygiene practices, for instance the wider availability of refrigeration, eating behaviours are more global and less based on individual cultural locations.

## STRENGTHEN YOUR LEARNING

1. In what ways may i] sweet, ii] salty, iii] bitter, iv] meat taste preferences have an adaptive survival value? Does research support such taste preferences being evolutionary?
2. Explain how food neophobia and taste aversions could also have an adaptive survival value. Does research support this point of view?
3. How might food companies exploit the human preference for salt?
4. Why might children find bitter-tasting medicines hard to swallow?
5. Explain the connection between taste aversion and biological preparedness.
6. Explain how SLT and operant conditioning can explain how taste preferences are learned. What evidence is there that food preferences can be learned?
7. How might observation and imitation of others' eating habits have an adaptive survival value?
8. Give an example of one food preference from your own cultural background and explain how this may have been learned.

*'A good meal ought to begin with hunger.'*
French proverb

# 7.2 Neural and hormonal mechanisms involved in the control of eating

We have already seen one biological factor upon eating behaviour, that of evolutionary influences. In this section we look at biological influences in the form of neural brain mechanisms and **hormonal mechanisms**, bodily chemical messengers that influence eating behaviour.

## Dual control theory

Lashley (1938) believed that **neural mechanisms** were involved in making decisions about when and when not to eat. He thought that there must be a brain mechanism involved in the motivation to eat and from experiments involving rats identified the **hypothalamus** brain area as playing a key role in controlling food intake. The **lateral hypothalamus** (LH) was identified as the 'hunger centre', initiating eating behaviour, and the **ventromedial hypothalamus** (VMH), as the 'satiety centre', producing a feeling of fullness that triggered cessation of eating (see Figure 7.8).

The hypothalamus is the body's control centre, playing a crucial role in many biological functions such as emotions as well as food/water intake. Just as a thermostat maintains temperature, the hypothalamus maintains the body's homeostasis (balance) by receiving messages from different parts of the body and making appropriate responses. This became known as **dual control theory** (DCT), based on the idea of a homeostatic perception of hunger and satiety (fullness), whereby when the level of glucose (blood sugar) is low, the liver sends signals to the lateral hypothalamus, creating a sensation of hunger that motivates an individual to eat. When food is eaten, glucose is released, activating the ventromedial hypothalamus, producing a sensation of satiety, which stops further eating.

### KEY TERMS

**Hormonal mechanisms** – chemical messengers within the body that influence eating behaviour

**Neural mechanisms** – the influence of brain components in regulating eating behaviour

**Hypothalamus** – a small brain structure associated with the regulation of eating

**Lateral hypothalamus** – a part of the hypothalamus associated with hunger and onset of eating

**Ventromedial hypothalamus** – a part of the hypothalamus associated with cessation of eating

**Dual control theory** – a homeostatic view of eating, whereby hunger motivates eating, which in turn leads to satiety and cessation of eating

Lateral hypothalamus (hunger centre)

Ventromedial hypothalamic nucleus (satiety centre)

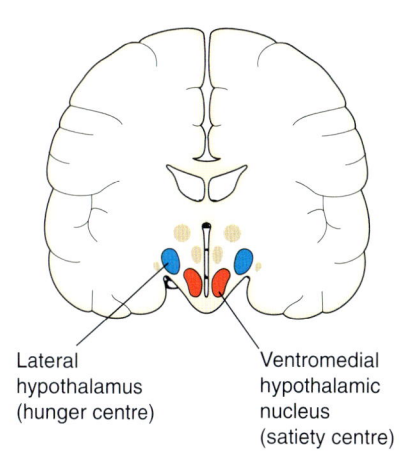

**Figure 7.8** The hypothalmic nuclei involved in the regulation of appetite

Therefore the hypothalamus helps maintain a constant internal environment (homeostasis). Which foodstuffs are eaten in response to low glucose levels depends on several factors, such as usual diet, culture, availability, habits, etc. Although research initially supported DCT, problems with the theory arose, such as the fact that rats were able to reach satiety even if their satiety centre was removed (by lesioning the VMH), and conversely rats with their hunger centre removed (by lesioning the LH) still became hungry.

## Research

Lashly (1938) and co-workers such as Brobeck (1946) performed a series of experiments in which rats were trained to negotiate a maze to gain food. Different parts of hungry rats' brains were lesioned to assess the effect on eating behaviour. **Lesions** to the lateral hypothalamus made animals stop eating spontaneously, while lesions to the ventromedial hypothalamus caused the rats to eat to excess, supporting the idea of the hypothalamus being the 'eating centre' of the brain, with the lateral hypothalamus being the 'hunger centre' and the ventromedial hypothalamus being the 'satiety centre'.

Hetherington & Ranson (1940) found lesions to the VMH led to hyperphagia (overeating) and weight gain. Anad & Brobeck (1951) found lesions to the LH led to aphagia (undereating) and weight loss, supporting DCT.

Stellar (1954) found stimulating the VMH decreased eating, but when lesioned increased eating, while the LH when stimulated and lesioned produced the opposite effects. This indicates, as predicted by DCT, that these two brain areas are the feeding and satiety centres.

Teitelbaum (1957) got rats to push a bar an increasing number of times to get food. Lesioned VMH rats initially work hard in line with DCT, but become less willing to work hard as more presses are required. It was also found that VMH lesioned rats are fussy eaters and eat less than normal rats if food tastes stale or bitter. These findings do not fit the predictions of DCT.

## Set point theory

A solution to the inability of the dual-point theory to explain the long-term effects of lesions to the LH and the VMH was **set point theory** (SPT). This suggests everyone has an individual metabolic set point, a certain weight their body is shaped towards, determined by the rate at which calories are consumed. Set points alter depending on several factors, including eating patterns and exercise. When people diet, leptin levels decrease, causing the hypothalamus to trigger 'hunger pangs' (see role of leptin, page 241). The set point for obese individuals is higher than for healthy individuals and lower for underweight individuals.

### Research

Han & Liu (1966) took rats that were obese through having VMH lesions and force-fed them to increase body weight even more. The rats then fed freely and lost weight, returning to the weight they were before force-feeding, i.e. back to their new increased set point, supporting SPT.

Powley & Keesey (1970) found rats that lost weight through starvation and then had lesions made to their LH did not lose further weight, supporting SPT as it indicates that the rats had slimmed down to a new set point before the lesions were created.

---

### KEY TERMS

**Lesions** – damage made to brain tissue in order to see the effects upon eating behaviour

**Set point theory** – that each individual is orientated biologically to a specific body weight

### Evaluation

- Perceiving the LH as a 'feeding centre' is oversimplified, as it is possible to recover from LH lesions and LH lesions also produce disruptions in aggression levels, sexual behaviour and reinforcement behaviour. Lesions to the nigrostriatal tract (NST), a brain structure that passes through the LH, can on their own produce aphagia (absence of eating) and adipsia (absence of thirst).

- The various signals sending information to the hypothalamus are only part of the complex systems regulating eating, as other factors apart from neural mechanisms play a role too, for instance biological rhythms. For example, rats become most active and start to eat after darkness descends, due to another area of the hypothalamus, the suprachiasmatic nucleus.

- Much research into neural mechanisms involves animal experimentation, creating problems of generalisation to humans. However, Quaade (1971) found stimulating the VMH of obese people made them hungry, similar to studies on rats. Also, findings from post-mortem studies lend support to animal studies suggesting findings are generalisable to humans.

- The notion of a biologically determined set point for body mass has experimental support and has been used to create practical applications in the form of therapies to treat the obese.

## The role of leptin and ghrelin

The role of the hypothalamus in controlling eating behaviour is complex. Apart from the LH and the VMH, the arcuate nucleus of the hypothalamus also plays a part. This region contains several different types of nerve cells, one of which manufactures the neuropeptide NPY, a very potent orexigen (appetite stimulator). Neuropeptides are minute proteins encoded by genes, which work as chemical messengers between neurons, or between the fat deposits of the body and the brain. The fat hormone **leptin** is a neuropeptide produced from fat cells and released into the blood to signal to the hypothalamus that calorific storage is high (in the form of fat deposits) and thus is associated with decreasing appetite. However, when people do not eat enough, fat is used up and fat cells stop producing leptin, causing leptin levels in the blood to fall. The hypothalamus detects the drop in leptin, interprets low leptin levels as a lack of calories and generates the sensation of hunger, stimulating an individual to eat more.

NPY neurons are also activated by **ghrelin**, a hormone secreted from the lining of the stomach, whose concentration in the blood falls after each meal and rises progressively until the next. The action of ghrelin upon the hypothalamus is to increase the sensation of hunger and thus stimulate eating. As leptin also helps stimulate hunger, it may be that leptin helps regulate ghrelin levels.

> **KEY TERMS**
>
> **Leptin** – a hormone produced by fat cells associated with the regulation of energy intake and expenditure
>
> **Ghrelin** – a hormone produced by the stomach associated with increasing appetite

## CLASSIC RESEARCH

### 'Effects of parabiosis of obese mice and mice with diabetes with normal mice' – Douglas Coleman (1973)

Douglas Coleman (1931–2014) was an only child with no playmates. Inspired by his father's job as an electrical repairman, Douglas amused himself by taking things apart to see how they worked, so it was not surprising that he became a scientist. Research in the 1950s had found that eating was restrained by levels of fat present in food, suggesting feeding was controlled by a negative feedback signal. This became known as lipostatic theory, which saw sensations of hunger deriving from lower fat levels, with leptin, a hormone derived from fat, playing a crucial role. Coleman confirmed this with his work on obese mice.

### Aim
To test lipostatic theory by using different genetic strains of mice.

### Procedure
Parabiosis, a technique that unites separate animals physiologically, was used in order to pair up different genetic strains of mice and involves the surgical joining of two mice by skin-to-skin anastomosis from the shoulder to the pelvic girdle. Wound healing and cross circulation are established in two to three days. Two forms of obese mice that were of different genetic mutations were used, 'ob' mice and 'db' mice (see Figure 7.9).

### Findings
When 'ob' mice were paired with normal mice, the obese mice lost weight.

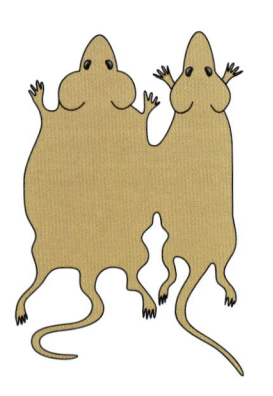

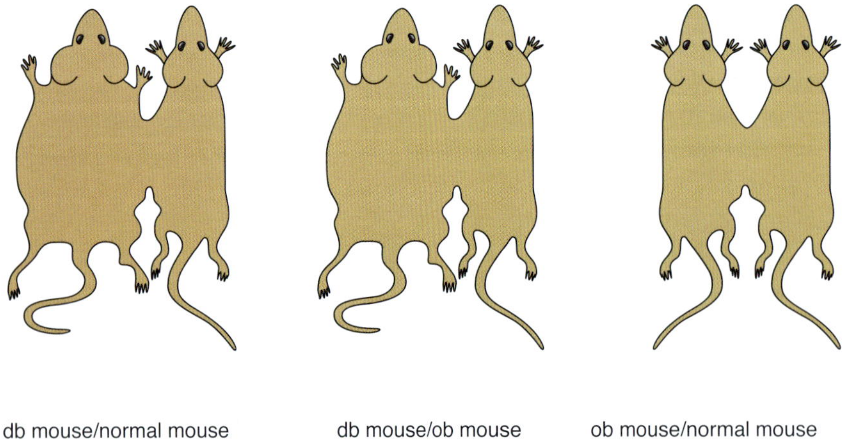

When 'db' mice were paired with normal mice, the normal mice starved to death after about one week, with their blood sugar concentrations declining to starvation levels.

When 'db' mice were paired with 'ob' mice, the 'ob' mice lost weight, blood sugar concentration in the ob mice declined, eventually reaching starvation levels. Survival time ranged from 20 to 30 days.

### Conclusions
The db mice produce a blood-borne satiety factor so powerful it induces normal mice partners to starve to death. The ob mice, like the normal mice, recognise and respond to the circulating factor provided by their db/db partners. Therefore db mice have a circulating factor that stops eating in ob and normal mice, but db mice are resistant to it.

When paired with normal mice, ob mice get a circulating factor from the normal mice and lose weight due to a decrease in hunger. However, the circulating factor is in insufficient amounts to be lethal.

db mice circulate a factor that their satiety centre in the VMH does not respond to, while ob mice have a normal satiety centre but produce inadequate levels of the satiety signal.

The circulating satiety factor (later named leptin) is a blood-borne hormone that functions in a negative feedback loop to control fat tissue by modulating appetite. Leptin is produced in fatty tissue, with the leptin receptor expressed mainly in the hypothalamus.

### Evaluation
- The research supports the lipostatic theory and displays the complexity of the mechanisms involved in the regulation of eating.
- The research confirms the key role that leptin plays in the regulation of hunger and appetite.
- The research was conducted on animals due to the ethical restraints on performing similar research on humans. Coleman justified his work by hoping that it would lead to effective treatments for diabetes.
- As the research was conducted on rats there are problems in generalising the results to humans.

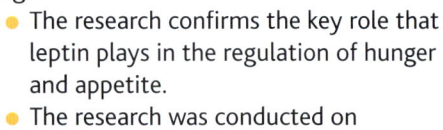

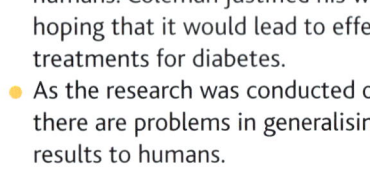

db mouse/normal mouse db mouse/ob mouse ob mouse/normal mouse

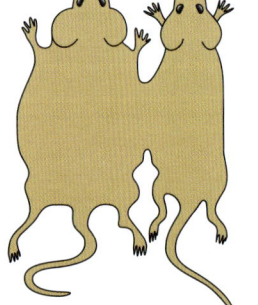

**Figure 7.9** Different parabiotic combinations

### RESEARCH IN FOCUS
Coleman had problems convincing others of his results and before they could be published his research had to be subjected to peer review. Outline the peer review process and explain why it needs to occur. What criticisms are there of peer review?

# Research

Baicy *et al.* (2007) found that leptin binds to NPY neurons in the arcuate nucleus brain area, decreasing the activity of these neurons, which signals to the hypothalamus to produce a sensation of satiety. This illustrates the key role leptin plays in controlling eating.

Malik *et al.* (2008) used ghrelin injections and fMRI scans on non-obese participants to measure brain activity responses to food and non-food images three hours after eating a standardised meal. Ghrelin increased response to food images in brain areas associated with hedonic feeding (feeding triggered by visual cues), suggesting that ghrelin works to increase appetite by stimulating brain areas involved in processing food cues.

Nakazato *et al.* (2001) found that ghrelin injections stimulated feeding and increased weight gain in normal rats and rats genetically deficient in growth hormone, demonstrating the important role of ghrelin in promoting eating and releasing growth hormone. As ghrelin was seen to influence NPY gene expression and decreased the influence of leptin, the findings additionally suggest that there is competitive interaction between ghrelin and leptin.

Shiiya *et al.* (2002) found that ghrelin levels in blood plasma were lower in obese participants and higher in anorexic participants than in normal-weight participants. Ghrelin levels also increased under conditions of low energy balance and decreased under conditions of high energy balance, supporting the idea of ghrelin being involved in the stimulation of appetite and feeding.

## Evaluation

- The main function of leptin may not be as a satiety signal to prevent overeating but may instead be a starvation signal when leptin levels are depleted, thus helping to maintain fat stores during times of food scarcity. Leptin may therefore help energy to be stored efficiently when food is plentiful and so has an evolutionary survival value.
- Identifying leptin as an important factor in the control of eating brought hopes that a leptin therapy could be developed to treat obesity. However, leptin injections, although achieving weight loss in some obese individuals, have not proven to be a universally effective treatment. Researchers believe that they need to identify the mechanisms at the molecular level by which leptin works if leptin therapy is to prove of use. Current thinking is that rather than being a therapy for weight loss, leptin may play more of a role in the prevention of weight regain.
- Although hypothalamic mechanisms are important in controlling hunger and satiety, they are not fully understood. For example, it is not clear how ghrelin and leptin reach targets in the brain, as both are large peptides that do not cross the blood–brain barrier readily. The degree to which leptin and ghrelin are working independently or in conjunction with each other is also not understood.

## STRENGTHEN YOUR LEARNING

1. Outline the dual control and set point theories of eating control and using research evidence explain which is more favoured.
2. Explain how the ventromedial hypothalamus and the lateral hypothalamus may be involved in controlling eating behaviour.
3. What are leptin and ghrelin? Outline their roles in lipostatic theory.
4. Use research evidence to assess the roles of leptin and ghrelin.
5. What other evaluative points can be made about the roles of leptin and ghrelin?

# ASSESSMENT CHECK

1. Briefly outline the role of leptin in the control of eating behaviour. **[3 marks]**

2. Discuss the role of learning in food preference. **[16 marks]**

3. Identify which two of the following statements concerning explanations of food preferences are true. **[2 marks]**
   - Evolutionary explanations see food preferences as being inherited.
   - Neophobia concerns an innate tendency to eat foods not experienced before.
   - Taste aversion concerns an innate tendency to dislike certain foods.
   - Cultural influences see specific food preferences as being found in all cultures.

4. Research into neural and hormonal mechanisms involved in the control of eating behaviour often uses non-human animals. Give two limitations of non-human animals in such research. **[2 + 2 marks]**

5. Three-year-old Velvet is poorly and her doctor has prescribed her a bitter-tasting medicine, but every time her father gives her a spoonful of the medicine she cannot swallow it.

   With reference to evolutionary explanations of food preferences, explain i] why Velvet cannot swallow the medicine, ii] how the medicine could be altered so that she could swallow it. **[2 + 2 marks]**

*'To lose confidence in one's body is to lose confidence in oneself.'*
Simone de Beauvoir (1949)

# Anorexia nervosa

**Anorexia nervosa** (AN) is characterised by an obsessive desire to lose weight by refusing to eat. AN has existed for a long time but has become more widespread in recent years. There are several theories, biological and psychological, for AN and different explanations may apply in different circumstances. AN can occur at various times of life and to differing degrees: 20 per cent of sufferers recover after one episode, 60 per cent continue to have periodic episodes, while 20 per cent will be hospitalised for lengthy periods. There are three main symptoms: 1) severe weight loss, 2) fear of weight increase and 3) a refusal to eat sufficiently to maintain body weight.

85 per cent of sufferers are female and 15 per cent are male. About 1 per cent of adolescent females will receive medical treatment as a diagnosed sufferer of the disorder. About 15 per cent of sufferers will die from starvation, suicide, electrolyte imbalances and organ failure.

> **KEY TERM**
>
> **Anorexia nervosa** – an eating disorder characterised by an obsessive desire to lose weight by refusing to eat

# 7.3 Biological explanations for anorexia nervosa

Biological explanations see AN as physically determined, through genetic, neural and evolutionary means.

## Genetic explanation

The **genetic explanation** sees AN as transmitted through hereditary means from the genetic material passed from parents to children. Evidence indicates an increased risk for individuals with close relatives with the disorder, which suggests that the disorder is in part genetically transmitted. However, the genetic explanation is seen as only a contributory factor in the causation of the disorder. What genes may do is to give individuals a level of inherited vulnerability to developing the disorder, with different individuals having differing levels of vulnerability. Whether a given individual goes on to develop AN would depend upon the presence of other factors, for example levels of environmental stress, types of family structure, etc. Study methods involve examining the incidence of AN among related individuals, such as twin studies, as well as gene-profiling studies that search for common genes among sufferers.

**Figure 7.10** Can psychology explain why people suffer from anorexia nervosa?

> **KEY TERM**
>
> **Genetic explanation** – that anorexia nervosa results from an inherited predisposition

### Research

Bulik *et al.* (2006) used a sample of 31,406 Swedish twin pairs to find the overall incidence of AN was 1.2 per cent for females and 0.29 per cent for males, with the heritability of the disorder calculated as 56 per cent, suggesting a significant genetic influence in the development of the disorder.

Kortegaard *et al.* (2001) assessed the level of AN among 34,000 pairs of Danish twins, finding the concordance rate for MZ (identical twins who share 100 per cent of genetic material) was 0.18 while for DZ (non-identical twins who share 50 per cent of genetic material) it was 0.07. In other words, if one MZ twin had anorexia then there was an 18 per cent chance the other twin would too, but if one DZ twin had the condition there was only a 7 per cent chance the other twin would. This supports the genetic explanation, while also suggesting a large role for environmental factors.

Hakonarson et al. (2010) compared DNA material from 1,003 mainly female AN participants and 3,733 non-sufferers, finding variants of the OPRD1 gene and HTR1D gene were commonly associated with the disorder. These findings confirmed those of earlier studies, supporting the idea of several genes contributing to an advanced risk of developing AN.

Scott-Van Zeeland et al. (2014) compared 152 genes in 1,205 women with anorexia and 1,948 without the condition and found that variants of the EPHX2 gene, which is involved with cholesterol function in the body, were more common in those with anorexia. The findings suggest a contributory role for this gene, though the results apply to female sufferers only.

## Evaluation

- Although research indicates that genes are a factor in the causation of anorexia, the fact that multiple genes are involved, as well as environmental factors, makes it difficult to identify and quantify the role of individual genes – many genes are involved, each having different levels of influence. These genes may also exert different levels of influence in different people.
- If genes were solely responsible for AN, concordance rates between MZ twins would be 100 per cent, and as they are not it confirms that other, non-genetic, factors are also involved, though an interaction between genetic and environmental factors seems most probable.
- The genetic explanation cannot account for why the disorder primarily affects females (a large number of homosexual males – above 20 per cent – also have AN), nor can it explain the heightened incidence of the disorder nowadays. The inheritance of genes from generation to generation has not greatly changed, yet the disorder has increased in prevalence.
- Genes may exert a non-direct influence upon the development of AN. Many sufferers display perfectionist personality characteristics and genes may be influencing such personality traits. For instance, Bachner-Melman et al. (2007) found three genes associated with AN are also associated with perfectionist personality.

## Neural explanations

*Material concerning abnormal biochemistry could be used in examination answers, as long as the link between abnormal biochemistry and neural explanations is explicitly made, for example the action of leptin upon the hypothalamus.*

**Neural explanations** involve the idea that AN is linked to defective brain structures. Early research focused on possible damage to the hypothalamus, but more recent research has concentrated on identifying specific brain mechanisms. One area of interest is the insula dysfunction hypothesis as the biological root of anorexia. This sees the insula brain area, part of the

**KEY TERM**

**Neural explanations** – that anorexia nervosa results from abnormally functioning brain mechanisms

cerebral cortex, as developing differently in anorexics. Various symptoms of AN are associated with dysfunction in several brain areas, with the common factor being the insula, which is responsible for more neural connections than any other part of the brain, including brain areas associated with AN. Contemporary research appears to back up the hypothesis.

Neural explanations also involve the idea that faulty biochemistry is related to the development of AN. The neurotransmitter serotonin is especially linked with the onset and maintenance of anorexia, though noradrenaline is also of interest, with its role in maintaining restriction of eating by influencing anxiety levels.

Leptin also attracts interest, as anorexics can have low levels of leptin, probably due to their low levels of fat. It is thought that leptin influences the regulation of the neuroendocrine system during starvation. Low leptin levels are also known to affect the hypothalamic-pituitary-gonadal axis, which leads to the amenorrhea (cessation of periods) often seen in anorexics.

## CONTEMPORARY RESEARCH

### Anorexia linked to disturbance in brain region – Tyson Oberndorfer et al. (2013)

Researchers are undecided as to whether anorexia is due to psychological factors, such as an obsession with body image, or biological factors, like a disturbance in the brain system that regulates eating behaviour. Oberndorfer et al. set out to investigate the degree to which brain structures play a role in the development of anorexia.

#### Aim
To confirm the findings of earlier studies indicating altered function of neural circuitry associated with appetite contributes to the reduced eating of anorexics.

#### Procedure
The participants were 14 female recovered anorexics and 14 non-anorexic females (recovered anorexics were used to avoid the confounding variable of altered nutritional state). (Fourteen recovered sufferers of bulimia nervosa were also studied for another aspect of the study.)

Participants fasted overnight and received a standardised breakfast of 604 calories, before having an fMRI scan as a control for satiety state.

fMRI scans were then used to test neurocircuitry by measuring brain responses to sweet tastes, where participants were given 120 doses of either sucrose or sucratose (to distinguish between neural processing of calorific and non-calorific sweet tastes).

#### Findings
Anorexic participants had greatly reduced responses to sweet tastes, especially the taste of sucrose, in the right anterior insula brain area (see Figure 7.11).

#### Conclusions
The findings confirm earlier studies suggesting a relationship between AN and neural processes in the insula brain

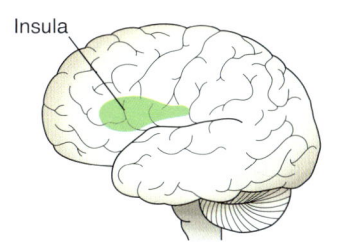

**Figure 7.11** Oberndorfer et al.'s research associated the insula brain area with anorexia nervosa

region, an area where taste is sensed and integrated with reward signals, which determines whether an individual feels hungry or not.

Altered functioning of neural circuitry appears to contribute to the restricted eating feature of anorexia.

The restricted eating and weight loss seen in anorexics may occur because the brain fails to accurately recognise hunger signals.

Anorexics appear to have altered balance or sensitivity in brain mechanisms that signal the calorific content of food.

#### Evaluation
- The findings may offer a practical application in the development of effective treatments for AN, such as enhancing insula activity in anorexics by using biofeedback or mindfulness training to adjust the brain's response to food stimuli. Alternatively, medications could be manufactured that enhance the reward response of food or decrease inhibition to food consumption in the brain's reward circuitry.
- The research does not determine whether faulty brain mechanisms cause anorexic behaviour or whether anorexic behaviour leads to changes in brain mechanisms. One way of addressing this would be to scan the brains of at-risk children to see whether their brains exhibit such faulty mechanisms.

> **YOU ARE THE RESEARCHER**
>
> Imagine that you are Tyson Oberndorfer and have just carried out his study comparing differences in brain structures between anorexics and non-anorexics. Explain how you would write up your practical report. To do this you will need to specify what the different sections of the report will be and what will go in each section.
>
> Why is it important to write up the report in this 'conventional' way?

## Research

Brooks (2012) used fMRI scans of anorexic and non-anorexic participants' brains and found heightened activity in the dorsolateral prefrontal cortex brain area of anorexics (a brain area associated with self-control that helps decrease impulsive behaviours) when they imagined eating plates of high-calorific food, like chocolate cake, but activity was not heightened when they imagined plates of inedible objects such as clothes pegs. This suggests that the brains of anorexics are regulating control over their desire to eat when confronted with food.

Bailer *et al*. (2005) used fMRI scans to compare serotonin activity in recovered female anorexics and female non-sufferers, finding heightened serotonin levels in several brain areas of the anorexics, especially those with the highest levels of anxiety. This suggests that prolonged disruption of serotonin levels produces heightened anxiety levels, which then trigger AN.

Nunn *et al*. (2012) reported that abnormal noradrenaline functioning is seen as being genetically determined, leading to high anxiety and insula brain area dysfunction that results in negative body image distortion. This gives rise to intense dieting, which helps reduce anxiety in the short term. Anxiety then increases again, illustrating how noradrenaline leads to a cycle of anorexia being maintained.

Grinspoon *et al*. (1996) compared leptin levels in 22 anorexic females and 23 female non-sufferers, finding leptin levels significantly lower in the anorexics and that leptin levels correlated positively with body weight and percentage of body fat. This supports the idea of leptin being related to AN.

Mayo-Smith *et al*. (1989) found that leptin and body fat mass levels were higher in healthy low-weight females than in anorexic females, supporting the idea that leptin levels are related to the low amounts of body fat in anorexics rather than their actual body weight.

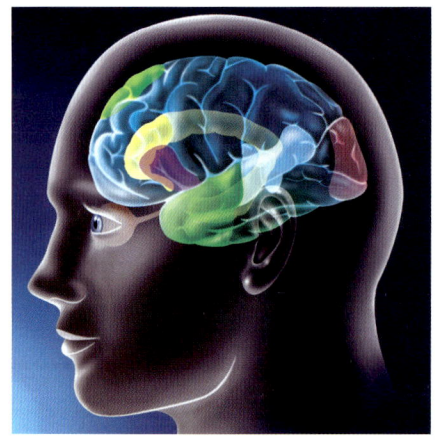

**Figure 7.12** The dorsolateral prefrontal cortex brain area is shown as light green in this image

## Evaluation

- Abnormal biochemistry, such as the levels of serotonin and leptin found in anorexics, may cause the onset of the disorder, but may instead be an effect of the malnutrition associated with AN.
- Current thinking on the role of leptin is that prolonged weight loss, as seen in anorexics, leads to a continual reduction in circulating leptin levels, rather than leptin levels causing the development of anorexia. Research interest in leptin now is focused more on the possible role for leptin as a therapy to treat AN.
- Much research into AN involves female participants, thus findings cannot be generalised to males, who differ in many ways physiologically from females. For example, males have different distributions and amounts of body fat, therefore the relationship between male anorexics and neurotransmitter levels may be different to that of female sufferers.
- Research, such as that by Nunn *et al*. (2012), illustrates that the abnormal biochemistry seen in anorexics may be under genetic control, suggesting a link between genetic and neural influences.

> **STRENGTHEN YOUR LEARNING**
> 1. What evidence is there that AN might be genetically transmitted?
> 2. What can the genetic explanation for AN not explain about the condition?
> 3. Outline the insula dysfunction hypothesis of AN. Does research support the hypothesis?
> 4. In what way can faulty biochemistry (neurotransmitters and hormones) be related to neural explanations of AN?
> 5. What has research suggested about the role of biochemistry in AN?
> 6. What other evaluative points can be made about biological explanations of AN?

# 7.4 Psychological explanations for anorexia nervosa

There are several psychological explanations of AN. The focus in this section is upon the **family systems theory** (FST), the social learning theory (SLT) and the cognitive theory.

## The family systems theory

### Minuchin (1979)

The FST sees families as intensely connected emotionally to each other, with family members seeking each other's attention and approval and continually reacting to each other's needs and moods. Thus families are interdependent units, where changes in the functioning of one member affects the functioning of other members, with AN seen as developing due to dysfunctional interactions between family members, and the development of AN often serving to prevent or reduce dissension within a family. For example, an adolescent fearing that arguments between parents may lead to divorce becomes anorexic to divert family attentions onto themselves, thus saving the marriage. In other words, the family is 'sick', but the anorexic becomes the 'fall guy' (takes the blame) for the family's problems, with the anorexic often fearing abandonment or worsening of the family's problems unless they accept their role.

## Enmeshment

**Enmeshment** involves dysfunctional interactions between family members inhibiting each family member's sense of individuality, for example where families are over-protective of their children, thus preventing any sense of independence developing. This tends to occur in families that do everything together and so adolescent children striving for independence restrict their eating as a form of protest. Enmeshment therefore occurs as a type of boundary between individuals being able to distinguish themselves as separate from family units. This occurs because in the families of some anorexics there is not enough flexibility to allow children to develop a sense of self.

**KEY TERMS**

**Family systems theory** – that anorexia nervosa results from dysfunctional patterns of family interaction

**Enmeshment** – a family interactive style that inhibits each family member's sense of individuality

### KEY TERM

**Autonomy and control** – the perception of anorexia nervosa as a struggle for self-management, identity and effectiveness

## Autonomy and control

Autonomy refers to the experience of choice and freedom in relation to oneself and others. It involves the development of control, identity, competence and effectiveness. The major aspect of achieving **autonomy and control** is to develop a sense of self.

An important part of the FST is that disturbances in the development of autonomy are a central feature of AN, which manifest themselves as distortions of body image, misperceptions of internal states and a paralysing sense of ineffectiveness.

Rosman & Baker (1978) described five qualities of dysfunctional families that hindered the development of autonomy: 1) enmeshment, 2) over-protectiveness, 3) rigidity of style, 4) conflict avoidance, 5) involvement of the anorexic in parental conflict.

## Research

Minuchin (1978) gave a standardised interactive task to 11 families of anorexics and 34 families of non-anorexics, finding the families of anorexics had higher levels of enmeshment, over-protectiveness, conflict avoidance and rigidity of style, supporting the idea of enmeshment and a lack of autonomy being features of AN in line with the FST.

Blinder *et al.* (1988) reported that although anorexic families seem ideal on the surface, closer inspection reveals little expression of affection and conflict avoided at all costs, although underlying tensions are often present. Parents also put high expectations on their children to compensate for the lack of love within their marriage, with anorexics going on to use their illness to try to unite their parents. These findings support the predictions of the FST.

Karwautz *et al.* (2003) used the Subjective Family Image Test to compare perceptions of family relationships between 31 pairs of sisters, where one sister had AN and the other did not, finding that the anorexics had lower levels of autonomy, related mainly to their relationships with their mothers (and to a lesser extent their fathers), supporting the idea of autonomy being a central feature of AN.

Strauss & Ryan (1987) used questionnaires, such as the General Causality Orientations Scale, to measure the degree of autonomy in 19 anorexics and 17 non-anorexic controls, finding anorexics had less sense of autonomy, poorer self-concept and more disturbed family interactions, supporting the FST, especially the idea of autonomy disturbance.

### Evaluation

- There tend to be heightened tensions within families of anorexics. However, rather than being a precipitating trigger for the development of AN, heightened tensions could easily be the result of having an anorexic in the family.
- Dysfunctional families like those described by the FST have always existed, so therefore it is difficult for this theory to explain the huge increase in AN throughout the population.
- Shapiro (1981) pointed out that deficiencies in autonomy are central to many abnormal conditions and that therefore it is not known how such deficiencies relate specifically to AN.
- Le Grange & Eisler (2008) report that for family therapies to be effective they have to be tailor-made to fit individual family circumstances, because uniform features of dysfunctional anorexic families do not really exist. Also treatments based around family therapies are more effective if they treat the family not as the cause of the disorder but as a valuable resource to help an anorexic recover from their disorder, thus weakening support for the FST.

*'Nothing tastes as good as skinny feels.'*
Kate Moss (2009)

# Social learning theory

**Social learning theory** sees learning occurring by social means, where an observation is made of someone being rewarded for their behaviour, with this behaviour then being imitated.

The SLT of AN is based around the idea that people wish to be popular and that imitating popular people's thinness will achieve this aim. Young people are seen as especially vulnerable, as they are searching for an identity and heightened self-esteem.

SLT can explain why AN occurs more in cultures where attractiveness is associated with being skinny and why it is more of a female disorder in those cultures, as low body weight is mainly associated with attractiveness in females. Similarly, it explains the relatively high incidence of AN in homosexual men, as gay men tend to value thinness more than heterosexual men do.

## Modelling

**Modelling** is an important aspect of SLT, where learning involves extraction of information from observations and making decisions about the performance of the behaviour. In this way learning occurs without noticeable changes in behaviour. There are three types of modelling stimuli: 1) a live model demonstrating desired behaviour (such as a skinny person being complimented); 2) verbal instruction by an individual of the desired behaviour (such as a skinny person talking about the positive aspects of being skinny, such as being complimented); 3) symbolic modelling through **media** presentations of the desired behaviour (such as images of skinny models in magazines).

Effective modelling depends on a) the amount of attention given to the observed behaviour, b) retention of a mental image of the observed behaviour, c) reproduction of the mental image and d) having motivation to imitate the behaviour.

## Reinforcement

Another important part of SLT is **reinforcement**. When an observed behaviour is imitated, others respond to this; if the response is rewarding, it increases the chances of the behaviour occurring again, as the behaviour has been reinforced (strengthened). Reinforcement can be external, such as gaining approval from others for losing weight, or internal, for instance feeling better about oneself. Reinforcements can also be positive, like receiving compliments for being skinny, or negative, like no longer being mocked for being chubby.

Vicarious reinforcement occurs when an individual imitates the behaviour of a model in an attempt to gain the reward that the model achieves through their behaviour, like the model being complimented for being skinny.

## Media

The media is a powerful force in SLT. In Western cultures the media portrays extreme thinness, such as through models in women's magazines, as being desirable. These images are observed and then imitated to the point at

> **KEY TERMS**
>
> **Social learning theory** – the perception of anorexia nervosa as being learned through observation and imitation
>
> **Modelling** – where learning occurs vicariously by experience through observation of others
>
> **Media** – public forms of communication
>
> **Reinforcement** – the consequence of a behaviour that strengthens (increases) the chances of it occurring again

which AN develops. This can help explain why women are more likely to be anorexic, as women are bombarded by more 'desirable' media images of thinness than men. It also explains why women who move from cultures where such media images do not occur to cultures where they do occur become more vulnerable to developing AN.

## Research

Bemis (1978) supported SLT by reviewing 20 years of 'Playboy' centrefolds and finding the weight of models progressively decreased. Additional support came from Garner & Garfinkel (1980) finding that Miss America beauty queen winners have become much slimmer over time.

DiDomenico & Andersen (1992) found that women's magazines had more articles and advertisements focused on losing weight than men's magazines, indeed magazines aimed at females aged 18–24 years had ten times more content concerning dieting than equivalent men's magazines, illustrating the power of the media as a social learning force.

Herzog *et al*. (1991) compared 43 homosexual and 32 heterosexual men on body satisfaction and weight issues, finding homosexual men had role models who were much lighter in weight than heterosexual role models, supporting the idea that heightened levels of AN among gay men can be explained by reference to SLT.

Mumford *et al*. (1991) found heightened levels of AN among Arab and Asian women who moved to Western cultures, which suggests that cultural pressures via the media were to blame, as media emphasis on dieting and female thinness is not found in their countries of origin. Lai (2000) supported this by finding AN increased among Chinese people in Hong Kong, as the region became more westernised.

**Figure 7.13** Research suggests that beauty queens have become increasingly slimmer over time, with the media encouraging girls to imitate such low-weight role models

### Evaluation

- SLT cannot explain why dieting continues after the point at which compliments for losing weight stop, or indeed when negative comments commence.
- SLT does not explain why only some women develop AN when all women are subjected to the same media images of thinness.
- If SLT truly can explain the development of AN through the observation and imitation of thin role models, then it suggests a practical application to counteract the disorder by the use of media images of desirable heavier women.
- SLT is better able than biological explanations or the FST to explain why the prevalence of AN has increased and why it occurs more in females and certain cultures (due to the increased promotion of thinness in Western cultures).
- SLT does not really consider the cognitive aspects of AN – for example, the faulty perceptions of body image that often underpin the disorder.

## The cognitive explanation

**Cognitive theory** sees AN as caused by a breakdown in rational thought processes, such as an individual wishing to attain an unreal level of perfection in order to be an acceptable person. This level of perception is seen as attainable by developing an extremely thin body type.

**KEY TERM**

**Cognitive theory** – that anorexia results from maladaptive thought processes

### KEY TERMS

**Distortions** – errors in thinking that negatively affect perceptions of body image

**Irrational beliefs** – maladaptive ideas that lead to the development and maintenance of anorexia nervosa

## Distortions

Distorted thought processes involve errors in thinking that negatively affect perceptions of body image. These **distortions** lead an individual to adopt strict, inflexible rules about eating, with any breaking of these rules leading to a sense of guilt and failure, thus lowering self-esteem and creating self-disgust, which in turn leads to even more severe anorexic behaviour.

## Irrational beliefs

**Irrational beliefs** are maladaptive ideas that lead to the development and maintenance of AN, with such irrational beliefs often resulting in anorexics misperceiving their body image and seeing themselves as fatter than they are. Anorexics will also possess flawed reasoning behind their eating habits.

Anorexics typically demonstrate 1) distortions in thinking and 2) errors in thinking, as outlined in Tables 7.1 and 7.2.

**Table 7.1** Distortions in thinking

| |
|---|
| Misperceiving the body as overweight when it is underweight |
| Basing self-worth on physical appearance only |
| Having flawed beliefs about eating and dieting |

**Table 7.2** Errors in thinking

| |
|---|
| All or nothing thinking, e.g. I ate a chip, now I will be fat |
| Overgeneralising, e.g. If I cannot restrict my eating I am a failure |
| Magnification/minimisation, e.g. Gaining any weight is not acceptable/My weight loss is not harmful |
| Magical thinking, e.g. If I weighed below five stone I would be happy |

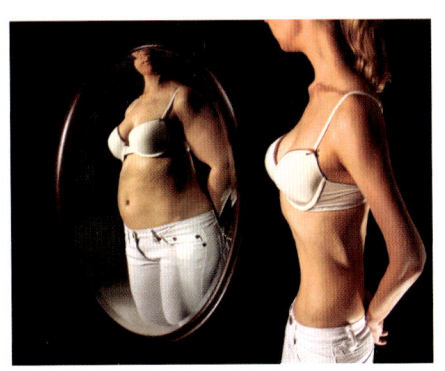

**Figure 7.14** Anorexics often have a distorted body image in line with the cognitive theory

## Research

Garner *et al.* (1982) compared 160 anorexic participants with 140 non-anorexic participants, finding that anorexics tended to overestimate their weight and body size, lending support to the cognitive theory. Further support came from Bemis-Vitouesk & Orimoto (1993), who found that anorexics have a consistent distorted body image and feel they must continually lose weight to be in control of their bodies, illustrating the key role that distortions play in the maintenance of AN.

Halmi *et al.* (2000) got 322 anorexics to complete the Multi-Dimensional Perfectionism Scale, finding they scored much higher on a need to be perfect than a similar non-anorexic control group. The higher the need for perfectionism, the more severe the symptoms of anorexia. This supports the belief of the cognitive theory that anorexics wish to attain an unreal level of perfectionism to be acceptable.

Steinglass *et al.* (2007) administered the Brown Assessment of Beliefs Scale (BABS) to 25 anorexics to identify the dominant belief that was inhibiting their eating and found 68 per cent had a main fear of gaining weight or becoming fat, with 20 per cent classed as delusional. This supports the idea of irrational thinking underpinning AN in line with cognitive theory.

Konstantakopoulos *et al.* (2012) used the BABS scale with 39 anorexics and found that 28.8 per cent had delusional body image beliefs that were associated with restricted eating and body dissatisfaction, again linking irrational thinking to the onset and maintenance of AN.

## Evaluation

- The cognitive theory, and research based upon it, does not clarify whether maladaptive thought processes are a cause of AN or a result of being anorexic.
- Cognitive behavioural therapies have a relatively high success rate in treating AN, giving a degree of support to the cognitive theory upon which they are based.
- Most females (and many males) express dissatisfaction with their bodies and many have been/are on diets, but only a few develop AN, which the cognitive theory cannot explain.
- The multiple factors of AN converge into two key elements, low self-esteem and a high need for perfectionism, both of which are explicable by reference to the cognitive theory.
- The cognitive theory does not consider other explanations, many of which are supported by research evidence. It may well be that different explanations can be combined to give a better understanding of the causes of AN. For instance, the high drive for perfectionism exhibited by many anorexics and which is a key part of the cognitive theory may be genetically transmitted.

## STRENGTHEN YOUR LEARNING

1. Outline the family systems theory of AN, including the role of enmeshment and autonomy and control.
2. What research evidence is there to support the family systems theory?
3. How can SLT explain why AN is more common in certain cultures and in certain groups of people, such as homosexual men?
4. What weaknesses are there of SLT as an explanation of AN?
5. Outline the cognitive theory of AN, including the role of distortions and irrational beliefs.
6. What distortions in thinking and errors in thinking are associated with AN? Give examples of your own for each one.
7. What research support is there for the cognitive theory?

## RESEARCH IN FOCUS

Research into the cognitive explanation of anorexia nervosa often uses questionnaires, such as the Brown Assessment of Beliefs Scale, generally finding that irrational thinking underpins the disorder. What would the strengths and weaknesses of investigating the cognitive explanation of anorexia nervosa be? What considerations should be made when constructing such questionnaires? In what ways would an experimental study be superior and inferior to a questionnaire?

# ASSESSMENT CHECK

1. Fifteen-year-old Janice comes from a close family who tend to do everything together. Janice's parents are very protective of her and her mum buys all Janice's clothes for her. Janice's parents have not been getting on very well recently and Janice is worried that they will get divorced. Over the last year Janice has lost a lot of weight and last month she was diagnosed as suffering from anorexia nervosa.

   Using your knowledge of the family systems theory and by reference to the scenario above, explain why Janice may have developed anorexia nervosa. **[4 marks]**

2. Discuss biological explanations of anorexia nervosa. **[16 marks]**

3. Explain what is meant by neural explanations of anorexia nervosa. **[2 marks]**

4. In terms of the social learning theory of anorexia nervosa, which one of the three following statements is true? **[1 mark]**
   - SLT is unable to explain why anorexia nervosa occurs more in certain cultures.
   - SLT sees anorexia nervosa as occurring through vicarious reinforcement.
   - Abnormal functioning of the hypothalamus is seen as causing anorexia nervosa.

5. A correlational study was performed that investigated the degree to which anorexia nervosa is genetic. MZ (identical) and DZ (non-identical) twins formed the sample, with the researchers recording the number of MZ twin pairs and DZ twin pairs who had both suffered from anorexia.

   Which statistical test would be used to analyse the data? Give three reasons for your choice of test. **[1 + 3 marks]**

*'We are digging our graves with our teeth.'*
Thomas Moffett (2009)

# Obesity

**KEY TERM**

**Obesity** – the condition of being chronically overweight

When fat accumulates to a body mass index (BMI) of 30kg/m², then a person is clinically obese. In Britain in 2011, 25 per cent of people were obese, with an estimated cost to the NHS of £6.4 billion per year. In the USA (with a 35 per cent **obesity** level), the condition is the second biggest cause of preventable death, being linked to cardiovascular diseases, diabetes, etc., with 9 per cent of health costs being attributed to the condition.

Symptoms include breathlessness, lethargy, difficulty in performing physical activities, excess fat in breast, abdomen and upper arm regions, sore joints and muscles, skin infections under folds of fat and varicose veins. Obese men have large waists and genitalia that appear disproportionately small. Obese women carry extra weight on their hips and have irregular periods. Conditions accompanying obesity include diabetes, heart disease, stroke and osteoarthritis. Obesity is influenced by biological and psychological factors.

# 7.5 Biological explanations for obesity

As with AN, biological explanations see obesity as physically determined, such as through genetic, neural and evolutionary means.

## Genetic explanations

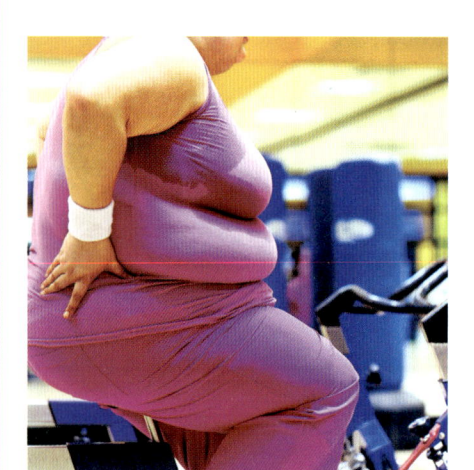

**Figure 7.15** Can obesity be explained by biological or psychological explanations?

There is an inherited genetic basis to obesity, as some individuals appear more genetically predisposed to become obese. There does not seem to be a single 'obesity gene', but instead those with multiple genes towards obesity are more vulnerable to developing the condition. The **genetic explanation** is generally tested by looking at the incidence of obesity among related individuals, such as twin studies, as well as gene-profiling studies that search for common genes among sufferers.

**KEY TERM**

**Genetic explanation** – that obesity results from an inherited predisposition

### Research

Stunkard *et al.* (1990) compared body-mass similarities between twins in a sample of 154 pairs of MZ (identical) twins reared together, 93 pairs of MZ twins reared apart, 208 pairs of DZ (non-identical) twins reared together and 218 pairs of DZ twins reared apart, finding the highest concordance rate between MZ twins reared together, but that the rate between MZ twins reared apart (0.68 concordance rate) was only slightly lower. This strongly suggests that body weight, and thus obesity, is heavily influenced by genes.

Sorensen & Stunkard (1994) compared the degree of obesity of adopted participants with their adoptive and biological parents, finding an individual's weight was more correlated with biological relatives, supporting the genetic explanation.

Frayling *et al.* (2007) found people with two copies of the fat mass and obesity gene FTO had a 70 per cent increased risk of becoming obese, while people with only one copy had only a 30 per cent increased risk, supporting a genetic explanation.

Willer *et al.* (2008) located six new genes associated with obesity. These variant genes increase the chances of being obese by up to 25 per cent, suggesting genetics does play a role in creating a predisposition to obesity.

### Evaluation

- Musani *et al.* (2008) suggest obese people may be more fertile, reproduce more and ultimately increase genes favouring obesity in the population.
- Genes cannot explain the upsurge in obesity. Genes have not changed, but environmental factors, such as the availability of food, have, suggesting environment plays the larger role.
- It is generally acknowledged that genes are one of a number of factors contributing to the onset and maintenance of obesity, but research needs to focus on how genes interact with these other factors to develop a better understanding of the disorder.
- The discovery of genes related to obesity may lead to effective gene therapies for the treatment of the condition.

## The evolutionary explanation

*The **evolutionary explanation** can be considered in essence an extension of the genetic explanation, as evolutionary influences upon obesity are genetically transmitted. If using material on the evolutionary explanation to answer questions on the genetic explanation this link should be made explicitly clear.*

Obesity may be an evolutionary hangover. In the Pleistocene era survival depended upon finding food that was not always plentiful or constantly available. Therefore selective pressure favoured individuals able to store excess energy as fat to see themselves through times of famine. Nowadays humans live in a world of constant, easily available food, but evolution causes bodies to behave as if they were still living in their ancestral past and because the gene pool has not substantially altered, genes that once favoured survival now favour obesity.

Fatty foods are preferred, as they are energy rich, and humans overeat in order to lay down fat stores that in ancient times would see them through the regular periods of food scarcity. Evolution also sees humans as preferring sedentary (lazy) lifestyles as in the EEA conserving energy was essential to survival. Modern humans continue to behave as if food supplies are irregular, resulting in dysfunctional overeating, and they over-eat foods that were not part of their evolutionary past, like liquid calories, because they do not trigger neural mechanisms that control appetite.

Evolution explains why some individuals are more vulnerable to dramatic weight increases, by reference to the thrifty gene model, which believes that in the EEA there was a selective advantage for people with insulin resistance as they would have been able to metabolise food more efficiently. This was advantageous in times of food scarcity, but now food is ever available, it leads to obesity.

### KEY TERM

**Evolutionary explanation** – that obesity results from the evolutionary tendency to store energy as fat for times of food scarcity

## Research

DiMeglio & Mates (2000) found participants given liquid calories, rather than an equal amount of solid calories, increased in weight, implying that liquid calories have caused the huge increase in obesity because humans are not shaped by evolution to cope with them.

Bray *et al.* (2004) believe high-fructose corn syrup (HFCS) causes obesity. Used as a drinks sweetener, its consumption in the USA increased by 1,000 per cent between 1970 and 1990, a time of greater obesity. Not a foodstuff familiar to our evolutionary ancestors, it is seen as not stimulating leptin and insulin production that normally act to regulate eating, thus leading to weight gain.

Rowe *et al.* (2007) found Pima Indians (Native Americans from central and southern Arizona) with high levels of obesity from a thrifty metabolism that allows them to metabolise food more efficiently. Once an advantage in times of food scarcity, it now leads to obesity, supporting the evolutionary thrifty gene hypothesis.

### Evaluation

- The idea that foodstuffs not present in the EEA are causing obesity is open to criticism due to the fact that obesity levels have also risen in countries where HFCS is not commonly used.
- The thrifty gene hypothesis explains why identifiable groups of people who do not have the gene are able to eat lots and not put on weight, for instance the people of the Nile delta where historically there were not food shortages.

## Neural explanations

It is worth remembering that there is a link between abnormal biochemistry and **neural explanations**, for example the action of leptin upon brain neurones.

The hypothalamus is the brain structure identified as playing the central role in the regulation of eating. Therefore neurological explanations focus on the idea that faulty functioning of the hypothalamus is associated with the development of obesity. Attention has focused upon the workings of the VMH, which in a normally functioning person acts as the satiety centre, informing an individual when they are full so that eating can cease. Research has also investigated specific mechanisms. For example, the action of leptin, a hormone produced by fat cells in the stomach in proportion to the amount of body fat, upon the proopiomelanocortin (POMC) and neuropeptide Y (NPY) neurones is seen as especially important. The amount of leptin influences these neurones, which regulate appetite.

Neurological factors are investigated by studying animals and faulty functioning brain structures and neurological mechanisms of obese individuals.

### Research

Reeves & Plum (1969) conducted a post-mortem on an obese female, finding her VMH had been destroyed, suggesting the hypothalamus is associated with the development of obesity. Friedman (2005) reports that

**KEY TERM**

**Neural explanations** – that obesity results from abnormally functioning brain mechanisms

**ON THE WEB**

Dr Jeffrey Friedman, who with Douglas Coleman pioneered work into the role of leptin in eating, presents the 2012 annual Sokol lecture on the biological basis of obesity. See it at **www.youtube.com**. Search for 'To eat or not to eat: Leptin and the biological basis of obesity – Sokol lecture Fall 2012'.

obese people do produce leptin, but its ability to suppress the neuron POMC is blocked, so their appetite stays high and they gain weight up to a point thought to be genetically determined, demonstrating the role of neurological factors in combination with genetics.

Stice *et al.* (2008) found obese people have a poorly functioning dorsal striatum, which leads to lessened dopamine signalling in the brain, causing them to overeat. This demonstrates the role of the neurotransmitter dopamine in determining obesity.

Yang *et al.* (2012) found that an increase in signalling in POMC neurons was positively correlated to age-dependent obesity in mice, suggesting neural factors may be able to explain why obesity increases with age.

### Evaluation

- Although there is some indication that abnormally functioning brain mechanisms can contribute to obesity, research indicates that the main biological factors are genetic and evolutionary ones.
- Much of the evidence linking neural mechanisms to obesity tends to be correlational and so it is not clear whether neural mechanisms are a cause or an effect of being obese.
- It was hoped leptin injections would prove an effective treatment for obesity, but they work for only a few people, casting doubt on the importance of leptin's role.
- Much research into leptin was done on mice and so the results may not be generalisable to humans.

### STRENGTHEN YOUR LEARNING

1. Is there a single gene for obesity? Explain your answer by referring to research evidence.
2. What do twin and adoption studies suggest about obesity? Refer to research evidence in your answer.
3. Why can genetics not be the only cause of obesity?
4. Explain why obesity may have an evolutionary cause.
5. By reference to the thrifty gene model explain why some people may be more at risk of developing obesity.
6. What does research suggest about neural mechanisms and obesity?

## 7.6 Psychological explanations for obesity

### Restraint theory

**Restraint theory** explains obesity as occurring through people attempting to lose weight by placing a self-imposed target upon food intake and then indulging in reduced eating to meet the target. However, rather than such behaviour leading to weight loss, in 80 per cent of cases it generally leads to overeating, weight increase and thus obesity. There is debate as to why this

### KEY TERM

**Restraint theory** – that obesity results from the placing of unsustainable limits on food intake

occurs. One point of view is that the self-imposed target is often unrealistic and attempting to diet in this way lowers mood and increases hunger and motivation to eat more. Another viewpoint is that the type of people likely to attempt restrained eating in this way are those with less self-control and who are thus more likely to display disinhibited eating, in other words individuals who are more vulnerable to becoming obese.

# Disinhibition

Disinhibited eating concerns overeating, eating too quickly and repeated lack of success with dieting. It is linked to having a high body mass index and thus obesity. Disinhibited eating occurs when individuals have opportunities to consume desirable foods and when under emotional distress. Disinhibited eating is often shown by anxiety-prone individuals, often those with poor interpersonal attachments, who rely more on external factors, such as food, for emotional control. Overall, therefore, **disinhibition** is a tendency to seek emotional comfort through overeating, leading to an increase in weight and ultimately obesity.

# Boundary model

### Herman & Polivy (1984)

The **boundary model** proposes that hunger motivates individuals to intake food above a set minimum level and that satiety motivates individuals to keep intake below a set maximum level. The distance between these levels is set by psychological factors, with dieters having a large range between their hunger and satiety levels because it takes longer for them to feel hungry and they need more food to reach satiety. The relationship to restraint theory is that once restrained eaters exceed their self-imposed eating target, they continue to eat until they reach satiety because their physiological set point boundary (see Biological explanations for obesity, page 256) overrides their self-imposed cognitive boundary, leading to overeating, with such individuals being at an increased risk of being obese.

## Research

Ruderman & Wilson (1979) found dieters ended up eating more food than non-dieters, suggesting restrained eating leads to weight increase rather than weight decrease. Further support came from Wardle & Beale (1988), who assigned 27 women to one of three groups, a diet group, an exercise group and a control group, for seven weeks, with food intake regularly assessed under laboratory conditions. Those in the diet condition ate more than those in the exercise and control groups.

Wilkinson *et al.* (2010) gave 200 adults with BMIs ranging from 17 to 41 the Three Factor Eating Questionnaire and the Experiences in Close Relationships Questionnaire to measure disinhibition and attachment style. Findings showed that anxiety-attachment style positively correlated with disinhibited eating and a high BMI, which suggests that disinhibited eaters are at risk of obesity because they attempt to reduce the anxiety experience associated with their attachment style by overeating.

Bryant *et al.* (2008) report that disinhibited eaters have lower self-esteem, low physical activity and poorer psychological health and also experience

**KEY TERMS**

**Disinhibition** – overeating through the loss of restraint over food intake

**Boundary model** – that obesity results from conflict between physiological and cognitive limits on food intake

lower success at dieting and incur greater weight regain, suggesting that disinhibition is strongly linked to vulnerability to obesity.

Herman & Polivy (1984) found dieters reported they could not be bothered to maintain dieting, as it took too much effort, suggesting a cognitive shift in thinking involving a breakdown of self-control or 'motivational collapse' in line with the boundary model.

### Evaluation

- Ogden (2009) reviewed research into restraint theory, concluding that if restraint is detrimental to the physical and psychological health of normal weight individuals, then it should not be used by overweight individuals vulnerable to becoming obese.
- Research supports the central idea that restrained eating leads to episodes of overeating and possible obesity. However, the theory cannot explain the minority of dieters who succeed in attaining weight loss through restrained eating. Also anorexics experience huge weight losses through restraint.
- Lowe & Kral (2006) reported that among restrained eaters there is an over-representation of people with a tendency for lack of self-control and disinhibited eating, which suggests that individuals who are more vulnerable to obesity indulge in restraint and thus see an increase in weight.
- Disinhibition is a major factor in weight gain leading to obesity because of the high daily number of overeating opportunities to be found in Western cultures.

> 'Eat, drink, and be merry, for tomorrow we may diet.'
> Harry Kurnitz (1955)

## Explanations for the success and failure of dieting

**Dieting** is a form of restrained eating involving voluntary restriction of food intake.

Wing & Hill (2001) define dieting success as 'successful long-term weight loss maintenance, involving the intentional loss of at least 10 per cent of initial body weight and keeping it off for at least one year'. According to this definition 20 per cent succeed. Dieters differ in the extent to which eating is restrained and for how long and these factors also affect success levels. The majority of dieters are women, of whom 87 per cent have dieted at some time.

There are many explanations for the success and failure of dieting, involving varied biological and psychological factors. However, these should be considered in conjunction with each other (multi-causal) rather than as individual explanations.

### Success

When diets succeed it is generally due to a combination of strategies that helps an individual lose weight in a realistic and attainable manner and then maintain the loss over an extended period. One means of accomplishing

**KEY TERM**

**Dieting** – restrained eating involving voluntary restriction of food intake

this is relapse prevention, which involves achieving a stable energy balance around a new lower weight. Relapse prevention involves learning to identify situations in which 'lapses' could occur and how to 're-focus' if and when they do, so that dieters do not return to pre-weight loss eating behaviours and lose the motivation and belief that a lower weight can be sustained.

Motivation and confidence, as well as incentives and social support, help determine success. Operant conditioning is used in the form of rewards acting as positive reinforcements to condition the desired weight-loss effect. For example, dieters might reward themselves with fashionable new clothes that fit their new body shape. The use of social networks is beneficial by using family and friends to provide support during the weight-loss time period. Weight Watchers is a dieting company that uses group meetings to actively encourage members to provide each other with social support, creating a positive social identity for individual dieters that fosters confidence and motivation to adhere to diets. Social learning theory is also used, by providing successful role models for dieters to observe.

These factors all increase the chances of success, but the process is dependent on setting achievable targets for the amount of weight loss and the time period in which it is to occur. The chances of success are maximised by not setting over-specific goals and the goal-setting process should consist of a series of short-term goals leading up to the ultimate long-term goal. Advice from health professionals is necessary to achieve this, and to avoid setting unrealistic targets dieters must establish a clear, objectively defined path to success in order to maintain motivation throughout the weight-loss process. If setbacks occur too often, even relapse prevention will not stop motivation declining and the person will abandon their diet. Initial targets are easily achievable, as reaching them increases confidence and motivation. Regular monitoring and feedback occur, with necessary readjustments being made. Although expert opinion is sought, individuals are involved in target setting to create a sense of 'ownership'.

Individuals who successfully diet share common behaviours that promote weight loss and its maintenance, and once weight loss has been maintained for two years the chances of long-term success increase dramatically.

**Figure 7.16** Successful dieting is dependent upon losing weight in a realistic and attainable way and maintaining the weight loss

### YOU ARE THE RESEARCHER

Design an experiment to test whether goal setting results in dieting success.

What would the IV and DV be? How would you operationalise failure/success? What experimental design would be used? How would you go about getting a self-selected sample? (Remember this is a study of dieters.)

Dieting is a sensitive area. How would ethical concerns be addressed through standardised instructions?

When analysing the results, what level of significance would be used and why?

## Research

Miller-Kovach *et al.* (2001) reported the social support methods that Weight Watchers offered were superior to individual dieting regimes over a period of two years.

Lowe *et al.* (2004) found an average of 71.6 per cent of Weight Watchers members maintained a body weight loss of at least 5 per cent, indicating that social support motivates people to not only lose weight but maintain the loss, too.

Bartlett (2003) found dieting success occurs best with a target of reducing calorific intake by between 500 and 1,000 **calories** a day, resulting in weight loss of about 1–2 pounds a week, supporting the idea that achievable goal setting is a strong motivational force.

Wing & Hill (2001) reported common behaviours leading to successful weight loss and its maintenance included a low-fat diet, constant self-monitoring of food intake and weight, and increased physical activity.

> **KEY TERM**
> **Calories** – the energy content of food

### PSYCHOLOGY IN THE REAL WORLD
#### Weight Watchers: the psychology of dieting

Weight Watchers, a private company founded in 1963, operates in 30 countries. Research suggests its weight-loss programmes are effective, due to the psychological factors at its core. The most important factor is the social support given to members. Positive role models in the form of successful dieters are provided, as well as vicarious reinforcement and the creation of a positive social environment that motivates members to believe they can succeed.

Weight Watchers also uses goal setting. Members are set target weights that are healthy and feasible. The long-term target weight is broken down into achievable short-term goals and by reaching each one members gain in confidence and motivation to continue. The programme includes a maintenance period where food intake is stabilised and weight is neither lost nor gained. For this members attain 'lifetime' membership, a status retained free of charge as long as they stay within 2lb of their maintenance weight.

Miller-Kovach *et al.* (2001) found the Weight Watchers programme more successful than self-help programmes over a two-year period, while Lowe *et al.* (2004) found that 72 per cent of members reaching their target weight maintained it over a five-year period, having lost initially at least 5 per cent of body weight. This suggests the programme is successful in losing weight and maintaining weight loss, highlighting the importance of incorporating psychological principles into successful dieting.

*'I've been on a diet for two weeks and all I've lost is two weeks.'*
Totie Fields (1965)

## Failure

Most diets fail, mainly because they are unsustainable, the prime factor being a lack of knowledge and the skills necessary to diet sensibly. Dieters set unrealistic targets, such as restricting themselves to too few calories per day, which they cannot continue for more than a short time. Also, many dieters who generally have spent prolonged periods becoming overweight expect to lose weight quickly, which again is not realistic. Although initial weight loss can be considerable, continued weight loss tends to slow down, which is perceived as less reinforcing and therefore the dieter's motivation to continue declines and they regain weight, which is even more demotivating.

The more restrictive the diet, the more likely it is that it will fail. Being on a low-calorie diet brings unpleasant side effects, such as lack of energy, dizziness and stress, which again leads to loss of motivation and abandonment of the diet. Dieters often perceive dieting as a temporary regime and once weight-loss targets are achieved they return to their old eating habits and regain weight. This results in constant weight fluctuations (yo-yo dieting) through a repetitive cycle of restrictive eating.

A biological role is played by the hormone ghrelin, which stimulates appetite, making hungry people even hungrier during dieting, as the body tries to address the weight loss by increasing the physiological desire to eat. This increases the chances of abandoning the diet.

Cognitive factors play a role, too, with a lessening of concentration associated with diets that fail.

## Research

Jeffery (2000) found obese people start regaining weight after six months due to failing to maintain behavioural changes, suggesting factors such as loss of motivation and social pressure have negative influences.

Cummings *et al.* (2002) found low-calorie diets stimulate appetite by increasing ghrelin production by 24 per cent, reducing the chances of losing weight, as individuals become more physiologically motivated to eat. This is supported by the success of stomach-reduction surgery being due to shrunken stomachs producing less ghrelin.

Williams *et al.* (2002) found individuals lacking concentration are unsuccessful with diets, as they lose focus on targets and strategies, indicating that cognitive factors play a role in abandonment.

D'Anci *et al.* (2008) found low-carbohydrate diets have a cognitive effect, reducing glycogen levels, which then leads to a lack of concentration. This suggests that certain types of diet influence cognitive factors and that cognitive processes are affected by biological factors.

### STRENGTHEN YOUR LEARNING

1. Why might people who restrain their eating actually become obese?
2. Why might people who are vulnerable to obesity be more likely to attempt restrained eating?
3. Explain the relationship between the set point theory (see page 240) and the boundary model.
4. What degree of research support is there for restraint theory (including disinhibition and the boundary model)?
5. Define success in dieting.
6. Explain what is meant by relapse prevention.
7. How might operant conditioning and SLT contribute to successful dieting?
8. What does research suggest about the reasons for diets failing?
9. What evaluative points can be made about the success and failure of diets?

### Evaluation

- Individual differences contribute to success rates. 'Low-restrainers' find dieting easy, while 'high-restrainers' find it difficult. Mensink *et al.* (2008) thinks high-restrainers are hyper-sensitive to food cues, thus likely to abandon diets. Stirling *et al.* (2004) found high-restrainers could not resist forbidden chocolate. However, it is not known whether being a high- or a low-restrainer is innate or learned.
- Nolen-Hoeksema (2002) found females on low-fat diets develop negative moods, which they address by overeating, with 80 per cent of these going on to develop clinical depression within five years, suggesting dieting can lead to a risk of developing mental disorders.
- Psychological research has contributed towards the formation of effective diets and weight-reduction programmes. Psychological knowledge, when applied properly, can lead to long-term effectiveness in the form of weight stabilisation around an ideal target weight. Such success can be measured in terms of people's heightened psychological well-being as well as reduced costs to the health services.
- Research into dieting can be seen as gender biased because it tends to focus on females, thus findings cannot be generalised to males. Some dieting behaviour has negative consequences, such as the development of anorexia nervosa, which although primarily a female complaint, has about a 15 per cent incidence of male sufferers, so it is important to understand male dieting behaviour as well.

# ASSESSMENT CHECK

1. Paul was overweight so decided to go on a diet. He placed a self-imposed limit on the amount of calories he could eat a day and was determined to stick to it. However, Paul found that he soon started to feel quite depressed and anxious and was very hungry all the time. Eventually he gave in to temptation, ate far more calories than his self-imposed limit allowed and actually ended up heavier than he was when he started the diet.

   Using your knowledge of restraint theory and making reference to the scenario above, explain why Paul is in danger of becoming obese. **[4 marks]**

2. Which of the two following statements relate to the neural explanation of obesity? **[2 marks]**
   - Neural explanation sees faulty functioning of the hypothalamus as being associated with the development of obesity.
   - Neural explanations of obesity focus on maladaptive thought processes.
   - Neural explanations see obesity as arising from the evolutionary tendency to store energy as fat for times of food scarcity.
   - Neural explanations see obesity as resulting from abnormally functioning brain mechanisms.

3. A team of researchers measured the amount of weight lost by participants receiving social support or on a self-help programme. The amount of weight each participant lost can be seen in the table below.

| Participant | Received social support | Followed self-help programme |
| --- | --- | --- |
| 1 | 4 | 2 |
| 2 | 12 | 3 |
| 3 | 4 | 7 |
| 4 | 12 | 0 |
| 5 | 4 | 3 |
| 6 | 6 | 3 |

   a) For participants receiving social support, calculate the mode.

   b) For participants following a self-help programme, calculate the mean. **[2 marks]**

4. Explain one reason for the success of dieting. **[3 marks]**

5. Outline and evaluate the genetic explanation of obesity. **[16 marks]**

Explanations for food preferences

Neural and hormonal mechanisms

Biological explanations for anorexia nervosa
Psychological explanations for anorexia nervosa

Biological explanations for obesity
Psychological explanations for obesity

**SUMMARY**

- Evolutionary explanations see food preferences as having an adaptive survival value, with important roles for neophobia and taste aversion.
- Food preferences can also be learned through experience via social and cultural influences.
- Neural and hormonal mechanisms are biological influences upon eating behaviour, with important roles for the hypothalamus, ghrelin and leptin.
- Genetic and neural explanations see anorexia nervosa as being biologically determined.
- The family systems theory sees anorexia nervosa as resulting from dysfunctional patterns of family interaction, with important roles for enmeshment and autonomy and control.
- The social learning theory sees anorexia nervosa as being learned through observation and imitation, with important roles for modelling, reinforcement and the media.
- The cognitive explanation sees anorexia nervosa as resulting from maladaptive thought processes, with important roles for distortions and irrational beliefs.
- Genetic and neural explanations see obesity as being biologically determined.
- Restraint theory sees obesity as resulting from the placing of unsustainable limits on food intake, with important roles for disinhibition and the boundary model.
- Dieting involves voluntary restriction of calories, with several reasons existing for success and failure.

# 8 Stress

## Introduction

Stress is a general response to demands made upon the body. Stress occurs when there is a lack of balance between the perceived needs of a situation and the perceived abilities of an individual to cope with those needs, for example not feeling able to meet the demands of your psychology examination.

Although stress has behavioural and cognitive components, stress responses are mainly physiological (bodily) ones. Stressors are the sources of stress (things that cause stress). If an individual is stressed due to owing money, stress is what the individual feels, while the stressor is owing money.

Specific focus will be upon:

1. The physiology of stress
2. The role of stress in illness
3. Sources of stress
4. Physiological measures of stress
5. Individual differences in stress
6. Managing and coping with stress.

## Understanding the specification

- When studying the physiology of stress the general adaptation syndrome, the hypothalamic-pituitary-adrenal system and the sympathomedullary pathway as well as the role of cortisol must be included, as they are explicitly listed on the specification.
- The specification requires that the study of the role of stress in illness should include immunosuppression and cardiovascular disorders, as again these are specifically listed.
- Sources of stress require focus on three areas: life changes, daily hassles and workplace stress (including the effects of workload and control).
- When studying measurements of stress, the Social Readjustment Ratings Scale, Hassles and Uplifts Scale and skin conductance response should be included, as they are explicitly listed in the specification.
- The study of individual differences in stress requires focus on personality types A, B, C and associated behaviours, as well as hardiness, including commitment, challenge and control.
- The specification's final focus is on managing and coping with stress, with a requirement to concentrate on i] the drug therapies of benzodiazepine and beta-blockers, as well as stress inoculation therapy and biofeedback, ii] gender differences in coping with stress, and iii] types of social support, including instrumental, emotional and esteem support.

These are the basic requirements of the specification. However, other relevant material is included to provide depth and detail to your understanding.

*'A crust eaten in peace is better than a banquet partaken in anxiety.'*
Aesop (540 BC)

## IN THE NEWS

### The Psychological Enquirer

Visitors to Cebu City Zoo in the Philippines are being offered snake massages to ease away stress after a hard day's sightseeing. The therapy involves lying down on a bamboo bed and being covered in four six-and-a-half-feet-long non-poisonous Burmese pythons weighing a combined total of 550lb (see Figure 8.1). A session lasts 10-15 minutes, with the slithering motion of the snakes said to be therapeutic and calming. The large snakes, which feed by crushing their prey and then swallowing them whole, are fed ten or more chickens each before each massage just to be on the safe side.

When individuals are stressed the neck, shoulders and lower back are especially tense. Snakes are not as efficient as a trained masseur who can apply specific pressures to targeted areas, but the large, heavy snakes provide a deep massaging effect as they crawl around a human body easing the muscular effects of stress.

Psychological research into stress helps form types of stress management, both biological, like drug therapies, and psychological, like hardiness training. Snake massage has a physical and psychological calming effect, but is probably not a therapy most people would wish to try.

**Figure 8.1** Snake massage is one of the more unusual forms of stress management

### ON THE WEB

To watch a video presentation of people being snake massaged at Cebu Zoo, go to **www.youtube.com** and search for 'Snake (pythons) massage comes to Cebu...travel, culture, fun...'. Not for those with a snake phobia!

### KEY TERMS

**Stressors** – internal and external sources of stress

**Stress** – lack of balance between the perceived demands of a situation and perceived abilities to cope with such demands

**General adaptation syndrome** – a description of the body's short- and long-term reaction to stress

**Hypothalamic-pituitary-adrenal system** – bodily system responding to chronic, long-term stressors, comprised of the hypothalamus, the pituitary gland and the adrenal glands

**Sympathomedullary pathway** – bodily system responding to acute, short-term stressors, comprised of the sympathetic nervous system and the sympathetic adrenal medullary system

**Cortisol** – a steroid hormone secreted from the adrenal glands in reaction to stress

*'The human body is robust. It gathers strength when it's in mortal danger.'*
Toni Morrison (2004)

## 8.1 The physiology of stress

**Stressors** can either be acute (short-term), for instance being confronted by a snarling dog, or chronic (long-term), such as pressures at work. Both types affect the body, though in different ways. The effects of **stress** upon the body have been explained initially by the **general adaptation syndrome** and later by the **hypothalamic-pituitary-adrenal system** and the **sympathomedullary pathway**. The hormone **cortisol** plays a vital role, especially with chronic stress.

### General adaptation syndrome

#### Selye (1936)

The general adaptation syndrome (GAS) describes the physiological reactions that occur in response to stress. There are three stages to GAS:

1 **Alarm reaction** – involves physiological changes associated with emotional reactions to stressors. The hypothalamus signals the sympathetic nervous system, which activates and stimulates the adrenal medulla to secrete adrenaline and noradrenaline, which help increase heart rate, blood flow and blood-sugar levels (this is commonly known as the fight-or-flight response).

2. **Resistance** – if the stressor continues the body recovers from the initial alarm and starts to cope with the situation. Sympathetic nervous system activity declines, thus adrenaline and noradrenaline secretion also declines but increases from another part of the adrenal gland, the adrenal cortex. The adrenal cortex is controlled by the amount of adrenocorticotropic hormone (ACTH) in the blood, which in turn is controlled by the hypothalamus. Levels of glucocorticoid hormones (mainly cortisol) are increased in blood sugar and these provide the energy (in the form of glucose) to resist the stress.

3. **Exhaustion** – if the stress continues, bodily resources become depleted so that the adrenal glands cannot function efficiently, blood-sugar levels drop and physical health is affected, e.g. high blood pressure, heart disease, ulcers, etc. can develop.

## Research

Selye (1950) gave a variety of stressors to rats, including exposure to extreme cold and heat, intense sound or light, forced exercise, and injections of various organ extracts. He found the stress reaction was identical, consisting of enlargement of the adrenal gland, shrinkage of the thymus, spleen and lymph glands, and ulcers in the stomach and small intestine. This suggests that there is one bodily stress response, supporting the notion of the GAS.

Timio *et al.* (1988) spent 20 years comparing nuns, protected from everyday stressors, with working women, who were not, to find the nuns' blood pressure was unchanged while the working women had heightened blood pressure. This supports the notion that long-term stress has negative effects on physical health in line with GAS.

Leshem & Kuiper (1996) reported that applying different types of stressors, such as heat, cold, drought, salt, etc., to plants produced a similar stress response of retarded growth and lower yields, which suggests that GAS can be applied to plants as well as animals, illustrating the biological underpinning of stress reactions.

### Evaluation

- GAS was the first theory to explain the physiological effects of stress and influenced a lot of later theories and research, especially into the negative effects of stress upon health.
- Much initial research was performed on rats, so it is difficult to generalise results to humans, whose stress responses have a greater emotional and cognitive input. Also rats are more passive in their response to stress – while humans generally respond more actively, i.e. humans try to find a way to lessen stressors, rats don't.
- Selye's belief that individuals respond in an identical way to all stressors is not true. Mason (1995) showed that stressors vary in the amount of adrenaline and cortisol they produce depending on the amount of fear and anger created by the stressors. There are also gender differences in stress reactions.
- Selye's experiments subjected rats to sustained forms of painful stress, such as surgical injury and rapidly altered temperatures. Many believe these techniques are ethically unacceptable, though Seyle thought them justified, as he hoped they would lead to therapeutic breakthroughs in treating stress-related illnesses.

### RESEARCH IN FOCUS

Hans Selye, in devising the *General Adaptation Syndrome* (GAS), conducted extensive research on animals, mainly rats, which involved exposing them to severe levels of stress. How might such research be seen as unethical? How also might it be possible to justify such research in terms of a *cost-benefit analysis*? Why also might the findings of such research not be generalisable to humans?

# The sympathomedullary pathway

The sympathetic nervous system (SNS) and the sympathetic adrenal medullary system (SAM) make up the sympathomedullary pathway (SMP). The SMP is concerned with acute (short-term) stressors.

Acute stressors activate the autonomic nervous system (ANS), which has two divisions:

1. The SNS, which is the 'troubleshooter'. It is highly responsive to stimuli and through activation is responsible for emotional states and heightened arousal.
2. The parasympathetic nervous system (PSNS), which is the 'housekeeper'. It is responsible for maintaining equilibrium and calming bodily processes.

These two divisions are opposing forces, interacting to produce the bodily state at any given time. The sympathetic division is the component primarily activated by stressors.

When exposed to an acute stressor, the SNS is activated and, simultaneously, the SAM system stimulates the release of the hormone adrenaline into the bloodstream from the adrenal glands in the adrenal medulla. This hormone prepares the body for the 'fight-or-flight' response by boosting the supply of oxygen and glucose to the brain and muscles and suppressing non-emergency processes like digestion.

## Research

Taylor *et al.* (2000) found that acute stress produces the fight-or-flight response in men but the 'tend-and-befriend' response in women. This different effect occurs as women produce more oxytocin, a chemical promoting relaxation and nurturing, suggesting a gender difference in the activation of the sympathomedullary pathway.

McCarty (1981) found that blood plasma levels of adrenaline and noradrenaline (another hormone) were equal in rats of varying ages before subjecting them to one minute of inescapable electric shocks to the feet, but that older rats had lower levels than younger rats after being shocked. This suggests that diminished responsiveness of the sympathomedullary pathway explains the reduced capacity of aged animals to adapt to stressful stimulation.

Horwatt *et al.* (1988) found that if animals are exposed to the same stressful stimulus each day for several weeks, a number of adaptive changes occur in the sympathomedullary pathway. These include the increased production and storage of catecholamines, fight-or-flight hormones produced in response to stress. If such animals are then exposed to a novel stressful stimulus, they display an exaggerated response of the sympathomedullary pathway compared with animals exposed to the same stressful stimulus for the first time. This suggests that acute stress responses develop differently due to previous stress experiences.

### ON THE WEB

To learn more about the 'tend and befriend' response in females, especially the evolutionary and biochemical explanations for such a unique female response to stress, go to **www.personalityresearch.org/papers/mccarthy.html** where you will find extensive coverage of Taylor et al's (2000) research. There is also coverage of research which suggests the response is found too in males who take on child caring responsibilities.

### Evaluation

- A gender difference in the activation of the sympathomedullary pathway may occur due to women's evolutionary role in caring for offspring. If women fought or fled when faced with danger, offspring would be placed in danger, reducing reproductive success. A better policy is to bond with other group members, most probably females.
- Studies on human stress responses were mainly conducted on men, as some researchers believed the monthly fluctuations in hormones experienced by women as part of their menstrual cycle would create stress responses that varied too widely to be considered valid. Therefore, such results cannot be generalised to women.
- Much research into the sympathomedullary pathway involves animals and thus presents a problem of extrapolation, as the stress-related behaviour of animals might not represent that of humans, with humans more likely to have a cognitive element to their stress responses.

## The hypothalamic-pituitary-adrenal system

Prolonged, chronic stress activates the hypothalamic-pituitary-adrenal system (HPA) (see Figure 8.2). This system is harder to activate than the SMP, being initiated by stressors continuous over a period of time. Such stressors alert the hypothalamus brain area to stimulate the release of the chemical messenger corticotropin-releasing hormone (CRH) into the bloodstream. This in turn stimulates the pituitary gland to release adrenocorticotropic hormone, which travels in the bloodstream to the adrenal glands just above the kidneys, triggering the release of stress-related hormones, the most important being cortisol.

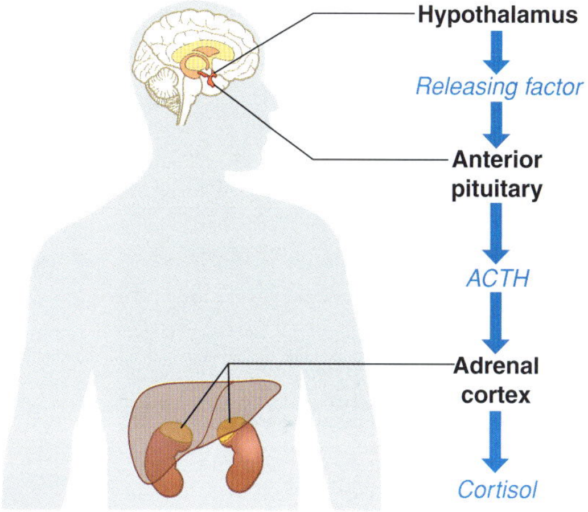

**Figure 8.2** The hypothalamic-pituitary-adrenal axis

### The role of cortisol

The production of cortisol, a glucocorticoid hormone, permits a steady supply of blood sugar, providing individuals with a constant source of energy, allowing the body to deal with stressors. Cortisol release increases the capability to tolerate more pain than usual, but also leads to impaired cognitive ability and reduced immune system performance.

### Research

Heim *et al.* (2000) found that women sexually abused as children exhibited increased pituitary-adrenal and autonomic responses to stress, measured by levels of ACTH and cortisol, compared with women who were not sexually abused in childhood. This suggests that pituitary-adrenal system hyper-reactivity due to corticotropin-releasing factor (CRF) hypersecretion is a consequence of childhood abuse. It is also suggested that CRF-receptor antagonists could be used to prevent and treat abnormal conditions related to early-life stress.

Newcomer *et al.* (1999) found that participants given levels of cortisol high enough to produce blood-sugar levels similar to those of people experiencing major stress events, like abdominal surgery, were poorer at recalling prose passages than participants given levels of cortisol only high enough to produce a stress reaction similar to minor surgery, such as having

### ON THE WEB

To view a short, informational animation display of the body's response to stress go to **www.youtube.com** and search for 'Stress response in animation'.

stitches out. This suggests that stressful stimulation of the pituitary-adrenal system has adverse effects on memory.

Watson *et al.* (2004) compared the pituitary-adrenal system functioning of 26 people with bipolar disorder (manic depression), 27 people with bipolar disorder in remission and 28 healthy controls. They found heightened cortisol levels in bipolar sufferers, including those currently in remission. This suggests that pituitary-adrenal system dysfunction may be involved in the disease process underlying bipolar disorder.

### Evaluation

- There are individual differences with response levels. Mason (1975) found that different individuals produce different levels of stress hormones when exposed to the same stressors.
- Prolonged activation of the HPA system can lead to Cushing's syndrome, which produces weight gain, memory and attention lapses as well as mood disruption. It is caused by extended exposure to high levels of cortisol, often resulting from lengthy periods of stress.
- People respond in more active ways to stressors involving cognitive and emotional factors. Symington *et al.* (1955) found that conscious terminal cancer patients experienced more stress than those in a coma, as they indulged in a more stressful appraisal of their condition.
- People who have had their adrenal glands surgically removed have to be given hormonal supplements in order to combat stressors, illustrating the crucial role of both the HPA system and the SMP in dealing with the physiological effects of stress.
- The biological explanation of stress allows accurate, objective measures to be made.

### YOU ARE THE RESEARCHER

Can you explain why for ethical reasons it would be difficult to conduct an experiment to examine the belief that chronic stress reduces the effectiveness of the immune system to fight off disease?

Design instead a correlational study to assess this belief. You will probably have to use, again for ethical reasons, a group of people who are naturally exposed to high levels of stress. What would your co-variables be? What type of statistical test could be used to analyse the data?

### STRENGTHEN YOUR LEARNING

1. Explain the difference between acute and chronic stressors.
2. Outline i) the GAS, ii) the SMP, iii) the HPA system and explain to what extent they are supported by research evidence.
3. What other evaluative points can be made about the body's physiological response to stress?

*'Take care of your body, it's the only place you have to live in.'*
Mara Lawton (2014)

# 8.2 The role of stress in illness

Small amounts of stress, which are enjoyed as satisfying challenges, contribute to good health; Selye called such stress eustress. However, for many people stress, especially prolonged stress that is not satisfactorily managed, can lead to serious illness, due to **immunosuppression** – the impaired ability of the immune system to fight illness and disease. **Cardiovascular disorders** – dysfunctions of the heart and blood vessels – are especially linked to immunosuppression.

### KEY TERMS

**Immunosuppression** – the impaired ability of the immune system to fight illness and disease

**Cardiovascular disorders** – dysfunctions of the heart and blood vessels

# Stress-related illness and the immune system

The **immune system** consists of billions of cells travelling through the bloodstream. These cells are produced in the spleen, lymph nodes, thymus and bone marrow (see Figure 8.3). They move in and out of tissues and organs, defending the body against antigens (foreign bodies), like bacteria, viruses and cancerous cells. The major type of cells are leucocytes (white blood cells), of which there are various types. Some immune cells produce and secrete antibodies, which bind to antigens and destroy them.

With chronic stress the immune system's ability to fight off antigens is reduced and infection becomes more likely. Stress does not actually *cause* infections but it increases the body's vulnerability to infectious agents by immunosuppression, the temporary reduction of immune system function.

Occasional production of cortisol and other corticosteroids does not harm the immune system, but if produced continuously, as with chronic stress, they interfere with leucocyte activity and the production of antibodies. Stressful events are linked to certain illnesses, such as cancer and chronic fatigue disorder, as well as infections like influenza. It seems, therefore, that although cortisol helps protect against viruses and heal injured tissues, too much cortisol suppresses the immune system, harming the very thing that protects us from infection.

## KEY TERM

**Immune system** – bodily system that defends against disease

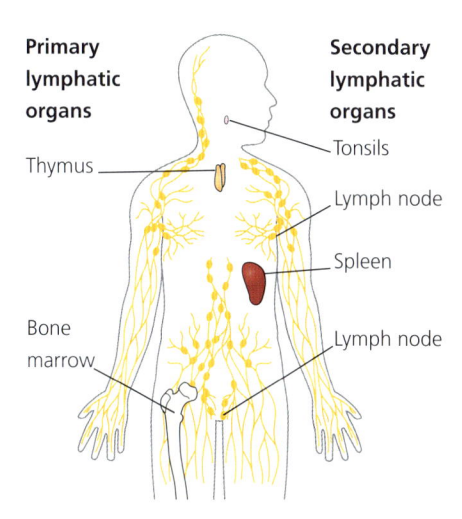

**Figure 8.3** The immune system produces cells in many parts of the body that help fight infection

## Research

Vaernes & Torjussen (1991) reported a study of Norwegian air force personnel that showed a relationship between perceived work stress and complaints related to immune system activity, demonstrating a link between work stress and immunosuppression.

Cohen *et al*. (1993) performed a research study centring on the cold virus. Of those given the virus, it was found that people were more likely to catch a cold if they displayed high stress scores, suggesting that stress depresses the efficiency of the immune system.

Evans *et al*. (1994) found that students who gave mildly stressful public presentations had increased levels of sigA, an antibody that improves the ability of the immune system to resist infection, illustrating how short-term stress can be beneficial to the functioning of the immune system.

Kiecolt-Glaser *et al*. (1995) gave small wounds to participants and measured how long they took to heal. The healing process took longer in women who cared for senile relatives. This was supported by other measurements of immune system functioning, indicating that prolonged chronic stress lessens immune system functioning.

### Evaluation

- The vulnerability of the immune system to chronic stress is influenced by individual differences, such as personality type, gender and age. Johnson & Sharma (2001) gave the toxin fumonisin B1 to rats, finding evidence of immunosuppression in females but not males, while Lindemann *et al*. (1978) found that immunosuppression as a result of physical stress increased with age in mice.
- Much evidence linking stress to immunosuppression is correlational, thus cause and effect relationships are difficult to identify, as other factors, like the unhealthy lifestyles of stressed individuals (such as smoking and drinking), may also be contributory factors.
- Changes in the functioning of the immune system take time to establish and may not be identifiable immediately by research. Longitudinal studies involving measurement of immune system functioning over an extended period would be required.
- Findings gained from research into stress and the immune system are used by health practitioners to help anticipate problems occurring as a response to stressful incidents and to develop appropriate therapies.

## CLASSIC RESEARCH

### Effect of immunosuppression in medical students – Janice Kiecolt-Glaser (1984)

Janice Kiecolt-Glaser is Professor of Medicine at Ohio State University. She has twice received the Award for Outstanding Contributions to Health Psychology and is best known for her work on the health consequences of stress. In this classic study she demonstrated how chronic stress leads to immunosuppression and increased risk of illness.

Figure 8.4 Janice Kiecolt-Glaser

#### Aim
To study the capability of the immune system in people facing stressful situations. The prediction was that immunosuppression, measured by the amount of natural killer cell activity, would be reduced when stress levels were high.

#### Procedure
Blood samples were taken from 49 male and 26 female volunteer first-year medical students one month before final exams and again after the first day of the exams. The blood samples were analysed for leucocyte activity, specifically how much natural killer cell activity, involved in fighting off viruses and tumours, was present.

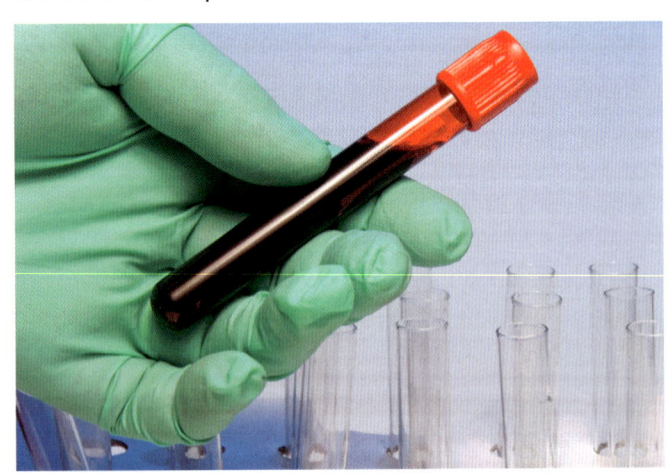

Figure 8.5 Blood samples can show immunosuppression

Questionnaires were also given, assessing psychiatric symptoms, loneliness and life events.

#### Findings
Natural killer cell activity was reduced in the second sample compared with the first. Immune responses were weakest in those scoring highly for loneliness, stressful life events and psychiatric symptoms, such as depression and anxiety.

### Conclusions

Chronic stress is associated with reduced immune function.

There are individual differences in levels of vulnerability to immunosuppression through chronic stress.

### Evaluation

- The stressors used were naturally occurring, as opposed to other studies using artificially induced stressors. In other words, the IV and DV were not artificially created.
- As the students were compared with themselves on the two occasions blood samples were taken, this controls for participant variables, such as personality.
- It is not certain whether the stressors caused changes in immune function; other non-controlled situational variables might play a part.
- The sample of volunteer medical students is potentially not representative of the general population.

*'Except for the occasional heart attack I feel as young as I ever did.'*
Robert Benchley (1943)

## Stress and cardiovascular disorders

The body is a physical structure requiring continual maintenance to stay healthy, but like prolonged exposure to storms damages a building, prolonged exposure to stress causes physical damage to the body. This is especially true of the heart and blood vessels, where prolonged stress can result in cardiovascular disorders (CVDs), such as hardened arteries, hypertension (high blood pressure) and coronary heart disease (CHD), which results from the arteries supplying the heart with blood becoming clogged up with fatty materials (see Figure 8.6).

Stress can lead to CVDs directly via activation of bodily stress systems or indirectly via stressed people's unhealthy lifestyles, for instance excessive drinking, drug-taking, poor diet and smoking.

### Research

Cobb & Rose (1973) compared the medical records of air traffic controllers (a highly stressful job) with those of other air traffic personnel and found that air traffic controllers had higher levels of hypertension, increasing the risk of heart disease. This supports the idea of chronic stress being linked to CVDs.

Krantz *et al.* (1991) looked at 39 people with myocardial ischaemia (a condition where the heart receives a reduced blood flow) and their reactions to low-level stress. Those with the highest myocardial ischaemia readings, when stressed, had the highest increases in blood pressure, suggesting a direct link between low-level cognitive stress and physiological reactions leading to cardiovascular damage.

Rozanski *et al.* (1999) found that some individuals are hyper-responsive to stressors, as the sympathetic branch of their ANS reacts more than in other people, leading to more damage of the cardiovascular systems. This shows that there are individual differences in people's reactions to stress and their levels of vulnerability to CVDs.

Melamed *et al.* (2006) reviewed clinical evidence to find that burnout, characterised by physical, emotional and cognitive fatigue, resulting from prolonged exposure to work-related stress, was associated with heightened levels of CVD and other cardiovascular-related ailments. The mechanisms responsible included immunosuppression, blood clots and poor health behaviours, such as excessive drinking. This illustrates the link between chronic stress and CVDs and suggests damage can occur directly through bodily systems or indirectly through unhealthy practices.

**ON THE WEB**

An hour-long National Geographic programme about stress, which includes excellent material on how stress affects health, can be found at **www.youtube.com**. Search for 'National Geographic: The science of stress'.

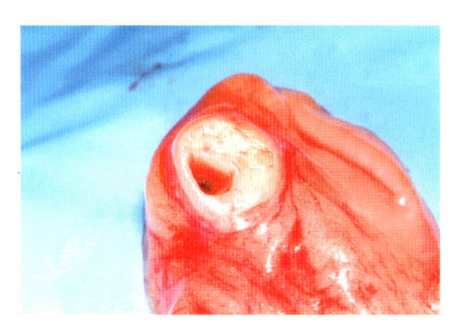

**Figure 8.6** Chronic stress can result in CHD from a build-up of fat lining the arteries that supply the heart with blood

## Evaluation

- As it would be unethical to conduct experiments into whether stress causes CVDs, much evidence is correlational, which means causality cannot be shown. Nor is it possible to identify specifically which factors are playing the largest contributory roles in the development of CVDs.
- In many cases it is probable that the direct effects of chronic stress, such as the over-activation of bodily systems, combine with indirect effects, like heightened smoking and drug taking, to increase vulnerability to CVDs. Cohen & Williamson (1991) found that chronic stress led to individuals smoking and drinking more, taking less exercise and not sleeping enough.
- With Krantz *et al.*'s (1991) study it may be that the patients with CVDs would show heightened myocardial ischaemia and blood pressure when relaxed as well as when moderately stressed. As no control was used to compare their behaviour when stressed and not stressed, it is not possible to know.
- As with immunosuppression there are individual differences, like personality (see page 289), gender and age, in levels of vulnerability to developing CVDs through exposure to prolonged stress. Vaccarino (2014) exposed 49 female and 49 male post-heart attack patients to a mild emotional stressor (speaking in public), finding females under 50 years of age had twice the levels of myocardial ischaemia than similar males. As the difference was not found in patients over 50, nor with physical stressors, it suggests younger women are more at risk of CVDs through emotional stress.

### STRENGTHEN YOUR LEARNING

1. Explain how the immune system works.
2. Explain how chronic stress can lead to immunosuppression. What evidence is there that this is true? What other evaluative points can be made about the relationship between stress and immunosuppression?
3. Outline and evaluate Kiecolt-Glaser's (1984) study of immunosuppression.
4. i] What is meant by cardiovascular disorders? ii] How can stress lead to CVDs both directly and indirectly? iii] To what extent does evidence support the idea that stress can lead to CVDs? iv] What other evaluative points can be made about the relationship between stress and CVDs?

### YOU ARE THE RESEARCHER

It seems to be that there are individual differences in the effects of stress upon immunosuppression. Select one area of individual differences, such as age, gender or culture and design an experiment to assess whether such individual differences exist.

What would be your experimental design? IV and DV? Why would a 1-tailed (directional) hypothesis be justified? Compose such a hypothesis, as well as a suitable null hypothesis. What type of graph would be used to display your data? Justify your choice. What statistical test could be used to analyse your data? Give 3 reasons for your choice of test.

# ASSESSMENT CHECK

1. Select from the descriptions A, B, C and D below to complete the table relating to stages of the general adaptation syndrome. One description will be left over. **[3 marks]**

   **A** Levels of cortisol are increased in blood sugar

   **B** Daily hassles occur which produce an increased level of stress

   **C** The sympathetic nervous system activates and stimulates the adrenal medulla to secrete adrenaline and noradrenaline

   **D** Bodily resources become depleted so that the adrenal glands cannot function efficiently

   | Stage | Description |
   |---|---|
   | Exhaustion | |
   | Alarm | |
   | Resistance | |

2. Daniel has had a lot of stress in his life for a long time and every time he is faced with stressful situations his alcohol and cigarette consumption seems to increase. Daniel has never been one for taking much exercise and he does tend to eat a lot of junk food. Recently Daniel hasn't been feeling very well and his doctor has told him that he has signs of coronary heart disease, a dangerous cardiovascular disorder.
   With reference to Daniel, explain the relationship between stress and cardiovascular disorders. **[4 marks]**

3. Research into stress and immunosuppression tends to use correlational studies. Explain why such studies cannot show cause and effect relationships. **[3 marks]**

4. Outline the role of cortisol in the body's response to stress. **[2 marks]**

5. Discuss the role of the hypothalamic-pituitary-adrenal system and/or the sympathomedullary pathway in the body's response to stress. **[16 marks]**

# 8.3 Sources of stress

## KEY TERMS

**Life changes** – occasional events incurring major adjustments to lifestyle

**Daily hassles** – everyday irritations that produce an overall elevated level of stress

**Self-report scales** – personal ratings of an individual's stress levels

Stressors can originate from many different varied sources, but psychologists are especially interested in those associated with major and minor **life changes**, as well as the **daily hassles** and irritations that people face. Workplace stress also attracts interest, as it is not only a common source of stress but costs industry a lot in terms of stress-related absences.

*'When we least expect it, life sets us a challenge to test our courage.'*
Paul Coelho (2005)

## Life changes

Life changes are occasional events resulting in adjustments to lifestyle, such as the death of a loved one or moving house. They can even be events people regard as enjoyable, such as Christmas or getting married. There is much variation in the impact life changes have. For instance, the ending of a relationship may be devastating for one person but a blessing for another. Equally, when expected life changes do not occur, for instance someone not getting a place at university, they can be stressful in their impact.

### Measuring life changes

**Self-report scales** try to measure the stressful effects of life events so that links between life changes and stress-related disorders can be investigated. The most well known is Holmes & Rahe's (1967) Social Readjustment Rating Scale (SRRS), a list of 43 stressful life events that can contribute to illness.

**Figure 8.7** Getting married is an occasional life event that can be very stressful

## CLASSIC RESEARCH

### The Social Readjustment Rating Scale – Thomas Holmes & Richard Rahe (1967)

Thomas Holmes found the visits of his mother-in-law so stressful that every time she came to stay he developed a cold. This observation got him thinking about the relationship between stressful life changes and vulnerability to illness and was the starting point for his attempt, together with Richard Rahe, to develop a means of measuring the impact of various life change stressors.

**Figure 8.8** Emotional stress can lead to physical ailments

#### Aim
To construct a method of measuring stress, with the prediction being that individuals are more likely to show symptoms of illness, both physical and psychological, following periods of stress and the greater the stress, the more serious the illness.

#### Procedure
The medical records of 5,000 patients were examined. A list of 43 life changes commonly occurring in the months prior to the onset of illness was compiled. One hundred judges were told that 'marriage' had been assigned a value of 500 and they were to assign a number to each of the other life changes, indicating how much readjustment was involved relative to marriage.

The average of the numbers assigned to each life change was divided by ten, with the resulting scores becoming the value for each change.

The amount of life stress a person experiences in a given period is measured by the total number of life change units (LCUs). These units are calculated by adding the mean values associated with each life change that individuals have experienced during that time.

### Findings
Most life changes were seen as less stressful than marriage, with only six events, like death of spouse, being rated as more stressful. People with higher LCU scores for the preceding year were more likely to experience physical illness the following year. For example, someone scoring over 300 LCUs had an 80 per cent chance of becoming ill, with health problems including sudden cardiac death, non-fatal heart attacks, tuberculosis, diabetes, leukaemia, accidents and sports injuries.

### Conclusions
Stress can be measured objectively as an LCU score. Stress can lead to illness. LCU scores can predict the chances of becoming ill, physically and/or mentally.

### Evaluation
- The 43 life changes listed are mainly negative, especially those with high LCU scores, so the SRRS may be confusing 'change' with 'negativity'.
- Some life events are ambiguous – for example, those referring to 'change in…' could be positive or negative.
- Brown (1986) argued it might not be change itself but unexpected, uncontrollable change that is stressful. When people were asked to classify undesirable life events on the SRRS, only those classified as 'uncontrollable' were correlated with later illness.
- Correlations do not indicate causality. Someone's general susceptibility to stress or their general level of health may also be important factors.
- Having a high LCU score suggests a health problem is imminent, but the nature of the health problem is not apparent. Different stress-related illnesses appear to be more or less associated with different forms of stressor.
- Holmes & Rahe did find a statistically significant correlation between LCU scores and subsequent measures of health, but the correlation was small. Therefore, the number and type of life changes experienced have some connection with subsequent health, but there is lots of variance and many individual differences in response to life change stressors not accounted for by the scale.
- A score for a particular life change indicates whether it is more or less stressful than other events, but does not say anything meaningful about the nature or extent of that particular event (see Table 8.1).

| Rank | Life change | Mean value |
| --- | --- | --- |
| 1 | Death of spouse | 100 |
| 2 | Divorce | 73 |
| 3 | Marital separation | 65 |
| 4 | Jail term | 63 |
| 5 | Death of close family member | 63 |
| 6 | Personal injury or illness | 53 |
| 7 | Marriage | 50 |
| 8 | Fired from work | 47 |
| 10 | Retirement | 45 |
| 11 | Change in health of family member | 44 |
| 12 | Pregnancy | 40 |
| 13 | Sex difficulties | 39 |
| 16 | Change in financial state | 38 |
| 17 | Death of close friend | 37 |
| 18 | Change to different line of work | 36 |
| 23 | Son or daughter leaving home | 29 |
| 27 | Begin or end school | 26 |
| 38 | Change in sleeping habits | 16 |
| 42 | Christmas | 12 |
| 43 | Minor violations of the law | 11 |

Table 8.1 A selection of life changes from the Social Readjustment Rating Scale (SRRS)

## Research

Rahe *et al.* (1970) gave the SRRS to 2,700 sailors to assess the number of life changes undergone in the previous six months. Then, during a six-month tour of duty, individual health records were recorded for each sailor and from this illness scores were calculated. A significant positive correlation between LCUs and illness scores of +0.118 was found, suggesting a link between life changes and physical illness.

Jacobs & Charles (1980) found that children with cancer were from families with higher life change scores than children with other illnesses, suggesting a link between stress and vulnerability to cancer and that certain illnesses are more influenced by stress than others.

Li-Ping Tang & Hammontree (1992) measured the occupational stress levels and life changes of 60 police officers over a six-month period, finding a significant association with absenteeism levels, again implying a link between life stress and illness.

### Evaluation

- Many studies are retrospective and reliant on accurate and full memory, with participants being asked to recall illnesses and stressful life changes that occurred in the past. This may produce unreliable data.
- Instead of life changes causing illness, it could be the other way round. Some life changes, like being sacked from work, might be an indication of an illness that is already developing.
- With the SRRS, each life change has a predetermined LCU score, but individuals may experience the same event differently. For example, the death of a friend could be less negative if that friend was suffering intense prolonged pain.
- Although they can have a major impact, compared with daily hassles, life events occur infrequently, therefore the cumulative effect of daily hassles, which are constant and repetitive, is a better predictor of stress-related illnesses.
- The SRRS does not distinguish between positive and negative life events and so as it may not be a true measure of life events and stress it can be accused of lacking internal validity. Martin (1989) found no relationship between positive life events, like 'outstanding personal achievement', and ill health.

*'I'm wanted at the traffic jam, they're saving me a seat.'*
Leonard Cohen (2012)

## Daily hassles

Life changes can be extremely stressful, but generally are rare. Most life stress comes from daily hassles, everyday irritations and annoyances that constantly infuriate, like queuing at the shops or being stuck in traffic. Daily hassles, due to their constant nature, are perhaps a better indicator of physical and mental states of well-being, because while life changes can activate big stress reactions, daily hassles tend to accumulate, producing a

**Figure 8.9** Being stuck in traffic jams on the way to work is an example of a stressful daily hassle

heightened level of stress, thus creating a serious risk of illness. Daily life also has uplifts (events that raise spirits, such as meeting friends) and these can neutralise the harmful effects of hassles.

## Measuring daily hassles

Self-report scales have been developed to try to assess the stressful effects of daily hassles, so that links between hassles and stress-related disorders could be investigated, such as Kanner *et al.*'s (1981) Hassles Scale, which has 117 negative items covering all aspects of daily life and an Uplifts Scale of 135 positive items.

Hassles were defined as: 'The irritating, frustrating, distressing demands that to some degree characterise everyday transactions with the environment. They include annoying practical problems, like losing things or traffic jams, and fortuitous occurrences, like inclement weather, as well as arguments, disappointments, and financial and family concerns.'

Daily uplifts were defined as: 'Positive experiences, like the joy derived from manifestations of love, relief at hearing good news, the pleasure of a good night's rest, and so on.'

## Research

Kanner *et al.* (1981) performed a study of 100 men and women, aged 45 to 64 years, over a 12-month period. They confirmed that hassles are correlated with undesirable psychological symptoms and that hassles were a better predictor of illness than life events. For instance, divorce creates stress by a number of hassles, like having to cook for oneself, handling money matters, etc. This suggests that daily hassles intervene between critical life events and health, with the collective impact of such irritations proving harmful to health. However, the effect of uplifts was unclear.

De Longis *et al.* (1988) studied stress in 75 married couples by giving them a life events questionnaire as well as the Hassles and Uplift Scales. No relationship was found between life events and health or between uplifts and health, indicating that stress is not related to these factors, although hassles did seem to be associated with next-day health problems.

Sher (2004) found that daily hassles were associated with increased cortisol levels in healthy individuals and that increased cortisol secretion caused by daily hassles contributes to the development of depressive disorders in vulnerable individuals. This implies that it is increased levels of cortisol, caused by the stress of daily hassles, that negatively affect health.

Courtois *et al.* (2007) used self-report scales to measure the influence of life events and daily hassles on teenage drinking and smoking (activities often related to heightened stress levels) and found that although life event scores were associated with greater levels of smoking and drinking, daily hassles were associated even more so, with teenagers smoking and drinking at an earlier age and in greater amounts with elevated levels of daily hassles. This supports the idea of daily hassles, through their repetitive and constant nature, raising vulnerability to illness more than life changes.

> **YOU ARE THE RESEARCHER**
>
> Design a questionnaire to assess the effect of daily hassles upon health. Some of your questions should be closed questions that generate quantitative data and use self-report scales (such as a Likert scale) to do so. However, you should also compose some open questions to generate qualitative data. How could you use content or thematic analysis to analyse such data? How could such a questionnaire be used to investigate possible differences in the way daily hassles affect different type of people, for example between people of different cultures?

### Evaluation

- Daily hassles may negatively affect health more, not just because they have a greater collective impact than occasional life events but because individuals receive more social support to lessen the effect of life events than they do with daily hassles. Flett *et al.* (1995) found that 320 students who read a scenario describing an individual who experienced either a life event or daily hassle rated those experiencing the life event as needing and receiving more social support.

- People in collectivist cultures give more social support to individuals when they are stressed and as social support lessens the effect of stressors, it suggests there will be cross-cultural differences in the effect daily hassles will have upon vulnerability to stress-related illnesses.

- Research tends to concentrate on whether life changes or daily hassles contribute most to stress-related illness. However, the two factors may actually influence each other so that the effects of daily hassles depend upon the impact of critical life events. For example, a person recently experiencing the death of a loved one may find daily hassles much more negatively impacting than usual.

- A practical application of research into daily hassles is the usefulness of findings and conclusions towards formulating effective stress management and coping strategies to deal with the ever-rising number of stress-related illnesses.

- A methodological problem in studying daily hassles is that participants are commonly asked to remember retrospectively hassles they have experienced and this is dependent upon accurate and full recall. A solution is to ask participants to keep a diary, where hassles and feelings of well-being are recorded on a daily basis.

### YOU ARE THE RESEARCHER

Research into life changes and daily hassles generally uses the correlational method. Design your own correlation into hassles and illness.

You will need to construct a list of daily hassles, for instance 'queuing in the cafeteria' or 'arguments with others'. For each hassle you will need to award a daily score, say 4 for extremely irritating, 3 for very irritating, 2 for irritating, 1 for slightly irritating.

Illness could be assessed by days absent.

How many participants will you need? How long would you have to conduct the study to get sufficient data? What type of graph would you need to construct to plot the data? Which statistical test would be used to analyse the data?

*'I love deadlines. I love the whooshing noise they make as they go by.'*
Douglas Adams (2000)

## Workplace stress

The modern workplace is a major, ever-increasing source of stress. This negatively impacts upon health, but also leads to poor performance at work, resulting in decreased productivity as well as increased absenteeism, accidents and high staff turnover levels. **Workplace stressors** can impact directly upon

**KEY TERM**

**Workplace stressors** – aspects of the work environment which have a negative impact on health

individuals' health and performance and indirectly through unhealthy lifestyle practices, such as heavy drinking. This has a high financial cost for industry and the health services, as well as a major cost in human terms to people's quality of life. Professional services organisation PwC estimates that the cost of absenteeism to industry in 2011 was around £28.9 billion.

It is therefore to everyone's benefit to identify the important factors, in order to reduce the impact of workplace stress upon individuals and to society as a whole. A non-stressed workforce would be a contented and productive workforce.

Important workplace stressors include environmental factors, predictability and role conflict and ambiguity. However, the two major workplace stressors we concentrate on here are **workload** and controllability of work role.

**Figure 8.10** The workplace can be a significant source of stress in many people's lives

## Workload

Workload involves the number of tasks and obligations individuals have to perform or complete within a specific amount of time. The heavier an individual's workload, the more stress they will experience. This is generally supported by research.

## Control

**Control** concerns the degree of influence individuals have over their workload and job requirements. It would be expected that the more control an individual has in their job, the lower their stress levels would be. However, evidence is somewhat contradictory.

## Research

Johansson *et al.* (1978) compared a group of high-risk-of-stress workers, whose jobs involved repetitiveness and high levels of responsibility and workload, with a low-risk group of cleaners from a Swedish saw-mill, on levels of stress hormones recorded in urine samples and days absent from work. The high-risk group had higher levels of stress hormones on work days than rest days and had higher levels of absenteeism than the cleaners. This suggests that work stressors create long-term physiological arousal, leading to stress-related illnesses and absenteeism.

Marmot *et al.* (1997) performed a five-year study of London-based civil servants, using questionnaires and health screenings for signs of heart disease. Employees with low job control were three times more likely to have heart attacks than those with high job control. This suggests that high job control is desirable in order to reduce the costs of work-related stress disorders. However, Caplan *et al.*'s (1975) research contradicts this, finding that ambitious individuals, like those in Marmot's study, were more strongly affected by workplace stressors. Therefore the results are not universally generalisable. Also, Marmot's study found no association between high workload and stress-related illnesses, contradicting Johansson's (1978) findings. However, Johansson's study focused on jobs with high levels of responsibility that were demanding in terms of requiring continuous concentration. Therefore Johansson's study may be a more valid measure of high workload.

Hobson & Beach (2000) examined relationships between working hours, perceived work stressors and psychological health in British managers. Managers at two factories completed questionnaires and work diaries. Hours of work were not directly related to psychological health, but were associated

### KEY TERMS

**Workload** – the number of tasks and obligations an individual has to perform or complete within a specific amount of time

**Control** – the degree of influence an individual has over their workload and job requirements

with individual perception of work stressors, which in turn were associated with measures of psychological health. This suggests that perceived workload is more important in determining psychological health than actual workload, implying a cognitive component to stress-related health risks.

Kivimaki *et al.* (2006) performed a meta-analysis of 14 studies involving more than 80,000 workers from Europe, Japan and the USA. They found that workers with high levels of workload were significantly more at risk of developing coronary heart disease, implying that workload is related to elevated health risks.

### Evaluation

- It is not really possible to isolate and test single workplace stressors, thus which workplace stressors are specifically related to stress-related illness and to what extent is difficult to assess.
- Not all workplace stressors are harmful, indeed the workplace presents opportunities to increase self-esteem, confidence and motivational levels and give individuals a sense of purpose and fulfilment, all factors which contribute to positive physical and psychological well-being.
- Different research methods produce different patterns of results. Usually questionnaires are used to assess the effects of workplace stressors, but questionnaires limit the stressors respondents can comment on. Interviews appear superior, as they give individuals more scope to report on individual experiences and thus identify other types of stressors, like interpersonal clashes for example.
- Research into workplace stressors does not account for individual differences, as individuals experience the same stressors in different ways and in varying amounts. This is related to each individual's perceived ability to cope with stressors, with those high in 'hardiness' more able to cope (see page 292). Also, different individuals are more affected by different degrees of job control and workload.
- The findings and conclusions drawn from studies of workplace stressors are quickly redundant, owing to the ever-changing demands of the workplace and its associated stressors. For instance, the increasing use of technology, lower job security and changing job practices place completely new demands upon employees that previous research does not reflect.
- Research suggests that employers can reduce workforce illness and absenteeism by lessening workplace stressors, for instance reducing workloads and giving employees more control over their jobs, a desirable outcome as it would increase employers' profits.

### RESEARCH IN FOCUS

Research into workplace stressors generally employs questionnaires, but when the alternative self-report method of interviews is used, different patterns of results are gained, with interviews identifying other stressors not included in questionnaires.

Why, therefore, might interviews be superior? (You may wish to refer to the evaluation feature box above for guidance.)

How might this affect the results of research into workplace stressors?

**PSYCHOLOGY IN THE REAL WORLD**

As the degree of control individuals have over their jobs is known to be related to vulnerability to stress-related illnesses, it follows that practical applications in the workplace that increase employees' sense of perceived control are desirable, as they reduce stress levels and absenteeism rates, making workers more contented and productive.

One such practical application is quality circles. Originally a Japanese idea, the concept was introduced to Britain by the Wedgwood Pottery Company in 1980. Quality circles consist of groups of workers given time away from their jobs to suggest and discuss ideas for improving their work tasks. If accepted, these changes are implemented by the workers themselves, who receive a share of any savings or boosts to profits. Quality circles lessen workplace stressors by increasing employees' controllability of their work role, while also reducing role conflict and ambiguity and improving environmental conditions.

When implemented properly quality circles enrich and empower the lives of workers, creating harmony and improved performance. Workers become happier, less stressed and less prone to absenteeism through stress-related disorders and all by the simple mechanism of giving workers more control over their job.

**Figure 8.11** The exterior of the Wedgwood Pottery Company

**STRENGTHEN YOUR LEARNING**

1. Explain the difference between life changes and daily hassles. Which has more effect on stress-related illnesses? Explain how both are measured.
2. Outline and evaluate Holmes & Rahe's (1967) study of life changes and stress.
3. Give evidence from two research studies that illustrate the relationship between i) life changes and stress (other than Holmes & Rahe), ii) daily hassles and stress. iii) What other evaluative points can be made about these relationships?
4. Outline the impact the workplace can have as a source of stress.
5. What have research studies suggested about the roles of workload and control as sources of stress? What other evaluative points can be made about workplace stressors?

*'If you cannot measure it you cannot improve it.'*
Lord Kelvin (1898)

# 8.4 Physiological measures of stress

As stress affects the body physically it presents ways of objectively measuring stress. Blood and urine are examined to assess the levels of stress hormones, such as corticosteroids like cortisol and catecholamines like adrenaline. Blood pressure also provides reliable measures of stress

**KEY TERM**

**Skin conductance response** – a method of measuring electrical conductivity within the skin as an indication of psychological and physiological arousal

levels, as blood pressure is higher when individuals are stressed. Another useful measurement is speech analysis. Stress increases respiration (breathing rate), which heightens sub-glottal pressure and in turn the pitch of a voice, as well as changes in the micro tremors of speech muscles. However, the physical measurement of stress attracting most interest is **skin conductance response** (SCR) (also known as galvanic skin response).

## Skin conductance response

SCR measures the skin's resistance to electricity. When individuals are stressed they sweat and this increases the skin's ability to conduct electricity. Therefore individuals have a higher SCR when stressed than when not stressed, and have higher SCR scores than other non-stressed individuals. SCR readings need to be taken in stressed and non-stressed states so that comparisons can be made. SCR readings are measured through use of a polygraph (more commonly known as a 'lie detector' – see Figure 8.12). This is a machine that records physiological measures such as blood pressure, pulse, respiration (breathing rate), as well as SCR. The use of a polygraph involves an individual sitting quietly for around 30 minutes so that a baseline score can be established to which readings are compared when the individual is stressed.

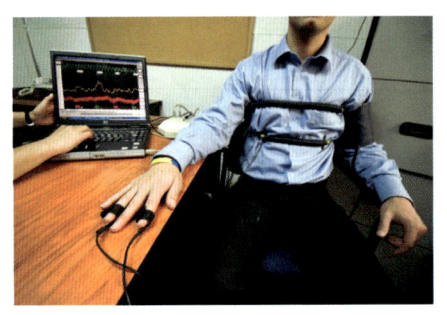

**Figure 8.12** Skin conductance response is measured by a polygraph, which requires a trained practitioner to operate

### Research

Khalfa *et al*. (2002) played different types of music to arouse the emotions of fear, happiness, sadness and peacefulness in participants and measured their reactions using SCR readings, which were greatest for the emotions of fear and happiness. This suggests that SCR readings can measure stress levels (as portrayed through fear), but cannot differentiate stress from other completely different emotional reactions such as happiness.

Villarejo *et al*. (2012) used a computer-operated stress sensor to measure stress levels in 16 adult participants, who were required to complete tests involving different levels of stress, for instance being relaxed, solving mathematical tests and exposure to anxiety-creating stimuli. It was found that SCR readings were able to detect participants' different stress levels with a success rate of 76.5 per cent, supporting the idea of SCR being a capable though not perfect method of measuring stress levels.

Reynaud *et al*. (2012) showed film excerpts including ones designed to elicit fear to 15 low neurotic and 18 high neurotic participants and found that SCR readings were higher in high neurotic participants, which suggests that SCR measurements have a useful role to play in displaying stress levels in different types of participants.

Kurniawan *et al*. (2013) found that trained operatives were able to differentiate between participants being lightly and more highly stressed (achieved by giving them light and heavy workloads) 70 per cent of the time using SCR readings, but 92 per cent of the time when using features of speech. This suggests that although SCR has some usefulness as a measurement of stress, speech analysis is superior.

### Evaluation

- One practical application of SCR could be the manufacture of measuring devices that recognise dangerous elevations in stress levels of individuals, so that they would be motivated to adjust their behaviour to achieve healthier stress levels. Indeed, biofeedback, a stress management technique, often utilises SCR measurements to indicate stress responses, with a view to helping individuals control their stress levels (see Biofeedback, page 294).

- SCR measurements are useful, as they can be used continuously throughout research and be relatively unnoticed by participants, meaning that they are a true measurement of stress levels. SCR readings are favoured by researchers, as they are easy to perform and of relatively low cost. Readings can be combined with recordings of heart rate, respiratory rate and blood pressure because they are all autonomic dependent variables. Analysis does, however, require trained practitioners.

- SCR readings are helpful to psychologists elsewhere. For example, Bogdonoff *et al.* (1961) used SCR readings in Asch-type studies of conformity (see Chapter 1 of Book One) to show that participants who did not conform to obviously wrong answers given by pseudo-participants had heightened levels of stress, allowing the researchers to conclude that conformity is healthy in terms of lowering stress levels.

- A negative aspect of SCR measurements is that they are affected by external factors, like temperature and humidity, leading to inconsistent readings. Internal factors, such as the taking of medications and alcohol, also have an effect. Responses can also be inconsistent even with the same stimulus levels, suggesting they are not a reliable form of measurement.

- Another drawback with SCR measurements is that raised by Bakker *et al.* (2011), who showed that SCR readings vary not only from person to person but from one day to another for the same person, again illustrating their lack of reliability in measuring stress levels.

### PSYCHOLOGY IN THE REAL WORLD

The Jeremy Kyle TV show (see Figure 8.13) makes much of its use of lie-detector tests to decide whether people are telling the truth about having cheated on their partners, etc. Lie detection is performed using a polygraph, which relies heavily on stress readings taken from measurements of SCR. Initial readings are taken during a relaxed phase to create a baseline score, which is then compared with readings when people are asked questions about their alleged unfaithfulness. If they are lying, SCR readings should increase.

However, although the American Polygraph Association claims an accuracy level of above 90 per cent, Lykken (1984) found that the actual accuracy rate is about 65 per cent, little better than the 50 per cent rate achieved by flipping a coin. Lykken also points out that although the test is reasonably efficient at detecting liars, it produces a 50 per cent 'false positive' rate in saying that honest people are liars.

As the consequences of being called a liar on TV shows like Jeremy Kyle's are so devastating, often resulting in shattered relationships, perhaps so much emphasis should not be placed on stress-related SCR readings, which are little different to the ancient Arabic test of detecting liars by pressing a heated knife blade to the tongue of the accused. If lying, their heightened stress made their tongue dry and it would blister – SCR works similarly by stress heightening sweat levels so that electricity conductivity is increased.

**Figure 8.13** The Jeremy Kyle Show uses SCR readings to detect whether people are lying, but how accurate are such readings?

### STRENGTHEN YOUR LEARNING

1. Explain how skin conductance response (SCR) is used as a physiological measure of stress.
2. Explain what research evidence suggests about the strengths and weaknesses of using SCR as a measurement of stress.
3. What other evaluative points can be made about SCR?

## ASSESSMENT CHECK

1. Jessica has a responsible job in a busy office. Recently the amount of work she has to do has increased dramatically and she is under pressure from her boss to get work completed to deadline. Although she works very hard she finds it frustrating that her boss constantly interferes, telling her how she should be doing her job.

    With reference to the scenario above, explain how the workplace can be a source of stress. **[4 marks]**

2. Place the letters 'LC' next to the following statement that relates to life changes and the letters 'DH' next to the statement that relates to daily hassles. One statement will be left over. **[2 marks]**
    - Occasional events which can have a stressful impact.
    - The use of instrumental social support to cope with stress.
    - Repeatedly being stuck in traffic on the way to work.

3. Stressful events are measured by the Social Readjustment Rating Scale, a list of 43 stressful life events that can contribute to illness. Death of a spouse scores a value of 100 life change units, while pregnancy scores a value of 40 life change units. Explain why life change unit scores can be argued to be an ordinal level of measurement. **[2 marks]**

4. Explain what is meant by skin conductance response. **[2 marks]**

5. Outline and evaluate the effects of workplace stress. **[16 marks]**

> *'Personality is to man what perfume is to a flower.'*
> Charles Schwab (1998)

# 8.5 Individual differences in stress

Although science studies what people share in common, humans are not identical and differ from each other in terms of inherited qualities and learning experiences. Personality, the traits (characteristics) that give individuals their unique identities, is one such important individual difference and research shows that the ways people perceive and respond to stressors are attributable in some part to differences in personality.

Psychologists refer to **personality types**, general categorisations that describe groups of people sharing similar traits. Much research into stress focuses on people categorised as having **Type A personality**, though **B, C and D personality types** have also been identified and investigated, along with **hardiness**. Psychologists are especially interested in connections between personality types and different forms of stress-related illnesses.

> *'Is everything as urgent as your stress would imply?'*
> Terri Guillemets (2008)

## Types A and B personality

Friedman & Rosenman (1959) were interested in the role non-physiological factors played in coronary heart disease (CHD), in particular the role of individual differences in the ways men deal with stressful situations (women were found to be less vulnerable). They discovered that a certain pattern of behaviour, Type A, was linked to an increased risk of developing heart disease. The key characteristics of this type are given in Table 8.2.

**KEY TERMS**

**Personality types** – broad characterisations describing categories of people sharing similar characteristics

**Type A personality** – personality type characterised by time urgency, excessive competitiveness and generalised hostility, incurring risk of heart disease

**Type B personality** – healthy personality type characterised by non-competitiveness, self-confidence and relaxation

**Type C personality** – personality type characterised by suppression of negative emotions, incurring risk of cancer

**Type D personality** – personality type characterised by distress, gloom, worry and lack of sociability, incurring risk of heart attacks

**Hardiness** – healthy personality type characterised by control, commitment and self-improvement

**Table 8.2** The key characteristics of people with Type A personality

| Characteristic | Description |
| --- | --- |
| Time urgent/impatient | Does several things at once<br>Constantly sets deadlines<br>Has low boredom threshold |
| Excessive competitiveness | Achievement orientated<br>Aggressive |
| Generalised hostility/aggressive | Easily irritated/provoked<br>Volatile<br>Displays self-anger |

Other Type A traits include insecurity about status and a need to be admired by their peers in order to feel good about themselves. Type A personality is associated with heightened risk of hypertension and CVD.

The researchers simultaneously described Type B personality. Type B men were described as having the same degree of ambition, but in a steady, non-competitive manner, and being much more self-confident, relaxed and easy-going, not driven to achieve perfection and much less hostile. Such individuals have no problem relaxing or doing nothing, something Type A men could never do. Type B man is more or less the direct opposite of Type A and is associated with low stress levels and therefore good health.

## Research

Friedman & Rosenman (1974) assessed the personality types of more than 3,500 healthy middle-aged men as part of a 12-year longitudinal study. Participants were asked questions relating to impatience, competitiveness, motivation for success, frustration at goals being hindered and their feelings towards being under pressure. High scorers were described as 'Type A' personalities while low scorers were described as 'Type B' personalities. Twice as many Type A personalities developed cardiovascular disorders as did Type B personalities, suggesting that personality traits are a risk factor in developing stress-related illness and that psychological factors can have physiological effects, through the harmful physical effects of stressors being mediated through psychological personality factors. Therefore stressors are not harmful in themselves: it is how people perceive and react to them that is potentially dangerous for health.

Matthews & Haynes (1986) found that coronary heart disease was most associated with the hostility trait of Type A men, especially those expressing high levels of hostility, supporting Friedman & Rosenman's findings and identifying the key trait related to CHD.

Hayes (2000) examined specific components and behaviours of the Type A personality, finding certain characteristics correlated more, or less, with specific forms of cardiovascular disorder. For example, angina sufferers were composed of Type A personalities that were impatient with other people and susceptible to feeling pressure at work, while those with heart failure tended to comprise Type A personalities with hasty personal habits and schedules. This suggests that it is particular traits of the Type A personality, rather than the personality type itself, that are related to specific heart conditions.

Forshaw (2002) supported Matthews & Haynes' findings that the Type A characteristic of hostility was the best single predictor of CHD and a better predictor than Type A personality as a whole. This suggests that it is the specific trait of hostility, rather than Type A personality, that increases the risk of developing stress-related illness, though it does not mean that hostility *causes* CHD, just as we could not claim that a Type A personality did.

### Evaluation

- Some researchers have failed to replicate Friedman & Rosenman's (1974) findings, but Miller *et al.* (1996) reviewed several studies, confirming the original results.
- Not all aspects of lifestyle were controlled in Friedman & Rosenman's study, so it may be other factors like hardiness (see page 292) that affect vulnerability to heart disease.
- While Type A men are more at risk of developing CHD, the risk is only relative: the vast majority of Type As do not develop CHD, while some Type Bs do.
- Ragland & Brand (1988) found that 15 per cent of Friedman & Rosenman's original sample had died of CHD, with age, high blood pressure and smoking proving to be significant factors, but little evidence of Type A personality being a risk factor. This suggests the original conclusions are unsupported.
- The Type A personality is too broad a description and it is more useful to think in terms of specific personality traits as stress-related risk factors, as suggested by Matthews & Haynes' and Hayes' research findings.
- Chesney & Rosenman (1980) found that control was an important factor that interacted with personality type to determine responses to stressors. Type A managers experienced greater anxiety when they were not in control, while other managers experienced greater anxiety when they were in control. The issue of perception of control in moderating stress outcomes may be worthy of further research.

**ON THE WEB**

If you want to know whether you have a tendency towards Type A personality, take the simple online test found at:

**http://stress.about.com/library/Type_A_quiz/bl_Type_A_quiz.htm**

Remember, though, that this is for your amusement, it is not a clinical diagnosis.

## Types C and D personality

Apart from types A and B personality, types C and D have also been proposed and their possible links to different forms of stress-related illnesses investigated.

Type C individuals are introverted, sensitive, thoughtful and inclined towards perfectionism, taking everything seriously and working very hard. They are conformist and thorough in everything they do and exceedingly dependable. However, because they tend not to express their emotions, are unassertive and try to please others even when it upsets themselves, they are easily stressed and prone to developing certain cancers, depression and illnesses associated with immunosuppression.

Type D individuals are people who like routine and not change. They shun responsibility, are highly obedient and are prone to worry and becoming irritable. Because they lack self-assurance and fear rejection they tend not to express their negative emotions and therefore become very stressed, making them prone to CVDs. Up to 53 per cent of cardiac patients are thought to have type D personality.

### Research

Morris *et al.* (1981) found that Type C women repress their emotions when stressed and are more likely to develop cancer. This was believed to be due to emotional suppression leading to a lowering of the immune system's effectiveness. This was supported by Greer & Morris's (1975) finding that women diagnosed with breast cancer showed significantly more emotional suppression than those with other, non-life-threatening breast disease.

Temoshok (1987) also found that Type C personalities were cancer prone, with such individuals having difficulty expressing emotion and suppressing or inhibiting emotions, especially negative ones like anger. This was backed up by Weinman (1995), who found it likely that such personality characteristics influenced the progression of cancer and the patient's survival time.

Denollet *et al.* (1996) found that up to 53 per cent of cardiac patients display Type D personality. This was supported by Denollet *et al.* (1998), who found Type D associated with a four-fold increased risk of sudden cardiac death, independent of traditional risk factors such as heavy smoking. These findings support the idea of Type D personality being linked with an increased risk of CVDs.

Schiffer *et al.* (2010) reviewed evidence relating to 6,000 cardiac disorder patients from 49 studies, to find a three-fold increase for Type D heart patients in risk of future CVDs, such as peripheral artery disease, angioplasty or bypass procedures, heart failure, heart transplantation, heart attack or death. This supports the idea that individuals with Type D personality are more vulnerable to CVDs.

*'Stress should be a powerful driving force, not an obstacle.'*
Bill Phillips (2010)

## Hardiness

Kobasa (1979) studied managers with stressful jobs in a company for three years, concentrating on identifying characteristics that distinguished those who became ill from those who did not. The findings allowed her to propose the hardy personality type, which she saw as having three key features:

1 **Commitment** – individuals who are committed to what they are doing and have a sense of self and purpose.
2 **Control** – individuals who feel a sense of personal control over what they are doing.
3 **Challenge** – individuals who see change as expected and normal and perceive stressors as challenges to be mastered.

Hardy personality type is associated with lowered physiological arousal in the presence of stressors, leading to a reduction in stress-related disorders. For this reason *hardiness training* has been developed as a form of stress management.

## Research

Kobasa (1979) measured the stress levels of 800 business executives with the SRRS, finding that individuals with equal stress levels had different illness levels. This suggests that some people had hardy personalities that afforded them a degree of protection against the effects of stress. Further investigation revealed that individuals with high stress and low illness levels scored high on control, commitment and challenge, which suggests that these characteristics are the important components of hardiness. This also implies that if people can be trained to be hardy, they will cope better with stress.

**Figure 8.14** What some people see as stressful, those with a hardy personality perceive as a challenge to be mastered

Sarafino (1990) found that people who undertook hardiness training developed lower blood pressure and felt less stressed, suggesting hardiness reduces the negative effects of stress and can be taught to people as a stress management technique.

Wiebe (1991) gave a stressful evaluative task to participants categorised as either low or high in hardiness. Those high in hardiness saw the task as less threatening and responded to it more positively. Males high in hardiness displayed less physiological arousal than males of low hardiness, though no differences in physiological arousal were noted in female participants. Though supporting claims for hardiness being related to lower experience of stress, the findings suggest some gender differences in arousal levels associated with hardiness.

Westman (2009) gave 326 Israeli Defence Force officer cadets a stress questionnaire at the start and finish of a training course and found that those displaying characteristics of hardiness experienced less perceived stress, supporting the idea that hardy personality type inoculates individuals against stress-related illnesses.

## Evaluation

- The studies into Type C women suffering from cancer might be considered unethical, as they may cause further distress to seriously ill women. However, the findings could be used to formulate effective strategies to reduce the chances of Type C women developing cancer.
- There is no evidence that people divide easily into separate personality types. Individuals may have elements of many of these characteristics and indeed labelling people could lead to self-fulfilling prophecies, where individuals adopt the characteristics ascribed to the label put upon them.
- It could be that hardiness does not exist. Funk (1992) believes a low hardiness score just means that a person is negative and it is this that results in the debilitating effects of stress. It could be that commitment and challenge are not as important as control in alleviating the effects of stress.
- As Kobasa's research was mainly done on wealthy managers, her results are not generalisable to other sections of society. However, subsequent research on soldiers, fire-fighters and students has backed up her findings.
- There are ethical concerns with conducting research that subjects participants to dangerous levels of stress. For this reason most research concentrates on stress that occurs in natural situations.

## RESEARCH IN FOCUS

The research carried out into Type C women (see research above) might be considered unethical, as it may cause additional distress to women already ill with cancer. However, such research might be considered ethical by reference to a cost–benefit analysis.

Explain what is meant by a cost–benefit analysis and how it might be applied in this instance.

## STRENGTHEN YOUR LEARNING

1. Outline the characteristics of individuals with types A, B, C and D and hardy personalities.
2. What has research evidence suggested about each personality type's link with stress-related illnesses?
3. What other evaluative points can be made about each personality type?

*'Give your stress wings and let it fly away.'*
Carin Hartness (2008)

*'How beautiful it is to do nothing, and then to rest afterward.'*
Spanish proverb

# 8.6 Managing and coping with stress

Modern life is increasingly stressful, with high costs to pay upon people's health and quality of life, as well as the cost to industry and health services in terms of stress-related illnesses. Heightened stress levels also lead to increased rates of violent crime. Therefore an understanding of stress that leads to practical applications in the form of stress management techniques that reduce stress levels is desirable.

There are two general types of **stress management**: biological methods, such as drug therapy, and psychological methods, including **stress inoculation therapy** and **biofeedback**.

## KEY TERMS

**Stress management** – physiological and psychological methods of reducing the negative effects of stress

**Stress inoculation therapy** – type of cognitive behavioural therapy that cognitively restructures emotional and behavioural responses

**Biofeedback** – the gaining of awareness and control over bodily functions in order to reduce stress levels

**Benzodiazepines** – anti-anxiety drugs that dampen down the activity of the nervous system, creating a sensation of calm and relaxation

**Beta-blockers** – anti-anxiety drugs that block the transmission of nerve impulses, to reduce heart rate and alleviate the physical effects of stress

## Drug therapy

Drugs are a biological and direct form of treatment that enter the bloodstream to reach the brain and affect the transmission of chemicals in the nervous system called neurotransmitters, facilitating communication between neurons (brain nerve cells).

Anti-anxiety drugs are used to treat stress, slowing down the activity of the central nervous system to suppress the physical symptoms of anxiety. They are often a starting point to treat stress-related conditions, with psychological methods added later on, when drugs have reduced symptoms sufficiently for psychological methods to have a positive impact. Two of the most commonly used anti-anxiety drugs are **benzodiazepines** (BZs) and **beta-blockers** (BBs).

### Benzodiazepines

BZs, like Valium and Librium, work by increasing the effect of the neurotransmitter GABA, which has a dampening, or quietening, effect on many of the brain's neurons. GABA works by allowing an increase of chloride ions into the neurons, making it more difficult for other neurotransmitters to stimulate them. This results in the slowing down of neural activity, creating a sensation of calm. The effect of BZs is to permit an even greater increase of chloride ions, boosting GABA's soothing effect. BZs also dampen the excitatory effect of the neurotransmitter serotonin, further slowing down the activity of the nervous system and adding to the feeling of relaxation.

BZs are for short-term use only, due to possible side effects like dependency, cognitive impairment and physical unsteadiness. They are a popular course of treatment, with more than two million people treated with them in Britain alone.

**Figure 8.15** Used to reduce stress levels, the benzodiazepine Valium is the world's most prescribed drug, but can be addictive

## Research

Havoundjian *et al.* (1986) induced stress in rats by getting them to swim. They found that the stress resulted in rapid increases in the amount of chloride ions in the benzodiazepine–GABA receptor complex in the cerebral cortical membranes, thus demonstrating the mechanisms by which acute stress operates. Such changes represent the compensatory response of an organism to stress-provoking changes in the environment and it is this response that BZ drugs have a moderating effect upon.

Davidson (1993) performed an assessment of BZ usage as a treatment for 75 patients diagnosed with social-anxiety disorder. Patients were randomly assigned to the drug or placebo treatment (a 'dummy' treatment with no clinical effect) for ten weeks, with drug treatment found to have an early and sustained positive effect – 78 per cent of patients improved, compared with only 20 per cent of placebo patients. Many drug-treatment patients reported the side effect of unsteadiness, with some forgetfulness and loss of concentration. A two-year follow-up study found a significant advantage in function among those treated with BZ drugs than a placebo, suggesting BZs are effective in the short and long term.

Zandstra *et al.* (2004) studied 164 short-term and 158 long-term users of BZs, finding that it was older, less well-educated, lonely patients, who tended to use avoidant-coping strategies to deal with stress, who were more likely to be long-term users. As long-term BZ usage is not seen as desirable, the findings suggest that patients with these characteristics should be treated with alternatives in the short term or be closely monitored if BZs are prescribed.

### Evaluation

- BZs are easy to take, cost effective and popular with patients due to the familiarity of taking pills for a multitude of uses.
- BZs were introduced to counteract high addiction rates in patients taking barbiturates. However, it became apparent that BZs too are addictive, even at low doses, with patients showing noticeable withdrawal symptoms when treatment ceased. The recommendation is that treatment with BZs should not exceed four weeks. However, there is a sizeable minority of patients using BZs long term, with the resultant risks of addiction.
- BZs are recommended as a short-term treatment only, not just because of addiction risks but also because the brain develops a tolerance, giving them only a brief effectiveness.
- A minority of patients experience side effects. However, these can be debilitating and include unsteadiness and cognitive impairments, especially impairment of long-term memory and lapses in concentration. Some patients even become aggressive and/or experience sexual dysfunction. This reduces the effectiveness of treatment, as patients experiencing side effects may stop taking the drugs before symptom reduction is achieved.
- Bernardy (2013) reviewed available evidence concerning US army veterans of the Gulf and Afghanistan wars to conclude that mounting evidence suggests that the long-term harm imposed by BZ use outweighs any short-term symptomatic benefits in patients with post-traumatic stress disorder. Lane (2010) also argues against their use, citing growing evidence that long-term usage incurs brain damage, especially to the cerebral cortex, resulting in short-term memory damage.

# Beta-blockers

BBs work by blocking the transmission of nerve impulses. Some nerve endings, when stimulated, release the neurotransmitter noradrenaline, activating beta-adrenergic receptors, tiny structures occurring on cells in various body parts, including the heart, brain and blood vessels. One effect of this is an increase in the force and the rate of the heartbeat. Beta-adrenergic receptors are also stimulated by the hormone adrenaline, released into the bloodstream from the adrenal glands in increased amounts when an individual is frightened or anxious, also resulting in an increased heart rate.

Beta-blockers 'sit' on beta-adrenergic receptors, blocking them from being stimulated. As a result, the force and rate of an individual's heartbeat are reduced, thus dampening down the physical effects of anxiety.

## CONTEMPORARY RESEARCH

### Behavioural stress accelerates prostate cancer development in mice – Kulik *et al.* (2013)

**Figure 8.16** Mice are often used in medical research

Being diagnosed with cancer and then treated for the disorder is stressful, reducing the ability of the treatment to cure the disease. As laboratory experiments involving stress and drugs are difficult to perform upon humans it is more usual for such research to be performed on animals, especially in the first instance. In this recent study Professor George Kulik and his team at Wake Forest Baptist Medical Centre used mice to investigate whether beta-blockers had a role to play in reducing the stress of cancer treatments.

#### Aim
To test the effects of behavioural stress in mice being treated with drugs for prostate cancer.

To assess whether beta-blockers improve the efficiency of drug treatment for cancer.

#### Procedure
**Study one.** Two types of 6–12-week-old male mice were used as participants, first mice that were implanted with human prostate cancer cells and second mice that were genetically modified to develop prostate cancer.

The first group of mice was treated with a cancer drug currently in clinical trials and the second group with bicalutamide, a drug currently used to treat prostate cancer.

Half of each group were stressed (either by immobilising them for one hour and subjecting them to the scent of fox urine or by injecting them with adrenaline to simulate the physiological response to stress), while half were kept calm and free of stress.

**Study two.** All mice were then given a beta-blocker to inhibit bodily release of adrenaline, with the effect of slowing heart rate, blood pressure and other bodily functions.

#### Findings
**Study one:** in both groups when the mice were kept stress free the drugs destroyed cancer cells and inhibited tumour growth. However, in the stressed mice cancer cells did not die and the drugs did not prevent tumour growth.

**Study two:** in all mice treated with beta-blockers, cancer cells were destroyed and tumour growth inhibited.

#### Conclusions
Stress reduces the effectiveness of anti-cancer drugs in treating cancer by stimulating the adrenaline-controlled signalling pathway, so that destruction of cancer cells does not occur.

Beta-blockers act to stop stress-induced tumour growth by blocking the adrenaline-controlled signalling pathway, so that destruction of cancer cells does occur.

#### Evaluation
- Providing beta-blockers to cancer patients with increased adrenaline levels due to stress could improve the effectiveness of anti-cancer drugs.
- The effects of beta-blockers on the same signalling mechanisms in humans being treated with anti-cancer drugs need to be tested to see whether they work in the same way.
- To increase their efficiency new cancer drugs should be designed that simultaneously target stress as well as cancer.
- The stress induced in the mice is designed to simulate that experienced in the presence of predators, which is somewhat of an automatic non-thinking response, rather different to the stress experienced by people told they have cancer whose stress will have more of a cognitive input, for instance having thoughts of dying, and be more of a chronic long-term stressor than an acute short-term one.
- The ethical concerns raised in breeding genetic strains of mice that develop cancer could be argued to be justifiable in terms of a cost–benefit analysis if the research results in increasing cancer survival rates.

# Research

Lau *et al.* (1992) performed a meta-analysis of studies assessing the effectiveness of beta-blockers against stress, finding them effective in reducing high blood pressure. They were found to reduce the risk of death by 20 per cent in patients with heart disease, suggesting that they are a lifesaver in some instances.

Gates (1985) tested the effectiveness of beta-blockers against stage fright in musicians. Thirty-four singing students were given different amounts of the beta-blocker nadolol or a placebo during end-of-term examinations. Low doses improved performance minimally, while high doses hindered performance significantly. This suggests BBs are effective in addressing performance anxiety, but only in small dosages.

Lindholm *et al.* (2005) used data from 13 randomised trials involving 105,000 participants to compare the effectiveness of beta-blockers against other anti-hypertension drugs, finding that the risk of strokes was 16 per cent higher with beta-blockers. There was no difference between the drugs in relation to heart problems and beta-blockers alone reduced the risk of strokes by 19 per cent compared with no treatment at all. This suggests that beta-blockers are effective in treating stress-related CVDs and reducing the risk of strokes, but that there are superior treatments for the prevention of strokes.

Beversdorf *et al.* (2005) stressed participants by getting them to speak publicly before an intimidating audience and then perform a mathematical task while being videoed. There was also a control condition of non-stressed participants who read aloud and counted out numbers while sitting alone in a room. Participants' cognitive flexibility was measured by performance on word-association tasks and unscrambling anagrams. Participants were also tested either with or without being given the BB propranolol. Stressed participants performed worse than non-stressed participants for cognitive flexibility, but stressed participants treated with the BB performed as well as the non-stressed participants, suggesting that BBs reduce the negative effects of stress upon cognitive performance.

## Evaluation

- BBs have an immediate effect, acting directly on the body to reduce heart rate and blood pressure, therefore are a desirable treatment against possible fatal cases of stress-related hypertension.
- Unlike BZs, BBs are not associated with dependency and addiction problems, but can have serious side effects, such as cold extremities, tiredness, nightmares and hallucinations.
- BBs have a purely physical action and are therefore more useful as an immediate, short-term treatment. They are not effective as a long-term treatment for stress conditions with more of a psychological element to them.
- Like many drug therapies, BBs do not address the cause of a problem, merely its symptoms. Therefore the medication only 'masks' effects and once treatment ends, symptoms return, suggesting drug treatments are not a cure.
- BBs are taken in tablet form and so are trusted by and familiar with people. Compared with other therapies they are cost effective, do not require a therapist to administer and so are often favoured by clinicians, even though better long-term therapies exist.

*'What doesn't kill you makes you stronger.'*
Friedrich Nietzsche (1888)

## Stress inoculation therapy

### Meichenbaum (1977)

Stress inoculation therapy (SIT) is a psychological form of stress management that involves cognitive restructuring, changing the way people think about themselves and their lives in order to alter their emotional responses and behaviour. SIT attempts to reduce stress through changing cognitions (thoughts). It believes that people find things stressful, as they think about them in catastrophising ways – misperceiving events in ways that make them seem more threatening and distressing than they really are.

The cognitive part of SIT involves individuals being trained to recognise stress symptoms and the behavioural part involves the use of skills to act upon the causes of stress.

SIT is like biological immunisation, where a small, harmless dose of an infectious disease is given to vaccinate an individual against an infection. SIT therefore allows an individual to become resistant to a stressor by exposing them to a small 'dose' of it, so that they can tolerate greater levels of the stressor later on. This is done by giving the individual a positive experience of the stressor.

SIT is used to treat acute, short-term stressors such as dental visits, chronic, long-term intermittent stressors like recurring headaches, chronic long-term continual stressors like medical illnesses, as well as anger control.

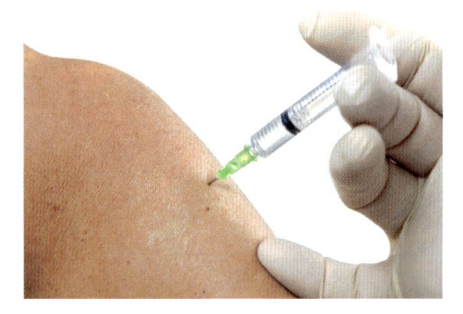

**Figure 8.17** SIT works like a vaccination, getting individuals to cope with small doses of stress so that they can deal with higher levels in real-life situations

SIT restructures the way an individual thinks in three phases:

1 **Conceptualisation** – the therapist gets the patient to think about how they deal with stressful situations and discuss how successful these strategies are. Negative self-statements that make stressful situations even more stressful, for instance *'I did badly with my essay therefore I will fail the exam'*, are identified.

2 **Skill acquisition and rehearsal** – the therapist helps the patient develop and practise coping statements to use in stressful situations that counteract their negative self-statements, like *'I am in control of this situation, it isn't in control of me'*. Other techniques include relaxation exercises to reduce physiological arousal and learning how to realistically assess situations.

3 **Application and follow-through** – patients visualise using stress-reduction techniques learned in the second phase and then use them in role-play exercises and lastly in real-life situations. Once the patient can cope with a relatively non-threatening situation, a more threatening one is presented and the process is repeated – for instance, imagining talking to people, then practising it in role play and finally talking to colleagues at break time.

### Research

Jay & Elliot (1990) developed a videotape for parents of 3–12-year-old children with leukaemia who were undergoing bone marrow treatment and lumbar punctures. One hour before treatment, parents were shown a film of a model parent employing self-statements, relaxation techniques and coping imagery rehearsal. The parents then practised these skills. Compared with parents receiving child-focused interventions, the SIT-treated parents showed significantly less anxiety and enhanced coping skills. This implies SIT to be an effective treatment for acute, short-term stressors.

Meichenbaum (2001) reports that SIT modelling films have successfully controlled anger in alleged rape victims when preparing them for forensic examination.

Holroyd *et al.* (1977) assigned 31 participants experiencing intermittent chronic tension headaches to an SIT group, a biofeedback group (see page 300) or a no-treatment control group. They found that only the SIT group showed substantial improvements in daily reductions of headaches, suggesting SIT is an effective treatment for chronic, long-term intermittent stressors and is superior to physiological treatment.

Holcomb (1986) assigned 26 psychiatric patients with severe stress and anxiety disorders to a) SIT, b) a combination of SIT and drug treatment or c) just drug treatment, finding SIT superior to drugs in reducing symptoms of depression, anxiety and distress. A three-year follow-up study revealed that patients from the SIT alone group required fewer admissions for psychiatric problems than other patients, suggesting that SIT is superior in treating stress-related disorders and that drugs actually hinder recovery.

## Evaluation

- Although some research shows SIT is effective in treating combat-based stress in the military, many studies find it ineffective. This may be due to the stigma associated with mental health issues in the military, with many soldiers only reluctantly undergoing treatment. Soldiers may hold the stereotypical view that psychological problems are the result of weaknesses in character and may hinder promotion chances. In addition, military SIT programmes tend to be delivered via an academic lecture format that is sometimes not appropriate or engaging for soldiers.
- SIT inoculates against future as well as current stressful situations, as it is effective over long periods and across different stressful situations. Patients continue to practise and apply skills they have learned to any type of stressful situations they come up against.
- SIT is not an easy option, requiring patients to be motivated and committed over long periods. This is not always an easy thing for individuals suffering from stress-related disorders to achieve.
- There are so many separate threads to SIT that it is difficult to work out which component – relaxation, cognitive appraisal, practical life skills and so on – is most important in addressing the negative effects of stress. It could just be relaxation.

**Figure 8.18** SIT has not proven useful to soldiers in combat situations, as it is not necessarily delivered in an appropriate way for them

### YOU ARE THE RESEARCHER

Design an experiment that tests how well SIT works. You will need an aim and a suitable experimental hypothesis. What would your IV and DV be? Consider why you would need a control condition.

How would the effectiveness of SIT be measured?

What statistical test would be used to analyse the data? Give three reasons for your choice of test.

# Biofeedback

Biofeedback is a behaviourist method of stress management involving training people to lower stress levels by using physical signals from their bodies. Patients are attached to a machine (see Figure 8.19) giving visual or auditory feedback about physiological activity, for instance whether heart rate is at a desired level. The biofeedback machine acts like a 'sixth sense', giving individuals an awareness of the physiological activity inside their bodies. This might involve a light flashing or a buzzer beeping every time they get stressed and their muscles tense. Patients learn to slow down the light or buzzer by relaxing their muscles. To do this they are taught relaxation techniques, such as breathing control, which help to dampen the physical effects of stress and bring them under personal control. Biofeedback allows patients to alter brain activity, blood pressure, heart rate and other bodily functions that are not usually under conscious control.

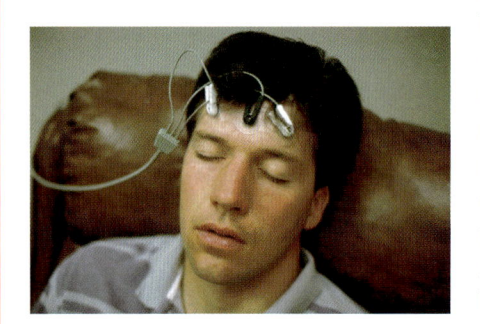

**Figure 8.19** Biofeedback involves being connected to a machine that gives feedback about physiological activity within patients' bodies

Patients are set targets, for instance reducing muscle tension, and the relaxation techniques help them reach their targets, reinforcing the behaviour (strengthening it, making it more likely to reoccur). This type of operant conditioning requires no conscious thinking to be learned and the patient transfers these new skills to real-life situations.

## Research

Bozsik *et al.* (1995) found that biofeedback and relaxation exercises helped 20 Hungarian elite biathlon competitors reduce the bodily stress levels created by vigorous cross-country skiing, so that they could control their fine-motor muscles in order to successfully shoot at targets. This suggests biofeedback has practical applications in reducing stress levels for competitive sportspeople.

**Figure 8.20** Biofeedback has proven useful in sports such as biathlon, which require control of bodily stress levels in order to be successful

Lemaire *et al.* (2011) gave biofeedback-based therapy to 40 medical doctors (a stressful occupation) three times daily for 28 days, with the participants' stress levels then monitored for a further 28 days. There was a similar control group who received no biofeedback. The stress levels of the biofeedback group decreased significantly and were maintained over the next 28 days, but no such improvements were seen in the control group. This suggests that biofeedback can reduce doctors' stress levels, improving their job capability.

Bouchard *et al.* (2012) found that a group of soldiers given one 30-minute session of biofeedback per day for three days while playing a stressful video shooting game had lower stress levels (measure by cortisol levels in saliva and heart rate) when undergoing a live simulated ambush where they had to apply first aid to a wounded soldier than a similar group of soldiers who received no biofeedback. This suggests that biofeedback is effective in reducing stress levels and has practical applications in combat situations for military personnel.

Zauszniewski *et al.* (2013) taught 20 grandmothers to use a biofeedback machine and relaxation techniques and got them to apply the therapy at home for four weeks. Data concerning stress and negative thoughts and emotions was collected by questionnaires and interviews. Significant improvements in stress levels were noted at 2, 8 and 14 weeks after using the therapy. As more and more grandparents experience increased stress from acting as full-time child carers, the findings suggest biofeedback can reduce and maintain reductions in their stress levels.

### Evaluation

- Biofeedback has successfully addressed a variety of stress-related physical disorders, illustrating its wide-ranging usage as a stress management technique.
- Biofeedback is not invasive and has no negative side effects or addictive qualities, giving it an advantage over drug therapies.
- Relaxation strategies learned through biofeedback can be continually applied in stressful situations, giving the therapy long-term usage.
- Attanasio *et al.* (1985) found that biofeedback works well with children, as they are more willing and try harder to achieve success, suggesting the therapy is suited to those motivated to reduce their stress levels.
- It is not fully understood how biofeedback works – it may be that its success is due to learning to relax, which leads to alleviation of stress symptoms, or it may be that patients acquire a greater sense of perceived control, which lowers stress levels.
- The treatment is relatively expensive, requiring specialist equipment and supervision. If the success of biofeedback is indeed due to relaxation, then such specialist equipment and supervision are unnecessary.
- It was originally hoped that biofeedback would give such control over bodily systems that it would do away with drug treatments and their negative side effects. Although biofeedback has proven that humans can exert some conscious control over seemingly involuntary bodily functions, there is a limit to which we can do this, meaning other stress management therapies have a role to play, too.

## Gender differences in coping with stress

There is a gender difference in the way males and females respond to stress that seems biologically based. Taylor *et al.* (2000) found that acute stress produces the 'fight-or-flight' response in men, but the 'tend-and-befriend' response in women, because females produce more oxytocin, a hormone released from the pituitary gland that promotes nurturing and co-operation. This gender difference affects the way males and females cope with stress.

Females use social support networks more, possibly because they are biologically wired at times of stress to be more caring and protective and thus are able to utilise social support. This means that they are generally more able to deal with stress than men. Females also generally have more social support, like close friendship groups, to call upon than males. Again this may be biological in nature, or because females are socialised (taught by society) to have more and closer friendship groups and to be able to express their emotions more openly.

Because females tend to express their emotions more openly they also use emotion-focused coping strategies more. Such strategies aim to reduce the negative effects of stress by making individuals feel positive about stressful situations. Some emotion-focused strategies are positive ones, like seeing stressful situations as opportunities for self-improvement, while others are negative, such as denying that the situation exists. Women have higher stress levels than men and this could be because they assess stressors as being more severe (or because they just have more stressful lives than men). This tends to result again in women dealing with stress in more emotionally focused ways.

Males are more reluctant to perceive or admit that stress affects them negatively, which affects the way they cope with stress – they are more reluctant to make necessary changes to their lifestyle or to manage their stress. Males are less likely to seek professional help from therapists and this again has a negative impact. Men use more problem-focused coping

**ON THE WEB**

A visual presentation of how biofeedback works (with sub-titles) can be seen at **www.youtube.com**. Search for 'Biofeedback for stress related health problems'.

**Figure 8.21** Females tend to have more social support to call upon in times of stress than males

strategies, where they confront stressors head on, for instance taking personal responsibility for dealing with the situation. Females are more likely to seek professional help and to use a multitude of strategies, while men are more likely to try to deal with stress by themselves or to reduce its effects through physical activity like sports.

## Research

Matud (2004) assessed gender differences in stress and coping strategies in 2,816 people, finding that women rated stressful life events as more negative and less controllable than men. This, coupled with the fact that women had more family- and health-related stressors, while men had more financial and work-related stressors, affected coping styles. Women used more emotional avoidance styles, while men were more emotionally inhibited. This suggests women cope less well with stress because they use more negative, emotion-focused strategies, though men's inability to express emotions could have long-term health impacts.

Garnefski (2004) administered the Cognitive Emotion Regulation Questionnaire to 630 males and females, finding that females used more emotion-focused strategies dwelling on thoughts and feelings associated with stressful situations and accorded more blame to themselves for stressful situations. Females also had higher levels of depression. This suggests females use more maladaptive emotion-focused strategies than males and that their higher rates of depression are linked to their less effective ways of coping.

Ptacek *et al*. (2014) found that females used more social support and emotion-focused coping strategies with an achievement-related stressor than males, who used more problem-focused coping strategies. This suggests that males and females are socialised and/or are biologically focused to deal with stressors differently.

Tamres *et al*. (2014) assessed evidence from several studies to find that females use a wider selection of coping strategies and are more likely to seek social support to deal with stressors. Females were also more likely to engage in negative emotion-focused strategies, which explains why they tended to perceive stressors as more severe than males did.

## Evaluation

- Findings of gender differences in coping strategies are often based on self-report measures that are prone to bias and therefore need validating by alternative methodologies.
- In Garnefski's study, 2,029 people were approached to participate, of whom 630 accepted (31 per cent). The sample may therefore be biased, for instance more severely depressed people may have been less willing to participate.
- The fact that women use emotion-focused strategies can have negative effects, as it delays dealing with the problem.
- Dividing the way that people cope with stress by gender is simplistic and may create self-fulfilling prophecies where people react in the way they think they ought to because of their gender. There are wide individual differences between people, meaning that many males and females will not cope with stress in gender-stereotypical ways.
- Gender differences in coping strategies may actually exist, as males and females have different types of stressors to deal with. Perhaps females use emotion-focused strategies more, as the types of stressors they deal with have more of an emotional content and impact, such as ill-health in loved ones.

*'It's the friends you can call up at 4 a.m. that matter.'*
Marlene Dietrich (1962)

# The role of social support in coping with stress

One important factor in how well individuals deal with stress is the degree of **social support** they get from family, friends, work colleagues, therapists, etc. The more social support individuals get, the better able they are to cope with stressful situations, with the social support acting as a buffer against the stressors. A lack of social support not only prevents individuals from dealing with stress, it can also lead to a sense of isolation and mental illness, such as depression.

What amount and types of social support an individual receives depends on several factors, such as the social networks that a person has and their gender, with females generally having wider social support systems. It also depends on cultural background, with certain cultures, like collectivist ones, having extended family networks that can provide heightened sources of support, such as instrumental, esteem and emotional support.

Stroebe (2000) identified five types of social support:

1 **Esteem support** – this occurs when an individual perceives that others value them and hold them in high regard. This strengthens feelings of self-value, which is particularly helpful in dealing with stressful situations, as it helps individuals feel competent enough that they can cope.

2 **Emotional support** – this occurs when an individual perceives that others care for them, have sympathy for and an understanding of their situation and can be depended upon to provide comfort.

3 **Appraisal support** – this occurs where others assist an individual to identify and understand their stressors and their effects on health, permitting a realistic view of stressful situations to be achieved.

4 **Informational support** – this occurs when others are able to give advice and guidance on how to deal with stressful situations, like that from a therapist, or feedback from others as to how an individual is coping.

5 **Instrumental support** – this occurs when others provide practical assistance, either indirectly, like helping out so that an individual has more time and energy to deal with a stressful situation, or directly, such as by helping to deal with the stressful situation themselves, for example loaning money to help cope with financial stressors.

## Research

Orth-Gomer *et al.* (1993) found that in a sample of 776 50-year-old healthy Swedish men born in 1933, the most common factors in those going on to develop CVDs was smoking and lack of social support, illustrating the importance of social support in counteracting the negative effects of stress. It was also found that only in men who lacked emotional support were the effects of stressful life events harmful, with such men five times more likely to die than those receiving emotional support, further highlighting the value of social support.

Stachour (1998) assessed the quantity and quality of social support for 37 participants. Quantity was measured by the number of interactions with

> **KEY TERM**
>
> **Social support** – the degree of assistance and resources available from others to help cope with stress

people within social support networks and quality by the administration of the Perceived Social Support from Friends and Family Measures questionnaire, which includes measures of emotional support, esteem support and instrumental support. It was found that participants with greater quality of social support were healthier, but no such relationship was found between health and quantity of social support, which suggests quality of support is more important than quantity.

Bolger & Amarel (2007) paired 35 female students, who were stressed by being told they had to make a speech that would be graded, with a female confederate each. The confederates gave either visible social support, by directly advising a participant on how to do the speech, or invisible social support, where the participant overheard them giving the same advice, but as an opinion to the researcher. Stress levels after social support was given were measured by questionnaire and it was found that invisible social support reduced stress levels more than visible social support. This suggests that social support that directly indicates to stressed people that they have the ability to deal with a stressor is less beneficial than support given more subtly.

## Evaluation

- Although social support generally helps individuals to deal with stress in a positive way, if different types of support are offered it can create confusion and overwhelm a person, making them less able to cope. Social support will also not be helpful if it is not perceived as such, or if the type of support makes the stressful situation worse, such as encouraging an individual to drink/take drugs to lessen their stress levels.
- Also different types of social support have been investigated it is difficult to isolate and test separate types, making it difficult to assess which types are most influential in helping individuals cope with stress.
- It is not fully understood how social support helps combat stress – it may be that social support raises self-esteem, enabling individuals to be more persistent in dealing with stress, or that social support lessens the impact of stressors.
- Different types of social support may be more helpful in different situations. For example, when stressed with high work commitments, instrumental support in the form of help babysitting the children may be best, while when faced with the stress caused by the breakdown of a relationship, emotional support may be best.

### STRENGTHEN YOUR LEARNING

1. How do i) BZs, ii) BBs work? What side effects are associated with these drugs?
2. What does Kulik's (2013) study suggest about the use of BBs?
3. What does other research suggest about the effectiveness of drug therapies? What other evaluative points can be made about drug therapies?
4. Outline how i) SIT, ii) biofeedback works.
5. How effective does research suggest both these therapies are? What other evaluative points can be made about SIT and biofeedback?
6. Explain why gender differences in coping with stress may exist.
7. What have research studies suggested about gender differences in coping with stress? What other evaluative points are there to consider?
8. Explain how different types of social support can affect how individuals cope with stress.
9. What have research studies suggested about the role of social support in coping with stress? What other evaluative points are there to consider?

# ASSESSMENT CHECK

1. A team of researchers assessed the ability of a beta-blocker to reduce the symptoms of stress in 20 participants who were given either the drug or a placebo. Stress levels were measured before and after treatment. The tables below summarise the participants' improvements in stress levels measured on a stress scale.

| Drug treatment participants | Stress improvement score |
| --- | --- |
| 1 | +10 |
| 2 | +15 |
| 3 | +10 |
| 4 | +20 |
| 5 | +12 |
| 6 | +18 |
| 7 | +5 |
| 8 | +7 |
| 9 | +13 |
| 10 | +10 |

| Placebo treatment participants | Stress improvement score |
| --- | --- |
| 11 | +3 |
| 12 | +4 |
| 13 | 0 |
| 14 | +2 |
| 15 | +4 |
| 16 | +8 |
| 17 | 0 |
| 18 | +1 |
| 19 | +4 |
| 20 | +4 |

   a) Calculate the mean stress improvement scores of both the drug and placebo conditions. **[2 marks]**

   b) Use the mean scores to plot the data on an appropriate graph. **[2 marks]**

   c) Give one reason for your choice of graph. **[1 mark]**

2. Manon is a talented young gymnast who performs well in training but badly in competition due to her high stress levels. Her heart rate becomes very high, she has difficulty controlling her breathing and she experiences uncontrollable tremors in her muscles.
   With reference to the scenario above, explain how biofeedback might help Manon cope with the stress of performing in public. **[6 marks]**

3. Place a letter 'C' next to the following statement that relates to Type C personality and a letter 'H' next to the statement relating to hardiness. One statement will be left over. **[2 marks]**
   - Personality type characterised by people who like routine and not change, who are highly obedient and prone to worry and becoming irritable.
   - Personality type characterised by people who take everything seriously and work very hard, who are thorough in all they do and who tend not to express their emotions.
   - Personality type characterised by individuals who are committed to what they're doing, who have a sense of control over what they're doing and perceive stressors as challenges.

4. Outline gender differences in coping with stress. **[3 marks]**

5. Outline and evaluate drug therapy in managing and coping with stress. **[16 marks]**

The physiology of stress

The role of stress in illness

Sources of stress

Physiological measures of stress

Individual differences in stress

Managing and coping with stress

**SUMMARY**

- Physiological reactions to stress are explained through the general adaptation syndrome, the hypothalamic-pituitary-adrenal system and the sympathomedullary pathway.
- Cortisol is a glucocorticoid hormone secreted from the adrenal glands that provides a steady supply of blood sugar to give the body energy to deal with stressors.
- Continual stress can lead to illness, especially through immunosuppression, where stress impairs the ability of the immune system to resist illness and disease.
- Continual stress can also lead to cardiovascular disorders, such as coronary heart disease.
- Life changes are occasional events incurring major adjustments to lifestyle, and along with daily hassles, everyday irritations that produce an overall elevated level of stress, they can increase vulnerability to stress-related illnesses.
- The workplace is a rich source of stressors, including an employees' workload and the degree of control they have over their job.
- Stress is measured through self-report scales like the Stress Readjustment Rating Scale and the Hassles and Uplifts Scale, as well as physiological measures such as skin conductance response.
- Vulnerability to different types of stress-related disorders is associated with different personality types, such as A, B, C, D and hardiness.
- Drug therapies to manage stress levels include benzodiazepines and beta-blockers, while psychological therapies include stress inoculation therapy and biofeedback.
- There are gender differences in coping with stress, due to socialisation processes, as well as biological influences.
- The ability to cope with stress is influenced by the degree and type of social support that individuals utilise.

# 9 Aggression

## Introduction

*'The tendency to aggression is an innate independent instinctual disposition in man ... it constitutes the powerful obstacle to culture.'*

Sigmund Freud (1913)

We can pick up from someone's body language when they are feeling aggressive towards us. It seems instinctive to do so. It is evident in their tone of voice, their stance and their actions. This chapter tackles the possible explanations of aggression (psychological and biological) and why someone may act that way. It also considers why aggression occurs in certain contexts, such as prisons, and how it can be influenced by the media.

Specific focus here will be upon:

1. Neural and hormonal mechanisms in aggression
2. The ethological explanation for aggression
3. Evolutionary explanations for human aggression
4. Social psychological explanations for human aggression
5. Institutional aggression in the context of prisons
6. Media influences on aggression.

## Understanding the specification

- The specification requires an understanding of the neural and hormonal mechanisms in aggression. You need to pay extra attention to the roles of the limbic system, serotonin and testosterone. You also need to be able to explain and evaluate the genetic factors with a focus on the MAOA gene.
- You need to know the ethological explanation of aggression and be able to make reference to innate releasing mechanisms and fixed action patterns. You should also understand the evolutionary explanations of human aggression.
- You should be able to explain and evaluate the frustration–aggression hypothesis, social learning theory and de-individuation.
- You need to understand explanations of institutional aggression, specifically both dispositional and situational explanations for why institutional aggression occurs.
- Finally, you will need to understand the effect the media, especially computer games, has on aggression and more specifically the role of desensitisation, disinhibition and cognitive priming.

These are the basic requirements of the specification. However, other relevant material is included to provide depth and detail to your understanding.

# IN THE NEWS

## ᴪ The Psychological Enquirer

### 'Harmless wedgie? Maybe not'

**Figure 9.1** John Hopoate came up with a novel form of aggression to put opponents off their game

Australian rugby league player John Hopoate had a reputation for unsettling and upsetting opposition players by any means possible and was suspended several times in 2000, once being charged with 'contrary conduct' for ten separate incidents in one game. But in 2001 Hopoate came up with an interesting and creative new type of aggression: shoving his fingers into the anuses of several opponents in order to 'affect their game'. Hopoate and his team mates tried to explain the behaviour as nothing more than a harmless 'wedgie', but opponents and the rugby league disciplinary board disagreed and John was charged with 'unlawful sexual connection'. He was later banned from rugby league and became a professional boxer.

John Hopoate's behaviour is an example of instrumental aggression, where aggression is deliberately used to gain a specific goal, such as putting your fingers up someone's bottom to 'affect' their game.

This suggests a cognitive input, where thought and planning are involved, much different from the use of hostile aggression, where aggression is a biologically controlled, unthinking response to a stimulus, like lashing out at someone who threatens you. This form of aggression seems more deterministic, as it suggests aggression is out of control of the individual. However, the calculated thought behind John Hopoate's actions illustrates that aggression can be controlled and used to achieve a set aim. Therefore Hopoate's actions are better explained psychologically.

## 9.1 Neural and hormonal mechanisms in aggression

The focus for this section is on how the brain and the biochemistry of the body can affect aggression levels. The **limbic system** is a key area of the brain thought to be involved in moderating aggression. Serotonin and **testosterone** are also implicated in the behaviour.

### The role of the limbic system

The limbic system is a central part of the brain involved in processing emotional responses. It is this area of the brain that is implicated in aggressive behaviour and it is also thought that the cortex works to mediate the level of aggression transmitted from that area. It is thought that this happens by moderating testosterone levels in response to environmental triggers. More specifically, the **amygdala**, which is part of the limbic system, is argued to have an important influence. If the amygdala malfunctions in any way due to a tumour, damage or atypical development then the levels of testosterone can be raised, making aggressive behaviour more likely.

**KEY TERMS**

**Limbic system** – a central area of the brain which has many functions, including processing of emotion

**Testosterone** – a steroid hormone that stimulates development of male secondary characteristics

**Amygdala** – an area of the brain within the limbic system which processes emotion

# Research

Siegel & Victoroff (2009) reviewed the research on the neurobiological and behavioural explanations of aggression (defensive and predatory). They found that both forms of aggressive behaviour seem to be controlled by the limbic system. They also found evidence that the cerebral cortex played an important role in moderating the extent to which aggression was expressed.

Raine *et al.* (1997) scanned the brains of 41 murderers and 41 controls. They found, using PET scans, that some had abnormalities in the way that their limbic systems functioned. This suggests that the limbic system could be implicated in aggressive behaviour.

Sumer *et al.* (2007) reported on a case study of a 14-year-old girl who, following an MRI scan, was diagnosed with a tumour in the limbic system. This was investigated due to epileptic seizures from the age of three and she was behaving in an aggressive manner, expressing anger and rage. When the tumour was treated with drugs, the patient returned to normal levels of aggression. This seems to suggest that the high levels of aggression could have been prompted by the tumour in the limbic system.

## Evaluation

- The role of the limbic system in aggressive behaviour is not clear cut. It should also be noted that the limbic system is made up of many components so it is not altogether clear which parts may be implicated. It could equally be that there is an interaction between components of the system.
- The research linking brain abnormalities to violence is only correlational – this means that there is only an indication of vulnerability to aggression. There are also people who have limbic system abnormalities who do not demonstrate violent behaviour and so causation cannot be ascertained.

# The role of serotonin

Various drugs such as Prozac, available for prescription, are thought to be related to lowering serotonin levels in some of the population, which is not the desired outcome. These have the unfortunate effect of depressing mood and increasing aggression in the individual. This has led to some drugs being withdrawn because of this effect on the serotonin levels on the person to whom the drug is administered.

However, the evidence base for the role of serotonin and its effect on aggression is mixed. Some studies show greater amounts of serotonin in the system increase aggression and others show the opposite effect.

The exact role it plays in aggression is unclear. Currently it is thought to mediate an individual's response to a situation. Activation in the brain's limbic region (which is the centre of the emotional response) is not controlled as much by the frontal cortex in individuals with low serotonin. This means, in essence, that an individual with low serotonin has less control over their emotional response, and this can lead to aggression (Crockett & Passamonti, 2011).

**KEY TERM**

**Serotonin** – a neurotransmitter thought to regulate feelings of well-being

**Figure 9.2** Serotonin increases aggression in crayfish

## Animal research

Work by Huber *et al.* (1997) demonstrated that increasing levels of serotonin in many species, from crayfish to humans, increases aggression. This perceived increase in aggression was observed in crayfish and in particular the length of time they continued fighting. Selected crayfish were infused with small amounts of serotonin while they moved around. Their behaviour was compared with crayfish that had serotonin at typical levels. It was observed that the crayfish whose serotonin levels were increased delayed the point at which they withdrew from fighting – they continued to fight beyond the point at which they would normally cease (see Figure 9.2). This seems to suggest that the level of aggression they were experiencing was greater or that their natural response were overridden. The broad effect across many species seems to suggest that its role is related to aggressive behaviour, and this could be an evolutionary adaptation.

There are issues with the fact that this study was conducted on crayfish and therefore the exact reason behind the apparent rise in aggression cannot be verified. Work on humans which measured aggressive behaviour has been conducted to test the relationship of serotonin to human aggression.

Crockett *et al.* (2009a and b) used the non-physical situation of game playing and moral dilemmas to observe behaviour. Some participants had their serotonin levels reduced by manipulation of their diets, others had their serotonin levels increased by being administered an SSRI drug, which increases serotonin levels. This was a temporary change. The participants who had been given the restrictive diet displayed a higher level of retaliation against their opponents, and the participants who had higher levels of serotonin responded to emotional moral dilemmas with increased compassion. These results together seem to suggest that serotonin in higher levels affects emotional responses and regulates social decision making.

This study, like the work of Huber *et al.* (1997), also suffers from a lack of validity. It was conducted on humans, but the measure of aggression was game playing, which could be said to lack the emotion involved in real life situations where aggression may occur.

## Human research

Cherek *et al.* (1996) found in their research that when men take drugs that increase their serotonin levels they display low levels of aggression. This suggests that there may be a causal link between serotonin levels and aggressive behaviour.

### Evaluation

- The Crockett & Passamonti study highlights why some people get aggressive when they have not eaten. This could be due in part to a depleted level of tryptophan, which is the dietary source of serotonin. Foods such as eggs and chickpeas are tryptophan rich.
- Much research into neural and hormonal mechanisms in aggression involves animals, which poses a problem for extrapolating to humans. This research is conducted on animals for ethical reasons, and availability of animals, but there is always an issue of using animal studies to explain human behaviour.
- Using biochemistry to explain aggression is a deterministic approach. There is a limited amount of control of the individual over their biochemistry and so, if aggression is explained this way, it is also saying that the individual does not have much control over how they act. This has implications for the legal system and punishing violent crimes.

# The role of testosterone

Testosterone is an androgen, or male hormone. Females also have testosterone in their bodies but in lower levels. Increased levels of testosterone are thought to be related to increased levels of aggression and of aggressive responses, such as provocation.

If a causal link is to be found then the mechanism behind how testosterone affects aggression levels needs to be documented. Some research on mice has suggested that the enzyme **aromatase** is implicated in the process. Aromatase is important in metabolising testosterone in the brain and is found in the limbic region of the brain such as the amygdala. So, if there are reduced levels of aromatase in those areas then the testosterone in the brain will not have enough enzyme for it to activate. This means it will have less effect and the response to emotional situations experienced by the amygdala will not prompt a reaction in the testosterone in the system. This reduces the likelihood of an aggressive reaction.

Another way in which the brain mechanism is thought to have an effect is that the level of testosterone affects the activity in the orbito-frontal cortex of the brain. If an individual has high levels of testosterone then the activity in the orbito-frontal cortex is reduced, which means that in an emotional situation there could be a heightened emotionally aggressive response.

Testosterone also influences the activity of serotonin in the brain and therefore can reduce serotonergic activity. As is evident from the previous section on the role of serotonin in aggressive behaviour, low levels of serotonergic activity are implicated in increased aggressive behaviour. It appears that testosterone does not just have an effect in isolation, it seems to mediate the effects of other biochemicals, too.

## Research

Connor & Levine (1969) experimented on rats and found that those that had been castrated when they were young had lower levels of testosterone and also displayed low levels of aggression as adults. When given testosterone injections, they still displayed passive behaviour. This was not the same for rats castrated when fully developed. If subsequently given testosterone they returned to pre-castration levels of aggression. This seems to suggest that sensitivity to testosterone is part of the developmental process.

Research by Higley *et al.* (1996) suggests that testosterone levels are not the only factor in aggressive behaviours. They found that testosterone can affect how aggressive an individual feels but that they will not necessarily act on that feeling. Therefore it could be concluded that testosterone levels may underpin the emotional response to a situation but that other factors such as social learning theory will affect whether the aggression felt influences the actual behaviour of the individual.

Ellis *et al.* (2009) in their *Handbook of Crime Correlates* reviewed the literature to establish the potential link of testosterone to violent crime. Their review seemed to suggest that there was a link, but that the relationship strength varied for gender and there was less of an effect for juvenile delinquency.

### KEY TERM

**Aromatase** – an enzyme which helps metabolise (or process) testosterone

## Evaluation

- Much of the research conducted in this field is on animals. This is problematic, for the same reasons stated in the serotonin research, in that the differences between human and animal aggression make extrapolation difficult. Human aggression has many different factors that affect it and as such it is more complex.

- Generalising from animal studies is also problematic because certain brain structures are involved with different types of aggression in different species. An example of this is the fact that the cingulate gyrus, an area of the brain, is linked to irritability in cats and dogs but is associated with fear-induced aggression in monkeys. This creates problems in generalising to humans as they have a different brain physiology.

- It is important to consider the measures used in research. Aggression is measured often through questionnaires or responses to hypothetical scenarios and therefore the predictive validity is poor. This means that someone may report high levels of aggression in a fake scenario on paper, but were it actually to occur in real life their response might be more passive. Testosterone can be measured using saliva samples and cerebro-spinal fluid, both of which are reliable measures. However, hormonal fluctuations occur throughout the day so test-retest reliability may be low.

- It is argued that testosterone may be able to explain only certain types of aggression. Simpson (2001) reports that testosterone is implicated only in inter-male aggression, but has no effect on other types of aggression.

- As most of the research is correlational it is important that it is recognised that testosterone levels rather than cause aggression may be a response to it and so caution should be taken when describing the role testosterone plays in aggression.

# IN THE NEWS

# Ψ The Psychological Enquirer

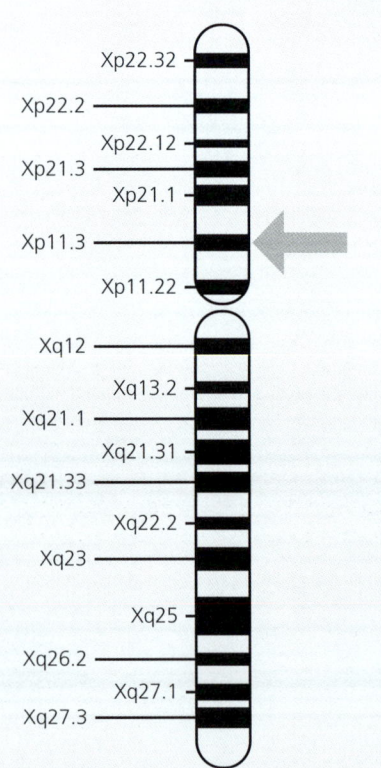

**Figure 9.3** An illustration of the MAOA gene

Davis Bradley Waldroup Jr lived in Tennessee, where in 2006, police were called to a disturbance. He was attacking his estranged wife when the police arrived and they also found the body of Leslie Bradshaw, who was a friend of Waldroup's wife.

Waldroup had gone to pick up his children from his estranged wife's home when the attack took place. The children were present. Reports state that the attack was committed in a calm and methodical manner. Waldroup was arrested and charged with murder and attempted murder.

However, his defence argued that he was not culpable for the crimes as he had the shortened version of the MAOA gene. This is nicknamed the 'warrior gene'. The gene is implicated in aggressive behaviour due to excessive amounts of certain neurotransmitters in the system. The expert defence witness, Dr William Bernet, found a match with the gene from a blood sample processed at Vanderbilt University's DNA lab, and stated that its presence, combined with the abuse Waldroup had suffered as a child, increased his chance of a violent offence by 400 per cent.

The jury found that Waldroup was predisposed to violent behaviour and the charge was reduced from murder to manslaughter. This allowed the defendant to avoid the death penalty, which would have been death by lethal injection. Instead he received 32 years in prison.

Waldroup is eligible for parole in 2026, when he will be 52 years old.

This is an example of how research into genetics can be used within the court system to account for behaviour. By saying that Waldroup had a genetic predisposition to violent behaviour meant that he could not be seen as culpable (to blame) for his violent acts, which has far-reaching implications for the legal system.

# Genetic factors in aggression

The neural and hormonal mechanisms implicated in aggression seem to suggest that biology is influential in aggressive behaviour. It is therefore no surprise that research is looking at the potential genetic influence on aggression.

It is entirely possible that high levels of testosterone or fluctuating levels of serotonin could be genetically determined. This then could mean that certain individuals or families could display higher levels of aggressive behaviour because of their predisposition to biochemical differences from the majority of the population.

Genes can determine levels of testosterone and the speed with which it is **metabolised**. They can also determine the physiology of the brain in terms of the number of receptors and how sensitive such receptors are. A different brain physiology determined by genetics may mean that the pathway between the limbic system and the frontal cortex is weak. These are all ways that our genetic make-up can potentially have an effect on the levels of aggression that we demonstrate in our behaviour.

Genetic influence is traditionally investigated through twin and adoption studies. Family studies are also used. However, these populations are naturally occurring and sometimes psychologists prefer to manipulate the situation in some way by using studies on animals that have been bred for the purpose of research. It is also common to use animal isolation studies as they effectively remove the influence of social behaviour and imitation.

As yet, no specific gene that causes behaviour has been identified. There does seem to be some evidence that individuals inherit a predisposition to being aggressive but that the genetic influence is not a certain influence. It can be mediated by the environment. In other words, the genotype may suggest that someone would be aggressive but the phenotype, after the environment has influenced the individual, may mean aggressive behaviour is not shown.

> **KEY TERM**
>
> **Metabolisation** – the processing of a biochemical by the body

# MAOA gene

The gene monoamine oxidase A (MAOA) has been implicated in aggression as it was found, almost by chance, that mice that possessed the gene were extremely aggressive. The gene is suggested to express itself through affecting levels of neurotransmitters.

MAOA is an enzyme that breaks down important neurotransmitters in the brain, including dopamine, noradrenaline and serotonin. The enzyme is controlled by the **MAOA gene**. There are variations of the gene found in humans, and these result in different levels of enzymatic activity. People with the low-activity form (which is called MAOA-L) produce less of the enzyme, while the high-activity form (MAOA-H) produces more of the enzyme.

Studies have found a correlation between the low-activity form of MAOA and aggression (see Research, below). Only about a third of men in Western populations have the low-activity form of MAOA and therefore have the higher levels of neurotransmitters because the excess amounts are not mopped up. There is also an environmental effect as the men who carry the shortened version of the MAOA gene do not automatically display aggressive

> **KEY TERM**
>
> **MAOA gene** – a gene which affects how neurotransmitters are metabolised

behaviour – this seems to occur only if they have been abused as children. Their chance of committing a violent crime is then increased.

Genes (strands of DNA) are not always activated; some are expressed only if combined with other genes and some may undergo mutation, a random change affecting an animal or human's anatomy and, hence, some aspects of its behaviour. It seems that aggressiveness is influenced by a variation in the MAOA gene, which is sensitive to social experiences early in development; therefore, its functional outcome depends on the environment. This indicates that an interaction of genetics and environment is at work in determining human aggression and that the phenotype differs from the genotype. Possessing the shortened version of the MAOA gene does not automatically make you a fighter.

## CLASSIC RESEARCH

### Abnormal behaviour associated with a point mutation in the structural gene for monoamine oxidase A – H.G. Brunner (1993)

**Figure 9.4** H.G. Brunner

Brunner syndrome was first described in 1993 by H.G. Brunner in his paper documenting the behaviour of five men in a family in the Netherlands. He found, through monitoring their urine samples, that they had an excess of monoamines (noradrenaline, serotonin and dopamine) in their bodies. This was caused by a monoamine oxidase A (MAOA) deficiency. They possessed a shortened version of the MAOA gene and therefore were not able to 'mop up' excess amounts of neurotransmitters.

Brunner found that all of the male family members had this genetic defect and that their behaviour was aggressive when they were under threat, frightened, angry or frustrated. These men also showed borderline mental retardation. Their behaviour was distinctive and anti-social as they demonstrated behaviours such as impulsive aggression, arson, attempted rape and exhibitionism.

### Evaluation

This case study has important implications for the legal system and how culpable someone is of any crime they commit. It should be noted, however, that this case study involves five males from the same family and as such is a specific and small sample.

The classic case study by Brunner shows how the MAOA gene can affect families that have the gene present in male members. The fact that, for this Dutch family, there was such a high relevance of aggressive behaviour supports the MAOA gene theory.

### ON THE WEB

There are a great many clips to watch on YouTube (**www.youtube.com**) on the warrior (MAOA) gene. Some films explain the action of the gene, others the effects it is reported to have on individuals, including Davis Waldroup Jr.

## Research

Moffitt *et al.* (1992) performed a study on 442 New Zealand males from birth to age 26, keeping a record of experiences of abuse and the presence of the shortened MAOA gene. It was found that those who had suffered abuse and had the low-activity version of the gene were nine times more likely to indulge in antisocial behaviour, including aggression.

Genetically engineered mice with low MAOA levels were studied by Cases *et al.* (1995). They found the mice had atypical serotonin levels and behaviour. As adult mice, they demonstrated increased levels of aggression and were aggressive during mating. This gives support to human studies suggesting that aggression is a direct result of MAOA deficiency and that the increased levels of aggression observed in humans with the gene are due mostly to the genetic defect.

### Evaluation

- The MAOA gene can only attempt to explain aggression in those individuals who possess the shortened version of the gene. This is thought to be one third of men in Western populations. It is often not expressed in women due to their chromosomal make-up. This means that aggression in two thirds of men and most women cannot be accounted for this way.

- It may be that this gene is present in a large number of individuals in the population due to the evolutionary advantages it bestows. It is possible that it gives a competitive edge and that risk-taking behaviour is more likely, which, although it does not sound helpful, can make someone stand out in the workplace. It may also be more attractive to the opposite sex and therefore makes reproductive success more likely.

- Interaction with the environment is clearly important as well as the gene. The presence of abuse makes the gene likely to express itself, so the presence of the gene alone cannot account for aggression. It is an incomplete explanation.

#### STRENGTHEN YOUR LEARNING

1. Explain the role of the limbic system in aggression.
2. Explain the role of serotonin in aggression.
3. Explain the role of testosterone in aggression.
4. Give an example of research that supports the role testosterone plays in aggression.
5. Name the three biochemicals thought to be affected by the MAOA gene.
6. What is a weakness of the argument that serotonin is implicated in aggression?
7. How does the MAOA gene affect the likelihood of aggressive behaviour?
8. Give an example of research that demonstrates the role of the MAOA gene.
9. Explain one criticism of the MAOA gene as an explanation of aggression.

## 9.2 The ethological explanation for aggression

**Ethology** is the study of animal behaviour. The study of animals can help us understand human aggression in three ways:

1. It helps define aggression and looks at how it occurs with other behaviours such as reproduction and threat.
2. The study of ethology, looking at animals in their natural setting, means we can understand the way it has helped the evolutionary process. This is more difficult with humans in the modern-day habitat.
3. When animal behaviour is studied in laboratory settings the conditions can be highly controlled, and this is not possible to the same extent with human participants.

**KEY TERM**

**Ethology** – the study of animal behaviour

One of the key ethological theorists on aggression is Konrad Lorenz, who published a book called *On Aggression* (1963).

## Innate releasing mechanism

Lorenz suggested that animals had an innate mechanism for aggression and that aggressive behaviour acted as a release. This drive, he argued, then built up until the next aggressive act was performed, when it was expended again. Lorenz argued that aggression was similar to food, drink and sleep in that it was a drive that needed to be satisfied. Just as with the other drives, a physiological deficit would build up and need to be satiated, like an itch that needs a scratch.

The **innate releasing mechanism** is the specific neural circuits hardwired into the brain which monitor the drive, such as aggression.

## Fixed action pattern

In ethology, the term **fixed action pattern** (FAP) is used to describe a sequence of behaviours that occurs throughout the species. In other words, almost all members of the same species act this way. It describes a universal (but species-specific) behaviour. FAPs are argued to be innate, which is understandable given how universal they are across a species.

An example of a fixed action pattern of behaviour involving aggression is the male stickleback fish. The FAP starts with the nesting behaviour in spring. Establishing territory around the nest is important to the stickleback so any other male sticklebacks that encroach on the territory are met with aggressive attacks. However, female sticklebacks are encouraged to stay so that they can lay eggs in the pre-prepared nests.

This behaviour was investigated by Tinbergen (1952) using models crafted to resemble male sticklebacks (with red bellies) and females (with swollen bellies). All male sticklebacks attacked the model designed to look like a male member of the species. This shows that the behaviour is invariant, i.e. all males do it, and it is a strong argument for the behaviour being innate.

It is argued that these fixed action patterns are adaptive because they increase evolutionary fitness. This means that with regard to aggression in humans it must increase fitness if it is to be regarded as a fixed action pattern. This has proven to be one of the issues in applying the theory to human aggression (see Evaluation, below).

### Research

The research of Cooper *et al.* (1989) and Cooper (2003) into aggression in Old World vipers and New World pit vipers showed that fixed action patterns occur in reptilian species. When they have bitten their prey both lizards and snakes use a chemical signal to help them locate the body later. This means that the aggressive or hunting act is always of use to them for survival and provides food, which supports the fact that it is innate and evolutionarily adaptive.

Sackett (1966) reared monkeys in isolation and provided them with pictures of monkeys playing, exploring and in threatening poses. As the baby monkeys matured they displayed reactions to the pictures of baby monkeys and threatening stimuli, suggesting that there is an innate mechanism to detect threat. This could then lead to aggressive behaviour.

> **KEY TERMS**
>
> **Innate releasing mechanism** – a proposed innate mechanism that prompts a behaviour following presence of a stimulus
>
> **Fixed action pattern** – the behaviour prompted by an innate releasing mechanism

> **ON THE WEB**
>
> Film footage of fixed action patterns in animals can be found on the internet. Search for 'fixed action pattern in animals' on YouTube. Not all are aggressive, but it is useful to see adaptive behaviours performed by animals.

Eibl-Eibesfeldt (1977) argued a number of patterns of aggression in men are highly ritualised and are similar to behaviour found in animals. He cited warfare as an example. However, he also felt that there is an element of control that we are born with, which prevents us from massacring other 'tribes' (groups of people). This suggests, certainly from Eibl-Eibesfeldt's point of view, that there is a distinction between the automatic processing of animals and the more considered processing of humans, so the ethological explanation has limited usefulness in explaining aggression in humans.

### Evaluation

- Research into the ethological theory of aggression is said to lack validity. This is because behaviour is defined as aggressive by its outcome, such as injuring or killing another creature. However, it could be argued that this is purely predatory behaviour and the aggressive intent is not present; it is a survival behaviour to get food. It is not often possible to gauge whether the act is aggressive in animals, as they cannot communicate how they feel.
- Generalising from animal research to human aggression is problematic. The environment in which an animal and a human develop is very different and for that reason there is no merit in generalising behaviours across species. Some species may well have an innate releasing mechanism and fixed action pattern because it is useful to them in their situation, but this cannot be said to be true for all humans.
- A key point of the ethological theory is that the behaviour is universal to the species. This is clearly not the case for humans as even within the same situation some will react aggressively, others will not. This makes the presence of an innate mechanism and a fixed action pattern unlikely.
- An issue with explaining human aggression this way is that it should confer an evolutionary advantage. It is possible this happens in some circumstances, but in others where, for instance, a female is scared, she will not want the aggressor as her partner. This reduces their chance of reproductive success and has not shown aggression to be an adaptive mechanism.

# 9.3 Evolutionary explanations for human aggression

Genes mutate and this can affect the behaviour of the individual. Most mutations are harmful and as such, the individuals who have them are unlikely to reproduce and pass mutated genes on to their children. However, sometimes mutations can be beneficial. They may help someone compete over limited resources, increase their chance of meeting a mate thus reproducing and helping them survive. Those that survive may do so because they have benefited from a mutated gene that allowed them to adapt to their environment and gave them an advantage over others.

The evolutionary explanation suggests that aggression serves an important function in terms of both individual survival and reproductive success.

**Figure 9.5** Stags rutting is a way of displaying their attributes to potential mates

It can help an individual to fight for resources if they are in short supply. It might also be, in the case of male aggression, that they appear more attractive to females as they would appear strong. Evolutionary psychologists would argue that this would be attractive to women because they would be able to protect offspring.

It is also argued that humans have a natural tendency for aggression and this goes some way to dominance over other species. The idea of men being aggressive with other men is similar to the rutting of stags (see Figure 9.5), in that it is a chance to display attributes and essentially to show off to females. The victor is more likely to gain a mate or mates to reproduce with. This means, it is argued, they will father more offspring and have a greater chance of furthering their genetic influence on subsequent generations.

Females tend to have stricter methods for choosing a mate because they have to consider the needs of their children. A potential mate is judged by how well he could provide for any offspring from the union. A man therefore has to display that he has access to plenty of resources to support the offspring. As aggression helps gain access to available resources it therefore can be beneficial to a man. However, so too is the attribute of sensitivity. Indeed, men who express aggression to a woman may equally be less likely to attract a mate as the woman may see him as a threat to offspring. Sensitivity, however, indicates that he will have a nurturing attitude to the children.

Jealousy provides an example of when aggression may be used to confer an advantage in evolutionary terms. Jealousy is when an individual fears losing the affections of a mate to another individual. There is therefore a potential threat to their relationship and it is argued that is why aggression is displayed in their behaviour.

The same is true for infidelity, which involves a sexual partner being unfaithful. This poses a potential threat to a relationship and the possibility of offspring from the other union. If a woman, for example, has been unfaithful then paternity of any subsequent offspring is not clear. Women are always certain of maternity, but a woman's adaptive problem is finding a mate willing and able to invest resources in her and her children in the long term.

There is much evidence to back up these claims, coming mainly from studies using forced-choice, hypothetical scenarios.

## Research

Research by Sadalla *et al.* (1987) suggests that women are attracted to dominant behaviour from men, supporting the idea that aggression in men can increase their chance of reproductive success. Interestingly, though, dominant behaviour may have enhanced their attractiveness, but it did not increase how much they were actually liked. It is possible that this shows that mate preference is based on survival rather than happiness.

Daly & Wilson (1988) found that homicide rates are much higher when a man's wife or partner is about to leave him, or when they have already left. It seems that the fear and jealousy involved in losing a partner can have aggressive consequences. This is evident when women have reported that their partners have said, 'If I can't have you, no one can.' This supports the idea that mate exclusivity is important to men.

Goetz *et al.* (2008) looked at men's violence against wives and partners and found that the motivation behind the violence was to punish and try to prevent them sleeping with another man. This ensures that any offspring can be said to be fathered by the partner and the man therefore does not spend time and resources on another man's child. This is further supported by Daly *et al.* (1982), who found that men were violent when they discovered that their wife or partner had been unfaithful.

### Evaluation

- There are cultural differences in homicide rates of husbands who kill their wives. If this act was to gain an evolutionary advantage then these rates would be consistent globally. As they are not, it can be argued that there are other factors involved and the aggression between partners is much more complex than the theory suggests.
- This type of theory is difficult to test as much of the research uses a forced option format. This loses the potential intricacies and complexities of the behaviours and means conclusions drawn lack detail and a full picture of the reasons behind the aggression. They may also lack validity.
- The evolutionary explanation for aggression seems to suggest that it is excusable and beyond a person's control. This has important consequences within the legal system and within society generally. It should not be used as an excuse for aggression. This makes the research socially sensitive and it should therefore be conducted with care.

### STRENGTHEN YOUR LEARNING

1. What is ethology?
2. Explain what is meant by the term innate releasing mechanism.
3. Explain what is meant by the term fixed action pattern.
4. Give an example of a fixed action pattern that might underpin aggressive behaviour in animals.
5. Explain a weakness of the ethological explanation for aggression.
6. What are the main features of an evolutionary theory?
7. What does evolutionary theory say is achieved by aggression?
8. What roles do jealousy and infidelity play in the evolutionary explanation for aggression?
9. Explain one weakness of the evolutionary theory of aggression.
10. Give an example of some research that supports the evolutionary theory of aggression.

# ASSESSMENT CHECK

1. Select from the definitions of psychological terms A, B and C below to complete the table relating to the key terms of ethological explanations of aggression. One definition will be left over. **[2 marks]**

    **A** A sequence of behaviours that is species specific

    **B** A term used to describe the study of animal behaviour

    **C** A behaviour that allows for a release of an innate drive

    | Key term | Definition |
    | --- | --- |
    | Ethological | |
    | Fixed action patterns | |

2. A research team was investigating the role testosterone plays in aggression in violent criminal behaviour. They measured the level of testosterone in both the offender and non-offender population using saliva samples. What inferential test could be used to test for a statistically significant difference? Justify your choice. **[3 marks]**

3. Read the item and then answer the question:

    The way some men fight if they think someone is chatting up their girlfriend is like two tom cats fighting in the street.

    Using your knowledge of the ethological explanation of aggression, explain why this human behaviour seems to be so similar to animal behaviour. **[4 marks]**

4. Briefly outline and evaluate the findings of one research study into the role of testosterone in aggression. **[4 marks]**

5. Describe and evaluate the genetic explanation for aggression. **[16 marks]**

# 9.4 Social psychological explanations for human aggression

## The frustration–aggression hypothesis

This theory for aggression is based on the work of Dollard *et al.* (1939). They suggested that aggression is a consequence of feelings of frustration. Frustration is the feeling you experience when you are trying to achieve something, i.e. working towards a goal, and there are barriers (real or imaginary) that are preventing you from realising your aim. It is an unpleasant feeling and needs to be relieved. Aggression, the theorists argue, allows that relief to happen.

An everyday example of this might be someone trying to find a parking space and when they finally do see one, a person coming the other way pulls into it. This leads them to shout abuse at the driver of the car who has taken the space. Dollard *et al.* would argue that the frustration felt by the person trying to park leads them to act in an aggressive manner towards the person who did get the space.

There are various factors that affect the likelihood of aggression occurring:

1 **The proximity to the goal.** If the individual is very close to achieving their goal then the likelihood of aggression occurring is much greater than if achieving the goal is much less imminent or attainable.
2 **Whether the aggression will remove the barrier that is causing the frustration.** If aggression will have no effect on removing the barrier it is less likely to occur. For example, if a piece of machinery breaks, aggression or violence towards it does not help the situation (although this does not always stop people!). However, if the person coming to fix the equipment is slow to arrive, the person waiting may get aggressive with them on the phone if they think it might speed them up.

## Research

Pastore (1952) tested the theory using scenarios where the frustration was brought about by 'justified' aggression such as a bus not stopping to pick up passengers. He found that levels of aggression expressed in justified frustration settings were lower than in unjustified settings. This suggests the source of the frustration is key to whether it leads to aggression or not.

Harris (1974) tested to see whether proximity to the goal had an effect on the level of aggressive behaviour shown. She used situations where queues occurred such as shops and her confederates pushed in front of people in the queue. If they were closer to the front of the queue they were more likely to react in an aggressive way than if they were towards the back of the queue. This supports the idea that proximity to achieving the goal is an important factor in whether aggression occurs.

**Figure 9.6** Harris found that people towards the front of a queue were more angry if someone pushed in

Buss (1963) examined whether different types of frustration would affect the likelihood of aggression occurring. He used three different types of frustration:

1. Failure to win some money.
2. Failure on a task.
3. Failure to get the grade you expect.

He found that all types of frustration prompted aggression and all three types prompted higher levels of aggression than a group that acted as a control group with no frustration. This clearly supports the theory.

> **Evaluation**
>
> - Not all types of frustration prompt aggression. The work of Pastore (1952) illustrated the difference in aggression levels for justified and unjustified aggression. This means that the source has some importance.
> - Aggression is also not always prompted by frustration. For example, someone may find themselves in a threatening situation and opt for fight rather than flight. This aggression could be seen to be self-preservation rather than frustration. The premeditated and planned aggressive acts of psychopaths and killers are not usually underpinned by frustration either. This suggests that there are other elements to aggressive behaviour.
> - Not everyone who experiences frustration reacts with aggression. It is also possible that someone may cry or withdraw rather than become aggressive. They may not feel anger and so react in a different way, reflecting their emotional state.
> - Much of the research for this theory is based on hypothetical situations as it is unethical to manipulate someone into feeling frustration and prompting aggression. This means that participants are saying how they think they would act in a scenario. This has low predictive validity because in reality they may act qualitatively differently.

# Social learning theory as applied to human aggression

*'Aggression only moves in one direction – it creates more aggression.'*
Margaret J. Wheatley (2002)

Social learning theory (SLT) is a learning approach to explaining behaviour and has its origins in behaviourism. It therefore believes that environmental influences, rather than genetic influences, underpin behaviour. SLT states that behaviour is learned from observing behaviour of a role model and imitating it. There are cognitive mediating factors which determine whether the behaviour is imitated or not, so behaviour is not imitated automatically. The theory suggests that aggression, like other forms of behaviour, is primarily learned. It does not agree with the idea that humans are born aggressive, and it argues that humans acquire aggressive behaviours in the same way as other social behaviours: through direct experience or by observing the actions of others.

SLT agrees with behaviourism that behaviour that is positively reinforced (in other words, rewarded) will be much more likely to be repeated again. If an individual observes that someone is rewarded for a behaviour they will also be more likely to imitate that behaviour. Reward that is observed is called vicarious reinforcement. In the case of aggression, if it becomes associated with a reward through observation (vicariously) the person will be more likely to be aggressive in the future. An example of this would be someone observing a playground bully using threatening behaviour to get money from another student. The aggression has been helpful to them, so the observer might imitate this behaviour in the future.

Social learning makes learning a quicker process as individuals do not need to behave a certain way to understand what the consequences might be. In the case of aggression it means that aggressive behaviour can be observed initially to test the likelihood of reward and then adopted if it appears to be rewarding.

Bandura (1997) acknowledged the role of biology in aggression, but said that social learning was useful for demonstrating when aggression might be used. The social learning therefore informs the observer of the context in which aggression might be expressed.

Behaviour is not automatically imitated. There are mediating cognitive processes which determine whether a behaviour is imitated or not. The processes are attention, retention, reproduction and motivation:

1 **Attention** – this is the initial process which must occur for the behaviour to be learned. The behaviour should catch the attention of the observer and it is perhaps easy to see how this would happen if it is an aggressive behaviour.

2 **Retention** – this follows attention and it happens when behaviour is memorable. If it catches the attention of the observer but they do not remember it then the behaviour will not be imitated, so remembering the behaviour is vital to the learning process. Again, aggressive behaviours are more likely to be remembered due to the emotion they evoke. This then means the memory of the behaviour is stored.

3 **Reproduction** – individuals must be capable of reproducing the model's behaviour and thus possess the physical capabilities and skill set needed to imitate the modelled behaviour. In the case of an aggressive act, even if it commands attention and is remembered, the observer must be able to physically reproduce the behaviour. Clearly, if they are not strong or big enough this will not happen.

4 **Motivation** – this is the final mediating cognitive process. It is essential that the observer wants to do the action or behaviour. For aggressive acts it may not be something they are happy doing, so they will not imitate what they have observed, whether it is attention grabbing, memorable or a physical possibility or not. This accounts for the individual differences between people who observe the same behaviour. Some will be happy to imitate it, others will not.

## CLASSIC RESEARCH

### Bandura, Ross & Ross (1961, 1963)

Bandura, Ross and Ross conducted several studies on the role of learning aggression from observing models. These studies formed the basis for Bandura's social learning theory. Two of these studies are outlined below.

### Study one: Bandura, Ross & Ross (1961)

The central apparatus used in these studies was a Bobo doll. A Bobo doll is inflatable and is weighted in the base so that when it is hit it will bounce back up again. The doll was used by Bandura *et al.* to test for aggression in children.

**Figure 9.7** Interactions with a Bobo doll

#### Aim
To test for aggression levels following observation of aggressive behaviour by a model. The term 'model' is used in this context to mean role model.

#### Procedure
The participants were 36 boys and 36 girls, aged between 3 and 5 years. The participants were divided into equal-sized experimental groups of six children each. Six children formed a control group. The children were brought to the experimental room individually and were invited to play a game as there were toys made available. An adult (the 'model') then entered the room and played with some of the toys.

There were two conditions that followed: aggressive and non-aggressive. In the aggressive condition the models performed aggressive behaviours such as punching the Bobo doll, hitting it with a plastic hammer and kicking it. The models also used verbal aggressive statements such as 'Pow', 'Sock him in the nose!' and 'He sure is a tough fella!' These statements were shouted to increase the perceived level of aggression.

The behaviour of the non-aggressive models was completely different. They ignored the presence of the Bobo doll and played quietly and gently with the other toys.

Prior to the observational part of the experiment the participants were placed in a 'mild aggression arousal' situation, which meant they were put in a room with some toys and allowed to play for two minutes. They were then told they could no longer play with the toys. This was designed to raise their levels of arousal, making them more receptive to observing and acting out aggressive behaviour.

There were both male and female models and the participants were observed in the room via a two-way mirror for 20 minutes after observing the behaviour of the model. Bandura *et al.* proposed that if children were observed to play aggressively with the Bobo doll it would be due to the effects of social learning.

The behaviour of the children in both aggressive and non-aggressive conditions was observed and the number of aggressive acts recorded. The observer was not aware which condition group the children were a member of while observing them to avoid experimenter bias.

#### Findings
There was a larger amount of aggression observed in children from the 'aggressive condition'. The results were statistically significantly different and this was for both physical and verbal aggression.

In 70 per cent of the children in the control and non-aggressive groups no aggressive behaviour was observed at all.

Both boys and girls were more influenced by the male model, although the level of verbal aggression was greater in girls who observed the female role model. The greater influence of the male model on aggressive behaviour was argued to be due to male stereotyped behaviour.

#### Conclusions
Bandura *et al.* concluded from the results that children could learn aggression from observing role models.

### Study two: Bandura, Ross & Ross (1963)

#### Aim
To see whether aggressive behaviour could be learned through observation of a film showing aggressive behaviour.

#### Procedure
The procedure was very similar to study one. However, the two key differences were that the children watched a film rather than live actors playing with the Bobo doll and all the models performed aggressive behaviours. The aggressive behaviour witnessed was on film.

Instead of two experimental conditions as there were in study one, there were three conditions:

1. 'Model-reward' condition – here the model was rewarded for abusing the doll by being given sweets and drinks, and called a 'strong champion'.
2. 'Model-punished' condition – here the model was punished for abusing the doll, being told off for 'picking on the clown'.
3. 'No consequences' (control) condition – here no reinforcement was given.

After watching the video the children were subjected to the 'mild aggression arousal' situation prior to being observed. Then, as in study one, they were taken to a room where there were toys to play with and observed for ten minutes. They were rated for aggressive behaviour in a similar way to study one.

In this study they were also offered a reward for imitating the behaviour they had just observed.

### Findings

In the 'model-punished' group there was significantly less aggressive behaviour demonstrated before being offered a reward to imitate the behaviour. Aggressive behaviour was not affected in the same way in the other two groups.

After a reward was offered for responding, children in all three groups then performed the aggressive behaviours to the same extent. Children in every condition learned aggressive behaviours.

### Conclusions

The likelihood of punishment is a good indicator for the likelihood of less aggressive behaviours being performed.

Reward for the children also affects the likelihood of aggression being performed but reward for the model does not increase the likelihood.

Aggression seen via the media can have an effect on aggression levels of the audience.

Social learning does occur in children.

### Evaluation

(Remember to focus your evaluation on the theory, so if there are flaws with the research then the theory is not as well supported as suggested.)

- The studies show a short-term effect on aggression levels. However, what is not clear is whether social learning can affect aggression levels long term. This was not tested. This therefore weakens the argument that social learning can explain both long- and short-term aggression as a theory.
- The experimental context means that the studies lack ecological validity. A Bobo doll is designed to be hit in a playful way, so this means that the internal validity of the measure could be criticised as the behaviour may have seemed aggressive when the intention was not. This means that the research is potentially flawed and weakens the support for social learning theory.
- The children were deliberately frustrated by the mild arousal situation. The frustration–aggression model states that aggression is more likely to occur if an individual is frustrated while trying to achieve a goal. This means that it could have been the frustration felt that increased the aggression rather than social learning, especially in the second study as all participants displayed aggression. It can be argued that the research actually supports the frustration–aggression hypothesis rather than the social learning theory. This weakens the research base support for social learning theory.

### ON THE WEB

Film footage from Bandura's Bobo doll studies can be accessed at YouTube (**www.youtube.com**). It is useful to watch in order to judge a level of aggression. This means you can evaluate the research which then can be used to evaluate the theory.

## Research on the media

Pinto da Mota Matos (2011) found that identification with an aggressive model from the television was linked to aggression in Portuguese students, suggesting that the process of social learning affected the level of aggression. This supports the use of social learning to explain some aggression (see Contemporary research, page 335).

When video gaming was studied by Cooper & McKay (1986), they found that there was a difference in the genders in susceptibility to acting more aggressively following the game. From their results it appeared that girls were influenced to a greater extent into acting aggressively than boys were. This would seem to suggest that the genders react differently to the social learning of aggression, certainly at the ages of 9–10 years.

Williams (1981) recorded the behaviour of children after the introduction of television to a remote area of Canada. He found that both verbal and physical aggression levels increased. This suggests the media to be a source of aggressive behaviour to children as observers.

## Research on environment

Guerra *et al.* (2003) looked at the effects exposure to violence in neighbourhoods could have on children aged 5–12 in terms of the level of aggression they demonstrated. An ethnically diverse sample of 4,458 children living in urban neighbourhoods was tested. It was found that imitation of violence did occur. This suggests that there is a long-term effect on the behaviour of children exposed regularly to violence in their environment.

In research by Bandura (1977) it was reported that people who live in areas with high crime rates have a greater likelihood of committing a violent crime than those who live in a low-crime area. This could be seen to support social learning theory as there will have been exposure to a greater number of aggressive acts in the high-crime area than where there is less crime. Caution should be exerted in automatically assuming this is the case though, as there are many other variables that can affect crime figures, such as stress, poverty and unemployment.

### Evaluation

- Research support is good for the concepts of SLT, and there is also extensive research to support the idea of aggression being learned through the environment. The work by Bandura, Ross and Ross in 1961 using the Bobo doll demonstrated a direct effect of observing aggressive behaviour leading to aggressive behaviour.
- Research into SLT has received criticism as it shows there is an immediate effect on the observer but it does not show whether this continues long term. This means that aggression over a lifetime may not have been learned this way.
- Aggression levels in a community can be affected by the environment as there are communities such as the Mennonites and Amish communities in the USA that are pacifist (peace loving). These communities believe that aggression is wrong and it is therefore not commonplace. This is a belief system, so if aggression was innate it would be likely to override an environmentally determined behaviour. As it does not, such communities provide strong evidence that aggression is learned.
- SLT is a useful theory for explaining why people become aggressive only in certain situations. This could be argued to be because they have only seen aggression reinforced in those specific contexts or because the mediating factors prevent aggression in certain circumstances. If it was due to a biological drive, aggression would not be so situation specific.

## De-individuation

De-individuation is a social psychological theory of aggression that occurs when an individual is part of a group or crowd. It states that aggression is more likely to happen when an individual experiences a loss of their sense of identity. As they no longer feel autonomous as an individual, the morals and beliefs that normally guide their behaviour are loosened and they adopt the morals of any group that they may be part of at that particular time.

It accounts for why someone may become part of an angry mob and act aggressively when they normally would not display this kind of behaviour. An example would be a football fan who gets involved in fights against the fans of the opposing team following a game. This person may not show any aggression for the rest of the week, but because they lose their identity temporarily when they become part of a crowd of fans they start to act with uncharacteristic aggression (see Figure 9.8).

The word 'de-individuation' was first used by Festinger *et al.* to describe this phenomenon in 1952 and there has been much subsequent research examining the idea.

This idea is not new. Work by Le Bon in 1895 examined how behaviour can change when an individual is in the crowd. He looked specifically at 'mob violence' during the French revolution and observed that people who were unlikely to act with violence in everyday situations became capable of violence and aggression when they were part of a mob. It could be argued that this is a unique property of a crowd, but Le Bon argued that it was necessary to look at the individual level to explain why this happened. He felt that the person loses their identity when they are mixed up among a crowd and their normal moral code does not apply. The larger the crowd, the greater the likelihood of this sense of identity being lost and therefore the more likely that aggression could follow. Their self-control and impulses that are normally moderated by internal standards rise to the surface. It was this behaviour that was examined further by Festinger.

However, there are psychologists who believe that the crowd behaviour occurs for more complex reasons. Zimbardo (1970) claimed that in addition to losing anonymity there is the role of drugs/alcohol, a reduced sense of responsibility and sensory overload. The effect of the crowd on an individual has many effects.

The idea of de-individuation was refined further by Diener in 1980. He felt that de-individuation was mediated by self-awareness. When someone is in a non-crowd situation their self-awareness acts as a regulator of their behaviour. However, in a crowd situation, the focus is outward, as there is lots of stimulation to attend to. This shifts the focus outwards and their self-awareness declines. This means that the regulator of behaviour is weakened and uncharacteristic behaviour is likely to occur.

This occurs especially when the crowd is at a sporting event. Not only does the individual have the stimulation from the crowd around them, but also, more often than not, they are focusing on a game and so self-awareness is diminished. This makes uncharacteristic behaviour such as aggression even more likely.

There are two types of self-awareness put forward by Prentice-Dunn & Rogers (1982): public self-awareness and private self-awareness. Public self-awareness is concerned with the appraisal of other people whereas private self-awareness is the awareness of one's own thoughts and feelings. Both of these can be affected by a crowd. In the case of public awareness the number of people appraising an individual is multiplied. There is also a feeling of diffusion of responsibility, so the focus is less on being responsible for one's own behaviour and a feeling that responsibility is shared by those around you. In general, the inhibitions that would normally moderate your behaviour lose their effect. With private awareness the decline in self-awareness occurs because the individual is simply distracted by the crowd. They 'lose' themselves. There are many environmental cues to focus upon and an individual prioritises those rather than focusing on themselves.

The result of this lack of self-awareness is de-individuation, which in turn leads to de-individuated behaviour, behaviour that is affected by the crowd rather than internal standards. De-individuation can also occur when the identity of the individual is hidden in some way. This type of de-individuation is less likely to lead to aggressive behaviour as there is still self-awareness and no distraction from being part of a crowd. However, research has shown that when someone's identity is hidden, their behaviour becomes less moral and they are more likely to cheat and act more selfishly (Zhong et al., 2010). This illustrates that identity is key to mediating behaviour.

**Figure 9.8** A football fan who behaves aggressively at a match may not be aggressive outside that situation

## Research

A meta-analysis was conducted by Postmes & Spears (1998) on 60 research studies and the general conclusion was that the evidence base for de-individuation is weak. The effects stated by de-individuation theorists are not widespread across all crowds.

The effects of de-individuation can also be positive. Hirsh *et al.* (2011) found that when in darkness an individual will experience de-individuation. However, this does not automatically lead to aggression; it may also lead to prosocial behaviour. This means that losing identity temporarily does not automatically mean there will be a negative effect – there may be positive behaviour, too. This also occurred when participants had consumed alcohol, so disinhibited behaviour displayed due to intoxication can also be positive. However, it should be noted that this research was not based on crowd behaviour and so it cannot be said that prosocial behaviour also occurs in a crowd.

Ingham (1978) argues that it is not de-individuation that causes the violence at football games. Football supporters follow rituals set within the group and it is these group norms, not de-individuation, that influence the behaviour.

### Evaluation

- There seems to be little argument that being in a crowd affects an individual's behaviour. However, the exact reasons behind this transformation are unclear and there appear to be many factors involved. It may be that the factors affect individuals differently, but with the same resultant behaviour.
- As de-individuation can occur in darkness, a practical application of research is to ensure areas are well lit. This will ensure that the sense of personal responsibility is not lost and that the likelihood of antisocial behaviour occurring is lowered. CCTV can have a similar effect, as people are often aware that they can be seen and identified. This will make them more accountable for their behaviour.
- It is possible that aggression occurs due to the anonymity of the victim rather than the loss of identity of the individual. Attacks on strangers do occur, so it could be that anonymity is an important factor in aggressive acts.
- De-individuation can only explain aggression that relates to specific contexts (i.e. where de-individuation can occur). Aggression does, however, occur outside these contexts so the theory can be seen to have a narrow application.

### ON THE WEB

The documentary 'Football hooligans and proud', shown by Channel 5, can be accessed at the Channel 5 website:

**www.channel5.com/shows/football-hooligans-and-proud/episodes/football-hooligan-proud**

It contains interviews with self-confessed football hooligans and offers some insight into why they do what they do.

### STRENGTHEN YOUR LEARNING

1. Who is a key theorist in the frustration–aggression hypothesis?
2. Explain what is meant by the frustration–aggression hypothesis.
3. Give one example of supporting research for the frustration–aggression hypothesis.
4. Explain how social learning theory can explain aggression.
5. What are the four mediating cognitive processes?
6. Give an example of how the mediating cognitive processes may stop an aggressive behaviour being imitated.
7. Explain a weakness of the social learning explanation for aggression.
8. Describe how de-individuation theory explains aggression.
9. Explain a weakness of the de-individuation theory for aggression.
10. Give an example of some research that supports the de-individuation theory of aggression.

# ASSESSMENT CHECK

1. Select from the descriptions of cognitive processes A, B, C and D below to complete the table relating to the mediating cognitive processes below. One description will be left over. **[3 marks]**

   **A** An aggressive behaviour is remembered

   **B** An aggressive behaviour is noticed

   **C** An aggressive behaviour will help achieve an aim

   **D** An aggressive behaviour is possible

   | Mediating cognitive process | Description of mediating cognitive process |
   | --- | --- |
   | Attention | |
   | Retention | |
   | Reproduction | |

2. A research team was examining the role time of day had on aggression. Two psychologists observed behaviour of selected children in the playground in both the morning and afternoon. They used behavioural categories to categorise and tally the behaviours.

   How could they check for reliability of the observers' data? **[2 marks]**

3. Read the item and then answer the question:

   Road rage in traffic jams is a problem; it can sometimes lead to arguments and fights between drivers.

   Using your knowledge of the frustration–aggression explanation of aggression, explain why these arguments and fights may occur. **[4 marks]**

4. Briefly outline and evaluate the findings of one research study into the social learning theory of aggression. **[4 marks]**

5. Describe and evaluate the de-individuation explanation for aggression. **[16 marks]**

# 9.5 Institutional aggression in the context of prisons

Aggression in prisons is a problem. In a report by the Prisons Inspectorate (the organisation that inspects prisons) into Feltham Prison in 2013, there was serious concern raised by the number and severity of violent acts every day. Feltham is a young offenders' institution, which is split into under 18s and young adults. It is acknowledged to be the most violent prison in the UK, with 300 acts of violence recorded in the six months prior to the report. That is about two a day. Those are the major incidents. The minor ones are unlikely to all be documented, so that statistic is, in reality, probably higher.

There are two main theories as to why aggression occurs in prisons at a higher rate than in the high street. These are the **situational model** and the **dispositional model**. Each looks to different sources of the aggression. The situational model attributes the aggression to the situation, and the idea that it is the conditions and deprivation that are the issue. The alternative dispositional model focuses on the characteristics of the prisoners themselves, arguing that they are violent and aggressive people and therefore bring the aggression into prison with them.

## Dispositional explanation

### Importation model

#### Irwin & Cressey (1962)

The **importation model** suggests that prisoners import their aggressive tendencies into prison with them and this is why the rate of violence is high. These aggressive characteristics may come from sources such as genetics, testosterone and serotonin levels and learned history from, for example, their background. Therefore the aggression that is evident in prison is no different to how the offenders act when they are in their home environment. It is therefore important to consider offenders' behaviour out of prison as well as inside an institution.

There are often factors that affect the offender both inside and outside of prison. An example of this is dependency or addiction to substances such as alcohol and illegal drugs. These can exacerbate aggressive behaviour and are not necessarily sorted out by putting someone in prison. It is also notable that the most violent prisons in the UK are young offenders' institutions. In the report by the Prisons Inspectorate that identified Feltham as the most violent prison it was also young offenders' institutions elsewhere in the country that came second and third.

The Prisons Inspectorate noted that there was a problem with gang culture in young offenders' institutions. This is likely to be an influence from the 'outside' and the offenders had encountered the gangs in their home environment.

> **KEY TERMS**
>
> **Situational model** – aggression occurs as a result of factors within the prison setting
>
> **Dispositional model** – this looks to the characteristics of an individual for an explanation as to why aggression may occur
>
> **Importation model** – aggression occurs due to the individual characteristics that prisoners bring into prison

**Figure 9.9** A person with aggressive tendencies will display them in prison as well as at home

There are three prison sub-cultures that influence inmates (Irwin & Cressey, 1962):

1. **Criminal/thief sub-culture** – this advocates a criminal 'code of honour', such as not telling on fellow inmates when they have committed a misdemeanour in prison. This sub-culture promotes honour, trust and loyalty as its key values. The members of this sub-culture will be hardened criminals, repeat offenders who re-enter the prison knowing that they will act this way. There is aggression within this group but it is not as dominant as in the 'convict sub-culture'.

2. **Convict sub-culture** – this has a strong power hierarchy. Much of the behaviour within this sub-culture is about position within the hierarchy and power. This group is the most likely to become aggressive as this is deemed necessary to exercise power over other inmates. Prisoners opting to join this sub-culture are often from deprived areas outside of prison and familiar with gang culture.

3. **Conventional or 'straight' sub-culture** – the individuals who are members of this sub-culture will be new to prison and probably likely to be one-time-only offenders. They will try to keep clear of the other two sub-cultures and have more in common with the prison guards. These prisoners are not generally aggressive.

> **YOU ARE THE RESEARCHER**
> It would be useful to know which sub-culture any inmate belonged to as it may help prison authorities work out which prisoners may be more aggressive. Think of some items you could include on a questionnaire to test membership of sub-culture. What would be problematic using such a method of classification?

These sub-cultures show how, in addition to personality characteristics, the background and learned history of a prisoner can affect whether they are likely to be aggressive and violent when put in prison.

## Research

Jiang & Fisher-Giorlando (2002) looked at the extent to which the importation model could explain prison violence. They also compared the explanatory power of the theory with the influences of deprivation and the prison environment. They concluded that the explanation was most useful in explaining violence against other inmates whereas the prison context was more useful for explaining violence against prison staff. This suggests that the idea has some validity but only in some incidents.

Kane & Janus (1981) found that the number of violent offences was related to the learned history of the offender. If a prisoner had previously had a lower level of education, a more serious criminal record and more time unemployed in their life then they were more likely to be aggressive and violent once put in prison. This is a clear indication of how the violence may have been imported due to the offender's previous experience.

The characteristics of age and ethnicity and how they relate to prison violence were examined by Kane & Janus (1981). They found that younger offenders and non-white prisoners were more likely to be aggressive while in prison. This could be due to the influence of gang culture and/or the marginalisation of ethnic groups. This supports the idea that outside influence affects aggression.

### Evaluation

- A strength of this idea is that it looks at prisoners in a more idiographic way rather than saying they are all the same. The work on sub-cultures is nomothetic to some degree, but the theory is essentially arguing that the effects of experience and predisposition are individual and therefore can explain well why some offenders are violent and others are not.
- The importation model suggests that rehabilitation should consider the home environment and the individual. This means that aggression should be dealt with by such programmes as anger management which reduces chances of recidivism (reoffending).
- DeLisi et al. (2004) found support for the importation model originating from gang culture. They studied the prison records of 831 US male inmates, assessing the relationship between prison violence and membership of street and prison gangs. They found a significant relationship between gang membership and prison aggression. This suggests that gang membership values are imported into prisons by gang members. This is further supported by the Prisons Inspectorate report of the violence in Feltham young offenders' institution (see page 330). They witnessed gang graffiti throughout the inmates' cells, suggesting very few inmates were not gang members.
- However, the influence of gang culture does not explain aggression in adult prisons so well. Poole & Regoli's (1983) study found that pre-institutional violence is the best predictor of inmate aggression in juvenile correctional institutions. This finding was not replicated in adult prisons in other studies and therefore cannot be generalised to explain aggression in all institutions or to support the importation model.

---

#### PSYCHOLOGY IN THE REAL WORLD
#### Prison solves problem of illegal mobile phones

The use of mobile phones in prison is banned. This is for obvious reasons, as it is a method of conducting 'business' (i.e. criminal activity) from within the prison walls. However, the lack of access to a phone can cause issues for inmates as they wish to contact loved ones, but often the number of landlines provided is insufficient to meet demand. This adds to the need to have access to a mobile phone in prison and consequently phones are smuggled in. The frustration felt by prisoners who cannot talk to family and friends can lead to violence, and reports from inmates and prison officers pinpoint frustration at being unable to contact family as being a precursor to violence.

Lowdham Grange, a prison in Nottingham, has installed landlines in the cells in the institution and prisoners can make calls at any time of the day. There is a restriction on the numbers allowed, however, and if they wish to make a call to a number it has to be checked first. There are only a few numbers permitted on each phone. This is an attempt to ensure phone calls are made only to landlines of family members.

The scheme has been well received. Statistics show that the prison is now safer as a consequence of this action.

*This is an example of how situational factors such as deprivation of access to phones can be dealt with by the prison service and this has the welcome effect of reducing aggression and violent acts as a consequence.*

**Figure 9.10** Prisoners are not allowed mobile phones during their incarceration

---

## Situational explanation

The prison context can also be regarded as a potential source of aggression. There are three specific types of factors that come from the environment within a prison:

- **Organisational** – this is the influence of rules and regulations that prisoners have to adhere to while serving their sentence. These can prompt aggression because of the expectation that all prisoners must follow them.

- **Physical** – the potentially cramped conditions, threatening environment and lack of comfort are argued to be factors in influencing aggressive behaviour.
- **Staff characteristics** – the attitude and behaviour of the staff can be influential in prompting aggression in inmates. For example, there could be a clash of personalities or an unwillingness of an offender to adhere to prison rules, eliciting a negative reaction from staff. These could lead to aggression against the staff or others.

# Deprivation model

The deprivation model is an example of how it is thought the prison environment can increase aggression in offenders. It relates to the organisational and physical indicators above.

The deprivation model sees the loss of key needs, such as frequent communication with loved ones outside of prison, as being the root to aggressive behaviour.

Sykes (1958) was the theorist to suggest that deprivation within prison could prompt aggression. It was argued that there were five types of deprivation that could influence behaviour: deprivation of liberty, deprivation of autonomy, deprivation of goods and services, deprivation of heterosexual relationships and deprivation of security. These were all factors in affecting behaviour and due to these factors, negative aggressive and violent behaviour increased.

These five deprivations are all considered in a little more detail below:

1. **Deprivation of liberty** – for some, this is seen to be the purpose of prison. It is meant to impinge on the liberties of the offender and during their sentence they are no longer allowed to go where they please, when they please. However, Sykes (1958) argued that this reinforced the feeling of rejection from society and so offenders became more likely to be antagonistic and aggressive.

2. **Deprivation of autonomy** – there is no independence for prisoners. They are expected to conform and they have no control over their day-to-day living. Even small choices such as choosing when to eat (that we take for granted in the non-prison environment) are not possible in prison. Inmates experience a feeling of helplessness and this, in turn, can lead to frustration and aggression. There is also a withdrawal of privileges from time to time which is often not explained to the inmates, so they feel angry and powerless.

3. **Deprivation of goods and services** – access to goods is severely restricted within prisons. A modern-day example and relatively new issue is access to mobile phones. This is prohibited and for most of the prisoners who used their mobiles extensively before entering prison the lack of access to a phone causes anger and resentment, which leads to violence (see Psychology in the real world: Prison solves problem of illegal mobile phones).

4. **Deprivation of heterosexual relationships** – a heterosexual prisoner has no access to companionship in prison and this can lead to frustration and consequently aggression. This is seen as a need for some, but it is not just the deprivation of the chance for sex that is the issue. The ability and need to form relationships and experience emotional intimacy with a person of the opposite sex are important.

> **YOU ARE THE RESEARCHER**
> If you were a prison psychologist you might be asked to research which of the five deprivations is most likely to trigger aggression in your prison. How would you do this? Try to think of a qualitative and a quantitative method. Which would be most reliable? Which would be most valid?

Withdrawal of this access, like the other deprivations, is argued to lead to increased violence.

5 **Deprivation of security** – the prison environment does not feel safe for most prisoners – they fear for their personal safety. This feeling of fear can lead to heightened awareness and defensiveness, which could make overreaction to incidents more likely.

All these potential areas of deprivation can be related theoretically to an increase in aggression in prisoners.

## Research

Lahm (2008) found in her research into inmate-on-inmate violence that both situational and dispositional factors played a part in prison violence. She looked at the incidences of violence experienced by 1,054 inmates across 30 prisons and found that the main predictors of violence were age and aggression level. These would seem to suggest that the importation model is the most powerful for explaining violence. However, she found that the level of overcrowding also played a part, so there is some evidence to suggest that situational factors are important, too.

Blomberg & Lucken (2000) found research evidence to support the idea that a lack of autonomy can contribute to aggression. In their research they found that prisoners often had to seek permission to perform acts such as eating and washing, which are key civil liberties. This leads to frustration and the deprivation of autonomy could therefore be a key factor in increasing aggression.

The lack of stimulation and focus brought about by being in prison were found by Cheeseman (2003) to link to aggression. The research found that aggression acted as a way of relieving stress due to the situation. The frustration–aggression hypothesis can be applied in this situation, with violence being an outlet for frustration. As the frustration is prompted by the situation inmates find themselves in, this can be argued to support the situational model.

Johnston (1991) also found that prison overcrowding leads to increased aggression. This means there is greater competition for the resources available. This competition elicits aggression and violence is an inevitable consequence of that aggression. The formation of gangs to help compete for resources fosters in-group/out-group conflict, leading to group aggression. These are all argued to be situational factors and therefore support the situational model.

### Evaluation

- Maslow's hierarchy of needs (see page 14) supports the idea that the situational effects in a prison could lead to aggression in inmates. The first step on the hierarchy, the physiological needs, cannot be met all the time due to the enforced regime of sleeping and eating and also the lack of opportunities to fulfil sexual needs. The safety needs are also not possible due to the lack of perceived safety within prison. This means that the drive to self-actualisation is prevented at the basic levels and can therefore lead to negative behaviour.
- In a modification of Zimbardo's prison study, Haslam & Reicher (2006) reported that it was not the adoption of the prisoner role that affected behaviour, it was the need to be part of a group. This suggests that the prison situation, which enforces the need for group behaviour to aid access to resources, is the reason behind the increased level of violence.
- Prison riots can both support and refute the situational model. They can occur when there has been a withdrawal of privileges or a lack of explanation as to why the daily routine has changed, but they can also flare up with apparently no reason whatsoever. This means the situational influence in violent behaviour cannot always be identified, or may not exist.

## The case for interaction

The research by Jiang & Fisher-Giorlando (2002) previously reported in the importation model research section illustrated that perhaps both types of influence, importation and situational, play a part in aggression. Their research picked up on the fact that it depends on who the aggression is directed towards that indicates which theory might explain the act better. Aggression towards fellow inmates seemed, in the research, to be better explained by the importation model and aggression towards prison officers seemed influenced to a greater extent by situational factors. It is not clear why this may be the case, but teasing apart the two possible sources of aggression is not easy. It seems likely that both contribute in differing amounts depending on the individual act.

> **STRENGTHEN YOUR LEARNING**
> 1 Explain what is meant by the dispositional explanation of aggressive behaviour.
> 2 How does the importation model explain aggression in prisons?
> 3 Give an example of research that supports the importation model of institutional aggression.
> 4 Explain one weakness of the dispositional explanation of institutional aggression.
> 5 Explain the situational theory of institutional aggression.
> 6 What are the main areas of deprivation argued to underpin institutional aggression?
> 7 Explain how deprivation can lead to aggression.
> 8 Explain a weakness of the situational explanation of institutional aggression.
> 9 Describe one research study that supports the situational explanation.
> 10 Explain why interaction might be the best explanation for institutional aggression.

# 9.6 Media influences on aggression

*'Video games are bad for you? That's what they said about rock 'n' roll.'*
Shigeru Miyamoto (1993)

The media has come under scrutiny as a possible source of prompting aggression. Media includes many possible channels, such as films, television and computer games. Computer games as a source of aggression are discussed in more detail in the following section.

## The effects of computer games

The first computer game was developed in 1958 and was an electronic tennis game for two players. However, it was not until the games became commercially available that the impact was researched. This was in the 1970s.

The primary concerns with regard to aggression were that exposure to violence in the games may have a desensitisation effect and that the people playing the games may receive positive reinforcement from using violence. It is perhaps a worry that this may reinforce violent behaviours in everyday life.

There is also the potential for exposure to violence affecting the moral judgement of those playing the games. They may not see it as inappropriate or wrong to use violence. Conversely, there is the argument that playing computer games is beneficial to the individual and society. A video game may provide an outlet for anger and relieve stress. The term for this effect is 'catharsis', which is a psychodynamic term describing the purging of strong emotion. In the example of computer games they would act as an outlet for anger.

## CONTEMPORARY RESEARCH

### Television and aggression – Pinto da Mota Matos, Alves Ferreira and Haase (2011)

Armanda Pinto da Mota Matos, Joaquim Armando G. Alves Ferreira and Richard Haase collaborated to examine the various factors that may contribute to media violence and the relative contribution to violence in children. There are many ways that the media can influence behaviour but finding out which, if any, is the most influential is problematic. This is what Pinto da Mota Matos et al set out to do.

#### Aim
To examine the roles of identification with violent TV heroes, enjoyment of TV violence and perceived reality in TV violence in subsequent aggression in children.

#### Procedure
722 students (353 boys and 369 girls) aged 9–16 years old were participants. They all came from schools in the centre of Portugal.

Data on variables such as age, socioeconomic status and school year was collected. In addition, the following measures were used:

**Exposure to TV violence:** children received a list of 23 genres of programmes and were asked to indicate how often they watched that particular type of genre on a four-point scale from Never to Always.

**Aggression:** children filled out a 20-item questionnaire called the 'Questionnaire of Aggressive Behaviour'. Each item was a hypothetical scenario, such as: 'You're in line for a glass of water. Some kid comes along and pushes you out of the line. What do you do?' For each scenario the participant was asked whether they would respond in a physically violent manner (would you hit him? Yes/No) or a verbally aggressive manner (would you yell at him? Yes/No).

**Enjoyment of TV violence:** children were given a questionnaire called, unsurprisingly, the 'Scale of Enjoyment of TV Violence'. It had 18 items asking them to indicate how much they enjoyed watching TV violence. The response scale was a four-point scale from I don't agree at all to I completely agree.

**Perceived reality in TV violence:** this was assessed too using a questionnaire with eight items. Four were about fictional programmes and four were about realistic programmes such as police shows. The participants were asked to rate how similar to real life these programmes were.

**Identification with violent TV heroes:** this was assessed by asking just one question to each participant: 'Who would you like to be if you could be a television character?'

As this was after the age of eight this was testing their wishful thinking rather than their judgement on similarity, which is how younger children would respond. The character chosen by the participant was then rated by the researcher on a three-point scale from not aggressive to very aggressive.

All these measures were statistically analysed by the researchers to see how the factors were all related.

#### Findings
The relationship to physical aggression was influenced by enjoyment of TV violence, perception of reality and identification with violent TV heroes.

The relationship to verbal aggression was mediated by enjoyment of TV violence but not by perception of reality and identification with violent TV heroes.

Children who watched more TV violence tend to identify with violent TV characters and show more physical aggression.

Overall there was a direct link between the exposure to TV violence and aggression (physical and verbal).

#### Conclusions
It can be concluded that exposure to TV violence is linked to aggressive behaviour and that there are several factors involved.

The identification with violent TV heroes supports the idea that social learning is a mechanism by which aggression can be imitated. The presence of a role model who is violent via the media does seem to indicate that children are influenced into taking the aggressive option in some contexts. This shows a more long-term link from social learning to aggression than the Bobo doll study (see page 324) demonstrates.

The fact that perception of reality of TV programmes is negatively related to aggression would also suggest that disinhibition could be occurring. Disinhibition (see page 339) is the feeling of being lost in the media, which then means an individual is more likely to act in an uncharacteristically aggressive way. If an individual's perception of reality is low then disinhibition is more likely to occur and influence the level of their aggression.

#### Evaluation
- Some of the measures involve hypothetical scenarios, which means the responses may not be typical of how the individual would act in everyday life. This means the predictive validity of some of the measures may be poor.
- The research is correlational, so cause and effect cannot be established, merely a relationship. This means that identification with a TV character and perception of reality are linked to aggression, but the psychological processes underlying that link are not tested in the research.

## Research

Ballard (1999) reports that the relatively recent development of new technology to enhance computer game experience such as a virtual world simulation may increase the emotion felt by the player. This may increase the likelihood of aggression.

Using brain scanning technology Matthews *et al.* (2006) found that adolescents who were playing violent computer games had decreased activity in the prefrontal lobe, which is associated with control. They also had increased activation in the emotion-centred areas of the brain such as the amygdala. This suggests violent computer games increase emotion and decrease control, which may lead to aggression.

The relationship between exposure to violent computer games and aggressive behaviour was investigated by Anderson & Bushman (2001). They conducted a meta-analysis of studies measuring the relationship and found that short-term exposure to video game violence was associated with temporary increases in aggression among all participants. This suggests a short-term relationship, but long-term effects were not tested so the relationship may be different.

The potentially positive cathartic effect of playing computer games was researched by Kestenbaum & Weinstein (1985). They found in a sample of adolescent males that the use of computer games actually helped them to release aggression and feel calmer. The research suggested that the games allowed an outlet that was socially acceptable for intense feelings experienced by this age group.

### RESEARCH IN FOCUS

The measures in this research are predominantly questionnaires. What are methodological issues with this? How reliable and valid are they?

The measure for aggression is also using a questionnaire format. This is clearly ethically the best way, but can you think of any other way aggression could be operationalised in the population used in this study?

### Evaluation

- The source of the research seems to affect the findings, which suggests research in this area is not objective and should be treated with caution. This was supported by Harris (2001), who reported that research conducted by the gaming industry found no relationship between video game violence and aggression.
- Cause and effect is difficult to establish in research. It is possible that any positive correlation between aggression and exposure to violent computer games is due to aggressive people choosing to play violent computer games as opposed to non-violent games.
- Most research examines the short-term effects of playing a violent computer game and therefore it is not clear how long the effect could last for. This has obvious implications for legislation.
- It can be argued that the effects do not affect all people equally. Young children who are still impressionable and are still developing their moral code may be more affected than adults.
- Aggression, hostility and desensitisation are all difficult constructs to measure. Inevitably self-report measures must be used due to ethical constraints and therefore the predictive validity and reliability of the measures is questionable. This has the effect of casting doubt over the validity of the findings in this area.

> **YOU ARE THE RESEARCHER**
>
> You have been given the task of investigating the effect computer games have on aggression levels in 11–14 year olds using an experimental design. What would your IV be? What would your DV be?
>
> How could both these variables be made as reliable as possible?

**KEY TERM**

**Desensitisation** – habituating to the violence seen in the media so that when it reoccurs at a similar level it has no emotional effect

**Figure 9.11** Horror films that seemed scary as a child might seem tame as an adult

# The role of desensitisation

Most people can remember watching horror films when they were young and being profoundly affected by what they saw. If they sit down to watch the same films when they are older they are often surprised by how tame the film appears. Psychologists call this **desensitisation** as the more someone is exposed to media that provokes fear, the less they are affected by that media. Their emotional response is reduced through exposure.

Desensitisation works in the same way with violence in films. People habituate to the level of violence and their emotional, cognitive and behavioural response is reduced. This means that when exposed to violence it prompts less of a response and the behaviour does not seem as bad as it would have done prior to desensitisation. Continual use of a computer game that exposes the player to violence can therefore reduce the impact and revulsion they may have for such violence. In theory, this then makes them more likely to act in a violent way because they have a reduced emotional reaction to it.

## Research

The occurrence of desensitisation in children was supported in research by Drabman & Thomas (1974). They found that children became more tolerant of violence in films as the amount of violence they watched increased, which suggests that there is a desensitisation effect.

If an individual sees a fight, would they be less likely to react and help if they have been desensitised? Bushman (2009) found that this was exactly what happened. When individuals who were playing violent video games for only 20 minutes saw someone injured in a fight they actually took longer to help than individuals who were playing non-violent games. This suggests that they were desensitised as the fight did not seem to affect them emotionally as much as the participants who were not being exposed to violence at the time. This suggests a short-term desensitisation effect.

In a study examining the relationship between exposure to violence and anti-social behaviour Belson (1978) found no evidence to suggest a link. The study of 1,500 teenage boys examined hours spent watching television violence and anti-social attitude. The lack of a link between the two suggests that desensitisation may not occur at all.

### Evaluation

- Research is mixed. Some indicates a desensitisation effect, other research finds no link. This means that the link between exposure to media violence and desensitisation may be more complex than originally thought.
- The fact that repeated exposure to violence in the media may provoke a diminished emotional response could mean that violent and aggressive behaviour may be less likely to occur. If someone has a lower level of arousal to a violent stimulus then it can be argued they may be less inclined to respond in a violent way. Violence and aggression are usually underpinned by high emotion.
- It is hard to establish a connection between media exposure and desensitisation. Media exposure is widespread and yet we are not all affected equally. Individual vulnerability in terms of level of emotion experienced may explain why some people are more desensitised than others.

# The role of disinhibition

**Disinhibition** means that uncharacteristic behaviour for the individual is demonstrated when playing a game. Ordinarily an individual would not act that way, but when in the virtual world of computer gaming a disinhibited person will act in a non-typical way. This could include displaying aggressive behaviours which are more intense than they would normally be. It can be argued, therefore, that playing a computer game may incite violence in someone who is a passive person in everyday behaviour.

This disinhibition effect when on a computer can be explained in several ways (Suler, 2004):

1. **Anonymity and invisibility** of the person is assured while playing a computer game. This means that responsibility for behaviour is perceived as reduced. This is a similar effect to de-individuation when an individual cannot be recognised because they are in the dark or their identity is obscured in some way (see page 326).
2. **Solipsistic introjection**, which is the feeling of becoming cognitively merged with the actor in the game. This occurs when an alter is selected to act within the virtual world and by playing as that alter the gamer becomes part of the alter. Therefore uncharacteristic behaviour may occur because the individual is not acting as himself/herself.
3. **Minimisation of authority** occurs in computer games as there is often no law enforcement or awareness of potential legal consequences as there might be in everyday life. This means that behaviour which would be classified as criminal is acted out as it is a virtual world.

> **KEY TERM**
>
> **Disinhibition** – the feeling of being within (or caught up in) the media and therefore acting in an uncharacteristic way

## Research

Hiltz *et al.* (1989) found that when pen names were used rather than actual names in computer conferencing there was more pro-social behaviour but it was not statistically significant. This seems to suggest little effect from being anonymous. However, it should be noted this was not aggressive behaviour so the effect may still apply in a media context.

Bandura, Underwood & Fromson (1975) examined the interaction between the dehumanisation of a person and reduced responsibility for an action (as would occur in disinhibition when playing computer games). They found that disinhibition in terms of responsibility prompted more punitive behaviour from participants and that the more dehumanised the person was, the more punitive the behaviour displayed by participants was. Although this was not in a computer game context, this finding suggests that when there is a diminished sense of responsibility, more aggressive behaviour can occur. However, the fact that opponents in computer games may not be human means that the raised level of aggression witnessed may be due to dehumanisation rather than disinhibition.

Josephson (1987) compared the effects of priming, social scripts (which is another word for a schema of a situation) and disinhibition. She put boys in groups of six to watch violent or non-violent television. The violent television was an ice hockey game. She also measured aggression levels by naturalistic observation. Priming was prompted by cues associated with violence. She found that violent television and the cues prompted higher levels of aggressiveness but only really in boys who were rated as normally aggressive by their teachers. The boys who were not rated as aggressive displayed low levels of aggression in the violent programme and priming conditions, potentially suppressing any aggression felt. This seems to suggest that a disinhibition effect did not occur as behaviour remained typical in both groups of boys. It is therefore possible that disinhibition occurs only in a computer-based context and not in other media contexts.

Pinto da Mota Matos and Haase (2011) found that perception of reality of TV programmes is negatively related to aggression. This suggests that disinhibition could be occurring, supporting the theory. (See page 336 for details of the study.)

### Evaluation

- It is likely that not all forms of media will evoke feelings of disinhibition and there is a bias in the research towards disinhibition in playing computer games. This suggests that disinhibition may apply only to certain forms of media and that the strongest effects are found in computer gaming.

- Effects from disinhibition seem to be contained in time to the period while playing the computer game. This means that the effect is relevant only while engaging with the media and that the effect is negligible while away from the computer game medium.

- The extent to which someone may become involved in the media they are experiencing will vary. So, disinhibition may occur only in people who are fully engaged in playing and are not easily distracted by external stimuli (for example, introverts). This narrows the number of people who can be affected this way. Applicability of the research is therefore not widespread.

## The role of cognitive priming

Cognitive priming is the idea that we may be exposed to cues on television or on computer games and that these cues can trigger behaviour in us. These cues can be anti-social, such as an aggressive act, or pro-social, such as helping behaviour. The effect of cognitive priming is therefore potentially immense. Many of us watch television regularly and play computer games, so there is exposure to cues on a daily basis. However, the effects of these cues are moderated to some extent by context. We do not blindly act out what we see and the cues will act as triggers only if the context is similar, which it rarely is.

It is possible that cognitive priming works in a more general sense to influence attitude and behaviour towards being pro- or anti-social. So, for example, we may watch an awards ceremony where people receive acknowledgement for the work they do helping others. This may inspire us, for a short time at least, to act compassionately. Conversely, the same can be said with anti-social programmes, in that they could have a negative effect on our behaviour and we may display more aggressive behaviour.

### Research

Anderson, Anderson & Deusser (1996) investigated the effects of the environment and cognitive priming on aggressive behaviour. They used images of guns as priming stimuli and varied the temperature of the room between hot, comfortable and cold. Aggression was measured by questionnaire, looking at hostile attitude and hostile thought. Interestingly, they found there were different effects on the hostility measures. Extreme temperatures increased the overall general hostility of mood and attitude and being shown images of guns actually primed hostile thoughts. This seems to suggest that the presentation of a cue can trigger a negative thought, but that the overall effect is short-lived and it does not affect the attitude or mood of the individual. This seems to relate to the length of time the individual is exposed to the stimuli.

Neuro-scientific evidence for priming was found in research by Murray et al. (2007). The researchers took fMRI brain scans of children watching violent and non-violent films, and found that those watching violence had increased activity in brain areas associated with emotion together with areas linked to personal memories. This seems to suggest that memories were formed which could later react to cues and prompt aggressive or violent behaviour.

Holloway et al. (1977) found that participants who 'overheard' a pro-social message on a radio in the waiting room before participating in a study involving bargaining were more co-operative in their bargaining than participants who did not hear the bulletin. This suggests a pro-social effect of the cognitive priming of good news.

Moriarity & McCabe (1977) found that children who witnessed sportspeople behaving pro-socially actually performed more pro-social acts themselves than those who did not see the sportspeople acting in a pro-social way. However, the children did not imitate the same behaviours, they just acted in a more pro-social way, which suggests that the effects of cognitive priming are not behaviour specific but do influence general conduct.

## Evaluation

- The research is mixed with regard to whether specific or general behaviours are affected by cognitive priming. There does seem to be an effect, but exactly how specific it is is unclear.
- It may be that cognitive priming has an effect on someone only if they have a predisposition to a certain type of behaviour due to their personality. The effects are likely to be subtle, so changing an aggressive individual into someone who is pro-social is unlikely with cognitive priming.
- The idea of cognitive priming can be seen to be simplistic. Social learning occurs only if the mediating processes are conducive to imitating a behaviour. It is likely that this is similar with cognitive priming, with the motivation, degree of impression and suitable context all being factors which mediate the effect the cue has.
- It is hard to establish cause and effect with cognitive priming. In general, it is true that the more violence someone is exposed to in the media, the more likely they are to be aggressive. However, this is correlational and therefore we can only establish that the two factors are related. It is possible that aggressive and violent people choose to watch more violent programmes, not that the violent programmes cause the violent behaviour.

## STRENGTHEN YOUR LEARNING

1 Give one example of research that demonstrates an increase in aggression when playing computer games.
2 Explain why computer games could be argued to decrease aggression.
3 Explain what is meant by desensitisation.
4 Explain how desensitisation might be argued to reduce aggression.
5 What is the difference between desensitisation and disinhibition?
6 Which type of media is most likely to induce disinhibition?
7 How can the disinhibition effect be explained?
8 With reference specifically to aggressive behaviour, what is meant by the term cognitive priming?
9 Describe one piece of research that supports the idea of cognitive priming affecting aggressive behaviour.
10 Explain one weakness of the cognitive priming theory of aggression.

# ASSESSMENT CHECK

1. Select from the types of deprivation A, B, C, D and E below to complete the table relating to the deprivation model of prison aggression. One type will be left over. **[4 marks]**

   **A** Deprivation of liberty

   **B** Deprivation of autonomy

   **C** Deprivation of goods and services

   **D** Deprivation of heterosexual relationships

   **E** Deprivation of security

   | Type of deprivation | Description of deprivation |
   | --- | --- |
   |  | There is a lack of luxury items in prison |
   |  | Prisoners sometimes do not feel safe |
   |  | Prisons are single-sex |
   |  | There is a lack of choice about how to spend the day in prison |

2. Researchers examining the effect that exposure to TV violence has on children used self-report questionnaires as their research methodology.

   Identify one type of reliability that may affect this research method and state how that could be dealt with by researchers. **[3 marks]**

3. Read the item and then answer the question:

   Some people argue that teenagers seem to be more aggressive than they usually are when they are playing computer games.

   Using your knowledge of disinhibition, explain why some people feel teenagers show high levels of aggression in this situation. **[4 marks]**

4. Briefly outline and evaluate the findings of one research study into the situational explanation of institutional aggression in prisons. **[4 marks]**

5. Describe and evaluate the role of desensitisation and/or cognitive priming on aggressive behaviour. **[16 marks]**

## SUMMARY

- The limbic system, more specifically the amygdala, is implicated in aggressive behaviour. The amygdala's role is emotion, which is thought to underpin most aggressive acts.
- Serotonin and testosterone are both biochemicals which seem to be involved in mediating aggressive behaviour. In the case of testosterone it seems to affect the activity in the orbito-frontal cortex.
- The MAOA gene affects the breakdown of dopamine, noradrenaline and serotonin. This seems to underpin some aggressive behaviour.
- The ethological explanation of aggression suggests that as humans, like animals, we have innate mechanisms which lead us to aggressive behaviour to help our chances of reproduction and survival. These are called the innate releasing mechanism and fixed action pattern.
- The evolutionary explanation for aggression states that aggression helps in terms of survival and reproductive success. It does this by competing for resources and overpowering rivals for suitable mates. It also helps ensure that any offspring are fathered by the man who will raise the children.
- The frustration–aggression hypothesis suggests that aggression is a by-product of frustration. Aggression can be a response when achievement of a goal is thwarted in some way.
- Social learning theory argues that aggression is learned by observing a role model being vicariously reinforced for aggressive behaviour. That behaviour is then imitated.
- The social learning theory states that not all behaviour is imitated. Mediating cognitive processes of attention, retention, reproduction and motivation affect whether the behaviour is imitated or not.
- De-individuation as a theory of aggression purports that the influence of being in a group means that an individual can act in an aggressive manner. This is thought to be due to the influence of group norms and a loss of identity, self-awareness and self-control.
- Institutional aggression in the context of prisons is problematic and there are two suggested explanations behind the higher incidence: dispositional and situational.
- The dispositional explanation argues that the high incidence of aggression in prisons is due to the characteristics that prisoners bring into the institution upon imprisonment. They have, it is argued, a predisposition to aggression due to personality and the home environment.
- The situational explanation argues that the high level of violence is due to the environment within the prison and the deprivation of liberty, autonomy, heterosexual relationships, goods and services and security. The deprivation prompts anger and frustration, which, in turn, makes aggression more likely.
- Media, and more specifically computer games, have the potential to influence aggressive behaviour. This can occur through exposure to violence and desensitisation, disinhibition and cognitive priming.

Neural and hormonal mechanisms in aggression

The ethological explanation of aggression

The evolutionary explanation for aggression

Social psychological explanations for aggression

Institutional aggression

Media influences on aggression

- Desensitisation occurs when the violence shown by the media means that an individual becomes less affected by what they see and their emotional, cognitive and behavioural response is reduced. This in turn means that aggression is more likely to occur as a consequence.
- Disinhibition can make aggression more likely as the individual loses their sense of self. This occurs in particular when playing a computer game. This is akin to de-individuation, although the presence of others is not necessary.
- Cognitive priming as a theory argues that the cues learned from and witnessed in the media mean that an individual may be prompted to act aggressively. Examples of cues are weapons such as guns.

# Forensic psychology

## Introduction

Forensic psychology considers crime. Psychology has the ability to offer insights into why someone might commit a crime, but also how crime might be prevented. This chapter will consider both of those aspects but will initially also look at defining and measuring crime.

Specific focus here will be upon:

1. Problems in defining crime
2. Offender profiling
3. Biological explanations for offending behaviour
4. Psychological explanations for offending behaviour
5. Dealing with offending behaviour.

## Understanding the specification

- For the section of the specification about problems in defining crime, you need to show an understanding of how crime is categorised and understand what constitutes a crime.
- There are many different ways of measuring crime. The ones you need to be able to speak about specifically are official statistics, victim surveys and offender surveys. Learn some examples of these and their advantages and disadvantages.
- The area of offender profiling has several different methods and the ones that are covered by the specification are the top-down approach (this includes organised and disorganised types of offender) and the bottom-up approach, which includes investigative psychology. Part of investigative psychology is geographical profiling, and this is mentioned in the specification.
- Regarding biological explanations of offending behaviour, you could be asked about a historical approach in this section, specifically atavistic form. You should also know more current biological theories, which include both neural and genetic explanations.
- There are many psychological explanations of offending behaviour, but for this specification it is stated you need to know Eysenck's theory of the criminal personality. You also need to understand cognitive explanations such as level of moral reasoning and cognitive distortions. This should include hostile attribution bias, minimalisation and differential association theory. Make sure you are also aware of the psychodynamic explanations for offending behaviour.
- The last section looks at treatment and prevention in dealing with offender behaviour. You need to be able to outline the aims of custodial sentencing and talk about psychological effects of custodial

sentencing. Recidivism is specified as a potential question topic. Finally, the treatments of behaviour modification in custody, anger management and restorative justice programme should be learned.

These are the basic requirements of the specification. However, other relevant material is included to provide depth and detail to your understanding. Don't forget also that you can be asked to evaluate any of the concepts. It is therefore important that research evidence to support or negate a topic is provided with your evaluation.

# 10.1 Problems in defining crime

## IN THE NEWS

### The Psychological Enquirer

#### Sleepwalking murder

**Figure 10.1** Can sleepwalking be used as a defence for murder?

Defining a crime is not always straightforward. There are circumstances where the individual is not seen as culpable because they were not in control of their actions.

An example of this is the case of Jules Lowe from Greater Manchester. In October 2003, after a heavy drinking session, he beat his elderly father to death, yet a jury found him not guilty of murder due to insanity. Apparently the attack on Edward Lowe, Jules' father, was prolonged and resulted in at least 90 injuries to the 83-year-old's body, which was punched, stamped on and kicked.

It would seem to be a clear case of murder, but Jules' defence was that he was sleepwalking at the time of the attack and therefore did not realise he was attacking his father. This state is called automatism. As Edward was a frail old man, he could not defend himself and was seemingly unable to wake his son.

The defence produced evidence from sleep tests to show that Jules Lowe did sleepwalk and that he could, in theory, have carried out the attack. The prosecution argued that the attack was due to his drunken state and that he was aware of what he was doing. The jury, however, believed that the evidence for automatism was convincing and Jules Lowe was admitted to a secure hospital unit to be monitored.

This case serves to demonstrate that definition of a crime is not clear cut. There may be circumstances where a person is not convicted even though they have actually carried out the act. There was no doubt that Jules Lowe had carried out the attack and killed his father, but the jury did not deem him culpable and therefore did not convict him.

Crime could simply be seen as any act that is against the law of the country in which it is committed. This is probably the definition that most people would suggest, if asked. However, the definition of crime is not so straightforward. The definition is only as good as the legal system it sits within, and is liable to change. Something could be a crime at one point in history, and not a few years earlier. People argue, therefore, that crime is socially constructed and is a reflection of the beliefs and attitudes of the society. This is supported by the idea that crime varies cross-culturally.

There are key crimes that are close to universal, such as murder and theft. However, even within these basic crimes there are cultural variations. There are four main issues that make crime difficult to define: culture, age, context and circumstance.

# Culture

Definitions of crime vary cross-culturally. This is unsurprising, as socially acceptable behaviour varies, too. Some countries accept that a man can marry more than one woman and therefore have several wives. The UK sees that as the crime of bigamy. Conversely, adultery is a felony (a serious crime) in five states in the USA: Massachusetts, Idaho, Oklahoma, Michigan and Wisconsin. This is also the case in many countries globally. It is not a crime in the UK, although it does give grounds for divorce.

These cultural differences clearly add weight to the argument that crime is socially constructed and there is no true definition of any act being criminal.

# Age

The idea that someone has committed a crime means that they should understand it is unacceptable. With young children this is not the case. It is obvious that if a baby hits their mother with an object they cannot be convicted of assault, but the age at which a child does realise the difference between right and wrong is difficult to ascertain.

The age of criminal responsibility varies from country to country. In the UK it currently stands at ten, having been increased from the age of eight in 1963. So, a ten year old can be tried in the criminal court in this country as they are deemed to know right from wrong and that they are committing a crime. This clouds the definition of a crime as it is not applicable to all people.

# Context

Historical context is very influential in defining crime. Clearly, the legal system changes its laws over time and so the position can arise where something previously deemed to be a crime by the legal system is no longer illegal through a change in the law.

An example of this is homosexuality. Until 1967 any homosexual acts, even between consenting adults, were criminal and the individuals could be prosecuted as such. This is no longer the case as homosexuality is not now against the law.

# Circumstance

It is argued that the law is clear and that there should be no argument over whether a crime has been committed or not. There are, however, circumstances in which the legal system can make allowances to take the situation and circumstance into account.

Within the UK legal system there are two core elements that should be present for it to constitute a guilty act, or crime: **actus reus** and **mens rea**. Actus reus essentially means that the crime should be a voluntary act. This means that the individual committing the act is in control of what they are doing. Mens rea is the intention to do the crime. In Latin it means 'guilty mind'. This means that the person, if committing a guilty act (actus reus), must also have intent to qualify it fully as a criminal act. So, actus reus is the action and mens rea is the psychological element of that behaviour.

To test these elements, consider a circumstance where a 'crime' has been committed and whether you would actually define it as a crime. Imagine, for example, a young man goes to a nightclub and because of the strobe lighting suffers an epileptic seizure. During the fit he thrashes around and hits someone who is helping him. It could be argued that he has assaulted the person, but it is pretty clear that no court would convict him in that circumstance. He was not in control (no actus reus) and he did not mean to do it (no mens rea). It can therefore be argued that it is not a crime. These key elements are important considerations for making the decision as to whether a crime has been committed or not. Would you say it was a similar situation if the young man was very drunk? In that situation would it be controlled and deliberate?

> **KEY TERMS**
>
> **Actus reus** – an act that constitutes a crime
>
> **Mens rea** – the intention to commit the act that constitutes a crime

# Ways of measuring crime

## Official statistics

The Office for National Statistics monitors crime rates throughout England and Wales. It collects data on several elements of crime, such as criminal damage and anti-social behaviour, drug crime, property crime, victims of crime, and violent and sexual crime.

Recent media reporting of crime statistics has focused on the coverage of the crime survey and levels of crime in society. Some types of crime can be difficult to measure. The ONS reports on various sources of crime that together give a fuller picture, but there is no official measure that combines sources into a single estimate of all crime in England and Wales.

### Police recording of crime

Police recording of crime is also used in the official statistics. These statistics are taken from the police computer systems and do not constitute the crimes that are eventually proven guilty, just the ones recorded.

This means that crimes that are not ever formally recorded by police are not included. The actual figure for more minor crimes could therefore be much higher. It also means that the figure could be misrepresentative because many crimes go unreported for many reasons, such as fear of reporting, lack of time, lack of faith in the system to catch the offender and social pressure.

## Victim surveys

### The Crime Survey for England and Wales (CSEW)

The CSEW examines the prevalence of crime and whether any trends are occurring in the general population, but does not claim to cover all instances of crime. It serves as a source for official statistics used to gauge crime levels.

It is a face-to-face survey asking people about their crime experiences. It is compiled using children as well as adults. The data is gathered from about 35,000 adults and 3,000 10–15 year olds who are interviewed each year. It can provide only an estimate of crime levels as it is a self-report measure. It does not cover everybody – there are some exceptions, such as people living in group residences (student halls or old people's homes). Other institutions are also not covered and anywhere in the public sector domain such as government offices and schools are exempted.

The survey varies from year to year in an attempt to keep abreast of crime trends. This is to keep it current and relevant. Over recent years the incidence of online criminal activity such as fraud has increased and the CSEW has had to adapt to take this into account, otherwise increases are not picked up.

The sample of people taking the survey is asked whether they have been victims of any of the following crimes: violence, robbery, theft and criminal damage. The survey includes motoring offences or possession of drugs offences, but these are classified as 'other crimes against society' as they do not have a clear victim. These are therefore sometimes excluded from headline statistics.

## Research

Figures from CSEW in March 2014 (released July 2014) estimate 7.3 million incidents of crime. This is a 14 per cent decrease from the year before and is the lowest estimate since 1981, when the survey began.

Despite the overall figures decreasing, shoplifting increased by 7 per cent and fraud increased by 17 per cent. Police-recorded crime remained the same as the previous year. However, in years prior to this the amount of police-reported crime had decreased year on year, which attracted criticism that the police were not recording crime accurately. If this was the case, then the current figures show this decline has been addressed. It also seems that this change is in certain crime areas such as violence and public order.

Sexual offences recorded by the police increased by 20 per cent from the previous year. This is argued to be because of Operation Yewtree, which was investigating sexual abuse by celebrities. As the media coverage was widespread, more victims approached the police to report sexual offences.

### Evaluation

- Figures from the official statistics have to be considered very carefully as some crime categories may be omitted.
- Self-report measures such as victim surveys are notoriously poor in reliability. Some people are reluctant to report crime, may forget they have been a victim of a minor crime or may lie. This ultimately means that much of the crime goes unreported. The unreported crime is known as the 'dark side' of crime and estimates on the amount of crime this represents vary wildly. It is, however, thought to be a significant figure.
- The victim survey is updated annually to keep abreast of trends and the emergence of new crimes (usually connected to new technology such as online fraud). This means that it attempts to include all possible crimes, even relatively new ones.

# Offender surveys

The Offending Crime and Justice Survey was conducted in England and Wales every year from 2003 to 2006 (inclusive). It covered self-reported offending and drug and alcohol use. It was a longitudinal survey to try to pick up on crime trends and patterns of offending behaviour and attitude. Offenders were asked about personal victimisation, recognising the offenders are also sometimes victims.

Offender surveys can also pick up on unreported crime from the official statistics and the method may give a more accurate picture of the 'dark side'.

In Scotland, an annual survey of prisoners and young offenders is carried out. They are asked not only about their current living conditions within prison but also about their offences. This offers some insight into why they may have committed a crime.

## CONTEMPORARY RESEARCH

### The 14th Prisoner Survey – Key points

#### Male offenders

- There was a decrease of 20 per cent in self-reported drug use from 2001 to 2013.
- 45 per cent of male prisoners stated that they were drunk at the time they committed their offence (although this was a slight reduction from the previous year of 4 per cent). This figure was, however, significantly larger for young offenders, with 68 per cent saying they were inebriated at the time.
- The young male offenders also reported a high rate of alcoholism, with 90 per cent of them drinking more than ten units a day when they were out of prison.
- One third of young male offenders were also members of gangs and 67 per cent of offenders carried a knife.
- 44 per cent said they had witnessed violence in the home.

#### Female offenders

- 50 per cent of female offenders reported being drunk when committing their offence. This was 5 per cent more than male offenders.
- 28 per cent of female offenders reported that drinking alcohol affected their employment.
- 28 per cent were worried that alcohol was going to be an issue for them when they were going to be released.
- As well as dividing by gender, the survey further divided the offenders into whether they had been in care, whether they were ex-servicemen and if they were older prisoners.

### Evaluation

- Offender surveys are self-report measures and therefore suffer from the same problems as all self-report measures in terms of reliability. However, it could be argued that offending behaviour is even more liable to inaccuracy due to the legal implications of giving a full picture.
- Asking offenders about the offences committed can give a good picture of the reasons behind their offending behaviour. This helps deployment of resources to areas which might prevent further crime such as alcohol dependence programmes. It also means that recidivism rates can be reduced.
- The offender surveys give the best chance of picking up on the dark side of crime because they have knowledge of exactly what crimes might be occurring when. This method is an official channel through to the criminal 'underworld' and can give a fuller picture and provide information that is otherwise inaccessible, much like undercover policemen and police informants do. This is a real strength of the method.

> **STRENGTHEN YOUR LEARNING**
> 1 Explain two factors in making the definition of crime problematic.
> 2 Outline one way of measuring crime.
> 3 Outline two strengths of using victim surveys to measure crime.
> 4 Outline two weaknesses of using official statistics to measure crime.
> 5 Explain why offender surveys are useful.

> **YOU ARE THE RESEARCHER**
> Imagine you are a researcher who has been given the job of establishing crime levels in a fictional city called Ollywood, which is the only settlement on an island in the Atlantic. How would you go about this task? Justify each choice of source of statistics.

## 10.2 Offender profiling

If we were to believe the media version of offender profiling then it would be described as a profiler going into a murder investigation room, looking at the evidence so far and saying who might have committed the crime, narrowing it down to where they live, with whom, their age, gender, etc. The police would then follow the profile and find the killer. This is the glamorous view, and it does happen. However, in most instances it is an investigative tool that is used alongside all the other ways of solving a crime. It sometimes works, it sometimes doesn't.

Broadly speaking, there are two types of profiling: top-down and bottom-up. Top-down methods are where the profiler has experience and can use the evidence at the crime scene to develop a profile of the likely criminal. The bottom-up approach is when research and statistics of similar crimes are used to develop a profile of the criminal based on previous convictions. The key difference between the two is the source of the profile. Top-down uses the experience (and intuition) of a profiler whereas bottom-up uses information on similar crimes.

The key questions that must be asked in profiling are:

1 What happened at the crime scene(s)?
2 Who would have committed that crime/those crimes?
3 What kind of personality would that person have had?

**Figure 10.2** What happened at the crime scene?

Jackson & Bekerian (1997) state that inferences about the criminal can be made from the scene(s) and that it is these which can enable a case to be solved.

The reason this can be argued is the modus operandi (MO) of the criminal, i.e. how they commit the crime, why they choose the situation, etc. Criminals often operate in a similar way and this reflects their personality. This is the core assumption of profiling. There is a core belief, implicit in this, that there is consistency in crime. For example, for profiling to work it needs to be assumed that the criminal's personality remains consistent. This then means that the MO will remain similar (because they will commit a crime the same way), thus the scene and any signatures (distinctive behaviours) left at the scene will be consistent.

## The top-down approach

As stated, this method uses the experience and intuition of a profiler to draw up a profile from the crime scene. It is most often used in violent crime such as murder. This is why it is often called crime scene analysis.

This approach to profiling emerged in the 1970s with the Federal Bureau of Investigation (FBI) and uses a seven-stage process to narrow down the number of possible suspects for a crime. It helps with the decision-making process to have seven aspects to consider (Ressler et al., 1988). Initially, though, all evidence needs to be collected from the crime scene, including photographs taken of the victim (if there is one) prior to the scene being disturbed. Then the seven decision-making tools are considered as follows.

### 1 Murder type

This asks whether the killing is an isolated incident. It could also be part of a number of killings, such as those committed by a serial killer, mass murderer or spree killer. A serial killer is classified as such if there have been three or more murders by the same person over a period of at least a month, with a period of 'down time' (i.e. no killing) between the murders. A spree killer is someone who has killed people in one time period (i.e. a day) in several locations. Mass murderers kill in only one location in one time period.

Initially a serial killer would be classified as a 'one-off' killer until more murders had been discovered/committed. This would give a very different picture of the perpetrator. However, when more than one murder takes place, an MO becomes apparent and the picture is more detailed. The difference in profiles between spree and serial/mass killers is noticeable, as serial killers choose their victim for their characteristics whereas spree killers do not tend to do this, so this is an important initial picture to establish.

### 2 Primary intent

This asks whether it was a deliberate, pre-meditated murder or not, which affects the profile development. It is possible that a murder is committed as a consequence of another crime, which elicits a very different picture of the criminal from someone who sets out to commit murder.

### 3 Victim risk

Some victims are classified as high risk and others as low risk due to their vulnerability. Children, old people and prostitutes (in countries where prostitution is not legal) are all examples of low-risk targets as they can offer little resistance. The motive for killing a low-risk target gives important information to a profiler.

### 4 Offender risk

This is how much risk the criminal actually took in committing the crime and, again, gives insight into who they are. To attack someone on a busy street in daylight is highly risky for the criminal and so, if they have chosen to do this, it tells the profiler the kind of person the police should look for.

## 5 Escalation

This aspect is the extent to which the crime has escalated from previous offences or the potential it has to escalate. This gives the profiler a pattern of behaviours and may help to pre-empt future crimes.

## 6 Time factors

The time of day crimes are committed gives a profiler clues to the criminal's daily routine and also feeds into the information about risk levels.

## 7 Location factors

This is similar to the time factors consideration, as it can inform the profiler about the criminal's environment, transport options and even where they might live.

From the seven decision-making tools a picture begins to emerge for the profiler, which helps to classify the criminal into 'organised' or 'disorganised'. The procedure for classifying into these categories has led this type of profiling to be called typological profiling. The distinction between the two types is shown in Table 10.1.

**Table 10.1** The distinction between organised and disorganised criminals

|  | Organised | Disorganised |
| --- | --- | --- |
| Behaviour towards victim | Victim targeted<br>Aggressive<br>Controls conversation | Victim selected at random<br>Crime unplanned<br>Avoids conversation |
| Crime scene detail | Weapon absent<br>Body hidden from view<br>Body transported from original point of murder<br>Crime scene orderly<br>Attempts to clear up | Weapon present<br>Sexual activity after death<br>Body left in view |
| Characteristics of criminal | High intelligence<br>Socially competent<br>Sexually competent<br>Skilled occupation<br>Monitors media coverage of crimes | Average intelligence<br>Socially immature<br>Sexually incompetent<br>Poor work history<br>Lives alone<br>Lives/works close to crime scene<br>No interest in media coverage |
| Background of criminal | High birth order (e.g. eldest)<br>Inconsistent discipline as child | Low birth order (e.g. youngest)<br>Harsh discipline as child |

The next step of the process is then for the profiler to compile the profile, taking all these factors into account. The profile will contain demographic and physical characteristics, a discussion of the likely behaviour of the perpetrator and any defining characteristics.

## CASE STUDY

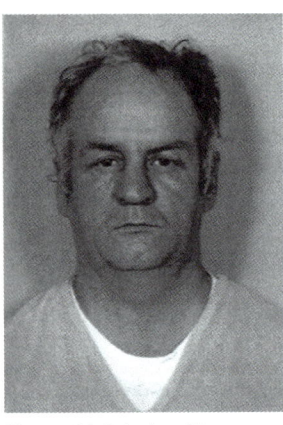

**Figure 10.3** Arthur Shawcross

In the USA, Arthur Shawcross had been in prison for murdering a ten-year-old boy and an eight-year-old girl. He was sentenced to 25 years in prison in 1972.

He served 15 years and was released in 1987. March 1988 marked the start of a long string of murders, where Shawcross chose prostitutes as his victims. Over two years he murdered 11 prostitutes and many of the bodies were found near the Genesee River in New York State. The victims were usually strangled, beaten and in some cases mutilated.

A criminal profiler called Gregg McCrary, from the FBI, was brought in to help with the investigation. Together with Ed Grant, an investigator, he visited crime scenes and looked at the case files. They thought that half the murders had a clear pattern, which suggested the same perpetrator. From the available evidence they suggested that the murderer was:

1. White.
2. Male.
3. In his late twenties/early thirties, although they stated that this was probably his mental age rather than his actual age.
4. A previous offender of violent crimes.
5. In a low-paid job.
6. The driver of a cheap, basic car.
7. Probably married.
8. Living or working near the Genesee River.
9. Keen on hunting or fishing.

As the murderer had started leaving bodies where they were and coming back to cut them up at a later date, McCrary and Grant suggested that the police should try to find a body before it was cut up. When one was found, they said the police should not remove it but instead should conduct a surveillance operation. McCrary and Grant thought that the murderer would revisit the body and that he could be caught this way.

This was exactly what happened. Shawcross went back to the body, which meant the police could arrest him.

The profile drawn up by McCrary and Grant was surprisingly accurate and the only aspect that was wrong was the age, as Shawcross was ten years older than they suggested. However, his mental age was younger, so in some ways this aspect was correct too.

Shawcross was found guilty, and although he pleaded insanity, the court found him to be sane and he received a 250-year prison sentence.

### Evaluation

- This case shows the accuracy level that can occur when typological (top-down) profiling is used. The profile, for this case, was very accurate.
- This is a case study and as such cannot be used to prove a profiling method correct universally.

### Evaluation

- There is a lack of theoretical foundation to this approach, which gives it a feel of an inexact science – more hunch than reasoning. In some people's view this reduces its credibility as it lacks the background research to say why it works. Reliance on intuition is problematic as personal emotion and memories can sway intuition.
- This method of profiling can only really be used in the crimes of murder and rape. This restricts its applicability, unlike the geographical approach, which looks at the pattern of crime rather than the crime type, making it more versatile.
- Having two main categories of criminal is very simplistic. It is likely that criminals do not fit neatly into either category, therefore making the prediction of their characteristics difficult. It is likely there will be more types, and the distinction is too restrictive.
- Each crime scene is unique and there are many different variables that should be accounted for. This makes the typological definition difficult to apply and this affects its accuracy.

## The bottom-up approach

This method builds a picture of the potential criminal from facts and figures collated from previous crimes of the same type. This removes the intuition element of the profiling.

## Investigative psychology

Investigative psychology is the term used to describe an approach fine-tuned in the UK by David Canter, who wanted to develop a method that used research as its basis. The fact that the analysis is based on statistical techniques makes the approach more objective.

There are essentially five assumptions of investigative psychology that underpin the crime, specifically what occurs between the victim and the offender:

1 **Interpersonal coherence** – this means that there is an assumption that behaviour is consistent across situations; more specifically, that everyday behaviour is similar to the way a crime is committed. For example, an aggressive person is more likely to commit an aggressive crime.
2 **Time and place** – these are similar to the time and location factors in the top-down approach where the positioning and timing of crimes give clues as to where the perpetrator might live or work.
3 **Criminal characteristics** – placing criminals into categories is a useful exercise to help the police.
4 **Criminal career** – this considers how far into their criminal experience offenders are, and how their pattern of crime might progress.
5 **Forensic awareness** – this highlights the fact that offenders who show an awareness of forensic investigation, e.g. by cleaning a crime scene, will probably have committed a crime before and been through the criminal justice system.

With these assumptions in place, investigative psychologists can work on a profile using statistical techniques. One example is geographical profiling.

## Geographical profiling

This specifically covers the location and timing aspects of a crime. This concurs with the assumption previously mentioned that these factors can give important clues to the living habits of the offender (Canter & Youngs, 2008).

There are four main principles which all help shape a profile using this method:

1 **Locatedness**. The location says a lot about the offender. Some crimes have several locations and they are all really important from a profiler's point of view. Locations include where the victim is met initially, where the attack occurs, where the victim is actually killed and finally where the body is disposed of. Of course, these might all be the same place, but if not, multiple locations can add to the profile accuracy.
2 **Systematic crime location choice**. This principle says that locations are not in any way random. Familiarity to the offender is important with this choice and means that the location is worthy of careful consideration.
3 **Centrality**. This principle states that there are two types of offenders: commuters and marauders. Commuters travel to commit the crime (but it is still likely to be somewhere familiar to them), while marauders commit crimes close to home. This centrality means that the crimes may cluster.
4 **Comparative case analysis**. This is the principle that other crimes should be considered as being committed by the same offender. The reason why this connection is actively sought is that the more crimes that

are committed by one particular person, the greater the accuracy and application of geographical profiling.

When these principles are applied to a location or series of locations they can help the police by narrowing down the pool of suspects, helping mobilise police resources for door-to-door enquiries and patrols.

## CASE STUDY

**Figure 10.4** John Duffy – the Railway Rapist

From 1982 to 1985 there was a series of rapes committed close to railway stations in the south east of England. At that point the perpetrators were nicknamed the Railway Rapists. Then thee women were killed, and it seemed the crimes were escalating. The offenders were renamed the Railway Killers and the police brought in Dr David Canter, a criminal profiler, who would, they hoped, be able to help them.

Evidence from the scene indicated that one of the perpetrators worked alone, so Canter applied his profiling theory and created an offender profile for the 'Railway Killer'. This profile included the personal characteristics and geographical information based on where the crimes were committed (see Table 10.2). The second column shows a comparison with John Duffy.

Following the help from Dr Canter, John Duffy, who had previously been questioned by the police, was arrested. Although he said he had not worked alone, it was not until 1997 that he gave the name of his accomplice and David Mulcahy was arrested.

Duffy was charged with a total of 11 rapes and 2 murders; Mulcahy was charged with 7 rapes and 3 murders. They will never be released from prison.

### Evaluation

- Canter's profile was very accurate, with 12 of the 17 suggested characteristics being correct. The geographical information was particularly invaluable.
- This is a case study so has limited value in providing evidence that this method of profiling works universally.

| Profile of personal characteristics | John Duffy |
|---|---|
| Poor relationship with women but has probably been married | Separated from his wife |
| Considerable sexual experience, potentially with bondage | Abusive to wife and tied her up during sex |
| A couple of close male friends | Two close male friends. David Mulcahy was a friend from school days |
| Experience with police or knowledge of procedures | He had a criminal record and combed the pubic hair of the victims to remove evidence of his own |
| Probably not physically strong | He carried out many of the offences with an accomplice, but was a martial arts instructor, which implies physical fitness He used restraints |
| Male in his mid-late twenties | He was 29 |
| Potentially semi-skilled work | Carpenter |
| *From the geographical information* | |
| Knowledge of the railway | He worked for the railways as a carpenter |
| Worked/lived near the crime scenes | He lived in Kilburn, which was central to the rapes and murders he committed |

**Table 10.2** A comparison of the profile characteristics and the actual characteristics of John Duffy

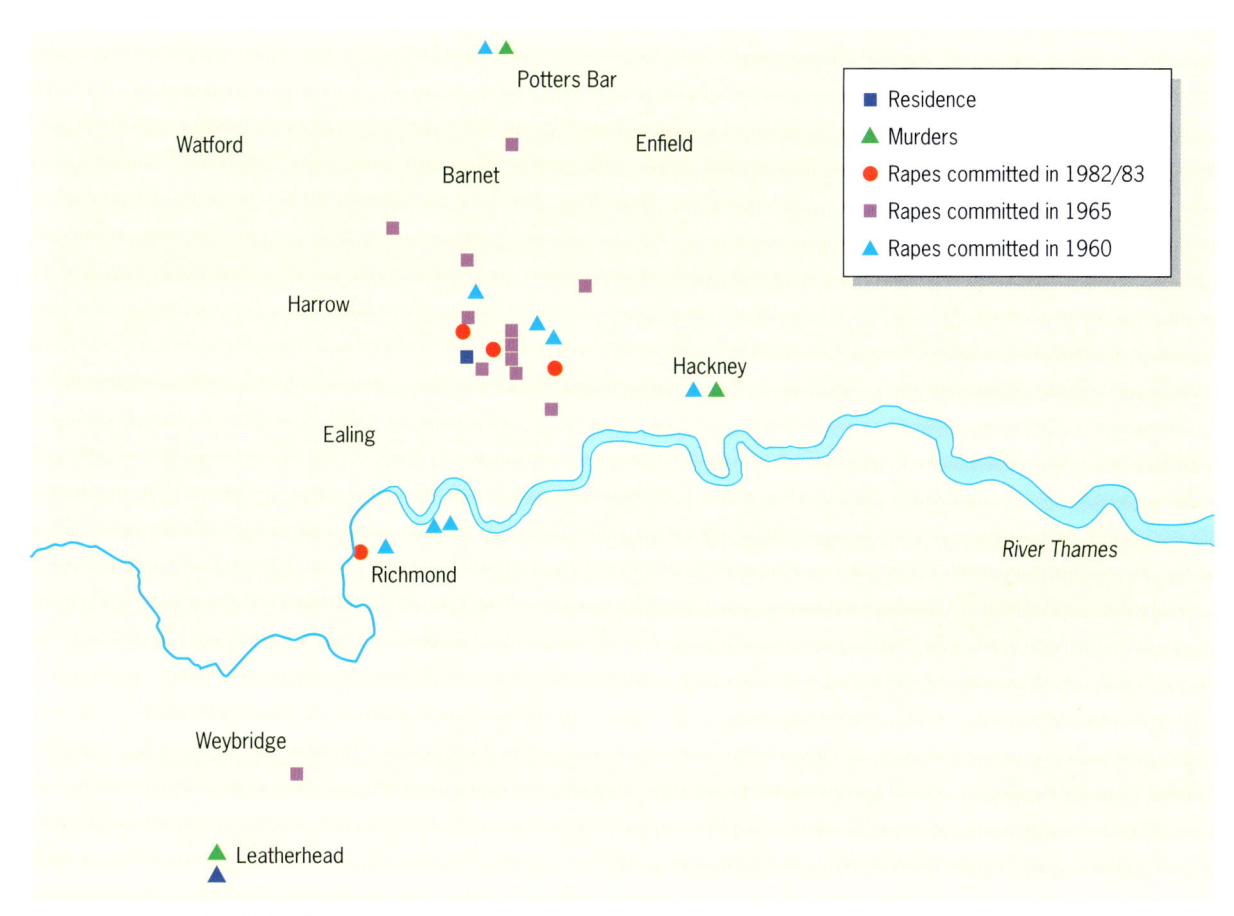

**Figure 10.5** Map of Duffy's offences

### ON THE WEB

A more detailed account of the John Duffy case can be found at:
**www.biography.com/people/john-duffy-17169740#synopsis**

## Evaluation

- The investigative psychology approach is based heavily on research and statistical likelihood. This means that it is seen to be more scientific than top-down approaches. This use of statistics and theory has removed intuition of the profiler from the process, which is argued to make it more reliable.

- Locations are important for the identification of the offender, but there are other considerations that need to be made, such as their psychological characteristics. Geographical profiling concentrates on location, which could miss important information if used in isolation.

- The technique requires statistical information from previous crimes, which is not always easy to gather. The problems of measuring crime show how imperfect the information might be in terms of coverage and so this means the evidence base on which this method functions is incomplete and/or inaccurate.

- Geographical profiling helps locate offenders of many different crimes. It can be used to locate the likely home of burglars given that they can concentrate their crimes in a familiar place, often not too far from where they live. This means the method can be widely applied across many different types of crime.

## Research on offender profiling

Snook *et al.* (2008) state that the number of cases using profiling to investigate the crime has increased. This seems to suggest that police officers are starting to recognise its credibility.

Pinizzotto (1984) identified that out of 192 requests for criminal profiles, only 17 per cent were actually useful for identifying the suspects. However, the same research from Pinizzotto showed that 77 per cent of the respondents indicated that the profiles had assisted them to focus on the investigations.

Abumere (2012) found more than 75 per cent of the British police officers who were asked said that the advice of the profiler had been useful to them in making predictions about the crime. For them the advice improved their understanding of the offender and others also stated that it supported their ideas and feelings about the offender. Police from the Netherlands stated that they found the advice from the profilers too general and others stated that the follow-up work needed was not financially viable. They also did not take advice from the profiler if it contradicted their own ideas.

Shanahan (2008) found the responses to questionnaires sent out by the Criminal Investigation Department, which were to evaluate the effectiveness of the criminal profiling in the department, were mainly negative. This was only when it had not worked effectively however – Shanahan found that most police officers still expressed confidence in criminal profiling and its potential to help them.

### Evaluation

- Research on the effectiveness of criminal profiling is mixed.
- Overall there is a suggestion that profiling is used by police but is seen as only one of the tools available to them when solving a crime and it is not the main method used.
- As criminal profiling is so often used in conjunction with other police work it is sometimes difficult to establish how much of a contribution it makes to an investigation. This makes its effectiveness impossible to measure.

### STRENGTHEN YOUR LEARNING

1. Explain the difference between top-down and bottom-up methods of criminal profiling.
2. Outline two strengths of top-down profiling.
3. Explain the difference between organised and disorganised types of offender.
4. Outline two weaknesses of using criminal profiling.
5. Outline one case study where criminal profiling has helped identify the victim.

# ASSESSMENT CHECK

1. Select from the characteristics A, B, C and D below to complete the table by classifying the action regarding factors affecting the definition of crime. One description will be left over. **[3 marks]**

   **A** Culture

   **B** Age

   **C** Context

   **D** Circumstance

   | Action | Factor affecting whether it is defined as a crime or not |
   |---|---|
   | An eight year old shoplifts a packet of sweets from the local shop | |
   | A mother steals powdered milk from a hospital because she says she cannot afford to buy it | |
   | A mother smacks her five-year-old child for running away from her in a crowded street | |

2. A researcher asked police whether they would use offender profiling to aid their investigations if they had the choice. They were asked to respond 'yes' or 'no'.

   What inferential statistical test could be used to test whether there was a statistically significant difference between the number who answered 'yes' and the number who answered 'no'? Justify your answer. **[2 marks]**

3. Briefly explain problems with measuring crime. **[2 marks]**

4. 'The legal system of this country and others can be confusing. Why are some acts seen as a crime and others not?'

   Using your knowledge of problems with defining crime, explain why some crimes vary so much within this country and abroad. **[4 marks]**

5. Outline what is meant by top-down offender profiling. **[2 marks]**

6. Describe and evaluate the effectiveness of offender profiling. **[16 marks]**

# 10.3 Biological explanations for offending behaviour

*'Once upon a time, a woman was picking up firewood. She came upon a poisonous snake frozen in the snow. She took the snake home and nursed it back to health. One day the snake bit her on the cheek. As she lay dying, she asked the snake, "Why have you done this to me?" And the snake answered, "Look, bitch, you knew I was a snake."'*

Natural Born Killers (1994)

## A historical approach (atavistic form)

An early historical perspective for explaining offending behaviour was suggested in the 1870s by an Italian criminologist called Cesare Lombroso. His work centred around the idea that criminals had distinguishing physical features which originated from a more primitive stage of development. In other words, they were less civilised and had more in common with evolutionary ancestors than people in the 1870s. For that reason he saw them as wilder and not suited to the culture and society in the late 1800s.

Lombroso called the features '**atavistic**'. He measured the physical features of Italian criminals and argued that they had measurements that distinguished them from non-criminals. These head and facial feature measurements, he said, demonstrated that they were from an earlier evolutionary stage of development and that criminals were born that way.

The data on the features was based on measurements from almost 4,000 criminals and also the skulls of almost 400 dead criminals. Examples of the atavistic features identified by Lombroso (see Figure 10.6) are:

- heavy brow
- large strong jaw
- large ears
- extra nipples or extra fingers/toes.

Lombroso argued that criminals were not to blame for their activities as their behaviour was determined by their physiology. This had implications for the criminal justice system as the assumption by the legal system was that they chose to act the way they did, whereas Lombroso was suggesting the opposite.

### Research

Goring (1913) conducted a study looking at some of Lombroso's proposed features. He tested Lombroso's findings by comparing 2,348 London convicts with a control group. Goring failed to replicate Lombroso's findings and concluded that criminal behaviour is not linked to physical appearance.

Hooton (1939) conducted a 12-year study comparing 13,873 male prisoners in 10 states in the USA with a control group of 3,023 men to investigate whether there were any physical differences. His publication of the results argued that criminal behaviour was due to biological inferiority and 'degeneration'. He also argued that a variety of unattractive physical

> **KEY TERM**
>
> **Atavistic form** – a possible explanation for criminal offending, centring on the idea that offenders may represent a more primitive evolutionary stage of development than their contemporaries. This may be shown in a range of facial and physical features

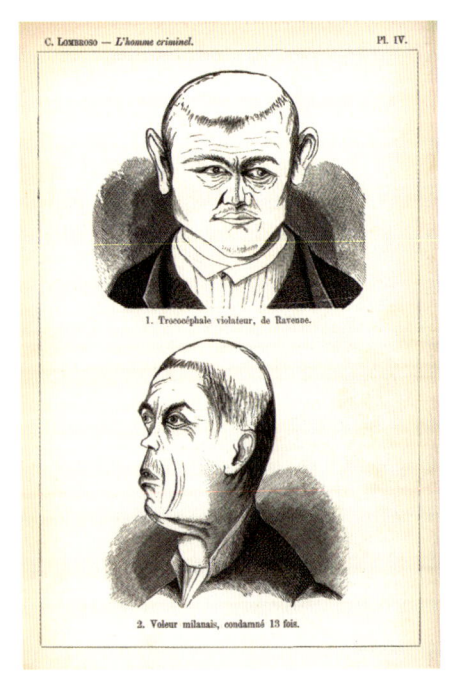

**Figure 10.6** Atavistic features identified by Lombroso (1876)

characteristics could be ascribed to criminals. These included sloping foreheads, protruding ears and narrow jaws. The characteristics described by Hooton differed from those outlined by Lombroso.

### Evaluation

- It is possible that the atavistic features Lombroso described are linked to criminality but not because of them being at an earlier stage of evolutionary development. Kaplan's (1980) self-derogation theory states that poor social interactions (which could be due to the way someone looks) can bring about criminal behaviours due to poor self-esteem and a reluctance to conform. Similarly, Agnew (1992) argued that unwanted and unpleasant interactions (again possibly due to appearance) can increase frustration and anger. This is called general strain theory.
- Lombroso's theory should be considered in its historical context to see how influential it has been. Prior to Lombroso's work criminality was often seen from a religious perspective and was attributed to bad spirits and devil influence. Lombroso's theory, although lacking the scientific rigour of today, was at least an attempt to bring explanations for criminality into the realms of science.
- Lombroso's methodology has been criticised because he merely measured the features of criminals and had no control group. Without a comparison with non-criminal controls it is difficult to draw conclusions and state that a feature is distinguishing. This was rectified by Goring and Hooton's work (see above) to some extent.
- Another issue with Lombroso's methodology is that his sample may have included people who had learning difficulties and this may have skewed the measurements taken as some learning difficulties have a physical effect on the facial features.
- The theory may have, in some way, contributed to criminals being stereotyped as looking a certain way. This is clearly unhelpful and perpetuates an idea that certain features are associated with criminal behaviour.

### ON THE WEB

A more detailed review of the atavistic form theory can be found at:

www.sagepub.com/schram/study/materials/reference/90851_04.1r.pdf

It was written by Cesare Beccalossi (2010) for publication in *The Encyclopedia of Criminological Theory*.

## Genetics

Genetics as an explanation for criminal behaviour is problematic as there is no criminal gene identified. However, there are twin, family and adoption studies that seem to indicate there may be genetic transmission of criminal behaviour.

### Twin studies

The concordance rate of twins for criminal behaviour gives an indication of the extent that offending behaviour could be seen to be heritable.

#### Research

In Table 10.3 there are two studies that show that the concordance rates of MZ (genetically identical) twins is greater than that of DZ twins (50 per cent genetically identical).

Table 10.3 Studies showing the concordance rates of MZ and DZ twins

|  | MZ concordance rate | DZ concordance rate | Sample size |
|---|---|---|---|
| Christiansen (1977) | 35% | 13% | 3,586 twin pairs |
| Raine (1993) | 52% | 21% | Review of 13 studies |

## Family studies

In the Cambridge Study in Delinquent Development (Farrington, 1996), 411 males living in London from nearly 400 families were monitored from age 8 to age 32 by using interviews, and from age 10 to age 40 in crime records. The conviction rates of these men were compared with convictions of their biological fathers and mothers, and close family members. The study found:

- 64 per cent of the families had at least one convicted person
- 6 per cent of the families accounted for 50 per cent of all the convictions
- convictions of one family member were strongly related to convictions of every other family member
- about 75 per cent of convicted fathers and convicted mothers had a convicted child
- approximately 75 per cent of families with convicted daughters also had convicted sons
- convictions of older siblings were more strongly related to convictions of the males than were convictions of younger siblings.

The conclusion was that offending is strongly concentrated in families and is demonstrated from one generation to the next.

## Adoption studies

Adoption studies allow the behaviour of an individual to be compared with both their birth and adopted parents. If their behaviour is similar to that of their adopted parents then the reason can be said to be environmental. However, if it is more like the behaviour of the biological parents it is attributed to a possible genetic influence.

A meta-analysis of 51 twin and adoption studies was conducted to estimate the extent of environmental and possible genetic influences on antisocial behaviour. The strength of family influences was lower in parent–offspring adoption studies than in both twin studies and sibling adoption studies. Overall, shared environmental influences seemed to equate to 16 per cent and non-shared environmental influences were 43 per cent.

### Evaluation

- Results from research seem to indicate that there are effects on offending behaviour influenced by the family. It is important to note though that these results merely illustrate that offending behaviour runs in families, and this does not automatically mean that it is due to genetic transmission. A study such as this cannot show how the results occurred – it could equally be social learning or other environmental influences.
- The stress of adoption could account for offending behaviour in adopted children and it is therefore difficult to say whether there is genetic transmission or not. Stress prior to birth can affect the

development of the foetus so even if the child is adopted very early, environmental influences pre-birth cannot be controlled for.
- It can be seen that in twin studies the concordance rate is higher when they are genetically more similar. This could be argued to show that there may be genetic transmission. However, it could equally be argued that as MZ (identical) twins are treated more similarly to each other than non-identical twins, this could account for the increased rate of concordance.

# Neural explanation

Neural explanations for offending behaviour have been proposed for both the biochemistry of the body and the brain physiology.

## Biochemistry

There are three biochemicals that are implicated in offending behaviour: noradrenaline, serotonin and dopamine:

- **Noradrenaline** is part of the fight-or-flight response and helps respond in a threatening situation. There is research to suggest that high levels are linked to violence and aggression and so, as a consequence, it is easy to explain some crimes as possibly being underpinned by the chemical imbalance.
- **Serotonin** regulates mood and impulse control. This means that in low levels it could be implicated in criminal behaviour as there will be more impulsivity. If a situation is particularly emotional then someone with low levels could easily react as they may have an impaired capacity to hold back.
- **Dopamine** is implicated in offending behaviour because of its link to addiction and therefore substance abuse. This makes crime more likely. Dopaminergic activity in the limbic system means that pleasure is experienced, and the greater the activity, the greater the feeling of pleasure. This makes addiction more likely. For a more comprehensive explanation of this process see page 407 in Chapter 11.

## Research

Higley *et al.* (1996) found that levels of testosterone were positively correlated with aggressiveness but not impulsivity, whereas levels of serotonin were negatively correlated with impulsive behaviour and extreme aggression, but not general aggression. This work was done on male non-human primates. These results seem to suggest how biochemical levels may underpin offender behaviour.

The relationship between serotonin and impulse control is complex. Other factors are involved. Krakowski (2003) argued through research that while serotonin was implicated in lack of impulse control and violence, to make a causal link is difficult. Krakowski proposed that it also depends on individual differences and the social context of the behaviour. For example, if an event occurs in a crowd it could prompt a different reaction from the individual than if he or she was alone, even if the levels of serotonin were the same.

Research by Brunner (see Classic research in Chapter 9, page 318) examined the effects of the MAOA gene, which alters the levels of neurotransmitters of those who have the shortened version of the gene. This then is linked to aggressive behaviour so could equally be applied to violent crime.

> **Evaluation**
> - It can be argued that the biochemical explanations are relevant more to everyday behaviour and that they may lead to offending behaviour in some circumstances. They may also underpin a mental illness and it is that which increases the likelihood of crimes being committed in some circumstances rather than the level of the chemical. This suggests the relationship is indirect.
> - Much of the research into neurotransmitters has been conducted on animals and for that reason there are issues of validity. Observing increased aggression in mice with higher levels of a neurotransmitter does not automatically extrapolate to humans committing a violent crime.
> - The biochemical explanations are reductionist and therefore can be seen to be simplifying criminal behaviour. It is likely that the issue is far more complex than the level of a biochemical in an individual's brain.

## Brain physiology

The idea that the physiology of the brain might be implicated in offending behaviour in some way has been suggested. The two key areas implicated in the brain are the limbic system and the way the brain develops.

### Limbic system

This is a central part of the brain and regarded as the primitive area. It is the centre where emotions are modulated and for this reason could be argued to be implicated in offending behaviour.

This is particularly the case with criminal psychopaths (or anti-social personality disorder). Psychopathy is a personality disorder with no clear cause. Psychopaths seem to have problems processing emotions and empathy. This leads to a lack of remorse or guilt if their actions affect others in a negative way. Not all psychopaths commit crimes, but it is argued that a fault in their limbic system means that lack of emotional reactions could lead to planned and organised offending behaviour as they lack remorse and are more self-serving as a consequence.

### Brain development

Work examining the role of brain development in offending behaviour has also centred around individuals with anti-social personality disorder (psychopathy).

Research by Raine *et al.* (2000) has suggested that the frontal lobe volume of people with anti-social personality disorder is less than those without. This reduced activity is argued to be why people with anti-social personality disorder do not feel guilt or appear to have a conscience. This means they do not have the 'brake' that stops the majority of the population from committing crimes against others.

### Research

Research by Kent *et al.* (2001) used fMRI scanning to ascertain any abnormalities in psychopathic brain activity during an emotion-based task.

When compared with criminal non-psychopaths and non-criminal control participants, criminal psychopaths showed much less activity in the limbic system. Psychopaths seem to use their frontal lobe to a greater degree in those situations, suggesting an element of planning and control.

Raine *et al.* (1997) investigated whether there was any difference between the brain activity of murderers and non-murderers. The sample was taken from 41 violent murderers who had claimed to be not guilty by reason of insanity. They had to be assessed for this reason. Using a PET scanner, Raine *et al.* found some differences in brain activity in areas linked to aggression such as the prefrontal cortex and areas of the limbic system.

Psychopathy is also linked to brain abnormalities in work done by Fallon (2013) (see the Debates section on page 53). This is further evidence to suggest that brain development and abnormalities can be implicated in criminal behaviour.

### RESEARCH IN FOCUS

Scanning brains for atypical brain structure and activity is one way to investigate the physiology of the brain as having an effect on offender behaviour. However, there are ethical issues with this.

What are the ethical issues of this kind of research? Why is the research socially sensitive? Is there any alternative?

### Evaluation

- It is argued that a clear link between abnormal processing and crime may not be appropriate. The functioning could be due to a brain trauma. Not everyone who receives a head injury commits crime though, even when the damage is comparable to the changed physiology in research. Cause and effect is therefore not clear as it does not affect people with brain physiology issues in the same way.
- The brain functioning issues may be due to abuse in the offender's childhood, for example if they were beaten as a child. This has implications for whether the offender is culpable or not as it could be argued it is beyond their control.
- Sample sizes for this kind of research are generally small for two reasons. First, the target population (e.g. psychopaths and criminals) is hard to access and second, using scanning is time consuming and expensive. This has an effect on the extent to which results can be generalised.

### STRENGTHEN YOUR LEARNING

1. Identify which neurotransmitters are implicated in offending behaviour.
2. Outline one study which supports the role of a neurotransmitter in offending behaviour.
3. Outline evidence to suggest that there is a genetic underpinning to offender behaviour.
4. Explain the atavistic form theory of offending.
5. What evaluative points can be made about the atavistic form theory of offending?

# 10.4 Psychological explanations for offending behaviour

*'It is a man's own mind, not his enemy or foe, that lures him to evil ways.'*
Buddha (approx 500BC)

## Eysenck's theory of the criminal personality

Eysenck's theory (1963) is actually a general theory of personality that has been very influential over the years. It is a trait theory, in other words it suggests that all personalities are made up of certain traits (characteristics) and the level you have of those traits determines your personality. His original work was based on servicemen, not criminals, but the theory has subsequently been applied to offending behaviour.

### The theory

Theory originally argued that there were two personality traits that existed along dimensions: 'extraversion' and 'neuroticism'. In 1976 Eysenck added 'psychoticism' as a third trait following his work with schizophrenics, as he felt there were elements of personalities that were not covered by the other two traits. The characteristics of each trait are as follows:

- **Extraversion** – an extravert is sociable, impulsive, expressive and risk taking. At the other end of the continuum, an introvert acts in the opposite way, being happy in their own company and more cautious.
- **Neuroticism** – an individual who scores high on the neuroticism scale will exhibit such behaviours as nervousness, anxiety and obsessiveness. The opposite end of the spectrum is described as 'stable' and they would have a calm demeanour and a more carefree attitude.
- **Psychoticism** – someone who measures high on the psychoticism scale would be insensitive, unconventional and lack a conscience.

The psychoticism dimension differed from the other two, Eysenck argued, as he felt most people would gain a low score on the measure for psychoticism. With extraversion and neuroticism he felt the distribution would be more even, with most people falling in the middle of the spectrum and equal numbers on each end of the continuum.

### Eysenck Personality Questionnaire

There are several measures for Eysenck's theory, one of the most widely used being the Eysenck Personality Questionnaire (EPQ). This has about 100 items in its full version and 48 in the shorter version. Examples for items measuring each personality trait are as follows:

- **Extraversion**
  – Do you like to talk a lot?
  – Are you rather lively?
- **Neuroticism**
  – Do you worry about things that might happen?
  – Are your feelings rather easily hurt?

**YOU ARE THE RESEARCHER**
Personality is often measured using a questionnaire format. However, there are issues with validity and reliability using this method. What are these issues? Can you think of an alternative method or way of combatting these issues?

- Psychoticism
  - Do you seem to get into a lot of fights?
  - Would you enjoy practical jokes that could sometimes really hurt people?

## Biological basis to the theory

Eysenck argued that there was a biological basis to personality and that the predisposition to certain traits was inherited. In terms of criminal behaviour this is essentially saying that criminals are born with a higher chance of becoming an offender.

The biological basis to extraversion, Eysenck argued, was the level of cortical arousal in the brain. The reticular activating system (RAS) modulates the level of activation. This is rather like a car ticking over at standstill – some hardly fire at all, other engines are more revved up. Eysenck argued that if the residual level of activation is low, then a person will seek stimulation from the environment to raise the level. This will mean the brain is functioning at its optimum. Extraverts seek stimulation from their environment, so Eysenck argued their brains had lower residual activation levels. Conversely, introverts withdraw from too much stimulation because, Eysenck argued, their brain arousal level needed to be reduced to function at its best.

With neuroticism, Eysenck suggested that the biological basis was due to the autonomic nervous system. Some people react swiftly and strongly to stress physiologically and Eysenck argued that those measuring high for neuroticism would react quickly and to a greater degree.

Eysenck's argument for a biological basis to psychoticism is not detailed, although he did mention that androgens (male hormones) such as testosterone might be implicated.

## Eysenck's theory applied to criminal behaviour

The basic ideas underlying Eysenck's theory are that:

- offenders demonstrate distinctive personality traits or behaviour patterns
- there is apparently a genetic basis for these personality traits
- development of conscience, which can stop offending behaviour, may be faulty.

With regard to the traits, he argued that people measuring higher were more likely to commit crime, but for different reasons. High extraverts are sensation seekers and for that reason the 'thrill' of committing a crime might make them drawn to such behaviour. High neurotics experience high levels of emotion, meaning they would be more likely to commit a crime in an emotionally charged situation. They are also more likely to be conditioned because of their responsive autonomic nervous system and therefore they could be conditioned to commit crime. Individuals scoring high on the psychoticism scale are more likely to commit crime as they are aggressive and lack a conscience. This means there will be less holding them back and concern for others will not prevent them.

## Research

In a study by Furnham (1984), 210 UK non-delinquents were tested for personality, anomie (level of moral guidance) and social skills. The best predictor of self-reported delinquency was psychoticism, then neuroticism, then anomie, followed by extraversion and finally social skills.

**ON THE WEB**

If you wish to test yourself on the Eysenck personality test, a free one can be found at:

**http://similarminds.com/eysenck.html**

Farrington (1992) found, however, that research depends on the measure used for level of offending behaviour. 'Official' offenders (i.e. those who have been caught and convicted) are high in neuroticism and low in extraversion whereas when a self-report measure is used for criminal activity, those who report criminal behaviour are actually low in neuroticism and high in extraversion.

Heaven (1996) conducted a longitudinal study monitoring 282 14 year olds over two years. Findings showed that psychoticism was the best predictor of later delinquency.

### Evaluation

- Research findings do not clearly support Eysenck's theory for all three traits. Most studies have suggested that offenders score higher on psychoticism and neuroticism. However, results for extraversion are mixed. This could be due to the kind of crime measured, as certain personalities may be drawn to specific types of crime. Extraverts, for example, may be more likely to be drawn to crimes that raise adrenaline levels, and if these are not part of the measure of the research then their criminal tendencies will be missed.

- The measure used can clearly affect results (see Farrington's research), therefore it is difficult to establish the exact nature of the relationship. This means that careful consideration of the measure used should be made prior to drawing any conclusions. Responses are also potentially variable depending on the mood of the individual, so both the validity and reliability are questionable.

- The argument that personality is inherited and therefore an individual is born with a predisposition to crime has far-reaching implications. The legal system is based on the idea that a person is in charge of their own actions and if their personality is fixed at birth this does not fit with that idea. It calls into question whether someone is actually culpable of a crime they commit.

- Eysenck has been criticised for the original sample that he used to develop his theory. It could be argued that it did not cover an adequate range of people and therefore specific personality types will have emerged as dominant.

## Cognitive explanations

### Level of moral reasoning

Developmental theories of moral development often state that moral reasoning is a stage process, whereby as someone matures their moral reasoning becomes more sophisticated. Piaget adhered to this view and also felt that an individual's moral development was completed by the age of nine or ten. This fits with the age of criminal responsibility in the UK.

However, in contrast, Kohlberg suggested a stage theory of moral development where some individuals did not progress past certain levels. This thus makes them more likely to commit a crime. He said that there are three levels of moral development and two stages within each one of those levels, as shown in Table 10.4.

**Figure 10.7** When do we understand the difference between right and wrong?

**Table 10.4** Kohlberg's stages of moral reasoning

| Level | Stage | Reasoning behind committing a crime |
|---|---|---|
| Pre-conventional morality (consideration of the self) | Punishment stage | The most basic reasoning: will I be punished? If punishment is not definite, a crime is more likely to occur |
| | Reward stage | This is all about what there is to gain from the behaviour. If the potential gains are good then the crime is more likely to occur |
| Conventional morality (consideration of society) | Good-boy or good-girl stage | This stage considers what other people would think. If the closest people are criminals then the crime is more likely to occur |
| | Law-and-order stage | This stage considers obedience to the law. Is the act illegal? Someone at this stage would be less likely to commit a crime |
| Post-conventional morality (own mind) | Social contract stage | Someone at this stage adheres to the law but may commit a crime in certain circumstances, where they may feel the law should not apply |
| | Ethical principle stage | This stage is where the individual has their own moral code and may commit a crime if they feel the law is unjust |

The argument is that an offender who is at a lower stage of moral development will be more likely to commit a crime as they are thinking about how it affects them rather than society.

## Research

Hollin *et al.* (2002) suggested that offenders were in a less mature stage of moral development than non-offenders.

Palmer (2003) looked at the association between moral development and offending behaviour and suggested that it is specific moral values that are associated with offending and that there is a relationship between the two. The implication of this is that intervention programmes should incorporate training to increase offenders' level of reasoning. This work on moral reasoning therefore has practical implications.

Ashkar & Kenny (2007) compared the moral reasoning level of juvenile sex and non-sex offenders to see whether there were differences in the maturity of reasoning. When asked about their reasoning in contexts similar to their crimes, both groups had a pre-conventional level of moral reasoning (see Table 10.4). However, they showed higher (conventional) levels when it was a context that was unrelated to their crimes. This suggests that 1) moral reasoning varies by context and 2) offenders have a lower level of moral reasoning which is specific to their offending type.

> **Evaluation**
> - This theory was developed using a dilemma scenario and therefore is argued to be low in predictive reliability. The way a participant responds on a questionnaire and what they say they would do in certain situations may differ greatly from what would happen in reality.
> - Kohlberg's theory was also based on data from boys only and is therefore gender biased. Gilligan (1982) developed a theory that proposed gender differences following her work looking at the moral development of women. She argued that women focus on how an action affects other people and that men consider fairness and justice. Given the varying rates of crime between men and women it may be that moral development in genders is different. Kohlberg does not take this into account.
> - Work by Walker (1989) showed moral development over time, as Kohlberg suggested. This can account for the incidence of anti-social behaviour in younger adults.
> - Moral reasoning can account, to some extent, for the individual differences in offending behaviour. It can explain, for example, why one person would commit a crime but someone else would not.

## Cognitive distortions

### Hostile attribution bias and minimalisation

Attribution theory is a cognitive theory that considers the reasons people ascribe to behaviour. They make either internal attributions (it's my choice) or external attributions (it's the fault of the others).

## Hostile attribution bias

Hostile attribution bias is a cognitive style which makes the assumption that other people's actions are in some way a negative reaction to the self. Imagine the scenario. Sarah is walking up to a group of friends at the school gates. They are busy talking and therefore do not greet her immediately. Many people would perceive that as being due to them being engrossed in conversation and that it is no indication of negative feelings towards Sarah at all. However, as Sarah has a hostile attribution bias she will interpret this as being a sign they do not like her or are angry with her. She may feel they no longer wish to be her friend. This misperception would lead her to feel upset and angry with them.

Research has shown that there is a relationship between hostile attribution bias and aggression (Spielberger, 1988). The way this occurs is thought to be due to the fact that cues from behaviour are misinterpreted, which then leads to a hostile response and, if the situation calls for it, an aggressive act.

It seems that hostile attribution bias is linked to some types of aggression and not others. Impulsive aggression is characterised by reactive outbursts in situations and it is this kind of aggression that shows a link to hostile attribution bias (Giancola, 1995). Other aggression, such as premeditated acts designed to be aggressive to achieve goals, does not seem to be underpinned or susceptible to hostile attribution bias. This is probably because there is not an immediate reaction to a misinterpretation of behaviour. Premeditated aggression is used as a tool to get the individual what they want.

In research, hostile attribution bias is measured using hypothetical vignettes which can be interpreted as hostile/ambiguous or benign. The individual then says how angry they think they would feel if faced with that scenario.

## Research on hostile attribution bias

Work by Gudjonsson (1984) created a measure for the attributions which offenders use to apportion blame for criminal behaviour. The measure was called the blame attribution inventory. This measured three things:

1  The extent to which offenders blame circumstances in the environment.
2  The extent to which they blame mental illness or a lack of self-control.
3  The extent to which they feel guilt or remorse.

Research using the measure (Gudjonsson & Singh, 1988) found that offenders differ in their attributions depending on the type of crime they have committed.

Crick & Dodge (1994) found evidence to support a relationship between hostile attribution bias and aggression in children and adolescents. This was in hypothetical situations, but they also found the relationship in actual situations, which shows that the theoretical explanation applies to everyday behaviour, too.

Epps & Kendall (1995) found that college students who had high scores for anger and aggression demonstrated a high level of anger and hostility when tested for hostile attribution bias, even when the situation they were tested on was benign (although their response was not as angry in these situations as when they could be interpreted as negative).

## Research on the link to violence

Holtzworth-Munroe & Hutchinson (1993) found a link between hostile attribution bias and domestic violence. They showed men vignettes of difficult marital situations and asked them to rate the woman's behaviour in each case. Men who had been violent towards their wives were more likely to think that the woman was being negative towards the husband and that her intentions were hostile. This seems to demonstrate a cognitive style that might underpin their violent and aggressive acts.

### Evaluation

- There is research support to demonstrate a link between hostile attribution bias and offending behaviour. For this reason it is regarded as one of the precursors of aggressive behaviour in children, adolescents and adults. This can then lead to criminal behaviour.
- The use of hypothetical situations in the measures for hostile attribution bias means that the measure could be argued to lack predictive validity. This means that the answer given may not be the response that would actually occur in that situation if it actually happened. There is then the possibility that some people who measure low on the scale for hostile attribution bias actually may interpret a situation as more hostile than recorded (or the reverse effect may occur with those who measure high on the scale).

- Hostile attribution bias cannot be used to explain all offending behaviour. As explained, it does seem to be linked to impulsive aggression but cannot explain planned aggression well at all. For this reason it can be argued to be a factor in offender behaviour but is by no means the full explanation.

## Minimalisation

Minimalisation (referred to as minimisation) is a type of cognitive distortion that serves to downplay criminal behaviour by the offender. It can be described as self-deception, where the offender does not accept the full reality of the situation and will attempt to rationalise what they have done. This involves such strategies as downplaying the effects of the crime, trivialising the acts and maybe even attributing some of the blame to the victim. This helps the offender deal with the guilt they experience.

### Research

Alvaro & Gibbs (1996) found that when they measured for cognitive distortions in anti-social young adults there was a strong relationship between the level of antisocial behaviour and minimalisation, indicating that offenders may use minimalisation with negative behaviours.

Maruna & Mann (2006) examined the idea that using minimalisation to downplay crimes serves as a useful strategy to deal with guilt. They also considered how treatment programmes in prisons often try to challenge that minimalisation. They argue that the focus should be on the offender taking responsibility for the future rather than for past demeanours, and that minimalisation is seen as a psychologically healthy strategy in non-offending contexts. This means that rather than being seen as an explanation for why someone commits a crime, minimalisation is more to do with how they cope afterwards.

Kennedy & Grubin (1992) looked at the use of minimalisation by convicted sex offenders. The offenders' accounts of their offences were used and the researchers rated the accounts for their degree of denial. The majority of the offenders attempted to excuse their behaviour by blaming someone else, usually the victim. A third of the offenders denied any involvement at all, and a quarter believed that their victim benefited in some way from the abuse. It seems that for certain crimes at least minimalisation is used extensively by the offenders.

### Evaluation

- Research has shown that there is a relationship between the amount minimalisation is used and the level of offending behaviour in the criminal population. This means the idea is well supported by data.
- It can be argued that it is a coping strategy for after a crime has been committed rather than an explanation for why someone might commit a crime. However, by downplaying crimes, the likelihood of reoffending increases.
- There is more evidence for the use of minimalisation in some criminal populations than others. This means its influence on crime may depend on the type of crime, for example the relationship between minimalisation and sex offences is strong.

# Differential association theory

The **differential association theory** was described in detail by Sutherland in 1939 and was very influential at that time in deviance and delinquency research. It is a theory that explains how people learn to become criminals from their environment. It takes an integrated stance, which means it recognises the differing factors playing a part in causation of crime and combines them in one theory.

The dominant message is that crime is learned. This occurs by learning the motivations, attitudes and drives of those engaging in criminal activity around them. It is the contact with lots of favourable messages towards committing crime that increases the likelihood of delinquency. Sutherland called these messages 'favourable differentiations'.

> **KEY TERM**
>
> **Differential association theory** – a learning theory of offending behaviour

## Research

Matsueda (1988) argued, following a review of the literature on differential association theory, that there needed to be much more research conducted to improve the theory's ability to predict offending behaviour. He also stated that one of the main problems with the theory was that the concepts were vague. Making the theory easier to test would, he said, have implications for public policy.

Alarid *et al.* (2000) tested 1,153 newly convicted criminals for the extent to which differential association theory could explain their offending behaviour. They found that differential association served as a good general theory of crime and that it could explain offending behaviour, especially in men. They therefore argued that it was necessary to look at the context of offending and use it to predict the likelihood of someone committing a crime.

### Evaluation

- The theory is seen as being too general. It has similarities with social learning theory but has none of the detail of the cognitive processes that might underpin criminal behaviour. It is a sociological theory though, so Sutherland did not feel that a cognitive level of explanation was necessary.
- It cannot explain all crimes, such as embezzlement, which are individualistic and seemingly not influenced by others. One-off crimes are also not well explained using this theory.
- It can explain the prevalence of crime in certain areas. High crime rates are evident for certain areas, usually urban areas, and this theory explains how crime becomes endemic in such areas.

# Psychodynamic explanations

There are three psychodynamic explanations for offending behaviour: the superego, maternal deprivation hypothesis and defence mechanisms.

### The superego

The superego develops around the age of four and serves as an individual's conscience. It is also the superego that has the ability to stop a behaviour. A strong superego will mean that the person feels guilt for their actions and this level of guilt means that they are unlikely to do something they think will affect others in an adverse way (for example, a crime).

This psychodynamic explanation says that if a superego has not developed properly then the conscience and ability to stop behaviour do not develop fully either, making the person more likely to commit a crime. There are three ways that a superego can underpin crime:

1 **Deviant superego**. This focuses on the concept of identification, which occurs during the phallic stage (see pages 130–131), when the superego is developing. The argument is that the small child identifies with the same-sex parent to resolve their Oedipus complex (in the case of boys) or their Electra complex (in the case of girls). Identification means adopting similar behaviour to the same-sex parent and clearly, if that behaviour is deviant in any way, the small child adopts similar behaviours and morals.

2 **Overdeveloped superego**. This superego has not had an issue with developing as such, it is more that the superego is very developed and therefore the individual feels large amounts of guilt most of the time. This would seem to suggest that the person is less likely to commit crime, but the psychodynamic argument is that crime serves as a release from the overwhelming feelings of guilt. However, this relief is argued to occur only when the criminal is caught and punished. The punishment is a way of relieving the conscience. In other words, the punishment makes the individual feel better.

3 **Underdeveloped superego**. An underdeveloped superego can occur if there have been issues for the individual between the ages of approximately four and six when the superego is developing. If it does not develop sufficiently, the ability to feel guilt and stop behaviour is impaired. This leaves the person to be dominated by their id impulses. The id is the part of the personality that acts in a selfish manner and pursues pleasure. This can clearly lead to criminal activity.

### Maternal deprivation hypothesis

In Bowlby's 1965 work *Child Care and the Growth of Love*, he argued that the early years were vital in shaping the adult personality. If they receive love and care from their primary attachment figure then they will grow to be able to develop strong positive attachments for the rest of their lives. However, if a child does not receive this secure start in life, they are likely to be affected for the lifespan with issues in forming relationships.

If there is disruption (for example, a separation) in the relationship with the primary caregiver, this is said to be maternal deprivation. This means the child will form a negative representation of the world as a hostile place and they will struggle to form attachments. This could, it is argued, lead to delinquent behaviour as they grow.

---

**YOU ARE THE RESEARCHER**

As the superego is a psychodynamic concept, it is tested using projective tests such as the ink blot test and using dream analysis. These methods are criticised for their validity. Why is the validity an issue?

> **CLASSIC RESEARCH**

### Bowlby's 44 thieves study of maternal deprivation (1944)

#### Aim
To test the maternal deprivation hypothesis by looking at a delinquent population to see whether separation had been experienced.

#### Procedure
Bowlby interviewed 44 juvenile delinquents who had been caught stealing from a psychiatric facility (the 'thieves') and 44 'controls' who were also at the facility but had not stolen (the 'controls').

Bowlby, as the psychiatrist, interviewed the children and mothers separately.

He interviewed the juveniles first to ascertain their personalities. Bowlby diagnosed affection-less psychopathy where there was a lack of affection for or empathy to others. He also established whether they felt a lack of guilt or shame at their actions and that informed the diagnosis.

The families were interviewed to determine whether the thieves had had prolonged early separations from their primary caregiver in their first two years of life.

#### Findings
The results were as shown in Table 10.5.

| Had they been involved in offending behaviour? | Yes | | | | No | |
|---|---|---|---|---|---|---|
| | 44 Thieves | | | | 44 Controls | |
| Diagnosed as affectionless psychopaths? | Yes | | No | | No | |
| | 14 | | 30 | | 0 | |
| Had they been separated from primary caregiver for 6+ months before the age of two? | Yes | No | Yes | No | Yes | No |
| | 12 | 2 | 5 | 25 | 2 | 42 |

**Table 10.5** Bowlby's 44 thieves study of maternal deprivation (1944)

#### Conclusions
The results seem to indicate that:

- if a child has experienced early separation from the primary caregiver for more than six months then the chance that they will become delinquent is greater
- if a child has experienced early separation from the primary caregiver for more than six months then they are more likely to be affectionless psychopaths.

Bowlby drew conclusions that the maternal deprivation can, to some extent, explain offending behaviour.

#### Evaluation
- This study was influential and supports the psychodynamic explanation of offending behaviour, but has been heavily criticised for its methodology and potential bias.

## Defence mechanisms

Defence mechanisms are used by the unconscious mind to reduce anxiety. This is because psychodynamic theorists believe that anxiety will weaken the ego, and the id or the superego will become dominant.

There are many documented defence mechanisms, but there are a few that are implicated in offending behaviour:

- **Displacement** – this is when the focus of a strong emotion is shifted from its actual target to a neutral target. In terms of offending behaviour an example of this might be a young man fighting a stranger in a pub because he is really angry with his parents.
- **Sublimation** – this is when a strong id impulse is expressed in a more socially accepted way, such as a football supporter wanting to murder but instead getting involved in football hooliganism. This still is not socially acceptable but is seen to be a diluted expression of the unconscious desire.

- **Rationalisation** – this is explaining behaviour in a rational and acceptable way when it is actually very negative. Offenders use this defence mechanism as a form of justification for their crime. An example would be a woman who kills prostitutes because she believes they are a threat to a civilised society.

### Evaluation

- There is a shortage of empirical research testing these ideas and therefore the ideas are not well supported. The concepts (e.g. phallic stage, superego) upon which they are based are also not empirically supported and this means the theoretical grounding on which the explanations are based is flawed.
- Research support for the maternal deprivation hypothesis comes from Bowlby's 44 thieves study. However, this is a retrospective study which was interpreted by Bowlby himself, so the results may be influenced by experimenter bias.
- Many of the theoretical concepts such as defence mechanisms are believed to generate from the unconscious mind and this means that they are untestable.
- There are many examples of individuals who have experienced problems in their early childhood and have not become criminals. This suggests that even if the explanations are correct, they are not complete.

### STRENGTHEN YOUR LEARNING

1. Explain Eysenck's theory of offending behaviour.
2. What strengths does Eysenck's theory have?
3. Outline evidence to suggest that the level of moral reasoning may affect offending behaviour.
4. Explain what is meant by hostile attribution bias.
5. Explain what is meant by minimalisation.
6. How does differential association theory explain offender behaviour?
7. How does the development of the superego affect offending behaviour?
8. Outline two weaknesses of the psychodynamic theory of offending.

# ASSESSMENT CHECK

1. Select from the stages A, B and C below to complete the table relating to the levels of Kohlberg's theory of moral understanding. One level will be left over. **[2 marks]**

   **A** Law and order stage

   **B** Punishment stage

   **C** Social contract stage

   | Levels of Kohlberg's theory | Stage of Kohlberg's theory |
   | --- | --- |
   | Pre-conventional morality | |
   | Conventional morality | |

2. A researcher measured the extraversion scores of offenders and non-offenders as part of their research. The mean of the non-offenders' scores on the scale developed by the researcher was 12 and the mean of the offenders' scores was 14 on the scale. The scale ran from 0–26.

   Sketch a graph to show the mean scores of each group. Label the axes and mark on the positions of the mean for each group. **[4 marks]**

3. 'It can be argued that criminals are born, not made.'

   Using your knowledge of the genetic explanation for offender behaviour, explain why some believe offenders are born with a predisposition to commit crime. **[4 marks]**

4. Outline one personality characteristic thought by Eysenck to be implicated in explaining offender behaviour. **[4 marks]**

5. Describe and evaluate the neural explanation for offending behaviour. **[16 marks]**

# 10.5 Dealing with offending behaviour

> 'To have once been a criminal is no disgrace. To remain a criminal is the disgrace.'
> Malcolm X (1957)

## The aims of custodial sentencing

**KEY TERMS**

**Custodial sentencing** – a prison sentence

**Deterrence** – a method of stopping someone doing something (in this context it is used regarding crime prevention)

**Rehabilitation** – to change the behaviour of an offender to being a non-offender

**Custodial sentencing** is when an offender is found guilty in court and as punishment spends time in a prison (or young offenders' institution). It would be easy to say that the sole purpose of custodial sentencing therefore is to punish the offender. However, it is argued to serve many functions for the offender, victim and society. These functions fall into four categories: **deterrence**, retribution, confinement and **rehabilitation**.

### Deterrence

This is the idea that prison serves to prevent criminals reoffending. It works on the simple, behaviourist principle that prisoners will learn that crime is punished and therefore they will not want to commit a crime again. Recidivism, which is reoffending, is discussed later in this chapter and can be used to measure whether the aim has been met or not.

### Retribution

This, as an aim, focuses on the feelings of the victim(s), their close family, friends and society generally. It is the idea that if the offender has 'hurt' someone else, they should pay for their actions in some way. By sending them to prison they lose their freedom and this is seen as a necessary consequence of their actions. It is sometimes argued that this is the main reason why prisons exist as statistics indicate that it does not serve to prevent reoffending.

### Confinement

While in prison or a young offenders' institution the offender is not free to commit other crimes. This aim is known as confinement. Some offenders, such as violent offenders or sex offenders, are seen to pose a threat to society. By putting them in prison for a period of time they are no longer a threat to society.

### Rehabilitation

It is argued that a prison sentence allows for rehabilitation of the offender so they are less likely to reoffend. Counselling and offender programmes are offered within prison. If successful, this offers the chance for the offender to sort problems or learn skills to mean that they are in a better position to lead a crime-free life once released.

**Figure 10.8** Custodial sentencing serves several purposes

> **Evaluation**
> - It appears, from recidivism rates, that the aims of deterrence and rehabilitation are not fulfilled by custodial sentencing as reoffending rates are high (see Recidivism, later in the chapter).
> - The idea that prison serves to rehabilitate is also questionable as it is seen as a potential source of information on how to commit crimes with more skill. It has even been named the 'College of Crime' by some commentators. This means that it possibly has the opposite effect to rehabilitation.
> - Retribution and confinement are argued to be the main reason we have prisons in society. They are not seen as a deterrent by some prisoners (Davis & Raymond, 2000) and so the focus of custodial sentencing moves to fulfilling the needs of the victim and society. They do provide a method of punishment that the legal system can administer and they ensure that the offender cannot commit more crime while they are incarcerated.

# The psychological effects of custodial sentencing

*'Solitary confinement is too terrible a punishment to inflict on any human being, no matter what his crime. Hardened criminals in the men's prisons, it is said, often beg for the lash instead.'*

Emmeline Pankhurst (1912)

The idea of psychological effects from a custodial sentence should come as no surprise. Indeed, the fact that prison is designed to act as a punishment means that it is predicted, by the principles of operant conditioning, to have an effect. However, there are other potential psychological effects, such as the offender becoming institutionalised, negative effects on mental health and potentially an increase in aggressive behaviour.

## Becoming institutionalised

Inmates can become institutionalised and this has an effect on their behaviour. The participants in Zimbardo's 1971 Stanford Prison Study (see Book 1, page 13) illustrated that individuals become influenced by the setting and lose their confidence to act.

Prisoners can also become institutionalised due to their background and living conditions they have 'on the outside'. If they are homeless or have a poor standard of living they might like the routine of prison and the fact that they have a bed, a roof over their head and food available to them. If this is the case then they will be likely to reoffend just so they can get back into prison.

The psychological effect of prison for some, then, is positive. Prison is not a punishment but acts more as a positive reinforcement for offending behaviour.

## Negative effects on mental health

The Stanford Prison Study (Zimbardo, 1971) showed how being incarcerated can have a negative effect on the well-being of the individual. There has been particular focus on the levels of suicide in prison as they stand at a higher rate than suicide rates out in the community (Crighton, 2006). Crighton & Towl (2008) observed that numbers of suicides among offenders in prison have increased of late in the UK. Factors suggested are overcrowding, low staff-to-offender ratio, lack of access to medical services and physical exercise, together with the increased risk of physical assault. It also appears that settling into the new environment is an issue as the risk of suicide among offenders is greater in the first 30 days of incarceration, so the adjustment required for some prisoners is evidently too much.

Another indication that prisoners' mental health is affected negatively is the fact that there are increasingly high levels of self-harm among offenders. This could be due to the frustration of being incarcerated and/or an attempt to regain control.

## Research

Zimbardo's Stanford Prison Study (1971) illustrates the effects incarceration can have on individuals. The mental health of one participant was affected so much that the participant had to withdraw from the study. This is potentially because of the withdrawal of freedom and treatment from the 'guards'. Caution should be used in generalising to real prisons from this study, however, as the setting was experimental and therefore ecological validity is low.

Snow (2006) examined the characteristics of prisoners who self-harm and compared them with those who are suicidal. She found that the offenders who self-harm are qualitatively different to those who commit or attempt to commit suicide in that the self-harmers display high levels of anger and stress whereas the ones who are suicidal withdraw and show signs of depression. Both, however, are displaying psychological effects of being in prison and a decline in mental health.

Cheeseman (2003) found that many aggressive incidents in prison occurred due to the need to relieve stress. This suggests that aggressive incidents in prison could be due to the surroundings being highly stressful, so the aggression is an effect of the circumstance.

Hollin (1992) stated in his research that there was evidence to suggest that prison became 'home' to some prisoners. The fact that they received three meals a day together with a bed and companionship was preferable to them than what they had to deal with outside of prison.

### Evaluation

- It is difficult to know whether the mental health issues within the prison are due to the context or whether they were already part of the individual. It could be that the offender committed a crime due to their mental health. It would therefore be an error to state that it is an effect of the prison setting. For example, aggressiveness could be due to the people who are put in prison, and they could have displayed high levels of aggression prior to incarceration. A full discussion of the reason behind aggression levels in prison can be found in Chapter 9, page 330.

• It is argued by some that a decline in mental health is necessary for the individual to be punished in prison. They state that is a necessary consequence of the situation and that if prison did not have a negative effect it would not be effective.

### PSYCHOLOGY IN THE REAL WORLD

#### Offenders with poor mental health

There is much research to suggest that the mental health of prisoners is, in part, what underpins high rates of recidivism.

In a report by Coid *et al.* (2007), the mental health of prisoners had a direct effect on recidivism rates. The researchers found that offenders in the UK who received treatment for their mental health problems while in prison were 60 per cent less likely to reoffend than untreated prison inmates. They were also significantly less likely to commit violent acts than untreated inmates. Indeed, Coid *et al.* found that they were 80 per cent less likely to commit violent acts.

There are moves globally to consider what the mental health of an offender is like as they start their prison sentence. Treatments are then put in place, where possible. There is also a move within the USA to introduce 'mental health courts', which are designed to treat mentally ill offenders who cannot plead guilty by reason of insanity. Offenders within these courts are sentenced and administered treatment but are not given custodial sentences.

**Figure 10.9** It is important to consider the mental health of offenders

# Recidivism

The rates for **recidivism** are a cause for concern. In the 'proven' reoffending statistics for October 2011 to September 2012 for England and Wales (published in July 2014):

- 573 000 adult and juvenile offenders were cautioned, convicted or released from custody
- 149 000 (26 per cent) of these committed a proven reoffence within one year. It is possible that more have committed offences but not been caught
- 438 000 proven reoffences were committed within a year, with an average of 2.9 offences per offender.

These rates are concerning as it appears the purpose of prison in terms of prevention of crime works for only some prisoners. There are several proposed ideas as to why recidivism rates might be high: becoming institutionalised, non-adherence to behaviourist principles and mental health/addiction issues.

### KEY TERM

**Recidivism** – reoffending following judicial punishment. Committing the same, or another, crime again

## Prisoners becoming institutionalised

There is an issue with prisoners getting used to being in prison and their day being organised. Their basic physiological needs are met and they have a sense of belongingness as there are fellow inmates in a similar position. If they come from a home environment where their daily life is a struggle, it is easy to see how offenders might reoffend to go back into prison.

When asked about what would help prevent recidivism, inmates report that support following release is the main way it can be prevented. Offenders state they need better employment prospects, help reintegrating into family life and relationship counselling.

## Non-adherence to behaviourist principles

Behaviourist principles state that the greatest amount of effect for punishment or reinforcement is if it is received at the same time as the action. This is time contiguity. Sentencing occurs some time later than the actual crime is committed, so the action and punishment do not coincide. The argument is that the connection between the two is therefore weaker. The strength of the association should be strong to be effective.

## Mental health and addiction issues

The likelihood of reoffending can be increased if an inmate's mental health is unstable. This could be prompted by the prison situation (see page 332) or they could already be suffering prior to conviction. Poor mental health, especially addiction disorders, is related to crime rates, so the problem, if not treated in prison, makes an offender vulnerable to reoffending (see Psychology in the real world, page 381).

# Research

Malott & Fromader (2010) conducted a survey with 102 Australian male offenders asking them about how they felt about release from prison and what they felt would reduce the likelihood of recidivism. They found that the offenders felt unsupported upon release and said that a greater level of accessible resources, treatment and/or support services after release would help reduce their recidivism. This supports the idea that offenders can feel institutionalised and that by reoffending they re-enter an environment that is organised for them rather than an unsupported outside environment.

Hanson & Bussiere (1998) looked at the reason why sexual offenders reoffended. The rates were low at 13.4 per cent, but the main indicators for the likelihood of reoffending were found to be lack of completion of treatment within prison and the level of sexual deviancy. They found that other factors, such as age, prior offences and level of juvenile delinquency, predicted recidivism, similarly to non-sexual offender populations. This indicates that clear groups can be identified at risk, which suggests the same underlying reasons for reoffending are occurring.

Cartier *et al.* (2006) researched the link between drug abuse and recidivism rates. They found a clear relationship between substance abuse and reoffending rates, although interestingly this was not linked to violent offences. This suggests that a mental health issue such as an addiction, if not treated within the prison system, can lead to reoffending.

> ### YOU ARE THE RESEARCHER
> Recidivism is clearly an issue in the UK. Imagine you have been given the job by the government to run a research project to establish why the rates are so high.
>
> How would you go about this? What method would you use to collect your data and why?

### Evaluation

- Self-report measures from offenders are problematic as offenders may not be able to reliably report why they have reoffended. There may be an inclination to adopt an external locus of control where they see issues with the system, rather than themselves, as being the reason they have reoffended. Trammel (2002), in her work looking at reoffending rates and locus of control, did indeed find that reoffenders were more likely to have an external locus of control.
- Although it can be said that custodial sentences do not work as deterrents, because of recidivism rates it is important to consider the other reasons why prisons are used. These include retribution and confinement. It is possible that recidivism rates are high and will remain so because society requires the offender to be kept out of society (confinement) and that they pay for their crime (retribution).
- It is important to consider that the recidivism rates may be due to the 'outside world' rather than prison and that until societal problems such as poverty and lack of support for mental health are addressed, the recidivism will remain high. Most research is centred on the prison rather than the post-release environment.
- Figures for recidivism are based on proven crimes that have been put through the court systems. The figure is likely to be higher as some reoffences will go undetected or will never reach court. Therefore, although rates are thought to be high, the numbers are inaccurate and will probably be greater.

## Behaviour modification in custody

Behaviour modification programmes are one of the methods used in rehabilitation of prisoners. Behaviour modification adheres to the principles of behaviourism, specifically operant conditioning. The idea is to increase the desirable behaviours and decrease the undesirable behaviours using positive reinforcement, negative reinforcement and punishment.

In the controlled conditions of a prison, reinforcement schedules can be imposed and there are a restricted number of options for reward. Most behaviour modification programmes are based around a token economy system. So, when good behaviour occurs, prisoners 'earn' tokens which can then be exchanged for desirable goods such as cigarettes or food. This kind of programme was first used with the mentally ill (see pages 216–217) and then in the 1960s the principle was applied to prisoners. This is simply using the principle of positive reinforcement to try to make sure the good behaviour continues and undesirable behaviour is stamped out.

There is also the threat of taking back tokens from prisoners when they have behaved badly. This is negative reinforcement and when working with the positive reinforcement of gaining tokens can be a powerful tool to modify behaviour.

### Research

Rice (1990) examined the outcomes from 92 prisoners on a token economy programme in a maximum-security psychiatric hospital and found two things: 1) that if it was effective for an individual then it continued to be so while in the institution, 2) the success shown within the institution had no influence on the offender's outcomes once released. This seems to suggest that it works for certain individuals only and only short term. It also means that the programme has no rehabilitative benefits.

Reppucci & Saunders (1974) found, through their research, that although the behaviour management programmes should, in theory, be easy to run, they are not. This was due to institutional pressures, limited resources and inconsistency with staff. There were instances of the 'rules' being adapted, which weakened the impact.

Hobbs & Tyllon (1976) found that introduction of a behaviour modification programme in three young offenders' institutions reduced the amount of undesirable behaviour within the institution when compared with an institution that had no such programme. This demonstrates the short-term benefits that behaviour modification can have.

### Evaluation

- Behaviour modification programmes work well in the short term but there is little evidence to suggest they work once the offender has left the institution. This means they have limited rehabilitative effect, which is not the aim of the programme. The reason for this lack of transfer to the 'real world' is probably due to prison being a very controlled environment. It is also probably because the reward (and punishment) needs to be administered immediately, which is not possible out of prison.
- Behaviour modification programmes have received criticism for contravening human rights. There is not an issue with the administration of positive reinforcement but with withholding such things as visits from relatives. These are seen as a right for prisoners and therefore withholding them is not a reasonable action within a civilised society.
- Behaviour modification takes little training or expense to use within an institution. This makes it one of the cheaper options available and it is also easier to introduce as there is less issue with staff being skilled to administer it, unlike other interventions such as anger management.

## Anger management

Anger management is a cognitive intervention that aims to help the offender control their feelings of anger. Many crimes have the emotion of anger as their root cause and so this intervention is designed to prevent anger prompting criminal acts.

The anger management training is based on the offenders learning and practising skills. This is focused on controlling impulses and anger. Anger management programmes follow a three-stage process:

1. **Cognitive preparation**. This is where an offender will spend time understanding what makes them angry and identifying triggers that are liable to make them react with anger. This means talking to an anger management therapist to remember experiences of anger and what led to that feeling. This is a very individualised part of the training as the cues for anger vary from person to person and it is vital to know what situation will make the angry feeling escalate.

**Figure 10.10** Anger management can be an important tool in crime prevention

It is recognised by anger management therapists that it is almost impossible to stop someone feeling angry, but it is possible to mediate the anger and prevent it from escalating.

2. **Skill acquisition**. The content of this second stage is dependent on the individual's response to the first. There are skills that can be taught, such as relaxation techniques and assertiveness techniques. Social skills training is invaluable as anger can stem from frustration at being unable to communicate in a social situation. This section is bespoke. It is individualised in line with the offenders' needs, which are identified from the first stage.

3. **Application training**. The final stage is designed to provide an opportunity for the offenders to practise their newly acquired skills. This can be done using role play in both realistic and imaginary situations. The idea is that offenders are prepared in future for situations that might have been an issue for them in the past. Using the new skills they have learned, the situation will no longer lead to criminal acts. They will be able to respond in a non-aggressive way.

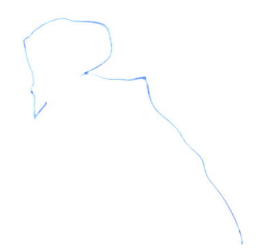

## Research

Research by Ireland (2000) showed that anger management programmes can be very successful. In the research, 50 prisoners completed two measures of anger both before and after completion of an anger management programme which involved 12 hours' worth of intervention spread out into 1-hour intervals over three days. The measures were a self-report questionnaire and a checklist of 29 problematic behaviours. There was also a control group of 37 prisoners (matched for offending behaviour profile) who did not have any intervention and completed the same measures. The results from the two groups were compared. There was a 92 per cent reduction in anger levels for the intervention group on at least one of the measures.

Howells *et al.* (2005) measured the success level of an anger management programme with violent offenders. They found that the programme reduced anger, but not to a statistically significant level. They also found that the level of anger reported prior to the intervention was an indicator of success, as was offenders' readiness to take part in the programme.

Koons *et al.* (1997) examined the factors that seemed to contribute the most to anger management interventions with offenders. They found that offenders and practitioners both suggested that an individualised programme was effective together with the way it was delivered by staff. It seems the trainers needed to be selected carefully to give the programme every chance of success.

### Evaluation

- Practising the skills in a role-play situation is argued to be too different from real life. The level and intensity of emotion are greater in a real-life situation, so the offender could find that the ability to apply the skill is hindered and they revert to their former behaviour.
- It is difficult to measure how successful an intervention has been. Levels of recidivism are one such measure, but there are many possible reasons why someone may reoffend, so any repeat of criminal behaviour may not be due to the failure of the anger management

programme. Using recidivism as a measure is also problematic because it only measures when a person is reconvicted. This means that the intervention may not be working on a day-to-day basis and this failure is not picked up.

- There is a lack of evidence that anger management programmes work well long term. It is possible that the effects are short term only and this means that the offender is in danger of reoffending at some point.
- Anger management gives the offender insight into how they think and can help them gain an understanding of problems in their thinking which have led them to offending behaviour in the past. It is possible that a cognitive intervention such as anger management can make them function better in everyday life because of the insight gained from the intervention.
- As with all cognitive interventions, an offender must be motivated and engage fully with the programme. It is difficult to change thought processes that are deeply entrenched, so motivation and a willingness to try hard are pivotal in its success. Some offenders do not have this focus and so for them the intervention does not work well.

## Restorative justice programmes

**Restorative justice** is a relatively new type of intervention with offenders. The aim is to make the offender realise the implications of their actions for the victim or victims and to improve their relationships with the victims and community by repairing the harm they have caused. This method also addresses some of the needs of the victim(s) to improve their recovery from the crime.

Restorative justice can be used instead of a custodial sentence, but it is also used alongside a custodial sentence in more serious crimes. The first step is to seek cooperation from both the victim and the offender. It will not work if one or other party is not interested in being involved. It should also not cause any further trauma to the victim, so it is important that they are happy to be involved.

Face-to-face meetings, mediation or indirect mediation are set up so that the offender and victim can communicate in a controlled setting. What happens in those meetings varies with the circumstance and the individuals involved. The victim is usually able to ask for answers to any questions they might have and to say what they want to say to the offender in a neutral setting.

There is also the potential to use practical reparation in restorative justice programmes. This means that the offender repairs the damage they may have done to property, for example painting over graffiti. This can be used when there is vandalism to property and it ensures that the community sees that the 'wrong' against the community is rectified.

### Research

Miers *et al.* (2001) examined the extent to which victims felt happy with restorative justice programmes. The majority of victims were happy with the outcome, although some were cynical about the offenders' sincerity and their motivation for taking part, i.e. they were doing it to reduce their sentence. Some also found that it made uncomfortable feelings resurface and some victims found it intimidating.

### KEY TERM

**Restorative justice** – where an offender meets with a victim and tries to make amends for the crime committed, thus helping the offender avoid further bad behaviour

**Figure 10.11** Restorative justice aims to make offenders realise the implications of their actions

Sherman & Strong (2007) looked at the perspective and judgement of the offenders. They found that the offenders said they had found it beneficial and there was a decrease in reoffending rates following the use of restorative justice.

Restorative justice compares favourably with other forms of punishment. There is research to suggest the reoffending rate is lower and both the victim and offender report higher levels of satisfaction with the technique (Latimer, Dowden & Muise, 2012).

### Evaluation

- Restorative justice is considerably cheaper than a custodial sentence so it is a popular option to sentencing by the court. It is also advantageous practically (in practical reparation cases) and psychologically helpful to the victim.
- There is potentially a problem with the satisfaction levels expressed by the victims and offenders. There is a self-selection bias in that both parties need to be willing to enter the programme. It may be that the restorative justice programme works really well for certain individuals but cannot be used for everybody. This limits the applicability of this type of punishment.
- There are high levels of attrition in the programme. This may be because both the victim and the offender find it harder to complete than they originally thought. It may also be, in the case of the victim at least, that it is not fulfilling what they wanted to achieve.

### ON THE WEB

A film of the victim's viewpoint of restorative justice programmes can be seen at **www.youtube.com**. Search for 'Victim's voice – restorative justice helps victims'.

Many YouTube clips on restorative justice programmes are available if you are interested in hearing what both the victims and the offenders have to say.

### STRENGTHEN YOUR LEARNING

1. Explain the aims of custodial sentencing.
2. What are the proposed psychological effects of custodial sentences for the offender?
3. Outline evidence to suggest why recidivism occurs.
4. Explain what is meant by behaviour modification of offenders.
5. Outline evidence to support the use of anger management with prisoners.
6. Explain what restorative justice programmes entail.

# ASSESSMENT CHECK

1. Select from the descriptions of therapist actions A, B and C below to complete the table relating to the stages of anger management. One description will be left over. **[2 marks]**

   **A** Offenders learn new skills to help them combat their feelings of anger

   **B** Offenders rehearse how they might act in a situation that might make them angry

   **C** Understanding of triggers to angry outbursts is established

   | Stages of anger management | Description |
   | --- | --- |
   | Cognitive preparation | |
   | Application training | |

2. To investigate the effectiveness of a behaviour modification programme, psychologists observed the behaviour of prisoners at meal times which they had noted was a particularly difficult time and a time when there was a higher than average number of violent incidents. They used behavioural categories to assess the number of aggressive acts both before and after the programme had been used.

   How could the psychologists test the data for reliability and what steps could be taken to ensure the data was as reliable as possible? **[1 + 2 marks]**

3. Read the item and then answer the question:

   Statistics show that the rate of recidivism in the UK is high, suggesting prison does not work.

   Using your knowledge of the reasons behind recidivism, explain why criminals reoffend. **[4 marks]**

4. Briefly outline and evaluate the effectiveness of anger management in treating offenders. **[4 marks]**

5. Describe and evaluate the use of behaviour modification in custody to deal with offending behaviour. **[16 marks]**

## SUMMARY

**Problems in defining crime**

- Defining crime is not a straightforward process. It can be affected by the culture, historical context, age of the perpetrator and the unique circumstances of the crime.

**Ways of measuring crime**

- Official statistics are one way of measuring crime, although the statistics cannot be totally accurate due to under-reporting of crime, inaccuracies of records and not all crimes being part of the statistics such as new technology crimes.
- Offender surveys are used to help compile information on crimes and to try to measure the 'dark side' of crime which is not traditionally picked up by official statistics. However, offender surveys are also inaccurate due to them being a self-report measure.

**Offender profiling**

- There are two types of offender profiling: top-down and bottom-up. Top-down profiling is where the experience and intuition of the profiler is used to build a profile and is sometimes called the typological approach. Characteristics of the profiler are derived from the crime scene.
- Bottom-up profiling uses geographical information and investigative profiling to build a picture of the offender. Previous information on similar crimes is used and the profile is not affected as much by the profiler conducting the investigation as with top-down profiling.

**Biological explanations of offending behaviour**

- Atavistic form is an early biological explanation for offender behaviour which is based on the idea that the physical features of an individual can show a genetic predisposition to be a criminal. This is due, it is argued, to the individual being less 'civilised' in evolutionary terms.
- Twin, family and adoption studies suggest there may be a genetic predisposition to offender behaviour. This is because concordance rates for monozygotic twins are higher than dizygotic twins, crime rates are greater in certain families and data from adoption studies suggests a genetic influence.
- There are three neurotransmitters that are implicated in offending behaviour; high levels of noradrenaline, low levels of serotonin and dopamine due to its links to addiction.
- The neural explanation for offending behaviour focuses predominantly on the limbic system and how it may affect processing of emotion and empathy. There is also some research that suggests that brain development in the frontal lobe is implicated in offender behaviour.

**Psychological explanations of offending behaviour**

- Eysenck's theory of personality suggests high levels of extraversion, neuroticism and psychoticism are linked to criminal behaviour. He also suggested that there was a biological underpinning to these characteristics.
- Kohlberg's levels of moral reasoning are also thought to be linked to the likelihood to commit crime. Those in the pre-conventional stage are thought to be more likely to become an offender as they think about themselves rather than others.

## Dealing with offender behaviour

- Attribution theory is a cognitive theory that considers the reasons people ascribe to behaviour. They make either internal attributions or external attributions. If attributions are external and hostile they are more likely to lead to criminal behaviour.
- Minimalisation is a form of self-denial which allows the offender to downplay the effects of their offences. It is a cognitive strategy which helps the offender deal with the guilt they experience. It seems to be evident in some groups of offenders more than others, for example research shows a strong presence of minimalisation in sex offenders.
- Differential association theory states that the environment a person grows up in predisposes them to crime. This is because some people are exposed to a higher number of positive messages (favourable differentiations) to committing crime.
- Psychodynamic explanations for offending behaviour focus on poor development of the superego. The superego can be deviant, overdeveloped or underdeveloped. Defence mechanisms such as displacement, sublimation and rationalisation are also implicated.
- The aims of custodial sentencing are deterrence, retribution, confinement and rehabilitation. However, the psychological effects include becoming institutionalised, negative impact on mental health and aggressive behaviour.
- Recidivism is a cause for concern in the UK. The main reasons thought to be accountable for the high recidivism rates are prisoners becoming institutionalised, non-adherence to behaviourist principles and mental health/addiction issues.
- Behaviour modification is based on behaviourist principles of operant conditioning and looks to reward good behaviour and punish poor behaviour in prison. This is often through the use of a token economy.
- Anger management programmes use cognitive techniques to alter offenders' thought processes so that they can cope better with their anger and avoid reoffending.
- Restorative justice programmes are a new technique of helping the victim come to terms with the crime and for the offender to realise the effects their crime has had on the victim, their family and society. This is facilitated by organised supervised meetings between the victim and the offender.

# 11 Addiction

## Introduction

Addiction has far-reaching consequences for an addict's life and affects the lives of the family and friends around them. It is a complex issue that requires understanding at both a biological and a psychological level.

Specific focus here will be upon:

1. Describing addiction
2. Risk factors in the development of addiction
3. Explanations for nicotine and gambling addiction
4. How to reduce addiction using treatments and theories.

### Understanding the specification

- You need to be able to describe addiction, specifically physical and psychological dependence, tolerance and withdrawal syndrome.
- It is important you can understand and evaluate the risk factors in the development of addiction, e.g. genetic vulnerability, stress, personality, family influences and peers.
- You need to be able to explain nicotine addiction with a special focus on brain neurochemistry, especially the role of dopamine, and learning theory. Cue reactivity needs to be learned well as this too could be asked about specifically.
- Similarly to nicotine addiction you need to learn the learning theory explanation for gambling addiction, including reference to partial and variable reinforcement. You also need to understand the cognitive explanation for gambling which must include cognitive bias.
- There are many ways of reducing addiction and you must know specifically drug therapy, behavioural interventions (which must include aversion therapy and covert sensitisation) and cognitive behavioural therapy.
- You need to be able to apply theory to reducing addiction, specifically the theory of planned behaviour and Prochaska's six-stage model of behaviour change.

These are the basic requirements of the specification. However, other relevant material is included to provide depth and detail to your understanding.

> 'Every form of addiction is bad, no matter whether the narcotic be alcohol or morphine or idealism.'
>
> Carl Jung (1962)

## IN THE NEWS

# Ψ The Psychological Enquirer

## Two mobile phone addicts treated in Spain

**Figure 11.1** Mobile phone addiction can be a problem

An increasing amount of research indicates that mobile phone addiction is the new form of addiction.

In Spain two children aged 12 and 13 were suspected of having an addiction to their mobile phones. Their parents sent them to a mental health clinic because they argued their children's reliance on their mobile phones was interrupting their daily life and hindering their ability to function.

The children had owned their mobile phones for 18 months and they initially had unrestricted usage of the devices. However, their parents had started to notice that their typical behaviour had changed. They had started to underperform at school and the parents reported they had also started lying to con money out of family members. This prompted the parents to seek treatment for their children. The children were treated over three months and had no access to their mobile phones in that time.

This story alludes to the potential problem of phone addiction globally. But how do we know if someone is addicted?
Look at these statistics from a study of cell phone addiction in college students (Roberts and Pirog, 2013):

- College students use their mobile phones 9 hours a day.
- 94.6 minutes a day were spent texting.
- 38.6 minutes a day were spent checking Facebook.
- 34.4 minutes were spent per day surfing the internet.
- 26.9 minutes a day were spent listening to music.

Do you use your mobile phone (if you have one) this often? When was the last time you checked it? Would you consider yourself addicted? Describing addiction is problematic, especially for new addictions that are not clinically defined such as mobile phone addiction. The criteria set out for substance addiction (below) describe how addictive behaviour may appear. Application to a behavioural addiction such as mobile phone usage is difficult even though many of the symptoms are similar, such as interference with important social, occupational or recreational activities.
Gauging whether someone is addicted relies on judgement so is therefore subjective. The fact that new addictions arise as technology advances also highlights the problems of describing addiction.

# 11.1 Describing addiction

*'Anything that you can become obsessed with, and you do so much that you don't do the things you need to do with family, friends, school, job - that can be an addiction. And texting absolutely can qualify.'*

Dale Archer (2010)

## Psychological and physiological dependence

Probably the best way to describe psychological and physiological dependence to a substance is to refer to the diagnostic manual to see what is now defined as addiction or dependence. This varies whether it is dependence on substance (like nicotine) or behavioural (like gambling). Alcohol is given separate diagnostic criteria.

DSM-5 states the following criteria to be diagnosed with substance dependence (mild to severe). There is a list of 11 symptoms, of which two need to be evident for diagnosis to be made. They also need to be present together in the same 12-month period. The 11 indicators are:

- Taking the substance in larger amounts or for longer than intended.
- Wanting to cut down or stop using the substance but not being able to.
- Spending a lot of time getting, using, or recovering from use of the substance.
- Cravings and urges to use the substance.
- Not managing to do what you should at work, home or school because of substance use.
- Continuing to use, even when it causes problems in relationships.
- Giving up important social, occupational or recreational activities because of substance use.
- Using substances again and again, even when it puts you in danger.
- Continuing to use, even when you know you have a physical or psychological problem that could have been caused or made worse by the substance.
- Needing more of the substance than you did originally to get the effect you want (tolerance).
- Development of withdrawal symptoms, which can be relieved by taking more of the substance.

The DSM-5 describes alcohol dependence separately, saying that two of the following 11 symptoms must be met:

- Missing work or school.
- Drinking in hazardous situations.
- Drinking despite social or personal problems.
- Craving for alcohol.
- Build-up of tolerance.
- Withdrawal symptoms when trying to give up the substance.
- Drinking more than intended.
- Trying to give up without success.
- Increased alcohol-seeking behaviour.
- Interference with important activities.
- Continued use despite health problems.

Addiction to gambling is also being classified under these disorders as it was felt that the symptoms and cause were similar to substance disorders. Gambling disorder is the only behavioural addiction that can actually be diagnosed in the DSM-5; however, several others are mentioned, such as internet dependence, as requiring further research before they are included as formal disorders.

Mobile phone addiction is thought to be a new addiction which may warrant inclusion in the diagnostic manual at a later date. It should be noted that caffeine is not deemed by DSM-5 to be a disorder, but, as with internet dependence, it is included as a potential disorder.

It is evident that the symptoms of a problem do not vary significantly from each other. Broadly speaking there are key behaviours such as over-use, taking the substance even when you know it is bad for you, problems maintaining everyday activities and ineffective efforts to stop. Tolerance and withdrawal are also a way to describe addiction.

If the dependence is purely physical, say, for example, on a pain killer, then the effects of withdrawal will be felt but the craving may not. This craving usually occurs when someone is also psychologically dependent and is much harder to treat as the craving remains for longer. They will actively seek out the drug again.

## ON THE WEB

In 2013 there was a total revision of the diagnostic Manual DSM-IV and the new version, called DSM-5, was published.

Information on how addictive disorder diagnosis has changed in the recent revision of the diagnostic manual can be found here:

www.dsm5.org/Documents/Substance%20Use%20Disorder%20Fact%20Sheet.pdf

### YOU ARE THE RESEARCHER

How would you design a study to check for mobile phone addiction? What criteria would you use to decide if someone is addicted? What research methodology would work well for this? What would its strengths and weaknesses be?

There are potential ethical implications for a study such as this. What ethical issues would you have to consider when designing your research and how could the finding cause ethical problems, too?

## KEY TERM

**Tolerance** – the need to take higher levels of a substance to get the same physical and psychological effects

## Tolerance

**Tolerance** of a drug is shown when an individual has to take more and more of the substance to gain the same effect as their initial experience.

This can be explained biologically by considering the idea of homeostasis (a state of acting and feeling normal). Our brain maintains homeostasis wherever possible. It is a balancing act, as, when we ingest a substance such as alcohol, it disrupts the balance. If we continue to drink alcohol regularly the brain readjusts what it considers to be homeostasis (normal levels). It 'raises the bar' so to speak.

This means that more alcohol (or substance) needs to be taken to gain some effect. This is because the body has become tolerant of the drug. This seems to occur in all drugs and across drug families, which is called cross tolerance.

There are two types of tolerance that have a different biological action. Metabolic tolerance is when the substance is metabolised quicker and therefore leaves the body quicker. The second type of tolerance is cellular tolerance and is when there are changes in the responsiveness of the neurons.

**Figure 11.2** Drinking larger amounts of alcohol will cause the brain to readjust, heightening tolerance

This is the brain's attempt to recalibrate to higher levels of the drug and this has the most profound effect on addictive behaviours.

The end result of tolerance in someone taking a substance is that the effects disappear more quickly and the amount needed to produce those effects increases.

## Withdrawal syndrome

**Withdrawal syndrome** occurs when an individual has been taking a drug, usually for some time, and when they do not have it in their system they start to experience unpleasant feelings and symptoms. Withdrawal occurs following tolerance as the brain has readjusted to the drug being in the system, and when it has dropped below the tolerance level the brain automatically seeks out the drug to bring the level back up. Remember the level is now higher due to tolerance.

Physical withdrawal syndrome can cause symptoms such as low mood, feeling nauseous and being achy. There might also be pain and flu-like symptoms. Some people may also shake or have a tremor. These symptoms depend on the individual and the drug type. Broadly speaking, withdrawal is the reaction of the body to no longer having the drug, and therefore the symptoms of withdrawal are the opposite to the feeling and symptoms induced by the drug. For example, if a drug makes you feel euphoric and makes you constipated then the withdrawal from that drug will lower your mood to depressive-like symptoms and give you diarrhoea.

The withdrawal levels can vary in severity (see Table 11.1) and this is determined by several factors:

1. **The drug used**. Each drug has a half-life. The half-life describes the amount of time it takes to eliminate half the drug from the body. The shorter the half-life of the drug, the more intense the withdrawal from it.
2. **Amount consumed**. If large amounts of a drug are consumed, then the withdrawal will be greater.
3. **Drug use pattern**. If the drug use is frequent and regular then it will be in the body for most of the day. This means the physical dependence will be greater and consequently the effects of withdrawal will be greater.

> **KEY TERM**
>
> **Withdrawal syndrome** – the reaction psychologically and physically of an individual when they no longer have a substance in their system

Table 11.1 A summary of the withdrawal effects of commonly used substances

| Drug | Withdrawal |
|---|---|
| Alcohol | Symptoms persist intensely for 24 hours with nausea, sweating and in some cases 'delirium tremens' (the DTs) causing confusion, agitation and aggression |
| Nicotine | Maximum intensity of symptoms from withdrawal starts at 24–48 hours and can last for weeks and months. Symptoms include irritability, loss of sleep and weight gain |
| Opioids | The symptoms can start six hours after taking the drug. Craving, sadness and physical effects are some of the unpleasant symptoms of withdrawal |
| Psychostimulants (e.g. cocaine) | Symptoms include depression, anxiety and disturbed sleep. The symptoms generally last 2–14 days |

## Research

Marks *et al.* (1997) found that alcoholics were more likely to have a higher nicotine dependence as they smoked more heavily. As a result, alcoholics may experience greater discomfort from nicotine withdrawal upon trying to give up smoking.

The amount of alcohol consumed on a regular basis affects the rate at which it is metabolised. A regular to moderate drinker will be able to metabolise 8g of alcohol in one hour but a heavy drinker may be able to metabolise twice that amount. Their tolerance is double that of a moderate drinker (Begg, 2001).

Work looking at physical dependence and tolerance in mice for nicotine showed that withdrawal prompted an increase in somatic signs such as paw tremors, backing and head shakes. Grabus *et al.* (2005) also found evidence for tolerance effects in that over a period of time there was an adjustment to the physical effects of nicotine such as body temperature, suggesting that the mice had become tolerant to the drug, thus requiring a higher level to induce similar responses.

### RESEARCH IN FOCUS
Research into tolerance and withdrawal can be conducted on human participants. There are, however, ethical issues in using human participants for this kind of work. What are they?

Can you suggest how they might be dealt with by researchers to minimise the issues? Is there any alternative method that can be used?

### Evaluation
- Tolerance and withdrawal are hard to research as the level of control in studies is poor. This is in part due to reliability of data as much requires self-report measures. There are also many variables which cannot be controlled for.
- Tolerance and withdrawal are affected by many individual differences such as the gender of the individual, their drug use behaviours, their age and their body weight. This makes it a difficult area to establish clear patterns.

### STRENGTHEN YOUR LEARNING
1. According to the DSM-5, how many symptoms must be evident from the list of 11 to be diagnosed with an addictive disorder?
2. How do the diagnostic criteria for alcohol dependence differ from those of substance dependence?
3. Which addictions are likely to be included in the next revision of the diagnostic manual?
4. Outline what the term tolerance means with respect to substance use.
5. What does the term 'withdrawal syndrome' in the context of substance or alcohol use mean?
6. Give two examples of signs/symptoms of alcohol withdrawal.
7. Give two examples of signs/symptoms of nicotine withdrawal.
8. Outline the findings of a piece of research which investigates tolerance to a drug/alcohol.
9. Outline the findings of a piece of research which examines withdrawal from alcohol or other substance.

# IN THE NEWS

## ψ The Psychological Enquirer

### Inquest into the death of Peaches Geldof: heroin overdose

**Figure 11.3** Peaches Geldof died from a heroin overdose

Peaches Geldof, 25, was a broadcaster, model and columnist who was discovered dead at her home on 7 April 2014.

The inquest ruled that she had died from a heroin overdose as 3mg of heroin was found in her system at the time of death. There was drug paraphernalia found near the body and in the house. The inquest ruled that the death was accidental as there was absolutely no indication of it being suicide.

Peaches had battled with addiction and had received treatment in the three years before her death. She had been taking the heroin substitute methadone and had also received counselling. Drugs tests in November 2013 showed that she was clean. However, at the inquest her husband stated that she had started to take the drug again, although she really did want to be drug free.

The heroin found in the house was of a purer quality than is generally found on the street. A forensic scientist explained that someone who had previously given up the drug would have lost their tolerance for it and therefore when a relapse occurs it is more likely for an overdose to happen as the previous levels of heroin taken would be excessive following a period of being clean.

Peaches Geldof was the mother to two young sons and married to Thomas Cohen, a musician.

This story illustrates the potential fatal consequences of substance addiction. Paula Yates, Peaches' mother, also died of an accidental overdose. The reasons behind Peaches' drug use are not known and we know there are many factors in influencing addiction ranging from genetics to stress. This section will consider the influences on addiction and later in the chapter there will be a commentary on how it can be treated.

*'No one is immune from addiction; it afflicts people of all ages, races, classes, and professions.'*
Patrick J. Kennedy (2009)

## 11.2 Risk factors in the development of addiction

### Genetic vulnerability

There is thought to be a genetic influence on development of addiction, much like many other behaviours. Nielsen *et al.* (2008) compared DNA from former heroin addicts and non-addicts, and they found a connection between the genetics of the individual and their genetic make-up.

However, it is absolutely necessary for there to be a gene–environment interaction for this to occur. The individual will plainly not become

> **KEY TERM**
>
> **Genetic vulnerability** – the idea that someone may be more likely to be an addict because of their genetic make-up

addicted if they are not exposed to the substance or the opportunity within their environment. Therefore, **genetic vulnerability** should be seen as an interaction.

Twin studies (see Research below) have been useful for picking up on a heritability component to addiction. So too have linkage studies of addiction to substances and genetic make-up. These have shown an association between genes and 1) alcohol (Foroud et al., 2000), 2) nicotine (Li et al., 2004) and 3) cocaine (Gelernter, 2005). Other linkage studies have found a similar relationship.

The way our genetics can increase our likelihood of becoming addicted is the way our body responds to a drug. We can be more susceptible to its positive or negative effects.

In the case of alcohol the way the genetic code affects the likelihood of addiction is the way in which alcohol is metabolised by the body. The first reaction of our body to alcohol is to metabolise it to acetaldehyde then to acetic acid. The acid gets released into our urine very quickly, otherwise we can feel nauseous. In about 50 per cent of people from Asia, their genetic code does not facilitate the release of the acetic acid into the urine so they feel nauseous when drinking alcohol. Clearly this means their chance of addiction is slim to none.

## Research

Tsuang et al. (1996) used data from the Vietnam Era Twin Registry to evaluate the genetic influence on addiction. They looked at the records of 3,000 male twins. To define addiction they deemed it to be at least weekly use of an illegal drug. The data showed that there was a significant difference in the concordance rates of MZ (identical) and DZ (non-identical) twins.

Kendler et al. (1997) found that the concordance rates for alcohol abuse in MZ twins were significantly higher than for DZ twins. The data was gathered from the Swedish Twin Registry and the sample size was large, at almost 9,000 twin pairs. The data had been collected over 40 years and the researchers found that the heritability figure stayed constant over time. This suggests that there is a genetic component to addiction.

Kendler & Prescott (1998) compared concordance levels of drug abuse among MZ and DZ twins. The classification of drug abuse was the criteria set out by DSM-IV and data from nearly 2,000 twins was used. They found concordance rates for using, abusing or being dependent on drugs were higher for MZ than for DZ twins. For cocaine use, concordance was 54 per cent for MZ twins against 42 per cent for DZ twins. For cocaine abuse, concordance was 47 per cent in MZ twins against 8 per cent for DZ twins. For cocaine dependence, concordance was 35 per cent in MZ twins against 0 per cent in DZ twins. These figures indicate there is a genetic link to use of drugs.

DiFranza (2008) found that 10 per cent of teenage smokers who went on to be nicotine addicts had strong cravings for smoking two days after first inhaling and 35 per cent within one month, suggesting that nicotine is strongly addictive, with long-term use not necessary for addiction. The fact that those who had cravings early on were 200 times more likely to become daily smokers suggests a genetic vulnerability. It seems that they are genetically more susceptible to feeling the effects of the drug.

Wan-Sen Yan et al. (2013) (see Contemporary research below) show that there is a link between stress and addiction.

### Evaluation

- There does seem to be a wealth of research indicating that there is a genetic vulnerability to addiction, although no concordance rates in twin studies have ever shown 100 per cent concordance, so it is clearly a genetic predisposition rather than a certainty.
- It appears that the genetic link to addiction varies across substances, which means that the vulnerability is not general but specific to certain substances. This in turn means that if an individual is never exposed to the substance they will never realise that they have that genetic vulnerability as they may not react in the same way to other substances.
- The role of the environment is also vital in considering genetics. This is particularly so with addiction as there are many factors which affect the predisposition to addiction such as exposure to the drug, availability, stress, family influence and peers.
- There may be a fundamental issue in drawing conclusions from twin studies as MZ twins are more likely to be treated similarly by parents than DZ twins. This means that concordance rate differences may be accounted for by upbringing rather than genetic similarity. This weakens the argument for a genetic vulnerability to addiction.

## Stress

It is easy to see why high levels of stress would make you more vulnerable to addiction. Turning to behaviours and drugs that give a temporary relief from stress is a sort of coping mechanism. Stress can be short term or long term and it is the long-term exposure to stress that could increase the likelihood of someone becoming addicted.

There would be mediating factors, however, so someone might experience high stress, but have a lot of social support and other ways of coping with it. It is possible that it is not the level of stress, but the ability to cope with it that predisposes someone to addiction.

There are higher levels of stress in cities or areas with a high population, and this is also related to addictive behaviour as the number of addicts is greater in urban overcrowded environments. However, cause and effect cannot be established as this is a correlation. The relationship is complex and it could be that addicts live in those kinds of areas because of the availability of drugs or cheaper living costs.

There is also the possibility that the two are related because addiction prompts high levels of stress due to the problems it causes or with money.

## Research

Wan-Sen Yan *et al.* (2013) (see Contemporary research below) show that there is a link between stress and addiction. The measure used was life changes which are linked to stress. However, it could be argued that the measure may lack validity.

Tavolacci *et al.* (2013) examined the risk factors in developing addiction at university. Their argument was that it was a stressful time and that this predisposed students to addictive disorders. They compared highly stressed students (using a perceived stress scale) with students who were feeling less stressed and found that high perception of stress was related to smoking regularly, alcohol abuse problems and risk of cyber addiction (addiction to the internet). This suggests that stress and vulnerability to addiction are linked, although a cause and effect relationship cannot be established through this research as it is correlational.

Sinha (2000) found in a review of research that stress plays an important role in perpetuating drug abuse and relapse. The mechanism was not made clear from the research, and ideas as to how this happened could merely be suggested.

Piazza *et al.* (1989) tested rats for vulnerability to addiction through stress. They achieved a state of stress in the rats by pinching their tails and found that rats were more likely to seek out and ingest amphetamines the more stressed they got.

### Evaluation

- There is an issue with establishing cause and effect through research. High stress levels may indeed be linked to the likelihood of becoming addicted, but they could equally be a by-product of being addicted.
- Stress research is often conducted on animals because of the ethical issues of using humans. This means that there are issues with applying the research to human behaviour. There is no way of knowing, for example, how stressed the animal feels or indeed if they are definitely stressed so it can be argued that there are issues with validity.
- Research in this field is useful in terms of developing a practical application. It is feasible that a vulnerability measure could be developed to help predict the likelihood of becoming addicted due to stress levels. A stress level could also be used to help predict the likelihood that someone might relapse, as relapses and stress levels are closely linked.

## CONTEMPORARY RESEARCH

### The relationship between stress, personality, family functioning and internet addiction in college students – Wan-Sen Yan *et al.* (2013)

**Figure 11.4** Wan-Sen Yan *et al.* studied cyber addiction in university students

There are various vulnerability factors implicated in addictive behaviour. This research by Wan-Sen Yan *et al.* examines the relative influence several proposed factors have on internet addiction. This could indicate a similar pattern with other addiction types such as substance abuse and gambling.

#### Aim
To examine whether there is a relationship between stress levels, personality traits, and family functioning in relation to internet addiction.

#### Procedure
1,065 college students were participants in the study, but due to incomplete data sets only 892 students were included in the analysis. 407 were male and 485 were female. They were selected from across five provinces in China.

Each participant was given five measures to complete designed to calculate the following constructs:

1. **Demographic variables.** A questionnaire was used to collect data on gender, age, education grade, university and province.
2. **Family functioning.** To measure how well the family of each participant functions, the researchers used the Family Adaptability and Cohesion Scale, a 30-item measure that looks at the adaptability and cohesiveness of the family, examining such things as the strength of the emotional bond between members and the level of connection between members.

3. **Addiction level.** The Chen Internet Addiction Scale was used for this purpose. It is a 26-item scale which considers compulsive use, withdrawal effects, tolerance, time management, interpersonal problems and health problems.
4. **Personality.** The Eysenck personality questionnaire was given to participants. This had 48 items with yes/no response options that measured the level of extraversion, neuroticism and psychoticism for each participant.
5. **Stress.** To measure stress levels the researchers administered the Adolescent Self-rating Life Events checklist which looks at the amount of life change the individual has been through in the last 12 months. There is a positive correlation between the number and degree of life changes experienced and stress.

### Findings

9.98 per cent (89 students) of the sample had severe internet addiction and 11.21 per cent (100 students) had mild internet addiction.

There was no link between the demographic variables and level of addiction.

The group with severe addiction had low family functioning levels.

The severely addicted group had higher levels of neuroticism and psychoticism and lower levels of extraversion.

Compared with the non-addicted participants, the severely addicted participants had higher scores on the life changes measure which suggests they were experiencing higher levels of stress. The mildly addicted students also measured higher than the non-addicted students, but only with regard to health and adaptation problems.

### Conclusions

It can be concluded from the results that there is a relationship between family functioning, personality type, stress and addiction.

### Evaluation

- The psychological processes underlying these factors were not in any way tested by this research. It is merely correlational, so only a relationship can be ascertained. This means that the factors could be vulnerability factors or they could equally be by-products of being addicted.
- The fact that there was missing data from so many students may mean that the sample is biased as it is essentially self-selecting. Exactly how this would affect the outcome is not known, but caution should be used in drawing conclusions from the figures showing the number who were severely/mildly addicted. It is possible this is higher in the college student population because internet-addicted individuals may be less likely to fill out the questionnaires as they have other priorities such as being on the computer. This means the exact relationship cannot be established.

## Personality

The role of personality in addiction is complex as cause and effect is difficult to establish. This means that it is not always clear whether the addiction has altered the personality or vice versa, i.e. has the individual's personality predisposed them to addiction?

It is argued that people who have pathological personalities are more likely to become addicts because the drug or behaviour they are addicted to initially offers them a relief. Pathological personalities are types who have a predominantly negative persona. Their personality means they may be more stressed and find life difficult. The temporary high gained from playing a fruit machine or drinking a vodka and tonic, for example, would make them more likely to keep doing it. This means ultimately that the personality triggers the addiction rather than the other way round.

### Addictive personality

Various theorists have proposed the existence of an addictive personality. Eysenck (1997) outlined a model that suggested that addictions occur because of personality type and the needs of the personality. He argued that those with high neuroticism levels were predisposed to addictions. Neuroticism is characterised by high levels of anxiety and irritability. He also added that high levels of psychoticism were linked to addiction because this meant that the individual was aggressive and emotionally detached so the high associated with drugs or certain behaviours helped this.

**Figure 11.5** Are certain personalities more predisposed to addiction?

Eysenck also argued that there was a biological basis to personality and therefore the personality was inherited. Following this argument through, it would seem to suggest that someone is born with a predisposition to their personality.

Cloninger's (1987) tri-dimensional theory of addictive behaviour suggests that there are three key traits – novelty seeking, harm avoidance and reward dependence – that make an individual liable to substance abuse.

Novelty seeking is the need for change and stimulation. Individuals will actively seek new environments and experience, almost as if they have a low boredom threshold. This element makes them more likely to seek out sensations from drugs.

Harm avoidance is the amount that a person worries and sees the negative elements of a situation. This can affect their likelihood of taking a drug and therefore becoming addicted to it.

Reward dependence in an individual is when someone reacts and learns from a rewarding situation quickly. This also predisposes them to addiction as the rewarding effects are experienced quickly and easily.

## Research

Howard *et al.* (1997) in a meta-analysis of the studies investigating Cloninger's tri-dimensional theory found that novelty seeking does predict alcohol abuse in teenagers and young adults. It also predicts anti-social behaviour in those alcoholics. However, harm avoidance and reward dependence do not seem as clearly linked to addictive behaviours and the relationship is less consistent.

Work by Zuckerman (1983) on sensation seeking shows a link between the need for novelty and addictive behaviours. Cloninger's novelty seeking and Zuckerman's sensation seeking are very closely linked so this supports Cloninger's ideas too.

Wan-Sen Yan *et al.* (2013) (see Contemporary research above) show that there is a relationship between personality characteristics and addiction. The research looked specifically at Eysenck's theory and found evidence to suggest that high levels of neuroticism, high levels of psychoticism and low levels of extraversion were linked to internet addiction. These findings support Eysenck's ideas, although the low levels of extraversion found in the study contradict Cloninger's theory that novelty seeking is a characteristic predisposing an individual to addiction. Extraversion is a personality characteristic that seeks out stimulation, so this would suggest that extraversion would be at a high level in addicts, if Cloninger's theory is correct.

### Evaluation

- There is evidence to suggest that personality traits are implicated in an individual's likelihood of becoming an addict. However, to argue that there is an addictive personality that is inherited seems less plausible.
- The possession of certain traits does not automatically mean that addiction will occur, it is merely a predisposition. There are lots of other factors involved that influence the behaviour.
- Evidence suggests that certain traits are high in predictive validity with regards to addictive behaviour. However, the research indicates only likelihood and cannot fully explain the mechanism or cause underlying the behaviour. This makes it incomplete.

# Family influences

There are two key ways that families can influence addictive behaviour: social learning and expectancies.

Social learning is the learning of behaviour by observation of role models in the environment. If the individual sees that model rewarded for their behaviour then the vicarious reinforcement is going to increase the likelihood of the observer imitating the behaviour. It is clear how that could occur with addictive substances within a family. However, it should be noted that the addiction is not the imitated behaviour, it is the desire to try the substance that is the influence.

Expectancies are the associations we make from observing the environment around us. In other words we may learn from our environment that *if* we drink a lot of alcohol *then* we will get ill (because we witnessed our older brother doing this). Another application is that *if* we smoke cigarettes *then* we will appear cool (because we saw a rock star doing this).

These expectancies are formed from our learning and experience, which in turn is often our home environment. They are a form of schema. This then can explain to some extent how our family can influence our likelihood of addiction. It can increase or decrease the likelihood of trying substances or behaviours and, as a consequence, can influence our chance of becoming addicted.

## Research

Akers & Lee (1996) found that the social learning process was important in explaining smoking behaviours in adolescents. They looked over five years at the smoking levels of 454 young adults aged 12 to 17 and found that social influences affected the smoking behaviours of these participants, to try smoking, continue smoking or quit smoking. One of the sources of social learning tested was family influences.

Christiansen *et al.* (1989) have shown that the expectancies of adolescents can be used to predict drinking problems in later life. When sampling a group of 11–14 year olds they found that the amount and how often they drank a year later was linked to their expectancies and beliefs. This research shows the importance of environmental influence on later behaviour, so the influence of the family is potentially significant.

Dunn & Goldman (1996, 1998) found that when they measured the expectancies of 7–18 year olds they mirrored those of adults. This suggests that the adults in a child's environment can heavily influence their attitude towards substance use and therefore potentially addiction.

Wan-Sen Yan *et al.* (2013) (see Contemporary research above) show that there is a relationship between the cohesiveness of the family and the likelihood of internet addiction.

> **Evaluation**
> - The relative influence of the family will vary depending on the age and the strength of relationship for an individual. It may be that at a younger age the influence of the family to try or abstain from a substance or behaviour could be much greater than in an older individual. Therefore family influence is not constant throughout the lifespan.
> - There is not a certainty that if a child observes a behaviour they will definitely imitate that behaviour. There are mediating cognitive processes that influence whether a behaviour is imitated or not. This means that motivations to behave a certain way, such as start smoking, are influenced by other sources which may counteract the family influence. For example, seeing a parent smoke is in no way a guarantee that the children will smoke too.
> - The relative influence of the family against all the other potential influences is very difficult to gauge as measurement is extremely difficult. All that can be said is that the family can influence behaviour and the likelihood to use a substance. However, how that influence compares with peer influence, for example, is difficult to ascertain.

## Peers

Given that social influence is often seen as the psychological explanation for initiation to addictive behaviours, the influence of peers is potentially great. However, as with many of the vulnerability factors, proving causation is problematic. It is just as possible choice of peer groups is influenced by addiction. So an addict might choose a peer group that allows them easy access to the focus of the addiction (i.e. drug) and they may choose a non-judgemental peer group.

Peers are influential at the intervention stage, too, as they can provide access to drugs and may encourage a relapse. It is argued that these social influences should be taken into account when designing and delivering an intervention programme to try to ensure maximum success levels.

### Research

In a longitudinal study by Bullers *et al.* (2001) it was found that selection of the peer group followed addiction in many cases and that it was the greatest influential direction. Social influence had less of an effect.

Leshner (1998) believes treatment strategies must include social context elements, such as peer groups, as well as biological and behavioural ones if they are to be successful, as recovered addicts may relapse when leaving a clinic due to the original social context still being in place.

Bauman & Ennett (2006) argued that much research states that peer influence is a reason behind substance abuse. However, upon reviewing the literature they found that often it was not tested as a construct and that it is possible that the influence level is overestimated.

Work by Kobus (2003) suggested, through reviewing the literature, that the effect of peer influence on smoking behaviour was more subtle than often thought and that the media, family and neighbourhood were also involved. They agreed with the idea of peer influence for both encouraging and deterring smoking but argued that the psychological processes behind the behaviour needed more research.

### Evaluation

- Peer group influences are just one of many social context effects. Others include such factors as economic and social deprivation, and all should be considered when assessing levels of vulnerability to dependency as dependency is rarely related to just one factor.
- It is difficult to ascertain the level of influence from peers. Distinguishing the influence of friends from that of family is impossible and therefore the exact amount someone is influenced by their peers is difficult to establish.
- The influence of peers is likely to be greater at different ages. The work of Rich-Harris (1998) states that peer influence increases during adolescence, so substance abuse in young adults is likely to be influenced by peers to a greater extent than parents.

### STRENGTHEN YOUR LEARNING

1. Explain why research shows there is probably a genetic vulnerability to addiction.
2. Outline one piece of research which shows there may be a genetic vulnerability to addiction.
3. What is the relationship between stress and addiction?
4. Outline the findings of one study that relates to stress and addiction.
5. How does Eysenck's theory of personality relate to addiction?
6. What three personality characteristics does Cloninger say are related to addiction?
7. What does research say about the family as a risk factor for development of addiction?
8. Outline the findings of a piece of research which show there is a relationship between family influence and addiction.
9. Describe one piece of research that shows that peer influence may be a risk factor for development of addiction.

# ASSESSMENT CHECK

1. Select from the behaviours A, B, C and D below to complete the table relating to possible symptoms of addiction. One description of a behaviour will be left over. **[3 marks]**

   **A** Adam used to buy one pack of cigarettes a week, now he buys three packs

   **B** Joanne is agitated if she is stuck in traffic and can't get home for a glass of wine

   **C** Simon has stopped going to play football on a Sunday

   **D** Susie always really fancies a cigarette with her pint of lager

   | Symptom of addiction | Behaviour |
   | --- | --- |
   | Cravings and urges to use the substance | |
   | Development of withdrawal symptoms | |
   | Taking the substance in larger amounts and for a longer period of time | |

2. To investigate the amount of alcohol drunk by secondary school students, researchers used a questionnaire, which gave a total of the reported units of alcohol in one week. The calculated measures of central tendency for the units consumed were, for the mean 4, for the median 5, and for the mode 5.

   Sketch a graph to show the distribution of units consumed. Label the axes and mark on the positions of the mean, median and mode. **[4 marks]**

3. Briefly outline what is meant by withdrawal syndrome. **[4 marks]**

4. Read the item and then answer the question:

   Amanda is really quite worried. Her father is a gambling addict and she has started to play bingo online a lot, like her friends.

   Briefly explain risk factors relevant to Amanda's playing of online bingo. **[4 marks]**

5. Describe and evaluate stress and/or personality as risk factors in addictive behaviour. **[16 marks]**

# 11.3 Explanations for nicotine addiction

## Brain neurochemistry: the role of dopamine

Dopamine is implicated in addiction as the addictive substance or behaviour prompts a 'high' through boosting the activity of the brain's reward system. This system is found in the centre of the brain and is a complex circuit of neurons that produces a high, like euphoria, which means the individual is tempted to take the drug again or repeat the behaviour.

The brain mechanism is basically a pathway of neurons that is activated by the neurotransmitter dopamine. The source of the activation is the ventral tegmental area (VTA), which has many dopamine neurons. This then triggers activation in the limbic system (specifically the nucleus accumbens) and this subsequently boosts activity in the prefrontal cortex.

This activity is called the 'common reward pathway', as it is associated with the feeling of euphoria. As the level of emotion experienced by this pathway is so high it explains how an addiction can be formed through repetitive behaviour. As time goes on, and through repeated usage, the level of drug needed to elicit the reaction becomes greater. This occurs due to a change in the neuronal structure in the pathway. This accounts for tolerance levels increasing in an individual and also why the individual craves the drug or wishes to carry out the behaviour. Addiction is the result.

## Research

Dani & Basi (2001) found that part of the reason nicotine is so addictive is because it acts upon the dopaminergic systems, which helps reinforce rewarding behaviour. This shows a direct relationship between the neural mechanisms in the brain and the rewarding effects felt while smoking.

Watkins *et al.* (2000) reviewed the research into the neurobiology of nicotine addiction. They found that dopamine release was reduced following chronic exposure to nicotine. This means that tolerance of the drug occurs due to the level of reward felt decreasing.

Chiara (2000) argues that dopamine is one of the main causes for the addictive nature of nicotine. The rewarding aspect of the drug such as the feeling of pleasure is released through dopaminergic activity and so is responsible for the addictive nature of the drug. If pleasure was not felt then the smoker would not continue to smoke over time.

### Evaluation

- The researchers argue that this is only part of the neural action and that dopamine is not the whole story. It is likely that the reason that nicotine is so addictive is due to several complex explanations.
- The role of dopamine could explain how there appears to be a genetic link to addiction. It is possible that the dopaminergic mechanism in some individuals leads them to feel the rewarding aspects of drugs to a greater level.

- The evidence base for research in this area is often using animals as a sample. This means the findings may not be generalisable to humans. They also potentially lack validity because the feelings associated with addiction and drug use cannot be measured successfully due to a lack of communication.
- The dopamine explanation for addiction is purely biological and, as a consequence, the psychological aspects of addiction are largely ignored. It is likely that dopamine, although implicated, is not the whole picture, and many levels of explanation should be considered. It can therefore be said to be reductionist.

**ON THE WEB**

There is a series of lectures available to watch on the brain and how it is affected by addiction. Go to **www.youtube.com** and search for 'Brain activity and addiction'.

# Learning theory as applied to smoking behaviour

*'Addiction isn't about substance – you aren't addicted to the substance, you are addicted to the alteration of mood that the substance brings.'*

Susan Cheever (2012)

Smoking behaviour is best explained by learning theory as a two-stage process involving social learning theory and operant conditioning.

## Social learning theory (SLT)

This is a sound explanation for how someone starts smoking. An individual observes role models smoking and experiences the vicarious reinforcement of social learning. This process is especially powerful in young people and this is also when most first experience smoking. Initiation of smoking is therefore well explained by peer pressure and social influences.

## Operant conditioning

Operant conditioning explains why smoking continues and is due to the positive reinforcement that nicotine induces. It can give a pleasant feeling and that is rewarding for the individual. The law of effect means this makes it more likely to keep reoccurring as positive reinforcement is involved.

# Cue reactivity

**Cue reactivity** with regard to smoking behaviour involves associations made through classical conditioning. For example cues in the environment such as sitting outside the pub on a summer's evening with a pint of beer in your right hand and a cigarette in your left, might lead to, an association forming between the pint of beer in your right hand and the need for a cigarette in your left hand. This means that the two go together and it is strange for the person not to smoke while drinking alcohol if they have learnt the association. In classical conditioning terms the pint glass serves as a conditioned stimulus to cue the craving for a cigarette. This association

**Figure 11.6** Observing role models or peers smoking may explain why someone starts smoking

**KEY TERM**

**Cue reactivity** – an example of classical conditioning where objects and environments become conditioned stimuli

makes giving up hard in certain environments and makes someone more likely to smoke, perpetuating the addiction.

## Research

Brynner (1969) found that media images of smoking create perceptions of it being attractive and tough. This increases the motivation for wanting to smoke, and if role models are smoking in the media, they could provide models for social learning in the audience. This lends support to SLT being implicated in smoking.

The US National Institute on Drug Abuse (NIDA) (2005) found that 90 per cent of US smokers started smoking as adolescents. This was attributed mainly to observing and imitating peers. This suggests that the decision to start smoking is due in part to social learning factors.

In research with monkeys, Goldberg et al. (1981) used a system where the monkeys had to press a lever to receive nicotine. The researchers found that the monkeys pressed the lever at a rate that was similar to the level that would be expected with cocaine. This suggests addictive behaviour and the idea that it is accessed for its reinforcing effect. Operant conditioning as an explanation for addiction therefore has research support.

Calvert (2009) reports that smokers shown cigarette packets experienced strong activation in the ventral striatum and nucleus accumbens brain areas, suggesting a biological explanation of craving behaviour. However, this also supports the idea of cue reactivity and the brain activation may show the neural basis for classical conditioning.

### Evaluation

- There is an extensive amount of research to show the role of social learning in initiation of addictive behaviours such as smoking. Other elements of learning theory cannot explain this first stage, which is pivotal in addictive behaviour. The individual must be motivated to try a behaviour initially for it to become classically or operantly conditioned. This suggests that social learning theory specifically is important in explaining addictive behaviour.
- Animal research is used to examine the effects of learning theory for addictive behaviour. There are issues with generalising this to human addiction, especially the cognitive elements of social learning theory. Caution should therefore be used in using animal research to explain why humans become addicted to a behaviour or substance as it might simplify the explanation.
- For more evaluation of how learning theory explains gambling specifically, see page 410.

### STRENGTHEN YOUR LEARNING

1. Explain how dopamine plays a role in nicotine addiction.
2. Outline one piece of research which shows the effects of dopamine on the brain and nicotine tolerance.
3. What is a weakness of the dopamine explanation for nicotine addiction?
4. What is a strength of the dopamine explanation for nicotine addiction?
5. How does social learning theory explain nicotine addiction?
6. How does operant conditioning explain nicotine addiction?
7. What does research say about the role of learning in nicotine addiction?
8. Outline the findings of a piece of research which show there is a relationship between operant conditioning and addiction.

# 11.4 Explanations for gambling addiction

Gambling behaviour can lead to an addiction. That addiction has far-reaching consequences for the individual and their family as it can result in the loss of their savings or even their home. It is also likely to massively increase debt levels, and figures show that a debt of £60,000 is not uncommon in someone with a gambling addiction (Downs and Woolrych, 2009).

**Figure 11.7** How can we best explain gambling behaviour?

The fact that gambling itself is not a drug that causes biochemical changes suggests that psychological explanations should be the main focus in trying to explain gambling behaviour. This section will consider the learning and cognitive approaches' explanations to gambling addiction.

## Learning theory as applied to gambling

Operant conditioning is one area of learning theory that is implicated in gambling addiction. The principles of operant conditioning state that if a behaviour is positively reinforced then it is more likely to reoccur. In the example of gambling, the positive reinforcement comes from the win but also the more subtle rewards such as excitement at the prospect of a win. This makes gambling an enjoyable process and, as such, it becomes positively reinforced.

It is noteworthy to remember that slot machines, for example, reinforce reward by playing cheers and claps when someone wins. It seems we are susceptible not only to the reinforcement of money, but also to appreciation from others (mechanical or not!).

However, operant conditioning also states that if a behaviour is punished then it will be less likely to reoccur. As gamblers do not always win, and in losing are therefore 'punished', it is hard to see perhaps why punishment does not extinguish the behaviour.

This can be explained in terms of contiguity. Contiguity is the term used in operant conditioning to explain the co-occurrence of an action and a reinforcement or punishment. The reward or positive reinforcement for gambling is immediate, so is 'time contiguous'. This means the association is greater. However, even though, for example, you can lose on a slot machine and therefore receive immediate punishment, the overall negative feeling does not arise until there has been a series of losses so the association is not as strong. The individual wins are also much bigger in magnitude than each loss so the punishment does not evoke such a strength of feeling.

## Partial and variable reinforcement

The schedules of reinforcement studied by Skinner's work on rats and pigeons are important in understanding how gambling behaviour can be encouraged. Figure 11.8 illustrates how this can occur.

Imagine you are standing at a slot machine with £1 change in 10p pieces in your pocket.

- **Fixed ratio reinforcement.** If the slot machine is set to give a prize every third time then you will use nine of your 10p pieces to get the three prizes you can win with your money. You will not put the final 10p piece into the machine because you know you cannot win.
- **Variable ratio.** If the machine is set to a variable ratio reinforcement schedule (as most of them are) you are more likely to put all your money in as you know that you can possibly win with every coin you put into the machine.
- **Fixed interval.** This is one of the least successful ratios of reinforcement for gambling because if you know or work out that you can only win every 20 seconds, for example, you will only put a coin into the machine every 20 seconds. This means the amount of money you use is minimal.

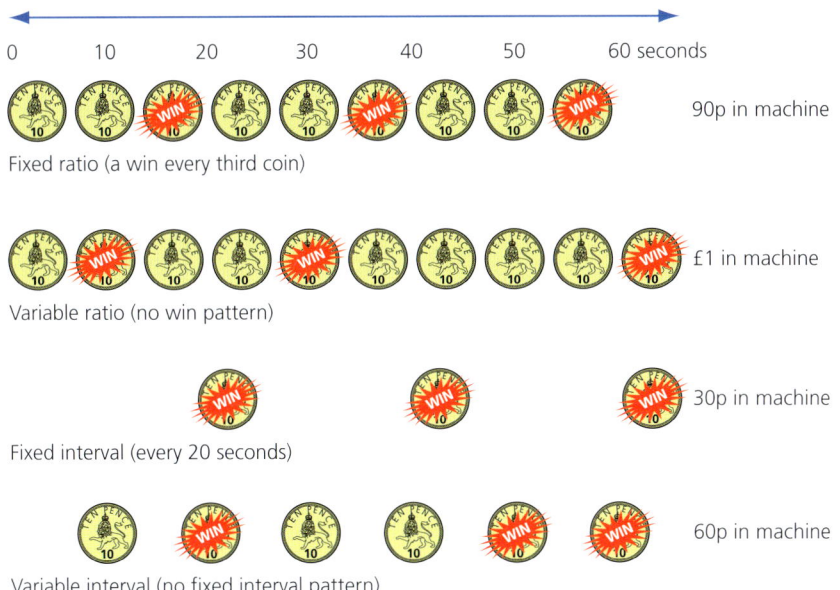

**Figure 11.8** Partial and variable reinforcement

- **Variable interval.** This schedule of reinforcement is much more likely to encourage people to gamble as there is no fixed pattern to predict from. This has a similar effect on gambling at a slot machine but coins are not entered with the same speed as with the variable ratio pattern. The response is steadier.

It seems that the schedule of reinforcement that is most likely linked to encouraging gambling and therefore more likely to encourage addiction is the variable ratio schedule. It is no surprise then that this is how slot machines are programmed to respond.

## Classical conditioning

To some extent classical conditioning can also be associated to gambling addiction, but to a lesser degree. It is possible that a positive association is made to the lights and sounds of an amusement arcade or casino due to the excitement that can be experienced. This can encourage someone to revisit a place to gamble to experience the positive emotions associated with it. This is especially the case if a positive event occurred on the initial visit to a place, such as a big win.

### Social learning

Social learning can be used to explain gambling addiction, though to a lesser degree, as is the case with classical conditioning. It is entirely plausible that a child or young adult, for example, could witness a parent receiving a big win in an amusement arcade. They will notice the happiness of the parent (attention), retain that memory (retention) and, when they have the money and opportunity, try using slot machines themselves (reproduction). The motivation would be to win too.

## Research

Blaszczynski & Nower (2002) looked at the possible origins of gambling addiction by reviewing the literature. They suggested that gamblers fell into one of three categories: behaviourally conditioned gamblers, emotionally vulnerable gamblers and antisocial impulsivist gamblers. The first group was deemed to have become addicted due to their learned experiences through conditioning and this therefore lends support to the theory. However, the fact that not all gamblers can be classified this way suggests that it serves as an explanation for only some addicts.

Parke & Griffiths (2004) investigated the idea of operant conditioning as an explanation for gambling addiction. They supported the idea that gambling is reinforcing due to the money, thrill and excitement, but they said that the fact that there is a sensation of a 'near miss' often experienced by gamblers makes it reinforced, even in times when there is a loss. This means that the behaviour is generally reinforced in both a win and an 'almost win', making it highly addictive.

Griffiths & Delfabbro (2001) reviewed the literature on gambling addiction and possible explanations for the behaviour. They found that any single explanation was insufficient and that an integrated theory of learning theory biology and the role of the environment should be developed. It seems that attributing gambling addiction to learning theory alone is only a partial explanation.

### Evaluation

- There is sound research support for learning theory as an explanation for addiction. However, it seems that just looking to operant conditioning, for example, is reductionist and more specifically an example of stimulus-response reductionism. There are many other factors involved in the behaviour.
- Learning theory cannot explain why one person may have a big win and not become addicted to gambling whereas another may be addicted. If learning theory is to be believed then any behaviour that is rewarded will be repeated. This is clearly not the case so the theory is flawed when considering individual differences.
- Operant conditioning cannot easily explain why someone would initially start gambling but can explain why they might get addicted to it. Social learning is able to explain the initial behaviour, so perhaps a more convincing explanation would be to combine the two learning explanations.

## Cognitive theory as applied to gambling: cognitive bias

The cognitive approach sees problem behaviour as a result of cognitive distortions or maladaptive thought processes. Gambling addiction is no exception. Cognitive theorists have looked to the thinking of the addict to explain how the addiction starts and how it becomes entrenched.

The mood of the individual is affected by these thought processes to the point where they mistakenly believe that the only way their mood can be lifted is to gamble, as that is the only way to feel happy. They also have a cognitive bias where they focus on the positive aspects of the behaviour (i.e. the wins) and downplay or ignore the negative side (i.e. the losses).

### Cognitive bias

The key to explaining gambling, according to the cognitive approach, is cognitive bias. Initially it was thought (Langer, 1975) that the bias was purely an 'illusion of control'. However, when Wagenaar (1988) reviewed all the literature he argued that gamblers gamble because their reasoning is biased in many ways, including control.

In his work he identified 16 cognitive distortions in the thoughts of gamblers. An example of some of these biases is included in Table 11.2.

Table 11.2 Some cognitive distortions of gamblers

| Distortion | Description |
| --- | --- |
| Availability | Memories of wins can be recalled more easily from memory than losses. |
| Confirmation bias | Focusing on information that is consistent with belief (such as being lucky). |
| Concrete information bias | This is when the gambler focuses on events such as big wins and downplays statistical facts or calculations of losses. |
| Hindsight bias | When gamblers look back and say they expected either the big win or loss, which gives them a feeling of control. This justifies gambling again because they control it. |
| Flexible attribution | When the gambler explains wins as due to his/her skill and losses to other people's influence. |
| Illusion of control | The feeling gamblers have that they can exert control over an uncertain outcome. |

These cognitive biases all serve to perpetuate gambling behaviour, leading to gambling addiction. This idea was tested by Griffiths (1994) – see Classic research.

## CLASSIC RESEARCH

### The role of skill and cognitive bias in fruit machine gambling – Griffiths (1994)

Gambling does not include ingesting a drug but addiction to it can have far-reaching and negative effects for the individual and their family. One explanation of why the addiction occurs and sets in is thought to be the cognitive biases they have. This is the focus of Griffiths' research.

#### Aim
To test the idea that gamblers think and behave differently to non-gamblers due to cognitive bias.

#### Procedure
The research was carried out in a natural setting in an arcade. Participants were 30 regular gamblers, who played once or more a week. These were compared with 30 non-regular gamblers, who played less than once a month. Each participant was given £3 to gamble on a fruit machine. Each gamble was 10 pence so they had 30 total gambles from the £3. They were given the objective of staying on the machine for 60 total gambles. They also had to try to win back the £3. If these objectives were met they were able to keep the money and continue gambling if they wished to do so.

Cognitive activity was measured as verbalisations uttered while participants played a fruit machine. The assumption was that they would speak their thoughts out loud. How skilful at gambling they thought they were was measured through a semi-structured approach.

#### Findings
Comments from regular gamblers seemed to indicate they thought they were more skilful than they actually were (see Table 11.3). The regular gamblers also made irrational comments, which seemed to indicate they thought the machine had a personality such as 'The machine doesn't like me'. They even seemed to think that the machine experienced moods, for example saying such things as 'Obviously the machine is being a bit of a bastard at the moment'.

| Content analysis of verbalisations | Non-regular players | Regular players |
| --- | --- | --- |
| Machine personification | 1.14 | 7.54 |
| Explaining losses as near wins | 0.41 | 3.12 |
| Talking to the machine | 0.90 | 2.64 |
| Referring to personal skill | 1.47 | 5.34 |

Table 11.3 Analysis of gamblers' and non-gamblers' verbalisations during play

When the regular gamblers lost they described them as near misses or near wins (see Table 11.4). Of the 30 regular gamblers 44 per cent achieved 60 gambles and one third continued until they had lost all the money. In comparison 22 per cent of the control group achieved 60 plays and two of them stayed on the machine until they had lost all the money.

| Belief that skill was involved | Non-regular players | Regular players |
| --- | --- | --- |
| Mostly chance | 19 | 10 |
| Equal chance/skill | 7 | 18 |
| Skill | 0 | 8 |

**Table 11.4** Analysis of gamblers' and non-gamblers' belief in skill or luck during play

### Conclusions

Regular gamblers have a misperception of their skill as being better than it actually is.

Regular gamblers have cognitive distortions about how close they come to winning and the nature of the machine they are using.

### Evaluation

- As the regular gamblers were more familiar with the machines their perception of skill may have been due to proficiency they felt at using the machine.
- This research potentially helps development of interventions as it gives an idea of the thought processes involved in gambling behaviour. Misperceptions can then be addressed by any intervention.

## Research

Joukhador *et al.* (2003) compared the cognitive styles of 52 social and 56 problem gamblers. They found that problem gamblers demonstrated more cognitive biases and irrational thinking than social gamblers. Interestingly, the use of denial showed no difference. Generally, however, the findings suggest that there is a distinct difference between the cognitive styles of those with a gambling problem and those without an addiction.

Rogers (1998) examined cognitive bias in gambling behaviour, more specifically buying lottery tickets. He found that there was cognitive bias in the reasoning behind buying a lottery ticket regularly such as a belief in personal luck, the illusion of control, unrealistic optimism and gambler's fallacy. This illustrates that cognitive biases are a key feature of all gambling behaviour.

Toneatto (1999) reviewed the literature on cognitive bias and found that there were key biases in the thinking of problem gamblers. These included an exaggeration of their own skill, downplaying the skill of other gamblers and gambler's fallacy. Gambler's fallacy is a misbelief that if something occurs more frequently than expected during a period of time then it will be less likely to occur later. This supports the idea that gambling addiction is driven by distorted beliefs.

### Evaluation

- The reliability of self-report has meant that the cognitive biases recorded in research have come under criticism. Delfabbro (2004) examined the literature on cognitive bias and argued that much of the biases recorded were difficult to falsify, idiosyncratic and context bound. It is a difficult area to research as it requires an element of introspection.
- When comparing the cognitive styles of problem and social gamblers a difference is observed. However, assuming that it is a distorted cognitive style that underpins addiction to gambling is problematic from such research. There is no way that a cause and effect can be established. It is also possible that the faulty cognitive style is a by-product of the problem and is a result of being an addict.

- The knowledge of how gamblers think and how their thoughts can be distorted is invaluable for treating the addiction. Cognitive therapy can help address the faulty thinking. Sometimes someone may not be aware that they have cognitive biases so a knowledge of some of the biases outlined by Wagenaar (1988) and subsequent work can help therapists design suitable interventions.

- There is also likely to be an influence from social factors involved in gambling becoming addictive. If someone is struggling with money the prospect of an easy win gives a quick solution to the problem. This may affect their desire to gamble in the first place. The cognitive approach does not focus on this aspect so perhaps a more complete explanation would be to combine cognitive and social factors.

### STRENGTHEN YOUR LEARNING

1. Explain how operant conditioning is connected to gambling.
2. Outline one piece of research which shows the effects of learning on gambling.
3. What is a weakness of the learning approach explanation for gambling?
4. What is a strength of the learning approach explanation for gambling?
5. How does cognitive theory explain gambling?
6. With reference to gambling, outline what cognitive bias means.
7. Outline one piece of research that investigated cognitive biases in gambling.
8. Outline the strengths of the cognitive explanation to gambling.

### YOU ARE THE RESEARCHER

Investigating cognitive biases is problematic due to the need for introspection. What are the validity issues with using introspection (where the individual reports what they are thinking)? If you used a questionnaire methodology instead, how would you compile the questionnaire? What terms might you include? How would the two methodologies compare in terms of validity?

## ASSESSMENT CHECK

1. Select from the statements made by an addict A, B, C and D below to complete the table relating to cognitive biases in addiction. One statement will be left over. **[3 marks]**

   A This machine is picking on me

   B I'm always winning

   C I expected last Sunday to be a bad day on the machines because it snowed

   D That win was because I play that machine regularly and am really good at it

   | Cognitive bias | Statement |
   | --- | --- |
   | Flexible attribution | |
   | Hindsight bias | |
   | Availability | |

2. Research into alcoholism frequently uses self-report measures such as questionnaires and interviews to ascertain the level of alcohol consumed.

   Explain what the issues of using this research method are for this type of study. **[3 marks]**

3. Briefly outline how the neurochemical explanation explains addiction to nicotine. **[4 marks]**

4. Read the item and then answer the question:

   Kristian loves to go to his local pub, The Bay Horse. He likes to drink pints but the main reason he goes to The Bay Horse every weekend is to play the 'King Cash' fruit machine. He thinks he is pretty good at it and says he knows when to play the machine to win more. He also describes himself as the luckiest man in Tadcaster, his home town.

   With reference to the item, briefly explain why Kristian plays the fruit machine so regularly. **[4 marks]**

5. Describe and evaluate the role of cue reactivity in explaining addiction to nicotine. **[16 marks]**

# 11.5 Reducing addiction

*'Life is very interesting…in the end, some of your greatest pains become your greatest strengths.'*

Drew Barrymore (1990)

## Drug therapy

Drug therapy is the biological method for treating addiction and is most commonly used with addiction to drugs such as alcohol and heroin. As the biochemical effects of each substance are different, the drug treatment used must necessarily also vary. For this reason this section will outline the drug treatments used for heroin, alcohol and nicotine.

### Heroin

Heroin withdrawal is very unpleasant. Drug therapy is therefore used for heroin addicts as a way of them coping with the withdrawal process. This means a heroin substitute is used in many cases. The drug methadone is a long-acting drug with a longer half-life than heroin, so is widely used as a substitute. It can be used to reduce the cravings and to gradually reduce the amount of opioid administered. Methadone is given once a day in the form of a syrup so the level of the drug in the bloodstream is kept fairly constant.

### Alcohol

Alcoholism is difficult to treat using drugs. The withdrawal symptoms from alcohol can sometimes require a patient to be hospitalised as they are so acute. There is no substitute like methadone for alcohol, so alcoholics need to be administered with a sedative to mimic the sedative effects of alcohol. The most commonly used sedative are benzodiazepines as they act to reduce the withdrawal symptoms. The dose is reduced steadily over several weeks until the alcoholic is deemed to be at a point where they can stop taking the drugs.

There is also a drug called Antabuse (disulfiram) which can be used to make the individual feel nauseous when they drink alcohol. The drug works to inhibit the release of acetic acid in the urine which would usually occur when alcohol is metabolised. This feeling of nausea is designed to break the positive association felt when drinking alcohol and can only be used when there has been a period without alcohol. The patient must not be in withdrawal. More detail about this treatment is included in the behavioural treatments section (page 419) as it is an example of a behaviourist treatment, working on the principles of operant conditioning, as well as a drug therapy.

### Nicotine

Cessation of smoking is a big industry. There are many products available over the counter which can help reduce addiction, such as nicotine gum, patches and electronic cigarettes. These nicotine replacement products are designed to slowly release nicotine into the system which should help the individual to fight cravings during a withdrawal period from cigarettes.

**PSYCHOLOGY IN THE REAL WORLD**
### Screening the older generation for addiction: November 2014

A nursing home in the Bronx, New York has decided that its residents need to be screened for addiction as they have noted that they are vulnerable at key times. One such potential time seems to occur when they are administered strong pain killers to reduce discomfort following surgery.

The nursing home targets recent patients who have had surgery for joint replacements or heart conditions. Other times when the nursing home believes they are vulnerable is when they have had a recent bereavement or life change such as retirement.

The residents are screened as part of their care programme, and if issues with addiction are picked up, they are offered help for their addiction.

## Research

Malcolm *et al.* (2006) compared how alcoholics responded to treatment with a drug called buspirone, which is a benzodiazepine. They compared the recovery rate with a group who received a placebo and found that there was no significant difference in the amount of alcohol consumed and anxiety levels. This means that it may be the belief that a drug can help, rather than its pharmacological action, that is beneficial.

McLellan *et al.* (1993) looked at whether it was sufficient to administer methadone alone as a treatment or whether it should be administered with psychotherapy and other support. They found that 69 per cent of the group that received methadone-only intervention had to be withdrawn from the study as they had eight consecutive positive urine samples indicating they were taking heroin. The groups that received methadone plus other interventions responded far better. This suggests that methadone treatment should be supplemented with other psychological interventions to be fully effective.

Fiore *et al.* (1994) conducted a meta-analysis of the effectiveness of nicotine patches for smoking cessation and found that it is an effective aid to quitting smoking. When compared with cessation rates in placebo patch wearers, they found that smokers with a nicotine patch were twice as likely to stop smoking. This suggests that the steady release of low levels of nicotine can lessen the cravings. Drug use can therefore aid nicotine addiction.

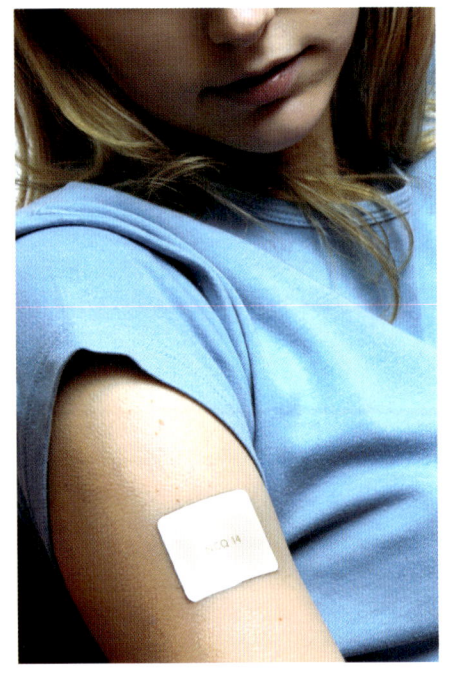

**Figure 11.9** Nicotine patches can be effective in helping people quit smoking

### Evaluation

- Research seems to suggest that, for some, drug therapy on its own is insufficient as an intervention. A combined approach with both biological and psychological interventions is likely to elicit the best outcome. This is not always an option, however, due to financial restrictions. It can therefore be argued that a combination of biological and psychological explanations gives the most holistic explanation for addiction.
- When drug substitution is used it removes the need for an addict to seek out a harmful and sometimes illegal drug. This means the addict can remove themselves from the criminal sources of the drug and focus on staying clean. This will improve their relationships and home life, which, in turn, will improve their chance of success in beating the addiction.

- Drug treatment for substance addicts is not suitable in all cases. This can be due to personal circumstances or because it could be physically harmful. Pregnant women may not be suitable for treatment because of possible harm to the foetus. However, drug treatment can be administered if it is felt that the risk to the foetus is less than the drug consumption habit of the mother. People suffering from addiction who are serving short prison sentences are sometimes not suitable for treatment because there needs to be a period of supervision, which may exceed the time in prison.

# Behavioural interventions

**Aversion therapy** is a behavioural intervention that works on the principles of classical conditioning. It is a relatively simple idea that has been used to treat many behaviours. With addiction it is used primarily with the addictions that have a biological agent, such as drugs, nicotine and alcohol.

The idea is that the pleasurable association with the addictive substance has to be broken and replaced with a negative association. That way the addict will no longer wish to have the substance as it elicits a negative association.

For example, if a practitioner wants to use aversion therapy for intervention with alcohol addiction they can use Antabuse, which is an emetic drug (it makes someone vomit). That serves as the unconditioned stimulus and the vomiting is the unconditioned response. Before treatment the alcohol is the neutral stimulus, although it actually prompts a positive response. When Antabuse is given at the same time as alcohol it becomes associated with it and becomes a conditioned stimulus. This essentially means that when the addict encounters alcohol after the treatment it is negatively associated with the vomiting, and so, even though the Antabuse is not present, the addict feels sick.

The process for doing this is detailed in Figure 11.10.

> **KEY TERM**
>
> **Aversion therapy** – a treatment used to reduce addictive behaviours broadly used on classical conditioning

```
Before conditioning        During conditioning        After conditioning

Antabuse ──▶ Vomiting      Antabuse ──▶ Vomiting                  Vomiting
(UCS)        (UCR)                                                (CR)
                                      ↗
Alcohol ──▶ Pleasure       Alcohol ┄┄                Alcohol ──▶
(NS)                                                 (CS)

Key
──▶ = prompts    ┄┄▶ = becomes associated with the UCS

UCS = unconditioned stimulus
NS = neutral stimulus
CS = conditioned stimulus
CR = conditioned response
```

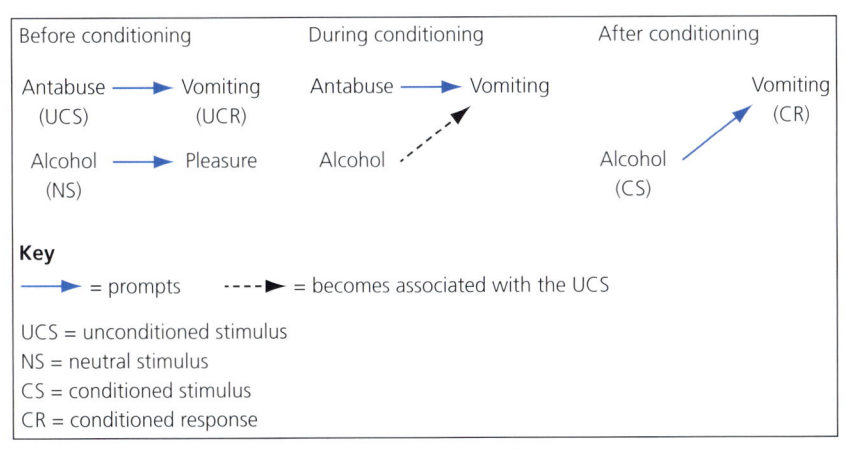

**Figure 11.10** Using Antabuse to treat alcohol addiction

This principle can be used to treat a variety of addictions although most often will be used for alcohol and smoking addiction.

## Research into aversion therapy and alcohol

Cannon & Baker (1981) tested whether 1) aversion therapy worked and 2) whether emetic drug aversion therapy was more effective than electric shock aversion therapy. They had 20 male alcoholic volunteers and assigned them to one of three groups: electric shock therapy, emetic drug therapy or no aversion therapy. They found that only the emetic drug therapy worked and the electric shock treatment was not effective. This indicates that aversion therapy can work but that the unconditioned stimulus used must be chosen carefully.

Howard (2001) tested how effective aversion therapy was with alcoholics. In a repeated measures design before and after the treatment he tested to see how confident the participants were that they would be able to refuse alcohol in social situations where they would normally drink it. He found they were more confident following treatment, so it appeared to have worked.

### Research into aversion therapy and nicotine

Curtiss *et al.* (1976) also examined how successful aversion therapy was in treating nicotine addiction. They had two groups, one that involved a discussion group and rapid smoking (to induce nausea) and the other that included discussion only. Five months after the treatment the researchers measured the smoking behaviour of the participants of both groups. They found both groups had decreased the amount they smoked but there was no significant difference in the effectiveness of the group who had received aversion therapy too. This means that the intervention was not successful with the participants in this study.

Danaher (1977) tested how effective aversion therapy could be with smokers. 50 habitual smokers were used as the sample and the intervention lasted three weeks. As an unconditioned stimulus the researchers used the smoke produced by the cigarettes and the smokers were asked to inhale deeply to the point that they felt sick. The treatment worked well for some participants but not others, which suggests that its effectiveness is specific to some individuals.

### Evaluation

- The ethics of this intervention have been challenged. The participants can be made to feel very unwell and this means that they are suffering physical harm. This means that the intervention is not now widely used in the UK.
- There is a risk that the negative association can be generalised to other stimuli inadvertently. This means that the participant may suffer from psychological harm as this is an unintended by-product of the treatment. Howard *et al.* (2001) tested this by measuring pulse rates of individuals receiving aversion therapy. They found that the pulse was raised only when they encountered the conditioned stimulus (addictive substance) so it may be that these fears are unfounded.
- Research (Danaher, 1977) shows that aversion therapy does not work with everybody. The principles of classical conditioning suggest that the treatment should work with everybody, as we all have the capacity to be classically conditioned. This suggests that there are individual differences which mean aversion therapy is only effective with some people, and has a limited usefulness.

## Covert sensitisation

This therapy adheres to the learning approach view of addiction, that it is learned and therefore can be unlearned. It is based on the principles of aversion therapy and uses classical conditioning.

### ON THE WEB

There are several videos available to watch online which show aversion therapy in action.

Although not applied to addiction, there is a classic clip from the 1970s of aversion therapy being used to stop a woman from eating junk food. You can watch it at **www.youtube.com**. Search for 'aversion therapy'.

Initially the patient is taught to relax. This means utilising relaxation techniques such as breathing exercises. The individual is then in a calm state for the next stage, removing agitation and anxiety so they can concentrate.

The next stage of the procedure involves classical conditioning and more specifically aversion therapy. However, unlike overt aversion therapy discussed above, which administers a drug to produce unpleasant feelings when someone ingests a drug such as alcohol, covert sensitisation uses the imagination of the individual. For this reason the treatment is sometimes called 'verbal aversion therapy'.

They are requested, in this therapy, to imagine bad consequences that might occur from their behaviour (this is the unconditioned response) and associate them with the drug they take. In the case of an alcoholic, alcohol would be the neutral stimulus before the therapy (although it is strictly not neutral as it induces pleasure). As covert sensitisation does not actually require the negative consequences to occur, it is really important that the imagined occurrence is as vivid and real as possible, otherwise the negative association will be too weak. For example, this therapy is often used with alcoholics. In treatment the alcoholic will be asked to imagine feeling sick when drinking alcohol. They will then be asked to further elaborate on that image by imagining actually being sick. To elicit a really negative response they would be encouraged to imagine vomiting over themselves somewhere public to maximise the negative feelings. In theory, the greater the negative emotion associated, the greater the success of the treatment. It is important that the therapist can really understand what will provoke a strong reaction from their client so that they can increase their chance of getting results.

## Research

Ashem & Donner (1968) looked at the efficacy of the treatment and found that 40 per cent of the patients receiving covert sensitisation for alcohol addiction were still abstinent six months after treatment, whereas none of the control group remained alcohol free in that time.

Maletzky (1974) found that covert sensitisation outperformed the use of a half-way house programme where patients spent time in rehab and then entered a half-way house to ease their reintroduction to their home life. It appeared to have a more enduring effect.

Fleiger & Zingle (1973) compared the use of individual covert sensitisation to problem-solving therapy which was administered in a group therapy situation. They found no statistically significant difference between the relapse rate at three months of the two treatments.

Gelder et al. (1989) reported that though covert sensitisation is preferable on humanitarian grounds, it is no more effective than aversion therapy, casting doubts on its suitability as a treatment. However, McConaghy et al. (1983) compared covert sensitisation as a treatment for gambling dependency against electrical aversion therapy, finding covert desensitisation to be more effective over a 12-month period, with 79 per cent of these patients, compared with 50 per cent of aversion patients, reporting control over, or not indulging in gambling, in a long-term follow-up study between two and nine years after treatment. This suggests that the treatment has long-term effectiveness.

### Evaluation

- This treatment does not have many of the ethical problems that other treatments such as aversion therapy have. This is because the negative consequences never actually happen to the client, they are imagined and not real, therefore the therapist is not compromised.
- The treatment is not suitable for everybody. The method only really works with highly motivated people and it is essential that they have a good imagination, otherwise the required level of emotional response will not be achieved.
- The treatment is adaptable to all addictions and other negative behaviours. This means that it can be fine-tuned to help in many situations.
- The therapist must really understand their client for it to work. The client's imagination is guided by the suggestions made by the therapist and if they do not understand what will really induce a negative reaction they will not be successful in treating the addiction.
- The treatment does not treat the motivations and root causes of the addiction. This means that the reasons why the person became addicted in the first place are not addressed and the potential for relapse is greater.

## Cognitive behavioural therapy

Cognitive behavioural therapy is an attempt to change the thought processes of the addict. It is also useful in that it helps the addict recognise what they are thinking prior to taking the drug, which raises self-awareness of potential triggers.

Part of the therapy is ensuring that the addict is equipped with skills to deal with triggers. These skills include drug-refusal skills, cognitive restructuring and relapse prevention training. However, more generic skills regarding relaxation, assertiveness and problem solving are also taught.

### Drug-refusal skills

Addicts find it difficult to say no to their addictive substance not only because of a physical addiction but also because of social pressures. This can clearly jeopardise their chances of giving up. Drug-refusal skills training can help equip them with specific strategies so that they can deal with situations where they are offered the drug. The therapy can involve role play of scenarios so that they are well rehearsed in dealing with the temptation and social pressures.

### Cognitive restructuring

This skill is hard work. It requires an addict to examine the thought processes that precede their addictive behaviour and to alter the way they think. In therapy the addict may recognise what triggers lead to their behaviours. The triggers cannot always be removed, so cognitive restructuring allows the therapist to offer alternative thought patterns that do not culminate in reverting to the addictive behaviour.

### Relapse prevention training

This is a more long-term technique of preventing a return to addictive behaviour. Some of the other forms of skill acquisition, such as learning relaxation skills (see below), work in the short-term, acute sense. While these are invaluable, it is important that there are strategies to help the addict avoid relapse in the future.

Relapse prevention training relates closely to the theory of planned behaviour (see page 425). In this training the practitioner talks to the addict about their beliefs in their addiction. This includes their attitude and motivation towards their treatment and their belief in themselves. If these beliefs are faulty or unhealthy then the practitioner will challenge their attitude. This has to be done in an individual way because of the varying attitudes addicts possess. Therapy such as this can improve the control the addict feels over their addiction, which makes them less susceptible to slipping back into addictive behaviour. If relapse is going to be prevented long term, the individual's faulty thinking will need to be addressed.

### Relaxation skills

Stress and anxiety can produce a physiological response. Some addicts will have previously self-medicated by, for example, taking a relaxant such as an opiate or by drinking alcohol. Being taught relaxation skills means they learn a physiological method for calming themselves down in a way that does not involve drugs. By practising these relaxation methods they then can relax themselves at the point they recognise they are in danger of using the drug again. This means the impulsive actions that lead to the addictive behaviour resurfacing are delayed, giving the addict a chance to rationalise their actions.

### Assertiveness training

Assertiveness training is a more generic version of the drug-refusal skills training. The trainer will teach the addict how to say no in situations where they feel pressure to conform. Assertiveness training uses non-verbal communication to ensure they say no with authority. This involves the use of powerful postures and authoritative tone of voice. This aspect of the training is clearly linked to confidence levels and so the trainer will try to boost the addict's confidence to speak up.

### Problem-solving techniques

Problem solving is seen as a key skill to treat addiction. This is because addicts will often relapse when confronted with everyday problems. The addictive substance acts as a prop to help them deal with problems they might encounter. Therefore, if they are taught strategies to stay focused on sorting the problem, and maybe even ways to enlist help, they will be better equipped to deal with issues as they arise. It is, ultimately, a way to reduce the stresses of day-to-day life by dealing with problems in a healthy way.

## Research

Young (2007) found that using cognitive therapy to treat internet addiction was highly successful. Her work was based in the USA at a centre for online addiction and focused on 114 participants. She used a self-report measure to establish such constructs as motivation, time management and social relationship success over a period of six months. In that time the participants received 12 sessions of CBT. Young found that most clients reported an excellent response to the treatment that was maintained six months later.

**ON THE WEB**

Relaxation skills are useful for everyone – not just addicts. There are many tutorials online to teach such skills. Search in YouTube for examples using 'relaxation skills'. This can also help you to describe the technique, if required, to explain what happens in Cognitive Behavioural Therapy.

Research into relapse prevention training has shown a good success rate. Chaney *et al.* (1978) conducted a randomised trial on alcoholics. There were 40 participants who were all ex-soldiers. They were randomly assigned to the skills training (relapse prevention), insight-oriented group (psychotherapy) or treatment as usual. The group that received the skills training spent fewer days drunk than the other groups and they also consumed less alcohol and spent less time drinking. This seems to suggest that cognitive therapy can be very successful in comparison with other treatments.

Haddock *et al.* (2003) examined the success of cognitive behavioural therapy with addicts who also suffered from schizophrenia. They found the treatment was highly effective and cost effective.

**Figure 11.11** Group therapy can be useful for overcoming addiction

### Evaluation

- There is research to suggest that cognitive therapy for addiction is successful. This supports the cognitive explanation for addictive behaviour as by addressing the addict's faulty thought processes, there is a change in the addictive behaviour. However, similar inferences could be made for the biological explanations for addiction due to the success of drug treatment.
- Cognitive behavioural therapy can be less successful in some cases due to the hard work that needs to be done between sessions. Maintaining a change in thought processes requires a great deal of effort on the part of the addict, so the dropout rate for such programmes can be high.
- It has been suggested that group cognitive therapy outcomes are better and that it is more effective when dealt with as a group. The cognitive theories of addiction find common misperceptions and shared cognitive distortions, so it is easy to see how this might work. The effectiveness of group therapy was evident with adolescents, who may be more likely to be affected and supported by the input of peers (Waldron & Kaminer, 2004).

### YOU ARE THE RESEARCHER

It is important for practitioners to have comparison of interventions for addictions so they have information about which intervention works best for people. How would you design an experiment that could compare any two intervention methods? What research design would you need to use? How could you gauge the effectiveness of each intervention?

There are also ethical implications and issues to consider in the design. What might those be and how could you address them?

Finally, how could you decide whether there was a statistically significant difference between the two interventions? If it is possible to test for significance, which test would you use?

> **STRENGTHEN YOUR LEARNING**
> 1. Explain how drug therapy is used for addiction.
> 2. Outline the details of one type of drug therapy for any substance.
> 3. What is a weakness of using drug therapy to treat addiction?
> 4. What is a strength of using drug therapy for treating addiction?
> 5. How does aversion therapy treat addiction?
> 6. Outline one piece of research into aversion therapy.
> 7. What is the difference between aversion therapy and covert sensitisation?
> 8. Describe how cognitive therapy can be used to treat addiction.
> 9. Outline some research that cognitive therapy is successful in treating gambling.
> 10. Outline a weakness of using cognitive therapy for treating gambling.

# 11.6 The application of theories of behaviour change to addictive behaviour

## The theory of planned behaviour

The theory of planned behaviour is a refinement of the model of reasoned action that stated that a change in addictive behaviour was underpinned by decision making processes. Ajzen (1991) developed the model to explain how beliefs affect behaviour change and it is a general model that can be related to many health behaviours, including addiction. In terms of addiction, the model may explain why someone might be successful in quitting addictive behaviours and why someone else might not.

The core idea of the model is that if we are to predict the outcome of a treatment programme we need to consider the beliefs, influences and motivation of an addict to the proposed change. There are four parts to the model:

1. **Attitude and behavioural beliefs**. Behavioural beliefs are the attitudes towards the behaviour. In the context of addiction this would be a recognition that the behaviour is having a negative effect on the addict and that giving up is a good idea. This is key to the process of recovery.
2. **Subjective norms and normative beliefs**. Normative beliefs are the beliefs of the group to which the addict feels they belong. If, for example, a drug addict was surrounded by friends who were also addicts and did not wish to give up, then the likelihood of the addict joining a treatment programme and staying on it would be diminished.
3. **Perceived behavioural control**. Control beliefs focus on the factors an addict believes are present and that may affect the treatment. It is very much their perceived idea of the situation and not the reality. So, for example, if they think that they cannot ensure they will attend

sessions or stay away from situations that challenge their resolve, the likelihood of the treatment working for them is decreased. This is not particularly what will happen, more what they believe will happen. It should be noted that Ajzen proposed that perceived control was linked directly to behaviour and could therefore be a predictor of behaviour on its own.

4 **Behavioural intentions**. The behavioural intentions are a combination of the other three factors. These all contribute to the level of intention, which is essentially the motivation to engage with the programme. This process is illustrated in Figure 11.12.

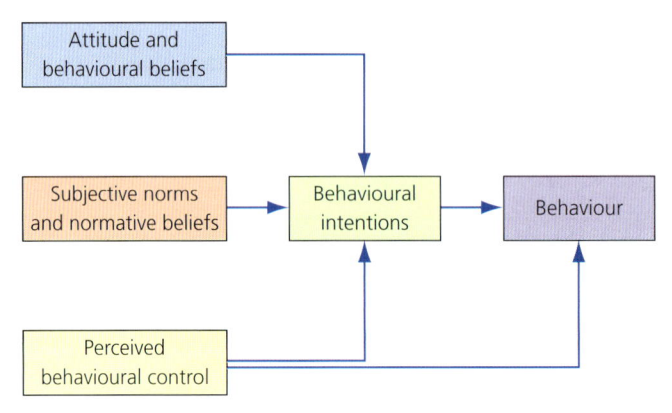

**Figure 11.12** Theory of planned behaviour (Ajzen, 1991)

The theory of planned behaviour is used by practitioners to predict the outcomes of potential treatment programmes. They can establish why someone wants to quit and the amount of resolve they have to do so. The first section of the model, which focuses on behavioural beliefs, is important to ensure they access the treatment initially. The second stage of normative beliefs ensures the social support is present and that negative peer and family influence can be dealt with. The final section of perceived control is a good indicator for the success of the programme. If an addict does not believe that they can stop their addictive behaviour, for example by stopping gambling or giving up smoking, then it is unlikely that they will.

## Research

Webb & Sheeran (2006) conducted a meta-analysis of 47 studies using the model. They found that the level of intention is linked to behavioural change, but that the link is small, so scoring high for intention with the model actually only prompts a small behaviour change. This suggests that the theory can explain behavioural change, but to a lesser degree than originally thought.

Godin & Kok (1996) reviewed how successful the theory was for predicting health-related behaviours generally. Their findings were positive, showing a significant correlation between the behaviours and the intention level predicted by the model. They also found that the level of perceived behavioural control made a significant contribution towards predicting the behaviours in half of the studies.

Oh & Hsu (2001) used a questionnaire to assess gamblers' previous gambling behaviour, their social norms, attitudes, perceived behavioural control (such as perceived gambling skills and levels of self-control), along with behavioural intentions. A positive correlation was found between attitudes and behavioural intentions and actual behaviour, supporting the model.

Walker et al. (2006) used interviews to assess whether theory of planned behaviour could explain gambling behaviour. They found that behavioural beliefs and normative beliefs were important, but that perceived behavioural control was not. Intention was, however, found to be a good predictor of behavioural change. This seems to support some elements of the model but not others.

### Evaluation

- The theory is used widely in health psychology and health economics (which looks at cost effectiveness of treatments). This suggests that practitioners acknowledge its validity and deem its predictive power as useful.
- There is no consideration of emotion within the model, which can influence the likelihood of behavioural change. This is especially the case with addiction, which is a vulnerable state and influenced by mood.
- A strength of the model is its acknowledgement of the role of peers in influencing behaviour. The previous section on peer influence in the development of addiction (see page 404) demonstrates how important their role can be. This influence does not stop once the behaviour is developed and therefore should be considered in predicting outcomes of behaviour change programmes.
- The model relies on self-report measures to gauge its effectiveness. This is a potential problem as the participants could be irrational and liable to downplay the level of their addiction. This means that the effectiveness measures may be unreliable.
- The practical application of this model is one of its strengths. Practitioners can use it to decide whether an intervention will be effective, and as such, time and money are not spent if it is not going to be effective for the individual.

## Prochaska's six-stage model of behaviour change to addictive behaviour

Prochaska's (1977) model offers an explanation for the process of changing from unhealthy to healthy behaviours. He and his colleagues felt that change of behaviour was often portrayed as an immediate jump from unhealthy to healthy and that in reality this was simply not the case. He argued that there are stages, a series of transitions in thinking and action, that lead to someone actually changing. He also argued that once their behaviour had changed, it was not a constant state and relapse could occur. Indeed, it could occur at any stage in the process.

The six stages are outlined in Table 11.5. There is also a quote of what someone in that stage might be expected to say.

**Table 11.5** Prochaska's six stages

| Stage | Outline of stage | Potential quote |
|---|---|---|
| 1 Pre-contemplation | This is when the individual will be aware that what they are doing is unhealthy, but they do not feel they need to do anything about it at this point | 'I am ok right now' |
| 2 Contemplation | In this stage individuals show an awareness that they need to take action, but they don't do it. It is often described as a stage of inertia, when people know the right thing to do but they do not act on it | 'I will change, tomorrow' |
| 3 Preparation | This stage is the first point at which action is taken. It is also important in that if the behaviour change is planned, it has a greater chance of succeeding. Behaviours at this stage are dependent on the aspect being changed, but they include things such as ensuring that there are no social events that might tempt a relapse in the early days, planning distractors to keep the individual busy, and deciding on rewards to keep motivation strong | 'I'm changing next month so I need to plan how I will do it' |
| 4 Action | This is when the plan is put into action. Smoking is stopped, alcohol is no longer drunk and this is the first time the person actually makes the change of behaviour. This stage lasts six months until it is deemed to be the next stage of maintenance. Relapse can happen at this stage | 'I have stopped' |
| 5 Maintenance | This stage can be lengthy, and starts to ensure that the initial enthusiasm and motivation do not wane. Maintenance strategies are employed, such as realising the benefits of adopting the healthier behaviour, rewarding oneself for stopping, and keeping focused on the long-term goal of termination. Relapse can still occur at this stage | 'I have still stopped!' |
| 6 Termination | Termination was added to a revision of the model in 1992. This is a stable state and is the point at which there is no longer any temptation and there is maximum confidence in the ability to resist the behaviour. Some people never achieve this stage, instead staying in the stage of maintenance for many years. However, this stage means the change is complete – relapse cannot occur | 'I will never do it again' |

The model is used to explain the change of all unhealthy behaviours to healthy ones, including addiction. The model also outlines what may make the person move on and progress from stage to stage. Variables suggested include self-efficacy (their confidence in their ability), helping relationships at home and in their social support network and reinforcement management (making sure the rewards from healthy behaviours are greater than those from unhealthy behaviours).

## Research

Smoking cessation programmes based on this theory can be successful. A meta-analysis of five studies by Velicer et al. (2007) showed that there was a robust 22–26 per cent success rate, which compares favourably with other interventions. The researchers also found no demographic differences in success (gender, age, etc.), therefore it would suggest that it suits all groups. They did find, however, that success was dependent on the smoking habits (e.g. frequency) of the individual.

Parker & Parikh (2001) looked at how successful Prochaska's theory was in aiding planning programmes of health-care interventions. They found the model performed well and helped facilitate the organising and planning of successful programmes.

A randomised control trial conducted by Aveyard et al. (2009) found that there was no increase in effectiveness if an intervention was tailored to the stages of change to the individual trying to stop smoking. This clearly contradicts the evidence found by Velicer et al. (2007).

### Evaluation

- Evidence on the effectiveness of the model is mixed. This can be seen from the Research section above.
- Noel (1999) developed a modified version of the model, which proposed that behavioural change is not linear and that the stages are more like 'influences'. So anyone going through a process of behaviour change has more or less influence from the stages at any one time. For example, someone may take action for most of the time but also have periods where they are judged to be in contemplation stage. It seems that the division between the stages may not be as clear cut as suggested by Prochaska. This idea is further supported in a 2002 review of the model (Littell and Girvin, 2002) where the discussion stated that the stages are not exclusive and therefore should not be seen as stages at all.
- Looking at change as a series of stages means that interventions can be designed to match the stage that the individual is currently in. This is argued to mean that interventions incorporating the model should work better than those that see it in a less dynamic way.
- The model has led to measures being developed to allow individuals to be classified as to which stage they are currently in. Perhaps the one which is the most widely used is URICA (University of Rhode Island Change Assessment scale), which measures the pre-contemplation, contemplation, action and maintenance stages. Adaptations have been made to make the scales more behaviour specific, depending on which unhealthy behaviour is being changed. This means that there has been a practical application to the theory, and that appropriate interventions can be administered depending on the stage.

#### STRENGTHEN YOUR LEARNING

1. Describe the theory of planned behaviour.
2. How can this theory of planned behaviour be applied to recovery from addiction?
3. Outline a piece of research that examines the effectiveness of the theory being applied to addiction.
4. What is a strength of applying the theory of planned behaviour to treat addiction?
5. What are the stages of Prochaska's six-stage model of behaviour change?
6. How is the model useful for treating addiction?
7. Outline some research which examines how effective Prochaska's model is when applied to changing behaviour.
8. What are the differences between the theory of planned behaviour and Prochaska's six-stage model of behaviour change?

# ASSESSMENT CHECK

1. Select from the statements made by an addict A, B, C and D below to complete the table relating to stages in the theory of planned behaviour. One statement will be left over. **[3 marks]**

   **A** I need to stop taking heroin, it is really bad for me

   **B** I am going to give up

   **C** My friends say the treatment doesn't work

   **D** I don't think I am going to be able to stop drinking until after Christmas

   | Stage in theory of planned behaviour | Statements |
   | --- | --- |
   | Attitude and behavioural beliefs | |
   | Subjective norms and normative beliefs | |
   | Perceived behavioural control | |

2. Researchers are interested in examining the point at which someone realises they are becoming addicted and intend to find people who may have a problem and don't realise.

   Explain what the issues of finding a sample are for this study. **[2 marks]**

3. Briefly outline how covert sensitisation can help reduce addiction. **[4 marks]**

4. Read the item and then answer the question:

   Replacing one drug with another to treat addiction is seen by some to be counter-productive.

   With reference to the item, briefly explain how drug therapy works and one limitation of its use. **[4 marks]**

5. Describe and evaluate the application of Prochaska's six-stage model to behaviour change in addicts. **[16 marks]**

## SUMMARY

**Describing addiction**

- Addiction can be described by using the diagnostic manual DSM-5. This suggests 11 possible symptoms of which two need to be evident. They must present together within the same 12-month period.
- Alcoholism must meet different criteria to be diagnosed. Internet dependence and caffeine addiction have not yet become part of the diagnostic manual.
- Tolerance is the name given to the need to ingest more and more of a substance for it to have an effect.
- Withdrawal is the effects that occur due to no longer taking the drug or substance. These vary depending on what the individual is addicted to.

**Risk factors in the development of addiction**

- Research indicates that there may be a genetic vulnerability to developing addiction. Much of the supporting research comes from twin studies.
- Stress seems to be implicated in addiction as the substance abuse or gambling may provide a means of escape from stressors.
- Eysenck and Cloninger both proposed that there may be elements of an individual that predispose them to addictive behaviour. These are suggested to be high neuroticism, novelty seeking, harm avoidance and reward dependence.
- Family influences may also make someone vulnerable to addiction due to the influences of social learning and expectancies. Peers have a similar effect. The relative influences of these two sources vary on the individual and their age.

**Explanations for nicotine addiction**

**Explanations for gambling addiction**

- Dopamine and, more specifically, dopaminergic activity is implicated in nicotine addiction due to the processing of reward from the substance or behaviour.
- The learning approach can explain nicotine addiction and gambling addiction through operant conditioning, social learning and cue reactivity (i.e. classical conditioning). It seems likely that an explanation combining these elements would have the best explanatory power.
- Partial and variable reinforcement play a part in the likelihood of developing an addiction with variable ratio and variable interval having the greatest effect.
- The cognitive approach argues that addiction to gambling can be explained by cognitive biases such as the gambler's fallacy, illusion of control and confirmation bias.

**Reducing addiction**

- Drug therapy can be used to treat addictions that are based on substance abuse. The drugs used depend on the drug addiction type. Nicotine and heroin rely on substitutes whereas alcohol relies on sedatives and Antabuse which is an integral part of aversion therapy.
- Aversion therapy works on the principles of classical conditioning where the pleasant feeling from taking a drug is replaced by an unpleasant association such as feeling sick. This association is induced by a drug or, in the case of nicotine addiction, by using the effects of the cigarette smoke.

### The application of the theory of planned behaviour and Prochaska's six stage model

- Covert sensitisation works on exactly the same principles as aversion therapy except that the unpleasant association is formed through the use of the addict's imagination. This method is more ethical than aversion therapy, although less effective generally.
- Cognitive behavioural therapy is based around teaching six skills to retrain distorted thinking; drug-refusal skills, cognitive restructuring, relapse prevention training, relaxation skills, assertiveness training and problem-solving techniques.
- The theory of planned behaviour is a model that predicts treatment success by examining the intention and control an individual perceives they have over their addictive behaviour. The motivation to succeed is also affected by their attitude and the attitude of those around them.
- Prochaska's six-stage model of behaviour change considers the stages somebody goes through before they have managed to make a permanent change in their behaviour, e.g. giving up addictive substances or behaviours. The six stages are pre-contemplation, contemplation, preparation, action, maintenance and termination.

# Glossary

**Absence of gating** – the lack of limiting factors upon the formation of virtual relationships that form barriers to the creation of physical relationships
**Absorption-addiction model** – where an individual's fascination with a media personality progresses to a delusion of a real relationship
**Accommodation** – altering existing schemas to fit in new experiences
**Actus reus** – an act that constitutes a crime
**Alpha bias** – the attempt to exaggerate the differences between the genders
**Amygdala** – an area of the brain within the limbic system which processes emotion
**Androcentrism** – 'male bias'. Men's behaviour is the standard against which women's behaviour is compared
**Androgyny** – co-existence of male and female characteristics within the same individual
**Anorexia nervosa** – an eating disorder characterised by an obsessive desire to lose weight by refusing to eat
**Aromatase** – an enzyme which helps metabolise (or process) testosterone
**Assimilation** – fitting new environmental experiences into existing schemas
**Atavistic form** – a possible explanation for criminal offending, centring on the idea that offenders may represent a more primitive evolutionary stage of development than their contemporaries. This may be shown in a range of facial and physical features
**Attachment theory** – the tendency for parasocial relationships to be formed by those with insecure childhood attachments
**Atypical antipsychotics** – a class of neuroleptic drugs produced later used to treat schizophrenia
**Autism** – a developmental disability characterised by problems in communicating and building relationships with others and in using language and abstract concepts
**Autonomy and control** – the perception of anorexia nervosa as a struggle for self-management, identity and effectiveness
**Aversion therapy** – a treatment used to reduce addictive behaviours broadly used on classical conditioning
**Avolition** – a general lack of energy resulting in loss of goal-directed behaviour
**Bem Sex Role Inventory** – a self-report measure of masculinity–femininity and gender role

**Benzodiazepines** – anti-anxiety drugs that dampen down the activity of the nervous system, creating a sensation of calm and relaxation
**Beta bias** – the attempt to downplay the differences between the genders
**Beta-blockers** – anti-anxiety drugs that block the transmission of nerve impulses, to reduce heart rate and alleviate the physical effects of stress
**Biofeedback** – the gaining of awareness and control over bodily functions in order to reduce stress levels
**Biological explanations for gender identity disorder** – the perception that gender identity disorder is physiologically determined
**Boundary model** – that obesity results from conflict between physiological and cognitive limits on food intake
**Calories** – the energy content of food
**Cardiovascular disorders** – dysfunctions of the heart and blood vessels
**Chromosomes** – structures of nucleic acids and protein found in the nucleus of most living cells that contain genetic information
**Class inclusion** – an understanding that some sets of objects or sub-sets can be sets of other larger classes of objects
**Cognitive behavioural therapy** – treatment of abnormality that modifies thought patterns to alter behavioural and emotional states
**Cognitive explanations** – the idea that the development of schizophrenia is related to maladaptive thought processes
**Cognitive theory** – that anorexia results from maladaptive thought processes
**Co-morbidity** – the presence of one or more additional disorders or diseases simultaneously occurring with schizophrenia
**Complementarity** – the ability of individuals to meet each other's needs
**Conditions of worth** – requirements an individual believes they must have to be loved
**Congruence** – when your selves are the same as each other
**Conscious mind** – the part of the mind we are aware of
**Conservation** – an understanding that changing the appearance of something does not affect its mass, number or volume
**Control** – the degree of influence an individual has over their workload and job requirements
**Core knowledge theory** – the belief that humans have an innate understanding of inanimate objects and their relationships with each other

**Cortisol** – a steroid hormone secreted from the adrenal glands in reaction to stress
**Cue reactivity** – an example of classical conditioning where objects and environments become conditioned stimuli
**Cultural influences** – eating practices that are transmitted to members of cultural groupings
**Cultural relativism** – the belief that it is essential to consider the cultural context when examining behaviour in that culture. There is no global right or wrong, it varies across cultures
**Culture bias** – the tendency to over-diagnose members of other cultures as suffering from schizophrenia
**Custodial sentencing** – a prison sentence
**Daily hassles** – everyday irritations that produce an overall elevated level of stress
**Decentring** – a movement away from egocentrism where children are increasingly able to see things from the viewpoint of others
**Defence mechanism** – a strategy to reduce anxiety
**Delusions** – a false belief that is resistant to confrontation with the truth
**Denial** – a refusal to accept the reality of a situation
**Desensitisation** – habituating to the violence seen in the media so that when it reoccurs at a similar level it has no emotional effect
**Deterrence** – a method of stopping someone doing something (in this context it is used regarding crime prevention)
**Diagnosis** – identification of the nature and cause of illness
**Diathesis-stress model** – the idea that individuals have varying genetic potentials for schizophrenia that combine with the degree of environmental stressors in their lives to form their actual amount of vulnerability to the disorder
**Dieting** – restrained eating involving voluntary restriction of food intake
**Differential association theory** – a learning theory of offending behaviour
**Discovery learning** – learning that occurs through active exploration
**Disequilibrium** – unpleasant state of imbalance that motivates a return to equilibrium
**Disinhibition** – the feeling of being within (or caught up in) the media and therefore acting in an uncharacteristic way
**Disinhibition** – overeating through the loss of restraint over food intake

433

**Displacement** – a strong emotion is displaced from its target onto a neutral object or person
**Dispositional model** – this looks to the characteristics of an individual for an explanation as to why aggression may occur
**Dissolution** – the process by which romantic relationships break down
**Distortions** – errors in thinking that negatively affect perceptions of body image
**Dopamine hypothesis** – that the development of schizophrenia is related to abnormal levels of the hormone and neurotransmitter dopamine
**Drug therapy** – chemical treatment of abnormality through tablets and intravenous means
**DSM-5** – diagnostic classification system produced in the USA
**Dual control theory** – a homeostatic view of eating, whereby hunger motivates eating, which in turn leads to satiety and cessation of eating
**Duck's phase model of dissolution** – that relationship breakdown occurs through a series of stages
**Dysfunctional thought processing** – the idea that the development of schizophrenia is related to abnormal ways of thinking
**Ego** – the part of the personality that delays gratification and balances the demands of the id and superego
**Egocentrism** – an inability to see a situation from another's point of view
**Electra complex** – the arousal in girls of unconscious sexual desire for their father and dislike of their mother
**Empiricism** – the nurture side of the debate
**Enmeshment** – a family interactive style that inhibits each family member's sense of individuality
**Equilibration** – the process of swinging between equilibrium and disequilibrium
**Equilibrium** – a pleasant state of balance
**Equity theory** – an explanation of relationship maintenance based on motivation to achieve fairness and balance
**Ethnocentrism** – the assumption that one ethnic group is superior to another or all others and that the behaviour in that group is the 'norm'
**Ethology** – the study of animal behaviour
**Evolution** – the process of adaptation through natural selection
**Evolutionary explanation** – that obesity results from the evolutionary tendency to store energy as fat for times of food scarcity
**Evolutionary explanation** – that certain foods are preferable as they have an adaptive survival value

**Family dysfunction** – the idea that dysfunctional family relationships and patterns of communication are related to the development of schizophrenia
**Family systems theory** – that anorexia nervosa results from dysfunctional patterns of family interaction
**Family therapy** – treatment of schizophrenia by alteration of communication systems within families
**Filter theory** – that choice of partners is affected by factors limiting the availability of those possible to select from
**Fixation** – if a conflict is experienced during development through one of the psychosexual stages, a fixation will affect the personality
**Fixed action pattern** – the behaviour prompted by an innate releasing mechanism
**Food preferences** – bias towards the consumption of certain foodstuffs
**Free will** – ability of an individual to choose a course of action or to act a certain way
**Freud's psychoanalytic theory of gender** – an explanation of gender development that sees gender identity and role as acquired during the phallic stage where the focus of libido moves to the genitals
**Gender** – the social and psychological characteristics of males and females
**Gender bias** – the tendency for diagnostic criteria to be applied differently to males and females and for there to be differences in the classification of the disorder
**Gender identity disorder** – a condition whereby the external sexual characteristics of the body are perceived as opposite to the psychological experience of oneself as male or female
**Gender schema theory** – an explanation of gender development that sees gender identity alone as providing children with motivation to assume sex-typed behaviour patterns
**General adaptation syndrome** – a description of the body's short and long-term reaction to stress
**Genetic explanation** – that anorexia nervosa results from an inherited predisposition
**Genetic explanation** – that obesity results from an inherited predisposition
**Genetic explanation** – transmission of abnormality by hereditary means
**Genetic vulnerability** – the idea that someone may be more likely to be an addict because of their genetic make-up
**Ghrelin** – a hormone produced by the stomach associated with increasing appetite

**Hallucinations** – the perception of something being real that does not truly exist
**Hardiness** – healthy personality type characterised by control, commitment and self-improvement
**Heredity** – the term for something being inherited, i.e. within the genes
**Hierarchy of needs** – the needs required to be in place before self-actualisation can be realised
**Holism** – the argument that behaviour should be viewed as a whole
**Hormonal mechanisms** – chemical messengers within the body that influence eating behaviour
**Hormones** – chemical messengers that are released into the bloodstream from glands
**Human reproductive behaviour** – the different mating strategies used by males and females
**Hypothalamic-pituitary–adrenal system** – bodily system responding to chronic, long-term stressors, comprised of the hypothalamus, the pituitary gland and the adrenal glands
**Hypothalamus** – a small brain structure associated with the regulation of eating
**ICD-10** – diagnostic classification system produced by the World Health Organization
**Id** – the part of the personality that seeks pleasure
**Ideal self** – the self you wish to be
**Identification** – the process of acquiring the characteristics of the same-sex parent
**Idiographic** – when an explanation considers the individual and argues that generalising from person to person is difficult because of their uniqueness
**Immune system** – bodily system that defends against disease
**Immunosuppression** – the impaired ability of the immune system to fight illness and disease
**Importation model** – aggression occurs due to the individual characteristics that prisoners bring into prison
**Influence of culture** – the effect of society upon gender development
**Influence of media** – the effect of mass communication upon gender development
**Innate releasing mechanism** – a proposed innate mechanism that prompts a behaviour following presence of a stimulus
**Interactionist approach** – the idea that schizophrenia results from a combination of psychological, biological and social factors

**Internalisation** – the incorporation of the same-sex parent into an individual's personality
**Irrational beliefs** – maladaptive ideas that lead to the development and maintenance of anorexia nervosa
**Klinefelter's syndrome** – a chromosomal condition that affects male physical and cognitive development
**Kohlberg's theory** – an explanation of gender development that perceives children as developing an understanding of gender in stages, with gender-role behaviour apparent only after an understanding emerges that gender is fixed and constant
**Lateral hypothalamus** – a part of the hypothalamus associated with hunger and onset of eating
**Leptin** – a hormone produced by fat cells associated with the regulation of energy intake and expenditure
**Lesions** – damage made to brain tissue in order to see the effects upon eating behaviour
**Life changes** – occasional events incurring major adjustments to lifestyle
**Limbic system** – a central area of the brain which has many functions, including processing of emotion
**MAOA gene** – a gene which affects how neurotransmitters are metabolised
**Matching hypothesis** – the idea that individuals are attracted to people of similar perceived attractiveness
**Media** – public forms of communication
**Mens rea** – the intention to commit the act that constitutes a crime
**Metabolisation** – the processing of a biochemical by the body
**Mirror neuron system** – a network of nerves in the brain that allows individuals to experience the actions of others as if they were their own
**Modelling** – where learning occurs vicariously by experience through observation of others
**Nativism** – the nature side of the debate
**Negative symptoms** – the displaying of behaviours involving disruption of normal emotions and actions
**Neophobia** – a dislike of new or unfamiliar foodstuffs
**Neural correlates** – that the development of schizophrenia is related to structural and functional brain abnormalities
**Neural explanations** – that obesity results from abnormally functioning brain mechanisms
**Neural explanations** – that anorexia nervosa results from abnormally functioning brain mechanisms

**Neural mechanisms** – the influence of brain components in regulating eating behaviour
**Nomothetic** – the idea that people can be regarded as groups and theories/explanations are therefore generalisable
**Obesity** – the condition of being chronically overweight
**Object permanence** – an understanding that objects that are not being perceived or acted upon still exist
**Oedipus complex** – the arousal in boys of unconscious sexual desire for their mother and fear and dislike of their father
**Oestrogen** – a group of steroid hormones which promotes the development and maintenance of female characteristics in the body
**Operations** – strings of schemas assembled in a logical order
**Oxytocin** – a polypeptide hormone which acts also as a neurotransmitter that controls key aspects of the reproductive system
**Parasocial relationships** – one-sided relationships occurring with media personalities outside of an individual's real social network
**Personality types** – broad characterisations describing categories of people sharing similar characteristics
**Perspective-taking** – the ability to understand from another's point of view
**Physical attractiveness** – the degree to which an individual's physical characteristics are considered aesthetically pleasing or beautiful
**Pleistocene era** (also known as the Environment of Evolutionary Adaptiveness or EEA) – time era when food preferences are seen as having evolved
**Positive symptoms** – the displaying of behaviours involving loss of touch with reality
**Pre-conscious mind** – the thoughts that occur just out of conscious awareness
**Psychosexual stages** – a series of stages that every individual develops through, from birth to puberty
**Real self** – who you actually are
**Recidivism** – reoffending following judicial punishment. Committing the same, or another, crime again
**Reductionism** – an explanation is reductionist when a single explanation or cause is suggested
**Rehabilitation** – to change the behaviour of an offender to being a non-offender
**Reinforcement** – the consequence of a behaviour that strengthens (increases) the chances of it occurring again

**Reliability** – consistency of diagnosis
**Repression** – highly emotional and unpleasant thoughts are buried deep in the unconscious mind
**Restorative justice** – where an offender meets with a victim and tries to make amends for the crime committed, thus helping the offender avoid further bad behaviour
**Restraint theory** – that obesity results from the placing of unsustainable limits on food intake
**Role-taking theory** – an explanation that sees perspective-taking developing through adopting the outlook of others in order to understand their feelings, intentions and thoughts
**Rusbult's investment model** – relationship satisfaction as dependent upon a consideration of perceived benefits, costs and the quality of possible alternative relationships
**Sally-Anne test** – a method of assessing an individual's social cognitive ability to attribute false beliefs to others
**Scaffolding** – tuition given by more knowledgeable others
**Schemas** – ways of understanding the world
**Schizophrenia** – a mental disorder characterised by withdrawal from reality
**Self-actualisation** – peak state of existence that any individual can attain
**Self-concept** – the way you see yourself
**Self-disclosure** – the revealing of personal information about oneself to another
**Self-report scales** – personal ratings of an individual's stress levels
**Serotonin** – a neurotransmitter thought to regulate feelings of well-being
**Set point theory** – that each individual is orientated biologically to a specific body weight
**Sex** – whether an individual is biologically female or male
**Sex-role stereotypes** – types of qualities and characteristics seen as appropriate for each sex.
**Sexual selection** – the selection of characteristics increasing reproductive success
**Similarity in attitudes** – the degree of likeness between individuals' viewpoints
**Situational model** – aggression occurs as a result of factors within the prison setting
**Skin conductance response** – a method of measuring electrical conductivity within the skin as an indication of psychological and physiological arousal
**Social cognition** – the understanding of information relating to members of the same species

**Social demography** – that choice of partners is limited to individuals of similar class, education and economic background
**Social exchange theory** – an economic explanation of relationship maintenance based on maximising profits and minimising costs
**Social explanations for gender identity disorder** – the perception that gender identity disorder is a condition learned via socialisation processes
**Social influences** – the impact of others upon an individual's food preferences
**Social learning theory** – explanation that sees gender development as occurring through the observation and imitation of models
**Social learning theory** – the perception of anorexia nervosa as being learned through observation and imitation
**Social support** – the degree of assistance and resources available from others to help cope with stress
**Socio-biological explanation** – a theory of relationships based on biological determinants
**Speech poverty** – a negative symptom of schizophrenia, characterised by brief replies to questions and minimal elaboration
**Stress** – lack of balance between the perceived demands of a situation and perceived abilities to cope with such demands
**Stress inoculation therapy** – type of cognitive behavioural therapy that cognitively restructures emotional and behavioural responses
**Stress management** – physiological and psychological methods of reducing the negative effects of stress

**Stressors** – internal and external sources of stress
**Superego** – the part of the personality that stops behaviour and becomes an individual's conscience
**Sympathomedullary pathway** – bodily system responding to acute, short-term stressors, comprised of the sympathetic nervous system and the sympathetic adrenal medullary system
**Symptom overlap** – the perception that symptoms of schizophrenia are also symptoms of other mental disorders
**Taste aversion** – an innate ability to dislike and avoid certain foodstuffs
**Testosterone** – a steroid hormone that stimulates development of male secondary sexual characteristics
**Theory of mind** – the ability to attribute mental states to oneself and others
**Token economies** – a method of behaviour modification that reinforces target behaviours by awarding tokens that can be exchanged for material goods
**Tolerance** – the need to take higher levels of a substance to get the same physical and psychological effects
**Turner's syndrome** – a chromosomal condition that affects female physical development
**Type I schizophrenia** – acute form characterised by positive symptoms and responsive to medication
**Type II schizophrenia** – chronic type characterised by negative symptoms and unresponsive to medication
**Type A personality** – personality type characterised by time urgency, excessive competitiveness and generalised hostility, incurring risk of heart disease

**Type B personality** – healthy personality type characterised by non-competitiveness, self-confidence and relaxation
**Type C personality** – personality type characterised by suppression of negative emotions, incurring risk of cancer
**Type D personality** – personality type characterised by distress, gloom, worry and lack of sociability, incurring risk of heart attacks
**Typical antipsychotics** – the original neuroleptic drugs created in the 1950s to treat schizophrenia
**Unconditional positive regard** – total acceptance received from another person
**Unconscious mind** – the thoughts that occur without any conscious awareness
**Validity** – accuracy of diagnosis
**Ventromedial hypothalamus** – a part of the hypothalamus associated with cessation of eating
**Violation of expectation technique** – a research method that uses the tendency for infants to look for longer at things that are not expected to test their knowledge of the properties of objects
**Virtual relationships** – non-physical interactions between people communicating via social media
**Withdrawal syndrome** – the reaction psychologically and physically of an individual when they no longer have a substance in their system
**Workload** – the number of tasks and obligations an individual has to perform or complete within a specific amount of time
**Workplace stressors** – aspects of the work environment which have a negative impact on health
**Zone of proximal development** – the distance between current and potential intellectual ability

# Index

## A

absorption-addiction model   99–100
Abumere (2012)   358
Abzug, Bella   115
accommodation   152
actus reus   348
acute onset schizophrenia   187
Adams, Douglas   282
addiction   32, 38, 43, 49, 54, 58, 363, 382, 391–429
   behaviour change theories, application of   425–9
   CBT and   422–4
   description of   393–6
   drug therapy   417–19
   explanations for gambling addiction   409–15
   explanations for nicotine addiction   407–9
   risk factors for   397–405
Adolescent Self-rating Life Events checklist   401
adoption studies   198, 199, 362
adrenaline   268–9, 270, 296
aetiological validity   190, 191
aggression   32, 35, 38, 43, 46, 49, 54, 58, 307–41
   ethological explanation for   315–17
   evolutionary explanations for human aggression   317–19
   genetic factors   32, 43, 49, 58, 312–15
   hormonal mechanisms   308, 311–12, 313
   institutional aggression in prisons   330–5
   media influences on   335–41
   neural mechanisms   308–11, 313–17
   social psychological explanations for human aggression   321–8
Agnew (1992)   361
Agnostic Zetetic   143
Aguiar & Baillargeon (1999)   166–7, 168
Ajzen (1977)   72
Ajzen (1991)   425–6
Akers & Lee (1996)   403
Akert (1992)   88
Alarid et al. (2000)   373
alarm reaction   268
Albrecht & Pepe (1997)   117
alcohol addiction   395, 396, 398
   aversion therapy   419–20
   drug therapy   417, 418
Allardyce et al. (2006)   191
Allen, Lily   154
Alonso & Rosenfield (2002)   117
alpha bias   30, 32
Altman & Taylor (1973)   72, 73
Alvaro & Gibbs (1996)   372
American Academy of Paediatrics (1998)   234

amygdala   308, 311
Anad & Brobeck (1951)   240
Anderson, Anderson & Deusser (1996)   340–1
Anderson & Bushman (2001)   337
androcentrism   29
androgyny   32, 37, 111–14
anger management   54, 384–6
animistic thinking   153
anonymity   339
anorexia nervosa (AN)   32, 37, 43, 49, 245–54
   biological explanations   245–8
   psychological explanations   249–54
anti-social personality disorder   364–5
antipsychotic drugs   211–15, 217
appraisal support   303
Archer, Dale   393
Archer & Lloyd (1982)   110, 136
Argyle (1977)   83
Argyle (1988)   82, 88
aromatase   311
Ashem & Donner (1968)   421
Ashkar & Kenny (2007)   369
Asperger's syndrome   176
assertiveness training   423
assimilation   151–2
atavistic form   360–1
Atkins et al. (2002)   180
attachment theories   44, 54, 102–3
Attanasio et al. (1985)   301
attractiveness   66, 75–6
atypical antipsychotic drugs   211, 212–15
atypical gender development   143–6
atypical sex chromosome patterns   120–3
Aubry et al. (1999)   129
authority, minimisation of   339
autism   58, 150, 169
   and mirror neuron system   179, 181
   and schizophrenia   195
   theory of mind as explanation of   174–7
automatism   346
autonomic nervous system (ANS)   270, 367
autonomy   250, 333, 334
aversion therapy   419–20
Aveyard et al. (2009)   428
Avis & Harris (1991)   173
avolition   188
Avramopoulos et al. (2013)   199
Ayllon & Azrin (1968)   220

## B

Bachner-Melman et al. (2007)   246
Bagnall et al. (2003)   212–13
Baicy et al. (2007)   243
Bailer et al. (2005)   248
Baillargeon (1987)   166
Baillargeon & DeVos (1991)   166
Baillargeon et al. (1985)   166
Baillargeon, Renée   150, 165–8
Baillie et al. (2009)   191

Bakker et al. (2011)   287
Ballard (1999)   337
Bandura (1977)   326
Bandura (1997)   323
Bandura, Ross & Ross (1961)   324
Bandura, Ross & Ross (1963)   324–5
Bandura, Underwood & Fromson (1975)   339
Bargh et al. (2002)   96
Barlow & Durand (2009)   222
Baron-Cohen (1993)   175
Baron-Cohen, Leslie & Frith (1985)   175–6
Barry et al. (1957)   141
Barrymore, Drew   417
Bartlett (2003)   263
Bartsch & Wellman (1995)   173
Bateson (1956)   205
Bateson et al. (1956)   205
Bauman & Ennett (2006)   404
Beauchamp (1987)   230
Beauvoir, Simone de   67, 108, 245
Beck et al. (1962)   189
Beck & Rector (2005)   206
Bee (2000)   139
Begg (2001)   396
behaviour change
   behaviour modification programmes   383–4
   six-stage model of   427–9
   theories of   425–9
Behavioural Assessment of the Dysexecutive Syndrome test   208
behavioural beliefs   425, 426
behavioural intentions   426
behaviourism   45–6; see also learning approach to psychology
Beijsterveldt et al. (2006)   144–5
Bell (1973)   230
Belson (1978)   338
Bem (1974)   113
Bem (1975)   112
Bem (1981)   127–8
Bem (1983)   112
Bem, Sandra   37, 114
Bem Sex Role Inventory (BSRI)   112–14
Bemis (1978)   252
Bemis-Vitouesk & Orimoto (1993)   253
Benchley, Robert   275
Bennett (2006)   145
Bentall (2003)   192
Benzel et al. (2007)   199
benzodiazepines (BZs)   294–5, 417, 418
Berg, Elizabeth   169
Berk (1994)   162
Berko (1960)   156
Bernardy (2013)   295
Bernstein & Webster (1980)   236
beta bias   30, 32
beta-blockers   295–7
Betall et al. (1991)   208
Beversdorf et al. (2005)   297
bias

cognitive   412–15
cultural   30–1, 32, 193–4
gender   28–30, 32, 194–5
Big 5 personality traits   53
biochemistry   35
biofeedback   300–1
biological approach to psychology   19, 20, 21, 22, 23, 24
biological determinism   35, 36–7
biological explanations for anorexia nervosa   245–8
genetic   245–6
neural   246–8
biological explanations
for gender identity disorder   144–5, 258–9
for obesity   256–9
for offending behaviour   360–5
for schizophrenia   198–204
biological reductionism   47
bipolar disorder   193, 195, 272
Birch (1992)   237
Birch et al. (1987)   234
Birch et al. (1998)   235
Birchwood & Jackson (2001)   191
Birkhead (1990)   70
Blaszczynski & Nower (2002)   411–12
Blinder et al. (1988)   250
Block (1979)   135
Blomberg & Lucken (2000)   334
blood pressure   285–6, 297
Bloom & German (2000)   174
body symmetry   66, 69
Bogdonoff et al. (1961)   287
Bolger & Amarel (2007)   304
Bombeck, Erma   211
Boos et al. (2012)   202
Booth (1975)   142
Bouchard et al. (2012)   300
Bourdieu (1984)   238
Bower & Wishart (1972)   155
Bowie & Harvey (2006)   207
Bowlby (1944)   375
Bowlby, John   44, 374
Bozsik et al. (1995)   300
brain physiology   35, 364–5
Branson, Tom   11
Bray et al. (2004)   258
Brehm (1992)   57, 58
Brewer & Mittelman (1980)   74
Brigham (1971)   75
Brobeck (1946)   240
Bronfenbrenner (1979, 1989)   30
Bronfenbrenner, Urie   32
Brooks (2012)   248
Brown (1986)   279
Brown Assessment of Beliefs Scale (BABS)   253–4
Brown et al. (2002)   122
Brune et al. (2011)   208
Brunner (1993)   314
Bryant et al. (2008)   260–1

Brynner (1969)   409
Buckley et al. (2009)   192
Buddha   366
Bulik et al. (2006)   245
Bullers et al. (2001)   404
Burchardt & Serbin (1982)   113
Bushman (2009)   338
Buss (1963)   322
Buss (1989)   69
Buss (1993)   67
Bussey & Bandura (1992)   137
Butzlaff & Hooley (1998)   205
Byrne (1961)   77
bystander behaviour   57

## C

Caesar, Julius   165
caffeine dependence   394
Calvert (2009)   409
Cambridge Study in Delinquent Development   362
Campbell (2000)   129
Campbell et al. (2002)   129
Canary & Stafford (1992)   83
cancer: and stress   291–2, 293
Cannon & Baker (1981)   420
Cannon et al. (2002)   222
Capaldi et al. (1989)   229
Caplan et al. (1975)   283
cardiovascular disorders (CVDs)   272, 284, 297
and stress   275–6, 289, 290–1, 292
Cartier et al. (2006)   382
Cartwright (2000)   69
case studies   8–9, 51, 132, 133
Cases et al. (1995)   314
Cashon & Cohen (2000)   167
Cassiodorus   230
Castle et al. (1993)   194
castration anxiety   7
causal explanations   36–7
CBT (cognitive behavioural therapy)   16, 216–17, 422–4
Celebrity Attitude Scale   99
celebrity worship syndrome (CWS)   100–1
cellular tolerance   394
centration   153
challenge   292
Chaney et al. (1978)   424
Charnley, Brian   188
Chavez, Cesar   30
Cheeseman (2003)   334, 380
Cheever, Susan   408
Chen Internet Addiction Scale   401
Chen Jen   204
Cherek et al. (1996)   310
Chesney & Rosenman (1980)   291
Chiara (2000)   407
childhood sexual abuse   271
Chisholm, Shirley   109
Christiansen (1977)   362
Christiansen et al. (1989)   403

chromosomes   115, 120–3
chronic onset schizophrenia   187
Clark (1952)   77
class inclusion   154
classical conditioning   35, 47, 235, 408–9, 411, 419–22
classification   52
DSM system   29, 52, 143, 188, 189, 190, 191, 393–4, 398
ICD-10 system   52, 188, 189, 191
of schizophrenia   186–96
Cloninger (1987)   402
Cobb & Rose (1973)   275
cocaine   395, 398
Cochrane (1977)   193
Cochrane (1983)   194
Cochrane & Sashidharan (1995)   194
Coelho, Paul   278
cognition   32, 37, 43, 48, 53, 58
cognitive approach to psychology   19, 20, 21, 22, 23, 24
cognitive bias   412–15
cognitive development stages   152–4, 155, 156
cognitive development theories   150–68
Baillargeon   150, 165–8
Piaget   150–7, 163
Vygotsky   150, 159–63
cognitive explanations
for anorexia nervosa   252–4
for gender development   125–9
for offending behaviour   368–70
for schizophrenia   206–7
cognitive priming   339–41
cognitive restructuring   422
cognitive schema theory   112
cognitive theories
for gambling addiction   412–15
for schizophrenia   206–7
cognitive therapy   19, 37, 415, 424
Cohen et al. (1993)   273
Cohen, Leonard   280
Cohen & Williamson (1991)   276
Coid et al. (2007)   381
Cole & Leets (1999)   102
Coleman (1973)   242
Colley (1994)   110
Collins & Miller (1994)   74
commitment   84–5, 292
compatibilism   34
computer games: effects of   335–7
concept formation   161
conditional positive regard   16
conditions of worth   16
confinement   378, 379, 383
congruence   15
Connor & Levine (1969)   311
conscious mind   2–3
conservation   153
contiguity   410
control   250, 283, 292, 317
control beliefs   425–6, 426

conventional/straight sub-culture 331
convict sub-culture 331
Coolidge et al. (2002) 145
Cooper (2003) 316
Cooper et al. (1989) 316
Cooper & McKay (1986) 325
core knowledge theory (CKT) 165–8
Cornwell & Lundgren (2001) 93
coronary heart disease (CHD) 275, 284, 289, 290
cortisol 49, 117, 222, 223
 and stress 268, 269, 271–2, 273, 281
Courtois et al. (2007) 281
courtship rituals 67, 68
Cousins, Norman 211
covert sensitisation 420–2
Crick & Dodge (1994) 371
Crighton (2006) 380
Crighton & Towl (2008) 380
crime
 definition of 346–50
 measurement of 348–9
Crime Survey for England and Wales (CSEW) 348–9
criminal personality theory 366–8
criminal responsibility 347
criminal/thief sub-culture 331
Crockett et al. (2009a and b) 310
Crockett & Passamonti (2011) 309
cross tolerance 394
Csikszentmihalyi, Mihaly 13
cue reactivity 408–9
cultural bias 30–1, 32, 193–4
cultural influences
 on food preferences 238
 on gender development 141–2
cultural relativism 31, 32
Cummings, Dominic 42
Cummings et al. (2002) 264
Curtiss et al. (1976) 420
Cushing's syndrome 272
custodial sentencing 378–81
cyber-bullying 92
cyber-stalking 92

D
Dainton (2003) 83
Daly et al. (1982) 319
Daly & Wilson (1988) 318
Danaher (1977) 420
D'Anci et al. (2008) 264
Dani & Basi (2001) 407
Daniels (1988) 13
Dapretto et al. (2006) 177, 179
Darwin, Charles 64–5
Dasen (1977) 156
Davidson (1993) 295
Davis (1990) 69
Davis et al. (1989) 213
Davis et al. (1991) 200
Davis & Raymond (2000) 379
de-individuation 49, 326–8

De Longis et al. (1988) 281
Deady et al. (2006) 116
decalage 153
decentring 154, 172
defence mechanisms 3–5, 375–6
Delfabbro (2004) 414
Delis Kaplan Executive Function System test 208
DeLisi et al. (2004) 332
DeLisi et al. (2005) 121
denial 4
Denollet et al. (1996) 292
Denollet et al. (1998) 292
Denton (1982) 230
deprivation 333–4
Derlega & Chaikin (1976) 74
Derlega & Grzelak (1979) 73
Descartes, René 40
descriptive validity 190, 191
desensitisation 338
Desor et al. (1973) 229
determinism 19–20, 34–8
deterrence 378, 379
deviant superego 374
Diamond (1992) 70
diathesis-stress model 222–3
Dickerson et al. (2005) 220
DiDomenico & Andersen (1992) 252
Diener, Ed 327
dieting 261–4
Dietrich, Marlene 303
differential association theory 49, 373
differential susceptibility hypothesis 223
DiFranza (2008) 398
Dijkstra & Barelds (2008) 78
DiMeglio & Mates (2000) 258
Dindia & Allen (1992) 74
discovery learning 162
disequilibrium 152
disinhibition 260–1, 339–40
displacement 4, 375
dissolution 86–7
Dollard et al. (1939) 321
domestic violence 371
Donaldson (1978) 155
dopamine 313, 363, 407–8
dopamine hypothesis: and schizophrenia 200–1
Downs and Woolrych (2009) 409
Drabman & Thomas (1974) 338
drug abuse 398, 382
drug-refusal skills 422
drug therapy
 for addiction 417–19
 for schizophrenia 211–15
 for stress 294–7
DSM-II classification system 190
DSM-III-R classification system 29
DSM-IV classification system 143, 191, 398
DSM-5 classification system 52, 143, 188, 189, 393–4

dual control theory (DCT) 239–40
Duck (1982) 86–7
Duck (1988) 84
Duck (2001) 86, 88
Duck, Steve 86–9
Dudley et al. (2008) 230
Duffy, John 356–7
Duffy & Rusbult (1986) 85
Dunbar (1995) 69
Dunn (1990) 234
Dunn (2012) 233
Dunn & Goldman (1996, 1998) 403
dysfunctional thought processing 208–9

E
early childhood experiences 2
eating behaviour 32, 37, 43, 45, 48, 53, 58, 227–64
 anorexia nervosa 32, 37, 43, 49, 245–54
 food preferences 228–38
 hormonal mechanisms 239–43
 neural mechanisms 239–43, 246, 258
 obesity 256–64
Eccles et al. (1990) 110
Edwards (1968) 116
ego 3
egocentric speech 161, 162
egocentrism 154, 155, 171, 172
Eibl-Eibesfeldt (1977) 317
Eisenberg et al. (1982) 129
Elbourne et al. (2001) 118
Electra complex 7, 131–2, 133
elephants: salt mining 228
Elliott (2002) 16
Ellis et al. (2009) 311
Elvevag & Goldberg (2000) 207
empiricism 40
enmeshment 249, 250
Environment of Evolutionary Adaptiveness (EEA) 229, 257, 258
environmental determinism 35
environmental (stimulus–response) reductionism 47
Epley et al. (2004) 171
Epps & Kendall (1995) 371
equilibration 152
equilibrium 152
equity theory 82–4
Erikson, Erik 8
Errington & Gewert (1989) 142
esteem support 303
ethical issues 54, 55–9
ethnocentrism 31
ethological explanation for aggression 315–17
eustress 272, 273
Evans et al. (1994) 273
Evans et al. (1997) 208
evolution 65
evolutionary explanations
 for aggression 317–19
 for food preferences 228–9

for obesity  257–8
for partner preferences  64–71
exhaustion  269
expectancies  403
Experiences in Close Relationships Questionnaire  260
extrapolation  23–4
extraversion  366, 367, 368, 402
Eysenck (1952)  9
Eysenck (1997)  401–2
Eysenck, Hans  43, 366–8
Eysenck Personality Questionnaire (EPQ)  366–7, 401

## F

Facebook  93, 138, 140
facial symmetry  66, 69
Fagot & Leinbach (1995)  135
Fallon (2013)  365
Fallon, James  55
Family Adaptability and Cohesion Scale  400
family dysfunction theory  43, 204–6
family studies  362
family systems theory  43, 249–50
family therapy  218–19
Farrington (1992)  368
Farrington (1996)  362
Fern, Fanny  131
Fernando (1988)  194
Ferrer (2013)  64
Festinger et al. (1950)  77
Festinger et al. (1952)  326
Fetherling, Doug  64
Fields, Totie  263
fight-or-flight response  268, 270, 301
filter theory  77–8
Finch & Standford (2004)  233
Finkelstein (2013)  118
Fiore et al. (1994)  418
Fischer, Martin H.  188
Fitch & Denenberg (1998)  117
fixation  6, 7, 8
fixed action pattern (FAP)  316–17
fixed interval reinforcement  410, 411
fixed ratio reinforcement  410, 411
Flaherty & Dusek (1980)  113
Flavell et al. (1986)  173
Fleiger & Zingle (1973)  421
Flett et al. (1995)  282
flow theory  13
fMRI (functional magnetic resonance imagery) brain scans  5–6, 341, 364–5
and anorexia  247, 248
and mirror neuron system  179, 180
and schizophrenia  201–2, 203
focus  14
focus on the self  15
Foley & Lee (1991)  233
food preferences  228–38
bitter/sour tastes  231–2
cultural influences  238

evolutionary explanation  228–9
meat eating  233–4
neophobia  234–5
salty taste preference  230–1
social influences  236–7
sweet taste preference  229–30
taste aversion  37, 235–6
forensic psychology  32, 38, 43, 49, 54, 58, 345–87
biological explanations for offending behaviour  360–5
dealing with offending behaviour  378–87
offender profiling  351–8
problems defining crime  346–50
psychological explanations for offending behaviour  366–76
Foroud et al. (2000)  398
Forshaw (2002)  290
Francis (2000)  137
Frankl, Viktor E.  34
Frayling et al. (2007)  256–7
free will  11, 12, 19–20, 33, 34, 35, 37–8
Freud, Anna  4
Freud, Sigmund  2–3, 4, 6, 7, 8, 30, 36
Little Hans case study  8–9, 132, 133
psychoanalytic theory of gender  130–3
Freund (1990)  162
Frey & Ruble (1992)  127
Friedman (1952)  132
Friedman (2005)  258–9
Friedman et al. (2007)  136
Friedman & Rosenman (1959)  289
Friedman & Rosenman (1974)  290
Frith (1989)  174–5
Frith & Frith (1999)  174
Fromm (1962)  82
frustration–aggression hypothesis  321–2
functional invariants  151
Funk (1992)  293
Furnham (1984)  367
Furnham (1996)  41

## G

GABA (neurotransmitter)  294–5
Gabriel (2008)  98
Gagnepain, Henson & Anderson (2014)  5–6
Galderisi et al. (2012)  194–5
Gallese (2001)  180
galvanic skin response  286–7
gambling addiction  394, 409–15
Garcia-Falgueras & Swaab (2008)  145
Garcia & Koelling (1966)  235–6
Garety et al. (2001)  208
Garnefski (2004)  302
Garner et al. (1982)  253
Garner & Garfinkel (1980)  252
Gates (1985)  297
gating  95–6
Geisel, Ted  51
Gelder et al. (1989)  421

Geldof, Peaches  397
Gelernter (2005)  398
Gelman (1979)  155
gender  43, 48, 53, 58, 107–46
chromosomes/hormones, role of  115–23
differences in stress management  301–2
psychoanalytic theory of  130–3
and self-disclosure  73–4
sex and gender  108–14
gender bias  28–30, 32, 194–5
gender constancy theory  125–7
gender development  125–46
atypical  143–6
cognitive explanations for  125–9
psychodynamic explanation for  130–3
social learning theory and  135–42
gender dysphoria, see gender identity disorder (GID)
gender identity  125–7
gender identity disorder (GID)  37, 58, 108, 138, 143–5
gender reassignment treatment  108, 143
gender research  17
gender schema theory  125
gender stereotypes  32, 112, 126, 127, 128–9, 135–6
media and  138–40
general adaptation syndrome (GAS)  268–9
general strain theory  361
general symbolic function (GSF)  152
genetic engineering  58
genetics  32, 35, 58
and addiction  397–9
and aggression  32, 43, 49, 58, 312–15
and anorexia  245–6
and gender identity disorder  144–5
Klinefelter's syndrome  120–1, 122–3
nature–nurture debate  20–1, 40–4
and obesity  256–7
and offending behaviour  361–3
and schizophrenia  198–9
Turner's syndrome  121–3
geographical profiling  355–6, 357
Gernsbacher & Frymiare (2005)  176
ghrelin  241, 243, 264
Giancola (1995)  370
Giles (2000)  98
Giles & Maltby (2006)  100
Gilligan (1982)  370
Gladue (1985)  144
Go et al. (2005)  232
Godin & Kok (1996)  426
Goel & Bale (2008)  116
Goetz et al. (2008)  319
Goldberg et al. (1981)  409
Goldman (1999)  192
Goring (1913)  360
Gottesman & Shields (1976)  198
Goudsblom (1992)  233
Grabus et al. (2005)  396

Gredler (1992)   162
Green & Fleming (1990)   146
Greer & Morris (1975)   291–2
Griffiths (1994)   413–14
Griffiths & Delfabbro (2001)   412
Grinspoon et al. (1996)   248
Gudjonsson (1984)   371
Gudjonsson & Singh (1988)   371
Guerra et al. (2003)   326
Guillemets, Terri   289
Gunnell & Ceci (2010)   76
Gunter (1986)   139
Guo et al. (2010)   224
Gurling et al. (2006)   199
Gurucharri & Selman (1982)   171
gynocentrism   32

## H

Haddock et al. (2003)   424
Hakonarson et al. (2010)   246
Halmi et al. (2000)   253
halo effect   75–6
Hambrecht & Häfner (2000)   195
Hamid, Mohsin   178
Han & Liu (1966)   240
handicap hypothesis   67
Hanson & Bussiere (1998)   382
Happe et al. (1996)   176
hard determinism   34
hardiness   289, 292–3
Hare et al. (2009)   145
Hare-Mustin & Marecek (1988)   30
harm avoidance   402
Haro et al. (2008)   195
Harper & Sanders (1975)   237
Harris (1974)   321
Harris (1989)   173
Harris (2001)   337
Hartness, Carin   294
Haslam & Reicher (2006)   334
Hassles Scale   281
Hatfield (1979)   81
Hatfield et al. (1984)   88
Havoundjian et al. (1986)   295
Hawking, Stephen   36
Hayes (2000)   290
Hayes (2004)   16
Hayling Sentence Completion Test   208
Healy (2000)   201
Heaven (1996)   368
Hedgecoe (2001)   199
Heim et al. (2000)   271
heritability equation   41–2
Herman & Polivy (1984)   260, 261
heroin   417
Herzog et al. (1991)   252
Hetherington & Ranson (1940)   240
Hewitt et al. (2013)   122
Heyes (2012)   181
Hickok (2009)   181
hierarchy of needs   14, 334
Higley et al. (1996)   311, 363

Hiltz et al. (1989)   339
Hines (2004)   145
Hirsh et al. (2011)   328
Hitopadesha (Sanskrit fables)   228
Ho et al. (2003)   203
Hobbs & Tyllon (1976)   384
Hobson & Beach (2000)   283–4
Hochschild & Machung (1989)   84
Hogarty et al. (1986)   223
Holcomb (1986)   299
holism   11, 21–2, 44–9
Hollin (1992)   380
Hollin et al. (2002)   369
Holloway et al. (1977)   341
Holmes & Rahe (1967)   278–9
Holroyd et al. (1977)   299
Holtzworth-Munroe & Hutchinson (1993)   371
homeostasis   239–40, 394
homosexuality   56, 251, 252, 347
Hooton (1939)   360–1
Hopoate, John   308
hormonal mechanisms
    for aggression   311–12
    of eating behaviour   241–3, 247, 248, 258–9
hormones   115–19
    adrenaline   268–9, 270, 296
    cortisol   49, 117, 222, 223, 268, 271–2, 273, 281
    and gender   115–19
    and gender identity disorder   144–5
    ghrelin   241, 243, 264
    leptin   241–3, 247, 248, 258–9
    noradrenaline   247, 248, 268–9, 270, 295–6, 313, 363
    oestrogen   117–18, 119
    oxytocin   118, 119
    testosterone   115–16, 119, 308, 311–12, 313
Horwatt et al. (1988)   270
hostile attribution bias   370–2
Howard (2001)   420
Howard et al. (1997)   402
Howard et al. (2001)   420
Howells et al. (2005)   385
Huber et al. (1997)   310
Hughes (1975)   155
human reproductive behaviour   65–6
humanistic approach to psychology   11–17, 19, 20, 21, 22, 23, 24, 54
Humphreys (1970)   56
Huston (1983)   135
Huston (1990)   139
Huston & Wright (1998)   139
Hyde, J.S. (2005)   17
Hyman (1921)   132
hypothalamic-pituitary-adrenal (HPA) system   271–2
hypothalamus
    and eating behaviour   239–43, 246, 258
    and stress   268–9

## I

Iacoboni et al. (2005)   180
ICD-10 classification system   52, 188, 189, 191
id   3, 374, 375
ideal self   15
identification   7, 131
idiographic approach   11, 22, 51–4
immune system: and stress-related illness   273–5
immunosuppression   272
importation model   330–2
Ineichen (1984)   193
infidelity   68, 85, 86, 92, 93, 318, 319
informational support   303
Ingham (1978)   328
Inhelder & Piaget (1958)   156
innate releasing mechanism   316
inner speech   160, 161, 162
Insel (2001)   118
Insel, Thomas R.   198
instincts/drives   2, 3, 6–8
institutional aggression   330–5
institutionalisation   379, 381–2
instrumental support   303
inter-rater reliability   189
internalisation   160
internet addiction   394, 400–1, 402, 423
investigative psychology   355
Ireland (2000)   385
Irwin & Cressey (1962)   330–1
Iversen (1979)   200

## J

Jackson & Bekerian (1997)   351
Jacobs & Charles (1980)   280
Jäger et al. (2003)   191
Jakobsen et al. (2005)   189
James, William   15
Jansson & Parnas (2007)   191
Jauhar et al. (2014)   217
Javitt (2007)   201
Javitt et al. (2000)   201
Jay & Elliot (1990)   298–9
jealousy   67, 68, 318
Jeffery (2000)   264
Jeremy Kyle TV show   287
Jeste et al. (1996)   192
Jiang & Fisher-Giorlando (2002)   331, 335
Johansson et al. (1978)   283
Johnson & Sharma (2001)   274
Johnston (1991)   334
Johnston & Ettema (1982)   140
Johnstone et al. (1976)   202
Josephson (1987)   339–40
Joshua et al. (2009)   208
Joukhador et al. (2003)   414
Jung, Carl   392

## K

Kahn et al. (2008)   214
Kane & Janus (1981)   331

Kanner *et al.* (1981)  281
Kaplan (1980)  361
Karwautz *et al.* (2003)  250
Kassin (1996)  88
Kavanagh (1992)  205
Kelley & Thibaut (1978)  84
Kelvin, Lord  285
Kendell & Jablensky (2007)  192
Kendler *et al.* (1997)  398
Kendler & Prescott (1998)  398
Kendrick (1982)  234
Kennedy & Grubin (1992)  372
Kennedy, Patrick J.  397
Kent *et al.* (2001)  364–5
Kerckhoff & Davis (1962)  77
Kessler *et al.* (2003)  200
Kestenbaum & Weinstein (1985)  337
Ketter (2005)  196
Kety & Ingraham (1992)  198
Khalfa *et al.* (2002)  286
Kiecolt-Glaser (1984)  274–5
Kiecolt-Glaser *et al.* (1995)  273
Kienlen *et al.* (1997)  102
Kintz, Jarod  80, 86
Kito (2010)  74
Kivimaki *et al.* (2006)  284
Kivran-Swaine *et al.* (2013)  139
Kleinke (1979)  73
Klinefelter's syndrome (KS)  120–1, 122–3
Knoblich *et al.* (2004)  207
Kobasa (1979)  292
Kobus (2003)  405
Kohlberg, Lawrence
 stages of moral reasoning  368–9
 theory of gender constancy  125–7
Konstantakopoulos *et al.* (2012)  254
Konstantareas & Hewitt (2001)  195
Koons *et al.* (1997)  385
Kortegaard *et al.* (2001)  245–6
Kosonogov (2012)  181
Krakowski (2003)  363
Krantz *et al.* (1991)  275, 276
Kulik *et al.* (2013)  296
Kulkarni *et al.* (2001)  195
Kurniawan *et al.* (2013)  286
Kurnitz, Harry  261
Kurzban & Weeden (2005)  69

## L

La Fromboise *et al.* (1990)  141
Lahm (2008)  334
Lai (2000)  252
Laing, R.D.  198
Lamb & Roopnarine (1979)  136
Lane (2010)  295
Lanfer *et al.* (2013)  238
Langer (1975)  412–13
Langlois & Downs (1980)  110, 136
Langlois & Roggman (1990)  69
Lashley (1938)  239
Lashly (1938)  240
Latané & Darley (1968a, 1968b)  57

Latifah, Queen  138
Latimer, Dowden & Muise (2012)  387
Lau *et al.* (1992)  297
Lawton, Gwlenis Maureen  136
Lawton, Mara  80
learning approach to psychology  19, 20, 21, 22, 23, 24, 35, 40
learning theory  410–12: *see also* operant conditioning
Le Bon, Gustave  327
Lee & Harley (2012)  30
Leff *et al.* (1985)  218
Le Grange & Eisler (2008)  250
Lemaire *et al.* (2011)  300
Lenhart & Duggan (2014)  93
Lennon, John  100
Leo (2006)  199
leptin  241–3, 247, 248, 258–9
Leshem & Kuiper (1996)  269
Leshner (1998)  404
Leslie (1987)  175, 177
Leslie & Frith (1988)  176
Lewin *et al.* (1984)  194
Li *et al.* (2004)  398
Li *et al.* (2010)  202
Lieberman *et al.* (2005)  213
Liem & Mennella (2003)  232
life changes  399, 418
 life change units (LCUs)  278–80
limbic system  308–9, 363, 364, 407
Lin & Rusbult (1995)  85
Lindemann *et al.* (1978)  274
Lindholm *et al.* (2005)  297
LinkedIn  139
lipostatic theory  242
Littell and Girvin (2002)  429
Lloyd *et al.* (1984)  201
Locke, John  40
Logue (1991)  229
Lombroso, Cesare  360–1
Lorenz, Konrad  316
Love, Jason  229
Lowe *et al.* (2004)  262–3
Lowe, Jules  346
Lowe & Kral (2006)  261
Lowney (1995)  56
Lubinski *et al.* (1981)  113
Lykken (1984)  287
Lysaker *et al.* (2008)  208
Lytton & Romney (1991)  110

## M

McCarty (1981)  270
Maccoby (1990)  137
Maccoby (1998)  128
Maccoby & Jacklin (1974)  126
McConaghy (1979)  126
McConaghy *et al.* (1983)  421
McCutcheon (2002)  99
McCutcheon (2006)  102
McCutcheon *et al.* (2002)  98, 99
McCutcheon *et al.* (2004)  98

McCutcheon *et al.* (2006)  102
McCutcheon & Houran (2003)  100–1
MacDougal (2005)  101
McFarlane *et al.* (2003)  219
McGarrigle & Donaldson (1974)  156
McGorry *et al.* (2002)  217
McGovern & Cope (1977)  193
McKenna (2002)  96
McKenna & Bargh (2000)  94–5
McKenna *et al.* (2002)  96
McLellan *et al.* (1993)  418
McMonagle & Sultana (2000)  220
McNaughton & Leyland (1990)  162
Malcolm *et al.* (2006)  418
Malcolm X  378
Maletzky (1974)  421
Malik *et al.* (2008)  243
Malinowski (1922)  132
Malott & Fromader (2010)  382
Maltby (2002)  101
Maltby *et al.* (2003)  101
Maltby *et al.* (2004)  101
MAOA gene  32, 43, 49, 58, 312, 313–15, 363
Marder (1996)  213
Marks *et al.* (1997)  396
Marmot *et al.* (1997)  283
Martin (1989)  280
Martin & Halverson (1981)  127–8
Martin & Halverson (1983)  128
Martin & Little (1990)  128
Martinez-Aleman & Wartman (2009)  140
Maruna & Mann (2006)  372
Maslow (1962)  11
Maslow, Abraham  12, 14
masochistic personality disorder  29
Mason (1975)  272
Mason (1995)  269
Mason *et al.* (1997)  191
Masters *et al.* (1979)  128
mate guarding  67, 70
mate preference  30, 32, 43, 318
maternal deprivation hypothesis  374–5
Matsueda (1988)  373
Matthews *et al.* (2006)  337
Matthews & Haynes (1986)  290
Matud (2004)  302
Maugham, W. Somerset  237
Mayo-Smith *et al.* (1989)  248
Mead (1935)  111, 141
Mead, Margaret  32, 141
Meadows (1988)  157
Meadows (1995)  157
media
 and aggression  335–41
 and gender development  138–40
 and social learning theory  251–2
 *see also* social media
Meichenbaum (1977)  298
Meichenbaum (2001)  299
Meiselman (1977)  229
Melamed *et al.* (2006)  275

Meloy (1998) 101
memories/memory 5–6, 271–2
Menella et al. (2005) 238
Mennella & Beauchamp (1996) 237
mens rea 348
Mensink et al. (2008) 264
mental health: negative effects of custodial sentencing 380–1, 382
mental health disorders: classification of 52
Merrit et al. (2008) 232
Mesch & Talmud (2006) 92
metabolic tolerance 394
metacognition 208–9
Metacognition Awareness Test 208
methadone 417, 418
Miers et al. (2001) 386
Milgram, Stanley 29, 57
Miller (1997) 70
Miller et al. (1996) 291
Miller, George 237
Miller-Kovach et al. (2001) 262, 263
Mills & Clark (1980) 81
Mills & Clark (1982) 84
minimalisation 372
Minuchin (1978) 250
Minuchin (1979) 249
mirror neuron system 150, 169, 177, 178–81
Mishna et al. (2009) 92
Miyamoto, Shigeru 335
mobile phone addiction 392, 394
Moffett, Thomas 256
Moffitt et al. (1992) 314
Moghaddam et al. (1983) 84
Money & Ehrhardt (1972) 116
Monroe, Marilyn 75
moral reasoning, level of 368–70
morality principle 3, 374
Morgan, C.L. 47
Moriarity & McCabe (1977) 341
Morris et al. (1981) 291
Morrisey 233
Morrison, Toni 268
Morrison & Turkington (2014) 224
mosaic Klinefelter's syndrome (MKS) 120
mosaic Turner's syndrome (MTS) 121
Multi-Dimensional Perfectionism Scale 253
Mumford et al. (1991) 252
Murray (1996) 222
Murray et al. (2007) 341
Murstein (1972) 76
Murstein et al. (1977) 82
Murstein & MacDonald (1983) 83
Musani et al. (2008) 257

## N
Nakazato et al. (2001) 243
National Institute on Drug Abuse (NIDA) (2005) 409
nativism 40

Natural Born Killers 360
natural selection 65, 66, 228–9, 232, 233
nature–nurture debate 20–1, 40–4, 46
  attachment theories 44, 54, 102–3
neophobia 234–5
neural explanations
  for anorexia 246–8
  for obesity 258–9
  for offending behaviour 363–4
  for schizophrenia 201–3
neural mechanisms
  in aggression 308–11, 313–17
  of eating behaviour 239–43, 246, 258
neuropeptides 241–3
neuroticism 366, 367, 368, 401, 402
Newcomer et al. (1999) 271–2
Newman & Taylor (1992) 237
nicotine addiction 395, 398, 403, 405, 407–9, 417, 418, 420, 428
Nielsen et al. (2008) 397
Nietzsche, Friedrich 298
Nilsson et al. (2000) 189
Noel (1999) 429
Nolen-Hoeksema (2002) 264
nomothetic approach 22, 51–4
noradrenaline 247, 248, 268–9, 270, 295–6, 313, 363
normative beliefs 425, 426
novelty seeking 402
Nunn et al. (2012) 248

## O
Oberndorfer et al. (2013) 247
obesity 43, 256–64
  biological explanations 256–9
  psychological explanations 259–64
object permanence 152, 165–8
O'Carroll (2000) 207
OCD (obsessive–compulsive disorder) 58
Oedipus complex 7, 130–1, 133
oestrogen 117–18, 119
offender profiling 351–8
  bottom-up approach 351, 354–5
  geographical profiling 355–6, 357
  top-down approach 351, 352–4
offender surveys 350
Offending Crime and Justice Survey 350
Office for National Statistics 348
Ogden (2009) 261
OGOD (one gene, one disorder) approach 41
Oh & Hsu (2001) 426–7
Olds (1981) 112, 114
online dating 91, 92
operant conditioning 35, 52
  and eating behaviour 237, 262
  and forensic psychology 379, 383
  and gambling addiction 410, 412
  and nicotine addiction 408, 409
  and stress 300
  token economies 220–1, 383–4
Operation Yewtree 349

operations 151
Ophoff et al. (2011) 195
opioids 395
Orlofsky (1977) 112
Orth-Gomer et al. (1993) 303
overdeveloped superego 374
oxytocin 118, 119

## P
Palmer (2003) 369
Pankhurst, Emmeline 379
parapraxes 36
parasocial relationships 97–103
parasympathetic nervous system (PSNS) 270
parents: influence on gender development 135–6
Parke & Griffiths (2004) 412
Parker & Parikh (2001) 428
Parker & Wampler (2003) 93
Parmas et al. (1993) 198
partner preferences: evolutionary explanation 64–71
Pastore (1952) 321, 322
Patino et al. (2005) 205
Pawlowski & Dunbar (1999) 69
Pedersen (2012) 215
peers
  and addiction 404–5
  influence on gender development 136–7
penis-baby making project 7, 131
penis envy 7, 131
Penton-Voak et al. (2001) 69
Peritz & Rust (1972) 70
Personal Orientation Inventory 13
personal therapy (PT) 216
personality 3, 53, 401–2
personality types 289–92
  hardy personality type 292–3
  Type A 289, 290, 291
  Type B 289, 290, 291
  Type C 291–2, 293
  Type D 289, 291, 292
perspective-taking 169–72
Peter et al. (2005) 94
Peters & Cantrell (1993) 113–14
Pew Research Internet Project (2011) 139
Pew Research Internet Project (2013) 91
Pew Research Internet Project (2014) 95
Phillips, Anthony 186
Phillips, Bill 292
physical attractiveness 66, 75–6
physiological measures of stress 285–7
physiology of stress 268–72
Piaget (1952) 155
Piaget (1960) 156
Piaget & Inhelder (1956) 154–5
Piaget, Jean 37, 43, 49, 150–7, 163, 368
Piaget & Szeminska (1941) 155
Piazza et al. (1989) 400
Pilling et al. (2002) 218–19
Pinizzotto (1984) 358

Pinto da Mota Matos (2011) 325
Pinto da Mota Matos, Alves Ferreira and Haase (2011) 336-7
Pinto da Mota Matos and Haase (2011) 340
Piper, John 97
pleasure principle 3, 374, 375
Pleistocene era 229, 257
Pliner & Loewen (1997) 234
Pliner & McFarlane (1997) 234
Plomin (1994) 41
Plutarch 160
police-recorded crime 348, 349
police-reported crime 349
polygraphs 286-7
Poole & Regoli (1983) 332
Postmes & Spears (1998) 328
Poulin-Dubois et al. (2002) 129
Powley & Keesey (1970) 240
pre-conscious mind 3
predictive validity 190, 191
Premack & Woodruff (1978) 172
Prentice-Dunn & Rogers (1982) 327
Price et al. (1986) 122
principle of parsimony 47
prisons: aggression in 330-5
private self-awareness 327
problem-solving techniques 423
Prochaska (1977) 427-9
proopiomelanocortin (POMC) 258-9
psychic determinism 36
psychodynamic approach to psychology 2-9, 19, 20, 21, 22, 23, 24, 36
psychodynamic explanations
  for gender development 130-3
  for offending behaviour 373-6
psychological and physiological dependence 393-4
psychological explanations
  for anorexia 249-54
  for obesity 259-64
  for offending behaviour 366-76
  for schizophrenia 204-9
psychometric tests 52
psychopathy 364-5
psychosexual stages 6-8
  Electra complex 7, 131-2, 133
  Oedipus complex 7, 130-1, 133
psychostimulants 395, 398
psychotherapy 2
psychoticism 366, 367, 368, 401, 402
Ptacek et al. (2014) 302
public self-awareness 327
Purcell et al. (2002) 101

## Q

QTL (quantitative trait loci) method 41
Quaade (1971) 241
quality circles 285
Queen Latifah 138
Quiery (1998) 135
Quigley et al. (2014) 122
Quintana et al. (1999) 172

## R

Rabban (1950) 126
Rack (1982) 194
Radford & Kirby (1975) 51
Rafferty (2013) 136
Ragland & Brand (1988) 291
Rahe et al. (1970) 280
Raine (1993) 362
Raine (1996) 56
Raine et al. (1997) 309, 365
Raine et al. (2000) 364
Raisanen & Hunt (2014) 45
Ramachandran, V.S. 150
Randrup & Munkvad (1966) 200
Rathod et al. (2005) 217
rational emotive therapy 216
rationalisation 376
Read et al. (2004) 189
Read & McDaniel (2008) 230
real self 15
reality principle 3
recidivism 378, 379, 381-3, 385-6
reciprocal determinism 35
reductionism 21-2, 44-9, 412
Reeves & Plum (1969) 258
rehabilitation 378, 379
Reichler-Rossler & Hafner (2000) 194
reinforcement 251, 410-12
Rekers (1995) 144
relapse prevention 261-2, 422-3, 424
Relate 89
Relationship Maintenance Strategies Measure (RMSM) 83
relationships 32, 37, 43, 48, 53, 58, 63-103
  Duck's phase model of relationship breakdown 86-9
  parasocial relationships 97-103
  partner preferences, evolutionary explanation for 64-71
  romantic relationships, factors affecting attraction in 72-8
  romantic relationships theories 80-5
  virtual relationships in social media 91-6
relaxation skills 423
reliability in diagnosis 189
Renold (2001) 137
Renzetti & Curran (1992) 110
Reppucci & Saunders (1974) 384
repression 4, 5-6
resistance 269
Ressler et al. (1988) 352
restorative justice programmes 54, 386-7
restraint theory 259-60, 261
Rethink Mental Illness self-help group 204
reticular activating system (RAS) 367
retribution 378, 379, 383
reward dependence 402
Reynaud et al. (2012) 286
Rice (1990) 383-4
Rich-Harris (1998) 405

Ridley (1993) 70
Riordan, Rick 82
risk factors: for addiction 397-405
Rizzolatti & Craighero (2004) 180
Rizzolatti et al. (1996) 180
Rizzolatti, Giacomo 178
Roberts and Pirog (2013) 392
Rogers (1998) 414
Rogers, Carl 12, 15, 16
role-taking theory 169, 170
Rollie & Duck (2006) 89
romantic relationships
  factors affecting attraction in 72-8
  theories of 80-5
Rose & Montemayor (1994) 114
Rosemann & Safir (2006) 96
Rosenhan (1973) 190
Rosman & Baker (1978) 250
Ross & Spinner (2001) 103
Roud Folk Song Index 125
Rowe et al. (2007) 258
Rozanski et al. (1999) 275
Rubin (1975) 93-4
Rubin (1983) 82
Rubin et al. (1985) 98
Ruderman & Wilson (1979) 260
Ruffman, Garnham & Rideout (2001) 176
Rusbult (1983) 81
Rusbult, Caryl 84-5
Rusbult et al. (1998) 85
Rusbult & Martz (1995) 81
Rzoska (1953) 235

## S

Sackett (1966) 316
Sadalla et al. (1987) 77, 318
Sally-Anne test 169, 175-6
Sapolsky, Robert 40
Sarafino (1990) 293
Sayers, Dorothy L. 28
scaffolding 160, 161
Schaffer (1996) 129
Schaffer (2004) 156, 163
schemas 151-2
Schiffer et al. (2010) 292
Schiller (1980) 238
schizophrenia 32, 35, 37, 43, 48, 53, 58, 185-224
  and autism 195
  biological explanations 198-204
  and bipolar disorder 193, 195
  CBT 216-17, 424
  classification of 186-96
  co-morbidity 192-3
  culture bias 193-4
  diagnosis 188-92
  drug therapies 211-15
  family therapy 218-19
  and flu 194, 222
  and fMRI brain scans 201-2, 203
  gender bias 194-5
  interactionist approach 216-24
  psychological explanations 204-9

symptom overlap   195–6
symptoms   187–8
token economies   220–1
Schizophrenia Commission (2012)   219
Schizophrenia Working Group of the Psychiatric Genomics Consortium (2014)   199
Schneider (1959)   187
Schöner & Thelen (2004)   168
Schooler et al. (2005)   213–14
Schouten et al. (2007)   94
Schultz & Selman (1990)   171
Schutzwohl & Koch (2004)   68
Scott-Van Zeeland et al. (2014)   246
Seavey et al. (1975)   110
Sedikides (2005)   82
self-actualisation   12–16
self-awareness   327
self-concept   15
self-derogation theory   361
self-disclosure   72–4, 93–5
self-esteem   15
self-harm   380
self-socialisation   126
Seligman, Martin   33
Selman (1971)   171
Selman (1980)   169
Selman & Byrne (1974)   171
Selman, Robert   169–72
Selye (1936)   268–9
Selye (1950)   269
Selye, Hans   30, 272
semiotics   161
sensation seeking   402
sensitivity   318
seriation   153
serotonin (neurotransmitter)   46, 201, 212, 247, 248, 294, 309–10, 311, 313, 363
Serper et al. (1999)   195
set point theory (SPT)   240–1
Seto (2004)   189
sex: and gender   108–14
sex-role stereotypes   109–11
sexting   94, 95
Sexton & Whiston (1994)   17
sexual dimorphism   65
sexual offences   349
sexual selection   65–6
sexy sons hypothesis   67
Shakeshaft et al. (2013)   42
Shanahan (2008)   358
Shapiro (1981)   250
shared attention mechanism (SAM)   173
Shatz et al. (1983)   173
Shawcross, Arthur   354
Sheffield et al. (1995)   13
Sher (2004)   281
Sherman & Strong (2007)   387
Shiiya et al. (2002)   243
Shipmon, Eric   91
Shostrum (1963, 1977)   13
Siegel & Victoroff (2009)   309

Silverstein et al. (2009)   220
Sim et al. (2006)   192
Simmons et al. (2003)   70
Simpson (2001)   312
Simpson et al. (2003)   120
Singer, June   111
Singh (1993)   70
Sinha (2000)   400
skin conductance response (SCR)   286–7
Slaby & Frey (1975)   126
Slater, Robert L.   115
Slater & Roth (1969)   188
Smith & Duggan (2013)   92
smoking, see nicotine addiction
snake massage   268
sneak copulations   67, 70
Snook et al. (2008)   358
Snortum et al. (1969)   132, 133
Snow (2006)   380
Snyder (1976)   200
social cognition development   169–81
  mirror neuron system in   178–81
  perspective-taking   169–72
  theory of mind (ToM)   172–7
social exchange theory (SET)   80–2
social explanations for gender identity disorder   143–5
social learning theory (SLT)   262, 322–6, 404, 408, 411, 251–2
  and gender development   135–42
social media
  Facebook   93, 138, 140
  virtual relationships in   91–6
social phobias   31
social psychological explanations for human aggression   321–8
Social Readjustment Rating Scale (SRRS)   278–80
social sensitivity   56–8
social speech   161
social support networks   301, 303–4
Söderberg et al. (2005)   189
soft determinism   34
solipsistic introjection   339
Sood et al. (2014)   110
Sorensen & Stunkard (1994)   256
Sorri et al. (2004)   199
speech analysis   286
speech poverty   188
Spielberger (1988)   370
Sprecher (1986)   84
Stachour (1998)   303–4
Stafford-Clark, David   186
Stanford Prison Study   379, 380
Stargardt et al. (2008)   214
Stefansson (1960)   230
Steinem, Gloria   135
Steiner (1977)   229
Steinglass et al. (2007)   253
Steinke et al. (2008)   138–9, 140
Steinke & Long (1996)   139
Stellar (1954)   240

Stephure et al. (2009)   92
Stever (1991)   101
Stever (2009)   103
Stever (2013)   103
Stice et al. (2008)   259
Stirling et al. (2004)   264
Stochholm et al. (2012)   121
Strauss & Ryan (1987)   250
stress   32, 37, 43, 49, 53, 58, 267–304
  and addiction   399–401
  adrenaline and   268–9, 270
  cancer and   291–2, 293
  and cardiovascular disorders   275–6, 289, 290–1, 292
  cortisol and   268, 269, 271–2, 273, 281
  and immune system disorders   273–5
  management of   294–304
  physiological measures of   285–7
  physiology of   268–72
  role of, in illness   272–6
  sources of   278–85
  work-related   275, 282–5
stress inoculation therapy (SIT)   298–9
stress management   294–304
  biofeedback   300–1
  drug therapy   294–7
  gender differences in   301–2
  social support networks   303–4
  stress inoculation therapy (SIT)   298–9
Stroebe (2000)   303
Stunkard et al. (1990)   256
Stuss et al. (2001)   180
Subjective Family Image Test   250
sublimation   375
Sudak (2011)   224
suicide   380
Suler (2004)   339
Sumer et al. (2007)   309
superego   3, 374
Sutherland, Edwin   373
Swami & Furnham (2006)   70
Swerdlow et al. (2005)   121
Sykes (1958)   333
Symington et al. (1955)   272
symmetry   66, 69–70
sympathetic adrenal medullary system (SAM)   270
sympathetic nervous system (SNS)   270
sympathomedullary pathway (SMP)   270–1

# T

Tager-Flusberg (2007)   177
taijin kyofusho syndrome   31
Takahashi et al. (2013)   207
Tamres et al. (2014)   302
Tan & Singh (1995)   77
Tang & Hammontree (1992)   280
Tarrier (2005)   217
Tarrier et al. (2000)   216
Tashiro & Frazier (2003)   88
taste aversion   37, 235–6
Tavolacci et al. (2013)   399–400

Tavris (1993)  29
Taylor (1986)  113
Taylor et al. (2000)  270, 301
Taylor et al. (2010)  77
Taylor et al. (2011)  76
Taylor & Hall (1982)  113
Teitelbaum (1957)  240
Temoshok (1987)  292
tend-and-befriend response  30, 32, 58, 270, 301
test-retest reliability  189
testosterone  115–16, 119, 308, 311–12, 313
theory of mind (ToM)  169, 172–7
theory of mind mechanism (ToMM)  175
theory of planned behaviour  423, 425–7, 428
Thibaut & Kelley et al. (1959)  81
Thompson (1975)  126
Thompson (2006)  98
Thorndike, Edward  52
Three Factor Eating Questionnaire  260
Tienari et al. (2004)  205
Tilo et al. (2001)  202
Timio et al. (1988)  269
Tinbergen (1952)  316
token economies  220–1, 383–4
tolerance  394–5
Toma et al. (2008)  69
Toneatto (1999)  414
Torrey et al. (1994)  198
trait theories of personalities  53
Trammel (2002)  383
transductive reasoning  153
tri-dimensional theory of addictive behaviour  402
trolling  92
Trower et al. (2004)  217
Tsuang et al. (1996)  398
Turner (1993)  98
Turner's syndrome (TS)  121–3
twin studies  41, 144–5, 198, 199, 245–6, 256, 361–2, 363, 398, 399
Type I/Type II schizophrenia  187
typical antipsychotic drugs  211–15

## U
unconditional positive regard  16
unconscious mind  2–3, 6–8, 36
underdeveloped superego  374
uniqueness  11, 12
universality  29, 30–1
Urberg (1982)  110
URICA (University of Rhode Island Change Assessment) scale  429

## V
Vaccarino (2014)  276
Vaernes & Torjussen (1991)  273
validity in diagnosis  190–2
Van Lange et al. (1997)  85
Van Leengoed et al. (1987)  118, 119
variable interval reinforcement  411
variable ratio reinforcement  411
variant structures  151
Varma & Sharma (1993)  198
Velicer et al. (2007)  428
verbal aversion therapy  421
vertical decalage  153
victim surveys  348–9
Villarejo et al. (2012)  286
violation of expectation (VOE) technique  165–8
virtual relationships  91–6
Vygotsky, Lev S.  32, 43, 49, 150, 159–63

## W
Wagenaar (1988)  413
waist-to-hip ratio  66, 70
Waldron & Kaminer (2004)  424
Waldroup, Davis Bradley  312
Walker (1989)  370
Walker (1997)  222, 223
Walker et al. (2006)  427
Walker & Selman (1998)  172
Walster et al. (1966)  75, 76
Walster et al. (1978)  83
Walster & Walster (1969)  76
Wampold (1997, 2006)  16
Wan-Sen Yan et al. (2013)  398, 399, 400–1, 402, 403
Wardle & Beale (1988)  260
Watkins et al. (2000)  407
Watson et al. (2004)  272
Watson, John B.  35
Webb & Sheeran (2006)  426
Wedgwood Pottery Company  285
Weight Watchers  262–3
Wertsch et al. (1980)  162
West & Sweeting (2002)  98
Westman (2009)  293
Weyandt (2006)  202
Whaley (2004)  193
Wheatley, Margaret J.  322
White-Traut et al. (2009)  118, 119
Whiting & Edwards (1988)  141
Wicker et al. (2003)  180
Wiebe (1991)  293
Wilkinson et al. (2010)  260
Willer et al. (2008)  257
Williams (1981)  325
Williams & Best (1990)  141
Williams et al. (2002)  264
Wimmer & Perner (1983)  173, 174
Wing & Hill (2001)  261, 263
Wiszewska et al. (2007)  132, 133
withdrawal syndrome  395–6
Wood et al. (1976)  161–2
Wood et al. (2002)  136
Wood & Middleton (1975)  161
workload  283
workplace stress  282–5
Wortman et al. (1976)  73

## X
Xiong et al. (1994)  218

## Y
Yang et al. (2012)  259
yo-yo dieting  264
Yoon et al. (2013)  202
Young (1966)  116
Young (2007)  423
Yum et al. (2009)  83
Yum & Hara (2005)  94

## Z
Zahavi (1975)  67
Zandstra et al. (2004)  295
Zauszniewski et al. (2013)  300
Zetetic, Agnostic  143
Zhao et al. (2008)  229
Zhong et al. (2010)  327
Zimbardo (1970)  327
Zimbardo (1971)  379, 380
Zimmerman et al. (1980)  237
Zimmerman et al. (2005)  217
Zinner (2002)  231
zone of proximal development (ZPD)  160, 161–2, 163
Zucker et al. (2008)  145
Zuckerman (1983)  402